Lecture Notes in Computer Science 3239

Commenced Publication in 1973
Founding and Former Series Editors:
Gerhard Goos, Juris Hartmanis, and Jan van Leeuwen

Giuseppe Nicosia   Vincenzo Cutello
Peter J. Bentley   Jon Timmis (Eds.)

Artificial
Immune Systems

Third International Conference, ICARIS 2004
Catania, Sicily, Italy, September 13-16, 2004
Proceedings

 Springer

Volume Editors

Giuseppe Nicosia
Vincenzo Cutello
University of Catania
Department of Mathematics and Computer Science
V.le A. Doria 6, 95125 Catania, Italy
E-mail: {nicosia;cutello}@dmi.unict.it

Peter J. Bentley
University College London
Department of Computer Science
Gower Street, WC1E 6BT, London, UK
E-mail: P.Bentley@cs.ucl.ac.uk

Jon Timmis
University of Kent
Computing Laboratory
CT2 7NF Canterbury, Kent, UK
E-mail: j.timmis@kent.ac.uk

Library of Congress Control Number: 2004111519

CR Subject Classification (1998): F.1, I.2, F.2, H.2.8, H.3

ISSN 0302-9743
ISBN 3-540-23097-1 Springer Berlin Heidelberg New York

Springer is a part of Springer Science+Business Media

springeronline.com

© Springer-Verlag Berlin Heidelberg 2004
Printed in Germany

Typesetting: Camera-ready by author, data conversion by PTP-Berlin, Protago-TeX-Production GmbH
Printed on acid-free paper   SPIN: 11320210   06/3142   5 4 3 2 1 0

Preface

Artificial Immune Systems have come of age. They are no longer an obscure computer science technique, worked on by a couple of farsighted research groups. Today, researchers across the globe are working on new computer algorithms inspired by the workings of the immune system. This vigorous field of research investigates how immunobiology can assist our technology, and along the way is beginning to help biologists understand their unique problems.

AIS is now old enough to understand its roots, its context in the research community, and its exciting future. It has grown too big to be confined to special sessions in evolutionary computation conferences. AIS researchers are now forming their own community and identity. The International Conference on Artificial Immune Systems is proud to be the premiere conference in the area. As its organizers, we were honored to have such a variety of innovative and original scientific papers presented this year.

ICARIS 2004 was the third international conference dedicated entirely to the field of Artificial Immune Systems (AIS). It was held in Catania, on the beautiful island of Sicily, Italy, during September 13–16, 2004. While hosting the conference, the city of Catania gave the participants the opportunity to enjoy the richness of its historical and cultural atmosphere and the beauty of its natural resources, the sea, and the Etna volcano.

In comparison to the previous two AIS conferences, at ICARIS 2004 we added some new and exciting features. First, there was a tutorial day, a new track where leading scientists presented the background and the future directions of the Artificial Immune Systems discipline. In particular, four extended tutorials were presented:

- the first was an introduction to Artificial Immune Systems by Dr. J. Timmis;
- the second tutorial, delivered by Dr. Filippo Castiglione, faced the immune system and related pathologies using in silico methodologies;
- the third tutorial, by Prof. R. Callard, described the modelling of the immune system;
- the last tutorial, offered by Dr. Leandro de Castro, illustrated the emerging engineering applications of Artificial Immune Systems.

There was also a plenary lecture, delivered by Prof. Alan S. Perelson, on the current state of the art of computational and theoretical immunology.

Moreover, the organizing committee devoted a special session to the topic "Immunoinformatics", run by Dr. Darren Flower. Immunoinformatics is a new discipline that aims to apply computer science techniques to molecules of the immune system and to use bioinformatics tools for a better understanding of the immune functions.

We had more submissions than ever this year, and because our acceptance rate is based purely on quality, we were able to accept only 59% of the submitted papers. More details: 58 papers were submitted, and each one was independently reviewed by at least three members of the program committee in a blind review process. So, in these proceedings you will find the extended abstract of the plenary lecture and 34 papers written by leading scientists in the field, from 21 different countries on 4 continents, describing an impressive array of ideas, technologies and applications for AIS.

We couldn't have organized this conference without these researchers, so we thank them all for coming. We also couldn't have organized ICARIS without the excellent work of all of the program committee members, our publicity chair, Simon Garrett, our conference secretary, Jenny Oatley, and, as local organizer, Mario Pavone.

We would like to express our appreciation to the plenary lecturer who accepted our invitation, to the tutorial speakers, and to all authors who submitted research papers to ICARIS 2004.

September 2004   Giuseppe Nicosia, Vincenzo Cutello
                                      Peter J. Bentley, and Jon Timmis

Organizing Committee

Conference Chairs	Jon Timmis (University of Kent, UK)
	Peter Bentley (University College, London, UK)
Local Chairs	Giuseppe Nicosia (University of Catania, Italy)
	Vincenzo Cutello (University of Catania, Italy)
Publicity Chair	Simon Garrett (University of Wales, Aberystwyth, UK)

Program Committee

Uwe Aickelin	University of Nottingham, UK
Paolo Arena	University of Catania, Italy
Lois Boggess	Mississippi State University, USA
Filippo Castiglione	Consiglio Nazionale delle Ricerche, Italy
Steve Cayzer	Hewlett-Packard (Bristol), UK
C. Coello Coello	CINVESTAV-IPN, Mexico
Dipankar Dasgupta	University of Memphis, USA
Leandro de Castro	Catholic University of Santos (Unisantos), Brazil
Darren Flower	Edward Jenner Institute for Vaccine Research, UK
Stephanie Forrest	University of New Mexico, USA
Alex Freitas	University of Kent, UK
Alessio Gaspar	University of South Florida, USA
Fabio Gonzalez	National University of Colombia, Colombia
Emma Hart	Napier University, UK
Yoshiteru Ishida	Toyohashi University of Technology, Japan
Colin Johnson	University of Kent, UK
Jungwon Kim	King's College, London, UK
Henry Lau	University of Hong Kong, P.R. China
Doheon Lee	KAIST, Korea
Wenjian Luo	University of Science and Technology, Anhui, P.R. China
Santo Motta	University of Catania, Italy
Mark Neal	University of Wales, Aberystwyth, UK
Peter Ross	Napier University, UK
Derek Smith	University of Cambridge, UK
Susan Stepney	University of York, UK
Alexander Tarakanov	St. Petersburg Institute, Russia
Andy Tyrrell	University of York, UK
Fernando von Zuben	University of Campinas, Brazil
Andrew Watkins	University of Kent, UK
Slawomir Wierzchon	Polish Academy of Sciences, Poland

Special Session on Immunoinformatics

Darren Flower	Edward Jenner Institute for Vaccine Research, UK
Vladimir Brusic	Institute for Infocomm Research, Singapore
P. Kangueane	Nanyang Technological University, Singapore

Tutorial Speakers

Jon Timmis	University of Kent, UK
Filippo Castiglione	Consiglio Nazionale delle Ricerche, Italy
Robin Callard	Institute of Child Health, London, UK
Leandro de Castro	Catholic University of Santos (Unisantos), Brazil

Keynote Speaker

Alan S. Perelson	Los Alamos National Laboratory, USA

Sponsoring Institutions

University of Catania, Faculty of Science
The academic network ARTIST
Department of Mathematics and Computer Science, University of Catania, Italy

Table of Contents

Special Session on Immunoinformatics

Theoretical and Experimental Studies on Artificial Immune Systems (Technical Stream)

Future Applications (Conceptual Stream)

Networks (Technical Stream)

Modelling (Conceptual Stream)

Distinguishing Properties of Artificial Immune Systems (Conceptual Stream)

Negative Selection Algorithm for Aircraft Fault Detection

D. Dasgupta[1], K. KrishnaKumar[2], D. Wong, and M. Berry

[1] Division of Computer Science, University of Memphis
Memphis, TN
[2] Computational Sciences Division, NASA Ames Research Center
Moffett Field, CA

Abstract. We investigated a real-valued Negative Selection Algorithm (NSA) for fault detection in man-in-the-loop aircraft operation. The detection algorithm uses body-axes angular rate sensory data exhibiting the normal flight behavior patterns, to generate probabilistically a set of fault detectors that can detect any abnormalities (including faults and damages) in the behavior pattern of the aircraft flight. We performed experiments with datasets (collected under normal and various simulated failure conditions) using the NASA Ames man-in-the-loop high-fidelity C-17 flight simulator. The paper provides results of experiments with different datasets representing various failure conditions.

1 Introduction

Early detection of a fault or damage of aircraft subsystems is very crucial for its control and maneuver during the flight [5, 15]. These events include sudden loss of control surfaces, engine failure, and other components that may result in abnormal flight operating conditions. Monitoring and detection of such events are necessary to achieve acceptable flight performance and higher flight survivability under abnormal conditions. There are several techniques available for aircraft fault accommodation problems [2-3, 11, 13] and for fault detection and isolation issues [6, 16]. This work investigated an immunity-based approach that can detect a broad spectrum of known and unforeseen faults. The goal is to apply the immunity-based fault detection algorithm to improve the fault tolerance capabilities of the existing Intelligent Flight Controller (IFC) architecture [11, 13].

Prior studies have established the benefits of intelligent flight control [2]. However, one area of weakness that needed be strengthened was the control dead band induced by commanding a failed surface. Since the IFC approach uses fault accommodation with no detection, the dead band, although reduced over time due to learning, was present and caused degradation in handling qualities. This also makes it challenging for outer loop control design. If the failure can be identified, this dead band can further be minimized to ensure rapid fault accommodation and better handling qualities [12, 13, 15].

G. Nicosia et al. (Eds.): ICARIS 2004, LNCS 3239, pp. 1–13, 2004.

2 Real-Valued Negative Selection (RNS) Algorithm

The negative selection algorithm [9] is based on the principles of self-nonself discrimination in the immune system (Fig. 1 shows the concept of self and nonself space). This negative selection algorithm can be summarized as follows (adopted from [7]):

- Define self as a collection S of elements in a feature space U, a collection that needs to be monitored. For instance, if U corresponds to the space of states of a system represented by a list of features, S can represent the subset of states that are considered as normal for the system.
- Generate a set F of *detectors*, each of which fails to match any string in S. An approach that mimics the immune system generates random detectors and discards those that match any element in the self set. However, a more efficient approach [8] tries to minimize the number of generated detectors while maximizing the covering of the nonself space.
- Monitor S for changes by continually matching the detectors in F against S. If any detector ever matches, then a change is known to have occurred, as the detectors are designed not to match any representative samples of S.

The above description is very general and does not say anything about the representation of the problem space and the type of *matching* rule is used. It is, however, clear that the algorithmic complexity of generating good detectors can vary significantly, which depends on the type of problem space (continuous, discrete, mixed, etc.), detector representation scheme, and the rule that determines if a detector *matches* an element or not. Most of the research works on the NS algorithm have been restricted to the binary matching rules like r-contiguous [9]. The primary reason for this choice is ease of use, and there exist efficient algorithms to generate detectors, exploiting the simplicity of the binary representation and its *matching* rules [8]. However, the scalability issue has prevented it from being applied more extensively.

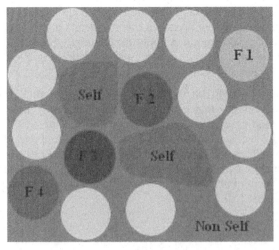

Fig. 1. The figure illustrates the concept of self and nonself in a feature space. Here F1, F2, etc. indicate different fault conditions represented by detectors.

We adopted a real-valued NS (RNS) algorithm, which tries to alleviate the limitations previously mentioned, while using the structure of the higher-level-representation to speed up the detector generation process. The real-valued NS algorithm applies a heuristic process that changes iteratively the position of the detectors driven by two goals: to maximize the coverage of the nonself subspace and to minimize the coverage of the self samples.

2.1 Details of the RNS Algorithm –Detector Generation Phase

The RNS detector generation starts with a population of candidate detectors, which are then matured through an iterative process. In particular, the center of each detector is chosen at random and the radius is a variable parameter which determines the size (in m-dimensional space) of the detector. The basic algorithmic steps of the RNS detector generation algorithm are given in Fig. 2, and some computational details of are illustrated in Figs. 3(a)-(d).

At each iteration, first, the radius of each candidate detector is calculated, and the ones that fall inside self region are moved (i.e. its center is successively adjusted by moving it away from training data and existing detectors). The set of nonself detectors are then stored and ranked according to their size (radius). The detectors with larger

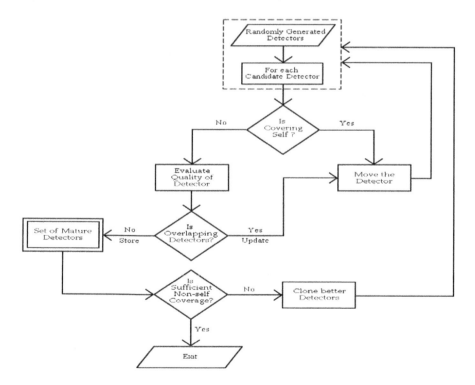

Fig. 2. Flow diagram showing the algorithmic steps for the real-valued negative selection algorithm.

radii (and smaller overlap with other detectors) are considered as better-fit and selected to go to the next generation. Detectors with very small radii, however, are replaced by the clones of better-fit detectors. The clones of a selected detector are
moved at a fixed distance in order to produce new detectors in its close proximity.
Moreover, new areas of the nonself space are explored by introducing some random
detectors. The whole detector generation process terminates when a set of mature
(minimum overlapping) detectors are evolved which can provide significant coverage
of the nonself space.

The purpose of the fault detection is to identify which states of a system are normal
(self) and which are faulty. The states of a system are represented by a set of control
variables which can exhibit the current and past system behavior. The actual values of
these variables are scaled or normalized in the range [0.0, 1.0] in order to define the
self-nonself space with a unit hypercube.

A detector is defined as $d = (c, r_d)$, where $c = (c_1, c_2,..., c_m)$ is an m-dimensional
point that corresponds to the center of a unit hypersphere with r_d as its radius. The
following parameters are used for the detector generation process:

r_s: threshold value (allowable variation) of a self point; in other words, a point at a
distance greater than or equal to r_s from a self sample is considered to be abnormal.

α: variable parameter to specify the movement of a detector away from a self sample or existing detectors.

ξ: maximum allowable overlap among the detectors, which implicates that allowing some overlap among detectors can reduce holes in the nonself coverage.

2.1.1   Calculating the detector radius: We used the *Minkowski distance* to measure
the distance *(D)* between two points x and y, which is defined as

$$D(x, y) = \left(\sum |x_i - y_i|^\lambda\right)^{1/\lambda}$$

where $x = \{ x_0, x_1,... x_{N-1}\}$ and $y = \{ y_0, y_1,... y_{N-1}\}$. The *Minkowski* distance with λ
$= 2$ is equivalent to *Euclidean Distance*.

This approach allows having variable size detectors to cover the nonself space. As
shown in Fig. 3(a), if the distance between a candidate detector, $d = (c, r_d)$ and its
nearest self point in the training dataset is D, then the detector radius is considered as
$r_d = (D - r_s)$. However, if a detector is close to any edge of the hypercube and has a
large radius, then only a portion of it is inside the space, and such a detector is referred to as an *edge* detector. If the value $r_d = (D - r_s)$ is *negative* then it falls inside the
self (radius); and this detector is expected to be discarded or moved in subsequent
iteration.

2.1.2   Moving detectors: Let $d = (c, r_d)$ represents a candidate detector and $d^{nearest} =$
$(c^{nearest}, r_d^{nearest})$ is its nearest detector (or a self point), then the center of d is moved
such that

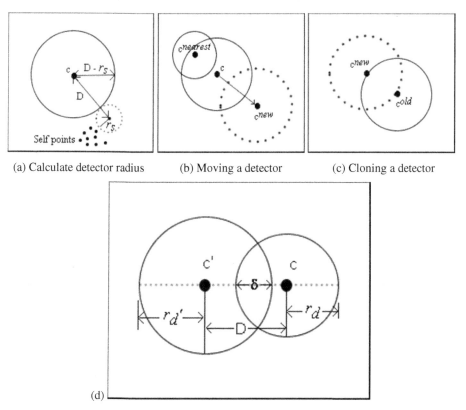

(a) Calculate detector radius   (b) Moving a detector   (c) Cloning a detector

(d)

Fig. 3. Illustrate different computational steps used during the detector maturation process. (a) Shows a way to calculate and update the radius of a detector (b) If a candidate detector overlaps with an existing detector (or self points), then the candidate detector (i.e. its center, c) is moved in the opposite direction to its nearest neighbor detector; (c) Given a mature detector, a clone is created at a distance equal to its radius, and the direction where it is created is selected at random. (d) The overlap between two detectors d and d' is computed in terms of the distance (D) between their centres (c, c') and radii (r_d, r_d').

$$ c^{new} = c + \alpha \frac{dir}{\left\| dir \right\|}, $$

where $dir = c - c^{nearest}$, and $\|\cdot\|$ denotes the norm of a m-dimensional vector (Fig. 3(b)). Accordingly, if a detector overlaps significantly with any other existing detectors, then it is also moved away from its nearest neighbor detector. In order to guarantee the convergence of this process, an exponential decay function is used for the moving parameter (α).

2.1.3   Detector Cloning and Random Exploration: At every generation, a few better-fitted detectors are chosen to be cloned. Specifically, let $d = (c^{old}, r_d^{old})$ be a detector to be cloned and, say $d^{clon} = (c^{clon}, r_d^{clon})$, is a cloned detector whose center is located at a distance r_d^{old} from d and whose radius is the same as that of the detector, d. Accordingly, the center of d^{clon} is computed as

$$c^{clon} = c^{old} + r_d^{old} \frac{dir}{\left\| dir \right\|}$$

$dir = c^{old} - c^{nearest}$ (see Fig. 3(c)), and where $c^{nearest}$ is the center of d's nearest detector.

In addition, a few less-fit detectors are replaced by random detectors at each generation. This process allows the exploration of new regions of the nonself space, which may need to be covered.

2.1.4   Evaluation of nonself detectors: Detectors which do not fall in the self region are sorted according to their size. A detector with large radius gets selected for the next generation population, if it has small overlap with existing detectors i.e. less than an overlapping threshold (ξ).

Accordingly, the overlapping measure W of a detector is computed as the sum of its overlap with all other detectors as follows,

$$W(d) = \sum_{d \neq d'} w(d, d'),$$

where $w(d, d')$ is the measured overlap between two detectors $d = (c, r_d)$ and $d' = (c, r_d')$; and is defined by $w(d, d') = \left(\exp(\delta) - 1 \right)^m$, m is the dimension of the feature space,

$$\text{and } \delta = \left(\frac{r_d + r_d' - D}{2 r_d} \right)$$

The value of δ is considered to be bounded between 0 and 1; and D is the distance between two detector centers c and c' as shown in Fig. 3(d). This overlapping measure seems to favor the detectors with bigger radii, i.e. detectors having larger coverage of the nonself space with minimum overlap among them. Accordingly, the closer the center of two detectors is, the higher the value of the overlapping measure $w(d, d')$.

2.2   Testing Phase: Detection Process

The detection process is straightforward -- the matured detectors are continually examined with new samples in test datasets. For example, the distance between a sample pattern, $p = (c_p, r_s)$ and a detector, $d = (c, r_d)$ is computed as $D(c_p, c)$, where $D(c_p, c)$ is the distance between the sample pattern and the detector calculated in the same way as in the detector generation phase. If the distance, $D < (r_s + r_d)$ then the detector d gets activated indicating possible fault.

3 Fault Detection in Aircraft Operation

There are many applications where the aircraft behavior monitoring for indicating flight subsystem fault/damage, detection of changes (in trends) in the operating condition, etc. appears to be very useful [12]. We used a C-17 man-in-the-loop simulation data for this study.

An aircraft typically has many dedicated primary and secondary control surfaces to maneuver the aircraft through space. In modern fly-by-wire aircraft, the pilot commands angular rates of the aircraft using a side stick device. Speed and altitude control is mostly achieved using auto pilot settings chosen by the pilot. The C-17 aircraft, in addition to four engines, has a stabilizer, four elevators, two ailerons, eight spoiler panels, four flap sections, and two rudders for control. In the figure shown below, the pilot stick commands are shaped by a reference model to generate body-axes roll, pitch, and yaw acceleration commands to the NASA Ames developed Intelligent Flight Controller [11, 13]. The sensory feedback to the controller includes the body-axes angular rates, airspeed, altitude, and angle-of-attack. An error vector, computed using the difference between commanded and sensed body-axes angular rates, is used to drive the intelligent flight controller. For this study, data generated through piloted simulation studies using the C-17 simulator are used.

We experimented with different detector generator schemes for real-valued negative selection algorithm for better detection of different faults. This fault detection system takes real-valued data set as input; extracts the important semantic information by applying data fusion and normalization techniques. The reduced information is then represented as a collection of strings, which forms the self set (normal patterns) that can be used to generate a diverse set of detectors. The set of detectors are subsequently used for detection of different type of faults (known and unknown faults). The aim is to find a small number of specialized detectors (as signature of known failure conditions) and a bigger set of generalized detectors for unknown (or possible) fault conditions. The output of the fault detection system will be provided to IFC for isolating the faulty control surface.

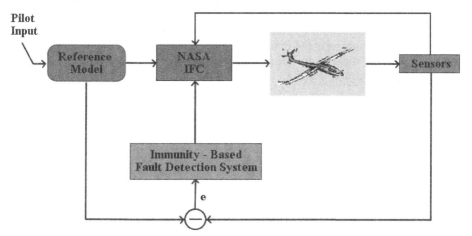

Fig. 4. The block diagram showing the integration of immunity-based Fault detection system and intelligent flight control (IFC) system.

4 Experiments and Results

The data from the simulator is collected at the rate of 30 Hz per second. Since the data is from man-in-the–loop simulation, there is an extra control (the human pilot) that simply cannot be removed from the data. We considered three sets of in-flight sensory information—namely, body-axes roll rate, pitch rate and yaw rate—to detect five different simulated faults. The error rates are measured from the desired output of the reference model and the actual sensed output (as shown in Fig. 4).

The training data set was created by taking all of the data until the moment of the failure. For both cases, this is a different amount of time which varies between 2-3 seconds. The test data were generated by windowing the data 1.5 seconds before and 1.5 seconds after the failure. As a result, the "normal" part of the test data looks similar to the training data for each case. It is to be noted that some of the entries are zero at the beginning of the data set, because the pilot has likely not entered a command to maneuver by then, and the aircraft would still be flying straight and level.

4.1 Preprocessing Data

First, data are normalized where the actual values of the variables are scaled or normalized to fit a defined range [0.0, 1.0] using the maximum and minimum (+/- 20% to normal data) value of each dimension in the data set. Any value above and below the defined *max* and *min* is considered as *1* and *0*, respectively. Data window shift—shifts the data based on the window shifting and data overlapping parameters. In these experiments, K-mean clustering is used to reduce the training dataset to improve the time complexity of the detector generation process.

4.2 Detector Generation Phase

The RNS algorithm takes as input a set of hyper-spherical detectors randomly distributed in the self/nonself space. The algorithm applies a heuristic process that changes iteratively the position of the detectors driven by the objective to maximize the coverage of the nonself subspace and to minimize their overlap, while not covering the self samples. The flow diagram for the proposed detector generation algorithm (RNS) is given in previous section (Fig. 2).

The aim is to find a small number of specialized detectors (as signature of known fault conditions) and other generalized detectors for unknown (or possible) fault conditions.

4.3 Testing Phase

After generating the detectors, the next step is to examine the effectiveness of detectors in identifying various faults. We used the same preprocessing steps and distance measure during the testing phase as was used in generating detectors. If a detector gets activated with current pattern, a change in the behavior pattern is known to have occurred and an alarm signal is generated regarding the fault. In particular,

- For each fault condition: Combine all (or as many as possible) activated detectors to form a small set of *specialized* fault detectors that can be *labelled* with specific fault type.

- For rest of the detectors: Use clustering method to form different clusters with cluster centre and radius of the cluster to be labelled as *probable (or possible)* fault detectors

Some of the generalized detectors can be used for detecting simulated faults during the testing phase, however, others may be considered as being useless and discarded. It is expected that a limited number of detector generated by NSA (initially) may not be sufficient to cover the entire space, so it may be necessary to change the number, their distribution and resolution in nonself space to provide system and condition specific fault detection capabilities.

4.4 Results

The sensor parameters considered for these experiments include body-axes roll angle rate, pitch rate and yaw rate, where both expected and observed values are monitored and error rate (e) is calculated. If these error rates are abnormal, the NS fault detection algorithm should detect them indicating possible failures. The following graphs illustrate results of experiments with different failure conditions.

Fig. 5 shows the error rate(e) for three sensory inputs that are considered as the normal operating conditions, and used to generate the detector set. Fig. 6 illustrates the performance of the detection system when tested with wing fault data, where this type of fault is manifested in roll error rate (starting at 300 time step). The graph also shows the number of detectors activated (upper bar chart) as significant deviations in data patterns appear. Fig. 7 displays similar results for the tail failure. It is to be noted that simulation data that have a full tail failure, show up first in the pitch axis as the pitch axis has very little coupling with the roll and yaw axes.

As this detector generation algorithm generates variably sized detectors to cover spaces within and outside self regions, Fig. 8 gives the number of detectors with different sizes in a typical run. In this case, more number of detectors is generated with radii ranging between 0.25-0.3. However, some of the detectors with larger radii are edge detectors, partially covering the nonself space.

Table 1 gives the statistical results of 10 runs for two different faults—tail and wing damage. Here the number of detector generated is 368; when tested on two faulty data sets, the detection rates of 89% and 92% are observed with relatively small false alarm rates.

Figure 9 shows the number of detectors activated for five different faults. We observed that a good number of detectors get activated in each fault case. There appears to be three possible reasons: first, because of allowing some overlap among detectors; second, faulty data may be clustered at several locations in the nonself space, and third, the same detectors may be activated for more than one fault cases. Figure 10 shows different false alarm rates with the change in number of detectors. It indicates that the false positive rate reduces as number of detectors increases; moreover, the increase in false negative is insignificantly small (up to 1.4%) at the same time.

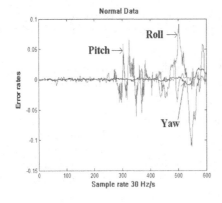

Fig. 5. Show error rates for three sensory inputs (roll, pitch and yaw) that are considered as the normal data pattern.

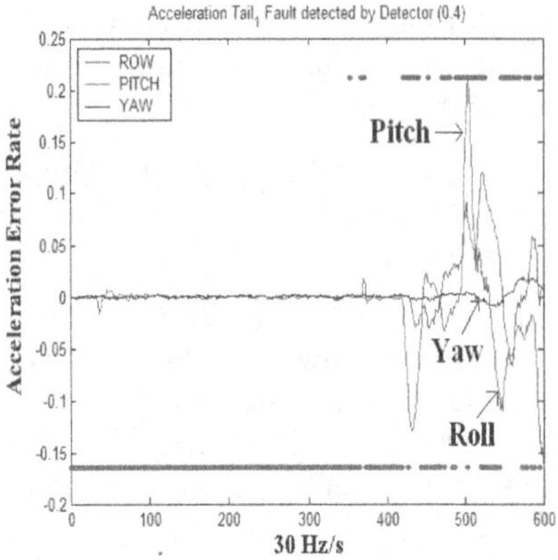

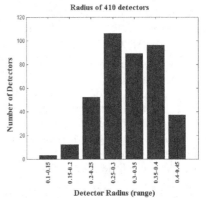

Fig. 6. Show the detection of a wing failure with number of activated detectors.

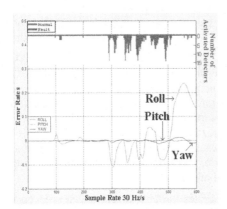

Fig. 7. Test results indicating the detection of Tail 1 failure.

Fig. 8. Indicates different sized detectors that are generated in a typical run.

Table 1. Table shows some statistics of testing two different faults (tail and wing failure).

Type of Faults	Performance			
	Detection date		False alarm rate	
	Mean	S.D.	Mean	S.D
Tail	89%	1.43	0.87%	0.45
Wing	92%	1.67	0.98%	0.32

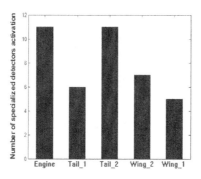

Fig. 9. Average number of detectors activated for each fault tested.

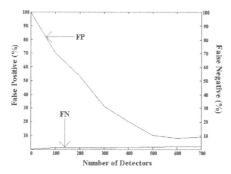

Fig. 10. Shows the false alarm rates (both false positive and false negative) with change in number of detectors.

5   Conclusions

There exist many techniques for aircraft failure detection [2-3,5-6,13,15]. One of the drawbacks of existing fault detection and isolation (FDI) based approaches is that they cannot detect unexpected and unknown fault types. The immunity-based approaches have been used in many applications including fault detection [1, 4, 17, 19, 20], anomaly detection [14, 18], etc. We investigated a real-valued negative selection algorithm that could detect a broad spectrum of known and unforeseen faults. In this work, once the fault is detected and identified, a direct adaptive control system would use this detection information to stabilize the aircraft by utilizing available resources (control surfaces). The proposed intelligent fault detection algorithm is inspired by the principles of the biological immune system. This fault detection algorithm is a probabilistic approach (motivated by the negative selection mechanism of the immune system) in order to detect deviations in aircraft flight behavior patterns. In particular, the detection system learns the knowledge of the normal flight patterns from sensory data, to generate probabilistically a set of (novel) pattern detectors that can detect any abnormalities (including faults) in the behavior pattern of the aircraft flight.

In summary, the proposed method works as follows:

Based on the dataset (given) of normal operating conditions, generate a set of fault detectors; the goal is, however, to evolve 'good' detectors that cover the nonself space.
- A 'good' detector:
  - o   It must not cover self space.
  - o   It has to be as general as possible: the larger the volume, the better.
- One detector may not be enough; instead, a set of detectors is required that can collectively cover the nonself space with minimum overlap.

During the testing phase, we used the data collected during different fault conditions:
- Detectors that get activated (match) for each fault are labeled as specific fault detectors. These constitute a set of specialized detectors for identifying different class of faults.
- It may be necessary to go through the detector optimization process: filter out some overlapping detectors, and merge some and generating new ones for better coverage.

Some faulty conditions can be simulated (by changing some crucial, monitored parameters) in order to check which generalized detectors get activated. These detectors can also provide the knowledge of possible (unknown) faults. The goal is to achieve a certain level of damage control under any known fault or unknown abnormalities.

The long-term goal is to use NSA to detect control surface area loss caused by damage (or failure) and other causes that may result in the departure of the aircraft from safe flight conditions. Once the failure is detected and identified, the Intelligent Flight Controller (IFC) then utilizes all remaining source of control power necessary to achieve the desired flight performance.

References

1.   M. Araujo, J. Aguilar and H. Aponte. *Fault detection system in gas lift well based on Artificial Immune System.* In the proceedings of the International Joint Conference on AI, pp. 1673 -1677, No. 3, July 20 - 24, 2003.
2.   Jovan D. Boskovic and Raman K. Mehra. *Intelligent Adaptive Control of a Tailless Advanced Fighter Aircraft under Wing Damage.* In Journal of Guidance, Control, and Dynamics (American Institute of Aeronautics and Astronautics), Volume: 23 Number: 5 Pages: 876-884, 2000
3.   Jovan D. Boskovic and Raman K. Mehra. *Multiple-Model Adaptive Flight Control Scheme for Accommodation of Actuator Failures.* In Journal of Guidance, Control, and Dynamics (American Institute of Aeronautics and Astronautics), Volume: 25 Number: 4 Pages: 712-724, 2002.
4.   D. Bradley and A. Tyrrell. Hardware Fault Tolerance: An Immunological Solution. In the proceedings of IEEE International Conference on Systems, Man and Cybernetics (SMC), Nashville, October 8-11, 2000.
5.   Joseph S. Brinker and Kevin A. Wise. *Flight Testing of Reconfigurable Control Law on the X-36 Tailless Aircraft.* In Journal of Guidance, Control, and Dynamics (American Institute of Aeronautics and Astronautics), Volume: 24, Number: 5 Pages: 903-909, 2001.

6. Y.M. Chen and M.L. Lee. *Neural networks-based scheme for system failure detection and diagnosis.* In Mathematics and Computers in Simulation (Elsevier Science), Volume: 58 Number: 2 Pages: 101-109, 2002.

7. D. Dasgupta, S. Forrest. *An anomaly detection algorithm inspired by the immune system.* In: Dasgupta D (eds) Artificial Immune Systems and Their Applications, Springer-Verlag, pp.262–277, 1999.

8. P. D'haeseleer, S. Forrest, and P. Helman. *An immunological approach to change detection: algorithms, analysis, and implications.* In Proceedings of the IEEE Symposium on Computer Security and Privacy, IEEE Computer Society Press, Los Alamitos, CA, pp. 110–119, 1996.

9. S Forrest, A. S. Perelson, L. Allen, and R. Cherukuri. *Self-nonself discrimination in a computer.* In Proc. of the IEEE Symposium on Research in Security and Privacy, IEEE Computer Society Press, Los Alamitos, CA, pp. 202–212, 1994.

10. F. Gonzales and D. Dasgupta. *Anomaly Detection Using Real-Valued Negative Selection.* In Genetic Programming and Evolvable Machines, 4, pp.383-403, 2003.

11. Karen Gundy-Burlet, K. Krishnakumar, Greg Limes and Don Bryant. *Control Reallocation Strategies for Damage Adaptation in Transport Class Aircraft.* In AIAA 2003-5642, August, 2003.

12. K. KrishnaKumar. *Artificial Immune System Approaches for Aerospace Applications.* American Institute of Aeronautics and Astronautics 41st Aerospace Sciences Meeting and Exhibit, Reno, Nevada, 6-9 January 2003.

13. K. KrishnaKumar, G. Limes, K. Gundy-Burlet, D. Bryant. *An Adaptive Critic Approach to Reference Model Adaptation.* In AIAA GN&C Conf. 2003.

14. F. Niño, D. Gómez, and R. Vejar. *A Novel Immune Anomaly Detection Technique Based on Negative Selection.* In the proceedings of the Genetic and Evolutionary Computation Conference (GECCO) [Poster], Chicago, IL, USA, LNCS 2723, p. 243, July 12-16, 2003.

15. Meir Pachter and Yih-Shiun Huang. *Fault Tolerant Flight Control.* In Journal of Guidance, Control, and Dynamics (American Institute of Aeronautics and Astronautics), Volume: 26 Number: 1 Pages: 151-160, 2003.

16. Rolf T. Rysdyk and Anthony J. Calise, Fault *Tolerant Flight Control via Adaptive Neural Network Augmentation,* AIAA 98-4483, August 1998.

17. Liu Shulin, Zhang Jiazhong, Shi Wengang, Huang Wenhu. *Negative-selection algorithm based approach for fault diagnosis of rotary machinery.* In the Proceedings of American Control Conference, 2002, Vol. 5, pp. 3955 -3960. 8-10 May 8-10, 2002.

18. S. Singh. *Anomaly detection using negative selection based on the r-contiguous matching rule.* In 1st International Conference on Artificial Immune Systems (ICARIS), University of Kent at Canterbury, UK, September 9-11, 2002.

19. Dan W Taylor and David W Corne. *An Investigation of the Negative Selection Algorithm for Fault Detection in Refrigeration Systems.* In the Proceeding of Second International Conference on Artificial Immune Systems (ICARIS), Napier University, Edinburgh, UK, September 1-3, 2003.

20. S. Xanthakis, S. Karapoulios, R. Pajot and A. Rozz. *Immune System and Fault Tolerant Computing.* In J.M. Alliot, editor, Artificial Evolution, volume 1063 of Lecture Notes in Computer Science, pages 181-197. Springer-Verlag, 1996.

A Hierarchical Immune Network
Applied to Gene Expression Data

George B. Bezerra[1], Leandro N. de Castro[1,2], and Fernando J. Von Zuben[1]

[1] Department of Computation and Industrial Automation, State University of Campinas
Unicamp, CP: 6101, 13083-970, Campinas/SP, Brazil
{bezerra,lnunes,vonzuben}@dca.fee.unicamp.br
[2] Graduate Program on Informatics, Catholic University of Santos
COPOP, R. Dr. Carvalho de Mendonça, 144, Vila Mathias, Santos/SP, Brasil
lnunes@unisantos.br

Abstract. This paper describes a new proposal for gene expression data analysis. The method used is based on a hierarchical approach to a hybrid algorithm, which is composed of an artificial immune system, named aiNet, and a well known graph theoretic tool, the minimal spanning tree (MST). This algorithm has already proved to be efficient for clustering gene expression data, but its performance may decrease in some specific cases. However, through the use of a hierarchical approach of immune networks it is possible to improve the clustering capability of the hybrid algorithm, such that it becomes more efficient, even when the data set is complex. The proposed methodology is applied to the yeast data and gives important conclusions of the similarity relationships among genes within the data set.

1 Introduction

The development of the DNA Microarray technique [11] has revolutionized the studies in functional genomics. By making it possible to measure the expression level of thousands of genes simultaneously, the DNA Microarrays provide resources for a more complete investigation about the role of the genes in the metabolic processes of an organism. The expression levels of a gene consist of indirect measures of the quantity of proteins it is producing, thus giving an indication of the biological state of the cell. Through the analysis of the expression data it is possible:
1. to determine the functional role of several genes;
2. to study the way the expression levels reflect processes of interest (such as the case of diseases);
3. to evaluate the effects of experimental treatments; and
4. to design tools for diagnosis based on the regularity of the expression patterns.

The microarray experiments usually produce very large quantities of gene expression data, thus making impracticable for any specialist to perform data inspection in a visual and intuitive manner. In order to perform knowledge extraction, a fundamental step in the analysis consists of identifying groups of genes that manifest similar expression profiles. In this way, it is possible to explore the inherent structure of the

G. Nicosia et al. (Eds.): ICARIS 2004, LNCS 3239, pp. 14–27, 2004.
© Springer-Verlag Berlin Heidelberg 2004

data, thus discovering possible correlations among genes and revealing hidden patterns. This problem is commonly known as gene expression data clustering, and it has already been treated by several different techniques, such as hierarchical clustering [6], self-organizing maps (SOM) [8], principal component analysis (PCA) [13] and k-means clustering [10].

To perform knowledge extraction of the expression data, we proposed the use of a hybrid algorithm, which is a combination of an artificial immune system (aiNet – Artificial Immune NETwork) and a tool from graph theory (Minimal Spanning Tree – MST) [1]. This algorithm has proved to be efficient in solving some benchmark clustering problems, obtaining in some cases betters results than other approaches more common in the literature, like SOM and hierarchical clustering [3]. However, in cases where the number of clusters is high and their shapes are arbitrary (this is frequently found in gene expression data), the proposed approach may still present good results, but may not be capable of solving the whole problem in a single run for a given set of user-defined adaptive parameters.

Some preliminary studies demonstrated that by using the hybrid algorithm in a hierarchical form it is possible to generate trees of immune networks capable of detecting clusters with arbitrary data distribution [2]. This method enhances the clustering capability of the hybrid algorithm, such that meaningful sub-clusters can be detected within a previously defined cluster. It has also been found that this approach alleviates the problem of setting up the initial values for some user-defined learning parameters.

This paper focuses on the use of a hierarchical approach that enhances the clustering capability of the hybrid algorithm, thus providing a useful tool for gene expression data analysis. This work is an extension of the works presented in [1] and [2].

The paper is organized as follows. Section 2 provides a description of the hybrid algorithm and discusses its operation. Section 3 refers to materials and methods, including gene expression data specification, similarity metrics used and parameter adjustment. In Section 4 the hybrid algorithm is applied to part of the data set without the hierarchical procedure. Section 5 describes the hierarchical methodology and discusses some modifications proposed by the authors. The final computational tests are presented in Section 6, where the hierarchical approach is applied to gene expression data, and the obtained results are discussed. The paper is concluded in Section 7 with some general comments and future trends.

2 The Hybrid Algorithm

The hybrid algorithm has two main stages in the clustering process. The first one consists of applying the aiNet, an immune inspired algorithm introduced by de Castro and Von Zuben [3,5], to the whole gene expression data. In this first step, the raw data set is explored and compressed by the aiNet, generating an antibody network that extracts the most relevant information contained in the data for clustering tasks. In the second step of the analysis, the MST is built on the resultant antibody network, and its inconsistent edges are then identified and removed, thus performing the network (data) separation into clusters. In this step, we use a special criterion that takes into account the relative density of points in the space to determine the edges of the tree to be pruned [14].

In other words, the aiNet representation introduces robustness to noise and reduces the redundancy of the data set, while the MST explores the inherent structure of the data points, detecting clusters that are continuous regions of the space containing a relatively high density of points. Clusters described in this way are referred to as natural clusters [7].

The combination of the properties presented by aiNet and the MST makes the hybrid algorithm a versatile clustering tool, even when the data set is complex, as in the case of gene expression data. A full and detailed description of the algorithm can be found in [3,5].

3   Materials and Methods

3.1   Gene Expression Data Set

The complete data set to be used in this work is composed of the expression levels of 2467 genes of the budding yeast *Saccharomyces cerevisiae*. The expression levels were measured in 8 different processes that totalize 79 experimental conditions. The values in the data table correspond to the transformed (log base 2) fluorescence ratio Cy5/Cy3. Due to difficulties in measuring, some values in the table are missing. The data was obtained from [6] and is available online at http://rana.lbl.gov/.

For the computational analysis, 9 out of the 10 clusters previously detected in [6] were chosen to be used. These clusters contain functionally related genes and they are B (spindle pole body assembly and function), C (proteasome), D (mRNA splicing), E (glycolysis), F (mitochondrial ribossome), G (ATP synthesis), H (chromatin structure), J (DNA replication), K (tricarboxylic), totalizing 135 genes. Table 1 shows the number of genes contained in each of them. These clusters are a benchmark data, and were already used by other authors, as in [12].

Table 1. Number of genes within each cluster

Cluster	B	C	D	E	F	G	H	J	K
Genes	11	27	14	17	22	15	8	5	16

The absent cluster, I, was not used because its genes were not specified in [6]. The fact of having previously known clusters is useful to evaluate the performance of the proposed technique and to make comparisons with other methods. However, the data is presented to the algorithm without their labels.

3.2   Similarity Metrics

The similarity metric used was the correlation coefficient [6]. Thus, those genes with similar behavior in parallel are privileged, not giving emphasis to the magnitude of the values. This is different of the Euclidean Distance, which takes into account the magnitudes. Let G_i be the expression level of gene G in experiment i. For two genes X_i and Y_i, the similarity measure S_i in a total of N experiments can be computed as follows:

$$S(X,Y) = \frac{1}{N} \sum_{i=1}^{N} \left(\frac{X_i - X_{offset}}{\Phi_X} \right) \left(\frac{Y_i - Y_{offset}}{\Phi_Y} \right) \tag{1}$$

where,

$$\Phi_G = \sqrt{\sum_{i=1}^{N} \frac{(G_i - G_{offset})^2}{N}} \quad , \ G \in \{X,Y\} \tag{2}$$

The value G_{offset} was chosen zero in all cases [6]. Missing values were omitted in the calculation of the similarity, and for these cases, N corresponds to the number of experiments that are actually included in the table.

As the aiNet algorithm was implemented to work with distances (dissimilarity metric), the following equation was used for the calculation of the distance D between two genes [12]:

$$D(X,Y) = 1 - S(X,Y) \tag{3}$$

Therefore, the maximum value for the similarity corresponds to distance zero.

3.3   Setup of Parameters for aiNet

The initial population of antibodies was generated by a random reordering of the elements in each column of the expression matrix (genes and its coordinates), rather than simply generating random numbers. Thus, a number of initial antibodies equals to the number of genes is created and these antibodies will then compete for the representation of the input data through the interactions of the aiNet algorithm. This was done to create an initial approximation between the network antibodies and the training data set, thus imposing some previous knowledge to the network.

The aiNet has some parameters to be defined in order to run the algorithm. Table 2 shows the combination of parameters used. These were obtained after some preliminary tests with the algorithm, though no exhaustive search of parameters or sensitivity analysis was performed. The reader interested in the aiNet sensitivity to the tuning parameters should refer to [5]. However, it is important to stress that most of these parameters assume their default values suggested in [5], such as n = 4, qi = 0.2, and N = 10. The main parameter that required tuning was σ_s, and some comments about how it influences the performance of the algorithm will be provided later.

Table 2. Values used for the aiNet parameters

Parameter	Value	
N	4	Number of antibodies selected to be cloned
It	20	Number of iterations
qi	0.2	Percentage of mature antibodies to be selected
σ_p	0.035	Natural death threshold
σ_s	0.01	Suppression threshold (initial value)

4   Computational Analysis with the Hybrid Algorithm

To demonstrate the potential of the proposed method, the hybrid algorithm was applied to part of the yeast gene expression data. The analysis was divided in two steps.
First, the MST was built directly on the raw data, rather than on the antibody network.
This was done to test the efficiency of the proposed criterion in the identification and
removal of the inconsistent edges of the tree. After that, the whole hybrid algorithm is
applied to the same data set, i.e., the aiNet preprocessing procedure is executed and
the MST is built on the resulting immune network.

In this part of the computational analysis only clusters C, E, F and H were used as
input data. The reason for this choice is to make a comparison with another method in
the literature that also uses the MST for gene expression data clustering [12]. In that
approach only these four clusters were analyzed.

The results obtained in this analysis are described in detail in [1]. In the first part of
the computational tests the MST was capable of correctly detecting the inherent inconsistencies that separate the four clusters, thus demonstrating the efficiency of the
proposed criterion for cutting the edges of the tree. However, the MST detected other
two inherent divisions in the data, giving origin to six clusters, rather than four. This
result is probably due to the noise present in the data set, to which the MST was susceptible.

The second step of the analysis came up with an interesting result. When the hybrid algorithm was applied to the same data, the four clusters were correctly identified, and the two extra inherent divisions detected by the MST were not there any-
more. These tests have shown that the data compression performed by the aiNet is
crucial for reducing the noise in the data, leading to better results of the technique.
The aiNet pre-processing is thus a fundamental step in more complex analyses as
well, mainly when the data sets are very large and have high levels of noise and redundancy. This is usually the case with bioinformatics data.

5   Hierarchy of Immune Networks

This section describes a methodology for a hierarchical approach using the hybrid
algorithm. Section 5.1 describes and discusses the original proposal of an algorithm
for the hierarchical analysis of aiNet and Section 5.2 presents some modifications on
the original algorithm proposed by the authors.

5.1   The Proposed Methodology

Though being sometimes superior to other techniques commonly applied to bioinformatics data sets, like self-organizing maps and hierarchical clustering, the hybrid
algorithm is not capable of solving the entire problem in a single run, particularly
when the number of clusters is very high and they present arbitrary data distribution.
This situation is faced when trying to apply the hybrid algorithm to all the 9 clusters
of the yeast data set. Finding the whole set of clusters is difficult, and may be very
time consuming.

In some preliminary studies [2] it was demonstrated that through a hierarchical approach it is possible to generate trees of immune networks capable of detecting clusters with arbitrary data distribution. The algorithm for this hierarchical approach is described in Algorithm 1.

Algorithm 1. Hierarchical procedure for data clustering.

1. *Parameter definition*: define the initial values for the relevant aiNet parameters σ_s (suppression threshold) and r (inconsistency ratio), and set up a decaying rate $0<\alpha<1$ for these parameters;
2. *aiNet learning*: run the aiNet learning algorithm with the given parameters.
3. *Tree branching*: each cluster detected by the MST constructed from the resultant aiNet generates an offspring aiNet in the next level of the tree, i.e., a new branch of the tree. The clusters already detected will indicate the portion of the data set to be attributed to each newly-generated branch;
4. *Parameters' updating*: reduce σ_s and r, e.g. by geometrically decreasing them by the factor α. If σ_s reaches $\sigma_{s(\min)}$, then go to step 6;
5. *Offspring network evaluation*: run each offspring network with the corresponding attributed portion of the data set;
6. *Tree convergence*: if the offspring network does not detect a novel cluster, the process is halted for that branch of the tree, and the tree expansion is completed at that branch. Each branch of the tree represents a cluster and a sequence of branches represents the hierarchy inherent to the data mapped into their corresponding clusters. Else, while a given offspring network (branch) of the tree is still capable of identifying more than one cluster, return to Step 4 and the process continues until no new cluster can be identified in any active branch.

The inconsistency ratio r cited in the first step of Algorithm 1 is the maximum ratio allowed between the length of a given edge and the sum of the lengths of the nearby edges on both sides of the selected edge of the MST.

The above algorithm can be described as follows. After the parameters have been defined, the aiNet is run with the whole input data set, and a first network is generated, named the *root network*. This network is a simplified representation, or internal image, of the input data, and it is responsible for detecting portions of the space relevant to clustering. Then the MST is built on this network, and after the cutting criterion is applied, some clusters will be identified. Each cluster detected in this step will further give origin to a novel network in a second level of the hierarchy. In the next step, the aiNet parameters σ_s (suppression threshold) and r (inconsistency ratio) are reduced by the factor α. The reduced suppression threshold makes the newly-generated aiNet to represent the attributed portion of the data set more accurately, thus forcing the antibodies to better match the antigens (data). With this more accurate representation, the aiNet discovers new portions of the data that may reveal clusters. By the reduction of the inconsistency ratio, the algorithm makes use of a more redundant representation to try to detect less apparent divisions in the data. The next step is to run the aiNet on each one of the detected clusters, generating sub-networks in which novel branched clusters may be found. This procedure continues until no more clusters are detected.

This methodology adapts to data sets presenting very complex and diverse characteristics, like those with lots of clusters with different density and irregular boundaries. In this kind of data, some clusters are easier to be detected by the hybrid algorithm, but others may need a fine tuning on the parameters (mainly on the suppression threshold) to be identified and removed. In general, suppression thresholds with high values detect more rough clusters, usually separating the data into large clusters. It is important to stress that these clusters are not always easy to detect. They may be masked by the noise and redundancy present in the data. However, by using high thresholds, the data representation assumes a robust form, thus revealing large classes, if they are present, within the data set.

Therefore, it becomes necessary to dynamically test several values of suppression thresholds on the same data set in order to determine the most significant clusters. This can be performed by iteratively applying the hybrid algorithm to the data for different levels of σ_s. However, the algorithm would have to be executed too many times and this would be very computationally expensive, mainly for low values of σ_s where there is low information compression.

By using a hierarchical approach, the clusters may be iteratively detected with a distinct value for σ_s at each level of the tree. Notice that σ_s is recursively reduced until the appearance of clusters or until a minimum value for σ_s is reached, as described in Algorithm 1. That is why (and how) sub-clusters can be determined from larger clusters already detected.

Another advantage is related to the computational cost. The number of data points is very high in the initial hierarchical steps. However, the suppression threshold is also very high, and thus the information compression. This gives origin to immune networks with a reduced number of antibodies, thus reducing the number of interactions within the aiNet learning algorithm and MST steps. Nevertheless, in the end of the hierarchical process, when σ_s assumes low values and the data compression is low, the number of genes tends to be very small, and the computational cost is still low.

As a final result, the hierarchical approach generates a tree of immune networks, or a tree of clusters, that corresponds to a hierarchical relationship between groups of data points. These relationships among clusters and sub-clusters can reveal degrees of similarity between genes or groups of genes within the data set, thus providing additional information relevant to the studies involving functional genomics.

5.2 Some Modifications on the Original Hierarchical Proposal

The hierarchical approach described above has proved to be useful in some simple test problems [2]. However, this approach can be improved in order to alleviate some problems identified when dealing with bioinformatics data sets. The main problem is that the hierarchy of immune networks is indirect, i.e., it is based only on the input data present in the clusters of each branch, and not on the antibodies of the networks.

At each new level of hierarchy, sub-groups of data are identified based on the division of the elements of a parent network. When a network is divided it produces sub-networks, each one representing a given portion (cluster) of the data set. To produce the next hierarchical level, the elements of each cluster are used as input data for the aiNet learning algorithm, which generates a novel immune network representing the data with a suppression threshold lower than its parent network. Note that at this step the sub-network that gave origin to the cluster is lost, and a new network is constructed based only on the elements of the cluster found. This means that the parental relation between a network and its offspring is indirect: a network gives origin to a cluster and the cluster gives origin to the offspring networks.

Two problems arise from this approach. The first is that at each level of the hierarchy a completely novel network is constructed based only on the input data. This means that a new convergence phase has to take place starting from initially random antibodies, as it is stated in the first step of Algorithm 1. The first iterations of this convergence phase are generally the most costly because the aiNet must produce antibodies that approximate the antigens (input data) starting from elements that may be completely different from them. The other problem is that if the information coming from the parent network is lost, the offspring network may become completely different from it. This may lead to an uncharacterized relation of hierarchy.

In summary, there is the need to define a way of taking advantage of the direct information coming from the parent networks. A simple solution is to use the antibodies of the parent network as an initial set of antibodies for the offspring network, rather than to start with random antibodies. By doing this, each input antibody will tend to produce offspring antibodies that are more accurate in relation to the antigens it represents, and in more number, because the suppression threshold has a lower value now. Therefore, we have now a direct hierarchical relation between the immune networks, because the offspring network is generated starting from its parent one. At a low level this is characterized by each antibody generating a number of mutated copies that represent the data more precisely.

Hence, the offspring networks are more similar, in terms of structure, to their parent networks. This also means that the convergence phase of the aiNet learning is drastically reduced, and the overall computational cost of the algorithm becomes much lower. Some preliminary tests confirmed these expectations, improving the clustering capability of the hybrid algorithm and convergence speed.

These ideas were inspired by a work of Herrero et al. [9], in which a hierarchical approach is used on an unsupervised growing neural network, and applied with success to gene expression data clustering. In that paper the way the neurons reproduce to compose a novel hierarchical level is similar (in topological aspects) to what happens with the antibodies in aiNet when they come directly from the parent network.

6 Hierarchical Analysis of the Yeast Data

The next step is to use the hybrid algorithm in a hierarchical form to the analysis of the yeast data. This analysis will give an indication of the performance of the algorithm based on its capability to detect previously known clusters. However, the results produced by the algorithm do not need to be exactly the same as those presented by Eisen et al. [6], where an average-linkage hierarchical technique was used. The hybrid algorithm will analyze the data to take its own conclusions about the gene relationships present in the data set. These novel information may be useful for biologists and other researchers.

In the gene expression analysis there are several techniques that have been used to find clusters within the data sets and the results produced by these techniques may be quite different in some cases. There is actually no consensus as to what is a good clustering. This is one of the reasons why so many techniques have been successfully applied to solve this problem. The final result of a clustering method must be analyzed and interpreted by a specialist in biosciences, and it is up to this specialist to define which results are most relevant in each case. Therefore, the most important contribution of the proposed hybrid algorithm in relation to the yeast data is to provide an alternative point of view on the relations of similarity among the genes.

The parameter configuration of the hybrid algorithm to be used in this analysis is the same as that presented in Section 3.3, with the exception of the number of iterations and the suppression threshold, which now became part of the hierarchical approach to the network. As previous knowledge is used in each hierarchy of the network, the number of iterations to run the algorithm can be reduced from it = 20 to it = 10. This is because the convergence phase is reduced when a direct parental relation between the immune networks is considered. Besides, with the hierarchical approach the number of genes to be presented to each network tends to be smaller when low suppression thresholds are used, thus the generated networks are also smaller.

The only remaining parameters to be determined are related to the hierarchical algorithm. These are the decaying rate α and the starting suppression threshold σ_s. The decaying rate was set up empirically by some preliminary tests with only part of the data. The value chosen was $\alpha = 0.5$, to be applied geometrically. The starting suppression threshold can be chosen to be any high value in which the root network is not branched. This is easily determined in the first runs of the algorithm. The value chosen was $\sigma_s = 0.08$.

With all the parameters set, the algorithm was then applied to the input data (135 genes, corresponding to clusters B, C, D, E, F, G, H, J and K). At the end of the branching procedure nine clusters were detected. It was interesting to note, however, that the detected clusters were not exactly the same as those identified in [6]. The tree branching reached four levels of hierarchy, and the lowest value of the suppression threshold that gave origin to clusters was $\sigma_s = 0.0025$. Fig. 1 (see Appendix) shows the entire hierarchical tree obtained, with a total of 14 clusters, with 9 of them as leaves of the tree. Table 3 shows the details of each cluster of the tree. The clusters in bold correspond to the leaves of the tree, i.e., did not give origin to any sub-cluster.

One interesting aspect to be highlighted is that the hierarchical relation between clusters and sub-clusters is independent of the suppression threshold used; the values of σ_s do not indicate the distance between clusters. Sometimes different values of σ_s occur in the same hierarchical level. A good example is what happens to the clusters in the fourth level of the tree. Note in Table 3 that although the four clusters are in the same level, clusters 2.4.1 and 2.4.2 were identified with a higher threshold, $\sigma_s = 0.005$, than clusters 2.1.1 and 2.1.2, with $\sigma_s = 0.025$.

However, the suppression threshold can provide other important information about the clusters. Note in Table 3 that the overall data compression was very high, mainly on the clusters that represent large portions of data, as in clusters 2, 2.1 and 2.4. Note also that these clusters are not terminal nodes of the tree, i.e., they can be further divided into sub-clusters. (If the average information compression is weighted by the number of genes in each cluster, regarding only the terminal nodes of the tree, the calculated value is 55.4%, which is still very satisfactory.)

Table 3. Details of the clustering results, including number of genes (n), information compression performed by aiNet (I.C.), the suppression threshold of the network that gave origin to the cluster (σ), and the piece of the original information it contains (Eisen Clusters). Clusters in bold did not produce any sub-cluster

	n	I.C. (%)	σ_s	Eisen Clusters
Cluster 1	17	64.7	0.04	E
Cluster 2	118	93.2	0.04	B,C,D,F,G,H,J,K
Cluster 1.1	**8**	**50.0**	**0.02**	**E'**
Cluster 1.2	**9**	**22.2**	**0.02**	**E"**
Cluster 2.1	35	91.4	0.02	C,H
Cluster 2.2	**5**	**20.0**	**0.02**	**J**
Cluster 2.3	**16**	**75.0**	**0.02**	**K**
Cluster 2.4	51	84.3	0.02	D,F,G
Cluster 2.5	**11**	**45.5**	**0.02**	**B**
Cluster 2.1.1	**27**	**70.4**	**0.0025**	**C**
Cluster 2.1.2	**8**	**75.0**	**0.0025**	**H**
Cluster 2.4.1	**37**	**21.6**	**0.005**	**F,G**
Cluster 2.4.2	**14**	**50.0**	**0.005**	**D**

Different levels of compression for a same value of suppression threshold indicate differences in density. This fact can be clearly observed between clusters 1 and 2. Note that cluster 1 (Eisen cluster E) has a much lower density than the rest of the data set. This is probably the main reason why it was identified first. As a consequence, a high level of data compression may indicate that the current value of σ_s is still very high, and by using lower values there is a large probability to find more clusters. Thus, the algorithm reveals another important relation between the clusters, that is, the lower density clusters tend to be detected first, and the higher density ones are found with lower values of σ_s. As an illustration, one can observe that, even for very low values of σ_s, clusters 2.1.1 and 2.1.2 still present a high compression, indicating that Eisen clusters C and H are those with the higher density in the whole data set. This additional information about the similarity among genes may help biologists to improve their interpretation of the expression data. Besides, this can be used to guide the application of aiNet in future works, by assisting the user to select more accurate parameters and to define a better stopping criterion for the network.

In this analysis the σ_s was decreased to the minimum value of 0.000625. At this level the data were represented so precisely by the network that lower values would probably find no more relevant information.

The final result of the proposed clustering method can be considered very satisfactory. Practically all Eisen clusters were correctly detected, with the exception of clusters F and G. These were identified as belonging to the same group, cluster 2.4.1. The hybrid algorithm did not find any inconsistencies that indicate the presence of natural sub-clusters. In fact, the expression profiles of Eisen clusters F and G are very closely related to each other, as depicted in Fig. 2.

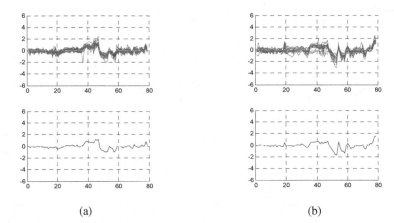

(a)   (b)

Fig. 2. Gene expression profiles and average expression profiles of (a) cluster *F* and (b) Cluster *G*. The *x*-axis indicates experiments and the *y*-axis represents the expression level

Note in Fig. 2 that the expression profiles of both clusters are very similar in most part of the experiments, but their average curves differ slightly in some points. However, with the exception of the last five experiments, the most relevant differences perceived in the average profiles occur in regions where the behavior of the genes is not clearly defined, i.e., there are some genes of cluster *F* that behave similarly to genes of cluster *G*, and vice versa, creating an interconnection between the two groups. This distribution does not admit inherent points of separation between *F* and *G*, therefore there is no natural sub-clusters. For more details the reader should refer to [1], where a similar conclusion is reported.

Another important aspect of the final result provided by the hybrid algorithm is the identification of two sub-clusters within the Eisen cluster *E*. This result indicates an important degree of relationship among genes that was not reported before by other approaches, as in [6,12]. Fig. 3 shows the expression profiles of the two clusters detected from cluster E.

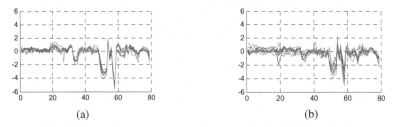

(a)   (b)

Fig. 3. Expression profiles of (a) cluster 1.1 (E') and (b) cluster 1.2 (E'')

Note in the figure that cluster E' presents a more dense distribution of points than cluster E'', i.e., cluster E' corresponds to a group of genes with more closely related expression profiles within cluster E. As explained before, the hybrid algorithm is capable of detecting clusters in the input data based on its density characteristics. In the above case, the algorithm detected a denser region in cluster E, thus revealing the presence of a subcluster.

7 Conclusion

This paper proposes the use of a hierarchical approach for a hybrid algorithm to the analysis of gene expression data. The hybrid algorithm is a combination of an artificial immune system, named aiNet, and a well known graph theoretical technique, called minimal spanning tree (MST).

The criterion for removing inconsistent edges of the minimal spanning tree used by the hybrid algorithm demonstrated to be more efficient in identifying natural clusters than simply removing the longest edges, an approach already presented in the literature. The hybrid algorithm performs clustering by interpreting and by preserving the key cluster features, while the approach proposed in [12] separates the data elements without taking into account the density of genes in the space. Furthermore, the data compression performed by the immune network preserves the structural properties of the clusters and plays a key role in the detection of important portions of the input space, being crucial for the analysis of complex data sets with high numbers of (noisy) data.

The hierarchical approach is widely discussed and some modifications to improve the performance of the original algorithm are proposed. The use of a direct parental relation of immune networks proved to be efficient for clustering gene expression data. Basically, it reduces the convergence time and overall computational cost of the algorithm. The proposed method achieved satisfactory performance in the benchmark problem tested. It was efficient in identifying previously known clusters in a benchmark data of the budding yeast *Saccharomyces cerevisiae*. It was also capable of detecting unknown sub-clusters within the data set, thus providing a new interpretation of the yeast data.

An important aspect observed in the hierarchical approach is that it provides degrees of relation between the clusters. The first one is a hierarchical topology that produces a branched tree of clusters and sub-clusters, where the data set is first separated into large classes and then into smaller ones. The second is additional information relative to the density of the clusters. The density can be estimated based on the values of the suppression threshold used on the clustering procedure. This kind of interpretation is not provided by other methods found in the literature, and it can be very relevant to gene expression data analysis.

References

1. Bezerra, G.B. & de Castro, L.N., "Bioinformatics Data Analysis Using an Artificial Immune Network", *Lecture Notes in Computer Sciences, Proc. of Second International Conference, ICARIS 2003*, pp.22-33, Edinburgh, UK, 2003.
2. de Castro, L. N. & Timmis, J. I., "Hierarchy and Convergence of Immune Networks: Basic Ideas and Preliminary Results", *Proc. First International Conference, ICARIS 2002*, pp. 231-240, 2002.
3. de Castro, L. N. & Von Zuben, F. J., "aiNet: An artificial Immune Network for Data Analysis", In Data Mining: A Heuristic Approach, H. A. Abbass, R. A. Saker, and C. S. Newton (Eds.), Idea Group Publishing, USA, Chapter XII, pp. 231-259, 2001.

4. de Castro, L.N. & Von Zuben, F.J., "The Clonal Selection Algorithm with Engineering Applications", GECCO'00 Proc. of the Genetic and Evolutionary Computation Conference – Workshop Proceedings, pp. 36-37, 2000a.
5. de Castro, L. N. & Von Zuben, F. J., "An Evolutionary Immune Network for Data Clustering", Proc. of IEEE SBRN – Brazilian Symposium on Neural Networks, pp. 84-89, 2000b.
6. Eisen, M.B., Spellman, P.T., Brow, P.O., & Botstein, D., "Cluster Analysis and Display of Genome-wide Expression Patterns", *Proc. Natl. Acad. Sci*, vol.95, pp. 14863-14868, USA, 1998.
7. Everitt, B., Landau, S. and Leese, M., *Cluster Analysis*, Fourth Edition, Oxford University Press, 2001.
8. Gomes, L.C.T., Von Zuben, F.J. & Moscato, P.A. "Ordering Microarray Gene Expression Data Using a Self-Organising Neural Network", Proceedings of the 4th International Conference on Recent Advances in Soft Computing (RASC2002), Nottingham, United Kingdom, pp. 307-312, December 2002.
9. Herrero, J., Valencia, A. and Dopazo, A., "A hierarchical unsupervised growing neural network for clustering gene expression patterns", Bioinformatics, 17:126-136, 2001.
10. Herwig, R., Poustka, A.J., Mller, C., Bull, C., Lehrach, H. and O'Brien, J., "Large-scale clustering of cDNA-fingerprinting data", Genome Res., vol. 9, pp. 1093-1105, 1999.
11. Shulze, A. & Downward, J. (2001), "Navigating gene expression using Microarrays – a technology review", *Nature Cell Biology*, vol. 3, pp. E190-E195.
12. Xu, Y., Olman, V. & Xu, Dong, "Minimum Spanning Trees for Gene Expression Data Clustering", Bioinformatics, vol. 18, pp. 536-545, 2002.
13. Yeung, K.Y.,, "Cluster Analysis of Gene Expression Data", Ph.D. Thesis, Computer Science, University of Washington, Seattle, WA, USA, 2001.
14. Zahn, C. T., "Graph-Theoretical Methods for Detecting and Describing Gestalt Clusters", IEEE Trans. on Computers, C-20(1), pp.68-86, 1971.

A   Appendix: Hierarchical Tree

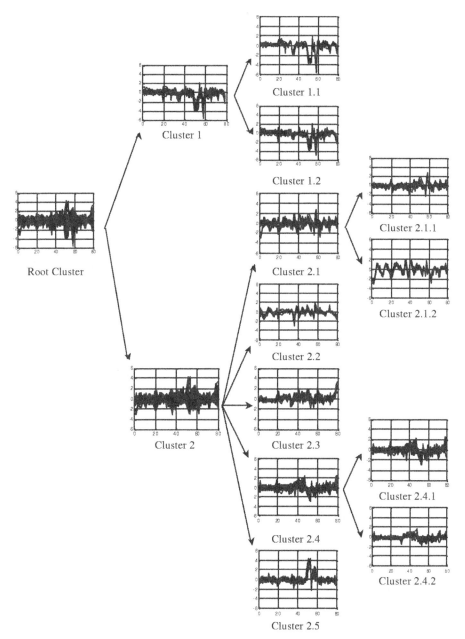

Fig. 1. Hierarchical tree for the yeast data with the expression profiles of all detected clusters. In all graphs, the x-axis indicates the experiments and the y-axis represent the expression level

Artificial Immune Regulation (AIR) for Model-Based Fault Diagnosis

Guan-Chun Luh, Chun-Yin Wu, and Wei-Chong Cheng

Department of Mechanical Engineering, Tatung University,
40 Chungshan North Road, 3rd sec. Taipei, Taiwan, R.O.C.
Tel: 886-2-25925252 ext.3410 ext. 806
{gluh,cywu}@ttu.edu.tw, d8701002@mail.ttu.edu.tw

Abstract. In this paper, a novel approach to immune model-based fault diagnosis methodology for nonlinear systems is presented. An immune-model based fault diagnosis architecture including forward/inverse immune model identification, the residual generation, fault alarm concentration (FAC), and artificial immune regulation (AIR). In this work, the artificial immune regulation was developed to diagnose the failures. A two-link manipulator simulation was employed to validate the effectiveness and robustness of the diagnosis approach. The results show that it can detect and isolate actuator faults, sensor faults and system component faults simultaneously.

1 Introduction

The development of effective and robust methods for fault diagnosis has become an important field of research in numerous applications, as can be seen from the relative survey literatures [1-4]. A fault diagnosis procedure typically consists of two steps, namely fault detection and fault isolation. The former indicates that an abnormal behavior has occurred while the latter identifies the type and location of the failures. The most relevant methods for fault diagnosis are model-based approaches [2,3]. The basic idea behind the model-based paradigms is to take advantage of the nominal model of the system to generate residuals that contain information about the faults. Residuals are quantities that are nominally zero and become nonzero in response to faults. However, the presence of disturbances, noise and modeling errors causes the residuals to become nonzero and thus interferes with the detection of faults. As a result, the residual generator needs to be designed so that it is unaffected by those unknown uncertainties.

After residual generation, a diagnostics mechanism fed with the residuals is implemented to determine the existence, the size and the source of faults in the plant. The center issue in fault diagnosis is to classify patterns corresponding to different faulty situations. The spirit of pattern recognition techniques finds the classification of features from the residuals. After partitioning the residual into clusters, there remain two fundamental questions that need addressing in any typical clustering scenario: (i) how many clusters are actually present in the data, and (ii) how real/good is the clustering itself. These questions are usually referred to as the cluster validity problem. That is,

G. Nicosia et al. (Eds.): ICARIS 2004, LNCS 3239, pp. 28–41, 2004.

whatever may be the clustering technique, one has to determine the number of clusters and also the validity of the clusters formed.

The immune system, a kind of information processing system with specific features of recognition, self-organizing, memory, adaptive, learning, has been adopted by a growing number of researchers to simulate the interactions between various components or the overall behaviors based on an immunology viewpoint [7-12]. It has been shown that artificial immune system provides various feasible approaches in engineering applications. In an early study of ours [13], a nonlinear system identification scheme with satisfactory robustness and efficiency was developed employing the features of the artificial immune system. However, no related investigation has been made into how the identified immune models might be applied to fault diagnosis. In this study, an immune-model based fault diagnosis methodology including the residual generation, residual filtering, fault alarm concentration (FAC), and artificial immune regulation (AIR) was developed to diagnose system failures. In addition, a two-link manipulator simulation was employed to evaluate the performance of the proposed diagnosis scheme.

2 Immune System

The natural immune system protects living bodies from the invading foreign substances, called antigens (Ag), including viruses, bacteria, and other parasites. The body identifies foreign antigens through two inter-related systems: the innate immune system and the adaptive immune system. The lymphocyte plays the most important role in the adaptive immune response. There are mainly two types of lymphocytes, namely, B-cells and T-cells. The former takes part in the humoral immunity that secretes antibodies (Ab) by clonal proliferation while the latter participates in cell-mediated immunity [14,15]. An immune response induced by an antigen generates antibodies that react specifically with the antigen. The antibody's receptor has a unique structure that allows a complementary fit to some features of a particular antigen. In addition, it can recognize different pathogen patterns and generate selective immune responses. Recognition is achieved by inter-cellular binding, which is determined by molecule shape and electrostatic charge. The binding of an antigen with an antibody can be represented as

$$Ab + Ag \xrightleftharpoons[k_-]{k_+} AbAg \qquad (1)$$

where k_+ is the forward (association) rate constant and k_- represents the reverse (disassociation) rate constant. The ratio of k_+ / k_- is a really measure of the affinity of the antibody for the epitope, called the association constant K expressed as following [15]

$$K = \frac{k_+}{k_-} \qquad (2)$$

These immune regulation controls are multiple and include feedback inhibition by soluble products as well as cell-cell interactions of many types that may either heighten or reduce the response. The objective is to maintain a state of homeostasis such that when the system is invaded by an antigen, enough response is generated to control the invader, and then the system returns to equilibrium state. However, its memory of that particular invader is retained so that a more rapid and heightened response will occur should the invader return [14].

Hightower *et. al.* [10] suggested that all possible antigens could be declared as a group of set points in an antigen space and the antigen molecules with similar shapes occupy neighboring points in that space. In addition, an antibody molecule can recognize some set of antigens and consequently cover some portion of that antigen space. Afterwords, Timmis *et. al.* [11] introduce a similar concept named Artificial Recognition Ball (ARB). Each ARB describes a multi-dimentional data item that could be matched to an antigen or to another ARB in the network by the Euclidean distance. Those ARBs located in the others' influence regions would either be merged to limit the population growth or pulled away to explore a new area.

3   Immune Model-Based Fault Diagnosis Scheme

In our previous works, a nonlinear system identification method was developed employing the features of the immune system employing different selecting mechanisms (Maximum Entropy Principle/orthogonal least-squares) [13,16]. The simulation results show that the identified immune models can achieve robustness and efficiency in identifying complex nonlinear systems. In addition, immune model based fault detection scheme has been proposed in study of ours [17]. The results show that a significant effectiveness has been achieved. Hence, artificial immune system could be expected to provide a feasible implementation for model-based fault diagnosis approach. Consequently, a novel fault diagnosis scheme is extended applying the identified immune model and the detection scheme.

Fig.1 shows the block diagram of the proposed immune model-based fault diagnosis consisting of immune model identification, fault detection, and isolation. A brief description of the immune model identification scheme and fault detection approach is presented briefly.

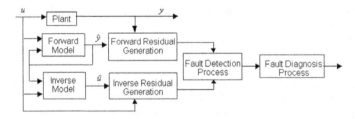

Fig. 1. The block diagram of the immune model-based fault diagnosis

3.1   Immune Model Identification

The problem of system identification is to find the structure of a nonlinear model and its corresponding coefficients. The structure could be treated as a nonlinear mapping from acquired pattern space to output space. The <u>N</u>onlinear <u>A</u>uto <u>R</u>egressive model with e**X**ogenous inputs (NARX model), proposed by Leontaritis and Billings [18, 19], provides a very concise representation for a wide class of nonlinear systems. Assumes that a general MIMO NARX model takes the following form:

$$\hat{y}(t) = f(y(t-1), \cdots, y(t-n_y), u(t-d), u(t-d-1), \cdots, u(t-n_u)) + e(t) \tag{3}$$

$$\text{where} \quad y(t) = \begin{bmatrix} y_1(t) \\ y_2(t) \\ \cdots \\ y_n(t) \end{bmatrix}, \quad u(t) = \begin{bmatrix} u_1(t) \\ u_2(t) \\ \cdots \\ u_m(t) \end{bmatrix}, \quad e(t) = \begin{bmatrix} e_1(t) \\ e_2(t) \\ \cdots \\ e_m(t) \end{bmatrix},$$

are the vectors of system outputs, inputs, and prediction errors, respectively; n_y, n_u are the maximum lags in the outputs and inputs, and $f(\bullet)$ is an unknown vector-valued nonlinear function in general. A polynomial expansion of $f(\bullet)$ adopted by Leontaritis and Billings is a convenient solution, but by no means the only choice. The regression vector takes the form $x(t) = [y(t-1), \cdots, y(t-n_y), u(t-1), \cdots, u(t-n_u)]^T$. This model is quite flexible; since n_y and n_u can each take arbitrary values.

In contrast to the series-parallel type model structure [20] presented in equation (3), this study uses parallel model structure [20, 21] whose model output $\hat{y}(k)$ is the function of the past values of the inputs and outputs of the identification model (rather than the plant).

$$\hat{y}(t) = f[\hat{y}(t-1), \cdots, \hat{y}(t-n_y), u(t-d), u(t-d-1), \cdots, u(t-n_u)] + e(t) \tag{4}$$

In addition, the regression matrix **X** and the output vector **Y** are constructed from the available input-output data pairs, and represented as $X^T = [x(1), x(2), ..., x(N_{Ag})]$, $Y^T = [y(1), y(2), ..., y(N_{Ag})]$, where N_{Ag} is the number of the data set. Hence the data set *S* can be represented as *S*=[**X, Y**], and each row S_j of *S* contains an input-output data pair: $s_j = [x_j, y_j]$, where x, y_j represents the system regression and output vectors respectively, and $j = 1, 2, ..., N_{Ag}$.

Therefore, the antigen space is defined as the input-output data set of unknown system. Let $\{s_j = (x_j, y_j) \mid x_j \in \Re^M, y_j \in \Re^N, j = 1, ..., N_{Ag}\}$ denotes the *j*th data set, and x_j, y_j represents the system regression and output vectors respectively. *M* and *N* indicate the associated dimensions of input and output training vectors. N_{Ag} is the number of the data set. And the regression vector takes the form $x(t) = [y(t-1), \cdots, y(t-n_y), u(t), \cdots, u(t-n_u)]^T$, where n_y, n_u are the maximum lags in the outputs and inputs. Each data set is treated as an antigen pattern, and the regression vector x_j, output vector y_j are defined as the antigen's epitope and the damage created by antigen respectively. For the purpose of efficiently neutralizing the antigen, different antigens require qualitatively different immune responses. The antigenic context has become correlated with the associated appropriate types of immune responses. Hence, the antibody's receptor is defined as $\{(p_i, q_i) \mid p_i \in \Re^M, q_i \in \Re^N, i = 1, ..., N_{Ab}\}$, where p_i denotes the shape vector of the receptor, q_i indicates the appropriate immune response, and N_{Ab} is the number of antibody. The affinity m_{ij}, defined as the matching ratio between the jth antigen epitope and the ith antibody receptor, is characterized as a Boltzmann-Gibbs distribution function [22]

$$m_{ij} = \frac{e^{-\beta_i d_{ij}}}{Z} \tag{5}$$

where β_i is a decay parameter controlling the distribution shape, and the area of coverage provided by an antibody is determined by β_i. And $d_{ij} = ||x_j - p_i||^2$ is the Euclidean distance between the jth antigen epitope vector and ith antibody receptor vector. The distance d_{ij} represents the structural similarity between antigen epitope and antibody receptor. The normalizing factor $Z = \sum_{i=1}^{N_{Ab}} e^{-\beta_i d_{ij}}$ is called the partition function. The affinity decreases monotonically with distance from the center.

The collective immune response function is represented as the following equation,

$$f(x_j) = \sum_{i=1}^{N_{Ab}} q_i m_{ij} = \frac{\sum_{i=1}^{N_{Ab}} q_i e^{-\beta_i d_{ij}}}{\sum_{i=1}^{N_{Ab}} e^{-\beta_i d_{ij}}} \tag{6}$$

Fig. 2 illustrates the scheme of the immune model. For the given inputs, the affinities will determine the relative influence to the overall output of the system. And the parameter q_i reflects the absolute contribution of the receptors. Analogy to our early work [16,17], the Gram-Schmidt orthogonal least-squares method is adopted in this paper to determine immune model structure p_i and the associated coefficients q_i.

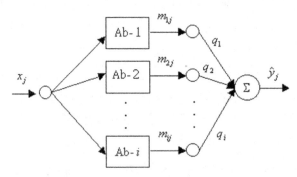

Fig. 2. The scheme of the immune model

3.2 Immune Model-Based Fault Detection

After the immune model has been generated, plant monitoring is followed by an online comparison between system behavior and model output. The comparison leads to the creation of residuals. Comparing the system output $y(t)$ with the associated model output $\hat{y}(t)$ leads to an output residual $r(t)$.

$$r(t) = y(t) - \hat{y}(t) \tag{7}$$

If the process data are significantly noisy, it can lead to either false alarms or non-detection of fault. The filtered residual and fault alarm concentration (FAC) is adopted for fault detection. To reduce the effects of modeling errors and noise further, the evaluation of the filtered residual $\tilde{r}(t)$ is formulated as

$$\tilde{r}(t) = \alpha \cdot r(t-1) + (1-\alpha) \cdot r(t) \tag{8}$$

where $r(t)$ is the output residual. α is a weighting parameter and $0 < \alpha < 1$. The larger value of α, the longer the detection period became. And the variance of the residual is reduced more at the longer detection.

As to the fault alarm decision making, the fault alarm concentration (FAC) is adopted and defined as

$$FAC = \Psi(\tilde{r}(t), r_{max}, r_{max} + \zeta) \tag{9}$$

where $\Psi(\cdot)$ is a smooth transition function from 0 (at r_{max}) to 1 (at $r_{max} + \zeta$) and ζ indicates an acceptable tolerance determined by heuristic knowledge. r_{max} denotes an appropriate lower threshold and $(r_{max} + \zeta)$ indicates the upper threshold for the normal system behaviors. In this study, r_{max} is defined as the maximum residual value created on a normal system during the process, and is presented as following

$$r_{max} = \max(\tilde{r}(t)), \quad \forall t \tag{10}$$

And ζ is defined as

$$\zeta = r_{max} \times 5\% \tag{11}$$

Then, while the residual value falls below the threshold no fault alarms, in that the residual value may be due to the modeling error or uncertainties, not due to a fault.

On the contrary, a fault must be appraised if the residual higher than the upper threshold as it is sure that this residual deviation is not due to parameter uncertainty. Obviously the interval threshold selection implies a trade-off between low false alarm rates and high sensitivity to fault [23].

3.3 Artificial Immune Regulation (AIR) Scheme for Fault Diagnosis

The main task in fault diagnosis is to classify the residuals into a number of distinguishable patterns corresponding to different faulty situation. The diagnostic knowledge base is automatically extracted based on the filtered residuals using the artificial immune regulation (AIR) scheme, which inspired by biological immune regulation process [14,15] and numerical clustering techniques [24, 25]. The scheme is presented as follows.

Consider a collection of filtered residual data $\{\tilde{r}_1, \tilde{r}_2, \cdots, \tilde{r}_n\}$ in n-dimensional space. Treating each data point as antigen and modifing the equation (3) to define the concentration of similar antigen $\tilde{r}_i$ as

$$C_i^1 = \sum_{j=1}^{n} \exp(-\bar{k}_+ \|\tilde{r}_j - \tilde{r}_i\|^2) \tag{12}$$

where k_+ represents the association rate constant and can be represented as following

$$\vec{k}_+ = \frac{1}{d_1^2} \tag{13}$$

where d_1 is the positive constant reflecting the radius of the influence. Obviously data points outside radial distance d_1 have little influence on the concentration. Consequently, a data point will have a high concentration value if it has many neighboring data points. After the concentration of each antigen has been computed, the antigen with the highest concentration is eliminated selectively at first. Let $\bar{r}_1$ be the location of the point and $\overline{C}_1$ be its concentration value expressed as

$$\overline{C}_1 = \max_{i=1}^{n}(C_i^1) \tag{14}$$

The immune regulation mechanism is then activated to eliminate the antigen. In order to reduce the effect of concentration around the point $\bar{r}_1$, significant antibody that react specifically with this antigen is induced by subtracting from concentraction. Then the concentraction of each antigen is revised by the formula

$$C_i^2 = C_i^1 - \overline{C}_1 \sum_{j=1}^{n} \exp(-\bar{k}_- \left\| \bar{r}_j - \bar{r}_1 \right\|^2) \tag{15}$$

where $k_- = k_+/K$ and C_i^2 is the concentration after elimination of the first antigen while C_i^1 is the original concentration. k_- represents the reverse (dissociation) rate constant, and K is the association constant. It is evident from equation (15) that the antigens similar to the first one have greatly reduced concentration value. This operation eliminates the effect of the antigen $\bar{r}_1$ over the other points, and localizing the second antigen with higher concentration. Thus, $\bar{r}_1$ becomes the receptor of first memory B-cell. After revision of concentration value of each antigen, the second antigen is selected with the highest value of C_i^2 defined below

$$\overline{C}_2 = \max_{i=1}^{n}(C_i^2) \tag{16}$$

Analogically, for the selection of N_{Ab} th antigen, revision of concentration value for each antigen is calculated as following:

$$C_i^{N_{Ab}} = C_i^{N_{Ab}-1} - \overline{C}_{N_{Ab}-1} \sum_{j=1}^{n} \exp(-\bar{k}_- \left\| \bar{r}_j - \bar{r}_{N_{Ab}-1} \right\|^2) \tag{17}$$

and the N_{Ab} th antigen is selected with the highest value of $C_i^{N_{Ab}}$ as

$$\overline{C}_{N_{Ab}} = \max_{i=1}^{n}(C_i^{N_{Ab}}) \tag{18}$$

The process goes on until the stop criterion (17) is satisfied.

$$\frac{\overline{C}_{N_{Ab}+1}}{\overline{C}_1} < \delta \tag{19}$$

where δ is a small fraction. This means that there are only very few points around this point and it can be omitted. Obviously the procedure generates N_{Ab} significant memory B-cells and each memory B-cell acts as a prototypical cluster center describing different characteristic mode of the system.

3.4 Partition Validity

Two well-known partition validity methods [26] are utilized in this study. Consider the end result of clustering can be expressed as a partition matrix U

$$U = [u_{ij}]_{i=1,\cdots,c;\, j=1,\cdots,n} \tag{20}$$

where c is a given number of clusters, u_{ij} denotes a numerical value range in [0,1] and represents the degree to which the data belongs to the cluster. Bezdek [27] defined the Partition Entropy (PE) to determine the degree of fuzziness in the partition

$$PE(U,c) = \frac{1}{n}\sum_{j=1}^{n}\sum_{i=1}^{c}|u_{ij}\ln u_{ij}| \tag{21}$$

And the Partition Coefficient (PC) is defined to measure the amount of overlap between clusters as following:

$$PC(U,c) = \frac{1}{n}\sum_{j=1}^{n}\sum_{i=1}^{c}u_{ij}^2 \tag{22}$$

According to the assumption that the clustering structure is better identified when more points concentrate around the cluster centers, the heuristic rules for selecting the best partitioning number c are

$$\min_{c=2}^{n-1}\{\min_{U\in\Lambda_c}[PE(U,c)]\} \tag{23}$$

$$\max_{c=2}^{n-1}\{\min_{U\in\Lambda_c}[PC(U,c)]\}$$

where Λ_c represents the set of all optimal solutions for a given c.

4 Simulations

To evaluate the performance of the proposed fault diagnosis schemes in real applications, a two-link manipulator simulation described by a set of nonlinear dynamic models is adopted. The dynamic equations of a two-link manipulator for shoulder and elbow are listed below [13].

$$[(m_1+m_2)\ell_1^2 + m_2\ell_2^2 + 2m_2\ell_1\ell_2\cos(\theta_2)]\ddot{\theta}_1 + [m_2\ell_2^2 + m_2\ell_1\ell_2\cos(\theta_2)]\ddot{\theta}_2 - 2m_2\ell_1\ell_2\sin(\theta_2)\dot{\theta}_1\dot{\theta}_2 \tag{24}$$
$$- m_2\ell_1\ell_2\sin(\theta_2)\dot{\theta}_2^2 + (m_1+m_2)g\ell_1\cos(\theta_1) + m_2g\ell_2\cos(\theta_1+\theta_2) + f_{c1} + f_{v1} = \tau_1$$

$$[m_2\ell_2^2 + m_2\ell_1\ell_2\cos(\theta_2)]\ddot{\theta}_1 + m_2\ell_2^2\ddot{\theta}_2 + m_2\ell_1\ell_2\sin(\theta_2)\dot{\theta}_1^2 + m_2g\ell_2\cos(\theta_1+\theta_2) + f_{c2} + f_{v2} = \tau_2$$

where τ_1 and τ_2 represent the joint torque, θ_1 and θ_2 represent the joint angle of the shoulder and elbow respectively. m_1 and m_2 indicate the mass of each link, ℓ_1 and ℓ_2 denote the length, and g is the gravity. f_{ci} and f_{vi} ($i = 1, 2$) are the Coulomb and viscous friction of the shoulder and elbow, respectively, and can be expressed as following

$$f_{C_i}(\dot{\theta}_i) = k_i \, \text{sgn}(\dot{\theta}_i) \qquad i = 1,2 \tag{25}$$

$$f_{v_i}(\dot{\theta}_i) = C_i \dot{\theta}_i \quad i = 1,2$$

In the simulations, the nominal values are given as $m_1 = 2$ kg, $m_2 = 1$ kg, $\ell_1 = 0.223$ m, and $\ell_2 = 0.2$ m. Coefficients of the frictions are defined as $k_1 = 2.5$ N-m, $k_2 = 1.5$ N-m, $C_1 = C_1 = 0.1$ N-ms. Two filtered uniform distribution signals were generated as torque inputs to excite the robot arm and the associated joint responses with a sampling interval of 0.005 sec. Note that normalization of the inputs and outputs have been applied to prevent input-output pair from being numerically dominant in the identification process. To evaluate the robustness of the proposed algorithm, two independent white noises (with signal-to-noise ratio (SNR) of 10/1) is added to the input-output data sequences. Both input and output measurements used for model identification are noisy data set. The simulation results can be referred to [13, 16].

4.1 Fault Detection

For the anomalous case, assume that each actuator is affected by diverse failure separately so that the joint torque of elbow and shoulder τ_1 and τ_2 are decreased as following after 10 seconds,

$$\tau_i(t) = \begin{cases} \tau_i(t) & ,t < 10 \\ 0.85\tau_i(t) & ,t \geq 10 \end{cases}, \ i = 1 \text{ or } 2 \tag{26}$$

Fig. 3 illustrates the one of the corresponding results of the evolution of the filtered residuals (both forward and inverse models) and their corresponding FAC values in the case of variations of τ_1. The filtered residuals and the FAC increase rapidly after 10 second, indicating the occurrence of fault. Clearly the proposed fault detection scheme is capable of detecting the presence of actuator failures and rejecting the modeling errors and noise while maintaining a reasonable sensitivity to faults as expected. In addition, Fig. 3(f) indicates the failure occurrence in shoulder actuator.

In addition to the sensor and actuator failures, faults may be raised due to the variation of system components such as the friction of the mechanical transmissions (Δk_1, Δk_2, ΔC_1, ΔC_2) or unexpected change of the load mass (Δm_1, Δm_2). Fig. 4 illustrates the one of the results when multiple-parameter faults ($\Delta m_1 = \Delta m_2 = 0.2$ kg, $\Delta C_1 = 0.4$ Nms, $\Delta C_2 = 0.1$ Nms) occur abruptly after 10 seconds.

These figures show that the filtered residuals and the associated FAC values of elbow and shoulder stay in normal situation before 10 seconds and then increase rapidly after 10 second. Based on these symptom generations, the underlying system faults can be detected and fault alarm is raised. However, it is impossible to distinguish and

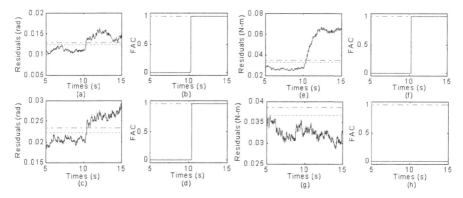

Fig. 3. Results of fault detection for actuator fault for the variation of τ_1

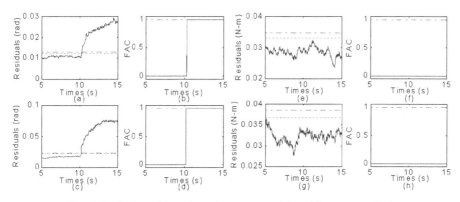

Fig. 4. Evolution of fault detection process with multi-parameter fault

classify the component faults as figures shown simply using the filtered residual or FAC values since they have the similar configurations. Moreover, it should have the same results if there have elbow and shoulder sensor faults at the same time. Therefore, the AIR scheme is proposed to diagnose the faults.

4.2 Fault Diagnosis

After the residual generation, the residual data contains a collection of n patterns constituting vectors in the 4-dimisional space. As described in early simulations, actuator faults can be apprized by FAC directly. In these cases the task's dimensionality can be reduced to 2-dimisional space for more convenient representation. The data will only contain a collection of the filtered residuals for system output y_1, and y_2.

The proposed AIR scheme produces a set of memory B-cells and their amount depends on the association rate constant k_+ as well as the disassociation rate constant k. In other words, the number of classification depends on the radius of the influence d_1 and the association constant K from equation (11) and (13). Consequently the values for the parameters utilized in AIR scheme need to be chosen firstly. Fig. 5(a) depicts

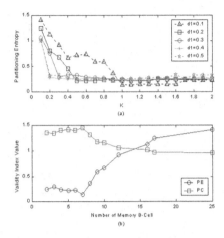

Fig. 5. The iteration for parameter selection

the partition entropy for different combination parameter-set of d_1 ranging from 0.1 to 0.5 and K from 0.1 to 2. After iterating calculation, the partition number is ranged from 2 up to 25 clusters for the manipulator case. Each choice of parameter set may leads to a different partitioning formation. In other words, different parameter set may yield identical number of clusters. In this study, the parameter set with the minimal value of PE is chosen as representative since the less the partition entropy means the better the performance has. Fig. 5(b) presents the relation between the number of clusters (memory B cells) and validity index value. As a result, the optimal values of validity index value are 0.1408 and 1.4511 for *PE* and *PC* respectively when the partition number equals 7 with the best parameter set: $d_1 =0.1$, and $K = 1$.

To evaluate the performance of the AIR scheme, the well-known fuzzy c-mean clustering (FCM) method [13,15] is adopted for comparison with *PE* and *PC* methods. Fig. 6 demonstrates the resultant classification for 7 different situations including normal (non-failure), ΔC_1 variation, ΔC_2 variation, Δm_1 variation, Δm_2 variation, ΔC_1, ΔC_2, Δm_1, Δm_2 variations, as well as sensor faults $\Delta \theta_1$ and $\Delta \theta_2$. The cluster validity measure results are tabulated in Table 1. Obviously, the performance of the proposed AIR scheme is better than that employing FCM method. In addition, Fig. 6 shows that the filtered residual data can be categorized into 7 meaningful clusters corresponding to different homogeneous regions without any prior knowledge. Apparently the proposed fault diagnosis scheme is able to diagnosis numerous faults and yield clear classification results. Consequently more data set can be collected to enhance reliability and safety in case of different kinds of symptoms with different fault sizes. Furthermore, the generation of additional symptoms can improve the depth of fault diagnosis.

Table 1. Comparison of the proposed scheme and FCM

	PE	*PC*
AIR	0.1408	1.4511
FCM	0.2996	1.3572

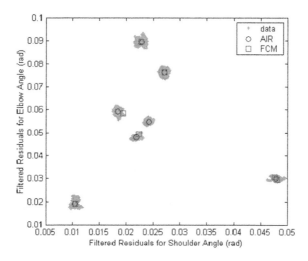

Fig. 6. The comparison result of the classification between IR scheme and FCM

5 Conclusions

In this paper, a novel artificial immune regulation scheme is proposed and integrated with the immune-model based fault detection approach for fault diagnosis. Therefore, the immune model-based fault diagnosis methodology consists of immune model identification, symptom generation, and diagnostic classification. The identified immune model provides a feasible robust model, and plant monitoring is followed by an on-line comparison between system behavior and model output. Subsequently residual is further filtered to reduce the effect of unknown uncertainties and the fault alarm concentration is employed to indicate the occurrence of faults. Based on the symptoms, the underlying faults are identified in the second level. The diagnostic knowledge base is automatically extracted based on data using the proposed immune regulation scheme. The main task in artificial immune regulation scheme is to classify the residuals into a number of distinguishable patterns corresponding to different faulty situations.

Several simulation examples on a two-link manipulator were conducted to evaluate the performance of the proposed methodology. The application of the proposed scheme to diagnosis of actuator, and system component faults yielded clear classification results. Conclusively, the proposed scheme could be expected to provide various feasible ideas for fault diagnosis applications.

Acknowledgement. The authors would like to acknowledge the National Science Council, Taiwan, R.O.C., for making this work possible with grant NSC90-2213-E-036-011.

References

1. Frank, P.M., and Birgit, K.S.,: New developments using AI in fault diagnosis. Engineering Applications of Artificial Intelligence, 10 (1), (1997), 3-14
2. Gertler, J.J.: Survey of model-based failure detection and isolation in complex plants. IEEE Control System Magazine, 8 (6), (1988), 3-11
3. Chen, J., and Patton, R.J.: Robust model-based fault diagnosis for dynamic systems. Kluwer Academic Publishers, Dordrechi. (1999)
4. Gertler, J.J.: Fault detection and diagnosis in engineering systems. Marcel Dekker Inc., New York, (1998)
5. Balle, P.: Fuzzy-model-based parity equations for fault isolation. Control Engineering Practice, Volume: 7, Issue: 2, (February, 1999), 261-270
6. Pakhira, M.K., Bandyopadhyay, S., and Maulik, U.: Validity index for crisp and fuzzy clusters. Pattern Recognition, Volume: 37, Issue: 3, (March, 2004), 487-501
7. Dasgupta, D.: Artificial Immune Systems and Their Applications. Springer-Verlag, Berlin Heidelberg, (1999)
8. Dasgupta, D., and Attoh-Okin, N.: Immunity-based systems: a survey. Computational Cybernetics and Simulation. in: IEEE International Conference on Systems, Man, and Cybernetics, (12-15, Oct. 1997), 369-374
9. de Castro, L.N., and Jonathan, T.: Artificial immune systems: a new computational intelligence approach. Springer-Verlag, Berlin Heidelberg, (2002)
10. Hightower, R., Forrest, S., and Perelson, A.S.: The evolution of emergent organization in immune system gene libraries. in: Proceedings of Sixth International Conference on Genetic Algorithms, (1995), 344-350
11. Timmis, J., Neal, M., and Hunt, J.: Data analysis using artificial immune systems, cluster analysis and Kohonen networks: some comparisons. in: IEEE International Conference on Systems, Man, and Cybernetics, (1999), 922-927
12. Knight, T., and Timmis, J.: AINE: an immunological approach to data mining. in: Proceedings of International Conference on Data Mining, (2001), 297-304
13. Luh, G.C., and Cheng, W.C.: Non-linear system identification using an artificial immune system. Proc. Instn Mech. Engrs, Part I, Journal of Systems and Control Engineering, 215 (2001), 569-585
14. Roitt, I., Brostoff, J., and Male, D.K.: Immunology, 5th ed. Mosby International Limited, (1998)
15. Benjamini, E., Coico, R., and Sunshine, G.: Immunology: a short course –4th ed., Wiley-Liss, (2000)
16. Luh, G.C., and Cheng, W.C.: Artificial Immune Network Based Nonlinear System Identification. The 20th National Conference on Mechanical Engineering, The Chinese Society of Mechanical Engineers, (2003), B01-34
17. Luh, G.C., and Cheng, W.C.: Identification of immune models for fault detection. Proc. Instn Mech. Engrs, Part I, Journal of Systems and Control Engineering, (in press)
18. Leontaritis, I.J. and Billings, S.A.: Input-Output Parametric Models for Non-Linear Systems Part I: Deterministic Non-Linear Systems. Int. J. Control, 41(2), (1985), 303-328
19. Leontaritis, I.J. and Billings, S.A.: Input-Output Parametric Models for Non-Linear Systems Part II: Stochastic Non-Linear Systems. Int. J. Control, 41(2), (1985), 329-344
20. Narendra, K.S. and Parthasarathy, K.: Identification and control of dynamical systems using neural networks. IEEE Transactions on neural network, 1 (1), (1990), 4-27
21. Luh, G.C. and Wu, C.Y.: Inversion control of non-linear systems with an inverse NARX model identified using genetic algorithms. Proc. Instn Mech. Engrs, Part I, Journal of Systems and Control Engineering, 214 (2000), 259-271
22. Baldi, P.F., and Soren, B.: Bioinformatics: The machine Learning approach. The MIT Press, (1999)

23. Schneider, H. and Frank, P.M.: Observer-based supervision and fault detection in robots using nonlinear and fuzzy logic residual evaluation, IEEE Transactions on Control Systems Technology, 4 (3) (1996), 274-282
24. Yang, T.N., and Wang, S.D.: Competitive algorithms for the clustering of noisy data. Fuzzy Sets and Systems, Volume: 141, Issue: 2, (January 16, 2004), 281-299
25. Velthuizen, R.P., Hall, L.O., Clarke, L.P., and Silbiger, M.L.:An investigation of mountain method clustering for large data sets. Pattern Recognition, Volume: 30, Issue: 7, (July, 1997), 1121-1135
26. Ronen, M., Shabtai, Y. and Guterman, H.: Hybrid model building methodology using unsupervised fuzzy clustering and supervised neural networks, Biotechnology and Bioengineering, 77 (4), (February, 2002), 420-429
27. Bezdek, J.C.: Pattern recognition with fuzzy objective function algorithms. New York: Plenum Press. (1981)

Optimal Circuit Design Using Immune Algorithm

Adem Kalinli

Erciyes University, Kayseri Vocational High School
Department of Electronics, 38039, Kayseri, Turkey.
kalinlia@erciyes.edu.tr

Abstract. Over the last years, there has been a great increase in interest in studying biological systems to develop new approaches for solving difficult engineering problems. Artificial neural networks, evolutionary computation, ant colony system and artificial immune system are some of these approaches. In the literature, there are several models proposed for neural network and evolutionary computation to many different problems from different areas. However, the immune system has not attracted the same kind of interest from researchers as neural network or evolutionary computation. An artificial immune system implements a learning technique inspired by human immune system. In this work, a novel method based on artificial immune algorithm is described to component value selection for analog active filters.

1 Introduction

In conventional approximation, components are assumed as ideal and in infinite values in designing analog electronic circuits. However, discrete components like that resistors and capacitor are produced in approximate logarithmic multiplies of defined number of constant values. Typically produced *preferred* values as known twelve series (E12) are 1.0, 1.2, 1.5, 1.8, 2.2, 2.7, 3.3, 3.9, 4.7, 5.6, 6.8, 8.2, 10, ... To reduce costs in design, discrete components are chosen from this series or other possible produced preferred values. Component values that obtained conventional approximations do not exactly converge with the produced preferred component values. Deviations from ideal are occurred as using component produced preferred that the nearest the ideal in implementing circuits. The occurring errors due to these deviations can be reduced by selecting nearer value components from such E24 series or using special value components that are obtained connecting couple of components in series or parallel. As a result of this, these approximations contain errors and will increase circuits dimension and cost.

In analog circuits, there are more components than important response parameters. Generally, conventional design methods show approximations; reducing freedom degree quantity to obtain directly applicable formulas by selecting defined certain components equal to each other or multiplies each other. The mean of this simplification in design methods is to make design that is near the ideal by excepting combinations of preferred component values. There will be generally a set of produced preferred values consisting of fewer design errors. To design in solution space that consists of all component values is rather than complex discrete searching problem. As a sample, in this study in completely discrete circuit that considering 8 components, if

G. Nicosia et al. (Eds.): ICARIS 2004, LNCS 3239, pp. 42–52, 2004.

components are selected from E12 series as choice that more than 40, search space will consist of $3x10^{13}$ points approximately [1]. For optimum design, computer based search on all possible combinations requires long computation time. For this reason, to define discrete component values an alternative method must be applied.

There has been a great increase in interest in studying biological systems to develop new approaches for solving difficult engineering problems in recent years. Artificial neural network, evolutionary computation, ant colony system, and artificial immune system are some of these approaches. In the literature, there have been several models proposed for neural network (NN) and evolutionary computation (EC). A well-known model of EC is genetic algorithm (GA), which is a stochastic optimisation algorithm, employed for combinatorial and continuous optimisation problems [2]. A simple GA has three main operators: crossover and mutation operators from genetic science and a selection operator simulating natural selection phenomena. GA can efficiently search large solution spaces due to its parallel structure and the probabilistic transition rules employed in the operators. However, a basic GA has two drawbacks: lack of good local search ability and premature convergence.

Ant colony optimisation (ACO) algorithm, which has global optimisation ability, is the artificial version of the natural optimisation process carried out by real ant colonies [3]. The main features of the algorithm are distributed computation, positive feedback and constructive greedy search. Therefore, the performance of ACO algorithm is good for local search due to the positive feedback and for global search because of the distribution computation features. In the literature, several models were proposed for ACO algorithm and the one of these is Touring ACO (TACO) algorithm [4]. In TACO algorithm each solution is represented by a vector of design parameters of which each is coded with a string of binary bits, i.e. a solution is a vector of binary bits. Therefore, artificial ants search for the value of each bit in the string, in other words they try to decide whether the value of a bit is 0 or 1.

An artificial immune algorithm simulates a learning technique carried out by human immune system [5-7]. However, the immune system has not attracted the same kind of interest from researchers as the NN or the EC. But, over the last few years, there has been increasing interest in the area of artificial immune system and their applications.

Although progress has been significantly made in automating design of certain categories of digital circuits, the design of analog circuits has not proved to automation. The heuristic algorithms and EC techniques, such as tabu search (TS), GA, simulated annealing (SA), and ACO algorithm, have attracted the attention of researchers in the field of analog circuits design in recent years. Various studies based on these algorithms have been realised to design analog circuits automatically. Horrocks et. al. successfully used GA to design active and passive filter circuits by using manufactured preferred component values [1,8-10]. There have been many studies used for analog circuit design with the help of SA and GA. However, there are few studies to minimize optimum layout and circuits dimension in VLSI circuits related to analogue circuit design using TS and ACO algorithm. [11-16]. Although the other algorithms have been used for designing some kind of analog circuit, immune algorithm has not been applied to component value selection for analog circuit, yet best of our knowledge.

In our previous work, we proposed an immune algorithm (IA) and tested its performance on a set of numeric test functions [17]. In this study, a novel method based on IA has been introduced to design analog active filters. IA is used for selection of active filter circuit component values. IA was compared to GA, TACO, and conventional methods in order to examine performance of the proposed method. Two forms of active filter with the second order state variable are considered to compare the performances. The first, resistance, capacitor and operational amplifier (opamp) are completely discrete circuit. The second is the semi-integrated form as exemplified by the AF100 from National Semiconductor [18]. In this form, the opamps and some of the passive components are integrated and the remaining discrete components are attached externally. In the examples, preferred values produced from E12 series for resistances and capacitors are considered. In the second section, the basic principles of the natural immune system and the IA are described. The third section presents the state variable active filter and the conventional design procedure. Section 4 describes how IA can be applied to component value selection for active filter. The simulation results are given in the Section 5 and the work is concluded in Section 6. IA also compares the performance of GA, TACO and the conventional method on considered circuit design problem.

2   Natural Immune System and Immune Algorithm Used

2.1   Natural Immune System

The natural immune system is a distributed novel-pattern detection system with several functional components positioned in strategic locations throughout the body. The main purpose of the immune system is to recognize all cells (or molecules) within the body and categorize those cells as self or non-self. The non-self cells are further categorized in order to stimulate an appropriate type of defensive mechanism. The immune system learns through evolution to distinguish between foreign antigens (e.g. bacteria, viruses, etc.) and the body's own cells or molecules. The lymphocyte is the main type of immune cell participating in the immune response that possesses the attributes of specificity, diversity, memory, and adaptability, there are two subclasses of the lymphocyte: T and B. Each of these has its own function. In particular, B-cells secrete antibodies that can bind to specific antigens. The immune system has evolved to mechanisms: innate (nonspecific) and adaptive (specific) immunity which are linked to and influence each other. Adaptive immunity consists of two branches: the humoral immunity, which is carried out by the Bcells and their products, and the cellular immunity by Tcells. Both branches follow a similar sequence of steps for defence. When an antigen enters the body, self-regulatory mechanisms determine the branch of the immune system to be activated, the intensity of the response, and its duration. Specifically, regulation of both immunity is conducted by a population of Tcells. T cells regulate immune responses by release of soluble molecules such as lyphokines, cytokines, interleukins in order to activate B cells [5,6]. The B cells originated in the bone marrow collectively form what is known the immune network. This network acts to ensure that once useful B cells are generated, they remain in the immune system until they are no longer required.

When a B cell of natural immune system encounters an antigen, an immune response is elicited, which causes the antibody to bind the antigen (if they match) so that the antigen can be neutralized. If the antibody matches the antigen sufficiently well, its B cell becomes stimulated and can produce related clones which are incorpo-

Randomly construct the initial B cell population
REPEAT
· Calculate the stimulation level of all B cells and select the highest stimulated B cell
· Calculate the similarity of all other B cells with the highest stimulated B cell
· Construct a sub-population by using the similarity values and applying a selection mechanism
· Apply somatic mutation operation to the sub-population
· Calculate the similarity of each B cell in the rest of network with all others and order these cells depending on their similarity values
· Remove some of the B cells stimulated at low level from the population
· Generate new B cells and insert some of them into the network
UNTIL (*generation = maxgeneration*)

Fig. 1. Main steps of the immune algorithm used

rated in to the immune network. The level of stimulation depends on both how well the B cell's antibody matches the antigen and how it matches other B cells in the immune network. If the stimulation level rises above a given threshold, the B cell becomes enlarged and starts replicating itself several times, producing clones of itself. To allow the immune system to be adaptive, the clones that grow also turn on a mutation mechanism that generates at high frequencies point mutations in the genes coding specifically the antibody molecule. This mechanism is called somatic hypermutation [7]. If the stimulation level falls below a given threshold, the B cell does not replicate and in time it will die off. Survival of the B cells produced by the bone marrow or by hyper mutation depends on their affinity to the antigen and to the other B cells in the network. The algorithm simulating the principles of natural immune system is called immune algorithm. The main steps of the immune algorithm used in this work are presented in Fig. 1.

2.2 Immune Algorithm Used

In the model used in this work, each B cell is represented with a binary string which is a possible solution to the problem. At the first step, an initial population of B cells is formed of the cells produced randomly. Then, all cells are evaluated for the problem and a fitness value is assigned to each cell in the population. Depending on the fitness values, cells are ordered and the cell with the highest fitness value is assumed as the antigen. Since the stimulation level of a cell depends on both the similarity with the antigen and the similarity with all other cells in the network, two different sub-populations are constructed based on these similarity values. Therefore, the similarity of all cells with the antigen is computed and the first sub-population is constructed of the cells with the highest match score with the antigen by using a K-Tournament selection scheme. After this selection operation each cell in the sub-population is mutated by applying a one-point mutation operator. The resulting mutated cells are only kept if they improve their own similarity with the antigen. After the first sub-population is formed, the similarity of each cell in the rest of network with all cells in the network is calculated and then these cells are ordered depending on their match scores. Some of B cells which are stimulated at low level are removed from the population. New B cells are randomly produced and those with the similarity above prede

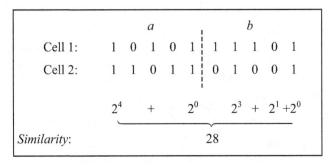

Fig. 2. Similarity calculation between two cells

termined level with the cells in the population are added into the network. These operations are repeated at each generation.

The similarity is calculated as shown in Fig. 2. In this example, each parameter (a, b) is represented with five bits. Therefore, a cell (solution) is a binary string with the length of 10 bits. Each bit in a sub-string used to represent a or b parameters has different weight in the similarity calculation. For example, the least significant bit has the minimum weight as the most significant one has the maximum weight.

3   The State Variable Active Filter

The state variable active filter (SVAF) is a different type of multiple-feedback filter, using three or four opamps. It has one input, and three outputs providing low-pass, high-pass, and band-pass filtering simultaneously. The basic design circuit for a SVAF is illustrated in Fig. 3. Detailed analysis of the circuit can be found in the literature, for example [1,19]. The low-pass output is assumed here to be the desired output.

The response of a second order low-pass circuit is completely specified by the three basic filter parameters: cutoff frequency ($w_0 = 2\pi f_0$), quality factor (Q), and pass-band gain (H). These quantities are given in, terms of the passive component values by the Eqn (1).

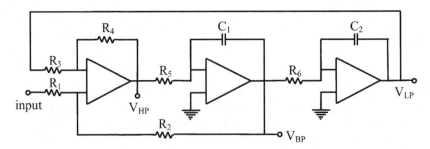

Fig. 3. Basic design for a state variable active filter

$$H = \frac{R_2(R_3 + R_4)}{R_3(R_1 + R_2)}$$

(1)

$$w_0 = \sqrt{\left(\frac{R_4}{R_3}\right)\left(\frac{1}{C_1 C_2 R_5 R_6}\right)}, \qquad Q = \frac{R_3(R_1 + R_2)}{R_1(R_3 + R_4)}\sqrt{\frac{C_1 R_4 R_5}{C_2 R_3 R_6}}$$

In this work, the specification chosen was $w_0 = 10000 \div 2\pi = 1591.55$ rad/sec, and $Q = \sqrt{2} = 1.41421$. The pass-band gain, H, can be easily compensated for by other cascaded analog circuits and it is not very critical in most applications. In the conventional design procedure, H is fixed at some value; however for the IA method described below it is unconstrained.

3.1 Conventional Design Procedure

In this work, the design method which is used by Horrocks and Spittle in Ref. [1] is considered as a conventional procedure. The explanation of this method is given below.

For the fully discrete circuit there are six resistors and two capacitors. Its values are to be chosen related to the specified values for w_0 and Q, and also H is important. The conventionally proposed method arbitrarily chooses to make both capacitors equal to C and all resistors except R_2 equal to R. Thus, Eqns (1) reduce the following.

$$w_0 = \frac{1}{RC}$$

(2)

$$R_1 = R_3 = R_4 = R_5 = R_6 = R, \quad C_1 = C_2 = C, \quad R_2 = (2Q - 1)R$$

(3)

Firstly, the procedure is to choose a pair of values for R and C to satisfy Eqn (2); then to calculate the circuit components using Eqns (3). For an exact design, a reasonable way is to choose a preferred value for R in the middle of the range. The values for the remaining R_2, and C then follow from Eqn (2) and (3). In general, these values have to be special non-preferred values, if an exact design is to be obtained. For a design using preferred values only the exact values can be rounded to the nearest preferred values [1].

For the semi-integrated circuit AF100, components R_1, R_5, and R_6 are connected externally, and the other five components, having fixed values, are integrated in the device. In the conventional design the user specifies the three performance parameters, H, w_0 and Q and solves for the three external resistor values by means of (1).

4 Application of the Immune Algorithm to the Problem

For the application of IA, each passive component of the considered circuit was represented with one location in each cell. Thus for the fully discrete circuit problem was used by having eight locations in each cell (see Fig. 4). Each of these locations was allocated a group of bits to identify a particular preferred value for that component. The number of bits allocated depends on the representation method. For the *one-bit* approach, one bit is allocated which allows a choice of from two preferred values that are nearest to the exact design values that emerged from the conventional design procedure described above. The number of bits is progressively increased in the *two-bit*, *three-bit*, and *four-bit* approaches. In the three-bit approach, three bits allow eight preferred values spreaded on either side of the exact values to be offered for selection by the IA. The purpose of these methods is to explore the effect of increasing the range of the search space.

In the *full evaluation* approach eight groups of six bits are used to specify any preferred value. Two of these bits signify the decade in the range 10^3 to 10^6 ohms for the resistors and 10^{-9} to 10^{-6} farads for the capacitors. Values outside of these ranges were judged to lead to unwanted practical effects such as stray capacitance effects or large signal currents. The remaining four bits are used to signify any of the twelve preferred values in the decade range. For the semi-integrated circuit the full evaluation approach has been applied using the same cell data structure as for the fully discrete circuit, but three rather than eight groups of six bits to specify the three externally connected components. Since each component value is represented with 6 bits in this work, the length of a solution in the form of binary string is 48 for the first circuit and 18 for the second circuit.

As a result of choosing preferred values for the components, the cutoff frequency and quality factor will deviate from the specification by Δw and ΔQ respectively. The aim is to keep these deviations as low as possible. The error criterion adopted here is

$$error = a_1 \frac{|\Delta w|}{w_0} + a_2 \frac{|\Delta Q|}{Q} \qquad (4)$$

where, a_1 and a_2 are constants and their values were chosen as 0.5. Thus, the acceptable design tolerances for cutoff frequency and quality factor are equal.

In this case, the components values of the circuits are successively adjusted by IA algorithm until the error is minimised. The performance of a solution is determined by using the following formula

$$fit(i) = \frac{1}{1 + error_i} \qquad (5)$$

where $error_i$ is the cost function value calculated by using the solution i.

The control parameter values of the IA were the number of cells in the network was 50 and the size of the both sub-populations was 20. At each generation, two least stimulated cells were removed from the population. 10 new cells are randomly produced and two of these new cells, which have the maximum similarity with the cells in the population, are inserted into the population.

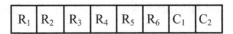

Fig. 4. Representing the component values in the string form

Table 1. Component values and performances of the conventional and IA methods

Parameters	Conventional [1]	Immune Algorithm				
		1 Bit	2 Bit	3 Bit	4 Bit	6 Bit
Q	1.37234	1.42119	1.41215	1.41358	1.41437	1.41423
w_0	1773.05	1585.86	1591.52	1591.52	1591.23	1591.55
R_1	4700	5600	3300	6800	2700	10×10^6
R_2	8200	10000	5600	15000	10000	56000
R_3	4700	4700	4700	5600	6800	2.7×10^6
R_4	4700	5600	3300	3900	2700	3.9×10^6
R_5	4700	4700	5600	4700	22000	1800
R_6	4700	5600	3300	3900	3300	2200
C_1	1.2×10^{-7}	1.5×10^{-7}	1.0×10^{-7}	1.0×10^{-7}	1.2×10^{-8}	1.2×10^{-6}
C_2	1.2×10^{-7}	1.2×10^{-7}	1.5×10^{-7}	1.5×10^{-7}	1.8×10^{-7}	1.2×10^{-7}
Error (%)	7.1824	0.4253	0.0737	0.0233	0.0155	0.0008

Table 2. Error values for various design methods

Methods	Errors (%)				
	1 Bit	2 Bit	3 Bit	4 Bit	6 Bit
IA	0.4253	0.0737	0.0233	0.0155	0.0008
TACO	0.4253	0.1442	0.0617	0.0355	0.0129
GA [1]	0.7260	0.3266	0.2187	0.0626	0.0010
Conventional [1]			7.1824		

5   Simulation Results

The results obtained by using conventional design method and the present novel approach for the first circuit is shown in Table 1. The design error achieved from the conventional method was 7.1824% [1].

The errors achieved from IA for the fully discrete circuit with various bits are shown in Table 1 as well. The results have been the clear evident that a very large reduction in design error was obtained. Even highly restricted one-bit approach IA produces a sixteen-fold improvement over the conventional method. For the full-evaluation approach, the design error is extremely low at 0.001%. Simulations with fully-evaluation approach by using TACO algorithm were also applied to this circuit problem. The performance of IA was compared with the results of TACO algorithm and GA. The results of GA have been taken from Ref [1]. The design results of these methods are given in Table 2. It is clearly seen that the designs obtained by using IA have lower error values.

In order to show the robustness of the proposed approach, frequency histograms of the results obtained for fifty different runs with different initial solutions by using IA, and TACO algorithm were drawn. Fig. 5 shows the histograms for the fully-discrete circuit. For the both algorithms, the total evaluation number was 500000.

In practical realizations, manufacturing tolerance in the components might mask these low error values. The design of active filters generally requires accurate components. Typically, resistors with 1 or 5% tolerances are used in discrete circuits more rarely in less critical applications 10 or 20% resistors will suffice. On the other hand,

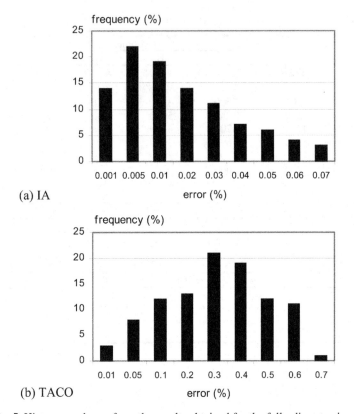

Fig. 5. Histograms drawn from the results obtained for the fully-discrete circuit.

capacitors with 10 or 20% tolerances are more readily available and are preferred to save cost [19]. 100 different trials were performed by adding tolerances maximum ±10% and ±1% to components values which are obtained with conventional and IA approaches in order to examine the effect of the manufacturing tolerances on design errors. Average values of the quality factors, cut-off frequencies, and errors obtained from these trials are given in Table 3. As it is seen in Table 3, lower design errors are obtained with IA also in case manufacturing tolerances are considered. It is also possible to realize designs close to the ideal case by selecting components with lower tolerances as 1%.

Simulation results obtained by different methods for the semi-integrated AF100 circuit are shown in Table 4. This circuit has five fixed internal components, indicated by parenthesis. The remaining three component values are available for choice by the IA. Because this is more restrictive than the fully discrete circuit, the error obtained is larger. Even so, the error value achieved from IA is less than GA, and is the same as TACO.

In the IA evolution of these designs, the pass-band gain, H, was unconstrained. The resulting pass-band gains, taken to be $H=1$ in the conventional design, range from 0.2854 to 2.1632 in the IA designs. These values would be acceptable for many applications. In the AF100 an extra opamp is included which can be used for adjusting the pass band gain.

Table 3. The results by considering manufacturing tolerances in the fully-discrete circuit

Parameters	Tolerance (10%)		Tolerance (1%)	
	Conventional	IA	Conventional	IA
Average Q	1.32457	1.41981	1.37106	1.41361
Average w_0	1786.57	1591.23	1773.23	1591.77
Average error (%)	10.1665	3.3366	7.2331	0.3463

Table 4. Component values and error values for AF100 circuit

Parameters	Conventional [1]	GA [1]	TACO	IA
Q	1.32008	1.44724	1.41521	1.41521
w_0	1610.80	1589.10	1610.81	1610.81
R_1	10000	68000	560000	560000
R_2	(100000)	(100000)	(100000)	(100000)
R_3	(100000)	(100000)	(100000)	(100000)
R_4	(10000)	(10000)	(10000)	(10000)
R_5	8200	390000	820000	820000
R_6	470000	10000	47000	47000
C_1	(1.0×10^{-9})	(1.0×10^{-9})	(1.0×10^{-9})	(1.0×10^{-9})
C_2	(1.0×10^{-9})	(1.0×10^{-9})	(1.0×10^{-9})	(1.0×10^{-9})
Error (%)	3.9055	0.7154	0.6403	0.6403

6   Conclusions

A novel method based on immune algorithm has been successfully presented for the component value selection of the analog active filter circuit. Significant reductions in design errors can be achieved with respect to the conventional approach. The performance of the proposed method was also compared with genetic algorithm and touring ant colony optimisation algorithm. Simulation results have shown that the immune algorithm could be efficiently used for components' value selection of the analog active filter. It is apparently seen in designing immune algorithm that expanding of the search space helps to achieve lower design errors. It has been also noticed that selecting components with lower tolerance series provides closer approximation to the ideal case.

It has been also expected that proposed method is applicable to the other analog circuits, which have greater complexity and are in various types.

References

1.   Horrocks, D.H., Spittle, M.C.: Component Value Selection for Active Filters Using Genetic Algorithms. Proc. IEE/IEEE Workshop on Natural Algorithms in Signal Processing, Chelmsford, UK, Vol.1 (1993) 13/1-13/6

2. Holland, J.H.: Adaptation in Natural and Artificial Systems, University of Michigan Press, Ann Arbor, MI (1975)
3. Dorigo, M., Maniezzo, V., Colorni, A.: Positive Feedback as a Search Strategy. Technical Report No.91-016, Politecnico di Milano (1991)
4. Karaboga, N., Kalinli, A., Karaboga, D.: Designing IIR Filters Using Ant Colony Optimisation Algorithm. Engineering Applications of Artificial Intelligence, Vol.17(3), (2004) 301-309
5. Farmer, J.D., Packard, N.H., Perelson, A.S.: The Immune System, Adaptation, and Machine Learning. Physica, Vol.22D (1986) 187-204
6. Hunt, J.E., Cooke, D.E.: Learning Using an Artificial Immune System. Journal of Network and Computer Applications, Vol.19 (1996) 189-212
7. Kepler, T.B., Perelson, A.S.: Somatic Hyper Mutation in B Cells: An Optimal Control Treatment. Journal of Theoretical Biology, Vol.164 (1993) 37-64
8. Horrocks, D.H., Khalifa, Y.M.A.: Genetically Derived Filters Circuits Using Preferred Value Components. Proc. of IEE Colloq. on Linear Analogue Circuits and Systems, Oxford UK (1994)
9. Horrocks, D.H., Khalifa, Y.M.A.: Genetic Algorithm Design of Electronic Analogue Circuits Including Parasitic Effects. Proc. First On-line Workshop on Soft Computing (WSC1), Nagoya University, Japan (1996) 71-78
10. Horrocks, D.H., Khalifa Y.M.A.: Genetically Evolved FDNR and Leap-Frog Active Filters Using Preferred Components Values. Proc. European Conference on Circuit Theory and Design, Istanbul, Turkey (1995) 359-362
11. Tao, L., Zhao, Y.C.: Effective Heuristic Algorithms for VLSI-Circuit Partition. IEE Proceedings G: Circuits, Devices and Systems, Vol.140, No.2 (1993) 127–134
12. Aguirre, M.A., Torralba, A., Ch´avez, J., Franquelo, L.G.: Sizing of Analog Cells by Means of a Tabu Search Approach. In Proceedings IEEE International Symposium on Circuits and Systems, Vol.1 (1994) 375-378
13. Lodha, S.K., Bhatia, D.: Bipartitioning Circuits Using Tabu search. Proceedings of 11th Annual IEEE International Conference ASIC (1998) 223-227
14. Sadiq, S.M, Youssef, H.: CMOS/BiCMOS Mixed Design Using Tabu Search. Electronics Letters, Vol.34, No.14 (1998) 1395-1396
15. Sadiq, S.M, Youssef, H., Barada, H.R., Al-Yamani, A.: A Parallel Tabu Search Algorithm for VLSI Standard-Cell Placement. Proceedings of the IEEE International Symposium on Circuits and Systems ISCAS 2000, Switzerland, Vol.2 (2000) 581-584
16. Kuntz, P., Layzell, P., Snyers, D.: A Colony of Ant-Like Agents for Partitioning in VLSI Technology. In: Proc. 4th Int. Conf. on Artificial Life (ECAL97), Husbands, P. and Harvey, I. (eds.), MIT Press (1997)
17. Karaboga, N., Kalinli, A., Karaboga, D.: An Immune Algorithm for Numeric Function Optimisation. 10th Turkish Symposium on Artificial Intelligence and Neural Networks (TAINN 2001), Dogu Akdeniz University, KKTC, June 21-22, (2001) 111-119
18. National Semiconductor Corp., Data Aquisition Data Book, National Semiconductors Corp., Santa Clara, CA, USA, (1993) 7.5-7.31
19. Schaumann, R., Valkenburg M.E.V.: Design of Analog Filters, Oxford University Press, (2001)

Towards a Conceptual Framework
for Artificial Immune Systems

Susan Stepney[1], Robert E. Smith[2], Jonathan Timmis[3], and Andy M. Tyrrell[4]

[1] Department of Computer Science, University of York
[2] The Intelligent Computer Systems Centre, University of the West of England
[3] Computing Laboratory, University of Kent
[4] Department of Electronics, University of York

Abstract. We propose that bio-inspired algorithms are best developed and ana-lysed in the context of a multidisciplinary conceptual framework that provides for sophisticated biological models and well-founded analytical principles, and we outline such a framework here, in the context of AIS network models. We further propose ways to unify several domains into a common meta-framework, in the context of AIS population models. We finally hint at the possibility of a novel instantiation of such a meta-framework, thereby allowing the building of a specific computational framework that is inspired by biology, but not re-stricted to any one particular biological domain.

1 Introduction

The idea of biological inspiration for computing is as old as computing itself. It is implicit in the writings of von Neumann and Turing, despite the fact that these two fathers of computing are now more associated with the standard, distinctly non-biological computational models.

Computation is rife with bio-inspired models (neural nets, evolutionary algorithms, artificial immune systems, swarm algorithms, ant colony algorithms, L-systems, …). However, many of these models are naïve with respect to biology. Despite the fact that these models often work extremely well, their naivety often blocks understand-ing, development, and analysis of the computations, as well as possible feedback into biology.

We propose that bio-inspired algorithms are best developed and analysed in the context of a multidisciplinary conceptual framework that provides for sophisticated biological models and well-founded analytical principles.

2 A Conceptual Framework

The next step in bio-inspired computation should both develop more sophisticated biological models as sources of computational inspiration, and also use a conceptual framework to develop and analyse the computational metaphors and algorithms.

G. Nicosia et al. (Eds.): ICARIS 2004, LNCS 3239, pp. 53–64, 2004.

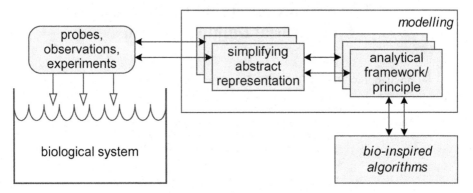

Fig. 1. An outline conceptual framework for a bio-inspired computational domain

Figure 1 illustrates a possible structure for such a conceptual framework. Here *probes* (observations and experiments) are used to provide a (partial and noisy) view of the complex *biological system*. From this limited view, we build and validate simplifying abstract representations, *models*, of the biology. From these biological models we build and validate *analytical computational frameworks*. Validation may use mathematical analysis, benchmark problems, and engineering demonstrators. These frameworks provide principles for designing and analysing *bio-inspired algorithms* applicable to non-biological problems, possibly tailored to a range of problem domains, and contain as much or as little biological realism as appropriate. The concept flow also supports the design of algorithms specifically tailored to modelling the original biological domain, permits influencing and validating the structure of the biological models, and can help suggest ideas of further experiments to probe the biological system. This is necessarily an interdisciplinary process, requiring collaboration between (at least) biologists, mathematicians, and computer scientists to build a complete framework.

An important observation is that none of the representation and modelling steps outlined above is *unbiased*. There are many possible probes, and many possible representations of the same systems even given the same probes, and they all provide different insights. In particular, models derived specifically for the goals of biological simulation may provide insights that are distinct from those that serve computational goals. It is very seldom that the modelling steps used in these distinct activities are examined for common properties, and comparative biases.

In many instances not all of the representational steps outlined above are taken. In particular, bio-inspired computational algorithms usually proceed directly from a (naïve) biological model to an algorithm, with little analytical framing of the representation's properties. Such "reasoning by metaphor" is a troubling aspect of these algorithms. Without the application of available analysis techniques to the simplified representations of biological systems, algorithms derived from these representations rely only on the (often weak) analogy to the biological system to support their use. We feel that it is important to recognize the distinct levels of the modelling process outlined above, to avoid naïve assumptions.

One example that *can* be described in terms of such a framework, at least partially, is John Holland's original adaptive system theories [Holland 1975; Goldberg 1989], founded on a simplified binary-encoded representation of genetics, and analytical principles of building blocks, k-armed bandit theories, the schema theorem, and implicit parallelism. Evolutionary computation theory has developed and deepened in the wake of this work, and it continues to influence the prescription of genetic algorithms. We propose that other bio-inspired computational domains, including Artificial Immune Systems, should be put on a similarly sound footing.

3 Instantiating for Artificial Immune Systems (AIS)

The natural immune system is a complex biological system essential for survival. It involves a variety of interacting cellular and molecular elements that control either micro- or macro-system dynamics. The effectiveness of the system is due to a set of synergetic, and sometimes competitive, internal strategies to cope with chronic and/or rare pathogenic challenges (antigens). Such strategies remodel over time as the organism develops, matures, and then ages (immuno-senescence). The strategies of the immune system are based on task distribution to obtain distributed solutions to problems (different cells are able to carry out complementary tasks) and solutions to distributed problems (similar cells carrying out the same task in a physically distributed system). Thus, cellular interactions can be envisaged as parallel and distributed processes among cells with different dynamical behaviour, and the resulting immune responses appear to be emergent properties of self-organising processes. Many theories abound in immunology pertaining to how the immune system remembers antigenic encounters (maintenance of memory cells, use of immune networks), and how the immune system differentiates between self and non-self molecules (negative selection, self-assertion, danger theory).

We can explicitly exploit the conceptual framework, in order to develop, analyse and validate sophisticated novel bio-inspired computational schemes, including those inspired by complex processes within the natural immune system. This work needs to be done; here we outline a suggested route.

3.1 A First Step: Interdisciplinary Research

AIS is a relatively new and emerging bio-inspired area and progress has been made from naively exploiting mechanisms of the immune system. Computer security systems have been developed, anti virus software has been created, optimisation and data mining tools have been created that are performing as well as the current state of the art in those areas.

However, as discussed above, in order to push forward the state of the art in this area, a greater interaction between computer scientists, immunologists and mathematicians is required. AIS are poorly understood on a theoretical level, and the metaphors employed have been typically limited: a deeper understanding of these systems is required as to their broader applicability, and a more radical view of their application is needed to break new ground in the research field, rather than reinvent old technology. In order for this emerging area of research to mature, a detailed investigation of the natural immune system properties and their interactions, coupled with sound theoretical development of corresponding AIS, and testing on hard real world problems, is needed. Such research is essential to ensure success of the area in being adopted as a serious alternative contender in the computational intelligence community.

In recent literature, it seems to be common that naïve approaches to extracting metaphors from the natural immune system have been taken, but this has not always been the case. The original AIS were developed with an interdisciplinary slant.

The work in [Bersini 1991,1992; Bersini & Varela 1994] are such cases. Clear attention to the development of immune network models is given, and these models are then applied to a control problem characterised by a discrete state vector in a state space $\mathfrak{R}^L$. Bersini's proposal relaxes the conventional control strategies, which attempt to drive the process under control to a precise target, to a specific zone of the state space. He instead argues that the metadynamics of the immune network is akin to a meta-control whose aim is to keep the concentration of the antibodies in a certain range of viability so as to continuously preserve the identity of the system.

There are other examples of interdisciplinary work, such as the development of immune gene libraries and ultimately a bone marrow algorithm employed in AIS [Hightower *et al* 1995], and the development of the now famous negative selection algorithm and the first application to computer security [Forrest *et al* 1994].

However, in more recent years, work on AIS has drifted away from the more biologically-appealing models and attention to biological detail, with a focus on more engineering-oriented approach. This has led to systems that are examples of the "reasoning by metaphor" outlined above. These include simple models of clonal selection and immune networks [de Castro & von Zuben 2000, 2001; Timmis 2000; Neal 2003], and negative selection algorithms [Bradley & Tyrrell 2002; Gonzalez *et al* 2003; Taylor & Corne 2003]. This is not a criticism of that work, but we are pointing out that these (and many more engineered solutions) may benefit from not only closer interaction with biologists, but also a more principled mechanism for the extraction, articulation, and application of the underlying computational metaphor.

[Freitas & Timmis 2003] outline the need to take into account the application domain when developing AIS. This seems reasonable when one considers the construction of the final solution. However, this stance will not hold completely when developing generic models and frameworks applicable to a variety of domains. The conceptual framework proposal here does not contradict the position taken in [Freitas & Timmis 2003], but rather complements it: once we have a well-developed conceptual framework, we can specialise it for various application domains in a justifiable way.

3.2 Adopting the Conceptual Framework for AIS

[de Castro & Timmis 2002] propose a structure for engineering AIS. The basis is a *representation* to create abstract models of immune organs, cells, and molecules, together with a set of *affinity functions* to quantify the interactions of these "artificial elements", and a set of *general-purpose algorithms* to govern the dynamics of the AIS.

The structure can be modelled as a layered approach (figure 2). To build a system, one typically requires an application domain or target function. From this basis, a *representation* of the system's components is chosen. This representation is domain and problem dependent: the representation of network traffic, say, may well be differ-

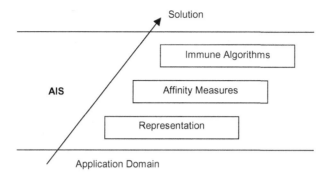

Fig. 2. A structure for AIS, from [de Castro & Timmis 2002]

ent from that of a real time embedded system. Once the representation is chosen, one or more *affinity measures* are used to quantify the interactions of the elements of the system. There are many possible affinity measures (which are also partially dependent upon the representation adopted), such as Hamming or Euclidean distances. The final layer involves the use of *algorithms*, which govern the behaviour (dynamics) of the system, such as negative and positive selection, clonal selection, the bone marrow algorithm, and immune network algorithms. Each algorithm has its own particular range of uses.

However, this layered structure is not complete from the conceptual framework perspective, which we believe is required to allow effective algorithms to be developed.

AIS algorithms in their current form can be classified as *population based* or *network based* [de Castro & Timmis 2002]. In the following sections, we adopt this initial breakdown, and in addition propose that AIS algorithms (in some cases) may benefit from asking questions such as: what is "self", or "danger". We propose how one might undergo a development of an AIS algorithms adopting the conceptual framework above.

3.3 Population Based AIS Algorithms

Three common algorithms in AIS, those of positive, negative, and clonal selection, are all based on *populations* of agents trained to recognise certain aspects of interest. (See [de Castro & Timmis 2002] for an overview.) There are similarities between the algorithms: positive and negative selection, for example, are merely two sides of the same coin. There are also differences: positive and negative selection involve essentially random generation of candidate recognisers, whilst clonal selection uses a form of reinforcement based on selection and mutation of the best recognisers.

Rather than describe how a population based AIS-specific framework might be developed, however, we defer discussion of these models to the meta-frameworks of section 4, and population based models in general.

3.4   Network Based AIS Algorithms

The original immune network theory [Jerne 1974] suggests an immune system with a dynamic behaviour even in the absence of non-self antigens. This differs from the biological basis of the clonal and negative selection algorithms, as it suggests that B-cells are capable of recognizing each other.

Several theoretical immunologists have been interested in creating models of immune networks in order to introduce new ways of explaining how the immune systems works [Perelson 1989; Farmer *et al* 1986]. This has been followed by a number of researchers who have translated some of these ideas into the computing domain, in applications such as optimization and control [Bersini 1991; Bersini & Varela 1994]. This work has also inspired the development of machine learning network models with applications mainly in data analysis [Timmis 2000; de Castro & Von Zuben 2001].

However, as we stated earlier, the later work has somewhat deviated from the biological model, being adapted to a particular problem. In addition, the immune network theory itself is controversial, and not widely accepted by immunologists. This has an impact on the AIS algorithm: if the biology is not correct, then one must re-examine it and understand what is *really* going on; this would hopefully shed light on the more complex nature of the immune systems, and the networks that are clearly present therein.

In order to achieve this understanding, the first step would be to probe the biological system from the perspective of interpreting the system as a *network* of interaction, cooperation and competition amongst molecules, cells, organs and tissues. The discovered properties could then be exploited in order to identify emergent behaviour and formulate a suitable mapping between biological properties and framework components. These components could then be used as the basis for the topology and dynamics of new computational and mathematical models, in addition to re-examining existing models such as [Perelson 2002; Romanyukha & Yashin 2003]. The resulting new models would allow a greater understanding of the operation of such systems to be developed in an artificial context. Within the context of immune networks, one could examine the danger theory [Matzinger 2002], context of response [Janeway & Medzhitov 2002; Kourilsky & Truffa-Bachi 2001], memory mechanisms [Sprent & Surh 2002], general alarm response or stress response [Padgett & Glaser 2003] and self/non-self recognition [Medzhitov & Janeway 2003]. Additionally, the constructive role of noise in biological systems, which is an intrinsic feature of such systems, could also be examined [Gammaitoni 1998].

From these biological models, suitable new computational metaphors could be created. An analytical framework could be created to include appropriate representations for components, methods of assessing interactions between components, and processes to act on components. The framework should also provide features that allow biological models to be represented and manipulated in a number of ways. The framework should permit the analysis and identification of generic properties, and an instantiation of the framework should permit the capture of properties relevant to the application being developed. In an iterative process, the framework algorithms should be implemented and tested in order to test and develop the biological metaphors prior to their implementation and experimental exercises on the intended platform.

Taking this fuller view of immune networks may yield AIS algorithms that truly mimic the qualities of the diversity of immune network memory mechanisms, and may inform us as to the scalability of immune networks, their ability to cope more effectively with noise, their open nature, and the level of interaction both within the network and external to the network. Biology would benefit from the resulting sophisticated models, too.

3.5 Self or Danger?

Immunologists are asking the question, does the immune system distinguish between self and non-self, or is there something more going on? Adopting the framework approach would allow AIS to adopt a principled approach to the review and analysis of such theories as danger theory [Matzinger 2002] and self-assertion [Varela *et al* 1998], and bring forth new and effective bio-inspired algorithms.

A more interdisciplinary slant has already begun in this area. For example, [Aicklen *et al* 2003] describe a large ambitious interdisciplinary project investigating novel ideas from immunology such as danger theory, with the application to computer security. Here the authors propose to observe the biological system by undertaking new experiments to identify key signals involved in cell death, and identify the functions of such signals and how these affect immune cells. The hope is that this research will shed light on how the immune system distinguishes self from non-self, in order to build effective immune-inspired computer security systems that no longer rely on the need to define *a priori* the self of the system. Although those authors make no reference to adopting a framework approach such as outlined above, we believe that it would to help ensure not only biologically-plausible algorithms, but effective and general solutions.

4 Meta-frameworks for Bio-inspired Computation

The earlier figure 1 shows potentially many representations of the same systems under the same observations, each of which may provide different insights. Such distinct representations, although common, are seldom examined for unifying properties. Once we have a conceptual framework, we can not only make such comparisons, we can go a step further: to examine and compare the separate conceptual, mathematical and computational frameworks, to develop more *integrated and generic frameworks*, and to expose essential differences.

To achieve this, we can apply the same conceptual model, at a higher level (figure 3). The key probes here are meta-questions. Just as the questions at the biological level influence the kinds of models developed, so the meta-questions influence the kinds of meta-models developed.

4.1 Meta-probes for Complex System Frameworks

What kind of meta-questions might we ask? Clearly, the questions asked influence the resulting framework. We have identified some initial areas thought to affect complex

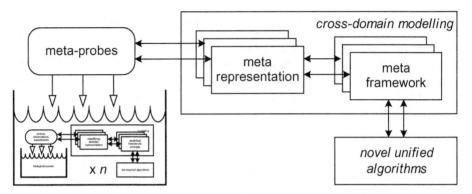

Fig. 3. An outline conceptual framework for integrating bio-inspired computational domains

behaviour in general; questions that address notions such as openness, diversity, inter-action, structure, and scale might lead to models of complex adaptive systems. The idea is to ask each question (suitably refined and quantified) across the range of frameworks being incorporated, and to use the answers as part of the input to build the meta-framework.

Openness: We do not want our computations to halt; we want continual evolution, continual growth, continual addition of resources: that is, *open*, *far-from-equilibrium* systems. How much openness is necessary? How is openness controlled by structure and interaction? How is system unity maintained in the presence of openness?

Diversity (heterogeneity) is present in all complex biological systems, and occurs in structure, behaviour, and interactions. When can we talk of an *average* agent? How much diversity is necessary within a level of a structure? between levels? What does it cost? How does it combat fragility?

Interaction: Agents interact with their environment and with each other. What are the features of interaction within structural levels? between levels? What is the bal-ance between computation and communication?

Structure: Biological systems have structure on a variety of levels, yet the levels are not crisply delineated. Are the levels we discern artefacts of our modelling framework? How can we recognise levels? When is a hierarchy an adequate structural model? How does structure affect interaction? What are the relationships between physical structures and information structures? What is the relationship with speciali-sation of function? with localisation of function?

Scale: Biological systems have a vast scale, a vast number of components. When and how does 'more' become 'different'? What are the critical points/phase transi-tions? How small can a system be, and still be emergent? When is a system too big? How important is multi-scale modelling? What are the relationships between scale and diversity?

Generic questions additionally apply to each meta-probe question area X: What is the role of X within a system? What is the balance between X and not-X at the peak of complexity? How and when does X emerge? How does X evolve? How does physical embodiment affect X? How can we exploit X?

4.2   A Meta-framework for Population Models

Many bio-inspired algorithms are based on *populations* of agents trained to perform some task, or optimise some function. The most obvious one is the area of evolutionary algorithms, based on analogy to populations of organisms breeding and selecting to become "fitter" [Mitchell 1996]. In AIS, there are the positive and negative selection, and clonal selection algorithms. Swarm algorithms and social insect algorithms [Bonabeau 1999] are based on populations of agents whose co-operations result in problem solving. Even a neural network could be viewed as a population of neurons cooperating to perform a recognition task.

Given the number of underlying commonalities, it seems sensible to abstract a meta-framework from individual population based models. (Since these individual frameworks themselves do not yet exist, this section is somewhat meta-speculative!)

What are the key properties of population models, and how are they realised in the various individual models? Here we outline just a few similarities and differences of these models, which could be used in constructing a population based meta-framework.

All these models contain a population of individual agents. Members of the population usually exhibit a range of *fitnesses,* where these *fitnesses* are used when calculating a new population: fitter individuals have a greater effect on the composition of the next generation than do the less-fit individuals. The aim is to find a population that is sufficiently fit for the task at hand.

In evolutionary algorithms (EAs), a population of *chromosomes* reproduces in a *fitness landscape*. Fitter individuals are *selected* more frequently, to breed the next generation. When described in these terms, the clonal selection algithm looks very similar: the population comprises a collection of *antibodies*, which proliferate in an *affinity landscape*. The higher affinity individuals are cloned more, and mutated less, when producing the next generation. Additionally, the lowest affinity cells are replaced by random cells (providing automatic diversity maintenance.) In swarm algorithms, a population of *particles* exists and adapts in a *fitness landscape*. Fitter individuals' properties are *copied* more by the next generation. In ant colony algorithms, a population of paths exist in a local fitness (path component length) landscape. The use of components from fitter (shorter) paths are reinforced (by "pheromones") in the next generation, which is then constructed by "ants" following pheromone trails.

In EAs, clonal AIS, and ant algorithms, the fitness of the entire population is evaluated and used for selection and construction of next generation. Swarm algorithm evaluate the fitness of each individual relative to the others in its *local neighbourhood*. (Some EA variants incorporate *niching*, which provides a degree of locality.)

In EAs, swarm and ants algorithms, the result is the fittest member of the final population. In clonal AIS, however, the result is the entire final population of detectors; the individual detectors are each partial and unreliable, yet their combined cooperative effect makes the full robust detector.

Such commonalities and differences as outline above, once exposed and analysed, can be used to suggest more general algorithms. For example, the natural diversity maintenance of clonal AIS suggests ways for similar mechanisms to be added to other population algorithms, in a less *ad hoc* manner than currently. Also, many population algorithms find themselves forced to add some form of *elitism* to preserve the best solution so far: clonal AIS is naturally elitist. One potentially interesting feature to explore is the relationship between the natural locality of swarm algorithms, and the locality inherent in AIS Danger Theory.

Such a combination of models permits many of the meta-probe question outlined above to be asked. *Diversity* is a key question: how to maintain diversity within a single population, but additionally, should there be different "species", too? *Interaction* with the environment (laying and sensing pheromones) is crucial in the ant algorithms, and with other agents (at least at the level of copying their behaviour) in swarm algorithms. Co-evolution, with its effect on mutual fitness landscapes, can be regarded as a form of interaction. What *scale*, that is, what population size, is appropriate? The probes also force us to think of new issues: is *openness* a relevant aspect? Should we be concerned with flows of agents into and out of the population (other than by internal mechanisms of generational breeding)? And is there any way to exploit *structure*, given the homogeneity of most population algorithms?

This somewhat simplistic meta-framework sketch is built on the correspondingly simplistic population models. More sophisticated population models developed in terms of full conceptual frameworks would doubtless lead to much richer and more powerful meta-frameworks.

4.3 A Meta-framework for Network Models

AIS networks, metabolic networks, auto-catalytic chemical reaction networks, intra-cellular protein interaction networks, inter-cellular cytokine, hormone and growth factor signalling networks, ecological food webs, are all examples of biological networks. Indeed, most biological processes operate through a complicated network of interactions, with positive and negative feedback control by factors that are themselves subject to similar controls. These networks function in a distributed fashion: most components have a variety of roles, and most functions depend on more than one component. This presumably underpins their robustness, whilst keeping the malleability required for adaptability and evolution. How this is achieved in practice is poorly understood.

Currently mathematical and computational descriptions of the structure of biological networks tend to be static (there is no time component to the architecture), closed (no inputs from the environment), and homogeneous (the types of nodes and connections are uniform, and new instances, and new kinds, of connections and nodes, are not supported). It will be necessary to develop novel mathematical approaches to model real complex biological networks. Developing these new mathematical models in the context of the proposed conceptual framework will provide mechanisms for evaluating their appropriateness and power.

5 Discussion and Conclusion

We have argued that bio-inspired algorithms would benefit from exploiting more sophisticated biological models, and from being based on sound analytical principles; we believe that biology could benefit from the resulting sophisticated models, too. We have outlined what we believe to be a suitable conceptual framework including these various components. We have suggested how AIS network models might fit into this framework.

We have additionally sketched how meta-frameworks, based on the same underlying structure, might be applied at higher levels to unify various kinds of bio-inspired architectures, and we have suggested how population based models, including AIS models, might form one such meta-framework. We do not expect that every individual model will fit perfectly into an integrated model: part of the development process will be to expose essential differences as well as to integrate common abstractions.

One exciting prospect of a unified meta-framework is the possibility of a *novel instantiation*, possibly using concepts from across a range of biological domains, and possibly using concepts from outside biology (since words like "Lamarck" and "teleology" need not be so necessarily dismissed in the artificial domain). This would allowing the building of a chimerical computational framework that is inspired by biology, but not restricted to any one particular biological domain.

Acknowledgements. The conceptual framework described in this paper was developed during the EPSRC-funded EIVIS project. We would like to thank the other members of the project for their invaluable contributions to some of the ideas in this paper: Andrew Anderson, Jim Austin, Brian Bell, Peter Bentley, David Broomhead, Robin Callard, Steve Furber, David Halliday, Andy Hone, Douglas Kell, Alan Murray, Jaroslav Stark, Stefan Wermter, David Willshaw, Xin Yao, Peter Young.

References

[1] U. Aicklen, P. Bentley, S. Cayzer, J. Kim, J. McLeod. Danger Theory: The Link Between AIS and IDS? In J. Timmis, P. Bentley, E. Hart (eds) *LNCS 2787,* 156-167, Springer, 2003

[2] H. Bersini. Immune Network and Adaptive Control. *Proc. First European Conference on Artificial Life*, 217-226. MIT Press, 1991

[3] H. Bersini. Reinforcement and Recruitment Learning for Adaptive Process Control. *Proc. Int. Fuzzy Association Conference (IFAC/IFIP/IMACS) on Artificial Intelligence in Real Time Control*, 331-337, 1992

[4] H. Bersini, F. J. Varela. The Immune Learning Mechanisms: Reinforcement, Recruitment and Their Applications. In R. Paton (ed) *Computing with Biological Metaphors*, 166-192. Chapman & Hall, 1994

[5] E. W. Bonabeau, M. Dorigo, G Theraulaz. *Swarm Intelligence: from natural to artificial systems*. Addison Wesley, 1999

[6] D. W. Bradley, A. M. Tyrrell. Immunotronics: Novel Finite State Machine Architectures with Built in Self Test using Self-Nonself Differentiation. *IEEE Transactions on Evolutionary Computation*, **6**(3) 227–238, June 2002

[7] L. N. de Castro, J. Timmis. *Artificial Immune Systems: A New Computational Intelligence Approach*. Springer, 2002

[8] L. N. de Castro, F. J. Von Zuben. The Clonal Selection Algorithm with Engineering Applications. *Workshop on Artificial Immune Systems and Their Applications, Genetic and Evolutionary Computation Conference*, 36-37, 2000

[9] L. N. de Castro, F. J. Von Zuben. aiNet: An Artificial Immune Network for Data Analysis. In H. A. Abbass, R. A. Sarker, C. S. Newton (eds) *Data Mining: A Heuristic Approach,* Chapter XII. Idea Group Publishing, 2001

[10] J. D. Farmer, N. H. Packard, A. S. Perelson. The Immune System, Adaptation, and Machine Learning. *Physica D* **22** 187-204, 1986

[11] S. Forrest, A. Perelson, L. Allen, R. Cherukuri. Self-Nonself Discrimination in a Computer. *Proc. IEEE Symp. on Research in Security and Privacy*, 202-212, 1994

[12] A. Freitas, J. Timmis. Revisiting the Foundations of Artificial Immune Systems. In J. Timmis, P. Bentley, E. Hart (eds) *ICARIS 2003*, LNCS 2787, 229-241. Springer, 2003.

[13] L. Gammaitoni, P. Hanggi, P. Jung, F. Marchesini. Stochastic Resonance. *Rev. Mod. Phys.* **70**(1) 223-287, 1998

[14] D. E. Goldberg. *Genetic Algorithms in Search, Optimization and Machine Learning.* Addison Wesley, 1989

[15] R. R. Hightower, S. A. Forrest, A. S. Perelson. The Evolution of Emergent Organization in Immune System Gene Libraries. In L. J. Eshelman (ed) *Proc. 6th Int. Conf. on Genetic Algorithms*, 344-350. Morgan Kaufmann, 1995

[16] J. H. Holland. *Adaptation in Natural and Artificial Systems.* University of Michigan Press, 1975

[17] C. A. Janeway Jr, R. Medzhitov. Innate immune recognition. *Ann. Rev. Immunol.* **20** 197-216, 2002

[18] N. K. Jerne. Towards a Network Theory of the Immune System. *Ann. Immunol. (Inst. Pasteur)* **125C** 373-389, 1974

[19] P. Kourilsky, P. Truffa-Bachi. Cytokine fields and the polarization of the immune response. *Trends Immunol.* **22** 502-509, 2001

[20] M. Neal. Meta-stable Memory in an Artificial Immune Network. In J. Timmis, P. Bentley, E. Hart (eds) *ICARIS 2003*, LNCS 2787, 168-180. Springer, 2003.

[21] P. Matzinger. The danger model: a renewed sense of self. *Science* **296** 301-305, 2002

[22] R. Medzhitov, C. A. Janeway Jr. Decoding the patterns of self and nonself by the innate immune system. *Science* **296** 298-300, 2002

[23] M. Mitchell. *An Introduction to Genetic Algorithms.* MIT Press, 1996

[24] D. A. Padgett, R. Glaser. How stress influences the immune response. *Trends Immunol.* **24** 444-448, 2003

[25] S. Perelson. Immune Network Theory. *Imm. Rev.* **110** 5-36, 1989

[26] S. Perelson. Modelling viral and immune system dynamics. *Nat Rev Immunol.* **2** 28-36, 2002

[27] A. Romanyukha, A. I. Yashin. Age related changes in population of peripheral T cells: towards a model of immunosenescence. *Mech Ageing Dev.* **124** 433-443, 2003

[28] J. Sprent, C.D. Surh. T cell memory. *Ann. Rev. Immunol.* **20** 551-579, 2002

[29] D. Taylor, D. Corne. An Investigation of the Negative Selection Algorithm for Fault Detection in Refrigeration Systems. In J. Timmis, P. Bentley, E. Hart (eds) *ICARIS 2003*, LNCS 2787, 34-45. Springer, 2003.

[30] J. Timmis. *Artificial Immune Systems: A Novel Data Analysis Technique Inspired by the Immune Network Theory*, Ph.D. Dissertation, Department of Computer Science, University of Wales, September. 2000

[31] F. Varela, A. Coutinho, B. Dupire, N. N. Vaz. Cognitive Networks: Immune, Neural and Otherwise. In A. S. Perelson (ed) *Theoretical Immunology, part 2*, 359-375. Addison-Wesley, 1988

Immunologic Responses Manipulation of AIS Agents

Henry Y.K. Lau and Vicky W.K. Wong

Department of Industrial and Manufacturing Systems Engineering
The University of Hong Kong
Pokfulam Road, Hong Kong, PRC
hyklau@hku.hk, vickywong@hkusua.hku.hk

Abstract. This paper presents a formal mathematical modeling of an AIS-based control framework. The control framework encapsulates how an AIS agent operates autonomously in a dynamic environment through imitating the properties and mechanisms of the human immune system. AIS agents operate under this control framework can manipulate their capabilities in order to determine appropriate responses to various problems. A methodology describes the responses manipulation of how the AIS agents decide different kinds of responses and generate new sets of knowledge is discussed. Through the responses manipulation, a non-deterministic and fully distributed system with agents that are able to adapt and accommodate to dynamic environment by independent decision-making and inter-agent communication is achieved.

1 Introduction

Artificial Immune System (AIS) is an engineering analogue to the human immune system. The human immune system is a self-organized and fully distributed multi-agent system with properties of specificity, diversity, memory management, self-organization and adaptive control. The characteristics of the immune system impart a high degree of robustness in implementing various engineering systems. These systems include parallel searching [1], detection systems [2], autonomous agents [3] and computing systems [4].

This paper extends the work of [5] for the development of an AIS-based control framework. The framework aims to operate various kinds of multi-agent systems. Previous results have shown that the control framework is more efficient in operating a fleet of Autonomous Guided Vehicles (AGVs) in an automated warehouse than the traditional centralized control [5]. This paper focuses on the development of strategic control for the AIS agents. These agents are employed with full autonomy in decision-making and communication by manipulating their capability. The internal behaviors of the AIS agents, which are decided by their perception of the environment, provide mutual understanding between the communicating agents and allow the AIS agents cooperated strategically.

A formal mathematical modeling is presented in this paper to describe the AIS-based multi-agent control framework. A detail methodology in capability manipulation is also described and this methodology forms the core of the AIS-based control framework. AIS agents are able to determine appropriate responses towards different

G. Nicosia et al. (Eds.): ICARIS 2004, LNCS 3239, pp. 65–79, 2004.
© Springer-Verlag Berlin Heidelberg 2004

problems and situations through manipulating their capabilities. Hence, agents under this AIS-based control are fully autonomous and adaptive.

This paper proceeds as follows. Section 2 reviews different AIS-based multi-agent systems. Section 3 illustrates a formal mathematical description of the AIS-based control framework. Section 4 presents the methodology of capability manipulation of the AIS agents. An illustrative example is given in Section 5 to demonstrate how responses are manipulated and new capabilities are generated.

2   The AIS-Based Multi-agent Control Framework

The immune system is a distributed multi-agent system with a collection of special-ized cells, tissues and molecules. Each of these components has distinct physical and functional characteristics that mediate resistance to infectious diseases. The immune components are highly interactive and involved in the immune response with a coor-dinated and specific manner.

Taking these properties of the immune system, various approaches have adopted AIS in the implementation of multi-agent control. The cooperative controls in [3] and [6] use group behavior mechanism of the immune system for autonomous mobile robots. A Distributed Autonomous Robotic System (DARS) that utilizes the AIS techniques shows a noticeable improvement in [7]. An autonomous navigation is developed in [8] to investigate an autonomous control system of mobile robots based on the immune network theory. Since AIS has found it popularity in developing vari-ous kinds of multi-agent systems, a control framework based on this biological meta-phor is proposed to operate a fleet of AGVs for automated material handling with an architecture (Figure 1) which defined the AIS-based control of an individual AGV [5].

The control framework provides a set of rules that guides and determines the be-havior of individual AIS agent in respond to the changing environment. Through the manipulations of the rules, unknown events and dynamic variations of the workplace can be investigated effectively. This paper presents a formal mathematical model to overview how the AIS agent is operated through the control framework. A detail analysis that describes the methodology for capability manipulation in giving out different responses is illustrated. These are the essential components of the proposed AIS agent that are lying within the dotted line area in the control framework shown in Figure 1.

3   Mathematical Modeling

The components of the AIS-based control framework in Figure 1 are formally de-scribed in this section. The control framework is defined for multi-agent based sys-tems. Inspired from the human immunity mechanisms, each AIS agent has its own behaviors and they cooperate via information communication and sharing in order to achieve common goals. Agents employed in the multi-agent system are abstracted as an independent agent that carries local information, searches for solution space and exhibits robust behavior to accomplish different goals.

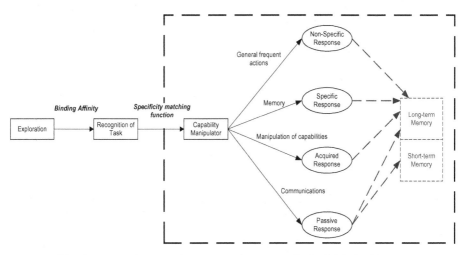

Fig. 1. The architecture of the control framework for individual AIS agent

The basic attributes of the AIS-based control framework includes a set of agents that is operated in the system, a set of goals that is located in the workplace, a sensory range (*SR*) of an agent that enables it to gain or receive information of the surrounding environment and a communication range (*CR*) that allows the agent to exchange information or messaging to each others.

A is a set of agents indexed by *j*:

$$A = \left\{ a_1, a_2, ..., a_j \right\} \qquad where \quad j = 1, 2, ..., n \qquad (1)$$

G is a set of goals indexed by *i*:

$$G = \left\{ g_1, g_2, ..., g_i \right\} \qquad where \quad i = 1, 2, ..., m \qquad (2)$$

The workplace environment, *Env*, is defined as:

$$Env = a_j \cup g_i \qquad \forall \ i, j \qquad (3)$$

3.1 Binding Affinity

The AIS agents employ Binding Affinity (*β*) in task recognition to identify and approach targeted task in a dynamic environment. The binding affinity is enumerated by the distance between an agent and a particular task (d_{ij}), task occurrence frequency (f_{ij}) and agent familiarity with such a task (r_{ij}). Binding affinity is formally modeled as follows:

Binding Affinity, *β*, is a function of d_{ij}, f_{ij} and r_{ij}:

$$\beta_{ij} = f(d_{ij}, f_{ij}, r_{ij}) \qquad (4)$$

$$\beta_{ij} = w_1 \left(d_{ij} \right)^{-1} + w_2 \left(f_{ij} \right) + w_3 \left(r_{ij} \right) \qquad (5)$$

where w_1, w_2 and w_3 are the weightings for the parameters d_{ij}, f_{ij} and r_{ij} respectively.

$d_{ij(E)}$ is Euclidean distance between an agent j and a goal i on a two dimensional plane:

$$d_{ij(E)} = \sqrt{(x_i - x_j)^2 + (y_i - y_j)^2} \tag{6}$$

f_{ij} is the frequency of occurrence of goal where O_i is the number of occurrence of goal i:

$$f_{ij} = \frac{O_i}{\sum\limits_{x=1}^{m} O_x} \tag{7}$$

r_i is agent familiarity with task that is defined by the agent-goal specificity matching, S_m, which is explained in Section 4:

$$r_{ij} = c_1(S_{m00}) + c_2(S_{m01}) + c_3(S_{m10}) \tag{8}$$

c_1, c_2 and c_3 are the weightings for the non-specific (00), specific (01) and acquired (10) capability chains respectively.

3.2 Communications Among the AIS Agents

The fundamental communication channels defined in our AIS-based control framework are designed for exchanging local information, messaging cooperation signals and transferring capability between the agents. The communications processes are primarily govern by the internal behaviors of the agents. In the AIS-based control, different behavioral states and their corresponding strategies that are analogous to the characteristics or mechanisms of the immune system are defined as shown in Table 1. These behavioral states allow agents to act according to and notify other agents' strategies during operations. Hence, these behavioral states form the basis for evaluating the feasibility of achieving a cooperative task through inter-agent communication. The state transition diagram given in Figure 2 underpins how individual agent behaves and executes different actions in response to the dynamic environment they are operating.

Agents of the AIS-based control framework cooperate by signaling each other through the 'request for' and 'respond to' help. This signal transmission is known as cooperation by stimulation and suppression. The AIS agents request for help by sending a 'help' signal to all agents that are within its communication range and regardless which agent is capable to offer help. On the other hand, there are no particular rules or algorithms defined to guide or restrict the agents in responding to the 'help' signal. This is similar to the human immune system where the immune cells are activated regardless of the type of antigens. The immune cells recognize a wide variety of antigens in the native conformation, without any requirement for antigen processing or display by a specialized system [9].

The prime concern to employ cooperation in the AIS-based control is to identify the current behavioral state of the responding agent so as to check if it is feasible to offer help. An agent who is in the Explore or Disperse states is capable to offer help and will be activated by the 'help' signal. Agent who is neither in the Explore or Dis-

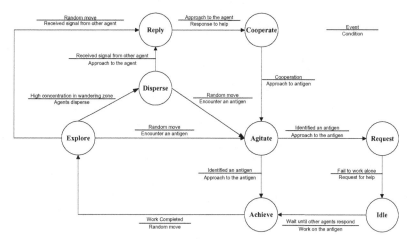

Fig. 2. A state transition diagram of an AIS agent

Table 1. Behavioral states of AIS agent

Behavioral State	Notation	Strategy
Achieve	Ach	To tackle the targeted goal.
Agitate	Ag	A goal has been found and the agent approaches the targeted goal.
Cooperate	Co	To offer help and participate in a cooperative work.
Disperse	D	To keep away from other agents if the number of agents is higher than a threshold value in a wandering zone. A wandering zone is defined as a region where none of the goals can be detected.
Explore	E	To explore the surrounding environment and search for goals randomly.
Idle	I	To wait for other agents for help in tackling a cooperative work.
Reply	Rp	To receive the 'help' signal from other agents.
Request	Rq	To request for help from other agents.

perse states will just ignore the request and continue the current job. In the meantime, the agent that is waiting for the help is being suppressed and change to Idle state until someone has responded. To allow such cooperation, it is necessary to establish a set of agents that are able to communicate with each other in the multi-agent system.

The jth agent that is within the communication range of the agent x (CR_x), $a_j^{CR_x}$, is defined as:

$$a_j^{CR_x} \triangleq \left| d_{xj(E)} \right| < CR_x \tag{9}$$

where $d_{xj(E)}$ is the Euclidean distance between agent x and agent j as given in equation (6).

The set of agents that is within the CR_x of agent x, A^{CR_x}, is defined as:

$$A^{CR_x} = \left\{ a_j \in a \mid a_j^{CR_x} \right\} \tag{10}$$

$$\exists A^{CR_x} \in a, \quad a_j^{CR_x} \wedge \neg(a_x) \tag{11}$$

The 'help' signal sent by agent x for the ith goal, h_j^i, is defined as:

$$h_j^i = (a_x, g_i) \qquad \forall \; A^{CR_x} \tag{12}$$

The 'response' signal sent by agent j with respect to agent x request, r_j^i, is defined as:

$$r_j^i = (a_j, g_i, h_j^i) \qquad \forall \; a_j^{cc_x}(E \vee D) \tag{13}$$

3.3 Basic Interactions Between the AIS Agents

Strategic behavioral changes of the AIS agents can be investigated through their interactions. There are two types of interactions between the agents of our AIS-based control framework. They are concentration constraint in the wandering zone and cooperation in teamwork.

As mentioned in Table 1, the number of agents within a wandering zone is restricted. This is to maximize the efficiency of the searching process and avoid overcrowding of agents in a multi-agent system. The concept of concentration constraint is inspired by the self-regulation theory of the human immunity. The theory is a balancing mechanism of antibody concentration that simulates and suppresses an immune response [10]. The immune system produces antibodies when antigen is presented and returns to equilibrium when antigen is eliminated.

Assuming that the number of agents that are exploring in the environment is n and the concentration threshold within the wandering zone is τ, the strategic changes of agents under the concentration constraint are as follows:

$$na(E) \rightarrow (n - \tau)a(D) \wedge \tau a(E) \qquad if \;\; n > \tau \tag{14}$$

$$na(E) \rightarrow na(E) \qquad if \;\; n < \tau \tag{15}$$

One of the significance of behavioral states is to illustrate how agents cooperate with each other. The pervious section has defined how agents can cooperate through communication. With the aid of the behavioral states, the change of agents' internal strategy can also be demonstrated. When agent x cannot complete the targeted task and needs cooperation from other agents, it will then send a 'help' signal to request for cooperation and change to the Request state, $a_x(\text{Rq})$.

The agent that may offer help and reply to agent x, $a_j^{CC_x}$, is defined as:

$$\forall a_j(Rp) \in a_j^{CC_x}, \quad a_j(E \vee D) \tag{16}$$

The cooperation processes with strategic behavioral control between the AIS agents are defined as:

$$[a_x(Rq) \wedge a_y(Ry)] \rightarrow [a_x(I) \wedge a_y(Co)] \tag{17}$$

$$[a_x(Rq) \wedge a_y(Ag)] \rightarrow [a_x(Ach) \wedge a_y(Ach)] \tag{18}$$

4 Responses Manipulation of the AIS-Based Control Framework

The AIS-based control framework presented in Figure 1 follows the idea of the human immune responses which consists of a sequence of actions. These sequential phases are antigen recognition, activation of lymphocytes, elimination of antigen and memory [9]. The core of the control framework is to manipulate different responses towards various problems encountered by the AIS agents. Four responses, drawing analogy from human immunity, have been identified in the response manipulation algorithm as specified in Figure 1. They are non-specific, acquired, specific and passive responses.

4.1 Capability Chain

The basic structure of all antibodies consists of two pairs of heavy and light chains. The heavy chains dedicate the class of antibody whereas the light chain is antigentically distinct and only one type of light chain is present in any single antibody molecule [11]. Imitating the structure of an antibody, a pair of heavy and light chains is abstracted to form a capability chain for each of the responses identified in the control framework. The heavy chain specifies the class of responses and uses as an indication for the respective response. The light chain consists of a sequence of atomic abilities and the atomic ability sequence is distinct for every response. On the other hand, an antigen of the system, for example a parcel to be moved, is represented by an antigen complexity chain. It has the same structure as the capability chain where the light chain is defined as antigen complexity. It specifies the required capabilities to handle the problem. In order to verify the feasibility of an agent to handle a task, specificity matching function is used to compare the light chains of both capability chain and antigen complexity chain. The structure of a capability chain and an antigen complexity chain is shown in Figures 3 and 4 respectively.

Figure 5 illustrates how the AIS agent determines an appropriate action in response to the encountering of an antigen autonomously. The agent initially considers if it is going to deal with an ordinary task or to response to a request. If the goal requires the achievement of a cooperative task, the agent will then communicate with the requested agent and perform a passive response. A passive response is similar to vaccination where the requesting agent will transfer necessary skills to the helper in order to complete the task. Contrarily, if the agent encounters an ordinary goal, the agent will initially check the capability of the non-specific and acquired chains. If nothing can be matched, the agent will then manipulate its atomic abilities in the non-specific chain to give out specific response.

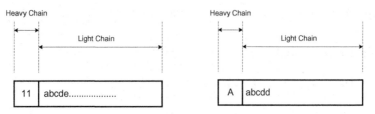

Fig. 3. A capability chain   **Fig. 4.** An antigen complexity chain

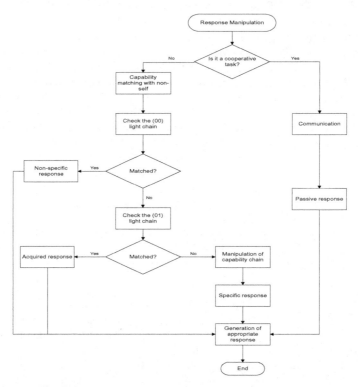

Fig. 5. Overview of the responses manipulation algorithm

The inter-relationship of the four capability chains is shown in Figure 6. The non-specific response deals with general and frequently occurred tasks. The sequence of atomic abilities is pre-defined during system development. Different types of system will have different notations for atomic abilities to specify the agents' actions. No capability manipulation is required for non-specific response. This response is an innate immunity which is the first general defense that provides resistance to antigens. For a distinct and specific task, the agents will generate a new set of knowledge through capability manipulation. This manipulation includes re-combination of atomic abilities from the non-specific response. The new capabilities will then go to the acquired response chain. This mechanism is equivalent to the secondary immunity where a faster and stronger response will be resulted in the next occurrence of the same antigen.

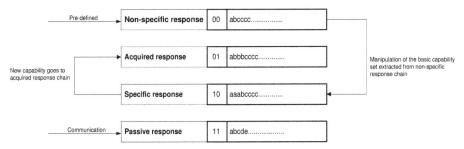

Fig. 6. Inter-relationship between the four capability chains

4.2 Specificity Matching Function

The specificity matching function utilizes the string matching algorithm [12]. This function is used to verify the feasibility of an agent to handle a particular task. In immunology, the activation of immune cells, lymphocytes, is triggered by recognition of antigens [9]. The lymphocytes recognize antigens structurally by their antigen receptors. Following this pattern recognition concept, string matching is used to recognize the required capabilities of the antigen complexity chain from the agent's capability chain. Hence, the light chains of both the agent and the antigen are compared to determine if the agent is competent to handle the targeted goal.

In specificity matching, non-specific (00) and acquired (01) capability chains are first being investigated since they give out faster responses by an absolute string matching method as illustrated in Figures 7 and 8. The absolute string matching determines if the whole string of an antigen complexity light chain can be found from the capability light chain and gives an absolute result of either matched or unmatched.

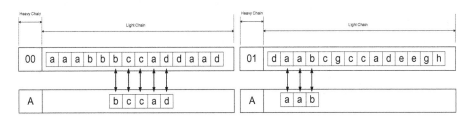

Fig. 7. Absolute string matching (1)   **Fig. 8.** Absolute string matching (2)

When an unmatched is resulted for both non-specific and acquired responses, specific response will then mediate to manipulate new knowledge that is capable to tackle the problem. The capability manipulation re-combines or re-arranges the elementary abilities of the non-specific capability chain to generate a new set of knowledge that is specific to the new problem. This process resembles that of the immature lymphocytes having receptor editing where receptors with self-specificity can make further re-arrangements of their light chains [13]. Figure 9 shows the sequential stages for capability manipulation.

A set of capability manipulation rules are used to determine how the atomic abilities in the non-specific (00) capability chain are manipulated to form new sets of

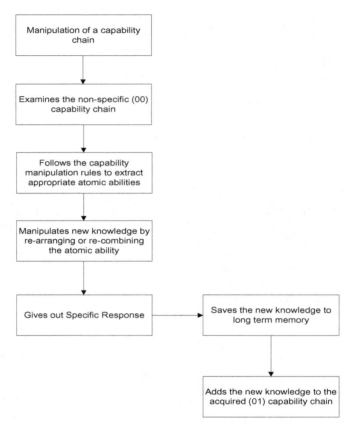

Fig. 9. The sequence of capability manipulation

knowledge. Not all generation of new capabilities will be successful. The atomic abilities of the non-specific capability chain should be qualified for a re-combination. All the capability manipulation rules must be satisfied and fulfilled in the listed order. The rules for capability manipulation are as follows:

Rule 1: Disjoin the antigen complexity light chain.

Rule 2: Compare the required capabilities of the antigen complexity individually with the capability chain. Check if all the disjointed required capabilities are found within the non-specific (00) capability chain.

Rule 3: Generate all possible combination of the required capabilities. These combinations are in the simplest form where minimum duplication of atomic capability is resulted.

Rule 4: Compare all the sets of disjointed required capabilities generated above with the capability chain. Extract all the matched sets.

Rule 5: Compute the matched sets by graph theory to find out the shortest path and to minimize the computational steps in re-arranging or re-combining a new set of knowledge that is capable to tackle the new problem.

The new knowledge developed by capability manipulation is appended to the acquired (01) capability chain after solving the problem. Addition of new capabilities to the capability chain has to avoid duplication of atomic ability and maintain a contigu-

1. If length of the new capability set, *newCap*, is equal to *n*, get *n* number of characters (*getChar*) from the end of the existing capability chain.
2. Match the strings *getChar* and *newCap* by absolute string matching.
3. If nothing is matched, delete the first character of *getChar*. This is done by shifting, $S_{(t-1)}$, the *getChar* pattern by *getChar = n-(t-1)* where *t=1* for the first string matching.
4. Match *getChar* with *newCap* by prefix string matching until *t=n*. This prefix string matching will return true (matched) only if the whole *getChar* pattern matches the prefix of the *newCap*.
5. When a matched is found, delete the first *(n-S)* characters of *newCap* and append the *newCap* to the end of the exiting capability chain.
6. Else if no match is found, append the whole *newCap* to the end of the existing capability chain.

Fig. 10. The append string algorithm

ous capability sequence of the existing chain. An append string algorithm, as given in Figure 10, is applied to attached the new capability set at the end of the exiting chain without duplication.

The procedures of adding new capability by the append string algorithm are illustrated diagrammatically by Figures 11 and 12. In Figure 11, nothing has been matched till *t=n=4*, therefore the whole set of new capability is appended to the end of the existing capability chain. On the other hand, in Figure 12, nothing has been matched when *t=1*. After the first shift (S_1), *getChar* becomes an 'ee' pattern. A matched is found when the *getChar* pattern is matched with prefix of the new capability set. Hence, the first two characters of *getChar*, which are 'ee', are eliminated from the new capability set. The remaining pattern of the new capability, which is the 'g' pattern, will then be appended to the existing capability chain.

5   An Illustrative Example of Responses Manipulation

The responses manipulation introduced previously is illustrated by an example in this section. For simplicity, we focus on how individual AIS agent determines different responses whereas cooperation among agents, indicated by the passive (11) capability chain, is not considered.

Capabilities of the AIS agents are classified into two main categories. They are simple capability and compound capability. Simple capability performs basic and straightforward action whereas compound capability deals with more complex and difficult tasks. Simple capability is represented by fundamental atomic ability such as 'a', 'b' 'c' and 'd'. Complex capability is a set of actions generated from the simple capability. For example, set of complex capability from 'a' and 'b' may include: {'aa', 'aaa', 'abb', 'abc'} and {'bb', 'bbb', 'baa', 'bca'}.

A simple example is illustrated the operation of the responses manipulation under the proposed scheme. The actual representation of what the capabilities are is not considered at this stage. Assuming the capability chains of agent *j* and the antigen complexity chains of Task I to IV are given by Figure 13 and Figure 14 respectively.

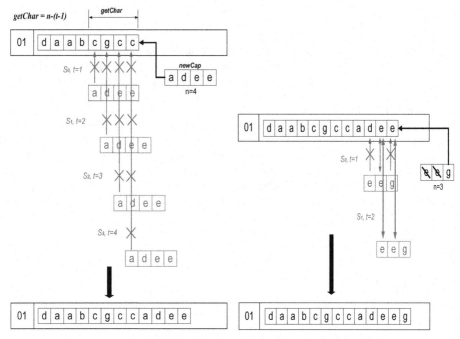

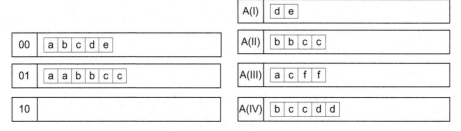

Fig. 11. Addition of new capability (Case 1)   **Fig. 12.** Addition of new capability (Case 2)

Fig. 13. Capability chains of Agent j **Fig. 14.** Antigen complexity chains of Task (I) to (IV)

To tackle a task, the AIS agent first investigates the non-specific (00) and acquired (01) capability chains with absolute string matching. For Task I, a match is found on the non-specific (00) chain. A direct and simple non-specific response 'de' is then carried out. Task II requires a set of capability 'bbcc' to tackle the problem. Nothing can be matched on the non-specific (00) capability chain. The acquired (01) chain is then examined. When a matched is found, the AIS agents then execute a direct and rapid 'bbcc' acquired response. The pseudo code is as follows.

Task III requires a set of capability 'acff'. Since this capability set cannot be found on both non-specific and acquired chains, the AIS agent needs to manipulate its capability in order to complete its task. The capability manipulation rules presented in Section 4.2 are followed. The set of capability 'acff' is disjointed and becomes 'a',

Pseudo code 1. Responses manipulation

```
nonChain = capabilities of the non-specific (00) capability
chain
acqChain = capabilities of the acquired (01) capability chain
taskChain = the capacities of antigen complexity chain

match = absoluteStringMatch(taskChain,nonChain)
if match = TRUE
 nonSpecificResponse()
else
 match = absoluteStringMatch(taskChain,nonChain)
 if match = TRUE
 acquiredResponse()
 else
 capabilityManipulation()
```

'c', 'f' and 'f'. According to rule 2, all the disjointed required capabilities are required to be referenced from the non-specific (00) capability chain to allow capability manipulation. The 'a' and 'c' are found, however, there are no 'f's presented in the non-specific (00) chain. Hence, this set of capability 'acff' is illegal to perform the specific capability manipulation. The AIS agent is therefore failed to handle Task III.

Similar to Task III, the required capability of Task IV 'bccdd' needs to be manipulated. The disjointed required capabilities of this set are 'b', 'c' and 'd' which is a legal set of capability for manipulation. Following Rule 3, there are 153 possible combinations of those disjointed capabilities from the set 'bccdd'. To re-arrange a new set of knowledge that is specific to Task IV, the 'bcd' pattern from the non-specific (00) capability chain is extracted for manipulation. New re-arranged patterns such as 'bc', 'cd', 'bd', 'bbc' and 'cdd' are generated. Through computation by graph theory, the pattern 'bc' and 'cdd' are re-combined to form the new set of capability 'bccdd' and give out specific response to solve Task III.

The new set of knowledge 'bccdd' is then appended to the acquired (01) capability chain. Following the append string algorithm given by Figure 10, 'bccdd' is the *newCap* with *n* equals to 5. *getChar* is 'abbcc' when *t=1* and *S=0*. No match is found until *t=3* and *S=2*. When there is a match, the first (n-S) characters, which are the first three characters 'bcc', are deleted from the *newCap*. The finalized *newCap* 'dd' is then appended to the acquired (01) capability chain without any duplication as shown in Figure 15.

The capability chains of agent *j* after finishing task I to IV are shown in Figure 16. The new capabilities acquired from handling Task IV are added to the acquired (01) capability chain. This leads to a stronger and faster response in reoccurrence of Task IV. Having different capability chains to perform specificity matching for responses manipulation allows the AIS agents to have a quick response in determining the strategy and technique to achieve goals. Intelligent and adaptable AIS agent that is flexible to new environment and in tackling various problems can thereby achieve through the immunologic responses manipulation.

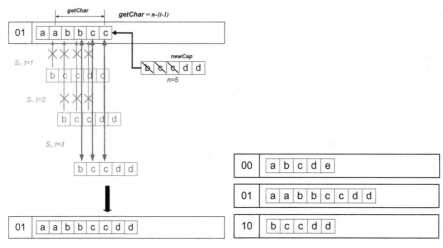

Fig. 15. The acquired (01) capability chain of Agent *j* after capability manipulation

Fig. 16. Capability chains of Agent *j* after operations

6   Conclusion

This paper extends and formalizes the work in [5] for the development of an AIS-based control framework. The control framework encapsulates how an AIS agent operates autonomously in a dynamic environment. A mathematical model is presented to formally describe the AIS-based control framework. Through the strategic behavioral study of the AIS agents, cooperation is evolved by mutual understanding and communication among them. On other hand, the response manipulation introduced in this paper presents the core idea of how an AIS agent can determine its capability towards different situations or problems. The work aims to develop a truly decentralized and non-deterministic multi-agent system where agents are self-organized, autonomous and intelligence in decision-making.

References

[1]   Fukuda, T., Mori, K. and Tsukiyama, M., Parallel Search for multi-Modal Function Optimization with Diversity and Learning of Immune Algorith, Artificial Immune Systems and Their Applications, D. Dasgupta Ed., Springer-Verlag, (1998) 210-219.

[2]   Kim, J. and Bentley, P., The Human Immune System and Network Intrusion Detection, 7th European Conference on Intelligent Techniques and Soft Computing (EUFIT '99), Aachen, Germany, (1999).

[3]   Lee, D.-W., Jun, J.-H. and Sim, K.-B., "Realization of cooperative strategies and swarm behavior in distributed autonomous robotic systems using artificial immune system", Systems, Man, and Cybernetics, *1999 IEEE International Conference*, Vol. 6, (1999) 614-619.

[4]   Sokolova, L., Index Design by Immunocomupting, ICRAIS 2003, (2003) 120-127.

[5]   Lau, H.Y.K. and Wong, V.W.K., Immunologic Control Framework for S=Automated Material Handling, ICRAIS 2003, (2003) 57-68.

[6]   Lee, D.W. and Sim, K.B., Artificial Immune Network-based Cooperative Control in Collective Autonomous Mobile Robots, IEEE International Workshop on Robot and Human Communication, (1997) 58-63.

[7]   Meshref, H. and VanLandingham, H., "Artificial Immune Systems: Application to Autonomous Agents", Systems, Man, and Cybernetics, *2000 IEEE International Conference*, Vol. 1, (2000) 61-66.

[8]   Michelan, R. and Von Zuben, F.J., Decentralized control system for autonomous navigation based on an evolved artificial immune network, Proceedings of the 2002 Congress on Evolutionary Computation, CEC '02, (2002) Vol. 2, p. 1021-1026.

[9]   Abbas, A. K. and Lichtman, A. H., Basic immunology: functions and disorders of the immune system, Philadelphia: W.B. Saunders Co., (2001).

[10] Elgert, K. D., Immunology: understanding the immune system, New York: Wiley-Liss, (1996).

[11] Eales, L.J., Immunology for life scientists: A basic introduction: A student learning approach, Chichester, John Wiley & Sons, (1997).

[12] Cormen, T.H., Leiserson, C.E., Rivest, R.L. and Stein, C., Introduction to algorithms, Cambridge, Mass London, Boston McGraw-Hill, 2nd Ed. (2001).

[13] Roitt, I.M., Brostoff, J. and Male, D., Case studies in immunology: companion to Immunology, 5th Edition, London Mosby, (1998).

Optima, Extrema, and Artificial Immune Systems

Andrew Hone[1] and Johnny Kelsey[2]

[1] Institute of Mathematics, Statistics & Actuarial Science, University of Kent,
anwh@kent.ac.uk,
http://www.kent.ac.uk/ims/people/anwh/index.htm
[2] Computing Laboratory, University of Kent, Canterbury, CT2 7NF, UK,
johnny_kelsey@yahoo.com

Abstract. We review various problems of extremization that arise in the calculus of variations, with wide-ranging applications in mathematics, physics and biology. Euler-Lagrange equations come from the extremum of an action functional, and we reformulate this as an optimization problem. Hence the task of solving systems of differential equations can be recast as the problem of finding the minimum of a suitable quantity, which is appropriate for the application of artificial immune system (AIS) algorithms. We also show how the problem of finding roots of polynomial functions is naturally viewed as another minimization problem. In numerical analysis, the Newton-Raphson method is the standard approach to this problem, and the basins of attractions for each root have a fractal structure. Preliminary investigations using the B-Cell Algorithm (BCA) introduced by Kelsey and Timmis suggest that the behaviour of AIS algorithms themselves can display fractal structure, which may be analyzed with dynamical systems techniques.

1 Introduction

Artificial immune systems (AIS) constitute a new paradigm in biologically inspired computing [5], [28]. This new paradigm has already been identified as being extremely useful in a wide range of actual and potential applications, including job shop scheduling, image alignment, analysis of bioinformatic data, fault detection, and many more [29]. Another standard application is function optimization (see [6], [13] for instance), which is particularly relevant for problems in molecular biology such as protein folding [23]. The aim of this short note is to suggest a whole range of new applications for AIS algorithms, as well as a possible approach to a rigorous analysis of their behaviour using the theory of dynamical systems. Here we should emphasize that, without the development of a substantial theory to justify the convergence properties of AIS, considerable caution is needed when applying them to new optimization problems.

There is a more general family of problems, which is concerned with *extremization* of functionals rather than simple function optimization, but which should nevertheless still be amenable to AIS techniques, and this larger family of

G. Nicosia et al. (Eds.): ICARIS 2004, LNCS 3239, pp. 80–90, 2004.
© Springer-Verlag Berlin Heidelberg 2004

problems is applicable to a huge range of situations in mathematics, physics and biology. We believe that the discussion of extremization problems is original in the context of AIS. Therefore, in the next section we provide basic background material on extremum principles, before explaining how to convert them into more standard optimization problems that can be solved via AIS methods. We also give a survey of important application areas where AIS might be employed for extremization problems in the future. The one-dimensional brachistochrone problem is used here as a pedagogical example, before moving onto its multivariate, multi-dimensional generalizations that arise in applications. We give a brief qualitative comparison of AIS optimization compared with some standard numerical analysis techniques, indicating why AIS may have some advantages in this area.

In the third section we consider a different problem, namely that of finding the roots of a polynomial. The traditional numerical scheme for solving this problem is the Newton-Raphson method, which leads to beautiful fractal patterns in the complex plane [25]. However, we show how this problem can be recast as another form of optimization, meaning that AIS can immediately be used to solve it. We have recently begun to use an implementation of the B-Cell Algorithm (BCA) introduced by Kelsey and Timmis [13] to solve a well known root-finding problem (the cube roots of unity), and we find that this also leads to apparently fractal structures in the complex plane. This strongly suggests that the behaviour of the BCA and other AIS algorithms might be analyzed using nonlinear dynamical systems, which we briefly discuss. The final section contains our conclusions and outlook for future work.

Before we launch into the main discussion, here it is convenient to summarize the main steps of the BCA as formulated in [13]. The algorithm seeks to minimize an objective function $g(p)$, as follows:

- Step 1: Create an initial random population P of individuals.
- Step 2: For each $p \in P$, evaluate $g(p)$ and create a clone population C.
- Step 3: Select a random member $c \in C$ and apply contiguous somatic hypermutation.
- Step 4: Evaluate $g(c)$; if $g(c) < g(p)$ then replace p by clone c.
- Step 5: Repeat steps 2-4 until a stopping criterion is met.

The significant novel feature of the BCA is the contiguous somatic hypermutation operator. The individuals $p \in P$ and $c \in C$ are represented by bit strings, and the hypermutation operator picks a segment of the string c of random length and then applies random mutation to this contiguous region. We describe how the above algorithm can be applied to the problem of finding zeros of a function in the third section below.

2   Extremum Principles

Extremum principles are ubiquitous in mathematics [11], with wide applications in areas ranging from genetic theory [21] to thermodynamics [30]. The most familiar example from single-variable calculus is the condition $f'(x) = 0$ for a stationary point, with the second derivative $f''(x) < 0$ or $f''(x) > 0$ ensuring a local maximum or minimum respectively; if $f''(x) = 0$ then there may be a saddle point. The general characterization of functions in terms of their behaviour near critical points is the subject of Morse theory [20].

Probably the most widespread type of extremum principles are those arising from the application of the calculus of variations [8]. One of the first historical examples of this sort is the brachistochrone problem posed by Johann Bernoulli the elder in 1696: given a particle sliding from rest along a path between two fixed points under the influence of gravity, find the plane curve such that the time taken is minimized. The solution curve (a cycloid) was obtained by both Johann and Jakob Bernoulli, and also by Newton, Leibniz and l'Hôpital. Nowadays the problem is usually solved directly through the use of the total time functional

$$T[y] = \int_{x_0}^{x_1} \sqrt{\frac{1 + (y')^2}{2g(y_0 - y)}} \, dx \equiv \int_{x_0}^{x_1} F(y, y') \, dx, \qquad y' = \frac{dy}{dx}, \qquad (1)$$

where $y(x)$ is the plane curve joining the points (x_0, y_0) and (x_1, y_1) and g is the acceleration due to gravity. To minimize the time it is necessary that the first variation of the functional T should vanish,

$$\delta T = 0,$$

which leads to the Euler–Lagrange equations

$$\frac{\partial F}{\partial y} - \frac{d}{dx}\left(\frac{\partial F}{\partial y'}\right) \equiv \frac{2(y_0 - y)y'' + (y')^2 + 1}{2\sqrt{2g}(1 + (y')^2)^{3/2}(y_0 - y)^{3/2}} = 0 \qquad (2)$$

The solution of the second order differential equation (2) is given parametrically in terms of (x_0, y_0) and another constant h by

$$x(\theta) = x_0 + (\theta - \sin\theta)/(2h^2), \qquad y(\theta) = y_0 - (1 - \cos\theta)/(2h^2).$$

Analogously to the condition $f''(x) > 0$ for a function of one variable, the positivity of the second variation $\delta^2 T$ ensures that the cycloid yields a minimum of the functional $T[y]$.

Given that the functional $T[y]$ has a minimum, then we can immediately formulate an optimization problem to derive a numerical solution. Since T depends on the function $y(x)$ and its derivative, we can replace the interval $[x_0, x_1]$ by a lattice of N points (for sufficiently large N) and set up a finite approximation scheme as follows:

$$y_0 = Y_0; \quad y_1 = Y_N; \qquad y(x_0 + j\epsilon) \approx Y_j, \quad j = 1, \dots, N-1, \qquad (3)$$

with

$$\epsilon = (x_1 - x_0)/N \ll 1.$$

Thus if the derivative of $y(x)$ at each lattice site is replaced by the forward differences

$$y'(x_0 + j\epsilon) \approx Y_j' = \frac{Y_{j+1} - Y_j}{\epsilon},$$

then the total time integral (1) can be crudely approximated by a sum:

$$T[y] \approx \tilde{T}[Y] := \sum_{j=1}^{N-1} \epsilon F(Y_j, Y_j'). \qquad (4)$$

Hence we arrive at a simple optimization problem:

Minimum time evaluation. *Given the end point values $Y_0 = y_0$, $Y_N = y_1$, find which intermediate values $Y_1, Y_2 \ldots, Y_{N-1}$ minimize the sum $\tilde{T}[Y]$ in (4).*

This optimization problem is clearly stated in a form suitable for AIS algorithms such as the BCA [13], but it could obviously be made more efficient by choosing a less crude finite difference scheme than the above. Moreover, as $N \to \infty$ the values Y_j should give successively better approximations to the function $y(x)$ sampled at a discrete set of points.

Although the brachistochrone problem concerns finding the minimum of a functional - in this case the total time given by (1) - the more general situation is that the *extremum* of some quantity is required, and in this general case ordinary optimization is insufficient. In physics perhaps the most important extremum principle of all is the *principle of least action*, also called Hamilton's principle. An early proponent of this notion was Maupertuis, who employed an extremality argument to solve a problem in statics [2]. The enormous generality of the least-action principle became apparent from the Lagrangian formulation of classical mechanics [9], as derived from the action functional

$$S[\mathbf{q}] = \int_{t_0}^{t_1} L(\mathbf{q}, \dot{\mathbf{q}}, t)\, dt. \qquad (5)$$

The variable t is the time, the vector $\mathbf{q}$ and its time derivative $\dot{\mathbf{q}}$ denote the generalized coordinates and velocities respectively, while the Lagrangian function L is just the difference of the kinetic and potential energies. We require that the action should be stationary with respect to variations that vanish at the initial and final times, so

$$\delta S = 0, \qquad \text{with} \quad \delta\mathbf{q}(t_0) = 0 = \delta\mathbf{q}(t_1). \qquad (6)$$

(This variational condition is explained in more detail below.) It then follows (after an integration by parts) that L must satisfy the Euler–Lagrange differential equations

$$\frac{\partial L}{\partial \mathbf{q}} - \frac{d}{dt}\left(\frac{\partial L}{\partial \dot{\mathbf{q}}}\right) = 0. \qquad (7)$$

The extremality condition (6) is truly fundamental, since once the Lagrangian L has been specified appropriately then all the classical equations of motion for a mechanical system (in particular, Newton's second law) are a direct consequence. The equations of motion are systems of coupled second order differential equations (ODEs) which in most cases cannot be solved explicitly, so one must resort to numerical integration schemes. Runge-Kutta methods are the most popular numerical ODE solvers, although an area of huge current interest is geometric integration [3], whereby the symmetries or geometrical properties of ODEs are preserved as much as possible. In particular, geometric integrators can be devised to preserve extremum principles.

To see how one might develop an AIS algorithm to solve (6), and hence obtain the solution of the Euler–Lagrange ODEs (7) *without* doing numerical integration, we consider in detail the exact meaning of $\delta S = 0$ within the calculus of variations [8]. The idea is that one should consider the action functional $S[\mathbf{q}]$ evaluated on the function $\mathbf{q}(t)$, and then look at the perturbation $\mathbf{q}(t) \rightarrow \mathbf{q}(t) + \delta\mathbf{q}(t)$ and evaluate $S[\mathbf{q} + \delta\mathbf{q}]$. The variation δS is just found by working out the change in S to first order in $\delta\mathbf{q}$, so we have

$$\delta S \approx S[\mathbf{q} + \delta\mathbf{q}] - S[\mathbf{q}] \tag{8}$$

to leading order. However, the solution to $\delta S = 0$ can lead to a maximum, minimum or a saddle point of the action $S[\mathbf{q}]$. To find an equivalent optimization problem, we can consider the following:

Minimization procedure. *Find the vector function $\mathbf{q}(t)$ such that the expression*

$$M[\mathbf{q}, \delta\mathbf{q}] = \left| S[\mathbf{q} + \delta\mathbf{q}] - S[\mathbf{q}] \right| \tag{9}$$

is a minimum for all (suitably small) perturbations $\delta\mathbf{q}$.

Because of the modulus signs in (9), we are guaranteed that the extremum of the action $S[\mathbf{q}]$ corresponds to the minimum of $M[\mathbf{q}, \delta\mathbf{q}]$. Also, because M is just given by the absolute difference of two action integrals (5), these can be approximated by a finite difference scheme similar to (4), by splitting up the time interval $[t_0, t_1]$ into a lattice.

The above minimization procedure using a discrete time lattice should provide a direct and simple way to apply AIS optimization algorithms (as in e.g. [6], [13]) to problems in mechanics. There are currently many challenging problems in numerical simulation of mechanical systems - in particular we should mention the Newton equations for molecular dynamics [18]. Finding the minimum of an appropriate quantity M as in (9) would also be relevant to problems in geometrical optics [17], using Fermat's principle of least time. However, possibly the most exciting application to physical problems would be in classical and quantum field theory.

Classical field theories are given by an action integral

$$S[\phi] = \int_V \mathcal{L}(\phi, \phi_\mu, \ldots)\, d^4x, \tag{10}$$

where the integration is taken over a region V of four-dimensional spacetime. In the formula (10), the Lagrangian density $\mathcal{L}$ is a function of the field ϕ, its first derivatives ϕ_μ ($\mu = 1, \ldots, 4$), and possibly higher derivatives. The appropriate variational principle for the classical field equations is

$$\delta S = 0, \qquad \text{with} \quad \delta\phi(\mathbf{x}) = 0 \quad \mathbf{x} \in \partial V,$$

so that the field variations $\delta\phi$ vanish on the boundary ∂V. Maxwell's theory of electromagnetism can be derived from an action of the form (10), as can Einstein's general theory of relativity [4].

The field theoretic action (10) is central to the path integral formulation of quantum field theory, as pioneered by Feynman [7]. The path integral allows the perturbative calculation of Feynman diagrams and quantum scattering amplitudes in gauge field theory [1]. The most important examples of gauge field theories are quantum electrodynamics (QED), electroweak theory, and quantum chromodynamics (QCD), which describe interactions involving the electromagnetic, weak and strong forces respectively. However, while perturbation theory in QED gives extremely accurate results, the situation in QCD is rather different: perturbation theory in QCD only works in the limit of high temperature (or equivalently, high energy), but at the low energies corresponding to ordinary nuclear matter it becomes impossible to make analytical calculations. To get around this problem, a major effort has been made to formulate QCD as a lattice gauge theory, replacing spacetime by a four-dimensional lattice and calculating with a discrete action using Monte-Carlo methods [15]. This is a hugely computationally intensive programme, and is the focus of the International Lattice Data Grid collaboration.

From the above it should be clear that there are some hugely important physical problems in which AIS optimization methods have the potential to play a role. Other areas where extremization principles apply are the maximum entropy and minimum energy principles in thermodynamics [27], and von Neumann's Minimax Theorem in game theory [31]. The latter only applies to two-person zero-sum games, and is usually solved using linear programming techniques [24], but it was proved by Nash [22] that there is a similar principle for n-person games (the Nash equilibrium). There are currently no general methods for finding Nash equilibria, so new computational approaches would be extremely desirable.

Very recently we became aware of the work [19] where neural networks have been applied to some simple problems in the calculus of variations. The approach taken by the authors of [19] is the standard method of Galerkin approximation, where it is assumed that the solution lies in some particular infinite set of functions, and then a finite truncation of this set is used to approximate it. There are various other mathematical techniques that are used for the numerical analysis of problems in optimization and control theory [16]; here we should mention the steepest descent method, variation of extremals, and quasilinearization. An in-depth knowledge of classical optimization is clearly a mandatory requirement for those wanting to apply AIS to extremization problems. However, here we would like to point out some possible advantages that the BCA (and other AIS) may have to offer:

- Unlike Galerkin approximation, the BCA does not assume the class of functions in advance.
- Steepest descent can be very slow to converge; the BCA method converges rapidly, at least compared with GAs [10].
- Variation of extremals and quasilinearization diverge if the initial approximation is poor; the BCA randomizes the starting point.

So far it seems that different AIS algorithms have only been compared with each other, or with equivalent genetic algorithms (as in [10]). Any serious evaluation of the BCA and other AIS algorithms will require proper benchmarking against classical numerical analysis techniques [16].

3   Roots of Polynomials and Fractals

We now move away from general extremum principles, and describe a situation where ordinary optimization (in fact, minimization) is applicable, namely the problem of finding roots of polynomials. Given a polynomial function $p(z)$ which takes a complex argument z (the case of real z is a special case), we are interested in solving the equation

$$p(z) = 0. \tag{11}$$

If p is of degree D then in the generic situation there will be exactly D solutions in the complex plane (i.e. provided there are no repeated roots). The traditional method for solving (11) is the Newton-Raphson method: start from a value z_0 which is near to one of the roots, and then calculate the successive iterates

$$z_{t+1} = z_t - \frac{p(z_t)}{p'(z_t)}, \qquad t = 0, 1, 2, \ldots$$

in the hope that they will converge to a solution. (The same method applies to an arbitrary differentiable function $p(z)$, but in that case there may be no solutions, or infinitely many.)

Let us take a concrete example, a cubic polynomial (of degree $D = 3$):

$$p(z) = z^3 - 1.$$

In this case the solutions of (11) are

$$z = 1, \qquad (-1 + \sqrt{3}i)/2, \qquad (-1 - \sqrt{3}i)/2, \tag{12}$$

the cube roots of unity, which lie at the vertices of an equilateral triangle in the complex plane. The Newton-Raphson iteration becomes precisely

$$z_{t+1} = z_t - \frac{(z_t^3 - 1)}{3z_t^2}, \tag{13}$$

However, the outcome of calculating the successive values z_t depends sensitively on the choice of the initial value z_0. For each root (12) there is a set of values of z_0 for which the Newton-Raphson method will converge to that root: this is called its *basin of attraction*. However, there are also periodic orbits which lie outside the basins of attraction. The basins of attraction are fractal sets, and beautiful fractal images are produced by assigning a colour to each root and then colouring the points in the plane according to which root they converge to [25].

There is an alternative way to calculate the roots of a polynomial, using an AIS function optimization algorithm. To do this, observe that

$$F = |p(z)|^2 = p(z)\overline{p(z)} \geq 0$$

(bar denotes complex conjugate), so F is non-negative and $F = 0$ precisely when $p = 0$ i.e. at the roots. Now writing the point in the complex plane as $z = x + iy$, in terms of its real and imaginary parts, we can think of F as a function of two real variables x, y, so

$$F(x, y) = p(x + iy)\overline{p(x + iy)}.$$

For example, for the case of the cubic considered above we have

$$F(x, y) = x^6 + 3x^4y^2 + 3x^2y^4 + y^6 - 2x^3 + 6xy^2 + 1,$$

and this polynomial function of two variables is non-negative and vanishes at the points (x, y) corresponding to the roots (12). Hence to find these roots we can apply an AIS algorithm to find the minimum of $F(x, y)$.

We have made a preliminary trial of this approach using the BCA algorithm introduced by Kelsey and Timmis [13], applied to the cube roots of unity problem. Remarkably, it appears that with the BCA, the basins of attraction of the roots still display some sort of fractal structure, with the complex plane divided up into striped regions of mostly the same colour (where "colour" corresponds to "root"). However, within each stripe there a yet further gradations of colour, so that by zooming on a particular region new granular structure is revealed. The data files for the colour plots thus obtained are too large to present here, but a sample output from the BCA applied to the solutions of $z^3 - 1 = 0$ can be downloaded from the internet site [12] (where basins of attraction of the three roots have been coloured red, green and blue). More colour plots have been generated and discussed in [14], and a detailed analysis of these results will be presented elsewhere. The granular structure apparent from [12] is possibly an artefact of the randomness inherent in the BCA (especially the somatic hypermutation operator), which contrasts with the Newton-Raphson fractals which come from a completely deterministic procedure.

The initial investigations above suggest that it may be possible to assign a fractal dimension to the sets obtained from iteration of the BCA (see [14] for more details), and that it may be appropriate to apply dynamical systems techniques in order to prove the convergence properties of this and other AIS algorithms. However, this will require further consideration of the stochastic nature of AIS, so that convergence can only be "on average" (in the sense of probability theory). The BCA appears to perform qualitatively better than genetic algorithms (GAs) when applied to function optimization, even for functions which vary sharply with respect to a control parameter [10]. It is a challenge for the future to perform rigorous benchmarking of the BCA: against GAs, against other AIS algorithms, and above all against classical optimization methods.

4   Conclusions

In summary, we propose that AIS algorithms have the potential to be useful in a wide range of new and important applications, including the following:

- Differential equations
- Molecular dynamics simulation
- Lattice quantum field theory
- Nash equilibria in n-person game theory

However, in order to be applied to such challenging problems, AIS will need to be carefully benchmarked against existing numerical schemes. Furthermore, some sort of rigorous theory is required to ensure their convergence to a solution (at least on average over several trials). Our brief discussion of the solution to polynomial equations suggests that the theory of dynamical systems and fractals may have something to offer in this regard. We conclude by pointing out that a dynamical systems approach to AIS convergence is not entirely without precedent, when one considers that the development of AIS was inspired by the dynamical description of biological immune systems in the work of Weisbuch, Perelson and others [26].

Acknowledgements. We are grateful to Thurston Park for inspiration, and to Jon Timmis for useful discussions. The referees' comments were also very helpful.

References

1. Bailin, D. & Love, A.: *Introduction to Gauge Field Theory*. Adam Hilger (1986)
2. Beeson, D.: *Maupertuis: an intellectual biography*. Voltaire Foundation, Taylor Institution, Oxford: Alden Press (1992)
3. Budd, C.J. & Iserles, A. (Eds.): Geometric integration: numerical solution of differential equations on manifolds. *Phil. Trans. R. Soc. Lond. A* **357** (1999) 943-1133.
4. Choquet-Bruhat, Y.: *Géométrie différentielle et systèmes extérieurs*. Paris: Dunod (1968)
5. de Castro, L.N. & Timmis, J.: *Artificial Immune Systems: A New Computational Intelligence Approach*. Springer-Verlag (2002)
6. Cutello, V. & Nicosia, G.: An Immunological Approach to Combinatorial Optimization Problems, in *Advances in Artificial Intelligence - IBERAMIA 2002*, F.J. Garijo, J.C. Riquelme, M. Toro (Eds.). Lecture Notes on Artificial Intelligence vol. 2527 (2002) 361–370.

7. Feynman, R.P. & Hibbs, A.R.: *Quantum Mechanics and Path Integrals*. New York: McGraw-Hill (1965)
8. Gelfand, I.M. & Fomin, S.V.: *Calculus of Variations*. Englewood Cliffs, New Jersey: Prentice-Hall (1963)
9. Goldstein, H.: *Classical Mechanics*. Reading, Massachusetts: Addison-Wesley (1950)
10. Hone, A., Kelsey, J. & Timmis, J.: Chasing Chaos, in *Proceedings of the Congress on Evolutionary Computation, Canberra, Australia*, R. Sarker et al. (Eds.), IEEE (2003) 413–419.
11. Hone, A.: Extremum principles, in *Encyclopedia of Nonlinear Science*, A.Scott (Ed.), Fitzroy Dearborn, Routledge (2004) in press; http://www.routledge-ny.com/nonlinearsci/
12. Postcript image of BCA applied to $z^3 - 1 = 0$ downloadable at http://www.kent.ac.uk/ims/publications/documents/banyan1.ps (scroll image to bottom of window)
13. Kelsey, J. & Timmis, J.: Immune Inspired Somatic Contiguous Hypermutation for Function Optimisation, in *Proceedings of Genetic and Evolutionary Computation Conference (GECCO) 2003*, Cantu-Paz et al. (Eds.), Lecture Notes in Computer Science **2723** (2003) 207–218
14. Kelsey, J.: An Immune System-Inspired Function Optimisation Algorithm, MSc thesis, University of Kent (2004)
15. Kenway, R.D.: Particles from scratch: the hadron spectrum from lattice gauge theory. *Contemporary Physics* **31** (1990) 325-333.
16. Kirk, D.E.: *Optimal Control Theory - An Introduction*. Englewood Cliffs, New Jersey: Prentice Hall Inc. (1997)
17. Kline, M. & Kay, I.W.: *Electromagnetic Theory and Geometrical Optics*. New York: Interscience Publishers, John Wiley & Sons (1965)
18. Kol, A., Laird, B. & Leimkuhler, B.: A symplectic method for rigid-body molecular simulation. *J. Chem. Phys.* **107** (1997) 2580-2588.
19. Meade, A.J. & Sonneborn, H.C.: Numerical solution of a calculus of variations problem using the feedforward neural network architecture. *Advances in Engineering Software* **27** (1996) 213–225
20. Morse, M. & Cairns, S.S. *Critical Point Theory in Global Analysis and Differential Topology*. New York: Academic Press (1969)
21. Narain, P.: On an extremum principle in the genetical theory of natural selection. *Journal of Genetics* **72**(1993) 59–71
22. Nash, J.: Non-Cooperative Games. *Annals of Mathematics* **54** (1951) 286–295
23. Nicosia, G.: Combinatorial Landscapes, Immune Algorithms and Protein Structure Prediction Problem. Poster at Mathematical and Statistical Aspects of Molecular Biology (MASAMB XIV) at Isaac Newton Institute, Cambridge, March 2004.
24. Owen, G.: *Game Theory*, 2nd edition. London: Academic Press (1982)
25. Peitgen, H.-O. & Richter, D.H.: *The Beauty of Fractals: Images of Complex Dynamical Systems*. Springer-Verlag (1986)
26. Perelson, A.S. & Weisbuch, G.: Immunology for physicists. *Rev. Modern Phys.* **69** (1997) 1219–1267
27. Prestipino, S. & Giaquinta, P.V.: The concavity of entropy and extremum principles in thermodynamics. *Journal of Statistical Physics* **111**(2003) 479–493
28. Tarakanov, A.O., Skormin, V.A. & Sokolova, S.P.: *Immunocomputing: Principles and Applications*. Springer-Verlag (2003)
29. Timmis, J., Bentley, P. & Hart, E. (Eds.): *Artificial Immune Systems*. Proceedings of ICARIS 2003. Lecture Notes in Computer Science **2787** Springer-Verlag (2003)

30. Velasco, S. & Fernandez-Pineda, C. 2002. A simple example illustrating the application of thermodynamic extremum principles. *European Journal of Physics* **23** (2002) 501–511

31. von Neumann, J. & Morgenstern, O.: *Theory of Games and Economic Behaviour.* New Jersey: Princeton University Press (1947)

An Immuno Control Framework
for Decentralized Mechatronic Control

Albert Ko, H.Y.K. Lau, and T.L. Lau

Intelligent Systems Laboratory
The University of Hong Kong
Pokfulam Road, Hong Kong SAR
aux1496@hkusua.hku.hk

Abstract. The Immune System is a complex adaptive system containing many details and many exceptions to established rules. Exceptions such as the suppression effect that causes T-cells to develop reversible aggressive and tolerant behaviors create difficulties for the study of immunology but also give hints to how artificial immune systems may be designed.
Presented in this paper is the General Suppression Framework, which models the suppression hypothesis of the immune discrimination theory. A distributed control system based on the proposed framework is designed to control a modular robot configured into a planar manipulator arm. The modules can generate emergent group behaviors by exhibiting aggressive or tolerant behavior based on the environment change. A MATLAB simulation program is developed to demonstrate the effectiveness of the suppression mechanism and a mechanical arm is constructed to verify the control actions of the mechanism. The ultimate ambition of this work is to understand how the suppression mechanism affects the discrimination system and in turn affect other integral parts of the artificial immune system.

Keywords: Artificial Immune Systems, Distributed Control, Multi-agents.

1 Introduction

Artificial Immune Systems (AIS) [4] that function like their biological counterparts is gaining researchers' attention from different disciplines. Lau & Wong [9] developed a control framework to improve the efficiency of a distributed material handling system. Segel & Cohen [12] examined how biological ideas can help to solve engineering problems, and inversely how the artificial system can inspire new conjectures to unrecognized methods by which the immune system is organized. de Castro & Timmis [3] presented the application of AIS in computer network security, machine learning, and pattern recognition. Tarakanov et al. [16] introduced Immunocomputing as a new computing approach based on the fundamental concept, the formal protein (FP). The virtual world, Tierra, created by Ray [11] contains virtual viruses and hosts that develop artificial immune systems to defend them. This work may not directly classify under AIS, but also share similar conceptual ideas. The term AIS was even mentioned in a novel [17] as early as 1992.

G. Nicosia et al. (Eds.): ICARIS 2004, LNCS 3239, pp. 91–105, 2004.

This paper presents the development of a new distributed control framework, named General Suppression Framework. The framework inspired by the suppression hypothesis in discrimination theory has a *Suppression Modulator* that contains many suppressor cells (*SC*) with different functions. To evaluate the effectiveness of the suppression mechanism, a seven-joint hyper-redundant planar manipulator is simulated in MATLAB and its mechanical counterpart is also constructed to verify the simulated motion and torque.

This paper proceeds as follows. Section 2 provides an overview of the Immune System. The overview focuses in bringing out the major concepts of the system and ignoring the details that may get in the way of seeing the big picture. Section 3 introduces the suppression hypothesis in discrimination theory and presents the General Suppression Framework. Section 4 discusses how the modules generate useful emergent behaviors using only simple local rules and how the suppression mechanism improves the efficiency of the system. The setup of the mechanical and simulated manipulator is also described in detail. Section 5 concludes the work in this paper and discusses future works to be taken.

2   The Immune System

The mother nature has inspired many fascinating systems to solve engineering problems [14], to name but a few, artificial neural networks [5] enable systems to learn effectively, genetic algorithm [2] creates diversified answers for complex problem, and swarm behavior inspired highly scaleable multi-agent systems [18]. Human Immune System [1] in its own stand is an extremely effective system that can identify abnormal activities, solve the problem using existing knowledge, and generate new solutions for unseen events; in short it is a network of players who cooperate to get things done. Strictly speaking Human Immune Systems consists of two major parts, the Innate Immune System (or sometimes called the Natural Immune System) and the Acquired (or Adaptive) Immune System. The General Suppression Framework presented in this paper is based on the acquired immune system.

Before going into the artificial version of the highly intricate Immune System, a basic understanding of how natural immunity protects our body would help to appreciate the intelligence embedded within the system and should also help the readers to see how the intelligent control of decentralized systems can benefit from Artificial Immune Systems (AIS) in the later sections.

Innate Immune System [10] consists of elements that are always present and available at very short notice to foil challenges from "foreign" invaders. These elements include skin, mucous membranes, and the cough reflex, which act as barriers to environmental invaders. Internal components such as fever, interferons, macrophages, and substances released by leukocytes also contribute to terminating the effect of invaders directly or to enhance the effectiveness of host reactions to them.

Acquired Immune System is a supplement to the innate system and presents only in vertebrates. The major recognition and reaction functions of the immune response are performed by T-lymphocytes (T-cells) and B-lymphocytes (B-cells) which exhibit specificity towards antigen. B-cells synthesize and secrete into the bloodstream antibodies with specificity against the antigen, the process is termed Humoral Immunity. The T-cells do not make antibodies but seek out the invader to kill, they also help B-cells to make antibodies and activate macrophages to eat foreign matters. Acquired immunity facilitated by T-cells is called Cellular Immunity.

Despite the many details in immunology theory, there are four unique functions that contribute to the operation of the entire system. These functions are:

Clonal Selection – This theory holds that each B-cell makes antibodies that fit only one specific type of antigen, called its "cognate" antigen. When the specific B-cell binds to its cognate, the B-cell proliferates to clone many copies of itself which recognize that same antigen. The newly cloned cells will become plasma B-cells and continue to produce and export huge quantities of antibodies and will continue to clone more B-cells. This simple action is recognized as one of the major concepts in immunology for its simplicity and high effectiveness.

Immunological Memory – After B and T cells have been activated and proliferated to build up clones and destroy the foreign invaders, most of them will die off but some of them will live to pass on their knowledge of the antigen. These leftover B and T cells become immunological memory of the system and therefore are called Memory Cells. These cells are much easier to activate than "inexperienced" cells and can spring into action quickly to protect the body.

Antibody Diversity – This is a modular design process which mix and matches segments of B-cell genes to create Modular diversity and Junctional diversity. The result of this mix and match strategy is a small number of gene segments can create incredible antibody diversity.

Discrimination – The most unique function of the immune system, perhaps the most important one too is to discriminate Non-Self Cells from Self Cells. Self Cells are the good cells that exist and work inside our body. Non-Self Cells are external elements that do harm to the system (antigen). The distinction and the recognition of foreign antigen is done by B-Cells and T-Cells, which allows the system to identify harmful bodies to respond (to kill) and leave the good bodies (self-cells) untouched.

3   The Framework

The *General Suppression Framework* developed in this research is based around the analogy of the immunosuppression hypothesis [15] in the discrimination theory. When a T-cell receptor binds to a peptide with high affinity presented by an APC (Antigen Presenting Cells), the T-cell recognized the antigen become mature and it has to decide whether to attack the antigen aggressively or to tolerate it in peace. An important decision factor is the local environment within which the T-cell resides. The present of inflammatory cytokine molecules such as interferon-gamma (INF-) [13] in the environment tend to elicit aggressive behaviors of T-cells, whereas the anti-inflammatory cytokines like IL-4 and IL-10 tend to suppress such behavior by blocking the signaling of aggression. In brief, a T-cell matured after recognizing an antigen does not start killing unless the environment also contains encouraging factors for doing so. In addition, after a mature T-cell developed a behavior, it will emit humoral signals to convert others to join. The mechanism is illustrated in Figure 1.

Our analogy infers each module (joint) of the modular robot or manipulator is an autonomous T-cell that continuously reacts to the changing environment and affects the functioning of other cells through the environment. The framework consists of five major components. The most notable difference between the natural mechanism

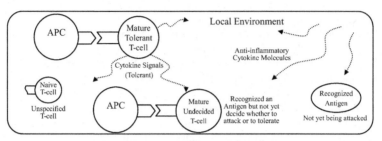

Fig. 1. Cell Suppression Mechanism.

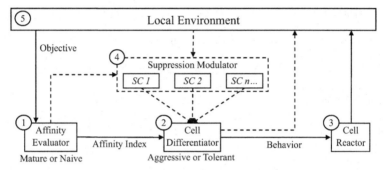

Fig. 2. The General Suppression Framework. Dashed lines represent humoral signal transmissions, where solid lines represent cellular signals.

shown in Figure 1 and the proposed framework shown in Figure 2 is that the T-cell's functions are divided into three separate components, the *Affinity Evaluator*, *Cell Differentiator* and the *Cell Reactor*. Delegating the three unique functions into separate components enables the system to be organized in modular manner and that when programming for an application, the result and effect of each component can be observed easier. The key functions of the five components are explained below.

(1) *Affinity Evaluator* – evaluates information in the *Local Environment* against the objective and output an affinity index. The function of this component is similar to the immune discrimination function, which helps to differentiate between self and non-self cells. *Affinity Evaluator* can affect the *(2) Cell Differentiator* in two ways, the first is to directly send a cellular signal that indicates the affinity level, the second is to send humoral signals to *Suppressor Cells (SC)* in the *(4) Suppression Modulator*. The cellular signals give a spontaneous effect that last only one cycle, whereas humoral signals can remain effective until another humoral signal is released to reverse or to neutralize the effect.

(2) *Cell Differentiator* – evaluates inputs from the *(1) Affinity Evaluator* and *(4) Suppression Modulator* to decide the type of behavior to adapt. The decided behavior is sent to *(3) Cell Reactor* using cellular signaling. The component can also send humoral signals directly to influence the *(5) Local Environment*. The functioning of the *(2) Cell Differentiator* is similar to the cell differentiation mechanism, in which cells develop aggressive or tolerant behavior in response to the type of cytokines present in the environment. When activated, these cells also release humoral signals to convert nearby cells to duplicate their behavior.

(3) Cell Reactor – reacts to the cellular signal from the *(2) Cell Differentiator* and execute the corresponding behaviors which take effect in the *(5) Local Environment*. This component is the part that actually does the killing like activated aggressive T-cells.

(4) Suppression Modulator – is a collection of *Suppressor Cells*, which response to different stimulations and exhibit specific suppression effects to *(2) Cell Differentiator's* decision process. The function of *Suppression Modulator* is comparable to the cytokine signaling mechanism which uses IFN- , IL-4, IL-10, etc. to perform intercellular communication and to cause the environment to inflame, so to elicit or suppress aggressive behaviors in the T-cells. In this framework, the *(4) Suppression Modulator* acquire information from the *(5) Local Environment* and the *(1) Affinity Evaluator*. This information is available to all Suppressor Cells within the modulator. There can be 0, 1, 2, 3, …, n number of *Suppressor Cells* and their response to stimulation may also influence other *Suppressor Cells* inside the modulator. When the number of *Suppressor Cell* is zero, the Modulator still exists but can no longer process information acquired from the *(5) Local Environment*, therefore all information will be fed directly to the *(2) Cell Differentiator*.

(5) Local Environment – is where interactions between different components take place. The importance of this component within the framework is to act as an interface that links to the *Global Environment* which contains other *Local Environments* with different sets of *Suppression Modulators*. In addition it provides a theoretical space to integrate the physical objects and the abstract system in an analyzable form.

4 Simulation and Implementation

The primary focus of this experiment is to exploit the T-cell suppression mechanism to control a modular robot [8] configured in the form of a multi-link hyper-redundant planar manipulator arm in decentralized fashion. Conventionally, a purpose-built articulated robot arm would have joints designed to provide the torque necessary for the task. i.e. a robot arm for lifting heavy parts would have a high-torque joint near to the base to manipulate the load and the links, whereas, the joint-torque near to the end-effector would be smaller because it is designed to carry the load only. Such robot arms are very unlikely to run out of joint-torque under designed working conditions (see Figure 3). However, when a modular robot configures into an articulated arm, the joint acting as the "base" can only exert as much torque as the joint acting as the "end-effector". Therefore the decentralized system must prevent each joint from exceeding its torque-limit while controlling individual modules to generate emergent behavior as a whole to reach the objective.

Ivanescu and Bizdoaca [6] have developed a hierarchical controller for hyper-redundant cooperative robots. The work effectively solved the force distribution problem but the system is only partially decentralized. Kimura et al. [7] developed a decentralized control algorithm for hyper-redundant manipulator that has failed joints. However, the system is not perfectly decentralized because it needs a core processor to supervise the system. In the remaining of this paper a fully decentralized system will be presented for controlling a hyper-redundant manipulator arm with limited joint torque.

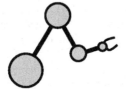 

Fig. 3. Purpose-built robot arms (Left) deliver larger torque at the base joint and smaller torque near at the end-effector. Modular robot arms have identical torque at each joint.

4.1 The Simulation

A simulation program concerning the control of a modular robot configured in the form of a planar hyper-redundant manipulator arm is constructed using MATLAB to demonstrate how the proposed framework can be applied to control a distributed system.

The planar manipulator arm (Figure 4) is constructed of seven modules. Each module has one degree-of-freedom and a motion range of +/- 90 degree from the center line (Figure 5). The system is completely distributed as each module has its own processing unit for logic evaluation and motion control. Each module constantly displays its local angle and joint torque for its immediate neighboring modules to see, conversely the module can read the same information from other modules. However, no active request of information is allowed. The working torque is set at 15 kg.cm (identical to the physical module), the module can adjust the joint angle freely under this limit, beyond which, the joint can no longer adjust itself and will not hold when the torque exceeds 20 kg.cm.

The seven modules are configured in such a way that module-one (md_1) is grounded as the base of the manipulator, followed by md_2, md_3, md_4, md_5, md_6, and md_7 is the end-effector equipped with a light sensor to track the light. The ultimate objective is to minimize the distance between the light source and the light sensor on md_7 without any joint exceeding the maximum torque limit. i.e. 20 kg.cm.

Theoretically, all modules possess the same ability but the sensors they carry differentiate their role within the system. In this simulation, the light sensor carried by md_7 allows the module to determine its distance from the light source, hence, giving it the ability to affect the entire system. However, it should be noted that other modules are also capable of producing similar effect if equipped with the necessary sensor.

The simulation consists of two separate programs, the main program, **msr_manipulator** contains the control algorithm, and the sub-program, **graphical_outputs** handles the arithmetic and produces the three output windows shown in Figure 4. The first window displays the motion of the manipulator and the location of the light source. The second window displays the joint torque of each module in kg/cm, and the third window displays the modules' local angle ranging from -90 to +90 degree.

The **graphical_outputs** plots and simulate the manipulator's motion by calculating the *Head*, *Joint* and *Tail* coordinates and the (AGA) *Accumulated Global Angle* (the angle between the *Head-Joint-Link* and the X-axis). A module's *Head* coordinate is

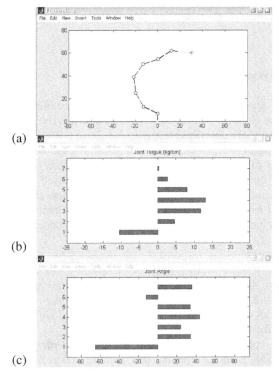

(a)

(b)

(c)

Fig. 4. The three simulator output windows showing the shape (a), the torque (b) and the local angle (c) of the simulated seven-link hyper-redundant manipulator.

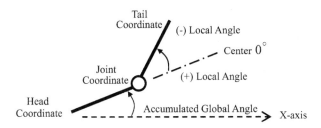

Fig. 5. An illustration of a single module in the simulation.

the same as the preceding module's *Tail* coordinate when docked, except for md_1's, which is grounded to the origin of the graph space (0, 0). The AGA of each module is calculated by the preceding module's AGA minus its *Local Angle*. The local *Joint* coordinate is found by converting its polar coordinate (σ, ρ) into Cartesian coordinate [x, y] in reference to the module's *Head* coordinate, where σ is the AGA in radian, and ρ is the length of the *Head-Joint-Link*. The converted coordinate is added to the linked *Head* coordinate to generate the global *Joint* coordinate in reference the origin of the graph space. The *Tail* coordinate is found by the same method by substituting *Local Angle* for AGA, and *Joint* coordinate for *Head* coordinate. When the locations of all components are known, the torque at each joint can be easily calculated by summing the moments created by the modules between itself and the hanging end-effector. In this simulation, the length of each link is 7 centimeter and the mass is 100 gram each.

4.2   The Control System

The control system applied to the manipulator is shown in Figure 6. This system is based on the General Suppression Framework, and also has five distinct components. Their specific functions are described below:

(1) *Affinity Evaluator* – is responsible for determining the affinity level according to the torque status of the neighboring modules. The affinity is highest when the torque loads of both neighboring modules plus the module itself are all under working limit, otherwise the affinity is low. Notice the information about the neighboring modules is obtained from the *(5) Local Environment*, this infers that each module is an independent unit and everything else, to the module's concern, belongs to the external environment.

(2) *Cell Differentiator* – is responsible for deciding the module's behavior by evaluating the affinity index from *(1) Affinity Evaluator* and the suppression index from *(4) Suppression Modulator*. In general, the cell becomes aggressive if the affinity index is high and become tolerant if the affinity index is low. However, the suppression index can act as a suppressant to force the (2) *Cell Differentiator* to become tolerant even when the affinity index is high.

(3) *Cell Reactor* – obtains instruction from the *(2) Cell Differentiator* and converts it into real action. This is the component that actually makes the module exhibit behaviors to influence the environment.

(4) *Suppression Modulator* – contains only one *suppressor cell* in this system. The *suppressor cell* reads in ls_dst from the light sensor and releases a humoral signal to suppress the *(2) Cell Differentiator* from choosing to become aggressive. The suppression signal's effect is strongest to those modules located furthest from the light sensor, and because the signal is in humoral form, it continues to affect the modules until another signal is sent to neutralize it. This suppression mechanism is simple but very useful for controlling systems that have the tendency to over react to occasional conditions.

(5) *Local Environment* – is where interactions between modules take place.

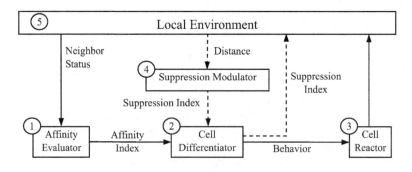

Fig. 6. The control system for the MSR manipulator based on the General Suppression Framework.

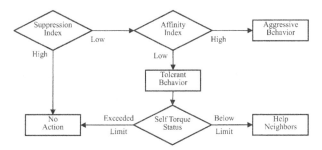

Fig. 7. Decision scheme in Cell Differentiator.

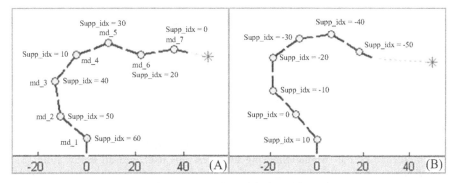

Fig. 8. When the distance from light source (ls_dst) is low (A) the initial suppression index is high. Conversely the initial suppression index is low (B).

The *Cell Differentiator* and the *Suppression Modulator* are the heart of the system; the former is responsible for integrating complex information from different sources into simple instruction, whereas the later plays an important role in turning intricate problems into quantitative outputs. The decision flow of the *Cell Differentiator* can be summarized using a simple flow chart as shown in Figure 7. Note that the suppression index can divert the decision straight to a behavior (No Action) without considering the affinity index level.

The suppression index (Supp_idx) grows stronger as the modules' location grows further from the signal origin (light sensor). When a module receives a suppression index, it adds a number (i.e. 10) to the index number and displays the result for the preceding module to consult. Since each module can only read information from the neighboring modules, the value of the suppression index will become higher as it passes from md_7 to md_1. The initial value can begin with any real number depending on the value of ls_dst, and all modules receiving a suppression index greater than zero will be affected. For example the suppression index in Figure 8(A) begins from 0 at md_7 and reaches 60 at md_1; therefore all modules except md_7 will be affected. In Figure 8(B), the suppression index begins from -50 at md_7; hence, only md_1 will be affected because it has a suppression index greater than 0.

The movement of the manipulator arm is indeed a reflection of the emergent behavior of the seven autonomous modules. Each module can exhibit aggressive or tolerant behavior; the decision is governed by two factors, the distance of light source from the light sensor (ls_dst), and the torque status of the neighboring modules in

Table 1. Status of neighbors in relation to self behavior. A module cannot exhibit aggressive behavior when its joint_torque has exceeded the limit.

Joint_torque Neighbor #1	Joint_torque Neighbor #2	Self Joint_torque	Self Behavior	Self Action
Good	Good	Good	Aggressive	Adjust Local Angle
Over limit	Good	Good	Tolerant	Help Neighbor #1
Good	Over limit	Good	Tolerant	Help Neighbor #2
Over limit	Over limit	Over limit	Tolerant	No Possible Actions

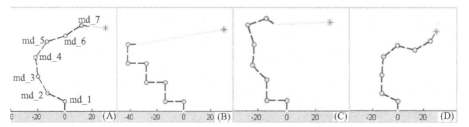

Fig. 9. In (A), if md_1, md_2 or md_3 adjust their *Local Angles* towards the positive direction even by one degree. Md_7 would get swung beyond the light source and must turn back to search again.

relation to the module's own. A module will not exhibit aggressive behavior unless the joint_torque of the two neighboring modules plus itself are all below limit (Table 1). The ls_dst is a signal from the sensor which acts as the suppressant to prevent over aggressive behaviors. A module will exhibit tolerant behavior if the joint_torque of itself or one or more of its neighbor has exceeded the limit. If a module in tolerant mode is still under its torque limit, it will attempt to help its neighboring modules to alleviate the torque load by adjusting its *Local Angle*.

To reach the furthest point, the system needs to adjust all modules' *Local Angles* to values that are as close to zero as possible. Following this logic, when the *Local Angle* of md_7 (the module equipped with the light sensor) is different from zero, its preceding module with aggressive behavior will adjust its *Local Angle* to absorb the difference. For the example in Figure 9(A), the *Local Angle* at md_7 is +30°; md_6 will increase its *Local Angle* slowly to facilitate md_7 to adjust to zero-degree while still pointing at the light source. At the same time, md_5 will adjust its *Local Angle* to absorb the angular differences at md_6. The same happens simultaneously in all other modules. Notice, that at this point, md_5 will adjust its *Local Angle* towards the negative direction because currently md_6 has a negative *Local Angle*. The movement is in fact counter productive as md_5 is moving the light sensor further away from the light source. However, this counter productive movement is compensated by md_4, md_3, md_2, and md_1 as their *Local Angles* are all adjusting towards the positive direction. The movement of md_5 will change as md_6 corrects the direction of its *Local Angle* after absorbing the angular difference in md_7.

The tolerant behavior is a balance of the aggressive behavior and is the safeguard mechanism that prevents all modules in the system from running out of joint_torque together and put the system into a dead loop. A tolerant module with its joint_torque under working limit, instead of adjusting its *Local Angle* to reach the goal, it would adjust its *Local Angle* towards the direction that alleviates the load on its neighboring modules. However, if the module becomes tolerant because its joint_torque is over limit, it can perform no action but to wait for its neighboring modules to come to the rescue.

4.3 The Experiment

The purpose of the experiment is to demonstrate how the suppression mechanism in the General Suppression Framework can assist the manipulator to reach the goal more effectively. The experiment consists of 10 preset test conditions and a total of 20 runs were performed. Each test condition is run twice, once with the Suppression Modulator in effect and once without. The position of the light source is fixed in all ten test conditions but the initial form of the manipulator changes after every two runs. As expected, when the manipulator first starts to approach the light source form its initial position, it behaved almost identical with or without the Suppression Modulator in effect. However, as the value of ls_dst decreases (approaching the light source), the manipulator without suppression requires many more extra steps to reach the goal. This is because when the light sensor is close to the light source (Figure 9(A)), the modules near to the end-effector (i.e. md_6 and md_7) require finer movement to approach the light source, but every minor movement of the modules near to the base (i.e. md_1 and md_2) would cause md_7 to swing beyond the position of the light source and causes the module with the light sensor to turn back and search for the light source again from another direction.

For the manipulator with Suppression Modulator turned on. The problem is easily solved because Suppression Modulator emits a suppression signal to limit the motion of the modules near to the base when approaching the light source. Therefore the modules near to the end-effector can approach the light source in fine motion. The suppression signal grows stronger as ls_dst decreases; hence, more modules near to the ground will slow down or even freeze. In the experiment, the Suppression Modulator usually needs to suppress three or less modules to reach the goal. The number of steps required for the manipulator with suppression mechanism to reach the goal, ranges from 30 to 75, which is approximately 1/2 to 1/3 of the steps required for the manipulator without suppression mechanism. In one of the test condition, the manipulator without suppression mechanism did not reach the goal even after 1000 steps, so the test was terminated and pronounced fail.

A side observation from the experiment is as with many other systems that exhibit emergent behaviors, wasted and counter productive effort occurs most often at the initial stage. Similar to a large group of ants transporting food to home, in the beginning, the ants travel between home and the food source using many different routes. Later, some ants begin to migrate to the routes that are more efficient and abandon the lesser ones. Finally the whole group will joint the most efficient route. The phenomenon is also noticeable in this system and the initial setting of the manipulator arm dictates how long it takes to overcome this initial period. Figure 9(B), shows a configuration that was willfully set to such a shape. The manipulator requires extra steps to reach the goal as most of the efforts were wasted at the initial stage to generate a more effective shape. Figure 9(C) shows how the manipulator arm begins to get out of the awkward shape and Figure 9(D) shows how the manipulator finally reaches the light source. This configuration took 72 steps (per module) to reach the goal, while the configuration in Figure 9(A) requires only 27 steps.

Fig. 10. The hardware set up of the seven-module MSR manipulator arm. Each module (joint) is controlled by a microcontroller.

4.4 The Hardware Implementation

A seven-module MSR manipulator arm is constructed to verify the computer simulated motion and to estimate the accuracy of the simulated torque (Figure 10). The arm consists of seven modules, each has one degree-of-freedom actuated by a standard hobby servomotor with built in potentiometer for position feedback. The brain of each module is a BrainStem® GP 1.0 microcontroller, which supports five 10-bit A/D inputs, five digital I/O, a GP2D02, and four high-resolution servo outputs that can also be used as input for position feedback. The 40 MHz RISC processor can execute 9000 instructions/second, and can be programmed using C, C++, or Java through the RS-232 serial port. The GP 1.0 can store eleven 1K programs and can run four programs simultaneously. The BrainStem® GP 1.0 runs on 5V DC and a separate 6V is supplied to the servomotor. Access to the microcontroller is through the console application which has an integrated compiler and a function library. The console application can be run on different platforms, including Windows, MacOS X, Palm OS, WinCE, and Linux.

The various I/O ports of the BrainStem® GP 1.0 are configured as shown in Table 2. Servo port #1 is set as a high-resolution output for controlling the servomotor using PWM (pulse-width modulator). Digital port #0 and #1 are used for reading the servo-horn position of the preceding and succeeding modules, digital port #2 is for reading suppression index from preceding module and digital port #3 is for output of suppression index to the succeeding module. The analog input port #0, #2, and #3 are used to estimate the torque in the self, preceding and succeeding servomotors.

The MATLAB generated manipulator arm motion is collected as data files and movie files. The data files include the servo position and the torque of the module in discrete form (i.e. the torque is not recorded continuously with respect to time). The hardware manipulator arm developed can reproduce the motion generated by MATLAB using the recorded servo position of each module. The local angle of each module at different time is stored as data file in the GP 1.0's RAM and can be recalled by the TEA (Tiny Embedded Application) program. The GP 1.0 has an internal clock and the motion regeneration program is written to instruct the servomotor to adjust its position every second according to the preloaded date in the RAM. The whole arm will therefore generate synchronized motion at one-second interval. Since this demon-

Table 2. The configurations of different I/O ports of the BrainStem® GP 1.0.

Servo I/O		Digital I/O		Analog Input	
		0	Preceding Position Input	0	Self Torque Sensing
1	Servo Control (Output)	1	Succeeding Position Input	1	Preceding Torque Sensing
2	*Not used*	2	Preceding Suppression Input	2	Succeeding Torque Sensing
3	*Not used*	3	Succeeding Suppression Output	3	*Not used*
4	*Not used*	4	*Not used*	4	*Not used*

stration does not concern with motion dynamics, the synchronization method used is acceptable for the sole purpose of comparing the mechanical arm motion against the computer simulated one.

The motion generated by the mechanical arm based on the position recorded from the MATLAB, closely resembles the movie recorded from the simulation. The most obvious difference between the simulated motion and the mechanical motion is the dynamics exhibited by the mechanical arm. Whenever the modules near to the ground (i.e. md_1 to md_3) adjust their angles, the module generates a dynamic inertia that is difficult for the plastic gear in the servomotor to absorb. After the base module (md_1) ground two plastics gears in two runs, the speed of the servomotor in the motion regeneration program was tuned down to help minimize the dynamic effect. In addition a metallic gear was installed to replace the plastic gear (Figure 11). These modifications apparently helped to solve the problem, and the arm could go thought the entire motion set without any further problem.

While reproducing the recorded motion, GP 1.0 records the torque after each angle adjustments into the RAM, and these data can be used to compare with the result obtained from the simulation program by referencing the relative local angle of each module. Despite the movement of the mechanical arm is very similar to the simulated movement. The recorded torque of the mechanical arm is very different from the simulated result. There are many explanations to this outcome, but the most likely reasons are that the assumed weight of each module is not distributed evenly between two sides of the joint and that the center of gravity is not at the middle of the link. A second explanation is that the dynamic effect of the inertia is still in effect when GP 1.0 records the torque that causes the torque measured from the mechanical arm differences from the simulated result.

Fig. 11. The ground plastic gear (front-left) is replaced by the new metallic gear on the right. The servomotor then has a full set of metallic gear.

5   Conclusion and Future Work

This paper focused solely in the suppression mechanism of the immune system and the effect it has on distributed systems. We have proposed the General Suppression Framework that emphasizes the use of suppressor cells to eliminate counter productive behavior. A distributed control system based on the General Suppression Framework is also developed to control a planar modular manipulator arm. The system is highly scalable as all communications are based on interactions with the environment. A MATLAB simulation program has shown the suppression mechanism can effectively prevent individual modules from committing counter-productive behavior when the value of ls_dst is low.

In our future work, we will develop more sophisticate suppressor cells to study the dynamic in a diverse group of suppressor cells. Currently the initial value of the suppression signal is determined by a set of heuristic rules based on the value of ls_dst. We are working to apply learning to allow the suppressor cells to generate more intelligent suppression signals based on the pattern of ls_dst changes. The storage, retrieval and selection of distributed immune memories generated during the learning process would probably bring new ideas in distributed data manipulation for behavior based systems.

In our analogy, suppression signals can exist in negative as well as positive forms, i.e. suppression and stimulation. Future work will investigate how the *Suppressor Modulator* can handle suppressions and stimulations simultaneously, like the biological immunosuppression mechanism. Apart from experimenting with the manipulator arm, we will apply the framework on an autonomous robot with multi-input and outputs to demonstrate the system's ability in continuously fusing suppressive and stimulative signals.

The mechanical hyper-redundant planar arm was constructed to verify the simulated motion and torque. Though the torque resulted from the mechanical arm is different than the simulated result, the mechanical and simulated motions are exceptionally identical. In this paper the manipulator arm was only used for visual analysis; control experiments were based entirely on the MATLAB simulation. However real-time hardware experiment will play a more significant role at later stages when the implementations of immuno memory and stimulation mechanism are completed. Future work will use the mechanical system to general real-time data for comparing with the simulated result. More schematic algorithms will be developed to harmonize the differences between real-time mechanical data and those from the simulation. It is hope that the conditioning scheme for real-time and simulated result would give new idea on how to bring AIS theories closer to practical engineering.

References

[1]   E. Benjamini, G. Sunshine, S. Leskowitz. Immunology: A Short Course. Wiley-Liss, New York, USA, 1996.
[2]   P.J. Bentley. Evolution Design by Computers. Morgan Kaufmann, Bath, U.K., 1999.
[3]   L.N. de Castro, and J. Timmis. Artificial Immune Systems: A New Computational Intelligence Approach. Springer-Verlag, New York, 2002.

[4]   D. Dasgupta. Artificial Immune Systems and Their Applications. Springer-Verlag, Germany, 1999.
[5]   M.H. Hassoun. Fundamentals of Artificial Neural Networks. MIT Press, Cambridge, Massachusetts, 1995.
[6]   M. Ivanescu, & N. Bizdoaca. A Two Level Hierarchical Fuzzy Controller for Hyperredundant Cooperative Robots. In Proc. of the IEEE *Intl. Conf. on Robotics & Automation.* 2000.
[7]   S. Kimura, M. Takahashi, and T. Okuyama. A Fault-Tolerant Control Algorithm Having a Decentralized Autonomous Architecture for Space Hyper-Redundant Manipulators. IEEE Transaction on Systems Man, and Cybernetics-Part A: Systems and Humans, vol. 28, No.4 pp. 521-528. 1998.
[8]   A. Ko, T.L. Lau, & H.Y.K. Lau. Topological Representation and Analysis Method for Multi-port and Multi-orientation Docking Modular Robots. To appear In Proc. of the IEEE *Intl. Conf. on Robotics & Automation.* 2004.
[9]   H.Y.K. Lau, and V.W.K. Wong. Immunologic Control Framework for Automated Material Handling. In Proc. of the *Intl. Conf. on Artificial Immune Systems.* 2003.
[10]   J. H. L. Playfair, B. M. Chain. Immunology at a Glance. Blackwell Science, Bodmin, Cornwall, 2001.
[11]   T.S. Ray. Overview of Tierra at ATR, in "Technical Information, no. 15, Technologies for Software Evolutionary Systems", ATR-HIP. 2001.
        <http://www.isd.atr.co.jp/~ray/pubs/overview/Overview.doc>
[12]   L. A. Segel, and I. R. Cohen. Design Principles for the Immune System and Other Distributed Autonomous Systems. Oxford University Press, Oxford, 2001.
[13]   J. Sharon. Basic Immunology. Williams & Wilkins, Pennsylvania, USA, 1998.
[14]   M. Sipper. Machine Nature: the Coming Age of Bio-inspired Computing. McGraw-Hill, New York, 2002.
[15]   L. Sompayrac. How the Immune System Works. Blackwell Science, pp. 99, Massachusetts, USA, 1999.
[16]   A.O. Tarakanov, V.A. Skormin, and S.P. Sokolova. Immunocomputing: Principles and Applications. Springer-Verlag, New York, 2003.
[17]   V. Vinge. A Fire Upon the Deep. Tor, New York, 1992.
[18]   M.J. Wooldridge. An Introduction to multiagent systems. John Wiley & Sons, West Sussex, England, 2002.

AIS Based Robot Navigation in a Rescue Scenario

Michael Krautmacher and Werner Dilger

Chemnitz University of Technology,
09107 Chemnitz, Germany
{michael.krautmacher,dilger}@informatik.tu-chemnitz.de

Abstract. An architecture for a robot control is proposed which is based on the requirements from the RoboCup and AAAI Rescue Robot Competition. An artificial immune system comprises the core component. The suitability of this architecture for the competition and related scenarios, including the modelling of the environment, was verified by simulation.

1 Introduction

1.1 RoboCup and AAAI Rescue Robot Competition

In the RoboCup and AAAI Rescue Robot Competition the following scenario is assumed:

'A building has partially collapsed due to earthquake. The Incident Commander in charge of rescue operations at the disaster scene, fearing secondary collapses from aftershocks, has asked for teams of robots to immediately search the interior of the building for victims.

The mission for the robots and their operators is to find victims, determine their situation, state, and location, and then report back their findings in a map of the building and a victim data sheet. These will immediately be given to human rescue teams preparing to extract all victims that are found.' [4]

In case of a disaster of that sort the risk to human rescuers is significantly reduced if this approach could be used. Provided the robots are quickly available, even the victim survival rate could be improved.

The RoboCup and AAAI Rescue Robot Competition is very demanding with respect to robot skills. In contrast to the competition rules of earlier years one of the skills that is increasingly demanded and honoured is robot autonomy.

In the competition, the exact task is to navigate in various mazes, to identify the "victims" therein and to provide a map or description of how to reach the victim. The difficulty of navigation in each maze increments: The very first scenario is 2D only, the second 3D and the third maze is an unstructured and fragile 3D environment.

Since a-priori knowledge of the mazes is disallowed, very adaptive and robust robot control systems have to be employed. However, no participating team has ever used an AIS as the central control component in their robot in this contest.

In this work it was examined if an AIS could be used and how environments like in the given scenario have to be modeled.

G. Nicosia et al. (Eds.): ICARIS 2004, LNCS 3239, pp. 106–118, 2004.

1.2 Robotics and Artificial Immune Systems

Autonomous robot navigation was recently investigated by A. Ishiguro, Y. Watanabe et al. [2]. They have published several papers on robot control using AIS, including the control of a movement of a robot leg and the control of a garbage-collecting robot.

Although they showed successfully an AIS can be used for control, their approach and results cannot easily be transferred to be used for the RoboCup Rescue robot control tasks for various reasons:

- In the scenarios used by Ishiguro and Watanabe the robot has a lot of a priori information about what it will encounter
- Macro commands like 'search for....' are used
- The environment used was simplified 2D, whereas a complex 3D environment has to be tackled in the Rescue scenario

A different approach was presented by E. Hart, P. Ross et al. [8]. They proposed a system capable of 'growing up', meaning it learns from experience and can hierarchically develop more complex behaviours from a basic set.

In the context of the RoboCup Rescue it has to be assumed there is not enough time available for a robot to start developing required behaviours and the general ability to do so is not necessary as a set of actions that is sufficient can be identified prior to the competition, even if the exact scenario is unknown.

In addition, the authors identified that the management of concentrations and immune network link weights is very difficult ('there is no straightforward way of quantifying the extent to which one RLA in the network should recognize another').

2 Architecture

2.1 Assumptions and Decisions

The amount of memory required to employ the architecture must be bounded, but may depend on the number of objects in the scenario and / or the volume of the scenario it is used in. It is assumed the robot is supplied with sufficient memory. The amount of processing power to enable real time decisions using the proposed architecture must be bounded, but may depend on the number of objects and / or the volume of the scenario. It is assumed the robot has sufficient processing power and data transfer handling capabilities.

It is assumed the robot is equipped with at least a short range sensor to gather data of the area in front of it and special sensors for identifying signs of human victims. It is assumed there is a primitive data abstraction mechanism available for the raw sensor data, i.e. object identification based on image processing, so the control system can be supplied with sets of tuples comprising a suspected object type and its position.

It is assumed the robot performs basic, complete actions. This means the robot decides on an action, executes it and when the execution is completed, the robot is no longer in motion. Exclusive usage of this type of action guarantees there are no dependencies between decisions of individual processing cycles; i.e. an action like "move forward by n units" falls into that category while "move forward at speed v" does not.

2.2 Functional Outline

A schematic representation of the proposed architecture is shown in figure 1. The raw sensor data is processed and individual objects as well as their positions relative to the robot are identified. This identification is not required to be exact, but can be fuzzy. The sensor information analysis component is assumed to be available; its realisation is out of the scope of this document. However, another AIS could be employed for this task.

The object information gathered by the sensors is combined with stored information; the result is saved back to the memory and also made available to the AIS. This process is completely transparent, so data from the memory and gathered by the sensors cannot be distinguished as such. This is useful for multiple purposes:

- it simplifies the interface to the AIS, especially if multiple sensors are used
- it enables the use of data of temporarily obscured objects
- effective data smoothing can be realised
- better determination of robot position and speed are possible

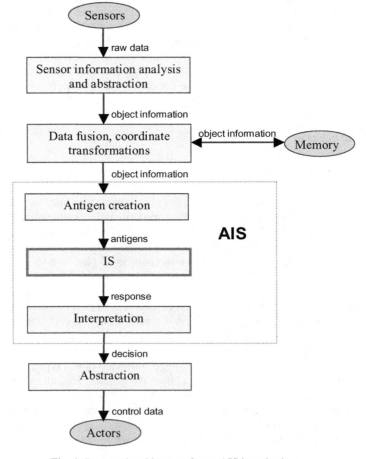

Fig. 1. Proposed architecture for an AIS based robot

All or at least a huge portion of the total "knowledge" about the environment are used for the AIS antigen creation. A set of antigens is created to represent the environment around the robot; this is effectively another data abstraction. However, all data that might be useful for an appropriate decision for an action is to be encoded in antigens. The exact technique to effectively achieve this is explained later in this document, however it has to be noted that the AIS can come to a decision on an action based on comparatively rich information in every situation.

The immune system response is interpreted and the associated action is executed. When the execution of the action is complete, the next processing cycle is started. If the ability to predict sensor data or the next situation exists (i.e. in the data fusion unit), it is possible to start the next processing cycle while the last action decided upon is still being executed. Although this could greatly improve the robots response with respect to time, this extension is out of scope of this work, as this is not related to the functioning of the AIS and should not have an effect in non real time scenarios.

The format of the object information can be different between individual components / layers, including the type of coordinate system used. The data fusion and coordinate transformation component is not required to have any intelligent behaviour, its main purpose is being an interface ensuring data compatibility and allowing a modular system.

Several additional useful features and extensions are omitted, like feeding back stored data to the sensor information analysis component.

3 Representation of the Environment

In most approaches the first simplification done is the reduction to a 2D only scenario. However, the ability to navigate in 3D scenarios may be essential for a final solution. This is definitely the case for the RoboCup Rescue scenario. Due to the high processing load induced by the conversion between coordinate systems especially for this approach a discussion of the underlying mathematical operations is crucial to ensure a 2D solution can be transferred to work in a 3D scenario.

3.1 Modelling

The exact representation of arbitrary real world objects and features is very complex. It would be necessary to be able to work with mixtures of volumes, surfaces, lines and points. In this approach all objects are reduced to sets of points, for simplicity. Objects occupying a small volume are modelled as single points, large surfaces or long lines are modelled as sets of points positioned in the respective shape.

The AIS controlling the robot is not affected by the choice of a global coordinate system, because all coordinates are transformed into the egocentric pseudo-coordinate system it is using. However, the choice determines the processing requirements for the transformation process:

- Using an allocentric coordinate system requires a transformation of all data stored and retrieved from the memory in every cycle, which involves shifting of the coordinate origin to the robot, the rotation of the coordinate system and the transition to the egocentric coordinate system.

- Using an egocentric coordinate does not necessarily require any transformations; however, *all* positions of objects present in the memory have to be updated every cycle. This can also cause cumulative positional errors.

It was decided to use an allocentric Cartesian global coordinate system. The coordinates of an object are given by the triple $(x_T \quad y_T \quad z_T)$. Robot coordinates are given by two triples $(x_R \quad y_R \quad z_R)$ and $(\xi_R \quad \eta_R \quad \varphi_R)$. (Note that for objects the index is "T" instead of "O" to avoid confusion) The first triple is the position of the robot in the global coordinate system, the latter indicates the tilting of the robot along the x-axis (ξ) and y-axis (η) and its rotation relatively to the orientation of the global coordinate system (φ). This is depicted in the following figure:

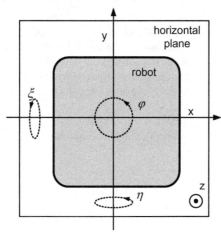

Fig. 2. Looking down on the robot

3.2   Conversion from Cartesian to Spherical Coordinates

For the creation of antigens (see section 4.1) a conversion to Cartesian coordinates is required. The following definition of the spherical coordinates based on Cartesian coordinates is used:

$$x = r \cos \varphi \cos \theta$$
$$y = r \sin \varphi \cos \theta \tag{1}$$
$$z = r \sin \theta$$

Basic solution:

$$r = \sqrt{x^2 + y^2 + z^2}$$
$$\varphi = \arctan \frac{y}{x} \tag{2}$$

$$\theta = \arcsin \frac{z}{\sqrt{x^2 + y^2 + z^2}} = \arcsin \frac{z}{r}$$

These formulas look rather simple, but the square root, arcsin and arctan operation are quite complex and not available as 'atomic operations' on most platforms. But the proposed design enables a range of simplifications in addition to supporting additional optimizations like using incremental calculation. One example is the antigen concentration produced by an object, which is a function of the distance r of the object, so $f(r) \equiv c(r) \equiv \tilde{c}(r^2) \equiv \tilde{c}(\tilde{r})$ with $\tilde{r} = x^2 + y^2 + z^2$, which consists of basic arithmetic operations, only.

To obtain the desired parameters r, φ, and θ, the coordinates of the object in the global coordinate system (allocentric) have to be transformed into coordinates relative to the robot (egocentric) first. This can be done by multiplying the vector pointing to the object with a single transformation matrix $\underline{\underline{T}}$ in homogeneous coordinates: $\left(x_{trans}\ y_{trans}\ z_{trans}\ k\right)^T = \underline{\underline{T}} \cdot (x\ y\ z\ 1)^T$. This matrix is a product of a rotation and a translation matrix and is identical for all object coordinates to be transformed in that cycle.

However, a matrix multiplication for every object vector means high processing load. An alternative is the combination of the calculations of the coordinate transformation and the change of the coordinate system:

$$r = \sqrt{\left(x_T - x_R\right)^2 + \left(y_T - y_R\right)^2 + \left(z_T - z_R\right)^2}$$

$$\varphi = \arctan\frac{y_T - y_R}{x_T - x_R} - \varphi_R \tag{3}$$

$$\theta = \arcsin\frac{z_T - z_R}{r} - \xi\sin\varphi - \eta\cos\varphi$$

It is also possible to ignore the tilting ξ and η of the robot; however, one has to bear in mind that this will have a major impact on the AIS if significant tilting occurs.

$$\theta_{alt} = \arcsin\frac{z_T - z_R}{r} \tag{4}$$

It is important to note that the exactness of the calculation does not need to be very high, so the trigonometric functions can be substituted with a few comparisons and *all* parameter calculations can be performed using basic arithmetic operations and comparisons only to generate the antigens described in section 4.1 (θ is approximated by the selection of a sector).

3.3 2D Scenarios

For a 2D scenario as implemented the derived equations can be used unchanged with input parameters z, ξ, and η set to zero, as there is no z-component for objects and robot and there is no tilting of the robot. This also means, there are no objects with a nonzero elevation angle.

$$r = \sqrt{\left(x_T - x_R\right)^2 + \left(y_T - y_R\right)^2}$$

$$\varphi = \arctan\frac{y_T - y_R}{x_T - x_R} - \varphi_R \tag{5}$$

$$\theta = 0$$

4 AIS Design

4.1 Antigens / Stimulation of the Immune System

All objects (modelled as sets of points) can be sources of antigens; they can all influence the immune system of the robot. Figure 3 shows an object that is within the sensor range; this results in the generation of at least one antigen, which is presented to the robot's immune system.

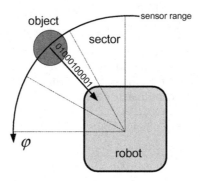

Fig. 3. Antigen from object within sensor range is created

The antigens provided to the robot's immune system are required to include information of object type as well as object position. In the case the scenarios are large and complex, a good transformation of object type and object position into antigens is crucial. If both properties were encoded in a fixed length antigen string, the position encoded would be the absolute one. This has some major drawbacks:

The size of the area to be navigated through may not be known and this, combined with a constraint on the minimal accuracy (resolution), does not allow antigens of fixed length. Even when the maximum size of the area is known, the length of the antigen string can be extremely high. Identical or similar objects at different positions emit completely different antigens, which is expected to have a negative impact on the minimal complexity of the immune system.

With relative position encoding, resulting in variable antigen strings, these problems can be at least partially avoided. However, this approach has negative properties, too. The coordinates of all known objects within a certain range have to be converted to relative coordinates in *every processing cycle* to generate correct antigen strings.

For this architecture, relative position encoding is chosen. The fundamental drawback mentioned cannot be fully overcome; however, the computation can be done relatively efficiently. The fundamental idea of encoding the distance of objects is shown in figure 4.

Object Type (fixed / static part)	Partial object position (variable / dynamic part)

Fig. 4. Proposed structure of an antigen

Although they are quite complex, spherical coordinates are the most promising, because they allow for easy encoding with a short variable part at a very high accuracy. This is partially due to a 'trick', as the distance between the robot and the object can be modelled with the antigen concentration (see below), so only the two angles φ and θ have to be encoded. A medium or even low resolution of about 12 sectors or less for these angles suffices.

A required property of the encoding is that the hamming distance monotonically increases with respect to the angle, which can be achieved quite intuitively with any popular encoding. However, it is also desirable to avoid a discontinuity at $\varphi = 0$.

For binary strings in a hamming shape space, there is a simple, suitable code, which is depicted in figure 5 (12 sectors, 6 bits). In the example given the hamming distance between each of the codes is proportional to the minimum $\Delta\varphi$ (linear / homogeneous sectorisation).

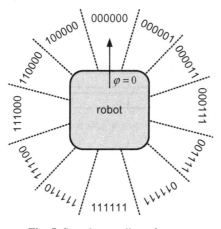

Fig. 5. Sample encoding of sectors

The antigen 'concentration' at the robot depends on the object type, a function f of the distance to the emitting object and a function g of the time that passed since the last encounter:

$$c = c_{0,id} \cdot f(r,id) \cdot g(\tau,r,id) \tag{6}$$

The object specific constant $c_{0,obj}$ is a measure of the general importance. The function f is a regression function, ensuring the objects very close to the robot get a higher weighing. The function g effectively is a measure for the assumed accuracy of the position of the object. This function can be $\equiv 1$ if the object is considered immobile or it is currently in the sensing range.

This approach differs from the one by Watanabe and Ishiguro in various aspects:
- In their model, a situation is characterised by a discrete number of antigens, each representing a state variable. In the proposed model, the situation is given by concentrations of several different antigens as shown in figure 6: The robot is obviously standing in front of a wall, an identified victim is not far away to its left and it knows of another victim to its right which is far away. In this approach, determining in what sort of situation the robot is currently in is considered being part of

the tasks of the AIS, so effectively it is also used for intelligent multi sensor data fusion.

- Their antigen is symbol based and comprises full relative, but symbolic position information (distance and direction of an object), which only offers reduced accuracy, compared to the proposed model.
- The distance of objects is modelled as a concentration of antigens and is almost perfectly continuous, the direction is supplied in a way that the antigens of objects located in *about* the same direction are always very similar. If their robot was either moved or rotated a few degrees, the scenario experienced by the robot would be either equal or quite different from the one sensed before.

The antigens are truly variable (or modular). The immune system can be supplied with antigens it has never encountered in the learning process. This even enables the modelling of uncertainties in object identification or position and robot malfunctions.

human	left	c = .30
wall	front	c = .50
empty space	back	c = .05
empty space	right	c = .10
human	right	c = .05

Fig. 6. Example: Set of antigens presented to the AIS

4.2   IS Structure

The immune principles of the AIS are largely identical to those used by Watanabe and Ishiguro. It uses the immune network model proposed by Farmer et al. [9]. The only other immune component modelled is the antibody, which consists of a condition (paratope), an associated action and a number of idiotopes.

Paratope	Action	Idiotope	Idiotope

Fig. 7. Antibody

The dynamic processes are modelled similarly, using difference equations (bilinear transformation of the original differential equations), which are only modified to handle multiple antigens per cycle. The meta dynamics proposed by Watanabe and Ishiguro can be adopted with very little change (bone marrow model).

5   Implementation

It was decided to simulate a system employing the proposed architecture directly, because a real robot was not available and those robot simulations available were not considered suitable, because they can not handle a scenario with the basic RoboCup Rescue competition scenario features which were identified:

- Various tiles
- Blocking objects
- Victims (human)
- Identified victims

These are used as a minimum set to start with. A basic maze using a block-world comprising of those features was designed, it is depicted in section 5.2.

5.1 Performance Rating

The performance rating proposed for the RoboCup and AAAI Rescue Robot Competition 2004 is very complex. In addition, although the official rating scheme seems to be fair in the context of the competition, it is not necessarily very good for rating the true performance of the robot. Nevertheless, a part of it applicable for the simplified scenario used has been implemented:

- 0.2 points per human part identified (all humans are modelled in six blocks / parts)
- 0.25 points loss for bumping (wall or victim)

The reinforcement strategy used deviates from this rating scheme to encourage additional behavioural attributes like exploring unknown areas without any signs of humans and avoiding useless scans and turns.

5.2 Implementation

It was chosen to use MATLAB for the simulation because operations on data vectors are handled very efficiently and can be implemented intuitively.

The scenario shown in figure 8 was used to evaluate the proposed architecture.

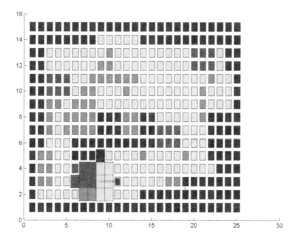

Fig 8. Scenario for the simulation of a rescue type environment

The objects modelled in this scenario are

- good tiles, depicted in light grey
- bad tiles, which can be crossed by the robot, depicted in dark grey
- impenetrable objects, which also block the robot's view, depicted in black
- unidentified humans, depicted in red

All objects which are actually known to the robot by either being in its sensor range or being stored in the robot's memory are shown slightly larger (there are no gaps between known tiles). The robot is depicted as a blue square with a dotted line indicating the direction it is currently pointing to. The robot's trail is marked with a black line and yellow markers indicate positions where the robot used its special sensors for detecting signs of human victims.

It has to be noted that the modelling of the environment performed here is relatively coarsely grained and completely block-oriented. These simplifications are used for simulation performance gain only, but they are considered acceptable because only the fundamental properties of the architecture are evaluated anyways.

The implementation supports two modes of operation:

- A training mode, in which the immune system is trained mainly by adjustment of the links between antibodies.
- An evaluation mode in which the network is evaluated according to the simplified RoboCup Rescue competition rating scheme.

The concentrations of the antibodies are dynamic regardless of the simulation mode. No meta-dynamics have been implemented. In the evaluation mode, the network links are static to enable a 'correct' rating of the network in the state it is supplied. This is problematic, as the network, including the antibody links, is to be optimised continuously.

The missing meta-dynamics are not a serious concern: To compensate their absence, a large number of potentially useful antigens is hand crafted at the beginning; these include all basic behaviours imaginable. Since all hand crafted antibodies can be useful, they are never deleted, but get 'memory cells': Their concentration is maintained at a very low, but constant level.

6   Results

Various experiments were conducted to find acceptable values for the numerous free parameters. Those parameters being free functions of another parameter were especially problematic. If the formula used for determination of antigen concentration enables antigen creation for a relatively high distance, the simulation (or the robot)is not only slowed down significantly, but the antibody concentrations need to be stabilised more rigorously. It is suggested to use a function that is $\equiv 0$ for $r > r_{max}$, where r_{max} is determined experimentally.

Another set of free parameters, namely the training step number and the reinforcement constant (learning rate) are more critical than in most other systems modelled; for each individual learning process an antibody link is updated, but there is no guarantee that this update improves the immune network overall. From early experiments

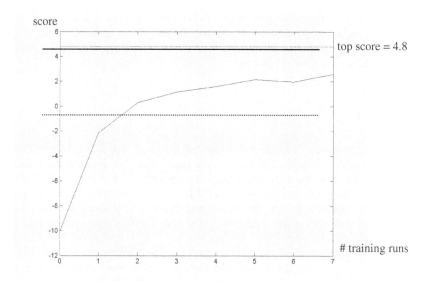

Fig 9. Performance of the robot according to the rescue scoring scheme

it was learned that about 400 simulated steps suffice to fully explore the area modelled and identify all human victims. To avoid bad training effects due to chasing the robot through a scenario which solely comprises known objects, this number was chosen to be the maximum of simulated steps for training. Every time this number of steps are processed, everything (except for the antibody network) is reset for another training run with a lower learning rate.

The performance of the system proposed was rated in an experiment with eight evaluation runs, the first with a completely untrained immune network (run 0) and the following with the respective numbers of training cycles. The learning rate was initialized with 10 and reduced with a factor of roughly $1/\sqrt{2}$ for every training run.

Figure 9 shows the robot's performance using the simplified scoring scheme introduced.

The screenshots of figure 10 show the results of two evaluation runs.

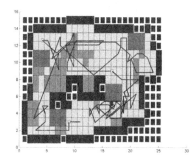 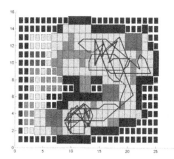

Result of two training runs with 400 steps each, score 0.3

Result of seven training runs with 400 steps each, score 2.6 (even though one victim was not found)

Fig 10. The results of two evaluation runs

Even though the performance gain seems to be quite promising, it can even be increased significantly by eliminating the determinism of the antibody link update mechanism, training and evaluating several immune networks in parallel and selecting the best network(s) after each set of runs.

7 Conclusion

The architecture proposed enables a simulated robot to navigate in an unknown environment. The implementation is still in a very early state, so it is not advisable to draw major conclusions; the experimental results obtained so far show that based on the proposed modelling of the environment an AIS can be a good solution to the problem of robot navigation in unstructured and unknown environments. We did not exhaust all features that are usually defined in AIS, thus is offers ways of extensions to this approach.

Depart from the proposal of the architecture, the most important issue is the research on the finding of acceptable defaults for the various free parameters. Several effects and implications have been identified and pointed out. On the basis of this work further research is necessary; several required and useful extensions have already been identified in this document.

A great challenge would be the realization of our approach on a real robot. To do this requires a lot of additional work. We hope that we can do it in the framework of a research cooperation that is in preparation at our university.

References

1. de Castro, L.N., Timmis, J.: Artificial Immune Systems: A New Computational Intelligence Approach. Springer-Verlag, London (2002)
2. Watanabe, Y., Ishiguro, A., Shirai, Y., Uchikawa, Y.: Emergent Construction Of Behavior Arbitration Mechanism Based On The Immune System. In: Proceedings of the IEEE International Conference on Evolutionary Computation (1998)
3. de Castro, L.N.: Artificial immune systems – Presentation Tutorial, ftp://ftp.dca.fee.unicamp.br/pub/docs/vonzuben/lnunes/demo.zip, (2000)
4. RoboCup and AAAI Rescue Robot Competition Rules - 2004 (Version 1). RoboCup-AAAI Rescue Robot Competition Rules (2004) (v1).pdf
5. Jacoff, A., Weiss, B., Tadokoro, S.: RoboCup Rescue Robot League Rules. RoboCupRescue2003Rules.pdf (2003)
6. Sieber, S.: Untersuchung qualitativer Repräsentationsformen im Rahmen des RoboCup Rescue. Diploma thesis, Chemnitz University of Technology, (2002)
7. de Castro, L.N., von Zuben, F.J.: aiNet: An Artificial Immune Network for Data Analysis. In: H.A. Abbas, R.A. Sarker, C.S. Newton (eds.): Data Mining: A heuristic Approach, Idea Group Publ., (2001) 231 - 259
8. Hart, E., Ross, P., Webb, A., Lawson, A.: A Role for immunology in "Next Generation" Robot Controllers. Proceedings of ICARIS 2003, Springer-Verlag, Berlin Heidelberg (2003), 46 - 56
9. Farmer, J.D., Kauffman, S.A., Packard, N.H., Perelson, A.S.: Adaptive Dynamic Networks as Models for the Immune System and Autocatalytic Sets, Ann. of the N.Y. Acad. of Sci., 504, (1987), 118 – 131.

Reactive Immune Network Based Mobile Robot Navigation

Guan-Chun Luh and Wei-Wen Liu

Department of Mechanical Engineering, Tatung University,
40 Chungshan North Road, 3rd sec. Taipei, Taiwan, R.O.C.
Tel: 886-2-25925252 ext.3410 ext. 806
gluh@ttu.edu.tw, g9001001@mail.ttu.edu.tw

Abstract. In this paper, a Reactive Immune Network (RIN) is proposed and applied to intelligent mobile robot learning navigation strategies within unknown environments. Rather than building a detailed mathematical model of immune systems, we try to explore the principle in immune network focusing on its self-organization, adaptive learning capability and immune memory. Modified virtual target method is integrated to solve local minima problem. Several trap situations designed by early researchers are employed to evaluate the performance of the proposed immunized architecture. Simulation results show that the robot is capable to avoid obstacles, escape traps, and reach goal effectively.

1 Introduction

Autonomous mobile robots have a wide range of applications in industries, hospitals, offices, and even the military, due to their superior mobility. Some of their capabilities include automatic driving, intelligent delivery agents, assistance to disable people, exploration and map generation for environmental cleanup, etc. In addition, their capabilities also allow them to carry out specialized tasks in environments inaccessible or very hazardous for human beings such as nuclear plants and chemical handling. They are also useful in emergencies for fire extinguishing and rescue operations. Combined with manipulation abilities, their capabilities and efficiency will increase and can be used for dangerous tasks such as security guard, exposition processing, as well as undersea, underground and even space exploration.

In order to adapt the robot's behavior to any complex, varying and unknown environment without further human intervention, intelligent learning algorithms including neural networks, fuzzy logic, and genetic algorithms, have been successively adopted to develop the behavior-based intelligent mobile robot. Intelligent mobile robots should be able to extract information from the environment, use their built-in knowledge about the environment to perceive, act and adapt within the environment. They move and plan their actions in the environment to accomplish objectives defined either extrinsically by a human programmer or intrinsically on the basis of a general objective of survival. As a result, path planning of intelligent robot behavior plays an important role in the development of flexible automated systems. The design goal for path planning is to enable a mobile robot to navigate safely and efficiently without collisions to a target position in an unknown and complex environment.

G. Nicosia et al. (Eds.): ICARIS 2004, LNCS 3239, pp. 119–132, 2004.

The navigation strategies of mobile robots can be generally classified into two categories, global path planning and local reactive navigation. The former such as artificial potential fields [1], connectivity graphs or cell decomposition [2] is done offline, and the robot has complete prior knowledge about the shape, location, orientation and even the movements of the obstacles in the environment. Its path is derived utilizing some optimization techniques to minimize the cost of the search. However, it has difficulty handling a modification of the environment, due to some uncertain environmental situation, and the reactive navigation capabilities are indispensable since the real-world environments are apt to change over time.On the other hand, local reactive navigation employing some reactive strategies to perceive the environment based on the sensory information and path planning is done online. The workspace for the navigation of the mobile robot is assumed to be unknown and consisting of static and/or dynamic obstacles. The robot has to acquire a set of stimulus-action mechanisms through its sensory inputs, such as distance information from infrared sensors, visual information from cameras or processed data derived after appropriate fusion of numerous sensor outputs. The action usually is a change in the mobile robot's steering angle and/or translation velocity to avoid collisions with the obstacles and reach the desired target. Nevertheless, it does not guarantee a solution for the mission, nor is the solution the optimal one.

Furthermore, a well-known drawback of reactive navigation is that the mobile robot suffers from local minima problems in that it uses only locally available environmental information without any previous memory. In other words, a robot may get trapped in front of an obstacle or wandering indefinitely in a region whenever it navigates past obstacles toward a target position. This happens particularly if the environment consists of concave obstacles and mazes, etc. Several trap escape algorithms, including the random walk method [1], the multi-potential field method [2], the tangent algorithm [3], the wall-following method [4], the virtual obstacle scheme [5], and the virtual target approach [6] have been proposed to solve the local minima problems. In the virtual target approach, the target is switched to a virtual location in the partial segment of the possible limit cycle path and is very effective in a simple U-shaped trap situation. Nevertheless, it failed to escape from recursive U-trap situations that may arise when the robot experiences a new trap while approaching the virtual target, and thus, a virtual-target-side concept [12] was proposed to get out of the trap situation. The most important solution to the local minima problems is the detection of the local minima situation during the robot's traversal.

Reactive behavior-based mobile robot responds to stimuli from the dynamic environment, and its behaviors are guided by local states of the world. Its behavior representation is situated at a sub-symbolic level that is integrated into its perception-action (*i.e.* sensor-motor) capacities analogous to the manifestation of the reflex behavior observed in biological systems. Several researches have focused on this kind of robot system and have demonstrated its robustness and flexibility against an unstructured world. A reactive behavior-based control system is now becoming attractive in the field of mobile robotics to teach the robot to learn its own.

In addition to the biologically inspired approaches such as neural networks, fuzzy logic and genetic algorithms providing various feasible applications mentioned above, immune networks have been implemented to mobile robotics as well. Lee *et al.* [8] constructed obstacle-avoidance and goal-approach immune networks for the behavior control of mobile robots. The results present more than 70% of the reaching probability on the usage of the artificial immune network. Additionally, it showed the advantage of not falling into a local loop. Ishiguro and his colleagues [9] proposed an immune-network based decentralized consensus-making mechanism and an off-line innovation mechanism that can be used to construct an artificial immune network suitable for adequate action selection. They applied behavior arbitration to an autonomous mobile robot for an example. KrishnaKumar and Neidhoefer [10] presented an adaptive neural control that is composed of several structures of the immune system. They addressed the using of neural networks with the concepts from the field of immunology in the modeling and adaptive control of complex dynamic systems. Luh and Cheng [11] applied an immunized reinforcement adaptive learning mechanism to an intelligent mobile robot and evaluated using a "food foraging work" problem. Moreover, an evolved artificial immune network [12] was proposed to navigate mobile robot to solve a multi-objective task: garbage collection.

It has been shown that the learning and adaptive capabilities of artificial immune systems have a great potential in the field of machine learning, computer science and engineering [13-14]. Dasgupta [13] summarized that the immune system has the following features: self-organizing, memory, recognition, adaptation, and learning. There are a growing number of researches investigating the interactions between various components of the immune system or the overall behaviors of the systems based on an immunology point of view. Immunized systems consisting of agents (immune-related cells) may have adaptation and learning capabilities similar to artificial neural networks, except that it is based on dynamic cooperation of agents [15]. Immune systems provide an excellent model of adaptive process operating at the local level and of useful behavior emerging at the global level [13]. Accordingly, artificial immune system can be expected to provide various feasible ideas for the reactive navigation of mobile robots.

A reactive behavior-based navigation mechanism was constructed for this study. The application task for the mobile robot was to navigate in an unknown and complex environment avoiding static obstacles and reaching a goal. In this paper, a novel Reactive Immune Network (RIN) was developed and implemented to navigate a mobile robot. Instead of building a detailed mathematical model of the immune systems, this study tried to explore the simple principle in immune networks focusing on its adaptive, learning capabilities.

2 The Biological Immune System

The most important function of a biological immune system is to protect living organisms from invading antigens such as viruses, bacteria, and other parasites; those antigens are initially identified by a combination of the innate and adaptive immune systems [16]. Fig. 1 depicts the model describing the relationship between components in the immune system. Phagocytes (part of the innate system) are capable of destroying numerous antigens on contact. The adaptive immune system uses lymphocytes that can quickly change in order to destroy antigens that have entered the bloodstream. A major difference between these two systems is that adaptive cells are more antigen-specific and have greater memory capacity than innate cell. Two main types of lymphocytes, namely B-cells and T-cells, play a remarkable role in both immunities. The former take part in the humoral immunity and secrete antibodies by the clonal proliferation while the latter take part in cell-mediated immunity. One class of the T-cells,

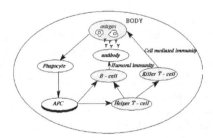

Fig. 1. Illustration of the biological immune system

called the Killer T-cells, destroy the infected cell whenever it recognizes the infection. The other class that triggers clonal expansion and stimulates or suppresses antibody formation is called the Helper T-cells. Lymphocytes float freely in blood and lymph nodes. They patrol everywhere for foreign antigens, then gradually drift back into the lymphatic system to begin the cycle all over again.

When an infectious foreign pathogen attacks the human body, the innate immune system is activated as the first line of defense. Innate immunity is not directed in any way towards specific invaders, rather against any pathogens that enter the body. It is called non-specific immune response. The most important cell in the innate immunity is a phagocyte, including monocyte, macrophage, etc. A phagocyte internalizes and destroys the invaders to the human body. Then the phagocyte becomes an Antigen Presenting Cell (APC). The APC interprets the antigen appendage and extracts the features, by processing and presenting antigenic peptides on its surface to the T-cells and B-cells. These antigenic peptides are a kind of molecule called MHC (Major Histocompatibility Complex) and can distinguish a "self" from other "non-self" (antigens) [17].

These lymphocytes will be able to sensitize this antigen and be activated. Then the Helper T-cell releases the cytokines that are the proliferative signals acting on the producing B-cell or remote the other cells. On the other hand, the B-cell becomes stimulated and creates antibodies when a B-cell recognizes an antigen. Recognition is achieved by inter-cellular binding, which is determined by molecular shape and electrostatic charge. The secreted antibodies are the soluble receptor of B-cells and these antibodies can be distributed throughout the body [17]. An antibody's paratope can bind with an antigen's epitope according to its affinity. Moreover, B-cells are also affected by Helper T-cells during the immune responses [18]. The Helper T-cell plays a remarkable key role for deciding if the immune system uses the cell mediated immunity (by Th1 Helper T-cells) or the humoral immunity (by Th2 Helper T-cells), and it connects the non-specific immune response to make a more efficient specific immune response. The Helper-T cells work, primarily, by secreting substances, known as cytokines and their relatives [36] that constitute powerful chemical messengers. The cytokines promote cellular growth, activation and regulation. In addition, cytokines can also kill target cells and stimulated macrophages.

When the maturation rate of a B-cell clone increases in response to a match between the clone's antibody and an antigen, affinity maturation occurs. Those mutant cells are bound more tightly and stimulated to divide more rapidly. Affinity maturation dynamically balances exploration versus exploitation in adaptive immunity [19]. It has been demonstrated that the immune system has the capability to recognize foreign pathogens, learn and memorize, process information, and discriminate between

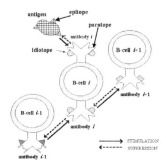

Fig. 2. Idiotypic network hypothesis

self and non-self [16, 19]. In addition, the immunity can be maintained even faced with a dynamically changing environment.

Jerne [20] has proposed the idiotypic network hypothesis (immune network hypothesis) based on mutual stimulation and suppression between antibodies as Fig. 2 illustrates. This hypothesis is modeled as a differential equation simulating the concentration of a set of lymphocytes. The concept of an immune network states that the network dynamically maintains the memory using feedback mechanisms within the network. The lymphocytes are not isolated, but communicate with each other among different species of lymphocytes through the interaction antibodies. Jerne concluded that the immune system is similar to the nervous system when viewed as a functional network.

3 Immune Network Reactive System

An immune network reactive system inspired by the biological immune system for robot navigation (goal-reaching and obstacle-avoidance) is described in this section. The architecture implies using a combination of both the prior behavior-based information and an on-line adaptation mechanism based on the features of the immune system. It consists of immune-related cells, and these cells interact with each other. This 'micro' level of cell interaction relationships may have adaptation and learning capabilities. For a reactive approach, it does not necessarily provide for very high optimization of all environments, instead that it should be robust in more general environmental changes [21]. The proposed mechanism, with the cooperation between B-T cells, can help the immune system adapt to the environment efficiently. It is difficult to decide exactly how well the system is doing globally, so evolutionary theories teach us that an appropriate response by the immune system should try to maximize an individual host's long-term averaged ability. It is emphasized here that self-improvement and stable ecological niche- approaching are the important goals of the 'macro' level of the system's behavior.

The immune network reactive system is depicted in Fig. 3. The antigen's epitope is a situation detected by sensors and provides the information about the relationship between the current location and the obstacles, along with target. The current state is defined as an antigen with a multiple combination of detected epitopes, including fusion measurements of distance sensors, as well as orientation of the goal. This

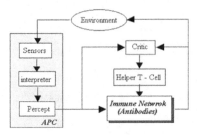

Fig. 3. The architecture of the immunized network reactive system

scene-based spatial relationship is consistently discriminative between different parts of an environment, and the same representation can be used for different environments. Therefore, this method is tolerant with respect to the environmental changes. The interpreter is regarded as a phagocyte and translates sensor data into perception. The antigen presentation proceeds from the information extraction to the perception translation. An antigen has several different epitopes, which means that an antigen can be recognized by a number of different antibodies. However, an antibody can bind with only one antigen's epitope. In the proposed mechanism, a paratope with a built-in behavior/steering direction is regarded as a B-cell and interacts with each other and with its environment. These B-cells are induced by recognition of the available antigens. Nevertheless, only one B-cell with the highest concentration will be selected to act.

The dynamic equations of the idiotypic network proposed by Farmer [22] are employed as a reactive immune network to calculate the concentration of antibodies, shown as the following equations:

$$\frac{dA_i(t+1)}{dt} = \left(\sum_{j=1}^{N_{Ab}} m_{ij} a_j(t) - \sum_{k=1}^{N_{Ab}} m_{ki} a_k(t) + m_i - k_i \right) a_i(t) \tag{1}$$

$$a_i(t+1) = \frac{1}{1 + \exp(0.5 - A_i(t+1))} \tag{2}$$

where $i, j = 0, 1, \cdots, N_{Ab}$ are the subscripts to distinguish the antibody types and N_{Ab} is the number of antibodies. A_i is the stimulus of antibody i, a_i is the concentration of antibody i, m_{ij} is the affinity between the ith and jth antibody, m_i is the affinity of antigen and antibody i, and k_i is the natural death coefficient. Equation (1) is composed of four terms. The first term shows the stimulation between the ith antibody and the jth antibody, while the second term depicts the suppressive interaction between the antibodies. The third term is the stimulus from the antigen, and the final term is the natural extinction term, which represents the dissipation tendency in the absence of any interaction. Equation (2) is a squashing function to ensure the stability of the concentration [9].

In the reactive immune network, antibodies are defined as the steering directions of mobile robots as shown in Fig. 4,

$$Ab_i \equiv \theta_i \qquad i = 1, 2, \cdots, N_{Ab} \tag{3}$$

where N_{Ab} is the number of antibodies, θ_i is the steering angle between the moving path and the head orientation of mobile robot. Note that $0° \leq \theta_i \leq 360°$. In addition,

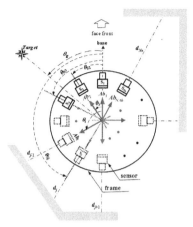

Fig. 4. Configuration of mobile robot and its relatives to target and obstacles

antigen represents the local environment surrounding the robot and its epitopes are a fusion data set containing orientation of goal position θ_g, distance between obstacles and the *jth* sensor d_j, as well as position of sensor θ_{S_j},

$$Ag_j \equiv \begin{bmatrix} \theta_g & d_j & \theta_{S_j} \end{bmatrix} \qquad j = 1,2,\cdots,N_s \qquad (4)$$

where N_s is number of sensors, $d_{min} \le d_j \le d_{max}$ and $0° \le \theta_{S_j} \le 360°$. Parameters d_{min} and d_{max} represent the nearest and longest distances measured by the range sensor respectively. It should be noted that different antigens (local environments) might have identical epitopes (fusion information from range sensors).

The potential-field method is one of the most popular approaches employed to navigate mobile robot within environments containing obstacles, since it is conceptually effective and easy to implement. The method can be implemented either for off-line global planning if the environment is known prior or for real-time local navigation in unknown environment using onboard sensors. The Artificial Potential Field (APF) approach considers a virtual attractive force between the robot and the target, as well as virtual repulsive forces between the robot and the obstacles. The resultant force on the robot is then used to decide the direction of its movements. In this study, the resultant force on the robot is defined as the m_i, the affinity value between the antigen/local environment and the *ith* antibody/steering angle,

$$m_i = w_1 F_{goal_i} + w_2 F_{obs_i} \qquad i = 1,2,\cdots,N_{Ab} \qquad (5)$$

The weighing values w_1 and w_2 indicate the ratio between attractive and repulsive forces. Note that $0 \le w_1, w_2 \le 1$ and $w_1 + w_2 = 1$. The attractive force F_{goal_i} of the steering direction (*i.e.* the *ith* antibody) is defined as follows:

$$F_{goal_i} = \frac{1.0 + \cos(\theta_i - \theta_g)}{2.0}, \qquad i = 1,2,\cdots,N_{Ab} \qquad (6)$$

Note that F_{goal_i} is normalized and $0 \le F_{goal_i} \le 1$. Obviously, the attractive force is at its maximal level ($F_{goal_i} = 1$) when the mobile robot goes straightforward to the target

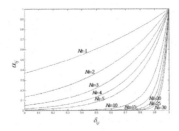

Fig. 5. Relation between α_{ij} and δ_{ij}

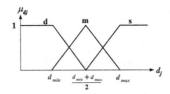

Fig. 6. Membership function and labels for measured distance d_j

(i.e. $\theta_i = \theta_g$). On the contrary, it is minimized ($F_{goal_i} = 0$) if the robot's steering direction of is opposite of the goal. The repulsive force for each moving direction (the ith antibody θ_i), is expressed as the following equation,

$$F_{obs_i} = \sum_{j=1}^{N_S} \alpha_{ij} \cdot \overline{d}_j \qquad (7)$$

where $\alpha_{ij} = \exp(-N_s \times (1 - \delta_{ij}))$ with $\delta_{ij} = \dfrac{1 + \cos(\theta_i - \theta_{S_j})}{2}$. The parameter α_{ij} indicates the weighting ratio for jth sensor to the steering angle θ_i while $\overline{d}_j$ represents the distance between the jth sensor and obstacles. The coefficient δ_{ij} expresses the affection and importance for each sensor at different location. Clearly, the information derived from the sensor closest to the steering direction is much more important due its biggest δ_{ij} value. Fig. 5 illustrates the relation between α_{ij} and δ_{ij} .

As Fig. 6 illustrates, the normalized obstacle distance for each sensor $\overline{d}_j$ is fuzzified using the fuzzy set definitions. The mapping from the fuzzy subspace to the TSK model is represented as three fuzzy if-then rules in the form of

$$\begin{array}{llll} \text{IF} & d_j \text{ is } \mathbf{f} & \text{THEN} & y = L_1 \qquad (8) \\ \text{IF} & d_j \text{ is } \mathbf{m} & \text{THEN} & y = L_2 \\ \text{IF} & d_j \text{ is } \mathbf{n} & \text{THEN} & y = L_3 \end{array}$$

where L_1, L_2, and L_3 are defined as 0.25, 0.5 and 1.0 respectively in this study. The input variable of each rule is the detected distance d_j of the jth range sensor. The antecedent part of each rule has one of the three labels namely, **s** (safe), **m** (medium) and

d (danger). Consequently, the total output of the fuzzy model is given by the equation below,

$$\overline{d}_j = \frac{\mu_{safe}(d) \cdot L_1 + \mu_{medium}(d) \cdot L_2 + \mu_{danger}(d) \cdot L_3}{\mu_{safe}(d) + \mu_{medium}(d) + \mu_{danger}(d)} \tag{9}$$

where $\mu_{safe}(d), \mu_{medium}(d), \mu_{danger}(d)$ represent the matching degree of the corresponding rule. The inputs to the TSK model are crisp numbers, and therefore, the degree of the input matches its rule is and computed using the "min operator".

Finally, the stimulation and suppressive interaction between ith and jth antibodies are defined as the following equations,

$$m_{ij} = \cos(\theta_i - \theta_j) \qquad i, j = 1, 2, \cdots, N_{Ab} \tag{10}$$

$$m_{ki} = \cos(\theta_k - \theta_i) \qquad i, j = 1, 2, \cdots, N_{Ab}$$

As mentioned previously, one problem inherent to the APF method is the possibility for the robot to get trapped in a local minima situation. Traps can be created by a variety of different obstacle configurations. To escape from the trap, the outbreak of local minima should be detected first. In this study, the comparison between the robot-to-target direction θ_g and the actual instantaneous direction of travel θ_i was adopted to detect if the robot got trapped. If the robot's direction of travel is more than 90° off-target (*i.e.* $|\theta_i - \theta_g| > 90°$), the robot starts to move away from the goal and is very likely about to get trapped. Various approaches for escaping trap situations were proposed as described previously. A modified virtual target method is proposed in this study to guide the robot out of the trap.

In the immunology, the T-cell plays a remarkable key role for distinguishing a "self" from other "non-self" antigens. The Helper-T cells work, primarily, by secreting substances, known as cytokines and their relatives [22] that constitute powerful chemical messengers to promote cellular growth, activation and regulation. Resembling the biological immune system, the interleukine can either stimulate or suppress the promotion of antibodies/steering directions depending on whether the antigen is non-self or self (trapped in local minima or not). Similar to the virtual target concept, an additional virtual robot-to-target angle θ_v (analogous to interleukine in the biological immune system) is added to angle θ_g whenever the trap condition ($|\theta_i - \theta_g| > 90°$) is satisfied,

$$\theta_g(k+1) = \theta_g(k) + \theta_v(k) \tag{11}$$

$$\begin{cases} \theta_v(k) = \theta_v(k-1) \pm \Delta\theta_g & \text{if } |\theta_i(k) - \theta_g(k)| \geq 90° \ \& \ \theta_v(k-1) = 0 \\ \theta_v(k) = \theta_v(k-1) + sign(\theta_v(k-1)) \cdot \Delta\theta_g & \text{if } |\theta_i(k) - \theta_g(k)| \geq 90° \ \& \ \theta_v(k-1) \neq 0 \\ \theta_v(k) = \max\{0, \theta_v(k-1) - sign(\theta_v(k-1)) \cdot \theta_c(k-1)\} & \text{if } |\theta_i(k) - \theta_g(k)| < 90° \ \& \ \theta_v(k-1) \geq 0 \\ \theta_v(k) = \min\{0, \theta_v(k-1) - sign(\theta_v(k-1)) \cdot \theta_c(k-1)\} & \text{if } |\theta_i(k) - \theta_g(k)| < 90° \ \& \ \theta_v(k-1) < 0 \end{cases}$$

where $\theta_c(k) = \theta_g(k-1) + \lambda$.

Parameters $k-1$, k, and $k+1$ represent the previous state, the current state and the future state respectively. Symbol "±" indicates that the location of the virtual target can be switched to either the right or the left side of the mobile robot randomly so that the robot has a higher probability to escape from the local minima in either direction. λ is

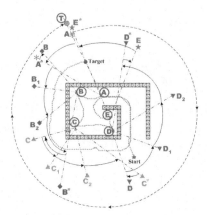

Fig. 7. Robot path and state of the indices along the trajectory

an adjustable decay angle. The bigger the value is, the faster the location of virtual target converges to that of the true one and the easier it is for the robot to get trapped in local minima again. A more detailed description of the proposed scheme and some practical considerations are elaborated below.

Fig. 7 shows the performance of the proposed strategy for the robot to escape from a recursive U-trap situation, which may make the virtual target switching strategy [6] ineffective suggested by Chatterjee and Matsuno [7]. The robot first enters a U-shaped obstacle and is attracted by the target, due to the target reaching behavior, until reaches the critical point Ⓐ. The variation of the distance between the target and the corresponding orientation of the virtual target over time is shown in Fig. 8. Clearly the orientation of goal θ_g is kept the same during this stage, however, the distance between the robot and the target is decreased quickly. The detection of the trap possibility due to the abrupt target orientation change at location Ⓐ (θ_g) makes the target shift to a virtual one A^* ($\theta_g - \Delta\theta_g$). In this study, $\Delta\theta_g$ is equal to 45°. Note that the switch-to-left or the switch-to-right of the virtual target (*i.e.* minus or plus $\Delta\theta_g$) is selected randomly. On the way Ⓐ→ Ⓑ, $\Delta\theta_g$ is decreased gradually according to equation (11) until a new local minimal is found at location Ⓑ. Again, the virtual target switches from A^* to B^*. Fig. 7 and Fig. 8 show that there are successive virtual target switching $A^* \to B_1 \to B_2 \to B^*$ when the robot moves around the left upper corner where it is tracked in a trap (satisfy condition $|\theta_i - \theta_g| > 90°$) three times. After passing through the critical point Ⓑ, the robot keeps approaching the virtual target until the third critical point Ⓒ. Concurrently, the associated orientation of the virtual target is decreased from B^* to C. Once more, it takes three times for the robot to escape from the trap situation in the left lower corner on the path Ⓒ→ Ⓓ (orientation of the virtual target $C \to C_1 \to C_2 \to C^* \to D$). Similar navigation procedures take place on the way Ⓓ→Ⓔ (orientation of virtual target $D \to D_1 \to D_2 \to D^* \to E \to E^*$). After escaping from the recursive U-shaped trap, it revolves in a circle and finally reaches target Ⓣ without any trap situations (orientation of virtual target θ_g decreases gradually from E^* to T illustrated with a dashed line). The trajectory illustrated in Fig. 7 is quite similar to the results derived by Chatterjee and Matsuno [7]. Fig. 9 shows another possible robot trajectory to escape the same trap situation, due to the random choosing of the "plus"

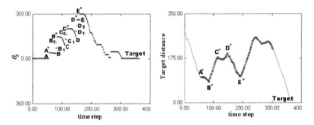

Fig. 8. Variation of virtual target orientation and relative distance of mobile robot

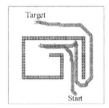

Fig. 9. Another possible trajectories to escape the same trap situation

or "minus" robot-to-target angle $\Delta\theta_g$ as equation (11) shows. Obviously, the mechanism for virtual target switching to the right or to the left ($\pm\Delta\theta_g$) increases the diversity and possibility of the robot escaping from the local minima problem.

4 Simulations and Discussions

Numerous simulation examples embraced by researchers [6-7] were conducted to demonstrate the performance of mobile robot navigation employing RIN to various unknown environments; in particular, the capability of escaping from the traps or the wandering situations described. Fig. 10 shows the performance of the proposed strategy for mobile robots to escape from loop-type and dead-end-type trap situations designed by Chatterjee and Matsuno [7]. It is assumed that the robot has eight uniformly distributed distance sensors and eight moving directions (forward, left, right, back, forward left, forward right, back left and back right). Compared with the results obtained in [12], the robot is capable of navigating through a similar path as Fig. 10(a) illustrated. In addition, Fig. 10(b) demonstrates another possible trajectory (escaping from the left side) due to the random selection scheme mentioned previously.

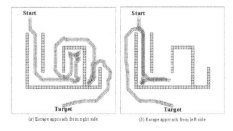

Fig. 10. Escape from loop type and dead-end type trap situation

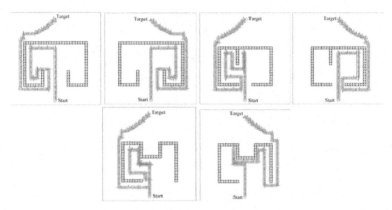

Fig. 11. Robot trajectories to escape from different trap situations designed in [7]

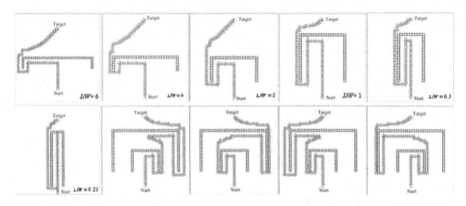

Fig. 12. Escape from U-shaped and double U-shaped traps

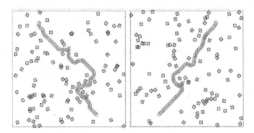

Fig. 13. Navigate in two environments filled with obstacles randomly generated

To validate the efficiency of the proposed strategy further, three trap environments adopted by Madhava *et. al.* [7] were simulated in this study. The simulation results show that the robot is capable of escaping all the traps as illustrated in Fig. 11.

The U-shaped trap problem is the most famous and utilized example in mobile robot navigation. Fig. 12 shows the path of the robot escaping from the U-shaped trap (with different length/width ratios) as well as the double U-shaped trap. Apparently, the robot is capable of escaping of U-shaped and double U-shaped environments.

Moreover, Fig. 13 shows the trajectories for the mobile robot to navigate in two environments filled with 100 randomly generated obstacles. Obviously, the immune network reactive system drives the robot to escape from the obstacles and reach the target safely.

5 Conclusions

An immunized network reactive system inspired by the biological immune system is developed for mobile robot navigation. In addition, a modified virtual target method is integrated to solve the local minima problem. Several trap environments employed in early studies are used to evaluate the performance of the strategy. Simulation results validate the flexibility, efficiency and effectiveness of the robot navigation architecture, especially solving the local minima problem.

References

1. Baraquand, J., Latombe, J.C., Monte-Carlo algorithm for path planning with many degrees of freedom, in: Proceedings of the IEEE International Conference on Robotics and Automation, Cincinnati, OH, (1990), 1712-1717
2. Chang, H., A new technique to handle local minima for imperfect potential field based motion planning, in: Proceedings of the IEEE International Conference on Robotics and Automation, Minneapolis, MN, (1996), 108-112
3. Lee, S., Adams, T.M., Ryoo, B.-Y., A fuzzy navigation system for mobile construction robots, Automation in Construction, 6 (1997) 97-107
4. Borenstein, J., Koren, Y., Real-time obstacle avoidance for fast mobile robots, IEEE Transaction on System, Man and Cybernetics 9 (5) (1989) 1179-1197
5. Park, M.G., Lee, M.C., Artificial potential field based path planning for mobile robots using a virtual obstacle concept, in: Proceedings of the IEEE/ASME International Conference on Advanced Intelligent Mechatronics, (2003),735-740
6. Xu, W.L., A virtual target approach for resolving the limit cycle problem in navigation of a fuzzy behaviour-based mobile robot, Robotics and Autonomous Systems 30 (2000) 315-324
7. Chatterjee, R., Matsuno, F., Use of single side refles for autonomous navigation of mobile robots in unknown environments, Robotics and Autonomous Systems, 35 (2001) 77-96
8. Lee, D.-J., Lee, M.-J., Choi, Y.-K., S., Kim, Design of autonomous mobile robot action selector based on a learning artificial immune network structure, in: Proceedings of the fifth Symposium on Artificial Life and Robotics, Oita, Japan, (2000), 116-119
9. Ishiguro, A., Kondo, T., Watanabe, Y., Shirai, Y., and Uchikawa, Y., Emergent construction of artificial immune networks for autonomous mobile robots, in: IEEE International Conference on Systems, Man, and Cybernetics, Orlando, Florida, (1997), 1222-1228
10. KrishnaKumar, K., Neidhoefer, J., Immunized Neuro control, Expert Systems With Applications 13 (3) (1997) 201-214
11. Luh, G.-C., Cheng, W.-C., Behavior-based intelligent mobile robot using immunized reinforcement adaptive learning mechanism, Advanced Engineering Informatics, 16 (2) (2002) 85-98
12. Michelan, R., Fernando, J.V., Decentralized control system for autonomous navigation based on an evolved artificial immune network, in: Proceedings, (2002), 1021-1026

13. D. Dasgupta, Artificial Immune Systems and Their Applications, Springer-Verlag, Berlin Heidelberg, 1999
14. L.N. de Castro, T. Jonathan, Artificial immune systems: A new Computational Intelligence Approach, Springer-Verlag, 1999
15. Y., The immune system as a prototype of autonomous decentralized systems: an overview, in: Proceedings of Third International Symposium on autonomous decentralized systems, (1997), 85-92
16. I. Roitt, J. Brostoff, D.K. Male, Immunology, 5th ed. Mosby International Limited, 1998
17. Oprea, M.L., Antibody repertoires and pathogen recognition: the role of germline diversity and somatic hypermutation, PhD Dissertation, Department of Computer Science, The University of New Mexico, Albuquerque, New Mexico, 1996
18. Carneiro, J., Coutinho, A., Faro, J., Stewart, J., A model of the immune network with B-T cell co-operation I-prototypical structures and dynamics Journal of theoretical Biological 182 (1996) 513-529
19. Dasgupta, D., Artificial neural networks and artificial immune systems: similarities and differences, in: IEEE International Conference on Systems, Man, and Cybernetics, Orlando, Florida, (1997), 873-878
20. Jerne, N.K., The immune system, Scientific American 229 (1) (1973) 52-60
21. R.C. Arkin, Behavior-based robotics, Cambridge, MIT Press, 1998
22. Farmer, J.D. , Packard, N.H., Perelson, A.S., The immune system adaptation, and machine learning, Physica 22-D (1986) 184- 204

A Fractal Immune Network

Peter J. Bentley[1] and Jon Timmis[2]

[1] Department of Computer Science, University College London. UK
p.bentley@cs.ucl.ac.uk
http://www.cs.ucl.ac.uk/staff/p.bentley/
[2] Computing Laboratory, University of Kent, Canterbury. UK.
j.timmis@kent.ac.uk

Abstract. Proteins are the driving force in development (embryogenesis) and the immune system. Here we describe how a model of proteins designed for evolutionary development in computers can be combined with a model of immune systems. Full details of a prototype system are provided, and preliminary experiments presented. Results show that evolution is able to adjust the mapping between input data and antigens and cause useful changes to the subnetworks formed by the immune algorithm.

1 Introduction

Human development (embryogenesis) is a highly evolved network of cellular and chemical interactions, which somehow manages to build and maintain our bodies throughout our lives (Wolpert et al, 2001). One of the processes built and maintained by development is our immune system. The human immune system is also a highly evolved network of cellular and chemical interactions, which somehow learns, predicts and correctly protects our bodies from invading pathogens and internal malfunctions.

Clearly, the features of immune systems are highly related to development. Indeed, immune systems can be considered to be a specialized form of development, which focuses on the removal of unwanted elements from us. Both work in much the same ways: genes produce proteins which control other genes, and determine the function of cells. In development, our genetic program causes cells to divide, move, differentiate, extrude substances, and signal other cells using special proteins. In immune systems, our genetic program causes immune cells to be created, to respond to signals from other damaged or infected cells, and to send and receive signals from each other.

Throughout, proteins are the driving force. Produced by genes, they activate or suppress other genes, they determine the fate of cells, and they act as signals, enabling cells to communicate with each other. It is the shape of these proteins that determines their function. Through a complex bio-chemical process of protein folding, every protein has a unique morphology which enables it to diffuse between cells, interact with other proteins, attach to receptors on cell walls, interact with genes, and perform thousands of other actions.

In an attempt to harness more of the capabilities of proteins, in this work we describe how a model of proteins based on fractals, designed for evolutionary develop-

G. Nicosia et al. (Eds.): ICARIS 2004, LNCS 3239, pp. 133–145, 2004.

ment in computers, can be combined with a model of immune systems. The *fractal immune network* maps data items to *fractal antigens*, creates *fractal recognition spaces* (similar to Artificial Recognition Balls) in dynamic networks, and forms all network links by emission and reception of *fractal cytokines*. The system is essentially a reconfigurable clusterer – the networks of fractal recognition spaces can be radically changed by changing the mapping from data to fractal antigens. The system evolves this mapping according to a fitness function, thus automatically providing desirable clusters and data classification, regardless of the data.

2   Fractal Proteins

Other work by the first author (Bentley, 2004; Kumar and Bentley, 2003) has focused on biologically plausible models of gene regulatory networks (GRNs) in the context of development (embryogenesis). In such models, genes define proteins, which trigger or suppress (i.e., *regulate*) the activation of the genes, causing dynamic, non-linear regulatory networks to form. By evolving the genes using a genetic algorithm, the resulting networks can be linked to sensors and functions and can be used for tasks such as function regression (Bentley 2004) or robot control (Bentley 2003a). In the context of a full developmental model, GRNs specify how cells divide, grow, differentiate and die, in order to produce a larger, more complex multicellular solution (Kumar and Bentley, 2003).

The recent work of (Bentley, 2004, 2003a,b) developed a new model of proteins to overcome various difficulties with previous models. Here, genes are expressed into *fractal proteins* – subsets of the Mandelbrot set that can interact and react according to their own fractal chemistry. The motivations behind this work are extensive and can briefly be listed as follows: (Further motivations and discussions on fractal proteins are provided in (Bentley, 2004, 2003b).)

1. Natural evolution extensively exploits the complexity, redundancy and richness of chemical systems in the design of DNA and the resulting developmental systems in organisms. Providing a computer system with genes that define fractal proteins gives the system complexity, redundancy and richness to exploit.
2. It is extremely difficult and computationally intensive to model natural chemical systems accurately in an artificial chemistry. Fractal proteins have many of the same properties as natural proteins, without any modelling overheads.
3. A fractal protein (with the infinite complexity of the Mandelbrot set) can be defined by just three genes.
4. The "fractal genetic space" is highly evolvable – a small change to a gene produces a small change to the fractal protein, while the self-similarity of fractals ensures that any specific shape can be found in an infinite number of places.
5. When fractal proteins are permitted to interact according to their morphologies, a hugely complex (and eminently exploitable) fractal chemistry emerges naturally.
6. Calculating subsets of Mandelbrot sets is *fast* so there is little overhead.

2.1 Mandelbrot Set

Given the equation $x_{t+1} = x_t^2 + c$ where x_t and c are imaginary numbers, Benoit Mandelbrot wanted to know which values of c would make the length of the imaginary number stored in x_t stop growing when the equation was applied for an infinite number of times. He discovered that if the length ever went above 2, then it was unbounded – it would grow forever. But for the right imaginary values of c, sometimes the result would simply oscillate between different lengths less than 2.

Mandelbrot used his computer to apply the equation many times for different values of c. For each value of c, the computer would stop early if the length of the imaginary number in x_t was 2 or more. If the computer hadn't stopped early for that value of c, a black dot was drawn. The dot was placed at coordinate (m, n) using the numbers from the value of c: $(m + ni)$ where m was varied from -2.4 to 1.34 and n was varied from 1.4 to -1.4, to fill the computer screen. The result was the infinite complexity of the "squashed bug" shape we know so well today. (Mandelbrot, 1982)

2.2 Defining a Fractal Protein

A fractal protein is a finite square subset of the Mandelbrot set, defined by three codons (x,y,z) that form the coding region of a gene in the genome of a cell. Each (x, y, z) triplet is expressed as a protein by calculating the square fractal subset with centre coordinates (x,y) and sides of length z, see fig. 1 for an example. In this way, it is possible to achieve as much complexity (or more) compared to natural protein folding in nature.

In addition to shape, each fractal protein represents a certain *concentration* of protein (from 0 meaning "does not exist" to 200 meaning "saturated"), determined by protein production and diffusion rates.

Fig. 1. Example of a fractal protein defined by ($x = 0.132541887$, $y = 0.698126164$, $z = 0.468306528$)

2.3 Fractal Chemistry

Cell cytoplasms and cell environments usually contain more than one fractal protein. In an attempt to harness the complexity available from these fractals, multiple proteins are merged. The result is a product of their own "fractal chemistry" which naturally emerges through the fractal interactions.

Fig. 2. Two fractal proteins (left and middle) and the resulting merged fractal protein combination (right).

Fractal proteins are merged (for each point sampled) by iterating through the fractal equation of all proteins in "parallel", and stopping as soon as the length of any is unbounded (i.e. greater than 2). Intuitively, this results in black regions being treated as though they are transparent, and paler regions "winning" over darker regions. See fig 2 for an example.

2.4 Fractal Development

Figure 3 illustrates the representation. Although not used here, fig. 4 provides an overview of the algorithm used in (Bentley, 2004, 2003a,b) to develop a phenotype from a genotype. Note how most of the dynamics rely on the interaction of fractal proteins. Evolution is used to design genes that are expressed into fractal proteins with specific shapes, which result in developmental processes with specific dynamics.

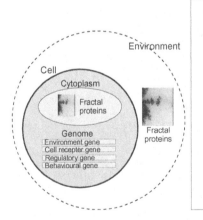

FRACTAL DEVELOPMENT

For every developmental time step:

    For every cell in the embryo:

        Express all environment genes and calculate shape of merged environment fractal proteins

        Express cell receptor genes as receptor fractal proteins and use each one to mask the merged environment proteins into the cell cytoplasm.

        If the merged contents of the cytoplasm match a promoter of a regulatory gene, express the coding region of the gene, adding the resultant fractal protein to the cytoplasm.

        If the merged contents of the cytoplasm match a promoter of a behavioural gene, use coding region of the gene to specify a cellular function.

        Update the concentration levels of all proteins in the cytoplasm. If the concentration level of a protein falls to zero, that protein does not exist.

Fig. 3. Representation using fractal proteins.

Fig. 4. The fractal development algorithm

3 Immune Networks

How the immune system remembers encounters with antigenic material has been a question immunologists have been asking for many years. A number of theories abound, from antigenic retention, to immune networks. A theory first proposed by Jerne (1974) suggested that B-cell memory was maintained via an Idiotypic network. This theory attempts to explain how B-cells survive even in the absence of antigenic stimulus. It is proposed that this is achieved by stimulation and suppression between B-cells via a network communicating via idiotypes on regions called paratopes; these are located on B-cell receptors. An idiotope is made up of amino acids within the variable region of an antibody or T-cell. The network acts as a self-organising and self-regulatory mechanism that captures antigenic information. Notable work in (Farmer et al. 1986) further explored the immune network theory and created a simple model of the Idiotypic network. This theory was further extended by (Perelson 1989). A network of B cells is thus formed and highly stimulated B cells survive and less stimulated B cells are removed from the system, as result is a meta-stable memory structure that exhibits interesting dynamics and properties.

Although it is now known that networks in the immune system are rather more complex than described in the immune network theory as described above, the ideas have led to a wide variety of immune-inspired algorithms to be created over the past few years (de Castro and Von Zuben, 2001), (Timmis and Neal, 2001), (de Castro and Timmis, 2002a) and Neal, 2003, to name a few.

3.1 A Meta-stable Artificial Immune Network

Work in Neal (2003) was based on an early artificial immune network model (AINE) devised for data clustering (Timmis and Neal 2001). The algorithm proposed in Neal (2003) allows for the creation of a network structure that captures the patterns (or clusters) contained within a constant input data stream. This algorithm has a number of attractive properties such as being able to identify new clusters that appear in the data stream, allows patterns to be remembered for long period of time without the need for re-enforcement from the input pattern and operates an adaptive memory mechanism that allows the network to be dynamic. It is this dynamic property of the network, that we wish to capture and augment with the use of fractal proteins. For the purposes of this paper, we will describe the system in terms of the representation or shape space of the system (coupled with an affinity function) and the algorithm used to control the population.

Representation and Shape Space

The immune system is made up of large number of B-cells and T-cells. These cells contain surface receptor molecules whose shapes are complementary to the shapes of antigens (invading material), allowing the cells to recognise the antigen and then elicit some form of immune response. Perelson and Oster (1979) first proposed the concept of *shape-space (S)*. Given that the recognition of antigens is performed by the cell receptors, shape-spaces therefore allow a quantitative description of the interactions of receptor molecules and antigens. As in the biological immune system, in a shape-space S, the degree of binding (degree of match or affinity) between an antigenic receptor or antibody **(Ab)** and an antigen **(Ag)**, is measured via regions of complementarity. Within an AIS the generalised shape of a molecule (m) of either an antibody **(Ab)** or an antigen **(Ag)**, can be represented as an attribute string (set of coordinates) $m = <m1, m2, ..., m_l>$ or many other forms of attributes, ranging from integers, binary values, or other more complex structures. Within the work of Neal (2003), a simple real valued shape space was employed.

The work of (de Castro and Timmis, 2002b) proposed that this notion of shape space could be used to model an antibody and an antigen. They also stated that what ever shape is chosen, will of course affect the way in which interactions are calculated between them, i.e. how their affinity will be calculated. Given that the Ag-Ab affinity is related to distance, they stated that this could be estimated via any distance measure between two strings or vectors. In the case of Neal (2003) the Euclidean distance measure was employed.

The Algorithm

Input data is presented continuously to the network, with each data item being presented to each Artificial Recognition Balls (ARB) in the network. Experiments demonstrated that once the network had captured the patterns in the data stream, then the data stream could be removed and the patterns would remain for a period of time, due to the network interactions of stimulation and resource allocation employed in the network (Neal, 2003).

Network Initialisation. The algorithm is initialised as a network of ARB objects. Each ARB represents a data vector, a stimulation level and a number of resources (used to control lifespan of the object). Links between ARBs are created if they are below the Network Affinity Threshold (NAT), which is the average Euclidean distance between each item in the data set. The initial network is a random selection of the data set to be learnt (or a set of randomly initialised vectors), the remainder makes up the antigen training set.

Stimulation. ARBs maintain a record of stimulation. In effect, this records how well the ARB matches a certain training data item and how well it matches neighbors within the network structure. The idea being that similarly occurring patterns will reinforce each other. It is worthy of note, that no suppression element is used in the equation, unlike the work of (Timmis and Neal, 2001). This is due to the fact, that with the resource allocation mechanism employed (see below) by the author, the suppression is no longer required.

Expansion. The system does not perform cloning or mutation in the same sense as many AIS algorithms (or indeed the natural immune system). In order to allow the network to grow, the affinity of an ARB to a training data item is required to be over a certain threshold, the *affinity threshold*. If this is the case, then a new ARB is created in the location of the antigen. This is effectively adding the new cell to the network representation of self.

Resource Allocation. Each ARB is assigned an initial number of resources. The resource level is used to indicate when the death of an ARB should occur, as if the resource level falls below a certain defined threshold, then the ARB is removed from the system: in effect, this is the algorithms population control mechanism. Simply put, each ARB is assigned a local number of resources, which is proportional to the stimulation of the ARB, minus a certain geometric death rate. This enables well-stimulated ARBs to survive in the network, and poorly stimulated ARBs to be removed.

4   A Fractal Immune Network

The concept proposed and partially investigated in this paper is to combine the ideas of fractal proteins with immune networks. Since fractal proteins have been shown to enable considerable benefits to developmental models, it is suggested here that similar benefits may be gained from their use in an immune network algorithm.

The combination of these ideas is relatively straightforward. Antigens, antibodies, and cytokines are all types of protein. The immune network relies on interactions between proteins. A Fractal Immune Network, therefore uses fractals to represent these proteins, and thus the network dynamics are created by interactions between different fractal shapes. (The immune network algorithm is based on (Neal 2003).)

4.1   Data to Fractal Antigen Mapping

To enable all interactions to take place in a fractal shape space, each data item of the incoming data stream is mapped to a fractal protein, which we term a *fractal antigen* $\mathbf{Ag}^f$. Each data item (comprising 4 values) is mapped to the (x, y, z) triplet (described in section 2) using equation [1]. Once mapped, the fractal antigen becomes a finite subset of the Mandelbrot set, and is stored as a bitmap. All operations in the network then take place using bitmap processing.

Mapping data to fractal protein (x, y, z)
$x = A_0 * \text{datum}_0 / \text{scale}_0 - B_0$
$y = A_1 * \text{datum}_1 / \text{scale}_1 - B_1$
$z = A_2 * \text{datum}_2 / \text{scale}_2 - B_2 + A_3 * \text{datum}_3 / \text{scale}_3 - B_3$ (1)

where:
  datum_i is the ith value of current data item
  A_i, B_i are mapping coefficients, evolved by the system
  (initial values for all $A_i = 1.0$, $B_i = 0.5$).
  scale_i is data range of values in ith column of data (assuming only positive values)

Clearly the mapping from data item to $\mathbf{Ag}^f$ is critical, so the algorithm incorporates a simple (1+1) Evolution Strategy (Bäck, 1996), which mutates the mapping coefficients every EVOLVEFREQ iterations (where EVOLVEFREQ is set to 1500 in the experiments to enable the entire data set to be presented 10 times). After mutating, the network is restarted. If the subsequent network scores a lower fitness, the coefficients are restored to their previous values before mutating again. Fitness of the network is calculated by presenting the entire dataset to the current network and using the fitness calculation shown in equation [2].

Fitness calculation for Evolution Strategy when evolving mapping coefficients:

$$F = | n_1 - class_1 | + | n_2 - class_2 | + n_3 + n_4 + nodes \qquad (2)$$

where:

n_1 is the highest number of data items from class 1 in a subnetwork p
n_2 is the highest number of data items from class 2 in a subnetwork q
(where p is not the same network as q).
n_3 is the number of data items from class 1 misclassified in subnetwork q
n_4 is the number of data items from class 2 misclassified in subnetwork p
class$_i$ is the ith class of data, see section 5.1 for an example.
nodes is the number of **FRS**s in the entire network minus five if that number is above five, zero otherwise.

4.2 Initialisation and Expansion

Initially, the network is presented with a small subset of the data (for the IRIS data used in the experiments, 10 out of 150 items are randomly picked). The data item is mapped to a fractal antigen as described above. Upon first encountering an **Ag^f**, the fractal immune network algorithm creates its version of an ARB at that point, if one sufficiently similar does not already exist: this represents the initial population of the network. For this system we refer to ARBs as "Fractal Recognition Spaces" or **FRS**s. Thus, each **FRS** is defined by a core **Ag^f** (which may subsequently match one or more fractal antigens). All fractal shapes are stored as bitmaps.

After the initialization, the network runs continuously, being presented with randomly chosen data items from the entire data set, and creating more **FRS**s if needed.

4.3 Stimulation

Should any **Ag^f** match an existing **FRS** closely enough (determined by measuring whether the difference between the bitmaps is below ANTIGENMATCHINGTHRESH-OLD), the **FRS** is *stimulated* according to equation [3].

Antigen stimulation S$_1$ calculation:

$$S_1 = 10 * (1 - d_{FRSAg} / \text{ANTIGENMATCHINGTHRESHOLD}) \qquad (3)$$

where:

S_1 is stimulation increase for **FRS** when **Ag^f** matched
d_{FRSAg} is matching distance between **FRS** and **Ag^f**
ANTIGENMATCHINGTHRESHOLD is the **FRS** matching threshold (set to 500)

If required, an optional feature of this algorithm in this situation creates a new **FRS** with a probability of 0.01 in addition to stimulating the existing one. The new **FRS** is a mutation (e.g. as caused by hypermutation in immune systems), created by merging the existing **FRS** with the current **Ag^f**. In this way, the core fractal protein becomes a "general" fractal antibody that will match more fractal antigens - the space of the **FRS** is widened or adjusted.

If the current **Ag^f** matches no exising **FRS**s closely enough, a new **FRS** is created as described in section 4.2.

In addition, **FRS**s in the network stimulate each other. Instead of explicitly maintaining a list of links between **FRS**s, this system makes dynamic network connections between **FRS**s, formed by the emission and reception of *fractal cytokines* **Ck**'s. To calculate the network stimulations, each **FRS** emits a **Ck**'s (simply a clone of the transmitting **FRS** bitmap) to every other **FRS**. This is bitwise masked by the receptor **Rc**' of the receiving **FRS** (simply a clone of the receiving **FRS** bitmap) thus ensuring that two similar **FRS**s will be able to "communicate" but dissimilar **FRS**s will never receive each others' signals. If the receiving **FRS** is mature, it compares the masked **Ck**' with itself – if the difference between the bitmaps is les than CYTOKINEMATCH-INGTHRESHOLD, then the stimulation of that **FRS** is increased, as defined in equation [4].

Network stimulation S_2 calculation:
$$S_2 = d_{FRSCk} \text{ / CYTOKINEMATCHINGTHRESHOLD} \tag{4}$$

where:
    S_2 is stimulation increase for **FRS** when masked **Ck**' matched
    d_{FRSCk} is matching distance between **FRS** and masked **Ck**'
    CYTOKINEMATCHINGTHRESHOLD is network matching threshold (set to 550)

An **FRS** is mature if its age is above MATUREAGE (set to the number of data items in the dataset) – needed when the "mutate FRS" option is activated to prevent excessive numbers of **FRS**s that match few or no **Ag**'s from overrunning the network.

    Each iteration, the stimulation for each **FRS** is calculated, summed, and a decay factor removed, see equation [5].

Total stimulation calculation:
$$S_{total} = S_1 + S_2 - C_{FRS} * \text{DECAYRATE} \tag{5}$$
$$\text{if } S_{total} >= \text{MAXNEWCONC } S_{total} = \text{MAXNEWCONC} - 1$$

where:
    S_{total} is stimulation from all **Ag**'s and masked **Ck**'s, reduced by decay
    C_{FRS} is concentration of current **FRS**
    DECAYRATE is decay rate constant (set to 0.1)
    MAXNEWCONC is maximum concentration increase each iteration (set to 100)

This is then scaled to prevent excessive new stimulation each iteration and added to the current concentration of the **FRS**, equation [6]. If this concentration drops below MORTALITY, the **FRS** is removed from the network. Figure 5 describes the fractal immune network algorithm.

Concentration update calculation:
$$C_{FRS} = C_{FRS} + S_{total} * (\text{MAXNEWCONC} - S_{total}) / \text{MAXNEWCONC} \tag{6}$$

Iterate until halted:
    For each new data item

            map data item to fractal antigen $\mathbf{Ag^f}$ according to eqn [1]

            present $\mathbf{Ag^f}$ to the fractal immune network:
            does $\mathbf{Ag^f}$ match an existing fractal recognition space **FRS**
            with difference less than ANTIGENMATCHINGTHRESHOLD?
            Yes: calculate stimulation S_1 of best matching **FRS** according to eqn [3]
                        *occasionally create new **FRS** by merging existing **FRS** shape with $\mathbf{Ag^f}$
            No: create new **FRS** with shape $\mathbf{Ag^f}$

            for every **FRS** in the network:
                    emit a fractal cytokine $\mathbf{Ck^f}$ to every other **FRS**
            for every *mature* **FRS** in the network:
                    mask all incoming $\mathbf{Ck^f}$'s with fractal receptor $\mathbf{Rc^f}$
                    does **FRS** match $\mathbf{Ck^f}$ masked by $\mathbf{Rc^f}$
                    with difference less than CYTOKINEMATCHINGTHRESHOLD?
                    Yes: calculate stimulation S_2 of **FRS** according to eqn [4]

            increase age of every **FRS**, when age > MATUREAGE **FRS** is mature.

            update concentration of every **FRS** according to eqn [6]
            has concentration fallen below MORTALITY?
            Yes: delete **FRS**
                        is there more than zero **FRS**s in the network?
                        No: halt processing

    Every EVOLVEFREQ **iterations, evolve mapping coefficients using eqn [2]and restart network.**

Fig. 5. The Fractal Immune Network algorithm. Algorithm constants are set as follows: ANTI-
GENMATCHINGTHRESHOLD = 500, CYTOKINEMATCHINGTHRESHOLD = 500, MATUREAGE = 150,
MORTALITY = 0.01, EVOLVEFREQ = 1500

5   Experiments

5.1   Experimental Motivation

From the beginning of this research it was clear that the mapping between data items
and fractal antigens would be critical. For example, if all data items were mapped to
almost identical fractal shapes, then the resulting network would be unable to distinguish between different classes of data. Contrast this with a good mapping from data
to $\mathbf{Ag^f}$, which would be able to amplify even minor differences between data and
enable useful clusters to form. Indeed, a good mapping would exploit the self-
similarity of fractals, enabling (when desirable) data items that might look different to
be correctly classified in the same class, and data items that might look similar to be
correctly classified in different classes.

It was for these potential benefits that an evolutionary stage was incorporated into the fractal immune algorithm, enabling the data-to-$\mathbf{Ag}^{f}$ mapping to be subtly modified over time, guided by a fitness function.

Here we present preliminary experiments to demonstrate the evolution of this mapping and provide evidence to demonstrate that it improves clustering by the fractal immune algorithm.

This IRIS dataset was employed (a set comprising data items of four values, in three classes with 50 items in each class). The first 50 items were treated as "class 1" by the fitness function, with the remaining 100 being treated as "class 2." The system was set up as described in previous sections, with all constants set to their default values. Evolution was permitted to proceed for 2000 iterations, where each iteration comprised the formation of a new network and the random presentation of the data set ten times. The option to create new merged "mutant" **FRS**s was active during evolution.

5.2 Results

Figure 6 illustrates a good result (judged by the fitness function) obtained by the fractal immune network using the default mapping coefficient values, before evolution. It should be clear that the network is malformed, with some areas excessively connected and other areas completely unconnected. Figure 7 shows the networks obtained after evolution, both with merging inactive, and with merging active. It should be evident that both show "healthier-looking" networks, with two clear subnetworks for each class of data, and fewer unconnected **FRS**s.

Table 1 shows the classification performance as measured by the fitness function of the fractal immune network. Evolution has clearly found an improved mapping, which increases the ability of the network to classify the IRIS data, (whether the merging **FRS** option is active or not). Although the results are not perfect, at this stage we are focusing on the ability of evolution to fine-tune the data-to-$\mathbf{Ag}^{f}$ mapping. From findings in other work (Neal 2003), the networks are likely to provide better results when given more iterations to converge. With improved, perhaps non-linear mapping functions, it seems likely that evolution would be able to exploit the fractal proteins further and increase accuracy.

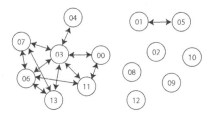

Fig. 6. Fractal Immune Network using default mapping coefficient values (merging inactive). **FRS**s are shown in arbitrary spatial positions.

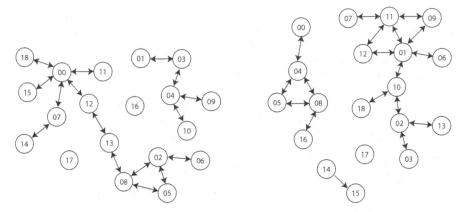

Fig. 7. Fractal Immune Network using evolved mapping coefficient values. Left: network obtained using no merging. Right: network obtained when new merged **FRS**s are permitted.

Table 1. Classification by the Fractal Immune Network. Note that **FRS**s within various subnetworks typically detect all data items, but only the two subnetworks that classify the largest amount of data in each class are shown here and used by the fitness function.

	Correct in class1	Correct in class 2	Incorrect in class 1	Incorrect in class 2
Default values	15 / 50	23 / 100	8 / 50	67 / 100
Evolved values, no merging	30 / 50	76 / 100	19 / 50	16 / 100
Evolved values, Merging	42 / 50	70 / 100	4 / 50	22 / 100

6 Conclusions

Proteins are the driving force in both development and immune systems. Here we have described the combination of fractal proteins (a model which has achieved great success within evolutionary developmental systems) with a network immune algorithm (which has also been demonstrated to great effect in the field of artificial immune systems). The model maps data items to fractal antigens, creates fractal recognition spaces in dynamic networks, and forms all network links by emission and reception of fractal cytokines. Experiments investigated the evolution of the mapping from data to antigens and demonstrated an improvement in cluster formation as measured by a fitness function. While not yet showing perfect results, these initial studies provide much promise. With a more advanced mapping stage and further analysis, the system provides the potential to enable the dynamics of this clusterer to evolve and thus automatically provide desirable clusters and data classification, regardless of the data.

Acknowledgements. Thanks to BAE Systems and Hector Figueiredo for providing support for this work. Thanks also to Johnny Kelsey for the idea of cytokines in the network algorithm.

References

1. Bäck, T. *Evolutionary Algorithms in Theory and Practice*. 1996. Oxford University Press, New York.
2. Bentley, P. J. Fractal Proteins. 2004. In Genetic Programming and Evolvable Machines Journal.
3. Bentley, P. J. Evolving Fractal Gene Regulatory Networks for Robot Control. 2003a. In Proceedings of ECAL 2003.
4. Bentley, P. J. Evolving Beyond Perfection: An Investigation of the Effects of Long-Term Evolution on Fractal Gene Regulatory Networks. 2003b. In Proc of *Information Processing in Cells and Tissues* (IPCAT 2003).
5. De Castro, L.N and Timmis, J (2002a). "An Artificial Immune Network for multi-modal optimisation". In proceedings of IEEE World Congress on Computational Intelligenece. Pp. 699-704.
6. De Castro, L.N and Timmis, J (2002b). "Artificial Immune Systems: A New Computational Intelligence Approach". Springer-Verlag.
7. de Castro, L. N. & Von Zuben, F. J. (2001), "aiNet: An Artificial Immune Network for Data Analysis", in *Data Mining: A Heuristic Approach*, H. A. Abbass, R. A. Sarker, and C. S. Newton (eds.), Idea Group Publishing, USA, Chapter XII, pp. 231-259.
8. Farmer, J. D., Packard, N. H. & Perelson, A. S. (1986), "The Immune System, Adaptation, and Machine Learning", *Physica 22D*, pp. 187-204.
9. Jerne, N. K. (1974), "Towards a Network Theory of the Immune System", *Ann. Immunol.* (Inst. Pasteur) 125C, pp. 373-389.
10. Kumar, S. and Bentley, P. J.. Computational Embryology: Past, Present and Future. 2003. Invited chapter in Ghosh and Tsutsui (Eds) Theory and Application of Evolutionary Computation: Recent Trends. Springer Verlag (UK).
11. Mandelbrot, B. *The Fractal Geometry of Nature*. 1982. W.H. Freeman & Company.
12. Neal, M. (2003), "Meta-stable Memory in an Artificial Immune Network", *LNCS 2787*. pp. 168-180. Timmis, J, Bentley, P and Hart E. (Eds). Springer-Verlag.
13. Perelson, A. S. (1989), "Immune Network Theory", *Imm. Rev.*, 110, pp. 5-36.
14. Perelson, A. S. & Oster, G. F. (1979), "Theoretical Studies of Clonal Selection: Minimal Antibody Repertoire Size and Reliability of Self-Nonself Discrimination", *J. theor.Biol.*, **81**, pp. 645-670.
15. Timmis, J. and Neal, M (2001). "A resource limited artificial immune system for data analysis" Knowledge Based Systems. 14(3-4).:121-130.
16. Wolpert, L., Rosa Beddington, Thomas Jessell, Peter Lawrence, Elliot Meyerowitz, Jim Smith. *Principles of Development, 2nd Ed.* 2001. Oxford University Press.

Nootropia: A User Profiling Model Based on a Self-Organising Term Network

Nikolaos Nanas[1], Victoria S. Uren[2], and Anne de Roeck[1]

[1] Computing Department, The Open University, Milton Keynes, MK7 6AA, U.K.
{N.Nanas,A.deRoeck}@open.ac.uk
[2] Knowledge Media Institute, The Open University, Milton Keynes, MK7 6AA, U.K.
{V.S.Uren}@open.ac.uk

Abstract. Artificial Immune Systems are well suited to the problem of using a profile representation of an individual's or a group's interests to evaluate documents. Nootropia is a user profiling model that exhibits similarities to models of the immune system that have been developed in the context of autopoietic theory. It uses a self-organising term network that can represent a user's multiple interests and can adapt to both short-term variations and substantial changes in them. This allows Nootropia to drift, constantly following changes in the user's multiple interests, and, thus, to become structurally coupled to the user.

1 Introduction

Artificial Immune Systems (AIS) have already been applied to the problem of filtering information according to an individual's (or a group's) interests. Information Filtering (IF) is typically based on a user profile, a representation of the user's interests, that is used to evaluate the relevance of information items, e.g. documents. This can be done in two complementary ways. *Content-based Filtering* is used to refer to the evaluation of an information item based on features that describe its actual content. *Collaborative Filtering*, on the other hand, is based on an information item's ratings by users in a community. The applications of IF include the removal of non-relevant items from an incoming stream, the automation of web search, the recommendation of information items (e.g. web pages, movies) and others.

Here we concentrate on content-based document filtering, but not on a specific application domain. The problem we are trying to address is user profiling for users with long-term interests. This implies that a user may be interested in multiple topics in parallel and that changes in them occur over time. In addition to short-term variations in the level of interest in certain topics, radical long-term changes are also possible. Occasionally, and at a slower time scale than short-term variations, interest in a specific topic can be lost and a new topic of interest can emerge. Therefore, a user profile has to be able to (a) represent multiple topics of interest and (b) adapt, based on user feedback, to both short-term variations and more substantial long-term changes.

G. Nicosia et al. (Eds.): ICARIS 2004, LNCS 3239, pp. 146–160, 2004.

The immune system, which we briefly describe in the next section, has the characteristic ability to distinguish between *self* (the organism's own molecules) and non-self (foreign molecules). This makes AIS particularly attractive for the problem of distinguishing information items that are relevant to the user (self) from non-relevant items (non-self). Nevertheless, existing approaches (section 3) have not directly tackled content-based document filtering according to a user's multiple and changing interests. For this purpose we introduce Nootropia[1], a model for user profiling that exhibits certain similarities to models of the immune systems that have been developed from the perspective of autopoietic theory. We describe these models in section 4. In section 5, we tackle the first of the above requirements. We describe the process for initialising a term network that can perform nonlinear document evaluation and hence can represent a user's multiple interests. To tackle the second requirement, we introduce in section 6 a deterministic process that allows the profile to adapt in response to changes in the user's multiple interests. In section 7, we argue that adaptation to both short-term variations and substantial changes in the user's interests is possible due to the term network's ability to self-organise. We also identify the similarities between Nootropia and the aforementioned models of the immune system. We conclude with a summary of the current work and plans for further research.

2   The Immune System

AIS are based on the biological immune system, which we describe, in simple terms, in this section. The general reader is thus introduced to concepts from immunology that are going to be used in the rest of this paper. Experts in AIS however, can skip this section.

The primary job of the immune system is to protect the host organism from foreign molecules. This is done in part by antibody molecules which are manufactured by *B-cells* (B-lymphocytes). Antibodies have specific 3-D structures that bind to foreign antigen molecules and thus signal their removal by other cells. The portion of the antibody molecule that can identify other molecules is called the *paratope*. When the paratope matches an antigen molecule sufficiently, the two attach leading to the antigen's removal. Paratopes can attach to specific regions on another molecule (antigen or antibody) that are called *epitopes*. Since the match between a paratope and an epitope does not have to be exact, a paratope may attach to an entire class of epitopes. So given enough antibody diversity the probability that an epitope is not recognised is very small [1]. In addition, when an antibody attaches to an antigen the corresponding B-cell is stimulated to clone and secrete more antibodies. This process which results in increased concentrations of useful antibodies is called *clonal selection*. The cloning process is not perfect, but is subjected to somatic mutation that results in slightly different B-cells and hence antibodies, which can be a better match to the invading antigen. Further diversity of antibody repertoire is maintained

---

[1] Greek word for: "An Individual's or a group's particular way of thinking, someone's characteristics of intellect and perception"

through replacement of a percentage of B-cells by new B-cells manufactured in the bone marrow. Overall, this is a very effective pattern matching mechanism capable of learning in the presence of different types of antigens.

However, an organism's immune system has to be able to differentiate between foreign molecules (non-self) and the organism's own molecules (self). *Self–non-self discrimination* is possibly done through *negative selection*, that triggers immature, freshly made B-cells that match the organism's molecules to be removed from the immune repertoire. Another possible explanation is based on Jerne's *idiotypic network theory*. Jerne's theory stresses, in addition to the matching between antibodies and antigens, the importance of the ability of antibodies to recognise other antibodies. An antibody type is reinforced when its paratope recognises the epitopes of other antibodies and suppressed in the opposite case. The antibody-to-antibody recognition can extent multiple levels, forming chains of suppression and reinforcement within complex reaction networks which regulate the concentrations of self-matching antibodies [2]. Not all antibodies in the immune repertoire join this network. There is evidence that the immune network comprises only 10-20% of the antibodies in the repertoire [3].

3   Related Work

It is the immune system's latter ability for self–non-self discrimination that makes it attractive for the problem of user profiling. As already mentioned, a user profile has to be able to discriminate between relevant (self) information items, like documents, and non-relevant (non-self). AIS that model various aspects of the immune system have already been applied to related problems. Chao and Forrest suggest the use of an AIS for filtering out information items that are non-relevant to an individual, or a group of people, and describe its application for filtering out computer generated graphics and music tracks broadcasted by an online radio [4]. They use a clustering-based model that includes antibody-to-antigen matching for recognising non-relevant information items and negative selection for supressing the action of antibodies that match relevant information. Twycross and Cayzer applied a co-evolutionary AIS to the problem of binary classification of documents [5]. Both antibodies that match relevant information items and antibodies that match non-relevant items have been explicitly encoded as binary vectors. Negative selection has been combined with clonal selection based on genetic operations similar to genetic algorithms. In [6], Greensmith and Cayzer propose extending the previous model to include weighted vectors and information extracted from a taxonomy to achieve document classification according to a fixed number of categories.

In addition to the above content-based approaches, AIS have been also used in collaborative filtering. They have been applied to recommend movies [7] and web sites [8] to a user based on the similarity between the user's preferences (usually expressed as a vector of rated items) to the preferences of other users. A user for which a prediction has to be made corresponds to an antigen and users with related preferences to antibodies. Clonal selection is applied to increase the concentration (strength) of antibodies that better match the antigen. A more interesting aspect of these systems is that they are based on the idiotypic network theory to encourage diversity between antibodies. An iterative algorithm is used to disseminate consentration between antibodies so that similar antibodies are suppressed. The goal is to achieve high concentrations of a diverse set of user's (antibodies) that share preferences with the target user (antigen).

The content-based evaluation of documents according to a user's multiple and changing interests has not yet been addressed by AIS. In this paper we approach this problem with a user profiling model that, although not strictly immune-based, has certain characteristics in common with models of the immune system that we discuss next.

4   Self-Organisation, Autopoiesis, and the Immune Network

Self-organisation refers to the spontaneous emergence of order in systems comprising many interrelated components. According to Capra [9] and Kelso [10] common characteristics of self-organisation include:

1. Due to the relations between multiple components self-organising systems are *nonlinear*. "The whole is more than the sum of its parts" (Aristotle *Metaphysics*).
2. Self-organising systems are *open* systems—energy and matter flow through the system—that operate far from equilibrium.
3. New structures and behaviours are generated in the self-organisation process.

Humberto Maturana and Francisco J. Varelas' *autopoietic theory* describes a model of self-organisation [11]. According to autopoietic theory a system's organisation is defined by its 'structure' (its components (nodes) and their relations (links)) and the processes that this structure performs, which continuously regenerate the structure that produces them. In the context of autopoietic theory, Varela's work contributes a different view of the immune system. The latter is no longer considered to be antigen driven. Rather the immune system is an *organisationally closed* network that reacts autonomously in order to define and preserve the organism's identity, in what is called *self-assertion* [12]. This is achieved through two types of change: variation in the concentration of antibodies called the *dynamics* of the system, and a slower recruitment of new cells (produced by the bone marrow) and removal of existing cells, called the *metadynamics*. While dynamics play the role of reinforcement learning, the metadynamics function as a distributed control mechanism which aims at maintaining the viability of the network through an on-going shift of immune repertoire [13].

One significant aspect of the immune network's metadynamics is that the system itself is responsible for selecting new cells for recruitment. As Vaz and Varela point out, it is this process of *endogenous selection* that results naturally to self-assertion [14]. According to this approach, a new cell is recruited if its structure matches closely that of existing cells. Different abstractions can be used for modeling the affinity between two cells. In [3], De Boer and Perelson used binary strings to represent antibodies and calculated the affinity between two antibodies as the Hamming distance between the corresponding strings. Stewart and Varela proposed an alternative model, where the affinity between two antibodies is a function of their respective position in a grid representation of shape-space [15]. The two models include, in common, the production of new antibodies by the bone marrow and symmetric affinities between antibodies. An antibody survives in the repertoire if its overall affinity to other antibodies lies within certain limits. No distinction between antibody and B-cell concentrations is made while foreign antigens are not included in the models. De Boer and Perelson showed that their network model has the ability to self-regulate both its size and connectivity. In Stewart and Varela's simulations, stable (but not static) patterns emerged as a result of the model's metadynamics. Both experiments indicate that specific antibodies, those with strong affinities to only a few other antibodies, tend to dominate over time.

Another concept within autopoietic theory that relates to the current work is that of *structural coupling* between a system and its environment (another system). Structurally coupled systems are mutually affective through feedback loops that perturb the plastic, self-organising structure of these systems and therefore the processes they perform [16]. Through structural coupling a system appears to respond, adapt, to changes in the environment. John Mingers suggests that a user may be considered to be structurally coupled to her environment, being academic, organisational or other [17]. Within this context, the user constantly interacts with a variety of information sources. The user develops in the process knowledge about and/or interest in certain topics and affects consequently the environment itself. Changes in the user interests are a result of these continuous feedback loops.

A user profile can become structurally coupled to the user as part of the user's broader information environment. Correctly evaluated relevant documents affect the evolution of the user's interests. In turn, changes in them are reflected in the user's feedback and cause the profile to adapt, thus affecting the document evaluation process. Continuous feedback loops occur between user and profile, as long as the profile is successful in attracting and maintaining the user's long-term involvement. Therefore, user and profile can become structurally coupled, but, as already discussed, this requires the profile's ability to drift, constantly following changes in the user's multiple interests. In Nootropia, we address this problem using a term network to represent a user's multiple interests and a deterministic process that adjusts this network in response to interest changes. In addition to its self-organising characteristics, this user profiling model exhibits similarities to the above models of the immune network. We describe Nootropia and identify these similarities in the following sections.

Table 1. Mapping of terminology

Immune System	Nootropia
immune network	term network
antibody	term
antibody concentration (production rate)	term weight
antibody-to-antibody affinity	term-to-term association
bone marrow	documents relevant to the user (self)

5   Multi-topic Profile Representation and Document Evaluation

To represent a user's multiple interests we use a weighted term network. We describe the process of initialising the network based on a set of user specified documents about various topics. We then introduce a directional spreading activation model to establish nonlinear document evaluation on this network. To be able to identify similarities between our model and the immune network models that we described in the previous section, we first need to map key concepts used in the following discussion to concepts from immunology. This is done in table 1.[2]

Given a set of documents about various topics, the network is initialised in three steps. Briefly:

1. Terms that are specific to the user's interests are extracted from the relevant documents using a term weighting method that we call *Relative Document Frequency* (see section 6.1 for details) [18]. Extracted terms populate the profile.

2. Associations between profile terms in the relevant documents are identified within a sliding window of 10 contiguous terms. Two profile terms are linked if they appear at least once within the window, i.e. within the same semantic context. A weight $w_{ij} \in (0, 1]$ is then assigned to the link between two extracted terms t_i and t_j using equation 1. fr_{ij} is the number of times t_i and t_j appear within the window, fr_i and fr_j are the number of occurrences of t_i and t_j in the interesting documents and d is the average distance between the two linked terms. Two extracted terms that appear next to each other have a distance of 1, while if l words intervene between them the distance is $l + 1$. The result of the first two steps is an associative term network with symmetric links between terms. A threshold on the weights of identified associations could be used to control the network's connectivity.

$$w_{ij} = \frac{fr_{ij}^2}{fr_i \cdot fr_j} \cdot \frac{1}{d} \tag{1}$$

3. Finally, we go a step further to order profile terms according to decreasing weight. The result of this last step is the formulation of a separate hierarchy for each general topic discussed in the documents.

---

[2] No distinction between B-cell and antibody concentrations is made.

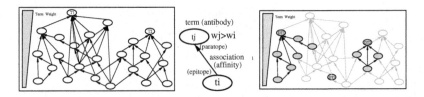

Fig. 1. Hierarchical Term Network: (left) deactivated network, (middle) term-to-term association (right) activated network

The left part of figure 1 depicts a network constructed from a set of documents about two overlapping topics. The two topics are reflected by two hierarchical sub-networks that share a small number of common terms. Each hierarchy can be identified by a term that is only connected to terms with lower weights (fig. 1(left): terms T1 and T2). This kind of "dominant" term can be used to identify the profile's "breadth", i.e. the number of general topics represented. A hierarchy's "size" on the other hand corresponds to the number of terms with decreasing weight that are connected explicitly or implicitly to the dominant term. A topic of interest discussed in the majority of the user specified documents will be reflected by a hierarchy with larger size. A hierarchy's size is therefore a measure of a topic's importance within the profile.

Document evaluation is formulated as a spreading activation model. Given a document D, an initial energy (activation) of 1 (binary indexing of documents), is deposited with those profile terms that appear in D. In the right part of figure 1 activated terms are depicted by shadowed nodes. Subsequently, energy is disseminated sequentially, starting from the activated term with the smallest weight and moving up the weight order. If and only if, an activated term t_i is directly linked to another activated term t_j with larger weight, then an amount of energy E_{ij} is disseminated by t_i to t_j through the corresponding link. In terms of the immune network, this is similar to the suppression of antibody t_i and reinforcement of antibody t_j, when t_j's paratope recognises t_i's epitope (fig. 1 (middle)). This implies that terms (antibodies) with larger weights are more likely to get reinforced (recognise other antibodies). This is an intrinsic characteristic of the document evaluation process that gives rise to the aforementioned hierarchies. E_{ij} is defined by equation 2, where E_i^c is t_i's current energy, w_{ij} is the weight of the link between t_i and t_j, and A^h is the set of activated terms higher in the hierarchy that t_i is linked to. The purpose of the normalization parameter $\sum_{k \in A^h} w_{ik}$ is to ensure that a term does not disseminate more than its current energy. The current energy of term t_i is $E_i^c = 1 + \sum_{m \in A^l} E_{mi}$, where A^l is the set of activated terms lower in the hierarchy that t_i is linked to. After the end of the dissemination process the final energy of a term t_i is $E_i^f = E_i^c - \sum_{k \in A^h} E_{ik}$.

$$
E_{ij} = \begin{cases} E_i^c \cdot w_{ij} & \text{if } \sum_{k \in A^h} w_{ik} \leq 1 \\ E_i^c \cdot \left(\dfrac{w_{ij}}{\sum_{k \in A^h} w_{ik}} \right) & \text{if } \sum_{k \in A^h} w_{ik} > 1 \end{cases} \tag{2}
$$

Similarly to the complete non-activated profile, activated profile terms define subhierarchies for each topic of interest discussed in the document. The dominant terms $DT1$, $DT2$ and $DT3$ can be defined as those activated terms that didn't disseminate any energy (fig. 1(right)). The number of dominant terms measures the document's breadth b, i.e. the number of interesting topics discussed in the document. For each dominant term the size of the corresponding subhierarchy is equal to the number of activated terms from which energy was received. The document's size d can thereafter be approximated as the number of activated terms that disseminated energy. Obviously, $b+d = a$, where a is the total number of activated terms.

One way to calculate a document's relevance score S_D, based on the final energies of activated terms (E^f), is using equation 3, where A is the set of activated profile terms, NT the number of terms in the document, and w_i is the weight of an activated term t_i. The factor $log(1 + (b + d)/b)$ favors documents with large size and small breadth.

$$S_D = \frac{\sum_{i \in A} w_i \cdot E_i^f}{log(NT)} \cdot log(1 + \frac{b+d}{b}) \tag{3}$$

The above establish a nonlinear document evaluation function that is defined by the hierarchical order of activated term's. An activated term's contribution to a document's relevance is more significant when it is strongly linked to other activated terms. A document's relevance score, and hence the possibility that it will be recommended to the user, increases when the document activates terms (antibodies) that formulate connected subhierarchies (chains of suppression and excitation) with large sizes, rather than isolated terms (e.g. term $DT3$ in fig. 1 (right)). In contrast to existing linear profile representation models, like the dominant Vector Space Model [19], Nootropia's nonlinearity enables the representation of multiple topics of interest with a single user profile. Comparative experiments between Nootropia and a traditional vector-based approach on a multi-topic filtering problem have produced positive results [20].

6   Profile Adaptation

Once the user profile is initialised it can be used to evaluate documents based on the user's current multiple interests. The most relevant documents are appropriately presented to the user (e.g. in decreasing order of relevance), who expresses her satisfaction or dissatisfaction of the evaluation results through relevance feedback. Changes in the user interest are thus reflected by changes in the content of feedback documents. The user profile has to be able to adapt to such changes and, in our case, this is achieved through a process comprising five deterministic, but interwoven steps.

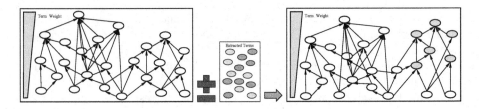

Fig. 2. Step 2: Redistribution of term weights

6.1 Step 1: Extract Informative Terms

The number of documents that received relevance feedback may vary from one to many. Here we concentrate on one relevant or non-relevant document. Nevertheless, the process may easily be generalised to more than one document. More specifically, the first of the five steps involves the weighting and extraction of terms. This process corresponds to the production of new cells by the bone marrow[3]. Given a feedback document D, after stop word removal and stemming[4], the online version of RelDF (equation 4) is applied to weight each unique term t in the document. In equation 4, n is the number of documents in a general, baseline collection that contain t and N is the total number of documents in that baseline collection. (The value 20 has been heuristically defined to account for the statistical insignificance of a single feedback document.) Only terms with weight (production rate) over a certain threshold are extracted. The term extraction process results in a set of weighted terms, some of which may already appear in the profile (existing antibody types in the immune network) and some may not (new antibody types).

$$RelDF_t^D = w_t^D = \frac{1}{20} - \frac{n}{N} \tag{4}$$

6.2 Step 2: Update Profile Term Weights

The second step of the adaptation process concentrates on those extracted terms that already appear in the profile (fig. 2: terms in light grey). For each such profile term t, equation 5 is used to calculate its updated weight (concentration) w_t' based on its initial weight w_t and its weight w_t^D in the feedback document (relevant or non-relevant). The weight of profile terms that don't appear in the extracted set remains unchanged.

$$w_t' = \begin{cases} w_t + w_t^D & \text{if } D \text{ relevant} \\ w_t - w_t^D & \text{if } D \text{ non-relevant} \\ w_t & \text{if } t \ni D \end{cases} \tag{5}$$

---

[3] As suggested in [2], the production of new cell types is not random.
[4] Common dimensionality reduction techniques

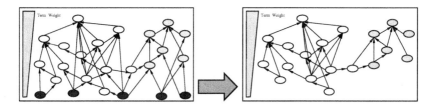

Fig. 3. Step 3: Removal of incompetent terms

Subsequently, in the case of a relevant document, we sum up the additional weights that have been assigned to the profile terms and then substract this sum evenly from all profile terms. This process is expressed by equation 6, where NP is the number of profile terms. The opposite takes place in the case of a non-relevant document. Therefore, given a profile with a specific set of terms (antibody repertoire), this last process assures that the overall weight of profile terms remains stable.

$$
w''_t = \begin{cases} w'_t - \dfrac{\sum_{t \in D} w^D_t}{NP} & \text{if } D \text{ relevant} \\[3mm] w'_t + \dfrac{\sum_{t \in D} w^D_t}{NP} & \text{if } D \text{ non-relevant} \end{cases} \tag{6}
$$

The above process implements the networks dynamics, a redistribution of profile term weights that may affect the ordering of terms. Figure 2 depicts this effect in the case of the example profile which represents two topics of interest and a document relevant to one of these topics. Profile terms that have been extracted from the relevant document have their weight reinforced while the weight of the rest of the profile terms decays. The reinforced terms climb higher in the hierarchy, while the rest of the terms fall lower.

6.3   Step 3: Remove Incompetent Profile Terms

A side-effect of the decrease in the weight of profile terms, which is caused either implicitly in the case of a relevant document, or explicitly in the case of a non-relevant, is that the weight (concentration) of some terms falls bellow zero. These terms, which have not been competent since entering the profile, or have become incompetent due to changes in the user's interests, are removed from the profile (fig. 3: black nodes). The sum of the initial weight–i.e. the weight with which a term had entered the profile (see next section)–of purged terms is evenly subtracted from all remaining terms (equation 7).

$$
w'''_t = w''_t - \frac{\sum_{t \text{ purged}} w^{init}_t}{NP} \tag{7}
$$

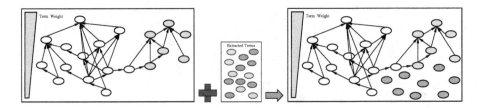

Fig. 4. Step 4: Adding new profile terms

6.4   Step 4: Add New Terms

At this step, we turn to terms extracted from a relevant document D that do not already appear in the profile (new antibody types). These terms are added to the profile (fig. 4: terms in dark gray) with initial weight equal to their weight in the document ($w_t^{init} = w_t^D$). A relevant document about a topic that is not already covered by the profile contributes a lot of new terms.

The last two steps implement the profile's metadynamics. Incompetent terms are removed from the profile and new terms are recruited. The number of terms in the profile (immune repertoire) is not fixed, but varies dynamically in response to changes in user feedback. Furthermore, weight enters the profile with the addition of every new term and is removed if and when the term is purged. As a result the profile becomes open to its environment. Weight flows through the system.

6.5   Step 5: Reestablish Links

In this last step we turn to links. For this purpose we refer back to the second step of the profile generation process (sec. 5). All of the parameters of equation 1 can be updated online for each relevant document D, using equations 8 to 10, where $dist_{ij}$ is the aggregate distance between terms t_i and t_j in the documents processed so far.

$$fr'_i = fr_i + fr_i^D \tag{8}$$
$$fr'_{ij} = fr_{ij} + fr_{ij}^D \tag{9}$$
$$d'_{ij} = \frac{dist'_{ij}}{fr'_{ij}} = \frac{dist_{ij} + dist_{ij}^D}{fr'_{ij}} \tag{10}$$

So after adding the new terms, the relevant document is processed using a window of size 10 to identify links between profile terms and update the above parameters using the aforementioned equations. Once links have been established and the parameters updated[5], the weight of new links and the updated weight of existing links is calculated using the original equation 1 of section 5. Figure 5 depicts this process.

---

[5] To overcome memory limitations one can either use normalisation or maintain in memory parameter values for the most recently processed documents

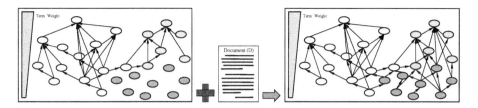

Fig. 5. Link generation and weighting

It is important to note that the generation of new links is an important part of the recruitment process. Due to the nonlinearity of document evaluation (see previous section), a term's survival in the profile does not depend only on its weight (concentration), but also on the strength of its links to other terms. Therefore, we may argue, that although not explicitly encoded, endogenous selection is an intrinsic part of the process.

7   Discussion

The above process adjusts the profile's structure in accordance with changes in the user interests. A comparison between the left part of figure 2 and the right part of figure 5 reveals an increase in the size of the hierarchy corresponding to the topic discussed in the relevant feedback document and a decline in the size of the hierarchy corresponding to the topic that did not receive positive feedback. Such variations in the size of hierarchies allow the profile to adapt to short-term variations in the user's interests. Furthermore, a new hierarchy may develop to account for an emerging topic of interest and a hierarchy that corresponds to a topic that is no longer interesting progressively disintegrates and is eventually forgotten. Note, that although negative feedback can be taken into account (section 6.2), it is not crucial for the profile's ability to forget. A topic can be forgotten if, in contrast to other topics, lacks positive feedback. Initial experiments using virtual users confirm that Nootropia can adapt to both short-term variations and occasional radical changes in the user interests. [21]. This ability allows Nootropia to drift, constantly following changes in the user's interests, in order to sustain the user's involvement (expressed as feedback). Structural coupling between user and profile is therefore possible.

Nootropia can tackle our initial user profiling requirements due to its self-organising characteristics. In contrast to a linear, vector-based representation, we employ a non-linear term network to represent a user's multiple interests. Adaptation is achieved using a deterministic process that calibrates the weight of profile terms, removes incompetent terms and recruits new candidate terms. In the process, the profile becomes open to its environment and operates far from equilibrium, constantly adjusting in response to changes in relevance feedback. As a result new structures (hierarchies) and new modes of behaviour (document evaluation) are generated.

Although our initial intention has not been to implement a model of the immune system, interesting similarities exist between Nootropia and models of the immune network that have been developed in the context of autopoietic theory (see section 4). In particular:

- The term network reflects the network of antibody-to-antibody recognitions.
- Chains of suppression and reinforcement between interrelated terms are formulated for document evaluation.
- Adaptation is primarily based on relevant feedback documents (antibody production by the bone marrow). It is not antigen driven.
- Dynamics are the result of term weight being redistributed towards terms that appear in relevant documents from the rest of the profile terms.
- Metadynamics result from the removal of terms with weight less than zero and the recruitment of new terms extracted from relevant documents.
- Although not explicit in the model, endogenous selection is an intrinsic part of the recruitment process. Only terms with strong enough links to other terms are likely to survive in the profile[6]

These similarities do not fully justify the characterisation of Nootropia as an AIS. Farmer has mapped AIS, neural networks, Holland classifier systems and autocatalytic chemical reaction networks into a general connectionist model and has identified similarities (and differences) between all of them [22]. Is Nootropia another instance of this general connectionist model? To answer this question further and more formal comparisons, like those performed by Farmer[7], have to be performed between Nootropia and the above models.

8   Summary and Future Research

We have presented Nootropia, a user profiling model for content-based document filtering, that uses a non-linear term network to represent a user's multiple interests and that self-organises in order to adapt to both short-term variations and substantial changes in them. Interesting similarities to models of the immune network that derive from autopoietic theory have been pointed out.

Nootropia's similarities to these models of the immune network and possibly to other models, like classifier systems, have to be explored further using more formal mathematical analysis. The dynamic nature of user interests and the statistical characteristics of written language provide an interesting background for performing such a comparison. Nevertheless Nootropia is not constrained to textual information. It is in principle applicable to any media for which features can be automatically extracted (e.g. music). Another possible application is collaborative filtering. Nodes in the network could represent users and links the affinity of their interests. Hybrid IF applications that combine content-based and collaborative filtering have also attracted our interest.

---

[6] As reported in [3], unpublished experiments also indicate, that the profile can control its size, and that networks with a small number of strong links are advantageous.

[7] See also [2] for a comparison of the dynamics of AIS and classifier systems

References

1. Perelson, A., Oster, G.: Theoretical studies of clonal selection: Minimal antibody repertoire size and reliability of self-non-self discrimination. Journal of Theoretical Biology **81** (1979) 645–670

2. Farmer, J.D., Packard, N.H., Perelson, A.S.: The immune system, adaptation, and machine learning. Physica 22D (1986) 187–204

3. Boer, R.J.D., Perelson, A.S.: Size and connectivity as emergent properties of a developing immune network. Journal of Theoretical Biology **149** (1991) 381–424

4. Chao, D.L., Forrest, S.: Information immune systems. Genetic Programming and Evolvable Machines **4** (2003) 311–331

5. Twycross, J., Cayzer, S.: An immune-based approach to document classification. Technical Report HPL-2002-292, HP Research Bristol (2002)

6. Greensmith, J., Cayzer, S.: An artificial immune system approach to semantic document classification. In Timmis, J., Bentley, P., Hart, E., eds.: 2nd International Conference on Artificial Immune Systems (ICARIS 2003). (2003) 136–146

7. Cayzer, S., Aickelin, U.: A recommender system based on the immune network. Technical Report HPL-2002-1, HP Laboratories Bristol (2002)

8. Morrison, T., Aickelin, U.: An artificial immune system as a recommender for web sites. In: 1st International Conference on Artificial Immune Systems. (2002)

9. Capra, F.: The Web of Life. Harper Collins (1996)

10. Kelso, J.A.S.: Dynamic Patterns: The Self-Organization of Brain and Behavior. MIT Press (1999)

11. Maturana, H.R., Varela, F.J.: Autopoiesis and Cognition. Dordrecht, Holland (1980)

12. Varela, F.J., Coutinho, A.: Second generation immune network. Immunology Today **12** (1991) 159–166

13. Bersini, H., Varela, F.: The immune learning mechanisms: Reinforcement, recruitment and their applications. In: Computing with Biological Metaphors. Chapman Hall (1994) 166–192

14. Vaz, N.M., Varela, F.: Self and non-sense: An organism-centered approach to immunology. Medical Hypotheses **4** (1978) 231–267

15. Stewart, J., Varela, F.J.: Morphogenesis in shape-space, elementary meta-dynamics in a model of the immune network. Journal of Theoretical Biology **153** (1991) 477–498

16. Quick, T., Dautenhahn, K., Nehaniv, C.L., Roberts, G.: The essence of embodiment: A framework for understanding and exploiting structural coupling between system and environment. CASYS'99 (1999)

17. Mingers, J.: Embodying information systems: the contribution of phenomenology. Information and Organization **11** (2001) 103–128

18. Nanas, N., Uren, V., Roeck, A.D., Domingue, J.: Building and applying a concept hierarchy representation of a user profile. In: 26th Annual International ACM SIGIR Conference on Research and Development in Information Retrieval, ACM press (2003) 198–204

19. Salton, G., McGill, M.J.: Introduction to Modern Information Retrieval. McGraw-Hill Inc. (1983)

20. Nanas, N., Uren, V., de Roeck, A., Domingue, J.: Multi-topic information filtering with a single user profile. In: 3rd Hellenic Conference on Artificial Intelligence. (2004) 400–409

21. Nanas, N., Uren, V., de Roeck, A., Domingue, J.: Nootropia: a self-organising agent for adaptive information filtering. Technical Report kmi-tr-138, Knowledge Media Institute (2004) http://www.kmi.open.ac.uk/people/nanas/kmi-tr-138.pdf.
22. Farmer, J.D.: A Rosetta stone for connectionism. In Forrest, S., ed.: Emergent Computation. MIT Press (1991) 153–187

Towards Danger Theory Based Artificial APC Model: Novel Metaphor for Danger Susceptible Data Codons

Anjum Iqbal and Mohd Aizani Maarof

Group on Artificial Immune Systems N Security (GAINS)
Faculty of Computer Science and Information Systems (FSKSM)
Universiti Teknologi Malaysia, 81310 UTM Skudai, Johor, Malaysia
anjum@siswa.utm.my, maarofma@fsksm.utm.my

Abstract. Danger Theory (DT) sets significant shift in viewpoint about the main goal of human immune system (HIS). This viewpoint, though controversial among immunologists, may enable artificial immune systems' (AIS) researchers to extract benefits of the theory for designing their systems and solving problems confronting with the conventional approach of self-nonself discrimination. Furthering recent pioneering concepts in the field, this paper aims to gain a distinct look for the data that DT based AIS processes. The proposed concept introduces a novel biological metaphor, DASTON, for observing danger susceptible data chunks/points' combinations. Preliminary analysis for DASTON identification gives hope for exciting future of the idea. It is an initial effort towards Artificial Antigen Presenting Cell (AAPC) modeling. The concept may initiate an argument that might contribute significantly for the body of knowledge in AIS research.

1 Introduction

U. Aicklein and S. Cayzer [6] presented the first paper proposing Polly Matzinger's Danger Theory (DT) [1][2][3][4][5] for Artificial Immune Systems' (AIS) research. The authors have elaborated important aspects of DT and motivated AIS researchers to follow this distinct approach, which may deliver more benefits to AIS research than Human Immune System (HIS) research. They have precisely pointed out the problems that HIS and AIS face with self-nonself (SNS) viewpoint. The DT, despite being controversial among immunologists, seems to bear intrinsic potential to scale up AIS. The researchers have initiated attempts [7][8][9] to gain benefits of the novel theory. They may extract useful knowledge for their research from the arguments among immunologists. U. Aicklein et al. [7] have established a team of experienced AIS researchers, which is designing an Intrusion Detection System (IDS) to prove the worth of their idea. The attempt of applying a novel AIS concept, danger theory, to IDS is in accordance with S. A. Hofmeyr's approach [26] that computer security systems have natural potential for elaborating AIS metaphors. The researchers are quite determined for their success, which would be independent of the DT arguments among immunologists. We, being infants in the field of AIS research, were looking for potential research area when came across the novel idea [6]. The idea of exploring DT, for its application to AIS, inspired us to such an extent that we jumped into this complex but exciting field of research.

G. Nicosia et al. (Eds.): ICARIS 2004, LNCS 3239, pp. 161–174, 2004.
© Springer-Verlag Berlin Heidelberg 2004

We are attempting bottom-up approach in our DT inspired AIS research. In our opinion, and as mentioned by others [1][6], APC is located at quite significant position in this context. APC is, perhaps, performing the most important tasks for HIS when looking from DT view point [6]. It may also provide appropriate analogies to simplify complexities of the novel domain. Therefore we consider artificial APC modeling for our research. Like [7], we aim to follow S. A. Hofmeyr's recommendation [26], for effectively elaborating our idea in computer security domain. The artificial APC in network based AIS may be considered analogous to a host based IDS contributing for overall system, like APC in HIS performing local danger detection and signaling for collaborative immune system activities. We will call our hypothetical artificial APC as MAP (Malicious Activities Presenter), to ease referencing in the following text. The MAP may be modeled with the conventional approach of self-nonself discrimination, like most of the existing AIS based IDSs. Our interest, however, is to follow the DT viewpoint for modeling MAP. We would rather like to dig into some deeper details of the phenomenon. The aim of this paper is to propose a novel concept, which we perceived after preliminary study and analysis of data. It is also to seek guidance from immunologists, genetists, and AIS researchers to better understand APC mechanisms for mapping these to our MAP.

Our current understanding of DT describes that danger signals are generated by the cells undergoing stress or those suffering from abnormal death (necrosis), the normal cell death (apoptosis) doesn't cause alerts for immune system [6][7]. There are some questions in our mind, for instance; In addition to cell stress or necrosis, are there any other causes for generating danger signals? What is the opinion of DT about HIS response while confronting potential suspects likely to produce danger at some later stage? Is there any mechanism for DT that proactively signals the presence of potential dangerous elements? These questions rise in our mind due to a person inheriting genes of a disease (potential danger elements) is more likely to develop disease (danger) than any other individual [10][11][12][13][14][15][16][17]. The genes that cause transfer of hereditary disease from parents to children are the genes that bear latent potential for producing danger in children at some later age. Without falling into further biological queries, as we are not immunologists, we expect that DT would be able to accommodate our queries. With this positive expectation from DT, we should move further into the depth of our main goal of modeling MAP. We want our MAP to process Data Codons (DATONs) (a genetics inspired name for data chunks/points' combination) and proactively observe the Danger Susceptible Data Codons (DASTONs) within healthy (normal) as well as sick (abnormal) data (details are given in the following sections). We believe that DASTONs will be able to offer a novel look towards data, input for DT based AIS. The strength of proposed metaphor lies in the biological mechanism from which it has been derived. This approach may enable us to device novel mechanisms for our MAP those are effective and closely analogous to nature.

The following sections contain essential information required to elaborate the concept (reader may follow references for further details). Section 2 throws light on already initiated efforts for DT based AIS research. Section 3 gives a brief overview of genomics and proteomics to establish foundation for the topic. The biological basis of the proposed metaphor - genetic susceptibility for danger (disease) - is described in section 4 and section 5 elaborates the mutual context of danger theory and genetics. Section 6 gives our abstractions from biology for the proposed concept. The preliminary analysis in section 7 is likely to support our metaphor. Finally, section 8 concludes the topic summarizing our current efforts and future trends.

2 Danger Theory Inspired AIS Efforts

After a century of study, the fundamental mechanisms of immunity and tolerance still remain elusive. In the 1940s and 1950s Burnet first proposed the concept of self-nonself discrimination in his clonal selection theory, which quickly became the central dogma of immunology for much of the ensuing 40 years [20]. S. Forrest et al. [28] and Jeffery O. Kephart [29] initiated ideas for AIS. Polly Matzinger [1][2][3][4][5] proposed the Danger Theory of immune system. U. Aicklein and S. Cayser [6] delivered the first inspiration for DT based AISs. Then some of the AIS researchers [7][8][9], who were previously working with conventional self-nonself viewpoint, focused to explore and verify DT potentials. Following sections briefly describe these efforts to highlight significance of DT based AIS research.

2.1 Intrusion Detection

The central challenge with computer security is determining the difference between normal and potentially harmful activity. The IDS designed on the principles of HIS would have the same beneficial properties as HIS like error tolerance, adaptation and self-monitoring. Current AIS have been successful on test systems, but the algorithms rely on self-nonself discrimination, as stipulated in classical immunology. U. Aicklein et al. [7] presented ideas about creating a next generation IDS based on DT. The danger theory suggests that the immune system reacts to threats based on the correlation of various (danger) signals and it provides a method of 'grounding' the immune response, i.e. linking it directly to the attacker. Little is currently understood of the precise nature and correlation of these signals. The research aims to investigate this correlation and to translate the DT into the realms of computer security, thereby creating AIS that are no longer limited by self-nonself discrimination. The project is expected to add to the body of knowledge in this area and AIS applications might scale up by overcoming self-nonself discrimination problems [6].

2.2 Self-Organizing Sparse Distributed Memories (SOSDM)

The Danger Theory based effort [8] presents improvements to original SOSDM algorithm [27] to make it more able to deal with dynamically changing environments. In the new model, antibodies emit a signal describing their current level of contentment monitoring the total level of contentment in the system provides a mechanism for determining when an immune response should occur, i.e. when new antibodies should be produced. It also provides a method of detecting catastrophic changes in the environment, i.e. significant changes in input data, and thus provides a means of removing antibodies. The original motivation behind SOSDM was to produce a system that could dynamically cluster data, and thus react to changes in the environment. If new clusters appear in the data-set, or clusters suddenly disappear, then the system should be able to detect these changes and react accordingly, by adding new antibodies or removing existing ones. Using the danger theory analogy, such extreme changes in environment would cause severe stress or trauma to cells which were previously content, causing them to undergo lytic cell death. Thus, Emma Hart and Peter Ross [8] model this in dSOSDM by monitoring the average change in cell contentment between two consecutive iterations. Simple experiments have shown that the immune systems produced do suffer uncontrollable expansion and can react to changes in the environment. The new system, dSOSDM, is shown to be more robust and better able to deal with dynamically changing databases than SOSDM.

2.3 Web Mining

A. Secker et al. [9] presented a concept to explore the relevance of Danger Theory to the application domain of web mining. The authors' interest in the idea of DT is that of a context dependant response to invading pathogens. They argue that this context dependency could be utilized as powerful metaphor for applications in web mining. An illustrative example adaptive mailbox filter is presented that exploits properties of the immune system, including the DT. They are of the view that dynamical classification task is well suited to the field of artificial immune systems, particularly when drawing inspiration from the Danger Theory. They also believe that a Danger Theory inspired approach to web mining could lead to the production of new and effective algorithms for knowledge discovery on the web. In their opinion the scalability of immune algorithms may be enhanced by initiating an immune response only when a local danger signal is present which may also yield an increase in result quality as the danger signal may be released in a context dependent manner.

3   Brief Overview of Genetics and Proteomics

A DNA sequence, shown in Figure 1(a), carries heredity information that is encoded sequentially on the double strands of the DNA with four different nucleotides: adenine (A), cytosine (C), guanine (G) and thymine (T). As shown in Figure 1(b), a DNA sequence can be divided into genes and intergenic spaces. The genes are responsible for protein synthesis. Three nucleotides in the base sequences, in the protein-coding regions of DNA molecules, form a triplet called codon that corresponds via an mRNA (messenger RNA) to an amino acid or an instruction. For eukaryotes (cells with nucleus) this periodicity has mostly been observed within the exons (coding subregions inside the genes) and not within the introns (noncoding subregions in the genes). Procaryotes (cells without a nucleus) do not have introns. Scanning the gene from left to right, a codon sequence can be defined by concatenation of the codons in all the exons. Each codon (except the so- called stop codon) instructs the cell machinery to synthesize an amino acid. The codon sequence therefore uniquely identifies an amino acid sequence which defines a protein. The introns do not participate in the protein synthesis. There are sixty-four types of codons for twenty amino acids and the initiation and termination instructions. Since several different codons called synonymous codons may correspond to an amino acid the mapping from codons to amino acids is many-to-one. The studies based on the spectral analysis have been attributed to the

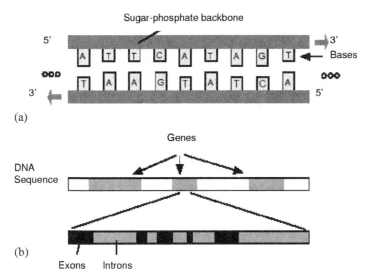

Fig. 1. (a) The DNA linearized schematic, and (b) various regions in a DNA molecule

fact that a codon composes of three nucleotides, and there exist protein structures and DNA folding. There are theories explaining the reason for such periodicity, but there are also exceptions to the phenomenon. Nevertheless, many researchers have regarded the period-3 property to be a good (preliminary) indicator of gene location. However, at the level of the functionality of DNA, it may be more appropriate to consider codons instead of nucleotides [22][23].

Recombinant DNA techniques have provided tools for the rapid determination of DNA sequences and, by inference, the amino acid sequences of proteins from structural genes. The proteins we observe in nature perform specific functions. The functional properties of proteins depend upon their three-dimensional structures (refer Figure 3 to have idea of protein structure). The three-dimensional structure arises because particular sequences of amino acids in polypeptide chains fold to generate, from linear chains, compact domains with specific three-dimensional structures. The folded domains either can serve as modules for building up large assemblies such as virus particles or muscle fibers or can provide specific catalytic or binding sites as found in enzymes or proteins that carry oxygen or that regulate the function of DNA. The amino acid sequence of a protein's polypeptide chain is called its *primary structure*. Different regions of the sequence form local regular *secondary structure*, such as alpha-helices or beta-strands. The *tertiary structure* is formed by packing such structural elements into one or several compact globular units called *domains*. The final protein may contain several polypeptide chains arranged in *quaternary structure*. By formation of such tertiary and quaternary structure amino acids far apart in the sequence are brought close together in three dimensions to form a functional region, an *active site*. Simple combinations of a few secondary structure elements with a specific geometric arrangement have been found to occur frequently in protein structures. These units are called *motifs*. Some of these motifs can be associated with a particular function such as DNA bindings; others have no specific biological function alone but are part of larger structural and functional assemblies [25].

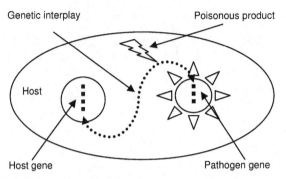

Fig. 2. The disease susceptible host genes are interacting with pathogen genes to produce poisonous products that cause disease (danger).

4   Genetic Susceptibility for Disease (Danger)

Although, it has been clear for many years that individual may differ markedly in their susceptibility to infectious diseases, recent advances in genomics have led to a dramatic increase in the power of techniques available to identify the relevant genes. Some infectious diseases were once regarded as familial before the identification of the causative micro-organism and early twin studies found that there was a substantial host genetic influence on susceptibility to diseases such as tuberculosis and polio. Today, it is clear that human genetic variation exerts a major influence on the course of disease caused by many infectious micro-organisms. Such host–pathogen gene interactions (Figure 2) are of general biological interest as they underlie the maintenance of much genetic diversity and such co-evolutionary interplay is often best studied in human infectious diseases where both the pathogen and the host genome are well characterized [15]. Following paragraphs provide examples from recent biological research to elaborate the concept of genetic susceptibility for disease (danger), hence strengthening the basis for our proposed metaphor.

The prion diseases are unconventional diseases. The agent is not a standard micro-organism, incubation periods can be several years and the most characteristic pathology is the accumulation of the prion protein, PrP. In humans they occur sporadically as Creutzfeldt–Jakob disease (CJD). PrP gene dependent susceptibility operates at two levels. Primary susceptibility demands that the organism produces the PrP protein. Secondary susceptibility stipulates that PrP protein has to have a susceptible amino acid sequence. The PrP protein gene contains about 255 codons. It is well conserved with common motifs found in PrP of very divergent genera. Amino acid variations are, however, common which makes it difficult to predict changes relevant to prion diseases. Despite this, definitions of susceptible sequence motifs have emerged [12]. Sheep represent an excellent model for studying the link between genetic controls of disease and the many variants of the PrP gene (PrP alleles). More than 20 ruminant PrP alleles have been described; several show major, some very subtle, effects on susceptibility. They are almost all associated with single amino acid substitutions. For example, the amino acid glutamine is encoded at codon 171 (see Figure 3) of sheep PrP and can be linked to susceptibility. If however arginine is encoded at position

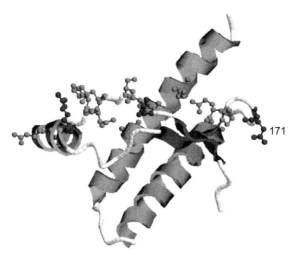

Fig. 3. The PrP protein structure is partly described which helps to link the position of amino acid changes associated with disease to protein structure. Amino acid positions genetically variable in sheep are highlighted in dark black.

171, as found in sheep, resistance is conferred. These sequence positions and genotypes appear to be of fundamental importance for assessing or predicting susceptibility. Humans encode a different amino acid in this position (glutamic acid). Perhaps this makes us less susceptible but not quite resistant to disease [12].

Similarly, the studies of [10][11][13][14][16][17][24] fortify the hidden potentials for disease or disease susceptibility.

5   The Danger Theory in Genetics Context

The immune system involves a highly developed network of cells and regulatory elements that must work together to protect the body without causing undue harm to the individual. It is unlikely that any one theory is capable of describing all observations related to this system [20]. However, the danger theory offers a stronger model than the classic SNS theory to describe some unrevealed mechanisms of the immune system.

The mechanisms of immune response during microbial infection became a major area of investigation subsequent to advances in understanding the potential role of innate immunity. It quickly became evident that the innate immune cells are endowed with multiple categories of receptors that discriminate between various microbe-associated motifs or exogenous danger signals. Crosstalk between the innate and adaptive immune systems subsequent to such pattern recognition events decisively influences the magnitude and profile of T and B cell responses. The innate immune system is rapid though less discriminative, but instructs the adaptive immunity that evolves more slowly and is composed of more efficient effectors with a vast repertoire acquired by somatic mutation. This multi-patterned recognition strategy that jointly employs innate and adaptive immunity shifted the immune discrimination paradigm from self/nonself to dangerous/nondangerous cognition. The poor immuno-genicity of purified proteins, induction of immune mediators by microbial motifs, and characterization of the activity of such mediators (cytokines, chemokines, and costimulatory molecules) on adaptive immunity all supported this concept [18]. Mature APCs play a critical role in the development of antigen-specific immunity. Whereas molecules derived from infectious pathogens most commonly stimulate APC maturation, recent studies indicate that factors, for example heat sock proteins (HSPs), released by dying host cells may also serve this function [19].

The study [18], delineates the role of noncoding RNA motifs as danger signals, with direct implications for understanding their role in controlling adaptive immunity during viral infections. The work of Ken J. Ishii et al. [19] suggests that double-stranded genomic DNA (dsDNA) provides a danger signal to the immune system, triggering macrophages and dendritic cells to mature phenotypically and functionally. APCs stimulated by dsDNA increased their expression of MHC class I/II and various costimulatory molecules. Moreover, the combination of dsDNA plus antigen triggered APC show improved primary cellular and humoral immune responses. These effects were dependent on the length and concentration of the dsDNA but were independent of nucleotide sequence. The study supports the hypothesis that "factors" released by dying host cells facilitate the induction of immunity against foreign and/or self anti-gens. The necrotic/apoptotic cellular debris promotes the development of autoimmune disease. The findings underscore the potential role of genomic DNA in the develop-ment or persistence of autoimmune disease. Yet, if immune recognition of dsDNA has been conserved, it must provide some benefit to the host. The dsDNA released following tissue injury/infection promotes APC maturation and thus facilitates the elimination of pathogens at the injury site. This mechanism might also improve host recognition of virus-infected APCs. During viral replication, pro-viral dsDNA com-monly accumulates in the cytoplasm of infected cells. By improving the presentation of viral antigens, APCs, the immune response elicited by dsDNA would facilitate the elimination of infected APCs and promote host survival [19].

The danger theory also offers a stronger model than the classic self-nonself (SNS) theory to describe gene replacement. Recent studies in gene transfer suggest that the innate immune system plays a significant role in impeding gene therapy. Brian D. Brown, and David Lillicrap [20] have chosen to apply Matzinger's danger model [1][2][3][4][5] to explain some of the observations reported in gene therapy.

6   The Novel Metaphor (DASTON)

The computational system components and processes may be mapped to different components and functions in biological systems in variety of ways. The success of all analogies between computing and living systems ultimately rests on our ability to identify the correct level of abstraction [30]. As the main focus of our perception in this paper is Danger Theory and the respective components and processes involved from both systems, computation and biology, therefore we are motivated to derive only those abstractions that deliver precise understanding of the perception we devel-oped from the literature in preceding sections. We abstract metaphors developing natural analogy in two distinct fields (Table 1, Figure 4). The novel metaphor, danger susceptible data codon (DASTON), differentiates our idea from others [7][8][9].

Table 1. The abstractions corresponding to the proposed metaphor

	Abstractions	
A	Biology	Computation
B	Danger	The behavior/feature/result of interest
C	Triplet of nucleotides (Codon)	Data chunk/points' combination (DATON)
D	Disease Susceptible Codon	Danger Susceptible DATON (DASTON)
E	Amino Acid	Specificity attributed to DATON
F	Motif	Specific functional domain in a Process
G	Protein	Process

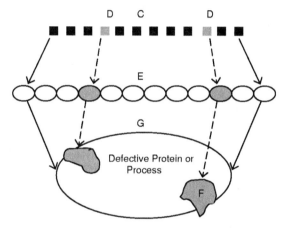

Fig. 4. The diagrammatic representation of abstractions as given in table 1; C - codon or DA-TON, D – danger susceptible codon or DASTON, E- amino acid or DATON specificity, F – motif or sub-process, and G – protein or process. Gray shaded components represent danger susceptibility and its results.

Codons in genetics may be abstracted as data chunks or combinations of various data points; we name them DATONs (data codons). The type and size of DATONs may depend upon the nature of application, data type, and depth of details required from the data. A specific attribute may be assigned to a DATON characterized like amino acid. A small group of DATONs, each bearing specific attribute, may represent a particular functionality domain in a process like motifs in protein. The clusters of these domains may then collectively exhibit the overall functionality of the whole process demonstrating a protein function in biology. In our effort for DT based MAP modeling we are focusing on Danger Susceptible DATONs (DASTONs), the DA-TONs that show elevated responses in cooperation with danger stimulating elements in their environment. This is like host-pathogen genetic interplay as described in section 4 (Figure 2). The definition of danger here also depends upon the type of application, data and details of information required from that data. In biology genetic susceptibility for disease (danger) can be used to forecast the likelihood of future danger that could be produced by defective genetic products (poisonous proteins) or host-pathogen genetic interplay. Similarly, in computational domain identification of DASTONs might enable us to guess the processes involved in their generation. The processes may actively cooperate with external instincts, under some circumstances, to produce danger. They may not be active in the absence of danger stimulating elements, but would be at higher potential to cooperate with these elements.

The idea [7] of detecting and estimating dangers, that is the intrusive activities, through necrotic and apoptotic signals should provide the instant danger information, while the identification of proposed DASTONs from system calls' sequences might enable us to proactively monitor the processes generating them hence avoiding or minimizing future dangers. The DT based study [8] uses the concept of Danger Theory to control the contentment and population of AIS components (antibodies). Here AIS components (antibodies) are being used to cluster various data components (antigens) from main data pool according to their affinity for the antibodies. On the other hand, we intend to identify DASTONs in data prior to its submission for main AIS processing and proposed AAPC should be responsible for successful identification of DASTONs. This clearly distinguishes our DT inspired approach from others [7][8].

7   Preliminary Analysis for DASTONs

To prove the worth of our perception, we have conducted preliminary analysis for DASTONs identification. Though, the metaphor, DASTON, can be mapped for a variety of computational applications and data types, we stick to our constrained application and data. The case study - intrusion detection - and the data - system call sequences - have potential to clearly illustrate the proposed metaphor (see Table 2) and also belong to significant application domain. There are a number of techniques available for system calls' analysis [31][32][33][34][35][36][37][38]. The DNA, codon, and other sequence analysis techniques can also be used [39][40][41][42]. In this preliminary effort we have conducted simple comparative analysis of normal and intrusion trace data available from the University of New Maxico web site [43]. It is like comparing healthy and diseased gene sequences to identify the disease (danger) susceptible codons. The system call pairs (DATONs), as shown in the plot of Figure 5, are of three types; a) present in both normal and intrusion trace data, b) present in normal data only, and c) present in intrusion trace data only.

In the plot, horizontal and vertical axes represent first and second members of the pairs (DATONs) respectively traversing system calls sequences from top to bottom, which is the order of their generation during the process. The first type of DATONs (a) that are present in both normal and intrusion trace data (shown as crosses) may represent normal function of some parts of the system, though suffering from attack. The second type of DATONs (b) that are present in normal data only (shown as circles), has not contributed for any dangerous activity and may be declared as safe DATONs. The third type of DATONs (c) that are present in intrusion trace data only (shown as dots), represent their significant cooperation with danger stimulating elements, that are the intrusive scripts. They are the DATONs of our interest and to whom we name DASTONs.

Table 2. Abstractions corresponding to danger susceptible system calls (the case study)

	Abstractions	
A	Biology	Computation
B	Danger	Intrusive activity
C	Triplet of nucleotides (Codon)	Pair of two adjacent system calls in a sequence (DATON)
D	Disease Susceptible Codon	Intrusion susceptible DATON (DASTON)
E	Amino Acid	Specificity attributed to DASTON regarding intrusion
F	Defective motif	The sub intrusive process domain
G	Poisonous protein	The major intrusive process

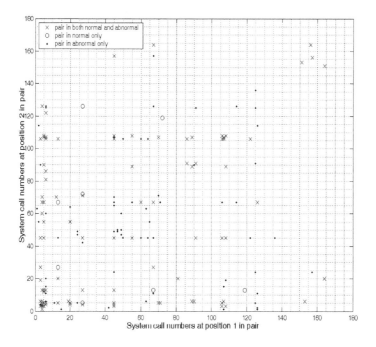

Fig. 5. Plot of normal and intrusion trace data for synthetic wu-ftpd; black dots are DASTONs those actively interacted with danger producing scripts.

8   Conclusions and Future Trends

The Artificial Antigen Presenting Cell (AAPC) would be a central component of Danger Theory based Artificial Immune Systems. We are following bottom-up approach to model our DT based AAPC. In our initial effort we are offering a novel look towards data that AAPC will process. This approach should be able to give better insight to serve the purpose of DT based AIS modeling. The proposed novel metaphor, DASTON, inherits its strength from genetics and proteomics. We believe that the ideas abstracted from natural systems bear potential to prove their strength. The preliminary analysis for observing DASTONs, presented in this paper, makes us hopeful about the exciting future of the idea. Our study for DASTONs will deliver its benefits to DT based AIS research in general and to system calls' analysis in particular. The identification of DASTONs might reduce the amount of data required for DT inspired processing. They might enable us to proactively measure the accumulative potential of danger at particular space and time. The DASTONs might also lead us to device mechanisms for better training and testing of Danger Theory based Artificial Immune Systems. Our future trend includes devising sophisticated mechanism for DASTONs identification. The mapping of concept to different AIS based applications and data should be a fruitful effort. Finally, we expect an exciting future of our DASTON.

Acknowledgment. The authors are grateful to Ministry of Science Technology and Environment (MOSTE) Malaysia for supporting this pioneering AIS research in Malaysia.

References

1. Polly Matzinger (2002), The Danger Model: A Renewed Sense of Self, Science, Vol. 296, pp. 301-305.
2. P. Matzinger (2001), The Danger Model In Its Historical Context, Scand. J. Immunol, Vol. 54, pp. 4-9.
3. Stefania Gallucci, Martijn Lolkema, and Polly Matzinger (1999), Natural Adjuvants: Endogenous Activators of Dendritic Cells, Nature Medicine, Vol. 5, No. 11, pp. 1249-1255
4. Polly Matzinger, The Real Function of The Immune System, Last accessed on 06-04-04, URL:http://cmmg.biosci.wayne.edu/asg/polly.html
5. Polly Matzinger (1998), An Innate sense of danger, Seminars in Immunology, Vol. 10, pp. 399-415.
6. Uwe Aickelin, and Steve Cayzer (2002), The Danger Theory and Its Application to Artificial Immune Systems, In Proceedings of the International Conference on Artificial Immune Systems (ICARIS, 2002), Edinburgh, UK.
7. U. Aicklein, P. Bentley, S. Cayser, J. Kim, and J. McLeod (2003), Danger Theory: The Link between AIS and IDS, In Proceedings of the International Conference on Artificial Immune Systems (ICARIS, 2003), Edinburgh, UK.
8. Emma Hart and Peter Ross (2003), Improving SOSDM: Inspirations from the Danger Theory, In Proceedings of International Conference on Artificial Immune Systems (ICARIS 2003), Springer LNCS 2787, pp. 194–203.

9. Andrew Secker, Alex A. Freitas, and Jon Timmis (2003), A Danger Theory Inspired Approach to Web Mining, In Proceedings of International Conference on Artificial Immune Systems (ICARIS 2003), Springer LNCS 2787, pp. 156–167.
10. Michael A. Lutz, Francine Gervais, Alan Bernstein, Arthur L. Hattel, and Pamela H. Correll (2002), STK Receptor Tyrosine Kinase Regulates Susceptibility to Infection with Listeria Monocytogenes, Infection and Immunity, Vol. 70, No. 1, p. 416–418.
11. S Roy, A V S Hill, K Knox, D Griffithsand, D Crook (2002), Association of Common Genetic Variant with Susceptibility to Invasive Pneumococcal Disease, BMJ Volume 324, page 1369.
12. Wilfred Goldmann (2003), The Significance of Genetic Control in TSEs, Microbiology-Today, Vol. 30/Nov. 03, pp. 170-171
13. Jennie Blackwell (2002), Genetics and Genomics in Infectious Disease, CIMR Research Report, Last accessed on 06-04-04,
    URL:http://www.cimr.cam.ac.uk/resreports/report2002/pdf/blackwell_low.pdf
14. Paul M. Coussens, Brian Tooker, William Nobis, and Matthew J. Coussens (2001), Genetics and Genomics of Susceptibility to Mycobacterial Infections in Cattle, On-line publication on the 2001 IAAFSC web site.
15. Adrian VS Hill (1999), Genetics and Genomics of Infectious Disease Susceptibility, British Medical Bulletin, Vol. 55, No. 2, pp. 401-413.
16. Sean V. Tavtigian1, et al (2001), A Candidate Prostate Cancer Susceptibility Gene at Chromosome 17p, Nature Genetics, Volume 27, pp. 172-180.
17. Jean-Laurent Casanova (2001), Mendelian Susceptibility to Mycobacterial Infection in Man, Swiss Med Weekly, Vol. 131, pp. 445–454.
18. Lilin Wang, Dan Smith, Simona Bot, Luis Dellamary, Amy Bloom, and Adrian Bot (2002), Noncoding RNA Danger Motifs Bridge Innate and Adaptive Immunity and are Potent Adjuvants for Vaccination, The Journal of Clinical Investigation, Volume 110, Number 8, pp. 1175-1184.
19. Ken J. Ishii, Koichi Suzuki, Cevayir Coban, Fumihiko Takeshita, Yasushi Itoh, Hana Matoba, Leonard D. Kohn, and Dennis M. Klinman (2001), Genomic DNA Released by Dying Cells Induces the Maturation of APCs, The Journal of Immunology, Volume 167, pp. 2602-2607.
20. Brian D. Brown, and David Lillicrap (2002), Dangerous Liaisons: The Role of "Danger" Signals in the Immune Response to Gene Therapy, Blood, Volume 100, Number. 4, pp. 1133-1139.
21. Dariusz W. Kowalczyk (2002), Tumors and the Danger Model, Acta Biochimica Polonica, Vol. 49 No. 2/2002, pp. 295-302.
22. Su-Long Nyeo and I-Ching Yang (2002), Codon Distributions In Dna Sequences of Escherichia Coli, Journal of Biological Systems, Vol. 10, No. 1, pp. 47-60.
23. P. P. Vaidyanathan and Byung-Jun Yoon (2002), Digital Filters for Gene Prediction Applications, URL: citeseer.nj.nec.com/vaidyanathan02digital, Last sighted on 01-05-2004
24. P. Denny, E. Hopes, N. Gingles, K. W. Broman, J. McPheat, J. Morten, J. Alexander, P. W. Andrew, and S. D.M. Brown (2003), A major Locus Conferring Susceptibility to Infection by Streptococcus Pneumoniae in Mice, Mammalian Genome, Springer, Volume 14, pp. 448–453.
25. Carl Branden, and John Tooze (1991), Introduction to Protein Structure, Garland Publishing Inc., New York and London.
26. Steven A. Hofmeyr and Sephanie Forrest (1999), Immunity by Design: An Artificial Immune System. In proceedings of the Genetic and Evolutionary Computation Conference (GECCO), CA, pp. 1289-1296.
27. Emma Hart and Peter Ross (2002), Exploiting the Analogy Between Immunology and Sparse Distributed Memories: A System for Clustering Non-stationary data, In Proc. of International Conference on Artificial Immune Systems (ICARIS 2002), pp. 49-58.
28. S. Forrest, et al. (1994), Self Non-self Discrimination in Computer, In Proceedings of the IEEE Symposium on Research in Security and Privacy. Los Alamitos, CA.

29. Jeffery O. Kephart (1994), A Biologically Inspired Immune System for Computer, In Proceedings of Artificial Life, Cambridge, M. A.
30. S. Forrest, J. Balthrop, M. Glickman and D. Ackley (2002). "Computation in the Wild." In the Internet as a Large-Complex System, edited by K. Park and W. Willins: Oxford University Press. July 18, 2002.
31. Dayle Glenn Majors (2003), Operating System Call Integrity of the Linux Operating System, Masters Thesis, University of Missouri–Rolla.
32. Anil Somayaji (2002), Operating System Stability and Security through Process Homeostasis, PhD Dissertation, The University of New Mexico, New Mexico
33. Niels Provos (2002), Improving Host Security with System Call Policies, CITI Technical Report 02-3, Center for Information Technology Integration, University of Michigan, Ann Arbor, MI
34. R. Sekar, M. Bendre, P. Bollineni, and D. Dhurjati (2001), A Fast Automaton-Based Method for Detecting Anomalous Program Behaviors, In Proceedings of the IEEE Symposium on Security and Privacy, Oakland, CA.
35. Midori ASAKA, Takefumi ONABOTA, Tadashi INOUE, Shunji OKAZAWA, and Shigeki GOTO (2001), A New Intrusion Detection Method Based on Discriminant Analysis, In IEICE Transactions on Information and Systems, Vol. E84-D, No. 5, pp. 570-577.
36. D. Wagner and D. Dean (2001), Intrusion Detection via Static Analysis, In Proceedings of the IEEE Symposium on Security and Privacy, Oakland, CA.
37. S. Li, and A. Jones (2001), Temporal Signatures for Intrusion Detection, In Proc. of the 17th Annual Computer Security Applications Conference, New Orleans, Louisiana.
38. C. Warrender, S. Forrest, and B. Pearlmutter (1999), Detecting Intrusions Using System Calls: Alternative Data Models, In Proceedings of the IEEE Symposium on Security and Privacy, pp. 133-145.
39. A.Som, S.Chattopadhyay, J.Chakrabarti, and D.Bandyopadhyay (2001), Codon Distributions in DNA, Physics, Vol. 1,
40. Ravi Vijaya Satya, Amar Mukherjee, and Udaykumar Ranga (2003), A Pattern Matching Algorithm for Codon Optimization and CpG Motif-Engineering in DNA Expression Vectors, In Proceedings of the Computational Systems Bioinformatics (CSB'03)
41. Su-Long Nyeo, And I-Ching Yang (2002), Codon Distributions In DNA Sequences of Escherichia Coli, Journal Of Biological Systems, Vol. 10, No. 1, pp. 47-60.
42. Michel Termier (2001), Genome Analysis and Sequences with Random Letter Distribution, In Proceedings of Algorithms Seminar, pp. 63-66.
43. Intrusion Detection Data Sets, URL:http://www.cs.unm.edu/~immsec/systemcalls.htm, Last sighted on 01-05-2004

Online Negative Databases

Fernando Esponda, Elena S. Ackley, Stephanie Forrest, and Paul Helman

Department of Computer Science
University of New Mexico
Albuquerque, NM 87131-1386
{fesponda,elenas,forrest,helman}@cs.unm.edu

Abstract. The benefits of negative detection for obscuring information are explored in the context of Artificial Immune Systems (AIS). AIS based on string matching have the potential for an extra security feature in which the "normal" profile of a system is hidden from its possible hijackers. Even if the model of normal behavior falls into the wrong hands, reconstructing the set of valid or "normal" strings is an $\mathcal{NP}$-hard problem. The data-hiding aspects of negative detection are explored in the context of an application to negative databases. Previous work is reviewed describing possible representations and reversibility properties for privacy-enhancing negative databases. New algorithms are described, which allow on-line creation and updates of negative databases, and future challenges are discussed.

1 Introduction

A striking feature of the natural immune system is its use of negative detection in which *self* is represented (approximately) by the set of circulating lymphocytes that fail to match self. The negative-detection scheme has been used in several artificial immune system (AIS) applications, and the benefits of such a scheme have been explored in terms of the number of required detectors [24,14,13,49, 50], success in distinguishing self from nonself [20,16], and the ease with which negative detection can be distributed across multiple locations. In this paper we explore a fourth interesting property of negative representations, namely their ability to hide information about self. This information hiding ability has interesting implications for intrusion detection as well as for applications in which privacy is a concern and where it may be useful to adopt a scheme in which only the negative representation is available for querying.

This paper extends results first presented in [15] which introduced the concept of a *negative database*. In a negative database, a collection of data is represented by its logical complement. The term *positive information* denotes the elements of the category or set of interest (e.g., self) while *negative information* denotes all the other elements of the universe. A negative database is then a representation of the negative information. In addition to introducing this concept, the previous paper showed that negative information can be represented efficiently (even though the negative image will typically be much larger than the

G. Nicosia et al. (Eds.): ICARIS 2004, LNCS 3239, pp. 175–188, 2004.

positive image), that such a representation can be $\mathcal{NP}$-hard to reverse (thereby hiding the exact composition of self), and that simple membership queries can be computed efficiently. For instance, a query of the form "is string x in the database" can be answered promptly, while a request of the form "give me all the strings in the positive image that start with a 1" cannot. However, the paper did not show that common database operations (such as inserts and deletes) can be performed easily on the negative representation or that a negative database can be maintained dynamically. Section 4 presents new algorithms that address these matters.

Many AIS used for anomaly detection represent the entity to be protected as a set of strings and, in parallel with the immune system, identification of anomalies is performed by an alternate set of strings (known as detectors) and a match rule that are designed not to match elements of self. In this context, there may be an additional incentive for negative detection using negative databases. When the negative information is represented as discussed in [15], it is provably hard to infer the positive image even if all the negative information is available. In the context of anomaly detection and security this provides an extra level of protection since it prevents someone from hijacking the detector set, deriving from it the normal profile of the system, and using that information to devise new attacks.

Section 2 reviews earlier work that is generally relevant to the topic of negative information; Section 3 reviews previous work on negative databases, showing that a negative representation can be constructed which occupies only polynomially more space than its positive counterpart, while retaining some interesting querying capabilities. Section 4 presents on-line algorithms, including how to initialize a negative database and how to perform updates. Section 5 considers the implications of our results.

2   Related Work

Negative representations of data have had several proponents in the past, especially in art where artists like Magritte and Escher have taken advantage of the so called figure-ground relationship. Examples can also be found in mathematics and statistics where sometimes it is easier to obtain an answer by looking at the complement of the problem we intend to solve and complementing the solution. For the purpose of this paper, however, we will review how negative representations of information have influenced the field of AIS.

As mentioned in the introduction, the natural immune system can be interpreted as representing data negatively. This observation has led to algorithm designs which take advantage of some of the inherent properties of negative representations. In particular, designers have taken advantage of the fact that negative detectors are more amenable to distributed implementations than positive detectors and that, for the purposes of anomaly detection, negative representations of data seem more natural. The negative selection algorithm whereby a set of negative detectors is created was introduced in [19]. Anomaly-detection systems based on these ideas can be found in [46,3,51,32,11,26,27,28]. Other applications have also been proposed that range from image classification to recommender systems [33,47,25,42,46,8,5,6]. We note that many AIS are not based on string matching and therefore are not directly affected by the results presented here; the interested reader is referred to [12,45].

Protecting information stored in a database from examination by unauthorized parties has been a concern since the inception of the field [41,40,44]. Some approaches relevant to the current discussion involve cryptographic protection of databases [17,43,48], multi-party computation schemes [52,23], the use of one-way functions [22,38], and dynamic accumulators [7,4].

Section 4 outlines an algorithm for generating and maintaining negative databases. These operations need to be adjusted in order to produce "hard" negative databases. There is a large body of work regarding the issues and techniques involved in the generation of hard-to-solve $\mathcal{NP}$-complete problems [30, 29,39,34] and in particular of SAT instances [35,9]. Much of this work is focused on the case where instances are generated without paying attention to their specific solutions. Efforts concerned with the generation of hard instances when there is a specific solution we want the instance to possess include [18,1]. Finally, the problem of learning a distribution, whether by evaluation or generation [31, 37], is also closely related to constructing the sort of databases in which we are interested.

3   Negative Databases

The notion of negative databases was introduced in [15], whereby for a given set of fixed length strings, called the positive database DB (*self*), all the possible records or strings not in DB are represented i.e. $U - DB$ (*nonself*) where U denotes the universe of all possible strings of the same length defined over the same alphabet. It was shown that the size of the resulting negative database, denoted NDB, can be constructed to be polynomially related to the size of DB, even though $(U - DB \gg DB)$ in the expected case. The intuition behind our compact representation is that there must be subsets of strings with significant overlaps, and that these overlaps can be used to represent these subsets succinctly. We have adopted the strategy of extending the alphabet over which strings are defined, in this case binary, to include an extra symbol $*$ known as the don't care symbol. A string exhibiting the $*$ at position i represents two strings; one with a 1 at position i and one with a 0 at position i with the remaining positions unchanged, as the following example illustrates. Position i in the string is referred to as a "defined position" if it contains either a 0 or a 1.

DB	$(U - DB)$	Negative Database
010	000	
011	001	*0*
110	100 $\Rightarrow$	
	101	1*1
	111	

Including this third symbol allows one entry (or record) in the negative database to represent several strings (records) in $U - DB$[1]. A string x is represented in NDB —meaning x is not in DB, if there is at least one string y in NDB that matches it, otherwise the string is in DB. Two strings are said to match if all of their positions match; the don't care symbol is taken to match everything.

Esponda, Forrest and Helman [15] give two algorithms for creating an NDB under the representation described above. One common feature is that both take as input DB —meaning DB must be held in its entirety at one time. Both operate by examining chosen subsets of bit positions to determine which patterns are not present in DB and must be depicted in NDB, the basic objective being to find the subsets of bit positions that serve to represent the largest number of strings in $U - DB$.

An interesting property of this representation concerns the difficulty of inferring DB given NDB. For an arbitrary set of strings defined over $\{0, 1, *\}$ determining which strings are not represented is an $\mathcal{NP}$-hard problem. To sustain this claim it is sufficient to note that there is a mapping from Boolean formulae to NDBs such that finding which entries are not represented by NDB (that is, which entries are in DB) is equivalent to finding satisfying assignments to the corresponding boolean formula, which is known to be an $\mathcal{NP}$-hard problem. The specifics of the proof can be found in Ref. [15], and an example of the mapping is given in Figure 1.

Boolean Formula	NDB
$(x_2$ or $\bar{x}_5)$ and	*0**1
$(\bar{x}_2$ or $x_3)$ and	*10**
$(x_2$ or $\bar{x}_4$ or $\bar{x}_5)$ and $\Rightarrow$	*0*11
$(x_1$ or $\bar{x}_3$ or $x_4)$ and	0*10*
$(\bar{x}_1$ or x_2 or $\bar{x}_4$ or $x_5)$	10*10

Fig. 1. Mapping SAT to NDB: In this example the boolean formula is written in conjunctive normal form and its defined over five variables $(x_1, x_2, x_3, x_4, x_5)$. The formula is mapped to an NDB where each clause corresponds to a record and each variable in the clause is represented as a 1 if it appears negated, as a 0 if it appears un-negated and as a * if it does not appear in the clause at all. In easy to see that a satisfying assignment of the formula such as $\{x_1 =$ TRUE, $x_2 =$ TRUE, $x_3 =$ TRUE, $x_4 =$ FALSE, $x_5 =$ FALSE $\}$ corresponding to string 11100 is *not* represented in NDB.

4   Creating and Maintaining Negative Databases

In this section we present an on-line algorithm for creating and maintaining a negative database under the representation discussed in Section 3. Negative databases should be viewed as logical containers of strings or detectors and it

---

[1] We consider DB to remain defined over the $\{0,1\}$ alphabet.

is important to point out that when the strings stored therein implement some partial matching rule, as is the case in AIS, removing or inserting a single string changes the definition of DB or $self$ according to the particulars of that match rule.

The algorithms discussed in this section have the flexibility to create negative databases with varying structures (see instance-generation models [35,9,10]), an implementation of the algorithms must make some restrictions in order to yield NDBs that are hard to reverse on average. The following are some properties, regarding string matching, that the algorithms take advantage of:

Property 1: A string y is subsumed by string x if every string matched by y is also matched by x. A string x obtained by replacing some of y's defined positions, with don't cares, subsumes y.

Property 2: A set of 2^n distinct strings that are equal in all but n positions match exactly the same set of strings as a single one with those n positions set to the don't care symbol.

4.1   Initialization

A natural default initialization of DB is to the empty set. And, the corresponding initialization of NDB would be to U—the set of all strings. As discussed in Section 3 an NDB contains strings defined over $\{0, 1, *\}$ so one possible initial state for NDB would be simply to store the string $*^l$, where l is the string length. This clearly matches every string in U, but doing so would trivially defeat our purpose of making it difficult for someone to know exactly what NDB represents. We need to make it hard to know what DB is, even when DB is empty.

The algorithm presented in Figure 2 creates a database whose strings will match any string in U (see example in Fig. 3). The rationale behind it comes from the isomorphism between NDBs and Boolean formulae (Sect. 3, Fig. 1). Hence, our algorithm is designed to potentially create the equivalent of unsatisfiable SAT formulas of l variables. The high-level strategy is to select m bit positions and create, for each possible bit assignment V_p of these positions, a string with V_p and don't care symbols elsewhere. A negative database created in this way will have 2^m records, each matching 2^{l-m} distinct strings, clearly covering all of U.

Figure 2 modifies this strategy to expand the number of possible NDBs output by the algorithm. The modifications are:

- Potentially add more than one string to match a specific pattern (line 3).
- Augment the original pattern with n other positions. This allows each of the l possible positions to be specified in the resulting pattern. However the choice of n has great impact on the complexity of the algorithm as line 6 loops 2^n times. A value of 3 will suffice to generate some types of 3-SAT formulas (see Fig. 1) while keeping the complexity reasonable.
- Using a subset of positions of the selected patterns to create an entry (line 7–8).

It is straightforward to verify using the properties laid out at the beginning of the section that the algorithm produces an NDB that matches every string in U.

The purpose of the current choices of k_1 and k_2, lines 3 and 7 respectively, is to give the algorithm the necessary flexibility to generate genuinely hard-to-reverse NDB instances. We return to this question in Section 5, as some restriction to these values might be warranted to produce hard instances in practice.

Empty_NDB_Create(l)
1. Pick $\lceil log(l) \rceil$ bit positions at random
2. for every possible assignment V_p of this positions{
3.   select k_1 randomly $1 <= k_1 <= l$
4.   for j=1 to k_1{
5.   select an additional n distinct positions
6.   for every possible assignment V_q of these positions{
7.   Pick k_2 bits at random from $V_p \cdot V_q$.
8.   Create a entry for NDB with the k_2
                chosen bits and fill the remaining $l - k_2$
                positions with the don't care symbol.}}}

Fig. 2. Empty_NDB_Create. Randomly creates a negative database that represents every binary string of length l.

Empty_NDB_Create(4)	Delete(1111,NDB)	Insert(1111,NDB)
000*	000*	000*
001*	001*	001*
01*0	01*0	01*0
01*1	01*1	01*1
10*0	10*0	10*0
10*1	10*1	10*1
111*	110*	110*
110*	11*0	11*0
	*110	*110
		11

Fig. 3. Possible states of NDB after successively performing initialization, deletion and insertion of a string.

4.2   Updates

We now turn our attention to modifying the negative database NDB in a dynamic scenario. The policies and algorithms used for selecting which strings should be added or retired remain application specific. It is worth emphasizing that the meaning of the insert and delete operations are inverted from their traditional sense, since we are storing a representation of what is *not* is some database DB. For instance, the operation "insert x into DB" would have to be implemented as "delete x from NDB" and "delete x from DB" as "insert x into NDB".

The core operation for both the insert and delete procedures, presented in Figure 4, takes a string x and the current NDB and outputs a string y that subsumes x without matching any other string in DB. The function starts by picking a random ordering π of the bit positions so as to remove biases from later choices. Lines 2–6 find a minimum subset of bits from the input string x such that no string outside $\{U - DB\}\bigcup\{x\}$ is matched. Step 4 of the algorithm ensures that inserting a don't care symbol at the selected position doesn't cause the string to match something in DB. Property 1, listed at the beginning of the section, establishes that the resulting string matches whichever strings the original input string x matched. Steps 7–9 create a string containing the pattern found in the previous steps plus possibly some extra bits, note that the added bits were part of the original input string x so it is automatically guaranteed that the result will subsume x. It is important to emphasize that, for an actual implementation of the algorithm, the value of t (line 7) might be restricted or even fixed to provide a desired NDB structure.

Negative_Pattern_Generate(x, NDB)

1.   Create a random permutation π
2.   for all specified bits b_i in $\pi(x)$
3.   Let x' be the same as $\pi(x)$ but with b_i flipped
4.   if x' is subsumed by some string in $\pi(NDB)$
5. $\pi(x) \leftarrow \pi(x) - i^{th}$ bit (set value to $*$)
6.   Keep track of the ith bit in a set indicator vector (SIV)
7.   Randomly choose $0 \leq t \leq |SIV|$
8. $R \leftarrow t$ randomly selected bits from SIV
9.   Create a pattern V_k using $\pi(x)$ and the bits indicated by R.
10. return $\pi'(V_k)^a$

---

[a] π' is the inverse permutation of π.

Fig. 4. Negative_Pattern_Generate. Take as input a string x defined over $\{0, 1, *\}$ and a database NDB and outputs a string that matches x and nothing else outside of NDB.

Insert into NDB. The purpose of the insert operation is to introduce a subset of strings into the negative database while safeguarding its irreversibility properties. Figure 5 shows the pseudocode of the insert operation, lines 1 and 2 enable the procedure to create several entries in NDB portraying x, as for the initialization of NDB shown in Fig. 2, the actual number of entries should be set to accommodate efficiency constraints and to preserve the irreversibility of NDB. Likewise steps 3 and 4 set some of the unspecified positions of x (if any) so that it may be possible for a set of strings representing x, that exhibit bits not found in x, to be entered in NDB (see property 2 at the top of the section). Finally the call to Negative_Pattern_Generate (see Sect. 4.2 and Fig. 4) produces a string representing x which is then inserted in NDB (see example in Fig. 3).

Insert(x, NDB)
1. Randomly choose $1 \leq j \leq l$
2. for $k = 1$ to j do
3.　　Randomly select from x at most n distinct unspecified bit positions
4.　　for every possible bit assignment B_p of the selected positions
5.　　　　$x' \leftarrow x \cdot B_p$
6.　　　　$y \leftarrow$ Negative_Pattern_Generate(x', NDB)
7.　　　　add y to NDB

Fig. 5. Insert into NDB.

Delete. This operation aims to remove a subset of strings from being represented in NDB. It is worth noting that this operation cannot simply be implemented by looking for a particular entry in NDB and removing it, since it may be the case that a string is represented by several entries in NDB and an entry in NDB can in turn represent several strings, some of which might not be our intent to remove. Figure 6 gives a general algorithm for removing a string or set of strings from being depicted in NDB, note that input x may be any string over $\{0, 1, *\}$ an thus many strings may cease from being represented by a single call.

The algorithm takes the current NDB and the string to be removed x as input, line 1 identifies the subset, D_x, of NDB that matches x and removes it. As mentioned previously, removing an entry that matches x might also unintentionally delete some additional strings. Lines 3–6 reinsert all the strings represented by D_x except x. For each string y in D_x that has n unspecified positions (don't care symbols) there are n strings to be inserted into NDB that match everything y matches except x. Each new string y'_i is created by using the specified bits of y and the complement of the bit specified at the ith position of x as the following example illustrates:

x	D_x	All but x
		111*0*
101001	1*1*0*	1*110*
		1*1*00

To see that this in fact excludes x from NDB, and nothing else, note the following: Each new string y'_i, by construction, differs from x in its ith position therefore none of the new strings match x. If a totally specified string $z \neq x$ is matched by $y \in D_x$ then z must have the same specified positions as y, now, since z is different from x it follows that it must disagree with it in at least one bit, say bit k, z will be matched by y'_k. Finally, observe that since y subsumes each new entry y'_i no unwanted strings are included by the operation (see example in Fig. 3).

Delete(x, NDB)
1. Let D_x be all the strings in NDB that match x
2. Remove D_x from NDB.
3. for all $y \in D_x$
4.   for each unspecified position q_i of y
5.   Create a new string y' using the specified bits of y and the complement of the bit specified at the ith position of x.
6.   Insert(y', NDB)

Fig. 6. Delete from NDB.

One very important fact to point out about this algorithm is that it may cause the size of NDB to grow unreasonably, even exponentially. It is important for any implementation to prevent the number of entries $|D_x|$ in NDB that match a particular, totally specified, string from being a function of the size of the negative database and/or to instrument a clean up operation that bounds the size of NDB.

5   Discussion

In this paper we have reviewed the concept of negative databases and introduced them as a means for storing strings or detector sets in the context of anomaly detection systems based on string matching. Negative representations of data can provide an extra level of protection for systems in which acquiring the detector set (the set of strings that detect anomalies) might produce a security breach. We described an algorithm for generating negative databases on-line that, unlike the previous work where the positive database was assumed to exist at one place and at one time in order to obtain its negative representation, allows for the negative representation to be updated dynamically.

In applications of AIS to anomaly detection, the set of detectors or strings typically implement a partial matching rule. This allows the system to include, in the definition of *self*, strings that have not been observed before (also known as a generalization), this contrasts with the previous negative database work where the negative information of a set is represented exactly. An important observation in regards to partial matching is that, for the irreversibility result to hold, it must be the case that the match rule complies with the generalized satisfiability problem [21] according to the isomorphism with Boolean formulas described in Section 3. Moreover, even though it was shown in [15] that finding DB given only NDB is $\mathcal{NP}$-hard, this does not mean that every NDB is hard to reverse. The algorithms presented in Section 4 have a series of free parameters that will need to be tuned in order to realize the irreversibility properties afforded by the negative representation. We have developed a preliminary version of the online algorithms presented here and those introduced in Ref. [15], referred to as the batch method. Quantitative results are still premature but some qualitative observations are relevant: Unlike the batch method, where the critical time cost is querying many negative patterns against the positive database, the online version spends its time querying the input record against the negative database. The negative database is typically larger than the positive database, and has been so in our tests.

The prototype, based on the algorithms in this paper is limited to records constructed from small two or three letter alphabets (16 to 24 bits). We have made a number of restrictions to the algorithms as a first step in understanding its effects and to limit the size of NDB and its running time. We constrained the number of passes through the Insert algorithm Fig. 5 to one (in line 1 $j = 1$) and kept $k1 = 1$ and $n = 3$ for the initialization phase (Fig. 2 lines 3 and 5 respectively). Further, both the processes of insertion and deletion cause NDB to grow in size, so it will be indispensable in the future to implement a clean-up operation that eliminates redundant strings.

In order to evaluate the difficulty of retrieving positive records given only NDB we convert NDB into a Boolean formula, taking advantage of the relationship an NDB has with SAT, and input it to a well-known SAT solver [36,2]. The solver returns the difficulty of obtaining a solution (specific to the particular heuristics used in the solver). One interesting observation is that the complexity of reversing the output of the on-line algorithm is significantly higher that that of the batch version. It appears that starting from an unsatisfiable formula and gradually adding satisfying assignments (adding records to DB, deleting them from NDB) is more challenging for the heuristics employed by the solver. Finally, our current implementation of the on-line algorithm can produce strings with a variable or constant number of specified bits. This latter restriction is in accordance with [35] and has, in our experience, greatly increased the complexity of reversing NDB.

Negative detection has been a trademark characteristic of artificial immune systems since they were first introduced and it is often lauded for its ability for distributed detection and its flexibility in detecting anomalies. Our research has led us to investigate the more general question of negative data representations and their properties. This led to the discovery that representing negative information in a certain manner exhibits an interesting and potentially useful property, namely that it makes it hard to recover the corresponding positive information. In the context of AIS for anomaly detection it adds an extra layer of security by making it hard to retrieve the profile of the system being monitored by simply analyzing the detector set. In other applications involving databases, it enhances privacy by naturally allowing only certain types of queries. Our current efforts are focused on the practical aspects of generating negative databases as well as in drawing out some additional properties that distinguish them from their positive counterpart.

Acknowledgments. The authors gratefully acknowledge the support of the National Science Foundation (CCR-0331580, CCR-0311686, and DBI-0309147), Defense Advanced Research Projects Agency (grant AGR F30602-00-2-0584), the Intel Corporation, and the Santa Fe Institute. F.E. also thanks CONACYT grant No. 116691/131686.

References

1. D. Achlioptas, C. Gomes, H. Kautz, and B. Selman. Generating satisfiable problem instances. In *Proceedings of the 7th Conference on Artificial Intelligence (AAAI-00) and of the 12th Conference on Innovative Applications of Artificial Intelligence (IAAI-00)*, pages 256–261, Menlo Park, CA, July 30– 3 2000. AAAI Press.
2. Boolean Satisfability Research Group at Princeton. zChaff. http://ee.princeton.edu/ chaff/zchaff.php, 2004.
3. M. Ayara, J. Timmis, R. de Lemos, L. N. de Castro, and R. Duncan. Negative selection: How to generate detectors. In J Timmis and P J Bentley, editors, *Proceedings of the 1st International Conference on Artificial Immune Systems (ICARIS)*, pages 89–98, University of Kent at Canterbury, September 2002. University of Kent at Canterbury Printing Unit.
4. J. Cohen Benaloh and M. de Mare. One-way accumulators: A decentralized alternative to digital signatures. In *Advances in Cryptology—EUROCRYPT '93*, pages 274–285, 1994.
5. D. W. Bradley and A. M. Tyrrell. The architecture for a hardware immune system. In D. Keymeulen, A. Stoica, J. Lohn, and R. S. Zebulum, editors, *The Third NASA/DoD Workshop on Evolvable Hardware*, pages 193–200, Long Beach, California, 12-14 July 2001. IEEE Computer Society.
6. D. W. Bradley and A. M. Tyrrell. Immunotronics: Novel finite state machine architectures with built in self test using self-nonself differentiation. *IEEE Transactions on Evolutionary Computation*, 6(3):227–238, June 2002.
7. J. Camenisch and A. Lysyanskaya. Dynamic accumulators and application to efficient revocation of anonymous credentials. In Moti Yung, editor, *Advances in Cryptology – CRYPTO ' 2002*, volume 2442 of *Lecture Notes in Computer Science*, pages 61–76. International Association for Cryptologic Research, Springer-Verlag, Berlin Germany, 2002.
8. D. L. Chao and S. Forrest. Generating biomorphs with an aesthetic immune system. In Russell Standish, Mark A. Bedau, and Hussein A. Abbass, editors, *Artificial Life VIII: Proceedings of the Eighth International Conference on the Simulation and Synthesis of Living Systems*, pages 89–92, Cambridge, Massachusetts, 2003. MIT Press.
9. S. A. Cook and D. G. Mitchell. Finding hard instances of the satisfiability problem: A survey. In Du, Gu, and Pardalos, editors, *Satisfiability Problem: Theory and Applications*, volume 35 of *Dimacs Series in Discrete Mathematics and Theoretical Computer Science*, pages 1–17. American Mathematical Society, 1997.

10. J. M. Crawford and L. D. Anton. Experimental results on the crossover point in satisfiability problems. In Richard Fikes and Wendy Lehnert, editors, *Proceedings of the Eleventh National Conference on Artificial Intelligence*, pages 21–27, Menlo Park, California, 1993. American Association for Artificial Intelligence, AAAI Press.

11. D. Dasgupta and F. Gonzalez. An immunity-based technique to characterize intrusions in computer networks. *IEEE Transactions on Evolutionary Computation*, 6(3), June 2002.

12. L.N. de Castro and J.I. Timmis. *Artificial Immune Systems: A New Computational Intelligence Approach*. Springer-Verlag, 2002.

13. P. D'haeseleer, S. Forrest, and P. Helman. An immunological approach to change detection: algorithms, analysis and implications. In *Proceedings of the 1996 IEEE Symposium on Computer Security and Privacy*. IEEE Press, 1996.

14. F. Esponda, S. Forrest, and P. Helman. The crossover closure and partial match detection. In Jonathan Timmis, Peter J. Bentley, and Emma Hart, editors, *Proceedings of the 2nd International Conference on Artificial Immune Systems (ICARIS)*, pages 249–260, Edinburgh, UK, Sep 2003. Springer-Verlag.

15. F. Esponda, S. Forrest, and P. Helman. Enhancing privacy through negative representations of data. Technical report, Univerity of New Mexico, 2004.

16. F. Esponda, S. Forrest, and P. Helman. A formal framework for positive and negative detection schemes. *IEEE Transactions on Systems, Man and Cybernetics Part B: Cybernetics*, 34(1):357–373, 2004.

17. J. Feigenbaum, M. Y. Liberman, and R. N. Wright. Cryptographic protection of databases and software. In *Distributed Computing and Cryptography*, pages 161–172. American Mathematical Society, 1991.

18. C. Fiorini, E. Martinelli, and F. Massacci. How to fake an RSA signature by encoding modular root finding as a SAT problem. *Discrete Appl. Math.*, 130(2):101–127, 2003.

19. S. Forrest, A. S. Perelson, L. Allen, and R. CheruKuri. Self-nonself discrimination in a computer. In *Proceedings of the 1994 IEEE Symposium on Research in Security and Privacy*, Los Alamitos, CA, 1994. IEEE Computer Society Press.

20. A. A. Freitas and J. Timmis. Revisiting the foundations of AIS: A problem oriented perspective. In Jonathan Timmis, Peter J. Bentley, and Emma Hart, editors, *Proceedings of the 2nd International Conference on Artificial Immune Systems (ICARIS)*, pages 229–241, Edinburgh, UK, Sep 2003. Springer-Verlag.

21. M. R. Garey and D. S. Johnson. *Computers and Intractability : A Guide to the Theory of NP-Completeness*. W.H. Freeman & Company, San Francisco, 1978.

22. O. Goldreich. On the foundations of modern cryptography. *Lecture Notes in Computer Science*, 1294:46–??, 1997.

23. S. Goldwasser. Multi party computations: past and present. In *Proceedings of the sixteenth annual ACM symposium on Principles of distributed computing*, pages 1–6. ACM Press, 1997.

24. F. Gonzalez, D. Dasgupta, and L. F. Nino. A randomized real valued negative selection algorithm. In Jonathan Timmis, Peter J. Bentley, and Emma Hart, editors, *Proceedings of the 2nd International Conference on Artificial Immune Systems (ICARIS)*, pages 261–272, Edinburgh, UK, Sep 2003. Springer-Verlag.

25. J. Greensmith and S. Cayzer. An AIS approach to semantic document classification. In Jonathan Timmis, Peter J. Bentley, and Emma Hart, editors, *Proceedings of the 2nd International Conference on Artificial Immune Systems (ICARIS)*, pages 136–146, Edinburgh, UK, Sep 2003. Springer-Verlag.

26. S. Hofmeyr. *An immunological model of distributed detection and its application to computer security.* PhD thesis, University of New Mexico, Albuquerque, NM, 1999.

27. S. Hofmeyr and S. Forrest. Immunity by design: An artificial immune system. In *Proceedings of the Genetic and Evolutionary Computation Conference (GECCO)*, pages 1289–1296, San Francisco, CA, 1999. Morgan-Kaufmann.

28. S. Hofmeyr and S. Forrest. Architecture for an artificial immune system. *Evolutionary Computation Journal*, 8(4):443–473, 2000.

29. R. Impagliazzo, L. A. Levin, and M. Luby. Pseudo-random generation from one-way functions. In *Proceedings of the twenty-first annual ACM symposium on Theory of computing*, pages 12–24. ACM Press, 1989.

30. R. Impagliazzo and M. Naor. Efficient cryptographic schemes provably as secure as subset sum. In IEEE, editor, *30th annual Symposium on Foundations of Computer Science, October 30–November 1, 1989, Research Triangle Park, NC*, pages 236–241, 1109 Spring Street, Suite 300, Silver Spring, MD 20910, USA, 1989. IEEE Computer Society Press.

31. M. Kearns, Y. Mansour, D. Ron, R. Rubinfeld, R. E. Schapire, and L. Sellie. On the learnability of discrete distributions. In *Proceedings of the twenty-sixth annual ACM symposium on Theory of computing*, pages 273–282. ACM Press, 1994.

32. J. Kim and P. J. Bentley. An evaluation of negative selection in an artificial immune system for network intrusion detection. In *Proceedings of the Genetic and Evolutionary Computation Conference (GECCO)*, pages 1330–1337, San Francisco, CA, 2001. Morgan-Kauffman.

33. P. May, K. C. Mander, and J. Timmis. Software vaccination: An AIS approach. In Jonathan Timmis, Peter J. Bentley, and Emma Hart, editors, *Proceedings of the 2nd International Conference on Artificial Immune Systems (ICARIS)*, pages 81–92, Edinburgh, UK, Sep 2003. Springer-Verlag.

34. R. C. Merkle and M. E. Hellman. Hiding information and signatures in trapdoor knapsacks. *IEEE-IT*, IT-24:525–530, 1978.

35. D. Mitchell, B. Selman, and H. Levesque. Problem solving: Hardness and easiness - hard and easy distributions of SAT problems. In *Proceeding of the 10th National Conference on Artificial Intelligence (AAAI-92), San Jose, California*, pages 459–465. AAAI Press, Menlo Park, California, USA, 1992.

36. M. W. Moskewicz, C. F. Madigan, Y. Zhao, L. Zhang, and Sh. Malik. Chaff: Engineering an Efficient SAT Solver. In *Proceedings of the 38th Design Automation Conference (DAC'01)*, June 2001.

37. M. Naor. Evaluation may be easier than generation (extended abstract). In *Proceedings of the twenty-eighth annual ACM symposium on Theory of computing*, pages 74–83. ACM Press, 1996.

38. M. Naor and M. Yung. Universal one-way hash functions and their cryptographic applications. In *Proceedings of the Twenty First Annual ACM Symposium on Theory of Computing: Seattle, Washington, May 15–17, 1989*, pages 33–43, New York, NY 10036, USA, 1989. ACM Press.

39. Odlyzko. The rise and fall of knapsack cryptosystems. In *PSAM: Proceedings of the 42th Symposium in Applied Mathematics, American Mathematical Society*, 1991.

40. G. J. Popek. Protection structures. *COMPUTER*, 7(6):22–33, June 1974.

41. J. H. Saltzer and M. D. Schroeder. The protection of information in computer systems. *Proceedings of the IEEE*, 63(9):1278–1308, September 1975.

42. S. Sathyanath and F. Sahin. Artificial immune systems approach to a real time color image classification problem. In *Proceedings of the IEEE International Conference on Systems, Man, and Cybernetics*, 2001.

43. B. Schneier. *Applied Cryptography: Protocols, Algorithms, and Source Code in C.* John Wiley and Sons, Inc., New York, NY, USA, 1994.
44. A. Silberschatz, H. F. Korth, and S. Sudarshan. *Database System Concepts (Fourth Edition).* Mc Graw Hill, 2002.
45. A. O. Tarakanov, V. A. Skormin, and S.P. Sokolova. *Immunocomputing:Principles and Applications.* Springer-Verlag, 2003.
46. D. W. Taylor and D. W. Corne. An investigation of negative selection for fault detection in refrigeration systems. In Jonathan Timmis, Peter J. Bentley, and Emma Hart, editors, *Proceedings of the 2nd International Conference on Artificial Immune Systems (ICARIS)*, pages 34–45, Edinburgh, UK, Sep 2003. Springer-Verlag.
47. P. A. Vargas, L. Nunes de Castro, R. Michelan, and F. J. Von Zuben. An immune learning classifier network for automated navigation. In Jonathan Timmis, Peter J. Bentley, and Emma Hart, editors, *Proceedings of the 2nd International Conference on Artificial Immune Systems (ICARIS)*, pages 69–80, Edinburgh, UK, Sep 2003. Springer-Verlag.
48. P. Wayner. *Translucent Databases.* Flyzone Press, 2002.
49. S. T. Wierzchon. Generating optimal repertoire of antibody strings in an artificial immune system. In M. A. Klopotek, M. Michalewicz, and S. T.Wierzchon, editors, *Intelligent Information Systems*, pages 119–133, Heidelberg New York, 2000. Physica-Verlag.
50. S. T. Wierzchon. Deriving concise description of non-self patterns in an artificial immune system. In S. T. Wierzchon, L. C. Jain, and J. Kacprzyk, editors, *New Learning Paradigms in Soft Computing*, pages 438–458, Heidelberg New York, 2001. Physica-Verlag.
51. P. D. Williams, K. P. Anchor, J. L. Bebo, G. H. Gunsch, and G. D. Lamont. CDIS: Towards a computer immune system for detecting network intrusions. In W. Lee, L. Me, and A. Wespi, editors, *Fourth International Symposium, Recent Advances in Intrusion Detection*, pages 117–133, Berlin, 2001. Springer.
52. A. Yao. Protocols for secure computation. In IEEE, editor, *23rd annual Symposium on Foundations of Computer Science, November 3–5, 1982, Chicago, IL*, pages 160–164, 1109 Spring Street, Suite 300, Silver Spring, MD 20910, USA, 1982. IEEE Computer Society Press.

Definition of MHC Supertypes Through Clustering of MHC Peptide Binding Repertoires

Pedro A. Reche[1,2*] and Ellis L. Reinherz[1,2]

[1] Laboratory of Immunobiology and Department of Medical Oncology,
Dana-Farber Cancer Institute
[2] Department of Medicine, Harvard Medical School,
44 Binney Street, Boston, MA 02115, USA.
TEL: +1-617-632-3412, FAX: +1-617-632-3351
reche@research.dfci.havard.edu

Abstract. MHC molecules, also known in the human as human leukocyte anti-gens (HLA), display peptides on antigen presenting cell surfaces for subsequent T cell recognition. Identification of these antigenic peptides is especially impor-tant for developing peptide-based vaccines. Consequently experimental and computational approaches have been developed for their identification. A major impediment to such an approach is the extreme polymorphism of HLA, which is in fact the basis for differential peptide binding. This problem can be miti-gated by the observation that despite such polymorphisms, HLA molecules bind overlapping set of peptides, and therefore, may be grouped accordingly into su-pertypes. Here we describe a method of grouping HLA alleles into supertypes based on analysis and subsequent clustering of their peptide binding repertoires. Combining this method with the known allele and haplotype gene frequencies of HLA I molecules for five major American ethnic groups (Black, Caucasian, Hispanic, Native American, and Asian), it is now feasible to identify supertypic combinations for prediction of antigenic peptide, offering the potential to gen-erate peptide-vaccines with a population coverage ≥95%, regardless of ethnic-ity. One combination including five distinct supertypes is available online at our PEPVAC web server (http://immunax.dfci.harvard.edu/PEPVAC/). Promiscu-ous peptides predicted to bind to these five supertypes represent around 5% of all possible peptide binders from a given genome.

1 Introduction

T cell immune responses are responsible for fighting viruses, pathogenic bacteria and the elimination of cancer cells, and arc triggcred by the recognition of foreign peptide antigens bound to cell membrane expressed MHC molecules via their T cell receptors (TCR)(reviewed in [1-3]. In the human, MHC molecules are also termed human leu-kocyte antigens or HLA. Traditionally, identification of T cell epitopes required the synthesis of overlapping peptides (15-20 mers overlapping 10 amino acids) spanning the entire length of a protein, followed by experimental assays on each peptide such as in vitro intracellular cytokine staining [4]. This method is economically viable only

---

[*] To whom correspondence should be addressed.

G. Nicosia et al. (Eds.): ICARIS 2004, LNCS 3239, pp. 189–196, 2004.
© Springer-Verlag Berlin Heidelberg 2004

for single proteins or pathogens consisting of a few proteins. As a result, computational approaches are used for the anticipation of antigenic peptides. Since T cells recognize antigenic peptides only in the context of MHC molecules [5], methods for the anticipation of antigenic peptides rely on the prediction of peptide-MHC binding. Peptides bound to the same MHC are related by sequence similarity [6, 7], and thus we have recently developed a method for the prediction of peptide-MHC binding based on the the the use of position specific scoring matrix (PSSMs) or profiles derived from aligned peptides known to bind to MHC [8] [9, 10].

A major complication to the development of T cell based immunotherapies (vaccines) using peptide antigens lies in the polymorphism of HLA molecules, which is the basis for their differential peptide binding specificity [10]. Because of the required HLA restriction and ethnic variation in HLA distribution [11], such epitope vaccines might not be effective across populations. Conversely, developing a broadly protective multi-epitope vaccine will require the targeting of a large number of HLA molecules for peptide-binding predictions, yielding an impractical large number of peptides to work with. Interestingly, groups of several HLA molecules (supertypes) can bind largely overlapping sets of peptides [12, 13]. A systematic selection of HLA supertypic peptide binders would allow the immune response to be stimulated in individual of different genetic backgrounds. Thus, identification of HLA supertypes would facilitate the practical development of epitope-based vaccines. Here we describe a method to define HLA supertypes based on the clustering of the predicted peptide binding repertoire of HLA molecules.

In this paper, we have applied the method to class I HLA molecules (HLA I), unraveling new peptide binding relationships, and defining new supertypes. Furthermore, using the HLA I allele and haplotype gene frequencies for five major American ethnicities (Black, Caucasian, Hispanic, Native American, and Asian), we have identified combinations of supertypes that when targeted for peptide predictions are able to give a population coverage 95%, regardless of ethnicity. One of these combinations comprises 5 supertypes and is available online at our PEPVAC web server (http://immunax.dfci.harvard.edu/PEPVAC/). The selected supertypes with the included alleles (in parenthesis) are the following: A2 (A*0201-07, A*0209, A*6802), A3 (A*0301, A*1101, A*3101, A*3301, A*6801, A*6601), A24 (A*2402, B*3801), B7 (B*0702, B*3501, B*5101-02, B*5301, B*5401), B15 (A*0101, B*1501_B62, B1502). The PEPVAC resource also allows the prediction of proteasomal cleavage using language models [14]. Identification of promiscuous peptide binders to these supertypes using PEPVAC reduces the total number of predicted epitopes without compromising population coverage, thus being useful for the design of multi-epitope vaccines.

2   Matherial and Methods

2.1   MHCI-Peptide Binding Repertoire

Peptide-binding repertoires of the 55 HLA I molecules considered in this study consisted of sets of peptides that were predicted to bind to the relevant HLA I molecules. Peptide binding predictions were obtained from a random protein of 1000 amino acids in length (swiss-prot amino acid distribution), using position specific scoring matrices

(PSSMs) obtained from aligned peptides known to bind to that HLA I molecule [9, 10]. The peptide binding repertoire for each HLA I molecule consisted of the 2% top scoring peptides, and thus was composed of 20 peptides. PSSMs used in this study were all obtained from peptides of 9 residues in length (9mers), and thereby predicted peptide binders were all 9mers.

2.2 Supertype Construction

HLA I supertypes were derived by clustering the peptide-binding repertoire overlap of HLA I as it is illustrated in Fig. 1. First, the overlap between the peptidebinding repertoire of any two pairs of HLA I molecules was computed as the number of peptides binders shared by the two HLA I molecules. Let that number be n_{ij}, where i and j, represent the peptide binding repertoire of the HLA I molecules i and j, respectively. Subsequently, a distance coefficient (d_{ij}) was obtained as follows:

$$d_{ij} = N - n_{ij} \tag{1}$$

Where N is the total number of peptides considered in the predicted peptide binding repertoire of any HLA I molecule, and is equal to 20 (peptide binding repertoire consisted 2% of top scoring peptides from a random protein of 1000 amino acids; see above). Thus, if the peptide binding repertoire between two HLA I molecules is identical, then $d_{ij} = 0$. Alternatively, if they share no peptides in common, then $d_{ij} = 20$. Consequently, a quadratic distance matrix was derived containing the d_{ij} coefficient for all distinct pair of HLA I molecules. Finally, clustering of the peptide-binding overlap was carried from this distance matrix using the clustering algorithms in the Phylogeny Inference Package (PHYLIP) [15], and the relationship were visualized in the form of a phylogenic tree.

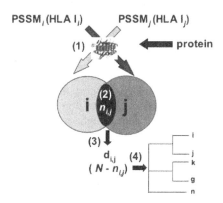

Fig. 1. Overview of the method followed for the identification HLA I supertypes. HLA I supertypes are identified by clustering their peptide binding repertoire (Materials and Methods).The method consists of 4 basis step. (1) Prediction of the peptide biding repertoire (*i,j* sets in figure) of each HLA I molecule from the same random protein using the relevant PSSMs in combination with the RANKPEP scoring algorithm [9]. (2) Compute the number of common peptides between the binding repertoire of any two HLA I molecules. (3) Build a distance matrix whose coefficients are inversely proportional to the peptide binding overlap between any pair of HLA I molecules. (4) Use a phylogenic clustering algorithm to compute and visualize HLA I supertypes (clusters of HLA I molecules with overlapping peptide binding repertoires).

3   Results and Discussion

3.1   Identification of HLA I Supertypes

Sidney, Sette and co-workers [12, 13](hereafter Sidney-Sette et al) described the first HLA I supertypes by carefully inspection of the reported peptide binding motifs of individual HLA alleles. While we acknowledge the pioneering work of these authors, the relationships between peptide binding specificities of HLA molecules may be too subtle to be defined by visual inspection of these peptide binding motifs. Furthermore, such sequence patterns have proven to be too simple to describe the binding ability of a peptide to a given MHC molecule [16, 17]. In view of these limitations, we have developed an alternative method to define HLA supertypes (outlined in Fig. 1 and described in Material and Methods). The core of the method consists of the generation of a distance matrix whose coefficients are inversely proportional to the peptide binders shared by any two HLA molecules (Fig. 1). Subsequently, this distance matrix is fed to a phylogenic clustering algorithm to establish the kinship among the distinct HLA peptide binding repertoires. Fig. 2 shows a phylogenic tree built upon the peptide binding repertoire of 55 HLA I molecules using a Fitch and Margoliash clustering algorithm [18]. In this representation, HLA I alleles with overlapping peptide binding repertoires (similar peptide binding specificities) branch together in groups or clusters, and we have identified as supertypes those clusters including alleles with at least a 20% overlap in their peptide-binding repertoire (pairwise)(highlighted in Fig. 2). It is important to indicate, that relationships between the HLA I peptide binding specificities noted in this study are restricted by the available HLA I binding repertoires obtained using our profiles, and relationships might shift in the future as the result of increasing the number of HLA I binding repertoires considered. As expected, our analysis indicates that the overlap between the peptide binding specificities of HLA I molecules is mostly confined to alleles belonging to the same gene. Nevertheless, it has also become apparent that peptidebinding overlap exists between alleles belonging to the HLA-A and HLA-B genes (Fig. 2, B15 cluster; B*4402 and A*2902; and A*2402 and B*3801). Relationships between the peptide binding specificities of HLA-A and HLA-B alleles (as well as new defined supertypes) would need experimental confirmation, but nevertheless it suggest that peptide-vaccine development would benefit from this inter gene cross-presentation. Cross-presentation of peptide in the context of two different HLA I genes might increase the frequency at which a peptide is recognized, thereby increasing its potential immunogenicity.

3.2   Supertypes and Population Coverage Studies

Supertypes defined in this study include the A2, A3, B7, B27 and B44 supertypes previously identified by Sidney-Sette et al. In our analysis, the alleles included in these supertypes match very well to those described earlier. However, there are discrepancies that extent beyond the limits imposed by the availability of profiles to obtain the peptide binding repertoire to specific HLA I alleles. The B27 supertype we defined here is more restricted than that proposed by Sidney-Sette et al, that also included the B*1509, B*1510, and B*3801 alleles, among others. The B7 supertype defined by Sidney-Sette et al. included the B*1508 allele, whereas in our analysis,

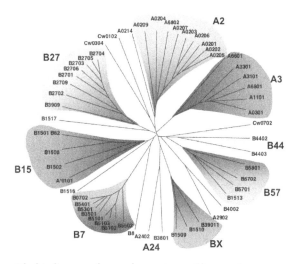

Fig. 2. *HLA I peptide binding overlap and supertypes.* Figures shows an unroot dendrogram built after clustering the overlap between the peptide-binding repertoire of the indicated HLA I molecules. The dendrogram reflects the relationship between the peptide-binding specificities of HLA I molecules. HLA I alleles with similar peptide binding specificities branch together in groups or cluster. The closer HLA I alleles branch, the larger is the overlap between their peptide-binding repertoires. Supertypes (shadowed with different colors) consist of groups HLA I alleles with at least a 20% peptide binding overlap (pairwise between any pair of alleles).

B*1508 cluster with the A*0101, and B*1501-02 alleles (Fig. 1, B15 supertype). Sidney-Sette et al also described a potential A24 supertype including the alleles A*2301, A*2402 and A*3001. We do not have profiles for the prediction of peptide binding to A*2301 or A*3001, but nevertheless with the available profiles the A*2402 binding specificity seems to be closer to that of B*3801. In addition, a new interesting peptide binding relationship includes that between the A*2902 and B*4002 alleles. Also, following our study we have defined two new supertypes, BX and B57. The BX supertype would include the alleles B*1509, B*1510 and B*39011, and B57 includes the alleles B*5801, B*5701-02, and B*1513.

Table 1. Cumulative phenotype frequency of defined supertypes

Supertype	Alleles	Blacks	Caucasians	Hispanics	*N.A.Natives	Asians
A2	A*0201-7, A*6802	43.7%	49.9%	51.8%	52.4%	44.7%
A3	A*0301, A*1101, A*3101, A*3301, A*6801, A*6601	35.4%	46.9%	41.5%	40.7%	47.9%
B7	B*0702, B*3501, B*5101-02, B*5301, B*5401	45.9%	42.2%	40.5%	52.0%	31.3%
B15	A*0101, B*1501_B62, B1502	13.06%	37.80%	16.75%	27.26%	21.04%
A24	A*2402, B*3801	15.5%	17.28%	25.85%	41.94%	35.0%
B44	B*4402, B*4403	10.4%	27.7%	17.15%	14.4%	10.1%
B57	B5701-02, B5801, B*1503	19.2%	10.3%	5.9%	5.8%	16.5%
ABX	A*2902, B*4002	7.4%	11.3%	19.1%	16.3%	16.3%
B27	B*2701-06, B*2709, B*3909	2.3%	4.8%	5.1%	16.9%	4.7%
BX	B*1509, B*1510, B*39011	3.1%	0.7%	4.2%	7.8%	4.1%

Cumulative phenotype frequency was obtained using the HLA I gene and haplotype frequencies published by published by Cao et al [19] corresponding to the indicated 5 American ethnic groups. Method for computing the cumulative phenotype frequency considered the disequilibrium linkage between the HLA-A and -B gene and was based on that reported by Dawson et al [20] *North American Natives.

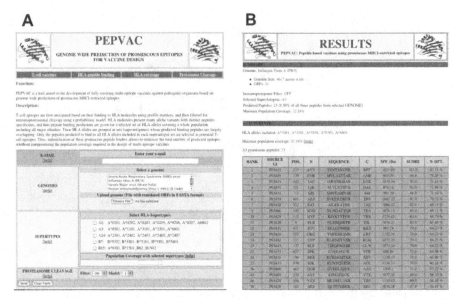

Fig. 3. *The PEPVAC web server.* A) PEPVAC input page. The page is divided into the following sections: E-MAIL, GENOMES, SUPERTYPES, AND PROTEASOMAL CLEAVAGE. Basically, the server allows the targetting of pathogenic organisms (GENOMES section) for the prediction of promiscuous peptide binders to any combination of the supertypes A2, A3, B7, A24, and B15. The CPF of the selected supertypes is calculated on-the-fly and shown on the relevant window. Prediction of proteasomal cleavage using three optimal language models are carried out in parallel to the peptide binding predictions (PROTEASOMAL CLEAVAGE section). B) PEPVAC result page. In the example shown, the A3 supertype was selected for peptide binding predictions from the genome of *Influenza A virus*. The result page first displays a summary of the predictions which reports the chosen selections, the number of predicted peptides and the minimum population coverage provided by the supertypic selection, followed by the predicted peptide binders to each of the selected supertypes. Peptides are ranked by score, and are predicted to bind to all alleles included in the supertype. Relevant information about each sorted peptide includes its protein source as well as its molecular weight. Peptides shown in violet contain a C-terminal residue that is predicted to be the result of proteasomal cleavage. If the proteasomal cleavage filter is checked ON in the input page, only violet peptides will be shown.

The cumulative phenotypic frequency (CPF) of the supertypes defined in this study is shown in Table 1. CPF was calculated by 5 distinct American ethic groups (Black, Caucasian, Hispanic, North America Natives and Asian), and it represents the population coverage that would be provided by a vaccine consisting of epitopes restricted by the alleles included in the supertype. The A2, A3 and B7 supertypes have the largest CPF in the 5 studied ethnic groups, and in fact, taken together, they provide a CPF close to 90%, irrespective of ethnicity. To increase the population coverage to 95% regardless of ethnicity it is necessary to include at least two more supertypes. Specifically, the supertypes A2, A3, B7, B15 and A24 or B44 represent the minimal supertypic combination with the largest population coverage. Note that the supertype B57, despite its quite large CPF, is not included in this minimal supertypic combination since alleles in the B57 supertype are in linkage disequilibrium with other alleles included in more prevalent supertypes.

3.3 Tool for the Design of Epitope-Based Vaccines

Prediction of promiscuous peptide-binders of supertypes that include highly prevalent alleles in the human population provides a head start to the development of broadly covering epitope-based vaccines. With that objective, we have implemented a tool that allow the prediction of promiscuous peptide binders to the supertypes A2, A3, B7, B15 and A24 (Fig. 1 and Table 1), which have a CPF greater than 95%, irrespective of ethnicity. We named this tool PEPVAC (Promiscous Epitopes based VACcines), and it is online at the site http://immunax.dfci.harvard.edu/PEPVAC/ hosted by the Molecular Immunology Foundation/Dana-Farber Cancer Institute. The web interface to PEPVAC (shown in Fig. 3A) allows targetting of any combination of the mentioned selected supertypes, displaying CPF of the selected supertypes.

MHCI-restricted epitopes derive from protein fragments generated by the protease activity of the proteasome, and it is thought that the C-terminus of any MHCIrestricted epitope is the result of the original proteasomal cleavage [21]. Consequently, in PEPVAC we have combined the predictions of promiscuous supertypic peptide binders using profiles, with probabilistic models that indicate whether a C-terminus of a given peptide is likely be the result of proteosomal cleavage. Probabilistic models for proteasomal cleavage were generated from a set of known epitopes restricted by human HLA I molecules, as indicated elsewhere [14]. Promiscuous peptide binders containing a C-terminal end predicted to be the result of proteasomal cleavage are shown in violet in the result page (Fig. 3. B). Threshold for the prediction of promiscuous peptide binders in PEPVAC have been fixed to provide a reduced and manageable set of promiscuous peptide-binders to each supertype. As an example, predicted promiscuous peptides to the above 5 supertypes from a genome such as that of *Influenza virus A* (4160 amino acids distributed in 10 distinct open reading frames (ORF)), represents only 5.51% (254 9mer peptides) of all possible peptides (4617 9mer peptides). Furthermore, this figure further contracts to 170 peptides (3.7% of all 9mer peptides from *Influenza virus A* genome) if only those peptides that are predicted to be cleaved by the proteasome are considered. Thus, PEPVAC is well fit to provide genome-wide predictions of promiscuous HLA I restricted epitopes at a practical scale for the development multi-epitope vaccines against pathogenic organisms and offering a broad population coverage.

Acknowledgments. This manuscript was supported by NIH grant AI50900 and the Molecular Immunology Foundation. We wish to acknowledge John-Paul Glutting for programming assistance.

References

1. Margulies, D.H., *Interactions of TCRs with MHC-peptide complexes: a quantitative basis for mechanistic models.* Curr Opin Immunol, Vol. **9** (1997) 390-5.
2. Garcia, K.C., L. Teyton, and I.A. Wilson, *Structural basis of T cell recognition.* Annu Rev Immunol, Vol. **17** (1999) 369-397.
3. Wang, J.-H. and E. Reinherz, *Structural basis of T cell recognition of peptides bound to MHC molecules.* Molecular Immunology, Vol. **38** (2001) 1039-1049.

4. Draenert, R., et al., *Comparison of overlapping peptide sets for detection of antiviral CD8 and CD4 T cell responses.* J Immunol Methods, Vol. **275** (2003) 19-29.
5. Zinkernagel, R.M. and P.C. Doherty, *Restriction of in vitro T cell-mediated cytotoxicity in lymphocytic choriomeningitis within a syngeneic or semiallogeneic system.* Nature, Vol. **248** (1974) 701-702.
6. Falk, K., et al., *Allele-specific motifs revealed by sequencing of self-peptides eluted from MHC molecules.* Nature, Vol. **351** (1991) 290-296.
7. Rammensee, H.G., T. Friede, and S. Stevanoviic, *MHC ligands and peptide motifs: first listing.* Immunogenetics, Vol. **41** (1995) 178-228.
8. Gribskov, M., A.D. McLachlan, and D. Eisenberg, *Profile analysis: detection of distantly related proteins.* Proc Natl Acad Sci USA, Vol. **84** (1987) 4355-4358.
9. Reche, P.A., J.P. Glutting, and E.L. Reinherz, *Prediction of MHC class I binding peptides using profile motifs.* Hum Immunol, Vol. **63** (2002) 701-9.
10. Reche, P.A. and E.L. Reinherz, *Sequence variability analysis of human class I and class II MHC molecules: functional and structural correlates of amino acid polymorphisms.* J Mol Biol, Vol. **331** (2003) 623-41.
11. David W. Gjertson and Paul I. Terasaki, E., *HLA 1998.* (1998).
12. Sette, A. and J. Sidney, *Nine major HLA class I supertypes account for the vast preponderance of HLA-A and -B polymorphism.* Immunogenetics, Vol. **50** (1999) 201-12.
13. Sette, A. and J. Sidney, *HLA supertypes and supermotifs: a functional perspective on HLA polymorphism.* Curr Opin Immunol, Vol. **10** (1998) 478-82.
14. Reche, P.A., J.-P. Glutting, and E.L. Reinherz, *Enhancement to the RANKPEP resource for the prediction of peptide binding to MHC molecules using profiles.* Immunogenetics, Vol. **Submitted** (2004).
15. Retief, J.D., *Phylogenetic analysis using PHYLIP.* 132 (2000) 243-58.
16. Bouvier, M. and D.C. Wiley, *Importance of peptide amino acid and carboxyl termini to the stability of MHC class I molecules.* Science, Vol. **265** (1994) 398-402.
17. Ruppert, J., et al., *Prominent role of secondary anchor residues in peptide binding to HLA-A2.1 molecules.* Cell, Vol. **74** (1993) 929-937.
18. Fitch, W.M. and E. Margoliash, *Construction of phylogenetic trees.* Science, Vol. **155** (1967) 279-84.
19. Cao, K., et al., *Analysis of the frequencies of HLA-A, B, and C alleles and haplotypes in the five major ethnic groups of the United States reveals high levels of diversity in these loci and contrasting distribution patterns in these populations.* Hum Immunol, Vol. **62** (2001) 1009-30.
20. Dawson, D.V., et al., *Ramifications of HLA class I polymorphism and population genetics for vaccine development.* Genet Epidemiol, Vol. **20** (2001) 87-106.
21. Craiu, A., et al., *Two distinct proteolytic processes in the generation of a major histocompatibility complex class I-presented peptide.* Proc Natl Acad Sci U S A, Vol. **94** (1997) 10850-5.

BcePred: Prediction of Continuous B-Cell Epitopes in Antigenic Sequences Using Physico-chemical Properties

Sudipto Saha and G.P.S. Raghava*

Institute of Microbial Technology, Bioinformatics centre
Sector 39A, Chandigarh, INDIA
raghava@imtech.res.in

Abstract. A crucial step in designing of peptide vaccines involves the identification of B-cell epitopes. In past, numerous methods have been developed for predicting continuous B-cell epitopes, most of these methods are based on physico-chemical properties of amino acids. Presently, its difficult to say which residue property or method is better than the others because there is no independent evaluation or benchmarking of existing methods. In this study the performance of various residue properties commonly used in B-cell epitope prediction has been evaluated on a clean dataset. The dataset used in this study consists of 1029 non-redundant B cell epitopes obtained from Bcipep database and equally number of non-epitopes obtained randomly from SWISS-PROT database. The performance of each residue property used in existing methods has been computed at various thresholds on above dataset. The accuracy of prediction based on properties varies between 52.92% and 57.53%. We have also evaluated the combination of two or more properties as combination of parameters enhance the accuracy of prediction. Based on our analysis we have developed a method for predicting B cell epitopes, which combines four residue properties. The accuracy of this method is 58.70%, which is slightly better than any single residue property. A web server has been developed to predict B cell epitopes in an antigen sequence. The server is accessible from http://www.imtech.res.in/raghava/bcepred/.

1 Introduction

The antigenic regions of protein that are recognized by the binding sites or paratopes of immunoglobulin molecules are called B-cell epitopes. These epitopes play a vital role in designing peptide-vaccines and in disease diagnosis. These epitopes provide information for the synthesis of peptides that induces cross-reacting antibodies, thereby promoting in the development of synthetic peptide vaccines [1]. The Bioinformatics approach of prediction of immunogenic epitopes remains challenging but vital. The inherent complexity of immune presentation and recognition processes complicates epitope prediction [2]. Number of methods has been developed for predicting B cell epitopes, which are based on physico-chemical properties of the amino acids [3]. Hopps and Woods [4] used hydrophilic analysis (on twelve proteins) to investigate the possibility that at least some antigenic determinants might be associ-

---

* Corresponding author.

G. Nicosia et al. (Eds.): ICARIS 2004, LNCS 3239, pp. 197–204, 2004.

ated with stretches of amino acids sequence that contain charged and polar residue and lack large hydrophobic residue. Parker et al. [5] use the modified hydrophilic scale based on peptide retention times during high-performance liquid chromatography (HPLC) on a reversed-phase column. Karplus and Schulz [6] suggested a link between antigenicity and segmental mobility and developed a method for predicting mobility of protein segments on the basis of the known temperature B factors of the a-carbons of 31 proteins of known structure. They utilize the flexibility scale for predicting the B-cell epitopes. Emini et al., [7] developed method for predicting epitopes based on surface accessibility of the amino acids. Kolaskar and Tongaonkar [8] derived their own scale of antigenicity based on frequency of residues in 169 experimentally known epitopes. Pellequer et al., [9] derived turn scales based on the occurrence of amino acids at each of the four positions of a turn using a structural database comprised of 87 proteins. The turn scales correctly predicted 70% of the known epitopes.

A number of computer programs have also been developed to assist the users in predicting epitopes in an antigen sequence. Pellequer and Westhof [10] developed program PREDITOP that utilize the 22 normalized scales, corresponding to hydrophilicity, accessibility, flexibility and secondary structure propensities. Another program PEOPLE [11] use combined prediction methods, taking into account physicochemical properties like b turns, surface accessibility, hydrophilicity and flexibility. PEOPLE have been applied for prediction of only two proteins, tropoelastin and antigen protein P30 of Toxoplasma gondii. The BEPITOPE [12] program aims at predicting continuous protein epitopes and searching for patterns in either a single protein or a complete translated genome. This program provide various options like i) selecting any residue property (e.g. hydrophilicity, flexibility, protein accessibility, turns scale); ii) graphical interface so that users can decide the antigenic region; and iii) combining two and more parameters.

It is not practically possible to evaluate all these methods and programs in their original form because many of these programs are not freely available, while some provides qualitative information (visualization etc.) rather than quantitative. Most of these programs are not automatic where you can give the query sequence and get the predicted epitopes. The selection of threshold is another problem. Thus, we have evaluated the various residue properties, which are commonly used in these existing methods rather than methods as such. As far as authors know, no study has been carried out in the past to evaluate these residues properties on large and uniform dataset of experimentally determined B cell epitopes. In this study, we have also evaluated two new properties, polarity and exposed surface area. The effect of combination of two or more properties on accuracy of predicting of B cell epitopes has also been determined in addition to individual properties.

It has been observed that the combination of two or more properties gives better accuracy than individual property, which agree with previous observations [12]. Based on these observations, a web server has been developed for predicting B cell epitopes in an antigenic sequence. This is almost similar to stand alone computer program BEPITOPE except that this is a web server, which allows on-line computation over Internet.

2   Materials and Methods

Data set: B-cell epitopes have been obtained from Bcipep database [13; See http://www.imtech.res.in/raghava/bcipep/ or
http://bioinformatics.uams.edu/mirror/bcipep/], which contains 2479 continuous epitopes, including 654 immunodominant, 1617 immunogenic epitopes. All the identical epitopes and non-immunogenic peptides were removed, yielding 1029 unique experimentally proved continuous B cell epitopes. The dataset covers a wide range of pathogenic group like virus, bacteria, protozoa and fungi. The final dataset consists of 1029 B-cell epitopes and 1029 non-epitopes or random peptides (equal length and same frequency generated from SWISS-PROT [14].

Measure of prediction accuracy: Both threshold dependent and independent measures have been used to evaluate the prediction performance. The threshold dependent measures include standard parameters such as sensitivity, specificity and accuracy. The parameter ROC has been used as threshold independent measure.

Brief description of existing methods:
Parker Method: In this method, hydrophilic scale based on peptide retention times during high-performance liquid chromatography (HPLC) on a reversed-phase column was constructed [5]. A window of seven residues was used for analyzing epitope region. The corresponding value of the scale was introduced for each of the seven residues and the arithmetical mean of the seven residue value was assigned to the fourth, (i+3), residue in the segment.

Karplus Method: In this method, flexibility scale based on mobility of protein segments on the basis of the known temperature B factors of the a-carbons of 31 proteins of known structure was constructed [6]. The calculation based on a flexibility scale is similar to classical calculation, except that the center is the first amino acid of the six amino acids window length, and there were three scales for describing flexibility instead of a single one. In the present study, 3Karplus scale has been used for prediction of the epitope region.

Emini Method: The calculation was based on surface accessibility scale on a product instead of an addition within the window. The accessibility profile was obtained using the formulae

$$Sn = (\prod_{i=1}^{6} \delta_{n+4+i}) (0.37)^{-6} \qquad (1)$$

Where Sn is the surface probability, dn is the fractional surface probability value, and i vary from 1 to 6. A hexapeptide sequence with Sn equal to unity and probability greater than 1.0 indicates an increased chance for being found on the surface [7].

Pellequer Method: This method is based on incidence of b turns [10]. The calculation was based on a turn scale and there were three scales for describing turns instead of a single one. A window of seven residues is used for analyzing epitope region. The corresponding value of the scale was introduced for each of the seven residues and the arithmetical mean of the seven residue value is assigned to the fourth, (i+3), residue in the segment. Gaussian smoothing curve was used, which assigns the residue weights in a window of seven residues (the weights were 0.05/0.11/0.19/0.22/0.19/0.11/0.05).

Kolaskar Method: In this method, 156 antigenic determinants (< 20 amino acids) in 34 different proteins were analyzed [8] to calculate the antigenic propensity (Ap) of residues. This antigenic scale was used to predict the epitopes in sequence.

Exposed surface scale and Polarity scale: The physico-chemical properties like exposed surface (15) and polarity [16] has also been evaluated in this study. A window of seven residues has been used for analyzing the epitope region. The corresponding value of the scale has been introduced for each of the seven residues and the arithmetical mean of the seven residue value is assigned to the fourth, (i+3), residue in the segment.

2.1 Normalization Procedure

Each property scale consists of 20 values assigned to each of the amino acid types on the basis of their relative propensity as described by the scale. In order to compare the profiles obtained by different methods, normalization of the various scales has been done. We have calculated the average of seven maximum and seven minimum values of a given physico-chemical scale and then calculated the difference between the two. The original values of the each scale are set between +3 to –3 by using the formulae

$$\text{Normalization Score} = \frac{AMS}{DS} * 6 \tag{2}$$

Where AMS refer to Average of seven maximum/minimum values from the physico-chemical scale and DS refer to difference between the maximum and minimum score. Normalization score are set to +3 (Maximum) and –3 (Minimum) by subtracting or adding additional values.

3   Results and Discussion

We have evaluated seven different physico-chemical scales as implemented in existing epitope prediction methods on the B-cell epitope dataset. The performance of all these methods are threshold dependent, so we select threshold value for each scale at which sensitivity and specificity are nearly equal. The performance of various property scales is shown in Table 1. As shown in Table 1 the performance of all the methods is poor and accuracy varies between 52.92% and 57.53%. It has been observed that flexibility as implemented by Karplus and Schulz [6], relatively perform better than any other property scale used in the past. We observe that some methods have higher sensitivity but lower specificity value or vice-versa (Table 1). This fact makes it difficult to compare the methods objectively. Therefore, we use a single threshold independent measure of performance called the Receiver Operating Characteristics (ROC), to assess the performance of the methods [17]. ROC plot, 1-specificity vs sensitivity from threshold –1.5 to 3 has been computed. It is clear from the ROC plot (Figure 1) that the flexibility property based method performs better in comparison to other methods.

Table 1. The performance of various residue properties in B-cell epitope prediction.

Physico-chemical Properties	Threshold	Sensitivity	Specificity	Accuracy% (Max)
Hydrophilicity [1]## (Parker et al., 1986)**	2.00	33	76	54.47
Accessibility[2] (Emini et al., 1985)	2.00	65	46	55.49
Flexibility [3] (Karplus and Schulz, 1985)	**1.90**	**47**	**68**	**57.53**
Surface [4] (Janin and Wodak, 1978)	2.40	37	74	55.73
Polarity [5] (Ponnuswamy et al., 1980)	2.30	2.8	81	54.08
Turns [6] (Pellequer et al., 199)	1.90	17	89	52.92
Antigenic Scale [7] (Kolaskar and Tongaonkar, 1990)	1.80	59	52	55.59
[3]+[1]	2.00	53	64	58.31
[3]+[1]+[5]	2.30	50	68	58.70
[3]+[1]+[5]+[4]	**2.38**	**56**	**61**	**58.70**
[3]+[1]+[5]+[4]+[6]	2.38	59	58	58.41
[3]+[1]+[5]+[4]+[6]+[2]	2.38	60	56	57.97

Residue property number, for each property a number is assigned. [3]+[1] means combination of Flexibility and Hydrophilicity.** Reference, which describes property scale used .

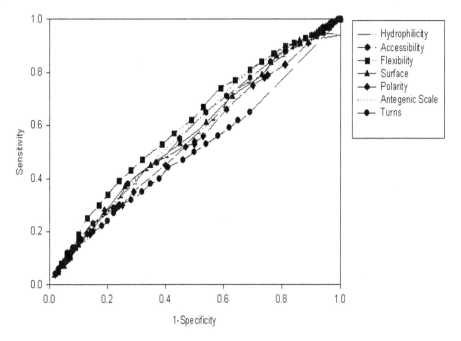

Fig. 1. ROC plot of various residue properties.

SUBMISSION FORM

Sequence name (optional) : Test

Paste your sequence below:
(Amino acid sequence in one lettercode. No header line)

Or Submit sequences from file :   Browse...

Threshold [-3 to 3] :

Hydrophilicity:	2.0	**Flexibility:**	1.9
Accessibility:	2.0	**Turns:**	1.9
Exposed Surface:	2.4	**Polarity:**	2.3
Antegenic Propensity:	1.8	**Combined:**	2.38

Select physico-chemical properties to use:
For multiple selection use Ctrl Key

Hydrophilicity (Parker et al., Biochemistry, 25, 5425 (1986))
Flexibility (Karplus et al., Naturwissenschaften, 72, 212 (1985))
Accessibility (Emini et al., J.virol., 55, 836 (1985))
Turns (Pellequer et al., Immunol.Lett., 36, 8 3(1993))

Clear fields   Submit sequence

(a)

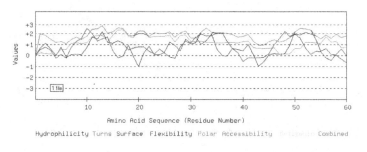

GRAPHICAL RESULT :: SEQ 1 to 60

(b)

Fig. 2. (a). The display of BcePred server submission form (b). The display of BcePred server graphical output

In order to see the effect of combination of properties, we have combined the best parameter, flexibility, with other properties one-by-one. It is found that on combination of hydrophilicity and flexibility, the algorithm performs marginally better (accuracy 58.31 %) than any single property or combination of any other two properties. After trying various combinations it is found that combination of properties hydrophilicity, flexibility, polarity and exposed surface performs better than any other combination at a threshold of 2.38. Though combination achieved accuracy 58.70%, sensitivity 56 % and specificity 61% but overall performance is quite poor. The results suggest that for a large dataset the performance of all methods or properties is much below than that is claimed. In past most methods were examined on small set of below than that is claimed. In past most methods were examined on small set of epitopes and property scales were derived from same epitopes (i.e., same training and testing dataset). It is important to have non-epitopes along with true epitopes to evaluate any threshold dependent method. Earlier non-epitopes were not used in any evaluation. Therefore, most methods never considered the possibility of over prediction. In the present study, we have considered random peptides obtained from SWISS-PROT as non-epitopes. We felt this as necessary since there is no existing database of B-cell non-epitopes.

3.1 Web Server

The server BcePred allows user to predict B cell epitopes in protein sequences. As shown in Figure 2a one can submit and can select any residue property or combination of two or more properties as well as threshold to be used for epitope prediction. It presents the results in graphical and tabular frame. An example of graphical output of BcePred is shown in Figure 2b. In case of graphical frame, server plots the residue properties along protein backbone, which assist the users in rapid visualization of B-cell epitope on protein. The peak of the amino acid residue segment above the threshold value (default is 2.38) is considered as predicted B-cell epitope. The tabular output is in the form of a table, which will give the normalized score of the selected properties with the corresponding amino acid residue of a protein along with the maximum, minimum and average values of the combined methods, selected.

Acknowledgment. We are thankful to Mr Biju Issac for assisting in graphic display of the output format of BcePred server. We also thank Mr Manoj Bhasin and Miss Harpreet Kaur for their help in writing web programs. We gratefully acknowledge the financial support from the Council of Scientific and Industrial Research (CSIR) and Department of Biotechnology (DBT), Govt. of India.

References

1. Nicholson.B.H.: Experimental determination of immunogenic sites. In "Synthetic Vaccines", Published by Blackwell scientific publications, London. (1994) 137-168.
2. Flower,D.R.: Towards in silico prediction of immunogenic epitopes. TRENDS in immunology, 24 (2003) 667-674
3. Pellequer,J.L., Westhof,E. and Regenmortel, M.H.V.: Predicting location of continuous epitopes in proteins from their primary structures. Methods in enzymology, 203 (1991) 176-201.
4. Hopp,T.P. and Woods,R.K.: Predictions of protein antigenic determinants from amino acid sequences. Proc. Natl. Acad. Sci. USA., 78 (1981) 3824-3828.
5. Parker,J.M.D., Guo,D. and Hodges,R.S.: New hydrophilicity scale derived from high-performance liquid chromatography peptide retention data: correlation of predicted surface residues with antigenicity and X-ray-derived accessible sites. Biochemistry, 25 (1986) 5425-5432.
6. Karplus,P.A. and Schulz,G.E.: Prediction of chain flexibility in proteins: a tool for the selection of peptide antigen. Naturwissenschaften, 72 (1985) 212-213.

7. Emini,E.A., Hughes,J.V., Perlow,D.S. and Boger,J.: Induction of hepatitis A virus-neutralizing antibody by a virus-specific synthetic peptide. J.Virol., 55 (1985) 836-839.
8. Kolaskar, A.S. and Tongaonkar,P.C.: A semi-emperical method for prediction of antigenic determinants on protein antigens. FEBS, 276 (1990) 172-174.
9. Pellequer,J-L., Westhof,E. and Regenmortel M.H.V.: Correlation between the location of antigenic sites and the prediction of turns in proteins Immunol.Lett., 36, (1993) 83-99.
10. Pellequer.J.L and Wasthof.: PREDITOP: A program for antigenicity prediction. J. Mol. Graphics., 11 (1993) 204-210.
11. Alix AJ. (1999) Predictive estimation of protein linear epitopes by using the program PEOPLE. Vaccine, 18, 311-314.
12. Odorico, M. and Pellequer, J.L. (2003) BEPITOPE: predicting the location of continuous epitope and patterns in proteins. J Mol Recognit., 16, 20-22.
13. Saha,S., Bhasin,M. and Raghava,G.P.S.: Bcipep: A database of B cell epitopes. (2004) (Submitted)
14. Bairoch,A. and Apweiler,R.: The SWISS-PROT protein sequence database and its supplement TrEMBL in 2000. Nucleic Acids Res., 28 (2000) 45-48.
15. Janin,J. and Wodak,S.: Conformation of amino acid side-chains in proteins. J.Mol.Biol., 125 (1978) 357-86.
16. Ponnuswamy,P.K., Prabhakaran,M. and Manavalan,P.: Hydrophobic packing and spatial arrangements of amino acid residues in globular proteins. Biochim.Biophys.Acta., 623, (1980) 301-316.
17. Deleo,J.M.: Proceedings of the Second International Symposium on Uncertainity Modelling and Analusis. IEEE. Computer Society Press,College Park, MD. (1993) 318-325 .

Integration of Immune Models
Using Petri Nets⋆

Dokyun Na, Inho Park, Kwang H. Lee, and Doheon Lee⋆⋆

Department of BioSystems, KAIST
373-1, Guseong-dong, Yuseong-gu, Daejon 305-701, Republic of Korea
dhlee@bisl.kaist.ac.kr

Abstract. Immune system has unique defense mechanisms such as innate, humoral and cellular immunity. These immunities are closely related to prevent pathogens from spreading in host and to clear them
effectively. To achieve those mechanisms, particular processes, such as
clonal expansion, positive and negative selection, and somatic hypermutation and so on, have been evolved. These properties inspired people
to open a new field, called artificial immune systems that mimics and
modifies immune behaviors to invent new technologies in other fields.
To explain immune mechanisms, many mathematical models focusing
on one particular phenomenon were developed. We developed an integrated immune model that enables to understand immune responses as
a whole and to find new emergent properties of the immune system that
could not be seen in separate models. We used a continuous Petri net as
modeling language, because of its easiness of modeling and analysis.

1   Introduction

The immune system is our defense mechanism against pathogens or abnormal
cells. Immune system consists of a few defense mechanisms such as innate [1,
2], humoral [3,4], and cellular immune responses [5,6,7,8], and many particular
processes, such as self-nonself discrimination [9,10], clonal expansion [3,11] and
somatic hypermutation [12]. Innate immunity is a first barrier to protect host
from pathogens [1,2]. In this response, for example, macrophages recognize common features of bacteria and clear them [13,14]. In humoral immunity, B cells
recognize foreign materials [15] called antigens(Ag). The antigen-recognized B
cells are induced to proliferate and differentiate into effector cells by helper T
cells(T_H) that were already activated by antigen-encountered antigen-presenting
cells(APC) [16,17]. Then effector B cells produce antibodies(Ab) to neutralize
Ag [18]. In cellular immunity, infected APC activates cytotoxic T cells (T_C), and

⋆ This work was supported by the Korean Systems Biology Research Grant (M1-
  0309-02-0002) from the Ministry of Science and Technology. We would like to thank
  CHUNG Moon Soul Center for BioInformation and BioElectronics and the IBM
  SUR program for providing research and computing facilities.
⋆⋆ To whom correspondance should be addressed.

G. Nicosia et al. (Eds.): ICARIS 2004, LNCS 3239, pp. 205–216, 2004.

then the activated T_C proliferates and differentiates into effector T cells [19]. After differentiation, these T_C recognizes and kills infected cells presenting viral peptides on their surface receptor, MHC class I[20]. These immune properties inspired to open a new field, called artificial immune systems, which applies the immune mechanisms to other fields. For example, by mimicking positive and negative selection processes in thymus, virus or network intrusion detection system was developed [21]. By using the selection processes and anergy-inducing process, a machine could be fault-tolerant [22]. By imitating affinity maturation and memorization during humoral immunity, machine could learn and find optimal solutions [23]. By using cross-reactivity of B and T cells, associative memory could tolerate memory errors [24].

To explain immunological phenomena, many models, which are based on cellular-automata(CA) [25] or differential equations [26,27], were developed. For example, IMMSIM [29] is a representative CA-based immune-specific simulator. Though CA-based models show individual properties of immune cells well, because of inefficiency in computation, this approach could not afford to simulate the whole immune system. Unlike CA-based models, differential equation-based models can show averaged properties of immune cells, so it can deal with whole immune system. But building and managing of models is not easy because of many variables and equations in a model.

Many mathematical models were developed, which explained one particular immunological phenomenon, such as germinal center formation [26,30], antigen presentation [31], cellular response against virus infection [32], humoral response against antigen [35], and innate immunity against bacteria infection [36]. Immune mechanisms are closely related in order to control and protect host from pathogens. For example, once T_{H1} is activated, the activated T_{H1} stimulates innate immune response and inhibits T_{H2} activation, thus inhibits humoral immune response, and *vice versa* [37]. Low and high Ag doses induces cellular immune response while intermediate Ag doses induce humoral immune response [38]. Virus and bacteria could induce both immune responses.

It is needed to develop a model including innate, humoral and cellular immunity to understand immune systems as a whole and to find out emergent properties which could not be seen in separate models. We developed a model using a Petri net for easy representation and modification for other uses.

2   Petri Nets

A Petri net is a graphical and mathematical modeling tool. In many fields, Petri nets are successfully used for concurrent, asynchronous, and parallel system modeling. Especially, Petri nets are used to represent biological pathways or processes [52]. Following is the definition of basic Petri net [50,51].

Definition 1. *A Petri net is a 5-tuple* $R = <P, T, F, W, M_0>$ *where* $P = \{p_1, p_2, \cdots, p_n\}$ *is a finite set of places,* $T = \{t_1, t_2, \cdots, t_n\}$ *is a finite set of transitions. The set of places and transitions are disjoint,* $P \bigcap T = \emptyset$. $F \subseteq$

(A)

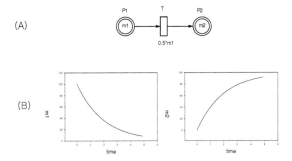

(B)

Fig. 1. Continuous Petri net. In the graphical representation of the Petri net (A), a circle represents a place and a rectangle represents a transition. Two graphs (B) show the change of value of places with respect to time

$(P \times T) \bigcup (T \times P)$ *is a set of arcs.* $W : F \rightarrow \{1, 2, 3, \cdots\}$ *is a weight function. And* $M_0 : P \rightarrow \{0, 1, 2, 3, \cdots\}$ *is the initial marking.*

The behavior of a Petri net is described in terms of changes of tokens in places according to the firing of transitions. If all of the input places of a transition have tokens more than the weight of arc between the transition and the place, the transition is enabled. Of the the enabled transitions, only one transition fire. After a transition is fired, the tokens of input places are removed as many as the weight of the arc. And the tokens of output places are added as many as weight of the arc.

Many extensions of the basic Petri net were developed. Among them, we use a continuous Petri net to reflect continuous aspects of immune system. The differences between the basic Petri net and the continuous Petri net are followings. In the continuous Petri net, place can have real value and transition fires continuously with some rate. The rate of transition is affected by the value of input places. Following is the definition of the continuous Petri net [53].

Definition 2. *A continuous Petri net is a 6-tuple* $R = < P, T, V, F, W, M_0 >$ *where* P, T, F, W, M_0 *are same to basic Petri net.* $V : T \rightarrow V(p_1, p_2, p_3, \cdots) \in R^+$ *is the firing speed function.*

In our immune model, places represent immune cells or external materials (e.g. antigen or virus) and transitions represent interactions (e.g. B cell activation by antigen).

3   Model

Our model includes simple innate immune response, T_{H1} and T_{H2} selection step, humoral immune response against antigens, and cellular immune response against infected cells.

3.1   Immune Cells

Dendritic cells(DC) and B cells are constantly produced from bone marrow, and naive T cells from thymus. We adjusted production rate of all immune cells to sustain the number of immune cells at steady state. When immunized, up to 1000 different B cells [35,39], and up to 500 different T_C cells could be activated [34]. We assumed that 200 different B and T cells exist at steady state, but they have same affinity to Ag. In case of naive T_H, because at normal condition there are about two fold greater T_H cells than T_C cell, it is assumed that there are 500 naive T_H cell at steady state [40].

3.2   Viral Infection

Virus in our model is an imaginary virus which infects and lyses host cells for reproduction. We assumed uninfected cells are produced constantly and virus could infect DC as same rate as the target cells, because DC expresses various proteins on their surface, which virus recognizes for invasion [41]. 100 virus particles are produced from each infected cell.

3.3   Innate Immunity

Innate immunity is the first defense system, when extracellular pathogens invade a host. This immune system is non-specific, but pathogen-recognized APC determines which type of helper T cell to proliferate depending on the level of Ag stimulation and type of Ag [42]. The T_H cells activated by APC are key regulators of immune responses.

Macrophages and dendritic cells are APC in innate immunity, but we simply assumed that there are only dendritic cells in innate immunity, because DC has more capability for antigen presentation. DCs could be infected by virus or could engulf and present them [41].

3.4   Helper T Cell Activation

When DC recognizes Ag or is infected by virus, the fate of DC is determined. In general, virus infected DC becomes to induce differentiation of T_{H0} to T_{H1} while Ag-engulfed DC becomes to induce T_{H0} to T_{H2} [41]. Though the fate of DC is determined by not only Ag type but also the level of stimulation [42], it is assumed that infected DC induces T_{H1} differentiation, and Ag-uptaken DC induces T_{H2} differentiation.

Once naive T cells are stimulated, they undergo a limited number of division. Naive T_C cells undergo division at least 8 times, and 15 times on average [43]. Because naive T_H cells divide fewer than T_C cells, we assumed that T_H cells undergo 10 divisions. The doubling time of T_H cell is known to be 11 hr [44]. In other words, T_H cells divide for about 5 days. As compared with T_C cell activation, T_H activation is not efficient, so we set the T_H activation rate to be less than the T_C activation rate. In order to induce T_{H2} activation, a greater level of signaling is required [42]. To satisfy this property, we adjusted T_{H2} activation rate to be less than T_{H1} activation rate.

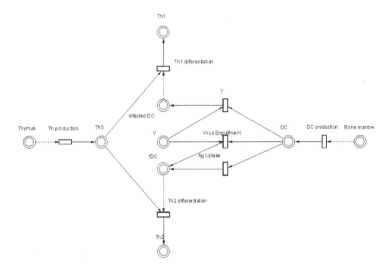

Fig. 2. A Petri net of innate immunity. In this diagram, death of immune cells and other immune responses are omitted. Ag uptake by or virus infection to DC, and T_H differentiations are shown. The reactions are simplified for easy understanding.

3.5 Cytotoxic T Cell Activation

When virus infects DC, infected DC activates T_{H0} to differentiate into T_{H1}, and then activated T_{H1} activates infected DC again. This activated DC now can activate naive T_C to differentiate into effector T_C [45].

Naive T_C cells are stimulated by an increased number of infected cell, and the stimulation level is saturable [32,33]. The level of stimulation is calculated by:

$$S(aDC) = \frac{aDC}{K + aDC} \tag{1}$$

S is the level of stimulation. aDC is infected DC which is activated by T_{H1}. K is the number of activated DC for half-maximum stimulation. We assumed that T cell and APC interaction follows above equation, and applied this stimulation equation to T_{H1} stimulation by DC, and B cell stimulation by T_{H2}.

When naive T_C receives stimulation signal, it delays about a day before starting proliferation [56]. Like T_H activation, once T_C cells are stimulated to undergo division, they divide 15 times on average even without the stimulation signal [43,46,47], and their division time is 6hr [55].

3.6 Killing Infected Cells

When effector T_C cell recognizes viral peptide on infected cells, T_C kills the infected cells. We assumed that the clearance rate of infected cell or infected DC follows the equation [48].

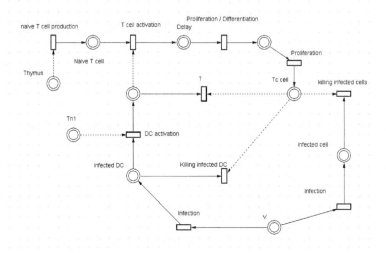

Fig. 3. A Petri net of cellular immunity

$$\text{Clearance rate} = \frac{K_C \cdot I \cdot T_C}{K_C + I + T_C} \tag{2}$$

The rate is proportional to avidity (K_C). High avidity T_C could clear infected cells more effectively than low avidity T_C. In our model, the T_C has high avidity, so K_C was set to be 7,800. Effector T_C kills not only infected target cells, but also infected DCs. Furthermore, because DC can present Ag on both MHC I and MHC II, we assumed that effector T_C could kill 10% of antigen-uptaken DC [41].

3.7   B Cell Activation

Like DC, B cell recognizes, engulfs and presents Ag. The Ag-presentation rate of naive B cell is proportional to Ag dose. This value was adopted from ref [35]. This Ag-encountered B cell is activated to proliferate by T_{H2}. As mentioned above, B cell and T_{H2} interaction follows APC-T cell interaction.

3.8   Ab Production and Ag/Ab Interaction

A plasma B cell produces 10^8 Ab/day [57]. Because 200 different B cells could be activated, 200 different Abs are produced. These Abs could bind to a single Ag. Therefore, we assumed that a single Ag could bind 200 different Abs. Since dissociation rate of Ag-Ab complex is relatively low [49], we ignore this reverse reaction.

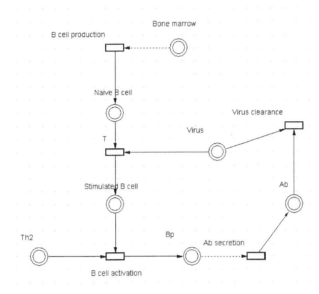

Fig. 4. A Petri net of humoral immunity

4   Results

In order to verify the model, it was applied to virus infection and immunosuppression phenomena.

First, LCMV virus infection was simulated by administering 1×10^5 viral particles and the results are shown in Fig.5. This virus replicated up to 6×10^6 particles, but due to high cytotoxicity of T_C, virus-producing cells were eliminated rapidly, and the number of virus also decreased. In Fig.5 A and B, the simulated and experimental data were shown. The number of T_C and T_{H1} cells from simulated and experimental results were not quantitatively same, but they showed qualitatively similar tendencies.

Second, immunosuppression by co-administered antibody was simulated and results are shown in Fig.6. Immunosuppression is that when antigen and antibody are co-administered, the number of antigen-specific B cell decreases rapidly and humoral response against the antigen diminishes [61]. One possible explanation is that, once B cells are stimulated, they need continuous signal from BCR(B cell receptor) for survival [62]. If they do not receive the survival signal, they eventually die by apoptosis [63]. In short, the co-administered antibody removes antigen, the source of survival signal, and then B cells, which do not receive the survival signal, die. In our simulation, 4×10^6 sheep red blood cell was administered as antigen. After one day post-administration of antibody, the number of B cell decreased (Fig.6A). As the antibody administered earlier, the degree of suppression increased (Fig.6A, B). The suppression ratio was calculated and our results were in good agreement with previous experimental results [58].

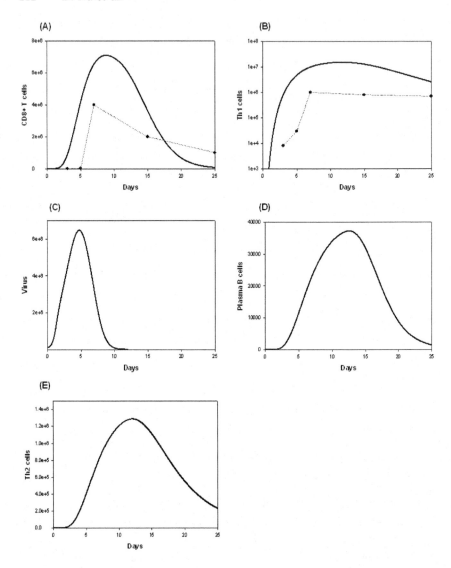

Fig. 5. LCMV infection profile. 1×10^6 LCMV particles were infected. (A) Cytotoxic T cell. Closed circles are data from previous experiment. (B) T_{H1} cell profile. (C) LCMV profile. (D) Plasma B cell profile. (E) T_{H2} cell profile.

5   Discussion

We developed the integrated immune model involving innate, humoral and cellular immunity, and used a continuous Petri net as a tool for developing and analyzing the model. The continuous Petri net could give more intuitive modeling environment than other modeling languages, such as differential equations or cellular automata.

(A)

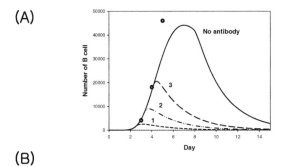

(B)

Day [a]	Antibody [b] Administration	Suppression ratio [c]	
		Simulation Results	Experimental Results
3	1	59 %	40-80 %
	2	100 %	90-100 %
4	1	13 %	20-30 %
	2	53 %	50-100 %
5	1	5 %	20 %
	2	20 %	20-25 %

Fig. 6. Humoral immune response profile when antigen and antibody are co-administered. (A) Numbers beside each curve are the number of days of antibody administration. Closed circles are the number of stimulated B cells from previous experiment when 4×10^6 SRBC was administered as antigen [58]. (B) Suppression ratios at indicated time were calculated. Experimental suppression ration was form [58].
[a] Indicated times are the number of days that data were calculated.
[b] The number of days that antibody was administered after antigen administration.
[c] suppression ratio $= \frac{Number\ of\ B\ cells\ when\ Ab\ was\ co-administered}{Number\ of\ B\ cells\ in\ control} \times 100$

Our model is not only for explaining a particular immune response, for example, immunosuppression, response against HIV [28] or infectious bacteria *M. tuboculosis* [59], but also for showing immune responses as a whole. Therefore, this model would give qualitative results rather than exact quantitative results.

Though we integrated many processes already known, because of lack of immunology knowledge, some processes rely on estimated parameters, or are missed in the model. For example, T_{H1}/T_{H2} balance hypothesis is still under debate [42], and the cytokine network [60] is not well established by experiment, so we simplified the T_H differentiation responses and removed cytokine dependent responses. As experimental results about immune processes increase, this model could have more chances to give precise results.

For many years, artificial immune systems were developed based on well known immunological processes such as clonal expansion, negative selection, and memory. Because these processes are closely related to eliminate pathogens effectively, complex network of these processes could give emergent properties that could be applied to artificial immune systems. By developing an integrated immune model, we could find out unknown emergent properties of immunity.

References

1. Fearon, D.T., Locksley, R.M.: The instinctive role of innate immunity in the acquired immune response. *Science* 272 (1996) 50-53
2. Dornand, J., Gross, A., Lafont, V .,Liautard. J, Oliaro, J., Liautard, J.P.: The innate immune response against *Brucella* in humans. *Veterinary Microbiology* 90 (2002)
3. McHeyzer-Williams, M. G.: B cells as effectors. *Curr. Opin. Immunol.* 15 (2003) 354-361
4. Baumgarth, N.: A two-phase model of B-cell activation. *Immunological Review* 176 (2000) 171-180
5. Dutton, R.W., Bradley, L.M., Swain, S.L.: T cell memory. *Annu. Rev. Immunol.* 16 (1998) 201-213
6. Lanzavecchia A.: Mechanisms of antigen uptake for presentation. *Curr. Opin. Immunol.* 8 (1996) 348-354
7. Dennert, G.: Molecular mechanism of target lysis by cytotoxic T cells. *Int. Rev. Immunol.* 14 (1997) 133-152
8. Rosen, H.R.: Hepatitis C pathogenesis: mechanisms of viral clearance and liver injury. *Liver Transplantation* 9 (2003) S35-S43
9. Surh, C.D., Sprent, J.: T-cell apoptosis detected *in situ* during positive and negative selection in the thymus. *Nature.* 372 (1994) 100-103
10. Cornall, R.J., Goodnow, C.C., Cyster, J.G.: The regulation of self-reactive B cells. *Curr. Opin. Immunol.* 7 (1995) 804-811
11. Mueller, D.L., Jenkins, M.K., Schwartz, R.H.,: Clonal expansion versus functional clonal inactivation: a costimulatory signaling pathway determines the outcome of T cell antigen receptor occupancy. *Annu. Rev. Immunol.* 7 (1989) 445-480
12. Wagner, S.D, Neuberger, M.S.: Somatic hypermutation of immunoglobulin genes. *Annu. Rev. Immunol.* 14 (1996) 441-457
13. Mond, J.J., Lees, A., Snapper, C.C.:T cell-independent antigens type 2. *Ann. Rev. Immunol.* 13 (1995) 655-692
14. Triantafilou, M., Triantafilou, K.: Lipopolysaccharide recognition : CD14, TLRs and the LPS-activation cluster. *Trends in Immunology* 23 (2002) 301-304
15. Pleiman, C.M., Dambrosio, D., Cambier, J.C.: The B cell antigen receptor complex-structure and signal-transduction. *Immunol. Today* 15 (1994) 393-399
16. Kidd, P.: Th1/Th2 balance: The hypothesis, its limitations, and implications for health and disease. *Altern. Med. Rev* 8 (2003) 223-246
17. DeFranco, A.L.: Molecular aspects of B-lymphocyte activation. *Ann. Rev. Cell Biol.* 3 (1987) 143-178
18. Robbins, F.C., Robbins, J.B.: Current status and prospects for some improved and new bacterial vaccines. *Am. J. Pub. Health* 7 (1986) 105-125
19. Rene A.W. van Lier, Ineke J.M. ten Berge, Laila E. Gamadia: Human CD+ T-cell differentiation in response to viruses. *Nature Rev. Immunol.* 3 (2003) 1-8
20. Trambas, C.M., Griffiths, G.M., Delivering the kiss of death. *Nature Immunol.* 4 (2003) 399-403
21. Kim, J., Bentley, P.J.: Towards an Artificial Immune System for Network Intrusion Detection: An Investigation of Clonal Selection with a Negative Selection Operator, *Proc. of the Congress on Evolutionary Computation,* (2001) 1244-1252

22. Bradley, D.W., Tyrrell, A. M.: The Architecture for a Hardware Immune System. *Proc. of 3rd NASA/DoD Workshop on Evolvable Hardware.* (2001) 193-200.
23. Knight, T., Timmis, J.: AINE: An Immunological Approach to Data Mining. *Proc. of the IEEE International Conference on Data Mining.* (2001) 297-304
24. Gibert, C. J., Routen, T. W.: Associative Memory in an Immune-Based System. *Proc. of the 12th National Conf. on Artificial Intelligence.* (1994) 852-857
25. Castiglione, F.: A network of cellular automata for the simulation of the immune system. *Int. J. Morden Physics C* 10 (1999) 677-686
26. Rundell, A., DeCarlo, R., HogenEsch, H., Doerschuk, P.: The humoral immune response to *Haemophilus influenzae* type b: a mathematical model based on T-zone and germinal center B-cell dynamics. *J. Theor. Biol.* 194 (1998) 341-381
27. Perelson, A.S.: Immunology for physicists. Reviews of Modern *Physics* 69 (1997)
28. Perelson, A.S.: Modelling viral and immune system dynamics *Nature Rev. Immunol.* 2 (2002) 28-36
29. Puzone, R., Kohler, B., Seiden, P., Celada, F.: IMMSIM, a flexible model for in machine experiments on immune system responses. *Future Generation Computer Systems* 18 (2002) 961-972
30. Kesmir, C., De Boer, R. J.; A mathematical model on germinal center kinetics and termination. *J. Immunol.* 163 (1999) 2463-2469
31. Agrawal, N.G.B., Linderman, J.J.; Mathematical modeling of helper T lymphocyte/antigen-presenting cell interactions: analysis of methods for modifying antigen processing and presentation. *J. Theor. Biol.* 182 (1996) 487-504
32. Davenport, M.P., Fazou, C., McMichael, A.J., Callan, M.F.C.; Clonal selection, clonal senescence, and clonal succession: the evolution of the T cell response to infection with a persistent virus. *J. Immunol.* 168 (2002) 3309-3317
33. DeBoer, R.J., Oprea, M., Antia, R., Murali-Krishna, K., Ahmed, R., Perelson, A.S.; Recruitment times, proliferation, and apoptosis rates during the CD8+ T-cell response to lymphocytic choriomeningitis virus. *J. Virol.* 75 (2001) 10663-10669
34. Bocharov, G.A.; Modeling the dynamics of LCMV infection in mice: conventional and exhaustive CTL responses. *J. Theor. Biol.* 192 (1998) 283-308
35. Funk, G.A., Barbour, A.D., Hengartner, H., Kalinke, U.; Mathematical model of a virus-neutralizing immunoglobulin response. *J. Theor. Biol.* 195 (1998) 41-52.
36. Marino, S., Kirschner, D.E.; The human immune response to *Mycobacterium tuberculosis* in lung and lymph node. *J. Theor. Biol.* 227 (2004) 463-486.
37. Koguchi, Y., Kwakami, K.; Cryptococcal infection and Th1-Th2 cytokine balance. *Intern. Rev. Immunol.* 21 (2002) 423-438
38. Hosken, N.A., Shibuya, K., Heath, A.W., Murphy, K.M., O'Garra, A.; The effect of antigen dose on CD4+ T helper cell phenotype development in a T cell receptor-$\alpha\beta$-transgenic model. *J. Exp. Med.* 182 (1995) 1579-1584
39. Edwards, B.M., Barash, S.C., Main, S.H., Choi, G.H., Minter, R., Ullrich, S., Williams, E., Fou, L.D., Wilton, J., Albert, V.R., Ruben, S.M., Vaughan, T.J.; The remarkable flexibility of the human antibody repertoire; isolation of over one thousand different antibodies to a single protein, BLyS. *J. Mol. Biol.* 334 (2003) 103-118
40. Mehr, R., Globerson, A., Perelson, A.S.; Modeling positive and negative selection and differentiation in the thymus. *J. Theor. Biol.* 175 (1995) 103-126
41. Guermonprez, P., Valladeau, J., Zitvolgel, L., Thery, C., Amigorena, S.; Antigen presentation and T cell stimulation by dendritic cells. *Annu. Rev. Immunol.* 20 (2002) 621-667
42. Rogers, P.R., Croft, M.; Peptide dose, affinity, and time of differentiation can contribute to the Th1/Th2 cytokine balance. *J. Immunol.* 163 (1999) 1205-1213

43. Foulds, K.E., Zenewicz, L.A., Shedlock, D.J., Jiang, J., Troy, A.E., Shen, H.; Cutting edge: CD4 and CD8 T cells are intrinsically different in their proliferative responses. *J. Immunol.* 168 (2002) 1528-1532
44. DeBoer, R.J., Homann, D., Perelson, A.S.; Different dynamics of CD4+ and CD8+ T cell responses during and after acute lymphocytic choriomeningitis virus infection. *J. Immunol.* 171 (2003) 3928-3935
45. Ridge, J.P., Rose, F.D., Matzinger, P.; A conditioned dendritic cell can be a temporal bridge between a CD4+ T-helper and a T-killer cell. *Nature* 393 (1998) 474-478
46. Badovinac, V.P., Porter, B.B., Harty, J.T.; Programmed contraction of CD8+ T cells after infection. *Nat. Immunol.* 3 (2002) 619-626
47. Kaech, S.M., Ahmed, R.; Memory CD8+ T cell differentiation: initial antigen encounter triggers a developmental program in naive cells. *Nat. Immunol.* 2 (2001) 415-422
48. Chao, D.L., Davenport, M.P., Forrest, S., Perelson, A.S.; A stochastic model of cytotoxic T cell responses. *J. Theor. Biol.* 228 (2004) 227-240
49. Dmitriev, D.A., Massino, Y.S., Sega, O.L.; Kinetic analysis of interactions between bispecific monoclonal antibodies and immobilized antigens using a resonant mirror biosensor. *J. Immunol. Methods* 280 (2003) 183-202
50. J. L. Peterson: Petri net theory and the modeling of systems. Prentice-Hall, Englewood Cliff, NJ, (1981)
51. T. Murata, Petri nets: Properties, analysis and applications, *Proc. IEEE* 77 (1989) 541-580
52. Mor Peleg, Iwei Yeh, and Russ B. Altman.: Modelling biological processes using workflow and Petri Net models. *Bioinformatics* 18 (2002) 825-837
53. H. Alla, R. David: A modeling and analysis tool for discrete event systems: continuous Petri net, *Performance Evaluation* 33 (1998) 175-199
54. Ridge J.P., et al. A conditioned dendritic cell can be a temporal bridge between a CD4+ T-helper and a T-killer cell. *Nature* 393 (1998) 474-478
55. Van Stipdonk, M.K., Lemmens, E.E., Schoenberger, S.P.,: Naive CTLs require a single brief period of antigenic stimulation for clonal expansion and differentiation. *Nat. Immunol.* 2 (2001) 423-429
56. Veiga-Fernandes, H., Walter, U., Bourgeois, C., McLean, A., Rocha, B.: Response of naive and memory CD8+ T cells to antigen stimulation *in vivo*. *Nat. Immunol.* 1 (2000) 47-53
57. Bachman, M.F., Kundig, T.M., Kalberer, C.P., Hengartner, H., Zinkernagel, R.M.: How many specific B-cells are needed to protect against a virus? *J.Immunol.* 152 (1994) 4235-4241
58. Karlsson,M.C.I., Getahun, A., Heyman, B.: Fc γ RIIB in IgG-mediated suppression of antibody responses: different impact in vivo and in vitro.*J. Immunol.* 167 (2001) 5558-5564
59. Simeone Marino, Denise E. Kirschner.: The human immune response to *Mycobacterium tuberculosis* in lung and lymph node. *J. Theor. Biol.* 227 (2004) 463-486
60. Wilson, M., Seymour, R., Henderson, B., Bacterial perturbation of cytokine networks, *Infection and Immunity* 6 (1998) 2401-2409
61. Heyman, Birgitta: Feedback regulation by IgG antibodies. *Immunology Letters* 88 (2003) 157-161
62. Pittner, B. T., Snow, E. C.: Strength of signal through BCR determines the fate of cycling B cells by regulating the expression of the Bcl-2 family of survival proteins.*Cell. Immunol.* 186 (1998) 55-62
63. Scott, D.W.: Activation-induced cell death in B lymphocytes. *Cell Research* 10 (2000) 179-192

MHC Class I Epitope Binding Prediction Trained on Small Data Sets

Claus Lundegaard[1], Morten Nielsen[1], Kasper Lamberth[2], Peder Worning[1], Christina Sylvester-Hvid[2], Søren Buus[2], Søren Brunak[1], and Ole Lund[1]

[1] Center for Biological Sequence Analysis, BioCentrum, Technical University of Denmark. Building 208, DK-2800 Lyngby, Denmark.
Tel: (+45) 45 25 24 26, Fax: (+45) 45 83 15 95
lunde@cbs.dtu.dk
[2] Department of Experimental Immunology, Institute of Medical Microbiology and Immunology, University of Copenhagen. Denmark

Abstract. The identification of potential T-cell epitopes is important for development of new human or vetenary vaccines, both considering single protein/subunit vaccines, and for epitope/peptide vaccines as such. The highly diverse MHC class I alleles bind very different peptides, and accurate binding prediction methods exist only for alleles were the binding pattern have been deduced from peptide motifs. Using empirical knowledge of important anchor positions within the binding peptides dramatically reduces the number of peptides needed for reliable predictions. We here present a general method for predicting peptides binding to specific MHC class I alleles. The method combines advanced automatic scoring matrix generation with empirical position specific differential anchor weighting. The method leads to predictions with a comparable or higher accuracy than other established prediction servers, even in situations where only very limited data are available for training.

1 Introduction

Cytotoxic T lymphocytes (CTLs) recognize foreign peptides presented on other cells in the body and help to destroy infected or malignant cells. The peptides are presented by the class I major histocompatibility complex (MHC), and the actual binding of the peptide to the MHC is the single most selective event in a larger antigen presentation process. The process also includes processing (cleavage) of proteins and transportation into the endoplasmic reticulum. These two steps, however, only filter out approximately 4/5 of all potential 9-mer peptides whereas a particular MHC class I allele only binds 1/200 potential peptides (Yewdell and Bennink 1999). The allele space of human class I MHCs (also called class I Human Leukocyte Antigens or HLAs) is highly diverse, and each allele binds a very specific set of peptides. All the different alleles can be divided into at least 9 supertypes, where the alleles within each supertype exhibit roughly the same peptide specificity (Sette and Sidney 1999). For nonamer peptides positions 2 and 9 are very important for the binding to most class I HLAs, and these positions are referred to as anchor positions (Rammensee et al. 1999). For some alleles the binding motif further have auxiliary anchor positions.

G. Nicosia et al. (Eds.): ICARIS 2004, LNCS 3239, pp. 217–225, 2004.

Peptides binding to the A*0101 allele thus have position 2, 3,and 9 as anchors (Kubo et al. 1994; Kondo et al. 1997; Rammensee et al. 1999). Several prediction methods have been proposed for discrimination between binders and non-binders, such as data derived weight matrices, including the publicly available BIMAS (Parker et al. 1994) and SYFPEITHI (Rammensee et al. 1999), weight matrices with optimized position weighting (Yu et al. 2002) and ANNs (Brusic et al. 1994; Adams and Koziol 1995). Other prediction algorithms have been developed to predict not only if a peptide binds, but also the actual affinity of the binding (Marshall et al. 1995; Stryhn et al. 1996; Rognan et al. 1999; Doytchinova and Flower 2001; Buus et al. 2003; Nielsen et al. 2003), and for affinity predictions ANNs outperform the simpler methods (Gulu-kota et al. 1997; Nielsen et al. 2003) but generally ANNs needs many examples in the training (Yu et al. 2002). Predictions in general tends to be more precise when more examples have been included in the training (Yu et al. 2002), but experimental data on peptides binding to HLA complexes are published in large numbers for just a few alleles. Here we will investigate the possibility to get reliable predictions even when data is limited. It have earlier been shown that a position weighted matrix were slightly better for A*0201 predictions than an unweighted matrix (Yu et al. 2002), but not to which extent such a weighting will influence the number of data needed to generate acceptable predictors.

2 Materials and Methods

Data sets: All 9-mer peptides assigned as binding to HLA class I alleles HLA-A*0101 (82 peptides), HLA-A*0201(450 peptides), HLA-A*0301 (63 peptides), HLAA* 1101 (77 peptides), and HLA-B*0702 (69 peptides) was extracted from the databases SYFPEITHI (Rammensee et al. 1999) and MHCPEP (Brusic et al. 1998). These pep-tides are in the following referred to as training sets. As evaluation sets we used pep-tides for which the affinities for the selected alleles had been measured (K. Lamberth, unpublished) using the ELISA method described by Sylvester-Hvid et al. (Sylvester-Hvid et al. 2002). The binders/non binders ratios were as follows using a threshold for binders of 500 nM: A*0101 (37/284), A*0201 (20/197), A*0301 (6/211), A*1101 (9/208). Furthermore peptides relevant to SARS (Sylvester-Hvid et al. in press) were used to evaluate matrices trained on peptides binding to the A*0101, A*0201, A*0301, A*1101, B*0702, B*1501 and B*5801 alleles. There was no peptide overlap (i.e., no identical peptides) between the training data and the evaluation sets. As inde-pendent evaluation sets for the alleles A*0101 and A*0201 we further used peptides extracted from the MHCBN 3.1 database (Bhasin et al. 2003) excluding peptides all ready present in the training sets. The same evaluation sets were also used to evaluate the prediction accuracy of both the BIMAS (Parker et al. 1994) and SYFPEITHI (Rammensee et al. 1999) prediction methods. SYFPEITHI predictions were per-formed using the web server (http://syfpeithi.bmiheidelberg. com), and BIMAS pre-dictions were performed as described at the web server, using matrices downloaded from the web site
(http://bimas.cit.nih.gov/cgibin/ molbio/hla_coefficient_viewing_page).

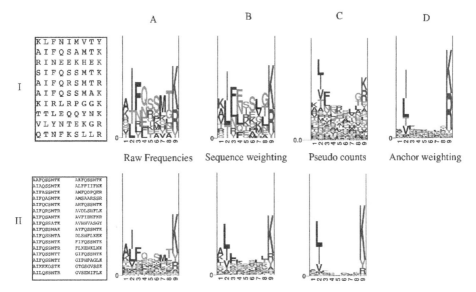

Fig. 1. Logos showing the information distribution after each step in the matrix calculation using few (I) or many (II) A*0301 training peptides. A) The distribution of amino acids at each position. B) After sequence weighting (Henikoff & Henikoff). C) After low count correction (Altschul + Henikoff & Henikoff). D) Extra weight on anchor positions when few peptides are used for training.

Matrix training: The selected peptides were stacked into a multiple alignment. Using an ungapped HMM like approach the log-odds weight matrix was calculated as $\log(p_{i,l}/q_i)$, where $p_{i,l}$ is the frequency of amino acid i at position l in the alignment and q_i the background frequency of that amino acid (Henikoff and Henikoff, 1994). The values for $p_{i,l}$ were estimated using sequence weighting and correction for low counts (Altschul et al. 1997, Henikoff and Henikoff 1992). A schematic view of the procedure is outlined in figure 1.

Increasing numbers of peptides were included to calculate the weight matrix. For each number of training peptides, 200 data sets were constructed, using the bootstrap procedure (Press et al. 1989), by randomly drawing the chosen number of peptides with replacement from the original data set of peptides.

Matrix evaluation: The score for a given peptide is calculated as the sum of the scores at each position. Predictions were made for the corresponding evaluation set by each of the 200 matrices of each train set size, and the predictive performance was measured in terms of both the linear (Pearson) correlation coefficients between the prediction output and log-transformed measured affinities (Buus et al. 2003) and the area under a Receiver Operating Characteristic (ROC) curve, the Aroc value (Sweet 1988). The final predictive performance is given as the simple average of the 200 values.

Sequence logos: The logos were calculated as described by Hebsgaard and coworkers (Hebsgaard et al. 1996), and visualized using the Logo program (Schneider and Stephens 1990).

A   B

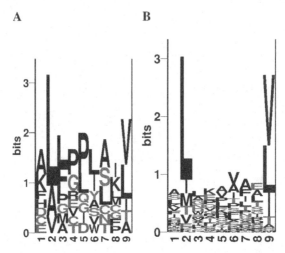

Fig. 2. Sequence logos generated by 10 (A) and 100 (B) randomly chosen A*0201 binding peptides.

3 Results

To visualize the problem one is facing when training a prediction method on limited amounts of data, we generated sequence weight logos for peptides binding to the A*0201 allele using 10 and 100 peptides. From the logo constructed using 10 random A*0201 binding peptides (fig. 2a), it can be seen that the importance of the anchor position 9 is not yet visible, while this feature is clearly apparent in the logo based on 100 sequences (fig. 2b). The amino acid preferences for the hydrophobic amino acids L and L/V at position 2 and 9 respectively is however present in both logos. It has been shown that a matrix method can generally benefit from anchor weighting (Yu et al. 2002). Based on the information content visualized with the logos in figure 2, a prediction method trained on very few data would very likely benefit even more by having prior knowledge about position specific weighting encoded.

To examine this hypothesis a weight matrix was generated for the A2 allele A*0201. Evaluated on 217 peptides with experimentally determined affinities to the A*0201 allele (K. Lamberth, unpublished), it was clear that at least 20 training peptides was needed to get a reasonably performance (Aroc>0,8, Pearson cc > 0.5), and at least 100 training examples to get values comparable to those obtained by public available prediction servers (Figure 3 A). In the work of Yu et al. (2002) several of the weights were scaled differently. Here, to make the approach more general applicable, only the weights on the anchor positions assigned in the SYFPEITHI database (Rammensee et al. 1999), position 2 and 9, were enhanced (biased) by a factor of 5. This approach resulted in a surprisingly good performance, even based on just a handful of training peptides (figure 3 A). The same approach was then used to train matrices with peptides belonging to the A*0101, A*0301, A*1101, and B*0702 alleles respectively, except that position 3 is an additional anchor position in the A*0101 allele and was thus also biased. In all cases reliable predictions were obtainable when evaluated on sets from K. Lamberth (unpublished) with matrices trained on no more

Table 1. Evaluation of 200 matrices made by selecting 5 or 20 peptides respectively, by the bootstrap method, or a single matrix generated by all available different peptides from MHCPEP and SYFPEITHI databases. Evaluation was performed with peptides extracted from the MHCBN 3.1 database, and SARS relevant peptides. *) The bootstrapping procedure was not used due to the small total number of peptides available. Instead all possible combinations of the available peptides were used to estimate the standard deviation. **) Predictions were made using the A03 predictor.

Allele	Matrix all peptides	Biased matrix 5 peptides	Biased matrix 20 peptides	Biased matrix all peptides	BIMAS	Syfpeithi
MHCBN peptides						
A*0101	1.000	0.992 ± 0.026	1.000 ± 0.002	1.000	1.000	1.000
A*0201	0.925	0.803 ± 0.024	0.830 ± 0.017	0.871	0.907	0.864
Sars peptides						
A*0101	0.963	0.986 ± 0.011	0.992 ± 0.004	0.997	0.951	0.987
A*0201	0.992	0.973 ± 0.015	0.978 ± 0.006	0.984	0.979	0.970
A*0301	0.912	0.855 ± 0.072	0.873 ± 0.028	0.877	0.857	0.829
A*1101	0.937	0.914 ± 0.038	0.948 ± 0.018	0.968	0.950	0.830
B*0702	0.983	0.972 ± 0.013	0.977 ± 0.009	0.985	0.990	0.990
B*1501*	0.928	0.932 ± 0.039	N.A.	0.955	0.893	N.A.
B*5801*	0.892	0.959 ± 0.008	N.A.	0.959	0.994	N.A.

than 5 training examples (Figure 3 B). Further B*1501 (a B62 allele) and B*5801 matrices were produced. All matrices were evaluated using the SARS relevant peptides (Sylvester-Hvid et al. 2004) and the independent evaluation sets obtained from the MHCBN 3.1 database (Bhasin et al. 2003). These sets were also predictable using biased matrices trained on very few peptides (Table 1).

4 Discussion

When trained on very few positive examples, matrices and other prediction methods do not contain sufficient information to distinguish between important and less important positions in the binding motif, and the predictions can thus be guided by increasing the relative weight on the positions in the motif that are known to be the generally most informative. This work shows that it is possible to obtain reliable predictions of MHC class I binding peptides, even when the allele in question is poorly investigated and few positive binding examples exist. Alternative ways to make MHC binding predictions when no or a few data are available is to use free energy calculations (Rognan et al. 1999) or threading approaches (Altuvia et al. 1995; Schueler-Furman et al. 2000). These types of methods may be optimal when no peptides are known to bind a given MHC molecule.

As new alleles constantly are being discovered, in humans as in animals, it is often important to be able to quickly assign these a general motif of binding peptides, e.g.,

A

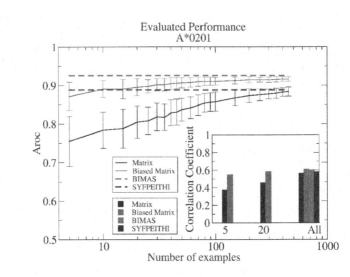

B

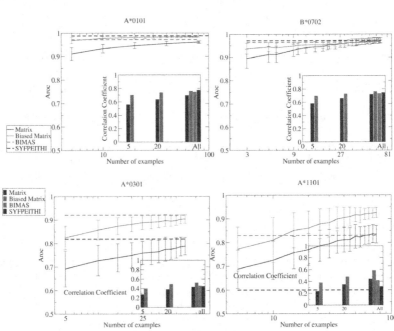

Fig. 3. Curves of the Aroc value (major graph) and the Pearson correlation coefficient (inserted graph) plotted against the number of positive examples randomly selected from the total pool of binding peptides. Each value is the simple average of 200 independent calculations with the indication of one standard deviation. The matrices were generated and evaluated with peptides binding to the alleles A*0201 (A) and A*0101, A*0301, A*1101 and B*0702 (B). SYFPEITHI A*1101 predictions were generated using the A03 predictor.

for transplantation purposes or veterinary vaccination programs. Also for future rational vaccine design it will be of great value to be able to scan for T cell epitopes as broad as possible. For this purpose the present method is a major advantage as only very few binders has to be identified to be able to deduce a reliable peptide profile. Having initial predictions driven by pure classification data (binders/nonbinders) furthermore enables us to select a limited set for which experimental binding affinity could be determined. These quantitative data can be used in an iterative process to train more advanced methods, such as artificial neural networks (ANNs), to an even better performance (Buus et al. 2003; Nielsen et al. 2003). If several slightly different quantitative ANNs are trained it is possible to use the degree of disagreement between the networks to select new peptides for experimental validation that would contain the most information for future trainings. Using such a scheme to select training data has been shown to lead to higher predictive performance by the use of fewer data (Buus et al. 2003; Christensen et al. 2003). The presented method will also be beneficial for other problems were some positions in the data are known to be especially important. As an example the general weighting approach have been used with success in the prediction of HLA class-II binding peptides (Nielsen et al. 2004).

Acknowledgements. This work was supported by the Danish MRC (grant 22-01-0272), the 5th Framework Programme of the European Commission (grant QLGT-1999-00173), the NIH (grant AI49213-02), and the Danish National Research Foundation.

References

Adams, H.P., and Koziol, J.A. 1995. Prediction of binding to MHC class I molecules. J Immunol Methods 185: 181-190.

Altschul, S.F., Madden, T.L., Schaffer, A.A., Zhang, J., Zhang, Z., Miller, W, and Lipman, D.J. 1997. Gapped BLAST and PSI-BLAST: a new generation of protein database search programs. Nucl. Acids Res. 25: 3389-3402

Altuvia, Y., Schueler, O., and Margalit, H. 1995. Ranking potential binding peptides to MHC molecules by a computational threading approach. J Mol Biol 149: 244-250.

Bhasin, M., Singh, H., and Raghava, G.P.S. 2003. MHCBN: A comprehensive database of MHC binding and non-binding peptides. Bioinformatics 19: 665-666.

Brusic, V., Rudy, G., and Harrison, L.C. 1994. Prediction of MHC binding peptides using artificial neural networks. In Complex systems: mechanism of adaptation. (ed. a.Y.X. Stonier RJ), pp. 253-260. IOS Press, Amsterdam.

Brusic, V., Rudy, G., and Harrison, L.C. 1998. MHCPEP, a database of MHC-binding peptides: update 1997. Nucleic Acid Res 26: 368-371.

Buus, S., Lauemøller, S.L., Worning, P., Kesmir, C., Frimurer, T., Corbet, S., Fomsgaard, A., Hilden, J., Holm, A., and Brunak, S. 2003. Sensitive quantitative predictions of peptide-MHC binding by a 'Query by Committee' artificial neural network approach. Tissue Antigens 62: 378-384.

Christensen, J.K., Lamberth, K., Nielsen, M., Lundegaard, C., Worning, P., Lauemøller, S.L., Buus, S., Brunak, S., and Lund, O. 2003. Selecting Informative Data for Developing Peptide-MHC Binding Predictors Using a "Query By Committee" Approach. Neural Computation 15: 2931-2942.

Doytchinova, I.A., and Flower, D.R. 2001. Toward the Quantitative Prediction of T-Cell Epitopes: CoMFA and CoMSIA Studies of Peptides with Affinity for the Class I MHC Molecule HLA-A*0201. J. Med. Chem. 44: 3572-3581.

Gulukota, K., Sidney, J., Sette, A., and DeLisi, C. 1997. Two complementary methods for predicting peptides binding major histocompatibility complex molecules. Journal of Molecular Biology 267: 1258-1267.

Hebsgaard, S.M., Korning, P.G., Tolstrup, N., Engelbrecht, J., Rouze, P., and Brunak, S. 1996. Splice site prediction in Arabidopsis thaliana pre-mRNA by combining local and global sequence information. Nucleic Acid Res 24: 3439-3452.

Henikoff, S., and Henikoff, J.G. 1992. Amino acid substitution matrices from protein blocks. Proc. Natl. Acad. Sci., USA 89: 10915-10919

Henikoff, S., and Henikoff, J.G. 1994. Position-based sequence weights. J Mol Biol 243: 574-578.

Kondo, A., Sidney, J., Southwood, S., del Guercio, M.F., Appella, E., Sakamoto, H., Grey, H.M., Celis, E., Chesnut, R.W., Kubo, R.T., et al. 1997. Two distinct HLA-A*0101-specific submotifs illustrate alternative peptide binding modes. Immunogenetics 45: 249-258.

Kubo, R.T., Sette, A., Grey, H.M., Appella, E., Sakaguchi, K., Zhu, N.Z., Arnott, D., Sherman, N., Shabanowitz, J., and Michel, H. 1994. Definition of specific peptide motifs for four major HLA-A alleles. J Immunol 152: 3913-3924.

Marshall, K.W., Wilson, K.J., Liang, J., Woods, A., Zaller, D., and Rothbard, J.B. 1995. Prediction of peptide affinity to HLA DRB1*0401. J Immunol 154: 5927-5933.

Nielsen, M., Lundegaard, C., Worning, P., Lauemøller, S.L., Lamberth, K., Buus, S., Brunak, S., and Lund, O. 2003. Reliable prediction of T-cell epitopes using neural networks with novel sequence representations. Protein Science 12: 1007-1017.

Nielsen, M, Lundegaard, C, Worning, P, Sylvester-Hvid, C, Lamberth, K, Buus, S, Brunak, S, and Lund, O. 2004. Improved prediction of MHC class I and II epitopes using a novel Gibbs sampling approach. Bioinformatics 20: 1388-97.

Parker, K.C., Bednarek, M.A., and Coligan, J.E. 1994. Scheme for ranking potential HLA-A2 binding peptides based on independent binding of individual peptide side-chains. J Immunol 152: 163-175.

Press, W.H., Flannery, B.P., Teukolsky, S.A., and Vetterling, W.T. 1989. Numerical Recipies in C: The Art of Scientific Computing, 2 ed. Cambridge University Press, Cambridge.

Rammensee, H., Bachmann, J., Emmerich, N., Bachor, O.A., and Stevanovic, S. 1999. SYFPEITHI: database for MHC ligands and peptide motifs. Immunogenetics 50: 213-219.

Rognan, D., Lauemøller, S.L., Holm, A., Buus, S., and Tschinke, V. 1999. Predicting binding affinities of protein ligands from three-dimensional models: application to peptide binding to class I major histocompatibility proteins. J Med Chem 42: 4650-4658.

Schneider, T.D., and Stephens, R.M. 1990. Sequence logos: a new way to display consensus sequences. Nucleic Acid Res 18: 6097-6100.

Schueler-Furman, O., Altuvia, Y., Sette, A., and Margalit, H. 2000. Structure-based prediction of binding peptides to MHC class I molecules: application to a broad range of MHC alleles. Protein Science 9: 1838-1846.

Sette, A., and Sidney, J. 1999. Nine major HLA class I supertypes account for the vast preponderance of HLA-A and –B polymorphism. Immunogenetics 50: 201-212.

Stryhn, A., Pedersen, L.O., Romme, T., Holm, C.B., Holm, A., and Buus, S. 1996. Peptide binding specificity of major histocompatibility complex class I resolved into an array of apparently independent subspecificities: quantitation by peptide libraries and improved prediction of binding. Eur J Immunol. 26: 1911-1918.

Sweet, J.A. 1988. Measuring the accuracy of a diagnostic systems. Science 240: 1285-1293.

Sylvester-Hvid C, Nielsen M, Lamberth K, Roder G, Justesen S, Lundegaard C, Worning P, Thomadsen H, Lund O, Brunak S, Buus S. 2004. SARS CTL vaccine candidates; HLA supertype-, genome-wide scanning and biochemical validation. Tissue Antigens 63: 395-400.

Sylvester-Hvid, C., Kristensen, N., Blicher, T., Ferré, H., Lauemøller, S.L., Wolf, X.A., Lamberth, K., Nissen, M.H., Pedersen, L.Ø., and Buus, S. 2002. Establishment of a quantitative ELISA capable of determining peptide - MHC class I interaction. Tissue Antigens 59: 251-258.

Yewdell, J.W., and Bennink, J.R. 1999. Immunodominance in major histocompatibility complex class I-restricted T lymphocyte responses. Annual Review of Immunology 17: 51-88.

Yu, K., Petrovsky, N., Schonbach, C., Koh, J.Y., and Brusic, V. 2002. Methods for prediction of peptide binding to MHC molecules: a comparative study. Mol Med. 8: 137-148.

Convergence Analysis of a Multiobjective Artificial Immune System Algorithm

Mario Villalobos-Arias[1,3], Carlos A. Coello Coello[2], and Onésimo Hernández-Lerma[1]

[1] CINVESTAV-IPN
Department of Mathematics
A. Postal 14-740
México, D.F. 07000, MEXICO
{mava,ohernand}@math.cinvestav.mx
[2] CINVESTAV-IPN
Evolutionary Computation Group
Depto. de Ingeniería Eléctrica
Sección de Computación
Av. Instituto Politécnico Nacional No. 2508
Col. San Pedro Zacatenco
México, D. F. 07300, MEXICO
ccoello@cs.cinvestav.mx
[3] Permanent Address:
Escuela de Matemática
Universidad de Costa Rica
San José, Costa Rica
mvillalo@cariari.ucr.ac.cr

Abstract. This paper presents a mathematical proof of convergence of a multi-objective artificial immune system algorithm (based on clonal selection theory). An specific algorithm (previously reported in the specialized literature) is adopted as a basis for the mathematical model presented herein. The proof is based on the use of Markov chains.

1   Introduction

Despite the considerable amount of research related to artificial immune systems in the last few years [3,10], there is still little work related to issues as important as mathematical modelling (see for example [13,11]). Other aspects, such as convergence, have been practically disregarded in the current specialized literature.

Problems with several (maybe conflicting) objectives tend to arise naturally in most domains. These problems are called "multiobjective" or "vector" optimization problems, and have been studied in Operations Research where a number of solution techniques have been proposed [9]. It was until relatively recently that researchers became aware of the potential of population-based heuristics such as artificial immune systems in this area [6,1]. The main motivation for using population-based heuristics (such as artificial immune systems) in solving multiobjective optimization problems is because such a population makes possible to deal simultaneously with a set of possible solutions (the

G. Nicosia et al. (Eds.): ICARIS 2004, LNCS 3239, pp. 226–235, 2004.

so-called population) which allows us to find several members of the Pareto optimal set in a single run of the algorithm, instead of having to perform a series of separate runs as in the case of the traditional mathematical programming techniques [9]. Additionally, population-based heuristics are less susceptible to the shape or continuity of the Pareto front (e.g., they can easily deal with discontinuous and concave Pareto fronts), whereas these two issues are a real concern for mathematical programming techniques [5,1].

This paper deals with convergence analysis of an artificial immune system algorithm used for multiobjective optimization.

The remainder of this paper is organized as follows. Section 2 briefly describes the general multiobjective optimization problem and introduces the basic definitions adopted in this paper. In Section 3, we briefly describe the specific algorithm adopted for developing our mathematical model of convergence. Then, in Section 4, we present our main results. A mathematical proof of such results is presented in Section 5. Finally, our conclusions and some possible paths for future research are presented in Section 6.

2   The Multiobjective Optimization Problem

To compare vectors in $\mathbb{R}^d$ we will use the standard *Pareto order* defined as follows.
    If $\boldsymbol{u} = (u_1, u_2, \ldots, u_d)$ and $\boldsymbol{v} = (v_1, v_2, \ldots, v_d)$ are vectors in $\mathbb{R}^d$, then

$$\boldsymbol{u} \preceq \boldsymbol{v} \iff u_i \leq v_i \, \forall \, i \in \{1, \ldots, d\}.$$

This relation is a *partial order*. We also write $\boldsymbol{u} \prec \boldsymbol{v} \iff \boldsymbol{u} \preceq \boldsymbol{v}$ and $\boldsymbol{u} \neq \boldsymbol{v}$.
    Let X be a set and $F : X \longrightarrow \mathbb{R}^d$ a given vector function with components $f_i : X \longrightarrow \mathbb{R}$ for each $i \in \{1, \ldots, d\}$.
    The multiobjective optimization problem (MOP) we are concerned with is to find $x^* \in X$ such that

$$F(x^*) = \min_{x \in X} F(x) = \min_{x \in X}[f_1(x), \ldots, f_n(x)], \qquad (1)$$

where the minimum is understood in the sense of the Pareto order.

Definition 1:
    A point $x^* \in X$ is called a *Pareto optimal solution* for the MOP (1) if there is no $x \in X$ such that $F(x) \prec F(x^*)$.
    The set

$$\mathcal{P}^* = \{x \in X \, : \, x \text{ is a Pareto optimal solution}\}$$

is called the *Pareto optimal set*, and its image under F, i.e.

$$F(\mathcal{P}^*) := \{F(x) \, : \, x \in \mathcal{P}^*\},$$

is the *Pareto front*.
    As we are concerned with the artificial immune system algorithm in which the elements are represented by a string of length l with 0 or 1 in each entry. In the remainder of the paper we will replace X with the *finite* set $\mathbb{B}^l$, where $\mathbb{B} = \{0, 1\}$.

3   The Artificial Immune System Algorithm

For our mathematical model, we will consider the artificial immune system (based on clonal selection theory [4]) for multiobjective optimization proposed in [2]. From here on, we will refer to this approach using the same name adopted by the authors of this algorithm: "Multi-objective Immune System Algorithm" (MISA for short). Next, we will focus our discussion only on the aspects that are most relevant for its mathematical modelling. For a detailed discussion on this algorithm, readers should refer to [2].

MISA is a technique in which there is a population that evolves as follows. The population is divided in two parts, a primary set and a secondary set; the primary set contains the "best" individuals (or elements) of the population. The transition of one population to another is made by means of a mutation rule and a reordering operation. First, several copies of the elements of the primary set are made; then, a "small" mutation (using a parameter or probability p_m) is applied to these copies, while a mutation with the parameter ρ_m is applied to the secondary set. These parameters are positive and less than $1/2$, i.e.

$$p_m, \rho_m \in (0, 1/2). \tag{2}$$

We model this algorithm with a Markov chain $\{X_k : k \geq 0\}$, with state space $S = \mathbb{B}^{nl}$, where $\mathbb{B} = \{0, 1\}$. Hence S is the set of all possible vectors of n individuals each one represented by a string of length l with 0 or 1 in each entry.

In our model, we omitted the clonation stage, and mutation is applied directly to the elements of the primary set. Note that if we use clones the probability of passing from a state to another is increased. Thus, our omission is not relevant to the model, since it does not affect our proof.

The chain's transition probability is given by

$$P_{ij} = \mathbb{P}(X_{k+1} = j \mid X_k = i).$$

We also write

$$P(i, A) = \mathbb{P}(X_{k+1} \in A \mid X_k = i).$$

Thus the transition matrix is of the form

$$P = (P_{ij}) = RM, \tag{3}$$

where R and M are the transition matrices of reordering and mutation, respectively.

Note that these matrices are stochastic, i.e. $R_{ij} \geq 0$, $M_{ij} \geq 0$ for all i, j, and for each $i \in S$

$$\sum_{s \in S} R_{is} = 1 \quad \text{and} \quad \sum_{s \in S} M_{is} = 1. \tag{4}$$

Suppose that the primary set has n_1 individuals, so that the secondary set has $n - n_1$ individuals. Let $i \in S$ be a state (population). Then we can express i as

$$i = (i_1, i_2, \ldots, i_{n_1}, i_{n_1+1}, \ldots, i_n),$$

where each i_s is a string of length l of 0's and 1's.

3.1 The Mutation Probability

In order to calculate the mutation probability from the state i to state j we use that the individual i_s is transformed into the individual j_s applying uniform mutation (i.e. each entrance of i_s is transformed into the corresponding one of j_s with probability p_m or ρ_m), as in the following scheme.

$$
\begin{array}{cccccc}
 & 1 & \cdots & n_1 & n_1+1 & \cdots & n \\
i & \boxed{i_1} & \cdots & \boxed{i_{n_1}} & \boxed{i_{n_1+1}} & \cdots & \boxed{i_n}
\end{array}
$$

$$\text{mutation} \downarrow \quad \cdots \quad \downarrow \qquad \downarrow \quad \cdots \quad \downarrow$$

$$
\begin{array}{ccccc}
j & \boxed{j_1} & \cdots & \boxed{j_{n_1}} & \boxed{j_{n_1+1}} & \cdots & \boxed{j_n}
\end{array}
$$

Thus, for each individual in the primary set of the population, the mutation probability can be computed as

$$p_m^{H(i_s,j_s)}(1 - p_m)^{l-H(i_s,j_s)} \;\; \forall s \in \{1,\dots,n_1\},$$

where $H(i_s, j_s)$ is the Hamming distance between i_s and j_s. For the secondary set we have

$$\rho_m^{H(i_s,j_s)}(1 - \rho_m)^{l-H(i_s,j_s)} \;\; \forall s \in \{n_1+1,\dots,n\}.$$

Hence the mutation probability from i to j is:

$$M_{ij} = \prod_{s=1}^{n_1} p_m^{H(i_s,j_s)}(1-p_m)^{l-H(i_s,j_s)} \prod_{s=n_1+1}^{n} \rho_m^{H(i_s,j_s)}(1-\rho_m)^{l-H(i_s,j_s)} \qquad (5)$$

3.2 Use of Elitism

We say that we are using *elitism* in an algorithm, in particular in MISA, if we use an extra set, called the *elite* set (or secondary population, as in [2]), in which we put the "best" elements (nondominated elements of the state in our case) of the primary set. This elite set usually does not participate in the evolution, since it is used only to store the nondominated elements found along the process.

After each transition we have to apply an *elitism operation* that accepts a new state if there is an element in the primary or secondary set that improves some element in the elite set.

If we are using elitism, the representation of the states changes to the following form:

$$\hat{i} = (i^e; i) = (i_1^e, \cdots, i_r^e; i_1, \cdots, i_{n_1}, i_{n_1+1}, \cdots, i_n)$$

where $i_1^e, \cdots, i_r^e$ are the members of the elite set of the state, r is the number of elements in the elite set and we assume that the cardinality of $\mathcal{P}^*$ is greater than r. In addition we assume that $r \leq n$.

Note that in general $i_1^e, \cdots, i_r^e$ are not necessarily the "best" elements of the state $\hat{i}$, but after applying the elitism operation on i^e, they are the "best" elements of the states.

Let $\hat{P}$ be the transition matrix associated with the new states.

Note that if all the elements in the elite set of a state are Pareto optimal then any state that contains an element in the elite set that is not a Pareto optimal will not be accepted, i.e.

$$\text{if } \{i_1^e, \cdots, i_r^e\} \subset \mathcal{P}^* \text{ and } \{j_1^e, \cdots, j_r^e\} \not\subset \mathcal{P}^* \text{ then } \hat{P}_{ij} = 0 \tag{6}$$

4   Main Results

Before stating our main results, we introduce the definition of convergence of an algorithm, where we use the following notation. If $V = (v_1, v_2, \ldots, v_n)$ is a vector, we denote by $\{V\}$ the set of entries of V, i.e.

$$\{V\} = \{v_1, v_2, \ldots, v_n\}.$$

Definition 2:

Let $\{X_k : k \geq 0\}$ be the Markov chain associated to an algorithm. We say that the algorithm converges if

$$\mathbb{P}(\{X_k\} \subset \mathcal{P}^*) \to 1 \text{ as } k \to \infty$$

In the case of using elitism, we replace X_k by X_k^e, wich is the *elite set* of the state (i.e. if $X_k = i$ then $X_k^e = i^e$)

Theorem 1:

Let P be the transition matrix of MISA. Then, P has a stationary distribution π such that

$$\|P^k - \pi\| \leq \left(1 - 2^{nl} p_m^{n_1 l} \rho_m^{(n-n_1)l}\right)^k \quad \forall k = 1, 2, \ldots. \tag{7}$$

Moreover, π has all its entries positive.

In spite of this convergence result, the convergence of MISA to the Pareto optimal set cannot be guaranteed.

In fact, from Theorem 1 and using the fact that π has all entries positive we will immediately deduce the following fact.

Corollary 1:

MISA does not converge.

To ensure convergence of MISA we need to use elitism.

Theorem 2:

The elitist version of MISA *does* converge.

5   Proof of the Results

We first recall some standard definitions and results.

Definition 3:
  A nonnegative matrix P is said to be *primitive* if there exists a $k > 0$ such that the entries of P^k are all positive.

Definition 4:
  A Markov chain $\{X_k : k \geq 0\}$ with transition matrix P, it is said to satisfy a *minorization condition* if there is a pair (β, μ) consisting of a positive real number β and a probability distribution μ on S, and such that

$$P(i, A) \geq \beta \mu(A) \ \forall i \in S, \forall A \subseteq S.$$

  The following result gives an upper bound on the convergence rate of a Markov chain that satisfies a minorization condition.

Lemma 1:
  Cosider a Markov chain $\{X_k : k \geq 0\}$ with transition matrix P and suppose that it satisfies a minorization condition (β, μ). Then P has a unique stationary distribution π. Moreover for any initial distribution we have

$$\|P^k - \pi\| \leq (1 - \beta)^k \ \forall k = 1, 2, \dots.$$

Proof see for example [7, pp. 56,57]

  We will use the next result to show the existence of the stationary distribution in Theorem 1.

Lemma 2:
  Let P be a stochastic primitive matrix. Then, as $k \to \infty$, P^k converges to a stochastic matrix $P^\infty = \mathbf{1}'p^\infty$, where $\mathbf{1}'$ is a column vector of 1's and $p^\infty = p^0 \lim_{k \to \infty} P^k = p^0 P^\infty$ has positive entries and it is unique, independently of the initial distribution p^0.
Proof [8, p. 123]

  The next lemma will allow us to use either Lemma 1 or Lemma 2.

Lemma 3:
  Let P be the transition matrix of MISA. Then

$$\min_{i,j \in S} P_{ij} = p_m^{n_1 l} \rho_m^{(n-n_1)l} > 0 \ \forall i, j \in S, \tag{8}$$

and therefore P is primitive. Moreover, P satisfies a minorization condition (β, μ) with

$$\beta = 2^{nl} p_m^{n_1 l} \rho_m^{(n-n_1)l}, \quad \mu(A) = \frac{|A|}{2^{nl}}, \ \forall A \subset S \tag{9}$$

where $|A|$ is the cardinality of A.

Proof

By (2) we have

$$p_m < \frac{1}{2} < 1 - p_m, \quad \rho_m < \frac{1}{2} < 1 - \rho_m.$$

Thus, from (5),

$$M_{ij} = \prod_{s=1}^{n_1} p_m^{H(i_s,j_s)}(1-p_m)^{l-H(i_s,j_s)} \prod_{s=n_1+1}^{n} \rho_m^{H(i_s,j_s)}(1-\rho_m)^{l-H(i_s,j_s)}$$

$$> \prod_{s=1}^{n_1} p_m^l \prod_{s=n_1+1}^{n} \rho_m^l$$

$$= p_m^{n_1 l} \rho_m^{(n-n_1)l}$$

On the other hand, by (3) and (4)

$$P_{ij} = \sum_{s \in S} R_{is} M_{sj}$$

$$\geq p_m^{n_1 l} \rho_m^{(n-n_1)l} \sum_{s \in S} R_{is}$$

$$= p_m^{n_1 l} \rho_m^{(n-n_1)l} > 0,$$

To verify (8), see that P_{ij} attains the minimum in (8) if i has 0 in all entries and j has 1 in all entries.

Now we will show that the pair (β, μ) given by (9) is a minorization condition for P. Indeed, from (8) we have

$$P(i, A) = \sum_{j \in A} P_{ij} \geq \sum_{j \in A} p_m^{n_1 l} \rho_m^{(n-n_1)l}$$

$$= |A| \, p_m^{n_1 l} \rho_m^{(n-n_1)l}$$

$$= \frac{|A|}{2^{nl}} \, 2^{nl} \, p_m^{n_1 l} \rho_m^{(n-n_1)l}$$

$$= \beta \, \mu(A)$$

and the desired conclusion follows.   ∎

Proof of Theorem 1

By Lemma 3, P is primitive. Thus, by Lemma 2, P has a stationary distribution π with all entries positive. Finally, using Lemma 1 and the minorization in (9), we get (7).   ∎

Before proving Theorem 2 we give some preliminary definitions and results.

Definition 5:

Let X be as in **Definition 1**. We say that X is *complete* if for each $x \in X \setminus \mathcal{P}^*$ there exists $x^* \in \mathcal{P}^*$ such that $F(x^*) \preceq F(x)$.

For instance if X is finite, then X is complete.

Let $i, j \in S$ be two arbitrary states, we say that i *leads* to j, and write $i \rightarrow j$, if there exists an integer $k \geq 1$ such that $P_{ij}^k > 0$. If i does not lead to j we write $i \nrightarrow j$.

We call a state i *inessential* if there exists a state j such that $i \rightarrow j$ but $j \nrightarrow i$. Otherwise the state i is called *essential*.

We denote the set of essential states by E and the set of inessential states by I. Note that

$$S = E \cup I.$$

We say that P is in *canonical form* if it can be written as

$$P = \begin{pmatrix} P_1 & 0 \\ R & Q \end{pmatrix}.$$

Observe that P can put in this form by reordering the states, that is, the essential states at the beginning and the inessential states at the end. In this case P_1 is the matrix associated with the transitions between essential states, R with transitions between inessential to essential states, and Q with transitions between inessential states. Also note that P^k has a Q^k in the position of Q in P, i.e.

$$P^k = \begin{pmatrix} P_1^k & 0 \\ R_k & Q^k \end{pmatrix},$$

and R_k is a matrix that depends of P_1, Q and R.

Now we present some facts that will be essential in the proof of Theorem 2.

Lemma 4:

Let P be a stochastic matrix, and let Q be the submatrix of P associated with transitions between inessential states. Then, as $k \rightarrow \infty$, $Q^k \rightarrow 0$ elementwise geometrically fast.

Proof   See, for instance, [12, p.120].   ■

As a consequence of Lemma 4 we have the following.

Corollary 2:

If $\{X_k : k \geq 0\}$ is a Markov chain, then

$$\mathbb{P}(X_k \in I) \rightarrow 0 \text{ as } k \rightarrow \infty,$$

independently of the initial distribution.

Proof

For any initial distribution vector p_0, let $p_0(I)$ be the subvector which corresponds to the inessential states. Then, by Lemma 4,

$$\mathbb{P}(X_k \in I) = p_0(I)'Q^k \mathbf{1} \rightarrow 0 \text{ as } k \rightarrow \infty.$$

■

Proof of Theorem 2

By Corollary 2, it suffices to show that the states that contain elements in the elite set that are not Pareto optimal are inessential states. To this end, first note that $X = \mathbb{B}^l$ is complete because it is finite.

Now suppose that there is a state $\hat{i} = (i^e; i)$ in which the elite set contain elements $i^e_{s_1}, \ldots, i^e_{s_k}$ that are not Pareto optimal. Then, as X is complete, there are elements, say $j^e_{s_1}, \ldots, j^e_{s_k} \in \mathcal{P}^*$, that dominate $i^e_{s_1}, \ldots, i^e_{s_k}$, respectively.

Take $\hat{j} = (j^e; j)$ such that all Pareto optimal points of i^e are in j^e and replace the other elements of i^e with the corresponding $j^e_{s_1}, \ldots, j^e_{s_k}$. Thus all the elements in j^e are Pareto optimal.

Now let

$$j = (j^e_1, \ldots, j^e_r, \underbrace{i^e_{s_1}, \ldots, i^e_{s_1}}_{n-r})$$

By Lemma 3 we have $i \to j$. Hence, with positive probability we can pass from (i^e, i) to (i^e, j), and then we apply the elitist operation to pass from (i^e, j) to (j^e, j). This implies that $\hat{i} \to \hat{j}$. On the other hand, using (6) $\hat{j} \nrightarrow \hat{i}$. Therefore $\hat{i}$ is an essential state.

Finally, from Corollary 2 we have

$$\mathbb{P}(\{X^e_k\} \subset \mathcal{P}^*) = \mathbb{P}(X_k \in E) = 1 - \mathbb{P}(X_k \in I) \to 1 - 0 = 1 \text{ as } k \to \infty.$$

This completes the proof of Theorem 2.   ∎

6   Conclusions and Future Work

We have presented a proof of convergence for the multiobjective artificial immune system algorithm presented in [2] and called MISA by its authors. The theoretical analysis of the approach indicates that the use of elitism (which is represented in the form of an *elite set* in the case of multiobjective optimization) is necessary to guarantee convergence. To the authors' best knowledge, this is the first time that this sort of mathematical proof of convergence is presented for a multiobjective artificial immune system.

As part of our future work, we plan to extend our theoretical analysis to other types of artificial immune systems [3]. We are also interested in defining a more general framework for proving convergence of heuristics that operate with base on a mutation operator. Such a framework would allow to prove convergence of a family of heuristics that comply with a certain (minimum) set of requirements, rather than having to devise a specific proof for each of them.

Acknowledgments. The first author acknowledges support from the Universidad de Costa Rica through a scholarship to pursue graduate studies at the Department of Mathematics of CINVESTAV-IPN. The second author acknowledges support from NSF-CONACyT project No. 42435-Y. The last author acknowledges partial support from CONACyT grant 37355-E.

References

1. Carlos A. Coello Coello, David A. Van Veldhuizen, and Gary B. Lamont. *Evolutionary Algorithms for Solving Multi-Objective Problems*. Kluwer Academic Publishers, New York, May 2002. ISBN 0-3064-6762-3.
2. Nareli Cruz Cortés and Carlos A. Coello Coello. Multiobjective Optimization Using Ideas from the Clonal Selection Principle. In Erick Cantú-Paz et al., editor, *Genetic and Evolutionary Computation—GECCO 2003. Proceedings, Part I*, pages 158–170. Springer. Lecture Notes in Computer Science Vol. 2723, July 2003.
3. Dipankar Dasgupta, editor. *Artificial Immune Systems and Their Applications*. Springer-Verlag, Berlin, 1999.
4. Leandro Nunes de Castro and F. J. Von Zuben. Learning and Optimization Using the Clonal Selection Principle. *IEEE Transactions on Evolutionary Computation*, 6(3):239–251, 2002.
5. Kalyanmoy Deb. *Multi-Objective Optimization using Evolutionary Algorithms*. John Wiley & Sons, Chichester, UK, 2001. ISBN 0-471-87339-X.
6. Prabhat Hajela and Jun Sun Yoo. Immune Network Modelling in Design Optimization. In D. Corne, M. Dorigo, and F. Glover, editors, *New Ideas in Optimization*, pages 167–183. McGraw-Hill, 1999.
7. O. Hernández-Lerma. *Adaptive Markov Control Processes*. Springer-Verlag, New York, 1989.
8. Marius Iosifescu. *Finite Markov Processes and Their Applications*. John Wiley & Sons, Chichester, UK, 1980.
9. Kaisa M. Miettinen. *Nonlinear Multiobjective Optimization*. Kluwer Academic Publishers, Boston, Massachusetts, 1998.
10. Leandro Nunes de Castro and Jonathan Timmis. *An Introduction to Artificial Immune Systems: A New Computational Intelligence Paradigm*. Springer-Verlag, 2002.
11. Rosa Saab, Raúl Monroy, and Fernando Godínez. Towards a model for an immune system. In Carlos A. Coello Coello, Alvaro de Albornoz, Luis Enrique Sucar, and Osvaldo Cairó Battis-tutti, editors, *MICAI 2002: Advances in Artificial Intelligence. Second Mexican International Conference on Artificial Intelligence*, pages 401–410, Mérida, Yucatán, México, April 2002. Springer. Lecture Notes in Artificial Intelligence. Volume 2313.
12. E. Seneta. *Non-Negative Matrices and Markov Chains*. Springer-Verlag, New York, second edition, 1981.
13. Alexander Tarakanov and Dipankar Dasgupta. A formal model of an artificial immune system. *BioSystems*, 55:151–158, 2000.

A Comparison of Immune and Neural Computing for Two Real-Life Tasks of Pattern Recognition

Alexander O. Tarakanov[1] and Yuri A. Tarakanov[2]

[1] St. Petersburg Institute for Informatics and Automation, Russian Academy of Sciences
tar@iias.spb.su
[2] A.F.Ioffe Physico-Technical Institute, Russian Academy of Sciences,
darkln2@mail.ioffe.ru

Abstract. This paper compares a new Immunocomputing (IC) approach with Artificial Neural Networks (ANN). We compare an IC algorithm of pattern recognition with Error Back Propagation (EBP) network. The comparison includes two real-life tasks of environmental monitoring and laser physics.

Keywords: Error Back Propagation, Immunocomputing

1 Introduction

Two types of biological systems, the neural system and the immune system of the vertebrates possess the capabilities of "intelligent" information processing, which include memory, the ability to learn, to recognize, and to make decisions with respect to unknown situations. The potential of the natural neural system as a biological prototype of a computing scheme has already been well-established as a field of ANN, or neural computing [4], [15], [16]. However, the computing capabilities of the natural immune system have only recently been appreciated as a field of Artificial Immune Systems (AIS) [2], [5]. The mathematical formalization of these capabilities forms the basis of IC as a new computing approach that replicates the principles of information processing by proteins and immune networks [13].

Some general discussions of similarities and differences between AIS and ANN were provided in [2], [5], [6]. Some theoretical and empirical comparison between immune and neural network models were provided in [3]. However, IC models of immune networks [11], [13] differ from those utilizing within AIS. Besides, no direct comparison between ANN and IC algorithms has yet been available. This paper investigates more specifically this area, which has been explored before in a rather conceptual way.

We compare the IC algorithm of pattern recognition, which uses mathematical properties of singular value decomposition (see, e.g., [8], [13]) with the EBP network [7], which implements the well-known back-propagation algorithm of training (see, e.g., [15], [16]). The EBP algorithm can be considered as a basic variant of training of multilayer ANN. To obtain an accurate comparison we also provide a simplified (basic) version of the IC algorithm, as described in the next section. This version considers only the (first-stage) mapping of raw data onto a formal space of so-called spatial formal immune network (sFIN) [11] without involving the (second-stage) processing by sFIN, as in the full version of the IC model of pattern recognition (see, e.g., [10]).

G. Nicosia et al. (Eds.): ICARIS 2004, LNCS 3239, pp. 236–249, 2004.

It worth also noting that our work does not use any general purpose data repository to test the algorithms. Instead of this, we use two real-life tasks, which have already been solved by the IC algorithm: computing of an ecological map of the big city [9] and predicting the optical power output of a laser diode [14].

Besides, we use both tasks because they differ strongly by the ratio of test patterns to training patterns: the first task has rather low ratio (11/391), whereas this ratio is rather high (15/19) for the second task.

Simply put, this paper tries to answer the following question: could we satisfactory solve such specific real-life tasks if we used EBP instead of the IC algorithm?

2 Immunocomputing Algorithm

2.1 General Description

Generally, real-life data are multi-dimensional and real-valued. In principle, sFIN is able to pattern recognition over such data [10]. However, more effective and visual data mining can be provided by using the concept of low-dimensional "shape space" proposed by [1]. An IC model of mapping real-life data to such formal space of sFIN has been proposed in [13]. This mapping is based on rigorous mathematical properties of SVD.

Using such mapping, consider a description (in pseudocode) of the basic IC algorithm of pattern recognition.

Basic IC algorithm of pattern recognition

```
Training
{
        Get training patterns;
        Form training matrix;
        Compute SVD of the training matrix;
}

Recognition
(
        Get pattern;
        Map the pattern to the formal space of sFIN;
        Find the nearest training pattern of sFIN;
}
```

Consider a brief description of this IC algorithm in mathematical terms.

2.2 Pattern Recognition

Define *pattern* as n - dimensional column-vector $X=[x_1,...,x_n]^T$, where x_1, ..., x_n are real values and "T" is symbol of matrix transposing.

Define *pattern recognition* as mapping $f(X) = \{1, ..., c\}$ of any pattern X, where integers $1,..., c$ are *classes*.

The task of pattern recognition can be formulated as follows.
Given:
  – Number of classes c;
  – Set of m training patterns: $X_1, ..., X_m$;
  – Class of any training pattern: $f(X_1) = c_1, ..., f(X_m) = c_m$;
  – Arbitrary n - dimensional vector P.
To find:
  Class of the vector P: $f(P)=?$

2.3 Training

1. Form training matrix $A=[X_1...X_m]^T$ of dimension $m{\times}n$.
2. Compute maximal singular value s and left and right singular vectors L and R of the training matrix by the following iterative (*evolutionary*) scheme:

$$L_{(0)} = [1 ... 1]^T,$$

$$R^T = L_{(k-1)}^T A , \; R_{(k)}=R/|R| , \text{ where } |R| = \sqrt{r_1^2 +...+ r_n^2} ,$$

$$L = AR_{(k)} , \; L_{(k)}=L/|L| , \text{ where } |L| = \sqrt{l_1^2 +...+ l_m^2} ,$$

$$s_{(k)} = L_{(k)}^T AR_{(k)} , \; k=1,2,...,$$

$$\text{until } \left| s_{(k)} - s_{(k-1)} \right| < \varepsilon , \tag{1}$$

$$s = s_{(k)} , \; L = L_{(k)} , \; R = R_{(k)} .$$

3. Store singular value s.
4. Store right singular vector R as "*antibody-probe*".
5. For any $i = 1,..., m$ store component l_i of left singular vector L and class c_i of corresponding training pattern X_i .

2.4 Recognition

6. For any n - dimensional pattern P compute its *binding energy* with R:

$$w(P) = P^T R / s$$

(remember that s is the computed singular value and R is the computed right singular vector of the training matrix A).

7. Select l_i , which has minimal distance (*affinity*) with w:

$$\min_i \left| w - l_i \right|, \; i = 1,..., m . \tag{2}$$

8. Consider class c_i as the required class of the pattern P.

2.5 Remarks

This core of the algorithm uses only maximal (first) singular value s and corresponding singular vectors L and R, which are computed in step 2 of the algorithm.

In general, we suggest using the first 3 singular values and corresponding singular vectors of the training matrix. They can be computed by the same iterative scheme (step 2) as follows.

2.1. Compute maximal singular value s_1 and corresponding singular vectors L_1 and R_1 of the training matrix by step 2.

2.2. Form matrix $A_2 = A - s_1 L_1 R_1^T$ and compute its maximal singular value s_2 and corresponding singular vectors L_2 and R_2 by step 2.

2.3. Form matrix $A_3 = A - s_2 L_2 R_2^T$ and compute its maximal singular value s_3 and corresponding singular vectors L_3 and R_3 by step 2.

Then compute three binding energies by step 6:

$$w_1(P) = P^T R_1 / s_1, \; w_2(P) = P^T R_2 / s_2, \; w_3(P) = P^T R_3 / s_3,$$

and select the class c_i on step 8 by minimal distance in three-dimensional Euclidian space on step 7:

$$\min_i \sqrt{(w_1 - [l_i]_1)^2 + (w_2 - [l_i]_2)^2 + (w_3 - [l_i]_3)^2}, \tag{3}$$

where $[l_i]_1$, $[l_i]_2$, $[l_i]_3$ are i-th components of left singular vectors L_1, L_2, L_3.

3 Back-Propagation Network

This kind of ANN is well-established and described in several sources (see, e.g., [15], [16]). In our numerical experiments we use EBP network [7] with $n+1$ input neurons, $n+1$ hidden neurons, and one output neuron.

Let $X_b = [x_1 \ldots x_n \, x_{n+1}]^T$ and $Y_b = [y_1 \ldots y_n \, y_{n+1}]^T$ be input and hidden vectors of ANN with bias values $x_{n+1} = -1$ and $y_{n+1} = -1$. Let X and Y be n - dimensional input and hidden vectors without bias. Let W and V be weight matrix of input layer of dimension $n \times (n+1)$ and weight vector of output layer of dimension $(n+1) \times 1$. Then for any n - dimensional input vector P the output value z of the network is computed by the following formulae:

$$Y = f_s(WP_b), \, z = f_s(V^T Y_b),$$

where P_b is the input vector added with bias component, and f_s is the unipolar sigmoidal activation function:

$$f_s(x) = 2 \, (1 + exp(-x))^{-1} - 1.$$

Training of the network consists in adapting weights of W and V by using the back-propagation algorithm. Training cycles are repeated until the overall error value drops below some pre-determined threshold:

$$\sum_i \left(z_i - z_i^*\right)^2 / 2 < \varepsilon, \tag{4}$$

where z_i^* is desired output for i-th training pattern X_i.

As activation function satisfies to the following inequalities: $-1 < f_S < 1$, we need to recompute any output z of the network at the stage of recognition to integer class c of input pattern as follows:

$$c = Entier\ (10z + 0.5).$$

4   Test-1: Ecological Atlas

4.1   General Description

The quality of the urban environment for human inhabitation is a very real issue. Its influence on the health of town-dwellers is widely known to be essential, though social processes also determine disease rates.

The maps presented in the ecological atlas of the City of Kaliningrad (formerly Koenigsberg) [9] have been taken from environmental monitoring and expert evaluations of the City. They characterize various aspects of environment as the pollution of air and waters, soil conditions, etc. However a city-dweller is influenced day to day by all the chemical, physical, climatic and other factors. It is therefore important to understand the complex impact of all these factors on a human organism in order to improve the environmental protection and emotional well being of the inhabitants.

The main ecological map is a complex appraisal of environmental conditions [9], which is based on, and summarizes the whole atlas.

4.2   Test Data

The test data for this real-life task are given by the following integer matrix M^*, which corresponds to the map of environmental conditions in Kaliningrad.

Matrix M^*:

```
0 0 0 0 0 1 1 1 1 1 1 2 1 0 0 0 0 0 0 0 0 0 0 0
0 0 0 0 1 1 1 2 1 1 1 2 2 2 2 3 4 4 0 0 0 0 0 0
0 0 0 0 0 1 1 2 2 1 1 2 2 1 1 1 2 2 2 0 0 0 0 0
1 1 1 1 1 2 3 2 2 3 2 4 4 3 2 2 3 2 2 2 0 0 0 0
1 1 1 1 2 1 1 1 1 4 5 4 5 4 3 2 3 3 3 3 0 0 0
0 0 2 2 3 2 2 2 2 4 5 4 4 4 4 2 1 2 1 1 0 0
0 0 1 1 1 3 4 3 2 3 4 5 5 4 5 3 2 1 2 1 1 1 0
0 0 1 1 1 1 3 2 3 4 5 5 3 4 6 4 4 4 3 1 1 1 0
0 1 1 1 2 3 4 4 4 3 5 4 5 6 5 5 4 5 4 3 2 0 0
1 1 1 3 2 3 3 3 4 4 4 5 5 6 5 5 5 5 4 3 3 0 0
1 1 4 4 4 3 3 2 3 4 4 3 4 6 5 6 5 4 4 3 1 0 0
0 0 0 0 0 0 0 0 3 4 3 4 3 3 3 5 4 3 4 2 1 2 1
0 0 0 0 0 0 2 3 3 4 3 3 2 3 4 3 3 2 3 2 1 1 1
0 0 1 1 0 2 3 3 3 3 4 3 2 3 3 2 3 3 2 2 1 1 0
0 1 1 2 3 3 3 3 0 0 0 0 0 0 0 2 3 0 0 0 0 0 0
1 1 1 1 3 0 0 0 0 0 0 0 0 0 0 0 0 0 0 0 0 0 0
1 1 1 0 0 0 0 0 0 0 0 0 0 0 0 0 0 0 0 0 0 0 0
```

Table 1. Maps of partial ecological factors

Map	Indicator	Factor	Scale
M_1	x_1	Geomorphology	0-5
M_2	x_2	Air	0-6
M_3	x_3	Water	0-7
M_4	x_4	Soil	0-7
M_5	x_5	Acoustic conditions	0-6
M_6	x_6	Electromagnetic fields	0-5

Table 2. Training set

$X_\#$	k_i	k_j	x_1	x_2	x_3	x_4	x_5	x_6	Class c*
1	1	1	0	0	0	0	0	0	**0**
2	1	6	1	1	4	7	1	1	**1**
3	5	9	1	2	2	4	2	1	**1**
4	6	11	3	6	4	1	2	2	**4**
5	7	10	3	2	5	1	4	2	**3**
6	7	14	5	3	4	3	4	3	**4**
7	8	15	4	2	6	5	6	4	**6**
8	8	16	4	2	4	6	2	5	**4**
9	10	14	4	3	7	6	5	3	**6**
10	10	16	4	3	5	5	4	3	**5**
11	13	14	1	3	3	4	5	3	**3**

This map had been computed by the IC algorithm based on expert opinions on the 11 most typical areas of the city as training examples (marked by bold in $M*$). After that, the map was corrected by analysts and published in the atlas [9]. Therefore, we can consider the matrix $M*$ as a probe for comparing the quality of several algorithms.

To compute this map, the whole city was divided into a 17×23 square grid with 1 km side by latitude (k_i) and longitude (k_j). Six maps M_1-M_6 of the partial ecological factors (indicators) were involved in the processing, as shown in Table 1.

Mark 0 (zero) of the scale means the absence of estimation in the corresponding square (the square is out of the city). Mark 1 means a good quality of the corresponding factor in the corresponding square. In general, the higher is the mark the worse is the quality of the factor.

The training set was given by experts in ecology as a set of the most typical areas of the city, for which experts assigned the values of index of general quality of environment in the scale 0-6. This training set is shown in Table 2.

4.3 Results of IC Algorithm

Training matrix $A = [X_1 \dots X_{11}]^T$:

0.0	0.0	0.0	0.0	0.0	0.0
1.0	1.0	4.0	7.0	1.0	1.0
1.0	2.0	2.0	4.0	2.0	1.0
3.0	6.0	4.0	1.0	2.0	2.0
3.0	2.0	5.0	1.0	4.0	2.0
5.0	3.0	4.0	3.0	4.0	3.0
4.0	2.0	6.0	5.0	6.0	4.0
4.0	2.0	4.0	6.0	2.0	5.0
4.0	3.0	7.0	6.0	5.0	3.0
4.0	3.0	5.0	5.0	4.0	3.0
1.0	3.0	3.0	4.0	5.0	3.0

Maximal singular value of the training matrix: $s = 27.757$.
Left singular vector:

$$L = [\,0.000\ 0.248\ 0.183\ 0.249\ 0.254\ 0.319\ 0.409\ 0.341\ 0.430\ 0.360\ 0.281\,]^T.$$

Right singular vector (antibody-probe):

$$R = [\,0.359\ 0.298\ 0.518\ 0.487\ 0.416\ 0.322\,]^T.$$

Complex map M_{IC} has been computed by the IC algorithm using first singular value s and corresponding singular vectors L and R, according to (2).

The following matrix shows absolute difference between the computed and the published complex maps $\Delta M_{IC} = |M_{IC} - M^*|$.

Matrix ΔM_{IC} :

```
000000000000100000000000
000010010001111100100000
000000011001100011100000
000001111010001101110000
000010000010000100000000
001101111101110110100000
000001011000001010100010
000000010111110010000010
000010100011100100011100
000010000010101011110000
001111110010101110000000
000000000101111111110010
000000100010100111010000
000001001100111110110010
000100000000000110000000
000000000000000000000000
001000000000000000000000
```

4.4   Results of EBP Network

Weight matrix W:

$$
\begin{array}{rrrrrrr}
1.635 & 0.802 & -0.401 & -0.609 & 1.020 & 0.672 & -0.547 \\
-0.081 & 0.100 & 0.347 & 0.010 & 0.386 & 0.254 & 0.398 \\
-0.647 & 0.101 & -0.915 & 0.186 & 0.998 & 0.293 & -0.235 \\
-1.467 & 1.142 & -4.928 & -1.381 & -1.796 & -1.898 & -3.908 \\
0.175 & 0.351 & 0.288 & -0.353 & 0.178 & 0.195 & 0.212 \\
0.893 & -2.261 & 0.911 & -0.056 & 1.588 & 1.677 & -0.643
\end{array}
$$

Weight vector V:

$$
1.208 \quad -0.033 \quad 1.085 \quad -1.158 \quad -0.172 \quad -1.920 \quad -1.235
$$

Difference map $\Delta M_{EBP} = \left| M_{EBP} - M* \right|$ computed by EBP network is the following.

Matrix ΔM_{EBP}:

```
0 0 0 0 0 0 0 0 0 1 0 1 1 0 0 0 0 0 0 0 0 0 0
0 0 0 0 1 0 0 0 0 1 0 0 1 0 1 0 1 2 0 0 0 0 0
0 0 0 0 0 0 0 0 0 0 1 1 0 0 0 1 2 2 2 0 0 0 0
1 0 1 1 1 0 1 0 0 0 0 0 0 0 0 0 0 1 0 2 0 0 0
1 1 0 0 2 1 1 1 0 1 0 1 1 0 1 0 0 1 0 1 0 0 0
0 0 0 1 0 0 0 1 0 1 0 2 2 1 1 0 0 0 0 1 0 0
0 0 1 1 1 1 0 1 1 0 0 0 0 0 1 1 0 1 0 1 1 0
0 0 1 1 0 0 1 1 1 1 1 1 1 0 0 0 1 0 2 0 1 1 0
0 1 1 1 2 1 1 0 0 0 1 1 1 0 0 0 1 0 1 1 1 0 0
1 1 1 0 0 0 0 0 0 0 1 0 0 0 0 0 1 1 1 1 1 0 0
1 1 2 2 2 1 1 1 0 0 2 0 1 0 1 1 0 0 0 0 1 0 0
0 0 0 0 0 0 0 0 1 1 0 1 1 1 1 1 1 1 1 1 0 1 0
0 0 0 0 0 0 2 1 0 0 1 0 0 0 1 1 1 0 0 1 0 0 1
0 0 1 1 0 1 1 1 1 1 1 1 0 1 1 0 1 1 1 2 1 1 0
0 1 1 1 1 1 1 1 0 0 0 0 0 0 0 0 1 0 0 0 0 0 0
1 1 1 1 1 0 0 0 0 0 0 0 0 0 0 0 0 0 0 0 0 0 0
1 1 1 0 0 0 0 0 0 0 0 0 0 0 0 0 0 0 0 0 0 0 0
```

5   Test-2: Optical Response of Laser Diode

5.1   General Description

Semiconductor laser diodes capable of generating high power picosecond optical pulses are required in a number of applications, including high resolution time-of-flight laser distance meters, laser tomography, etc. One of the promising ways of generating such optical pulses is the gain-switching method. In [14] we proposed the gain-switched GaAs/AlGaAs double-heterostructure laser diode with one potential barrier incorporated into the active region, and showed that the optical power in this barrier could be increased significantly. We also suggested that presence of several potential barriers would give rise to additional emitted optical power. Computer simulation for the structure with 3 barriers shows that the optical responses of the structure depend strongly on the parameters of all the barriers, and this dependence is far less evident than for a structure with 1 or 2 barriers.

To construct a laser diode, we should first prove that the chosen structure is optimal. It is evident that creating and testing different structures is a very expensive process which takes too much time. On the other hand, conventional methods of simulation of laser dynamics (e.g., computational physics) are so time expensive, that it is also impossible to test sufficient quantities of varying data. Therefore, to predict the structure of a laser diode which would provide us with the maximum output of optical power, and to capture this dependence, novel computational approaches are necessary.

Table 3. Optical power of different laser diode structures

$X_#$	x_1	x_2	x_3	x_4	x_5	Class c* (optical power)
1	40	40	30	30	40	1
2	40	20	40	30	40	1
3	40	30	55	40	40	1
4	30	40	40	30	55	1
5	40	30	40	30	40	2
6	40	40	40	30	55	3
7	40	40	30	40	40	3
8	40	20	30	40	40	4
9	40	30	40	55	40	4
10	40	30	40	40	40	4
11	55	40	40	30	30	4
12	30	40	40	30	30	5
13	40	40	40	30	40	6
14	55	40	40	30	55	6
15	40	40	40	30	30	7
16	30	40	40	30	40	1
17	40	40	40	20	40	1
18	40	40	40	40	40	3
19	40	20	40	40	40	4

5.2 Test Data

The test data for the laser diode structure with 3 barriers is given in Table 3. This data was obtained using the computational physics method also proposed in [14]. The experimental results for such structures do not yet exist. However, the computational results for a simpler structure, which has only 1 internal barrier, correspond well to the experimental structures.

As stated above, the optical power depends on the properties of the internal barriers in the laser diode. The input data composes these barriers, as well as being the emitters, namely the percentage of aluminium in ternary solution AlGaAs, which defines the energy offset of these barriers. Therefore, the indicators are defined as follows:
- x_1 and x_5 are aluminium percentages in emitters of electrons and holes, respectively;
- x_2, x_3, and x_4 are aluminium percentages in 1st, 2nd and 3rd internal barriers respectively.

The class (index) number corresponds to the output optical power in a response to the nanosecond current pulse with amplitude of 3.2 A as follows: class 1: 0-2 Wt; class 2: 2-3 Wt; class 3: 3-4 Wt; class 4: 4-5 Wt; class 5: 5-6 Wt; class 6: 6-7 Wt; class 7: more than 7 Wt.

We used the first 15 structures in Table 3 as a training set (marked by bold).

5.3 Results of IC Algorithm

Training matrix $A = [X_1 \dots X_{15}]^T$:

$$
\begin{array}{ccccc}
40.0 & 40.0 & 30.0 & 30.0 & 40.0 \\
40.0 & 20.0 & 40.0 & 30.0 & 40.0 \\
40.0 & 30.0 & 55.0 & 40.0 & 40.0 \\
30.0 & 40.0 & 40.0 & 30.0 & 55.0 \\
40.0 & 30.0 & 40.0 & 30.0 & 40.0 \\
40.0 & 40.0 & 40.0 & 30.0 & 55.0 \\
40.0 & 40.0 & 30.0 & 40.0 & 40.0 \\
40.0 & 20.0 & 30.0 & 40.0 & 40.0 \\
40.0 & 30.0 & 40.0 & 55.0 & 40.0 \\
40.0 & 30.0 & 40.0 & 40.0 & 40.0 \\
55.0 & 40.0 & 40.0 & 30.0 & 30.0 \\
30.0 & 40.0 & 40.0 & 30.0 & 30.0 \\
40.0 & 40.0 & 40.0 & 30.0 & 40.0 \\
55.0 & 40.0 & 40.0 & 30.0 & 55.0 \\
40.0 & 40.0 & 40.0 & 30.0 & 30.0 \\
\end{array}
$$

Singular values of the training matrix:

$$s_1 = 330.447, \; s_2 = 33.024, \; s_3 = 28.799 .$$

Left singular vectors:

$L_1 = [\; 0.244 \; 0.233 \; 0.278 \; 0.265 \; 0.245 \; 0.280 \; 0.256 \; 0.231 \; 0.276 \; 0.258 \; 0.265 \; 0.229$
$\qquad 0.258 \; 0.301 \; 0.243 \;]^T$,

$L_2 = [\; -0.226 \; 0.189 \; 0.297 \; -0.288 \; 0.004 \; -0.289 \; -0.002 \; 0.367 \; 0.564 \; 0.228 \; -0.110$
$\qquad -0.107 \; -0.181 \; -0.292 \; -0.108 \;]^T$,

$L_3 = [\; 0.039 \; -0.138 \; 0.052 \; -0.484 \; -0.022 \; -0.338 \; 0.031 \; -0.200 \; -0.042 \; -0.030 \; 0.601$
$\qquad 0.235 \; 0.094 \; -0.118 \; 0.381 \;]^T$.

Right singular vectors (antibody probes):

$R_1 = [\; 0.478 \; 0.407 \; 0.458 \; 0.402 \; 0.484 \;]^T$,
$R_2 = [\; -0.005 \; -0.610 \; 0.150 \; 0.740 \; -0.240 \;]^T$,
$R_3 = [\; 0.422 \; 0.333 \; 0.157 \; -0.023 \; -0.828 \;]^T$.

The following classes $(c_{IC})_i$: $i = 1, \dots, 19$ have been computed by the IC algorithm, according to (3):

$$c_{IC} = \{1, 1, 1, 1, 2, 3, 3, 4, 4, 4, 4, 5, 6, 6, 7, 1, 1, 3, 4\}.$$

Note that all the computed classes correspond to the classes c^* of Table 3 obtained by the computational physics method. Therefore, the IC algorithm gives no recognition errors $\Delta c_{IC} = |c_{IC} - c^*|$ for this test.

5.4   Results of EBP Network

Weight matrix W:

$$\begin{matrix} -11.921 & -16.744 & 21.104 & 2.008 & 7.414 & 0.900 \\ 1.573 & 3.664 & -0.798 & -7.312 & -0.731 & -0.295 \\ 0.457 & 2.665 & -2.604 & -3.183 & 2.698 & -1.270 \\ 0.349 & 0.380 & 2.388 & 1.420 & -0.853 & 1.070 \\ 6.097 & 7.449 & -16.291 & 1.515 & -2.004 & 0.917 \end{matrix}$$

Weight vector V:

$$-2.682 \quad -3.557 \quad 1.589 \quad -1.014 \quad -6.425 \quad 6.058$$

The following classes $(c_{EBP})_i$ have been computed by EBP network:

$$c_{EBP} = \{1, 1, 1, 1, 2, 3, 3, 4, 4, 4, 4, 5, 6, 6, 7, 3, 3, 7, 3\}.$$

The recognition errors $\Delta c_{EBP} = |c_{EBP} - c*|$ for the EBP network are as follows:

$$\Delta c_{EBP} = \{0, 0, 0, 0, 0, 0, 0, 0, 0, 0, 0, 0, 0, 0, 0, 2, 2, 4, 1\}.$$

5.5   Test of Possible Overtraining

An additional experiment has been done with data of Test-2 to check whether rather high recognition errors could be caused by possible overtraining of EBP network. For this purpose, we changed the training set of Table 3 as follows:

Table 4. Modified training set for Test-2

$X_\#$	x_1	x_2	x_3	x_4	x_5	Class c* (optical power)
1	40	40	30	30	40	1
5	40	30	40	30	40	2
6	40	40	40	30	55	3
8	40	20	30	40	40	4
12	30	40	40	30	30	5
13	40	40	40	30	40	6
15	40	40	40	30	30	7

Apparently, such EBP network can not be overtrained, because any class corresponds just to one training pattern. The following results have been obtained for such EBP network.

Weight matrix W:

$$\begin{matrix} -1.020 & -1.157 & -1.421 & -3.597 & -0.347 & -2.735 \\ 0.918 & 1.591 & 2.296 & 4.909 & 0.574 & 3.612 \\ 0.625 & 0.746 & 1.234 & 1.998 & -0.006 & 1.697 \\ 0.146 & -0.057 & -0.808 & -0.513 & 0.587 & -0.171 \\ -2.355 & -3.037 & -3.122 & -6.893 & 3.738 & -2.504 \end{matrix}$$

Weight vector V:

$$-2.621 \quad 3.497 \quad 1.449 \quad 0.059 \quad -4.939 \quad 1.588$$

The recognition errors $\Delta c_{EBP} = |c_{EBP} - c^*|$ for such EBP network are as follows:

$$\Delta c_{EBP} = \{0\ 3\ 9\ 1\ 0\ 0\ 6\ 0\ 6\ 5\ 5\ 0\ 0\ 1\ 0\ 2\ 6\ 6\ 4\}.$$

Total error for such EBP network (without overtraining) is 54, whereas total error for the case with possible overtraining is just 9 (see Table 5).

Therefore, the low performance obtained with EBP network might not be due to overtraining.

6 Discussion

Comparative performance of EBP and IC algorithms for the above tests is given in Table 5.

Training time is determined by the same error value $\varepsilon = 1.0e - 8$ for both algorithms, according to (1) and (4). Note that both algorithms have no recognition errors on training sets. However, training time of the EBP network is far longer than that of the IC algorithm.

Note that maximal difference between the computed by the IC algorithm and the published complex maps does not exceed the value of 1: max(ΔM_{IC})=1, whereas max(ΔM_{EBP})=2 for Test-1. Note also, that max(Δc_{IC})=0, whereas max(Δc_{EBP})=4 for Test-2.

Summarizing all the elements of the matrix ΔM_{IC}, we obtain the total difference 117, whereas the total number of squares in the map is 391. Thus, we obtain mean difference per square lower than 1/3.

We consider this value as a quantitative measure of quality of the IC algorithm. Therefore, we can consider the results obtained by the IC algorithm as completely satisfactory, because the mean difference from the expert evaluations is lower than a half of the index scale unit per square. Note, that total difference for the matrix ΔM_{EBP} is equal to 170, which is 1.45 times more adverse than that of the IC algorithm.

Table 5. Performance of IC and EBP algorithms

Algorithm	IC	EBP	IC	EBP
Test	Test-1	Test-1	Test-2	Test-2
Training patterns	11	11	15	15
Training time (for Pentium-4 1.8 GHz)	<1 s	45 s	<1 s	120 s
Errors on training set	0	0	0	0
Test patterns	391	391	19	19
Total errors on test set	117	170	0	9
Mean error per pattern	0.30	0.43	0.00	0.47
Maximal error on test set	1	2	0	4

Therefore, we can answer the question stated in Introduction as follows: the EBP algorithm could in principle solve both tasks [9] and [14], but at least 1.4 times worse (by mean error) than the IC algorithm. However, such solutions could not be considered as satisfactory because the maximal errors of the EBP algorithm is 2-4 times worse than those of the IC algorithm.

Apparently, such results could be explained by the fact that EBP network provides continuous output, whereas the discrete output of the IC algorithm is better suited to pattern recognition. It worth also noting that any repeat of training of an EBP network gives a different weight matrix and weight vector. This feature makes EBP network somewhat "unpredictable", whereas singular values and vectors of any matrix are the same for any repeating of the training by the IC algorithm. A possible way of improving the performance of neural computing has been proposed in [12].

Acknowledgments. This work was partially supported by EU project IST-2000-26016 "Immunocomputing". First author acknowledges also the support of EOARD under project # 017007 "Development of mathematical models of immune networks intended for information security assurance". The idea to compare IC algorithm with EBP network belongs to Prof. Gerard Weisbuch (Dept. of Physics, Ecole Normale Superieure, Paris). We also thank Dr. Salvatore Parisi (Dept. of Informatics, Universita degli studi di Milano) for his valuable suggestions and applications of the IC algorithm.

References

1. de Boer, R.J., Segel, L.A., Perelson, A.S.: Pattern formation in one and two-dimensional shape space models of the immune system. J. Theoret. Biol. 155 (1992) 295-333
2. de Castro, L. N., Timmis, J.: Artificial Immune Systems: A New Computational Intelligence Approach. Springer, London (2002)
3. de Castro, L. N., von Zuben, F.J.: Immune and neural network models: theoretical and empirical comparisons. Int. J. Comp. Intelligence and Applications 1(3) (2001) 239-257
4. Cloete, I., Zurada, J. M. (eds): Knowledge-Based Neurocomputing. MIT Press, Cambridge (2000)
5. Dasgupta, D. (ed): Artificial Immune Systems and Their Applications. Springer, Berlin (1999)
6. Dasgupta, D.: Artificial Neural Networks and Artificial Immune Systems: Similarities and Differences. Proc. IEEE Int. Conf. on Systems, Man and Cybernetics. Orlando, October 12-15, (1997)
7. Error Back Propagation Program. Available: http://ci.uofl.edu/zurada/ece614/index.html
8. Horn, R., Johnson, Ch.: Matrix Analysis. Cambridge University Press (1986)
9. Kuznetsov, V. I., Gubanov, A. F., Kuznetsov, V. V., Tarakanov, A. O., Tchertov, O. G.: Map of complex appraisal of environmental conditions in Kaliningrad. Kaliningrad: Ecological Atlas. Kaliningrad (1999)
10. Melnikov, Yu., Tarakanov A.O.: Immunocomputing model of intrusion detection. Lecture Notes in Computer Science, Vol. 2776. Springer, Berlin (2003) 453-456
11. Tarakanov, A.O.: Spatial formal immune network. Lecture Notes in Computer Science, Vol. 2723. Springer, Berlin (2003) 248-249
12. Tarakanov, A. O., Penev, G. D., Madani, K.: Formal neuro-immune network. Neural Networks and Soft Computing, Physica-Verlag, Berlin (2002) 644-649

13. Tarakanov, A. O., Skormin, V. A., Sokolova, S. P.: Immunocomputing: Principles and Applications. Springer, New York (2003)
14. Tarakanov, Yu. A., Ilyushenkov, D. S., Chistyakov, V. M., Odnoblyudov, M. A., Gurevich, S. A.: Picosecond pulse generation by internal gain switching in laser diodes. J. Appl. Phys. 95(5) (2004) 2223-2228
15. Wasserman, P. D.: Neural Computing: Theory and Practice. Van Nostrad Reinhold, New York (1990)
16. Zurada, J. M.: Introduction to Artificial Neural Systems. West Publishing Co., Boston (1992)

An Artificial Immune System Based Visual Analysis Model and Its Real-Time Terrain Surveillance Application

György Cserey[1,2], Wolfgang Porod[1], and Tamás Roska[2]

[1] Department of Electrical Engineering, University of Notre Dame,
275 Fitzpatrick Hall, Notre Dame Indiana 46556, USA
{gcserey,porod}@nd.edu
[2] Faculty of Information Technology, Pázmány University, Budapest and
Computer and Automation Research Institute
of the Hungarian Academy of Sciences,
Kende utca 13-17, Budapest, H-1111, Hungary
roska@sztaki.hu

Abstract. We present a real-time visual analysis system for surveillance applications based on an Artificial Immune System inspired framework [10] that can reliably detect unknown patterns in input image sequences. The system converts gray-scale or color images to binary with statistical 3x3 sub-pattern analysis based on an AIS algorithm, which make use of the standard AIS modules. Our system is implemented on specialized hardware (the Cellular Nonlinear Network (CNN) Universal Machine). Results from tests in a 3D virtual world with different terrain textures are reported to demonstrate that the system can detect unknown patterns and dynamical changes in image sequences. Applications of the system include in particular explorer systems for terrain surveillance.

1 Introduction

The detection of important objects, patterns or dynamic changes in real time is a difficult problem for machine visual systems (such as those used for surveillance, robots, etc.), where there is no human decision-maker present, since the image database becomes too big to handle efficiently. The problem becomes intractable on autonomous robots with limited computational resources, where standard imaging algorithms are not applicable because of their high computational demands. Yet, for many surveillance tasks, such as those performed by video surveillance systems to record strange and important events at a bank or in the street, being able to send an event detection message as fast as possible is essential.

Recently, many pattern recognition approaches have been proposed for supervision systems to detect or classify patterns based on different theoretical models and processing methods [16,17,18,19]. While these systems are capable of classifying scenes based on motion information of trajectories or labelling

G. Nicosia et al. (Eds.): ICARIS 2004, LNCS 3239, pp. 250–262, 2004.

of events and interactions, none of them is capable of carrying out all of the needed tasks, like preprocessing, feature extraction, learning and recognition in real time. *Artificial Immune Systems* (AIS) mimic the human immune system that has refined capabilities and methodologies to build efficient algorithms that solve engineering problems such as those mentioned above. Moreover, our immune system possesses important properties (eg. diversity, noise and fault tolerance, learning and memory and self-organization) which give it an advantage compared to other standard methods.

In this paper, based on the original CNN-UM simulation of immune response inspired spacial-temporal algorithmic framework, we present an AIS-based image terrain pattern analysis approach that is intended to solve the real time dynamical pattern recognition and detection problem in 2D image sequences using techniques analogous to natural immune systems. Humans monitor their environment with eyes and process its input image flow through their retina and relay the result to the brain for further evaluation. In our experiments, we utilized a parallel array processor, the *Cellular Nonlinear Network* (CNN) universal machine [6,7,8,9] for visual processing. This fast processor runs not only the sensory pre-processing algorithm, but the learning and recognition methods too, which in cooperation with digital algorithms allows for fast applications.

In Fig. 1, we would like to show the basic idea. This is a simple example where the detection is based on the tail type of the objects (airplanes). During initialization our system was taught not to detect planes with the first type of tail (Fig. 1a). Then, during the recognition phase, the planes which have the same tail, will not be detected, but any other type of tail, like the second set of tails (Fig. 1b, the unfamiliar ones), will be detected.

Fig. 1. After the initialization phase (a), known input patterns keep the system tolerant and during the recognition phase (b) unknown objects can cause detection, if they can be differentiated from the unimportant noise.

The organization of this paper is as follows: after a quick review of recent AIS approaches for pattern recognition and a brief introduction to the applied methods of AIS in Section 2, a detailed overview of our proposed system is presented focusing mainly on the AIS methods in Section 3. We discuss the properties, the mathematical representation and the algorithm. Section 4 explains a terrain surveillance application with results of the experiments and observations. In Section 5 the new aspects and time measurements of this research are presented. Finally in Section 6, the results are summarized, conclusions drawn, and plans for future work given.

2   Background on Pattern Recognition Using Artificial Immune Systems

2.1   Human and Artificial Immune System

The human immune system is an elaborate system with complex mechanisms for defense against antigens. Antigens are all materials that can be specifically recognized as an offensive (pathogen) or non-offensive (non-pathogen), and specifically responded to by the immune system [13]. The basic components of this biological system are the B and T lymphocytes, they intervene during the adaptive immune response and are accountable for the detection and elimination of offensive materials. From the point of view of pattern recognition, a very important characteristic of T and B-cells is that they have surface receptor molecules for recognizing antigens.

Some of important processes and properties of the immune system from our model's point of view are briefly summarized in following:

- *Bone marrow* is the major site of production of blood cell types including lymphocytes. Special environment is also provided for antigen-independent differentiation of B-cells by this soft issue.
- *Thymus* is a lymphoid organ, whose environment is provided for antigen-independent differentiation of T-cells. Immature T-cells migrate from the bone marrow to the thymus, some of them differentiate into immunocompetent cells by positive selection and those who have strong recognition of self-peptides are purged out by the negative selection method.
- *Positive and negative selection*: All T-cells bind to the antigens through self-peptide complexes (MHC, see [13]). Only those T-cells, which are capable of recognizing the self-peptide complexes, are stimulated for maturation by the positive selection, and the process of negative selection purges the auto-reactive T-cells from the repertoire.
- *Clonal selection* is one of the basic properties of an adaptive immune response where only those cells proliferate and differentiate into effector cells which are capable of recognizing an antigen stimulus.
- *Immune memory*: After the first infection, high affinity, long living lymphocytes are stored and persisted in a resting state to give stronger response after the next infections.

"Artificial immune systems (AIS) are adaptive systems, inspired by theoretical immunology and observed immune functions, principles and models, which are applied to problem solving" [2]. For the AIS, immune cells and molecules are represented by data items which take apart in some general-purpose algorithm that models specific interactions and aspects of the immune systems. The repertoires of the data items are usually generated by bone marrow models. The models of thymus are used to select repertoires capable of performing non-self/self-peptide discrimination. In the theory of AIS [1,2], antigens, lymphocytes and any molecules have a generalized shape m in shape-space S. This generalized shape can be represented as an attribute string - set of binary or other coordinates - of length L. Therefore any molecule string m can be regarded as a point in an L-dimensional shape-space. The interaction of an antigen and a peptide is assessed via a common (Euclidean, Manhattan, Hamming, etc.) D distance measure, which is also called affinity measure, between their proportional strings. Usually a relation is defined between the distance D and the recognition region V_ε proportionally to the recognition threshold or cross-reactivity threshold ε. If the D distance measure between data items is larger than ε, then a successful recognition is assumed between the items.

2.2   Applied Pattern Recognition Methods with AIS

The field of pattern recognition is mainly focused on building systems which are able to identify patterns in given measurement or observation data. Sub-disciplines are feature extraction, error estimation, classification, syntactical pattern recognition. The main applications are classification, image processing, character or handwriting recognition, speech analysis, human person identification, diagnosis and industrial applications.

To overview the main pattern recognition areas using AIS, we can give some fields based on the literature of [2,4], where general AIS approaches were to be applied. Each chemical reaction, which maps a set of reactants into a set of products, can be identified by a spectrum, see [20]. We worked with a binary Hamming shape-space, and our AIS was combined with a genetic algorithm to recognize specific spectrums. We proposed an affinity function where the weight of each bit was chosen according to a spectrum characteristic. Another area is the surveillance of infectious diseases [21]. Their AIS was developed for analysis and understanding at the dynamics of the plague. Pattern recognition applied in other different medical areas. A general data classification system was designed for medical data analysis [22]. In the area of data mining, an immunological algorithm was proposed [23] to discover rules classifying samples belonging to small disjuncts, which correspond to rules covering a small number of examples. In [4], a genetic algorithm and computational implementation of AIS was proposed to solve a color image recognition and classification task.

In the following, we will present our approach to image pattern recognition that was designed to solve efficient feature extraction, clonal selection, mutation processes and overcome real-time speed limitations.

3   Model and Algorithm

3.1   Comparison of the Methods and Parameters

Our model defines the antigens and T-lymphocytes as two data items with different characteristics and goals. These data items are elements of a shape-space, which can be represented by nxn sized binary (black and white) matrixes. Colors can be coded with 1 (black) and -1 (white) numbers. Each antigen is usually a

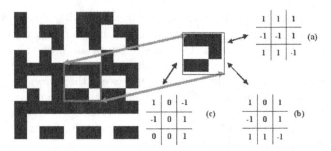

Fig. 2. If in the position of *1*s black pixels and in the position of *-1*s white pixels are found, the matching is successful, while pixel color in the position of the *0*s is indifferent. Therefore (a) and (b) give successful matching while (c) is unsuccessful.

3x3 or *5x5* subpattern of a binary picture which is subtracted from the input image flow by a special feature extraction method. These patterns (2D-strings) can be recognized by our T-lymphocytes, called match-templates [14]. They are usually *3x3* or *5x5* matrixes and contain *1, -1* and *0* numbers. During the interaction between templates and patterns, if in the position of *1*s black pixels and in the position of *-1*s white pixels are found, the matching is successful, while pixel color in the position of the *0*s is indifferent. An example can be seen in Fig. 2.

We used a simple bone marrow model to create an initial template set [11]. The elements of this matrix set (*1, -1* and *0*) were generated randomly with equivalent probability. This method was applied in our application but also there are other strategies to initialize the starting template set. One can be to predetermine the number of *0* or otherwise 'don't care' elements. Other important attributes, like age (length of life), efficiency (number of successful matching) and specificity (number of *0* elements) were also initialized during our method.

Basically our algorithm has an initialization and recognition phase, where the former models the function of thymus. Our thymus model is based on a template runner, which tested all the elements of the initial template set on a learning input flow using a negative selection algorithm. The templates, which were able to match more than a given number of sub-patterns of the initial input flow, were selected out. In the recognition phase we use the same template runner module, but for a different purpose. If any members of the template set are able to match the actual pattern with a given threshold, a detection message is generated. The steps of the algorithm can be followed in Fig. 3, continuing our "fighter tail" example. For clonal selection, the mutation is provided through a loop-back from the result of the template-runner to the template-set.

In our model the S shape-space has 9 or 25 dimensions, because the sub-pattern matrixes can be represented by 25 or 9 long binary vectors and the templates correspond to 25 or 9 long vectors (coordinates can be -1, 1, or 0). The distance measure between an antigen ($Ab = \langle Ab_1, Ab_2, ...Ab_L \rangle$) and a template $Ag = \langle Ag_1, Ag_2, ...Ag_L \rangle$ is

$$D = \sum_{i=1}^{L} \delta_i, \; where \; \delta_i \begin{cases} 1 \; if \; Ab_i = Ag_i \; or \; Ab_i = 0 \\ 0 \; if \; Ab_i \neq Ag_i \end{cases} \tag{1}$$

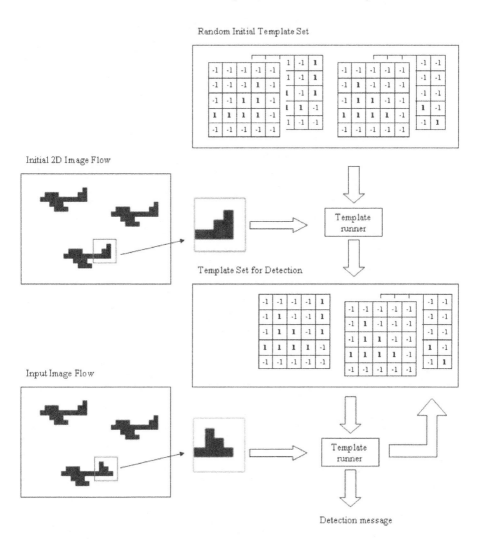

Fig. 3. AIS based algorithm framework for a simple example. The random initial template set is generated by the bone marrow model. After negative selection of the initial 2D image flow, the template set is prepared for detection. In the recognition phase, in case of any members of the template set are able to match the actual pattern with a given threshold, a detection message is generated. The influence of mutation is provided by a loop-back from the template-runner to the template-set.

Our match template class does the recognition if and only if the D distance is L, where L equals to the dimension of the actual S shape-space. Contrary to common AIS, where the molecules usually are represented by similar vectors, the sub-patterns and template vectors generally differ in our model. There are "don't care" elements in the templates, whose position are fixed within their vectors. Therefore, we could not give a definition of affinity as other AISs have. If a match-template has d "don't care" elements, it can detect 2^d different sub-patterns. The more 'don't care' elements it has, the more different sub-patterns are, which are detected. Therefore, the affinity of a template can be characterized by the number of the 'don't care' elements. This affinity is called template affinity α. This affinity has a similar effect to the usual affinity or cross-reactivity threshold in AIS. A sub-pattern can be matched successfully by $2^L = \sum_{\alpha=0}^{L} \binom{L}{\alpha}$ different match-templates, where α is the affinity, defined formerly. The maximum number of sub-patterns that can be recognized by a template set is $\sum 2^{\alpha_i}$, where the α_i is the template affinity of ith template of the template set. During the recognition phase a successful template is cloned changing one of its *0* elements to *-1* or *1*, therefore the clones are more specific. The lifetime of a template is extended if it is successful and its specificity reaches a given threshold. Parallel to the recognition process, the actual template repertoire can be expanded with new templates using negative selection. It is also beneficial to refresh the template repertoire replacing the unsuccessful old templates with low template affinity ones.

The parallel notions between the immune system and our AIS visual analyzer model can be found in Table 1.

Table 1. Mapping between the immune system and the our AIS visual analyzer model.

Immune System	AIS Visual Analyzer Model
Antigen	Sub-patterns in pictures of 2D image flows
T-lymphocyte	Template matrixes
Memory cell	Specialized template with several recognition
Recognition	Template matching between the matrixes
Life of an organism	Number of interactions
Affinity measure	Number of 'don't care' elements

3.2   Feature Extraction Method

Because the input frames of a visual 2D image sequence can be gray-scale or color, we need a conversion method which transforms the input image into a binary one. Let us suppose that the input image is gray-scale and the size of the templates is 3x3. In the algorithm, the input image is threshold nine times at different levels. Each element in the 3x3 binary pattern is defined by a given threshold result. Practically, each threshold result is AND-ed to its mask to select its position in the 3x3 sub-pattern. The masks define disjunct sets on the picture. All these masked binary images are logically OR-ed to give the output result. The detailed algorithm can be found in [12]. If the input image is gray-scale the algorithm sub-samples the original input and sets the binary value of the sampled pixels into the pixels of the output binary image. If the input is color, we can combine the different color channels (red, green, blue) as above,

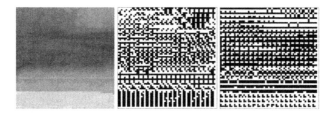

Fig. 4. Conversion results of different type input images. The original version of the left image was colorful. In the middle there is result of the gray-scale to binary conversion. In the right side, the result of the color to binary conversion can be seen.

but each input channel defines only three binary pixels in the pattern. Sample conversion results can be seen in Fig. 4.

3.3 Theoretical Aspects

In this section, we give an approximation based probability analysis of the needed computational power, estimating the size of the template set. As we know, in the case of the *5x5* sized matrixes, the number of different patterns is $2^{25} =\sim 33$ million. The probability that a random template contains 0 don't care elements, or in other words, that it can match only one pattern, is

$$\frac{2^{25}}{3^{25}} \tag{2}$$

The probability that a random template can match exactly 2^k patterns is

$$\frac{\binom{25}{k} 2^{25-k}}{3^{25}} \tag{3}$$

If we summarize this formula by multiplying with the appropriate values we can get the mean value:

$$\sum_{k=0}^{25} \frac{2^k \binom{25}{k} 2^{25-k}}{3^{25}} = \frac{2^{25}}{3^{25}} \sum_{k=0}^{25} \binom{25}{k} = \frac{4^{25}}{3^{25}} \cong 1328.8 \tag{4}$$

This is the mean value of how many patterns will be covered by a template. Therefore, the theoretical value of the size of the template set is around 25000. If we use 3x3 sized templates, based on a similar proof the size of the template set should be at least around 39. It is not proved that this set will cover all of the same sized sub-patterns, but it gives a good order of magnitude. It must be noted, that any sub-patterns can be recognized by special decomposition of 3x3 templates [15]. The templates can overlap each other without inconsistency, which means that -1 and 1 are not allowed in the same overlapped position. Only one of the overlapped values can be other than 0. An example of overlapping decomposition can be seen in Fig. 5. In this case where the pattern contains 14 pixels the size of the template set should be around 292.

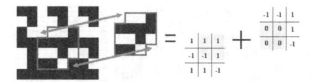

Fig. 5. A decomposition of the bordered pattern by two 3x3 templates. Note that the overlapping area is darker and contains "don't care" elements.

4   Application

Our development focused on a real time application that is able to detect unknown objects, patterns and geological formations based on their textures. It can be used in visual systems where autonomous surveillance is needed or where there is no human presence. It is a helpful additional property of existing surveillance systems subject to unexpected occasions and give detection warnings. For example, it could be a useful complementary function on Mars rovers because due to the long distances real time remote control is unfeasible.

Our test application was implemented in the Aladdin Pro environment using a cellular nonlinear network chip, called Ace4k [8,9]. The input images were generated in a 3D virtual environment by a Pentium IV. personal computer. The relative movement of the camera, direction, camera orientation speed and altitude was controllable manually. A screen-shot is presented in Fig. 6. The size of the input image was 64x64 because our hardware can process images of this size paralelly. Therefore, we cut out a part of the original input for processing. This sub-image was converted to binary patterns by the above presented feature extraction methods.

The template runner worked with a 3x3, randomly generated template set, whose size was between 100 and 500. A texture or image was detected by a template if the number of the successful matching of the template with the sub-patterns was more than the given parameter value.

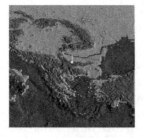 

Fig. 6. On the left side the map of the virtual environment can be seen. In the middle the white arrow shows the position of the camera whose input image can be seen on the right side in gray-scale. The small window is the actually processed area.

4.1   Parameter Definitions

The most relevant parameters in our real-time experiments are summarized in Table 2.

Table 2. The most relevant parameters in our AIS visual analyzer model.

Parameter name	Meaning and values
InitSetSize	The size of the template set, usually between 100 and 500.
InitMethod	The initial method can be random creation or loading stored data.
ImmuneProcessLevels	Learning phase, recognition phase or combined phase.
Agelimit	Length of the non-active state after successful matching.
FeatureExMethod	Color or gray-scale feature extraction method.
FeatureExThreshold	Value usually between 1 and 400.
MatchThreshold	Needed threshold value for successful matching, usually between 1 and 100.
Mutation	True or false.
MutationValue	Probability value of mutation between 0 and 1.

4.2   Experiments

In the first experiment, we used the initialization and recognition phases separately. In the initialization phase, all the templates of the initial set was run on some input images of the actual view of the virtual world. The size of these input images was *64x64*. They usually contained some typical texture patterns, eg. texture of mountains, ocean or forest. During the process, in case of successful matching the template was selected out from the set. During the recognition phase the algorithm detected all textures, which were not members of the initial input flow. But those sub-patterns, which the system has been taught with, have not been detected. Detection results can be seen in Fig. 7.

Fig. 7. The first and third images are different inputs. White dots on the second and fourth image show the result of the detection. In the first case the desert, in the second case the sky was already taught to the system. Note that different colors can be detected with the same template set.

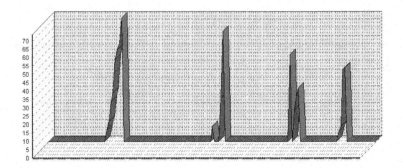

Fig. 8. The horizontal coordinates show the time based on the the input frames. The vertical value is the label of the actual template. Different peaks appear when the texture of the environment manly changed and at least one template has detected a new pattern. The first peak came when we reached the mountains, the second shows the water, third is ground again and the last one ocean again.

In the second experiment, the initialization and recognition part periodically followed each other. If any template had a detection, it was selected out temporarily. For a longer period if this template has detection, it was not allowed to send detection message. We assumed that if something was detected by this template, then the next few detections carry no new information, therefore it is not worth sending a warning message. The dynamics of this process can be seen in Fig. 8.

4.3   Observations

The time measurements of the algorithm are summarized in Table 3. The difference of the speed between the gray-scale and color method is caused by the data transfer in memory, as the color images are 3 times bigger than the gray-scale ones. These results show that our algorithm can run in real time even if we use the combination of two *3x3* templates for sub-pattern detection.

Table 3. Speed and time measurements of our visual analyzer algorithm.

Input image	Size of template set	Speed [msec] for a frame	Nr of million matches / sec
Color	100	25.641	15
Color	250	33.333	27
Color	500	52.632	36
Gray-scale	100	21.277	18
Gray-scale	250	28.571	31
Gray-scale	500	47.619	40

5   Conclusions and Future Work

In this paper, we presented a real-time visual analysis system for surveillance applications based on an Artificial Immune System (AIS) that can reliably detect unknown patterns in input image sequences. Our system is implemented on specialized architecture (the Cellular Nonlinear Network (CNN) Universal Machine) and its CMOS implementation. Results from tests in 3D virtual world with different terrain textures are reported to demonstrate that the system can detect unknown patterns and dynamical changes in image sequences. Applications of the system include in particular explorer systems for terrain surveillance. In the future, we would like to extend our system with robust classifier modules. Also, our aim is to further develop our mutation algorithm.

Acknowledgements. The support of MURI grant of the Office of Naval Research and the multidisciplinary doctoral school at the Faculty of Information Technology of the Pázmány P. Catholic University, are gratefully acknowledged.

References

1. Dasgupta, D.: Artificial Immune Systems and Their Applications. Springer-Verlag, Germany (1999)
2. de Castro, L. N., Timmis, J.: Artificial Immune Systems: A New Computational Intelligence Approach. Springer, UK, (2002)
3. Hofmeyr, S.A., Forrest, S.: Architecture for an Artificial Immune Evolutionary Computation. (2000) 7(1):45–68 http://www.cs.unm.edu/ steveah/
4. Satyanath, S., Sahin, F.: Artificial Immune Systems Approach to a Real Time Color Image Classification Problem. Proceedings of the SMC2001, IEEE International Conference on Systems, Man, and Cybernetics, Vol 4, (2001) pp.2285–2290, Arizona, USA.
5. Chao, D.L., Forrest, S.: Information Immune Systems. In Proceedings of the First International Conference on Artificial Immune Systems (ICARIS), (2002) pp. 132–140
6. Roska, T., Chua, L. O. : The CNN Universal Machine: An analogic array computer. IEEE Transactions on Circuits and Systems-II, Vol. 40, (1993) pp. 163-173
7. Chua, L.O., Roska T.: Cellular neural networks and visual computing, Foundations and applications. Cambridge University Press, (2002)
8. Zarandy, A., Rekeczky, Cs., Szatmari, I., Foldesy, P.: Aladdin Visual Computer. IEEE Journal on Circuits, Systems and Computers, Vol. 12(6), (2003)
9. Liñán, G., Espejo, S., Domínguez-Castro R., Rodríguez-Vázquez: ACE4k: An analog I/O 64 x 64 Visual Microprocessor Chip With 7-bit Analog Accuracy. Intl. Journal Of Circuit Theory and Applications, Vol. 30, May-June (2002), pp. 89–116
10. Cserey, Gy., Falus, A., Roska, T.: Immune Response Inspired CNN Algorithms for Many-Target Detection. in Proc. ECCTD '03, Krakow (2003).
11. Cserey, Gy., Falus, A., Porod W., Roska, T.: An Artificial Immune System for Visual Applications with CNN-UM. ISCAS 2004, Vancouver, (2004) paper accepted.
12. Cserey, Gy., Falus, A., Porod W., Roska, T.: Feature Extraction CNN Algorithms for Artificial Immune Systems. IJCNN 2004, Budapest, (2004) paper accepted.

13. Falus, A.: Physiological and Molecular Principles of Immunology. in Hungarian, Semmelweis Press, Budapest, (1998)
14. Roska, T., Kék, L., Nemes, L., Zarándy, Á., Brendel M., Szolgay P. (ed): CNN Software Library (Templates and Algorithms), Version 7.2. Analogical and Neural Computing Laboratory, Computer and Automation Research Institute, Hungarian Academy of Sciences (MTA SzTAKI), DNS-CADET-15, Budapest, (1998)
15. Kék, L., Zarándy, Á.: Implementation of Large-Neighborhood Nonlinear Templates on the CNN Universal Machine. International Journal of Circuit Theory and Applications, Vol. 26, No. 6, (1998) pp. 551–566
16. Antani, S., Kasturi, R., Jain, R.: A survey on the use of pattern recognition methods for abstraction, indexing and retrieval of images and video. Pattern Recognition, 35 (2002) pp. 945–965
17. Egmont-Petersen, M., de Ridder, D., Handels, H.: Image processing with neural networks–a review. Pattern Recognition, 35 (2002) pp. 2279-2301
18. Ivanov, Y., Stauffer, C., Bobick, A., Grimson, W.E.L.: Video Surveillance of Interactions. Proc. Second IEEE Int. W/S on Visual Surveillance, (1999) pp. 82–89
19. Hayashi, A., Nakasima, R., Kanbara, T., Suematsu, N.: Multi-object Motion Pattern Classification for Visual Surveillance and Sports Video Retrieval Int. Conf. on Vision Interface, (2002)
20. Dasgupta, D., Cao, Y., Yand, C.: An Immunogenetic Approach to Spectra Recognition. Proc. of the Genetic and Evolutionary Computation Conference, (1999) pp. 149–155
21. Tarakanov, A., Sokolova, S., Abramov, B., Aikimbayev, A.: Immunocomputing of the Natural Plague Foci. Proc. of the Genetic and Evolutionary Computation Conference, Workshop on Artificial Immune Systems and Their Applications, (2000) pp. 38–39
22. Carter, J.H.: The Immune System as a Model for Pattern Recognition and Classification. Journal of the American Medical Informatics Association, (2000) pp. 28–41
23. Carvalho, D.R., Freitas, A.A.: An Immunological Algorithm for Discovering Small-Disjunct Rules in Data Mining. Proc. of the Genetic and Evolutionary Computation Conference, (2001) pp. 401–404

Exploring the Capability of Immune Algorithms: A Characterization of Hypermutation Operators

Vincenzo Cutello[1], Giuseppe Nicosia[1,2], and Mario Pavone[1]

[1] Department of Mathematics and Computer Science
University of Catania
V.le A. Doria 6, 95125 Catania, Italy
{cutello,nicosia,mpavone}@dmi.unict.it

[2] Computing Laboratory, University of Kent, Canterbury, Kent CT2 7NF

Abstract. In this paper, an important class of hypermutation operators are discussed and quantitatively compared with respect to their success rate and computational cost. We use a standard Immune Algorithm (IA), based on the clonal selection principle to investigate the searching capability of the designed hypermutation operators. We computed the parameter surface for each variation operator to predict the best parameter setting for each operator and their combination. The experimental investigation in which we use a standard clonal selection algorithm with different hypermutation operators on a complex "toy problem", the trap functions, and a complex NP-complete problem, the 2D HP model for the protein structure prediction problem, clarifies that only few really different and useful hypermutation operators exist, namely: inversely proportional hypermutation, static hypermutation and hypermacromutation operators. The combination of static and inversely proportional Hypermutation and hypermacromutation showed the best experimental results for the "toy problem" and the NP-complete problem.

Keywords: Clonal selection algorithms, hypermutation operators, hypermacromutation operator, aging operator, trap functions, 2D HP protein structure prediction problem.

1 Introduction

Immune Algorithms (IA's) based on the clonal selection principle [1], are a special kind of immune algorithms [2,3] where the clonal expansion and the affinity maturation are the main forces behind the searching process. The hypermutation operator explores the actual fitness landscape by introducing innovations into the population of potential solutions to a given optimization problem. Hence, it is reasonable to test its effectiveness on any kind of IA, in particular, and evolutionary algorithm, in general. The clonal selection algorithm used in this research work is a modified version of a previous immune algorithm [4]. It has significant new features, hypermutation and aging operators [12], to face hard

G. Nicosia et al. (Eds.): ICARIS 2004, LNCS 3239, pp. 263–276, 2004.

problems, allowing us to experimentally compare the different types of hyper-mutation operators. To this end, we ran many experiments to properly tune the parameter values of each hypermutation operator, and in doing so, deter-mining the corresponding parameter surfaces. Following the advice reported in [5], we test the class of hypermutation operators on a toy problem and a NP-complete problem. This pair of computational problems (for sake of completeness the author's advice in [5] is to use a real-world application as well), are robust test beds to analyze theoretically and experimentally the overall performance of evolutionary algorithms. We choose a complex, yet rarely used toy problem, trap functions, and a complex NP-complete problem, the 2D HP model for the protein structure prediction problem with a particular search space, the funnel landscape. We will tackle the trap functions and the 2D HP model for the pro-tein structure prediction problem to assess the performances of the developed hypermutation operators. The experimental results reported in this article prove the good performances of the designed IA when it uses inversely proportional, or static, hypermutation coupled with hypermacromutation operator. Moreover, we will show that the hypermacromutation procedure is an useful variation op-erator to extend the regions of parameter surfaces with high success rate values, and, in particular, it helps in improving the regions where the hypermutation operator by itself performs poorly.

2   The Clonal Selection Algorithm

The IA we work with, uses only an entity type: the B cells. The B cell population, $P^{(t)}$, represents a set of candidate solution in the current fitness landscape at each time step (or generation) t. The B cell, or the B cell receptor, is a string of length ℓ, where every variable is associated either to one bit, or an integer, or a floating point, or a high level representation of data depending upon the given computational problem that the IA is facing. At each time step t, we have a B cell population $P^{(t)}$ of size d. The initial population, time $t = 0$, is randomly generated. The Algorithm uses two main functions:

- *Evaluate(P)* which computes the affinity (fitness) function value of each B cell $x \in P^{(t)}$.
- *Termination_Condition()* which returns true if a solution is found, or a max-imum number of fitness function evaluations (T_{max}) is reached.

It also uses three immune operators: cloning, hypermutation and aging; and a standard evolutionary operator: ($\mu + \lambda$)-selection operator.

Static Cloning Operator. The cloning operator, simply clones each B cell *dup* times, producing an intermediate population P^{clo} of size $d \times dup = Nc$. Throughout this paper, we will call it *static cloning operator*, as opposed to a *proportional cloning operator* [6], that clones B cells proportionally to their antigenic affinities. Preliminary experimental results using such an operator (not shown in this paper), showed us frequent premature convergence during the population evolution. In fact, proportional cloning gives more time steps to B cells with high affinity values, and the process can more likely be trapped into local minima of the given landscape.

Hypermutation Operators. The hypermutation operators act on the the B cell receptor of P^{clo}. The number of mutations M is determined by a specific function, *mutation potential*, that is, for each B cell at any given time step t. It is possible to define several mutation potentials. We tested our IA using static, proportional and inversely proportional hypermutation operators, hypermacro-mutation operator, and combination of hypermutation operators and hyperma-cromutation. The three hypermutation operators and the Hypermacromutation operator mutate the B cell receptors using different mutation potentials, depending upon a parameter c. If during the mutation process a constructive mutation occurs, the mutation procedure will move on to the next B cell. We call such an event: *Stop at the first constructive mutation* (FCM). We adopted such a mechanism to slow down (premature) convergence, exploring more accurately the search space. A different policy would make use of $M-$mutations $(M-mut)$, where the mutation procedure performs all M mutations determined by the potential for the current B cell. The mutation potentials we used are:

(H1) *Static Hypermutation*: the number of mutations is independent from the fitness function f, so each B cell receptor at each time step will undergo at most $M_s(\boldsymbol{x}) = c$ mutations.

(H2) *Proportional Hypermutation*: the number of mutations is proportional to the fitness value, and for each B cell $\boldsymbol{x}$ is at most $M_p(f(\boldsymbol{x})) = (E^* - f(\boldsymbol{x})) \times (c \times \ell)$, where E^* is the minimum fitness function value known for the current instance problem. The shape of $M_p(f(\boldsymbol{x}))$ is a straight line.

(H3) *Inversely Proportional Hypermutation*: the number of mutations is inversely proportional to the fitness value. In particular, at each time step t, the operator will perform at most $M_i(f(\boldsymbol{x})) = ((1 - \frac{E^*}{f(\boldsymbol{x})}) \times (c \times \ell)) + (c \times \ell))$ mutations. In this case, $M_i(f(\boldsymbol{x}))$ has the shape of an hyperbola branch.

(M) *Hypermacromutation*: the number of mutations is independent from the fitness function f and the parameter c. In this case, we choose at random two integers, i and j such that $(i + 1) \leq j \leq \ell$ and the operator mutates at most $M_m(\boldsymbol{x}) = j - i + 1$ values, in the range $[i, j]$.

Aging Operator. The aging operator eliminates old B cells from the populations $P^{(t)}$, $P^{(hyp)}$ and/or $P^{(macro)}$, so to avoid premature convergence. To increase the population diversity, new B cells are added by the *Elitist_Merge function*. The parameter τ_B sets the maximum number of generations allowed to B cells to remain in the population. When a B cell is $\tau_B + 1$ old it is erased from the current population, no matter what its fitness value is. We call this strategy, *static pure aging*. During the cloning expansion, a cloned B cell takes the age of its parent. After the hypermutation phase, a cloned B cell which successfully mutates, i.e. with a better fitness value, will be considered to have age equal to 0. Thus, an equal opportunity is given to each "new genotype" to effectively explore the fitness landscape. We note that for τ_B greater than the maximum number of allowed generations, the IA works essentially without aging operator. In such a limit case the algorithm uses a strong elitist selection strategy.

$(\mu + \lambda)$-selection with birth phase and no redundancy. A new population $P^{(t+1)}$, of d B cells, for the next generation $t+1$, is obtained by selecting the best B cells which "survived" the aging operator, from the populations $P^{(t)}$, $P^{(hyp)}$ and/or $P^{(macro)}$. No redundancy is allowed. Thus, each B cell receptor is unique, i.e. each genotype is different from all other genotypes. If only $d' < d$ B cells survived , the *Elitist_Merge* function creates $d - d'$ new B cells (*Birth phase*). Hence, the $(\mu + \lambda)$-selection operator (with $\mu = d$ and $\lambda = Nc$; or $\lambda = 2Nc$ if both variation operators are activated) reduces an offspring B cell population (created by cloning and hypermutation operators) of size $\lambda \geq \mu$ to a new parent population of size $\mu = d$. The selection operator chooses the d best elements from the offspring set and the old parent B cells, thus guaranteeing monotonicity in the evolution dynamic.

The properties of each immune operator is relatively well understood: the cloning operator explores the attractor basins and valleys of each candidate solution; the hypermutation operators introduce innovations in *exploring* the current population of B cell; the aging operator creates diversity during the searching process. The selection evolutionary operator directs the search process toward promising regions of the fitness landscape and *exploits* the information coded within the current population. While selection is a universal, problem- and algorithm-independent operator, hypermutation, and in general mutation and crossover, operators are specific operators, that focus on the structure of the given landscape. Here, we analyze the exploring capability of a class of hypermutation operators using a classical $(\mu + \lambda)$-selection operator, a simple cloning operator and a static pure aging process to stress the property of each hypermutation operator. Below we show the pseudo-code of the proposed Immune Algorithm (the boolean variables H, HM control, respectively, the hypermutation and the hypermacromutation operator).

Immune Algorithm$(\ell, d, dup, \tau_B, c, H, HM)$
$Nc := d * dup;$
$t := 0;$
$P^{(t)} := $ Initial_Pop();
Evaluate($P^{(0)}$);
while ($\neg$ Termination_Condition()) **do**
    $P^{(clo)} := $ Cloning $(P^{(t)}, Nc);$
    if (H) **then** $P^{(hyp)} := $ Hypermutation $(P^{(clo)}, c, \ell);$
        Evaluate($P^{(hyp)}$);
    if (HM) **then** $P^{(macro)} := $ Hypermacromutation $(P^{clo});$
        Evaluate $(P^{(macro)});$
    $(P_a^{(t)}, P_a^{(hyp)}, P_a^{(macro)}) := $ Aging$(P^{(t)}, P^{(hyp)}, P^{(macro)}, \tau_B);$
    $P^{(t+1)} := (\mu + \lambda)$-Selection $(P_a^{(t)}, P_a^{(hyp)}, P_a^{(macro)});$
    $t := t + 1;$
end_while

3   First Test Bed: The Trap Functions

The trap functions are complex *toy problem*, that can help in understanding the efficiency and the searching capability of evolutionary algorithms [5]. Toy problems such as ones-counting, Basin-with-a-barrier, Hurdle-problem, play a central role in understanding the dynamics of algorithms [7]. They allow algorithm designers to devise new tools for mathematical and experimental analysis and modelling. One can tackle toy problems to build-up a fruitful intuition on how the algorithms work. In this paper we used the trap functions to show the main differences between the hypermutation operators. The trap functions [8], simply, take as input the number of 1's of bit strings of length ℓ :

$$f(x) = \widehat{f}(u(x)) = \widehat{f}\left(\sum_{k=1}^{l} x_k\right) \tag{1}$$

An IA to face this toy problem would naturally use B cell receptors of bit string. For our experiments we will use two trap functions: a *simple trap function* and a *complex trap function*. The simple trap function is defined as follows:

$$\widehat{f}(u) = \begin{cases} \frac{a}{z}(z-u), & \text{if } u \leq z \\ \frac{b}{l-z}(u-z), & \text{otherwise.} \end{cases} \tag{2}$$

There are many possible choices for the parameters a, b and z. We choose the values used in [8]: $z \approx (1/4)\ell$; $b = \ell - z - 1$; $1.5b \leq a \leq 2b$; a a multiple of z. The simple trap function is characterized by a global optimum (for a bit string of all 0's) and a local optimum (for a bit string of all 1's) that are the each other *bit-wise* complement.

The complex trap function, how we will see, is more difficult to investigate, since there are two directions to get trapped. Its definition is the following:

$$\widehat{f}(u) = \begin{cases} \frac{a}{z_1}(z_1 - u), & \text{if } u \leq z_1 \\ \frac{b}{l-z_1}(u-z_1), & \text{if } z_1 < u \leq z_2 \\ \frac{b(z_2-z_1)}{l-z_1}\left(1 - \frac{1}{l-z_2}(u-z_2)\right) & \text{otherwise.} \end{cases} \tag{3}$$

We note that for $z_2 = \ell$ the complex trap function becomes the simple trap function. In this case, the possible values of the parameter z_2 are determined by the following equation $z_2 = \ell - z_1$. An *ad hoc* operator that mutates all the bits of the string does not obtain the global maximum of the complex trap function. The experimental results are shown in the next tables, where the following notation is used: $S(type)$ and $C(type)$. S and C mean, respectively, Simple and Complex trap function, while *type* varies with respect to the parameter values used by simple and complex trap functions: type I ($\ell = 10, z = 3, a = 12, b = 6$), type II ($\ell = 20, z = 5, a = 20, b = 14$), type III ($\ell = 50, z = 10, a = 80, b = 39$), type IV ($\ell = 75, z = 20, a = 80, b = 54$), type V ($\ell = 100, z = 25, a = 100, b = 74$). For the complex trap function $z_1 = z$ and $z_2 = l - z_1$.

All the reported experimental results have been averaged over 100 independent runs, allowing at most $T_{max} = 5 \times 10^5$ fitness function evaluations (FFE)

Table 1. The best results obtained by IA with static, proportional, inversely proportional hypermutation and hypermacromutation with $M-$mutations ($M-mut$) strategy.

Trap	Static	Proportional	Inversely	Hypermacro M-mut
S(I)	**100**, *576.81*	**100**, *604.33*	**100**, *504.76*	**100**, *4334.94*
	$\tau_B = 25$, $c = 0.9$	$\tau_B = 100$, $c = 0.2$	$\tau_B = 5$, $c = 0.3$	$\tau_B = 1$
S(II)	**34**, *82645.85*	**100**, *50266.61*	**97**, *58092.70*	**5**, *5626.8*
	$\tau_B = 20$, $c = 1.0$	$\tau_B = 25$, $c = 0.8$	$\tau_B = 20$, $c = 0.2$	$\tau_B = 50$
S(III)	**0**	**0**	**0**	**5**, *174458.6*
				$\tau_B = 50$
S(IV)	**0**	**0**	**0**	**0**
S(V)	**0**	**0**	**0**	**0**
C(I)	**100**, *389.67*	**100**, *404.94*	**100**, *371.15*	**100**, *1862.09*
	$\tau_B = 100$, $c = 0.6$	$\tau_B = 50$, $c = 0.1$	$\tau_B = 10$, $c = 0.2$	$\tau_B = 5$
C(II)	**100**, *36607.15*	**100**, *22253.70*	**100**, *44079.57*	**56**, *84001.29*
	$\tau_B = 15$, $c = 0.1$	$\tau_B = 25$, $c = 0.3$	$\tau_B = 10$, $c = 0.2$	$\tau_B = 50$
C(III)	**1**, *15337.00*	**0**	**2**, *236484.50*	**1**, *185318*
	$\tau_B = 50$, $c = 0.7$		$\tau_B = 25$, $c = 0.1$	$\tau_B = 50$
C(IV)	**0**	**0**	**0**	**0**
C(V)	**0**	**0**	**0**	**0**

and with $c \in \{0.1, 0.2, ..., 1.0\}$, and $\tau_B \in \{1, 5, 10, 15, 20, 25, 50, 100, 150, 200, \infty\}$. The population size $d = 10$ and the duplication parameter $dup = 1$ were set to minimal values to stress the real searching capability of the used hypermutation operators. The Hypermacromutation operator is a random procedure independent from the parameter c, for this reason we vary only the τ_B parameter. Tables 1 and 2 show the best results obtained by IA in terms of Success Rate (SR) and Average number of Evaluations to Solutions (AES). Each entry in the tables indicate, in the first row, SR (in bold face) and AES (in italic), and in second row, the best parameter values that allowed the hypermutation operators to reach the best results. In table 1 we report the performances of IA when working with each hypermutation operator alone: static, proportional, inversely proportional hypermutation and hypermacromutation with $M-$mutations ($M-mut$) strategy (hypermacromutation performs all M mutations determined by the mutation potential). IA works better when it uses hypermacromutation. Indeed, this operator is the only one that solves the simple trap function type III and IV. The other operators are practically the same with the inversely proportional slightly better than static and proportional hypermutation.

Table 2 shows the results obtained by IA using both perturbation operators (columns $2-4$), while the first column reports the IA with hypermacromutation FCM (Stop at the first constructive mutation) only.

If we compare the hypermacromutation $M-$mut (table 1 fourth column) versus hypermacromutation FCM (table 2 first column), it is clear how the

Table 2. The best results obtained by IA with hypermacromutation FCM, and combinations of static, proportional, inversely proportional hypermutation and hypermacromutation FCM.

Trap	Hypermacro FCM	Static+Macro	Proportional+Macro	Inversely+Macro
S(I)	**100**, *1495.90*	**100**, *452.94*	**100**, *834.01*	**100**, *477.04*
	$\tau_B = 1$	$\tau_B = 25$, $c = 0.2$	$\tau_B = 50$, $c = 0.2$	$\tau_B = 15$, $c = 0.2$
S(II)	**28**, *64760.25*	**99**, *37915.17*	**100**, *51643.11*	**100**, *35312.29*
	$\tau_B = 1$	$\tau_B = 25$, $c = 0.1$	$\tau_B = 20$, $c = 0.7$	$\tau_B = 100$, $c = 0.2$
S(III)	**15**, *15677.53*	**100**, *18869.84*	**1**, *243038.00*	**100**, *20045.81*
	$\tau_B = 100$	$\tau_B = 50$, $c = 0.1$	$\tau_B = 20$, $c = 0.2$	$\tau_B = \infty$, $c = 0.1$
S(IV)	**24**, *40184.83*	**100**, *37871.71*	**0**	**100**, *42082.00*
	$\tau_B = 200$	$\tau_B = 25$, $c = 0.1$		$\tau_B = 25$, $c = 0.2$
S(V)	**27**, *139824.44*	**100**, *78941.79*	**0**	**100**, *80789.94*
	$\tau_B = 1$	$\tau_B = 100$, $c = 0.1$		$\tau_B = 50$, $c = 0.2$
C(I)	**100**, *826.78*	**100**, *367.67*	**100**, *644.67*	**100**, *388.42*
	$\tau_B = 50$	$\tau_B = 10$, $c = 0.1$	$\tau_B = 10$, $c = 0.1$	$\tau_B = 10$, $c = 0.2$
C(II)	**96**, *54783.25*	**100**, *24483.76*	**100**, *23690.82*	**100**, *29271.68*
	$\tau_B = 15$	$\tau_B = 10$, $c = 0.2$	$\tau_B = 50$, $c = 0.3$	$\tau_B = 5$, $c = 0.2$
C(III)	**39**, *112533.18*	**27**, *172102.85*	**1**, *147114.00*	**24**, *149006.5*
	$\tau_B = 15$	$\tau_B = 20$, $c = 0.1$	$\tau_B = 50$, $c = 0.1$	$\tau_B = 20$, $c = 0.1$
C(IV)	**5**, *227135.80*	**2**, *99259.00*	**0**	**2**, *154925.00*
	$\tau_B = 15$	$\tau_B = 25$, $c = 0.5$		$\tau_B = 15$, $c = 0.4$
C(V)	**2**, *353579.00*	**0**	**0**	**0**
	$\tau_B = 15$			

Stop at first constructive mutation strategy improves the performance of the hypermacromutation operator and, in general, of all hypermutation operators. In fact, we adopt this strategy for all hypermutation operators, a simple scheme to prevent the premature convergence during the search process of IA. Moreover, the proportional hypermutation performs poorly whether or not combined with the hypermacromutation operator.

Finally, the usage of coupled operators, static and inversely proportional hypermutation with hypermacromutation (see table 2), is the key feature to effectively face the trap functions. The results obtained with this setting are comparable to the results gained in [8], where the authors, though, in their theoretical and experimental research work, use only cases C(I), C(II) and C(III) for the complex trap function.

4   Second Test Bed: The Protein Structure Prediction

A possible approach to model the protein folding problem is the well-known Dill's lattice model (or HP model) [9]. It models proteins as two-dimensional (2D) *self-avoiding walk chains* of ℓ monomers on the square lattice (two resides cannot occupy the same node of the lattice). There are only two monomer types: the H and the P monomers, respectively for hydrophobic and polar monomers. In this model, each H–H topological contact, that is, each lattice nearest-neighbor H–H contact interaction, has energy value $\epsilon \leq 0$, while all other contact interaction types (H–P, P–P) have zero energy In general, in the HP model the residues interactions can be defined as follows: $e_{HH} = - \mid \epsilon \mid$ and $e_{HP} = e_{PH} = e_{PP} = \delta$. When $\epsilon = 1$ and $\delta = 0$ we have the typical interaction energy matrix for the standard HP model [9]. The native conformation is the one that maximizes the number of contacts H–H, i.e. the one that minimizes the free energy function. This model has a strong experimental justification. During the folding process of real protein the hydrophobic residues tend to interact with each other, forming the *hydrophobic kernel* of the native structure, while the hydrophilic resides are on the external surface of protein, forming the interface with the watery environment. The HP model has the great practical advantage of formalizing the protein primary structure as a binary sequence s of H's and P's (i.e., $s \in \{H, P\}^{\ell}$) and the conformational space as a square lattice. It is worth to say that is possible to extend the model on triangular 2D lattices and on 3D lattices. Finding the global minimum of the free energy function for the protein folding problem in the 2D HP model is NP-hard [10]. In general, the HP model is used by biologists to study the theoretical properties of the folding processes while computer scientists use its hard instances to analyze the performance of designed algorithms. In this section, we run the IA with the HP model as hard benchmarks. We used the first nine instances of the *Tortilla 2D HP Benchmarks*[1] to test the searching capability of the designed IA.

The input protein is a sequence $s \in \{H, P\}^{\ell}$, where ℓ, the length, represents the number of amino-acids. The B cell (or B cell receptor) is a sequence of *relative directions* [11] $r \in \{F, L, R\}^{\ell-1}$; where each r_i, is a relative direction with respect to the previous direction (r_{i-1}), with $i = 2, \ldots, \ell - 1$, (i.e., there are $\ell - 2$ relative directions) and r_1 the non-relative direction. Hence, we obtain an overall sequence r of length $\ell - 1$. The sequence r detects a *self-avoiding* conformation, i.e. a 2D conformation suitable to compute the energy value of the hydrophobic-pattern of the given protein. Hence $f(\boldsymbol{x}) = e$ is the energy of conformation coded in the B cell receptor $\boldsymbol{x}$, with $-e$ the number of topological contacts $H - H$ in the 2D lattice. It is worthwhile to note here, that all the implemented operators try to mutate each B cell receptor M times, maintaining the self-avoiding property.

The parameter surfaces of hypermutation operators. To understand the searching ability of single or combined hypermutation operators, when changing the parameter values, we performed a set of experiments on a PSP instance, *Seq2*, *hhpphpphpphpphpphpphpphh*, ($\ell = 24$ and minimum energy value known $E^* = -9$). We chose the instance *Seq2*, because *Seq1* is a relative easy instance. Indeed, for each combination of hypermutation operators there are many parameter settings which produce $SR = 100$ (experimental results not shown in this paper). The hydrophobic pattern *Seq2* is a good trade-off between complexity instance and time needed to perform a complete experimental analysis to discover the best parameter setting for each hypermutation operator. The duplication parameter

---

dup varies from 1 to 10 and the constant *c* from 0.1 to 1.0. As a function of *dup* and *c* we show either the success rate (SR) or the average number of evaluations to solutions (AES). The 3D plots obtained are the characteristic *parameter surfaces* for each combination of the hypermutation operators.

We set the population size to a minimal value $d = 10$, to stress the property of each operator when working with few points in the conformational space. This strategy gives us a good measure of the "real" performance of the single hypermutation procedures. The aging parameter τ_B was set to 5. This value produces almost always the best convergence rate, or similar behavior for all hypermutation operators (simulation results not shown in this paper). Moreover, the *Termination_Condition()* function allowed at most $T_{max} = 10^5$ fitness function evaluations and we performed for each value pair of the parameters, 100 independent runs.

Using the SR and AES values, our experimental protocol has the following four objectives:

1. to plot the characteristic parameter surface of each hypermutation operator,
2. to analyze the joint effects of hypermacromutations and hypermutations,
3. to determine the best hypermutation operator or the best combination operators,
4. to find the best setting of parameter values for each operator and combination of operators, that is, the best delimited region on the parameter surfaces that maximize the SR value and minimize the AES value.

Figure 1 (left plot) shows the parameter surface of the static hypermutation operator; the region with high success rate values is for $dup \in \{2, \ldots, 10\}$ and $c \in \{0.1, \ldots, 0.4\}$. In this area the static hypermutation has an average $SR > 80$. For $c > 0.5$ the SR decreases softly. IA obtains the best performance, $SR = 98$, for $dup = 3$ and $c = 0.1$ and a computational average effort of $AES = 29131, 28$.

In figure 1 (right plot) we report the parameter surface of the proportional hypermutation operator. For this operator the region with high SR is a straight

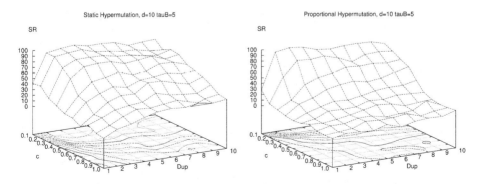

Fig. 1. SR as a function of the values *dup* and *c* for the Static Hypermutation Operator (left plot) and Proportional Hypermutation Operator (right plot) on sequence 2.

line, $c = 0.1$. For $c > 0.1$ the SR decreases quickly, with a high slope. For $dup = 3$ and $c = 0.1$ the IA reaches the highest success rate, $SR = 96$, with $AES = 32958, 87$.

Figure 2 (left plot) shows the performance of the inversely proportional hypermutation operator. There is a large region with high SR values ($dup \in \{2, \ldots 10\}$ and $c \in \{0.2, \ldots, 1.0\}$), with an average $SR > 75$. The highest peak, $SR = 93$, is obtained for $dup = 4$ and $c = 0.5$ with $AES = 29721, 4$.

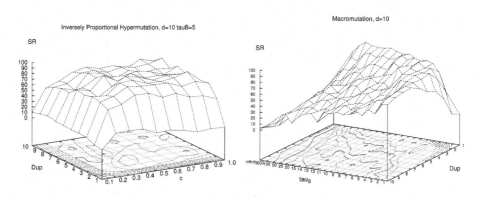

Fig. 2. SR versus parameter values dup and c for the Inversely Proportional Hypermutation Op. (left plot) and Hypermacromutation Op. (right plot) on sequence 2.

The parameters surface of the Hypermacromutation operator is shown in figure 2 (right plot). The operator does not use the parameter c, hence we vary the cloning parameter dup from 1 to 10 and the aging parameter τ_B in the set $\{1, 2, 3, \ldots, 15, 20, 25, 50, 100, 200, \infty\}$. We note that setting the parameter τ_B at a value higher than the possible number of generations, is equivalent to giving the B cell an infinite life, that is, we turn off the aging operator. When $\tau_B = \infty$ one has the worst SR values (2–8). For $dup = 1$ and $\tau_B \in \{6, \ldots, 50\}$ we have high SR values (with the best SR value 96 for $\tau_B = 20$). For $dup = 2$ we have high SR values when $\tau_B \in \{3, \ldots, 25\}$. Increasing dup we obtain high SR only for $\tau_B \in \{1, 2\}$.

To show the effects of combining the hypermacromutation operator with the above described three hypermutation operators, we overlap the two parameters surface generated by IA with just one hypermutation operator, with the results of combining hypermutation and hypermacromutation operators. Figure 3 shows the parameters surface of the Static Hypermutation Operator in terms of SR and AES. In the left plot, we illustrate how the combination of hypermacromutation and static hypermutation outperforms the static hypermutation operator along, in the region where it performed poorly ($c \geq 0.5$).

Moreover, the computational effort of the IA with both operators is smaller than the IA with only the static hypermutation operator (fig. 3 right plot). This is the general behavior of the designed IA when we use the combination

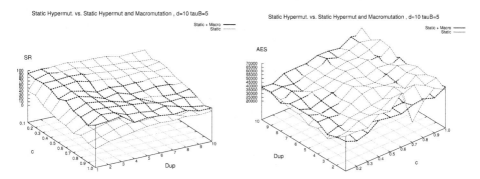

Fig. 3. SR (left plot) and AES (right plot) versus parameter values *dup* and *c* for the sequence 2. The surface parameters of Static Hypermutation operator and the combination of Static Hypermutation operator and Hypermacromutation Operators.

of hypermutation and hypermacromutation operators (see fig. 4). The hypermacromutation operator makes the IA less sensitive to parameter values. It extends the region with high SR and raise the overall parameters surface. For the proportional hypermutation operator (see fig. 4 (left plot)), this phenomenon is particularly evident, in fact the operator alone, performs poorly. Whereas, when we add the hypermacromutation we observe a clear improvement in the IA performance.

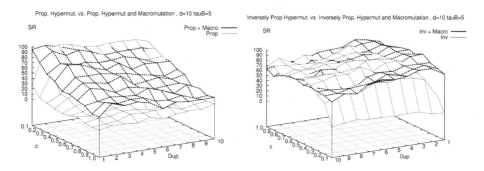

Fig. 4. Combination of hypermutation and hypermacromutation operators.

In the right plot, we show the surface parameters of inversely proportional hypermutation operator and the combination of inversely proportional hypermutation operator and hypermacromutation operators(upper surface): the hypermacromutation extends the region with high SR values and in particular improves the region where the inversely proportional hypermutation operator alone performed poorly ($c \in \{0.1, 0.2\}$ and $dup \in \{1, 2, 3\}$).

Table 3. The SR and AES of all hypermutation operators and their combination on the sequence $1, 2, 3, 6, 9$. The acronym *b.f.* stands for *best found* (result b.f. by IA).

Sequence	1	2	3	6	9
Length	20	24	25	50	20
E^*	−9	−9	−8	−21	−10
Static $(5, 0.1)$	**100**	**100**	**100**	**76.6**	**100**
	15915,63	*29702,6*	*96211,9*	*425199,82*	*26004,86*
Prop $(3, 0.1)$	**100**	**100**	**100**	*b.f. -19*	**100**
	14954,33	*36254,56*	*132119,64*		*21775.06*
Inv Prop $(5, 0.6)$	**100**	**100**	**83,33**	**40**	**100**
	21252	*48756,56*	*135694,32*	*513626,33*	*18547,96*
Macro $(1, \tau_B = 15)$	**100**	**100**	**100**	**16,67**	**100**
	25418,83	*39410,9*	*79592,1*	*469941,2*	*27852,13*
Static+Macro $(3, 0.3)$	**100**	**100**	**96.66**	**80**	**100**
	24362,93	*33496,83*	*89598,31*	*394373,08*	*29148,5*
Prop+Macro $(2, 0.1)$	**100**	**100**	**100**	**30**	**100**
	19355,73	*25627,5*	*69555,07*	*548883,44*	*30683,47*
Inv P+Macro $(2, 0.4)$	**100**	**100**	**100**	**53,33**	**100**
	14443,7	*39644,1*	*95146,97*	*538936,43*	*17293,87*

Experimental Results. To assess the overall performance of all hypermutation operators, we tested them using the tortilla benchmarks. Using the region with high SR value for the protein sequences *Seq1* and *Seq2*, we tried to predict suitable parameter values for each hypermutation operator. In practice, we take the centroid, a pair (dup, c), that maximizes SR and minimizes the AES value. Table 3 shows the SR and AES values of each operator for the protein sequences *Seq1*, *Seq2*, *Seq3*, *Seq6* and *Seq9* (the "simple" protein instances). Table 4 shows the SR and AES values of each operator for the protein sequences *Seq4*, *Seq5*, *Seq7* and *Seq8* (the "complex" protein instances).

Near the operator names, we put the parameter values (dup, c) with the best average performance for all the benchmark instances. The table contains the *SR* and *AES* values. We performed for each instance, 30 independent runs and allowed at most $T_{max} = 10^6$ fitness function evaluations (FFE). All operators reach $SR = 100$ for the protein sequences *Seq1*, *Seq2* and *Seq9* (the simplest instances of benchmark). For the protein configuration *Seq3*, the Inversely Proportional operator and the combination of Static Hypermutation and Hypermacromutation operator obtain respectively $SR = 83, 3$ and $SR = 96, 6$. Most likely these operators, given the current parameter settings, need a higher T_{max} value. For protein sequence *Seq6*, only three operators obtain a *SR* value higher than 50% (Static, Static and Hypermacromutation, and Inversely Proportional and Hypermacromutation). We note that only the proportional hypermutation operator does not reach the minimum energy value $E^* = −21$, since it gets trapped in a local minimum $E^* = −19$. In table 4 we show the overall performance on the complex instance of the tortilla benchmark. All operators reach the minimum energy value $E^* = −14$ for the protein conformation *Seq4*, on av-

Table 4. The SR and AES of hypermutation operators and their combination on the sequence $4, 5, 7, 8$. The acronym *b.f.* stands for *best found* (result b.f. by IA).

Sequence	4	5	7	8
Length	36	48	60	64
E^*	-14	-23	-36	-42
Static $(5, 0.1)$	**20** *304971.33*	*b.f. -22*	*b.f. -35*	*b.f. -39*
Prop $(3, 0.1)$	**3,33** *355512*	*b.f. -19*	*b.f. -32*	*b.f. -31*
Inv Prop $(5, 0.6)$	**10** *462321*	*b.f. -22*	*b.f. -34*	*b.f. -38*
Macro $(1, \tau_B = 15)$	**16,67** *466177,4*	**6,67** *483651,5*	*b.f. -34*	*b.f. -36*
Static+Macro $(3, 0.3)$	**23,33** *347078,14*	*b.f. -22*	*b.f. -34*	*b.f. -38*
Prop+Macro $(2, 0.1)$	**26,66** *375700,25*	*b.f. -22*	*b.f. -34*	*b.f. -37*
Inv P+Macro $(2, 0.4)$	**23,33** *388323,43*	*b.f. -22*	*b.f. -34*	*b.f. -39*

erage with $SR \in \{3, 33, \ldots, 26, 66\}$. There is a clear improvement when IA runs using a combination of hypermutation operators and the hypermacromutation operator. In the remaining protein sequences, no operator obtains the minimum known energy value E^*, except for the *Seq5* where the hypermacromutation operator reaches $E^* = -23$ with $SR = 6, 67$. In the sequence *Seq7* only the Static Hypermutation operator overtakes the conformation with energy value nearest the best known $E^* = -36$. Whereas for the instance *Seq8*, the Static Hypermutation operator and the combination of Inversely Proportional Hypermutation and Hypermacromutation operators achieve the best value ($b.f. = -39$). By inspecting the performance of each operator, it emerges how the static hypermutation, hypermacromutation and the combination of inversely proportional hypermutation and hypermacromutation achieve the best results.

In [12] is reported the comparisons with the state-of-art algorithms for the 2D HP PSP problem. The shown results suggest that the IA with hypermacromutation and aging operators is comparable to and, in many protein instances, outperforms the best algorithms.

5   Conclusions

In this paper we propose a modified version of an IA for a toy problem, trap function, and a NP-complete problem, 2D HP protein structure prediction problem, using simple cloning operator, static pure aging and seven types of different hypermutation operators. Moreover, the used standard IA adopts the *Stop at first constructive mutation strategy* to improve the performance of hypermacromutation operator and in general of all hypermutation operators; we set this strategy for all hypermutation operators, a trick to try to prevent the premature convergence during the search process. For both problems the usage of coupled operators, static and inversely proportional hypermutation with hypermacromutation is the key feature to effectively face the different computational problems; while the proportional hypermutation operator with or without hypermacromutation almost always performs poorly. In particular, for the NP-complete problem, for each hypermutation operator we determined the characteristic parameter surface and the best delimited region on the parameter surfaces that maximizes the SR value and minimizes the AES value. This region has been used to predict the best parameter value setting for all operators and their combinations. When overlapping the parameter surfaces with and without hypermacromutation, we discover that this new kind of perturbation operator makes the IA less sensitive to parameter values setting, and, in general, it improves the performance in terms of SR and AES values.

References

1. Cutello V., Nicosia G.: The Clonal Selection Principle for in silico and in vitro Computing. In L. N. de Castro and F. J. Von Zuben editors, Recent Developments in Biologically Inspired Computing, (to appear) (2004)
2. Dasgupta D. (ed.): Artificial Immune Systems and their Applications. Springer-Verlag, Berlin, Germany (1999)
3. De Castro L. N., Timmis J.: Artificial Immune Systems: A New Computational Intelligence Paradigm. Springer-Verlag, London, UK (2002)
4. Cutello V., Nicosia G., Pavone M.: A Hybrid Immune Algorithm with Information Gain for the Graph Coloring Problem. GECCO '03, Lecture Notes in Computer Science, pp.171-182, 2723 (2003)
5. Goldberg D. E.: The Design of Innovation: Lessons from and for Competent Genetic Algorithms. Kluwer Academic Publishers, Vol. 7, Boston (2002)
6. De Castro L. N., Von Zuben, F. J.: Learning and optimization using the clonal selection principle. IEEE Trans. on Evol. Comp., 6(3), pp. 239-251, (2002)
7. Prugel-Bennett A., Rogers, A.: Modelling GA Dynamics. Proceedings Theoretical Aspects of Evolutionary Computing, Springer, (2001)
8. Nijssen S., Back, T.: An analysis of the Behavior of Simplified Evolutionary Algorithms on Trap Functions. IEEE Trans. on Evol. Comp., 7(1), pp.11-22, (2003)
9. Dill K. A.: Theory for the folding and stability of globular proteins. Biochemistry, 24(6), pp. 1501-9 (1985)
10. Crescenzi P., Goldman D., Papadimitriou C., Piccolboni A., Yannakakis M.: On the complexity of protein folding. J. of Comp. Bio., 5(3), pp. 423-466 (1998)
11. Krasnogor N., Hart W. E., Smith J., Pelta D.A.: Protein Structure Prediction with Evolutionary Algorithms. GECCO '99, 2, pp. 1596-1601, Morgan Kaufman (1999)
12. Cutello V., Nicosia G., Pavone M.: An Immune Algorithm with Hyper-Macromutations for the 2D Hydrophilic-Hydrophobic Model. CEC'04, 1, pp. 1074-1080, IEEE Press (2004)

Exploiting Immunological Properties for Ubiquitous Computing Systems

Philipp H. Mohr, Nick Ryan, and Jon Timmis

Computing Laboratory, University of Kent, UK
{phm4,nsr,jt6}@kent.ac.uk

Abstract. The immune system exhibits properties such as learning, distributivity continual adaptation, context dependent response and memory during the lifetime of a host. This paper argues that such properties are essential for the creation of future context-aware and ubiquitous systems where the need for such properties is becoming increasingly clear. To that end, we present an immune inspired system, which draws heavily on the immune network metaphor to create a meta-stable context-aware memory system that could be delivered in small hand-held devices.

1 Introduction

Locating the information, tools, and other resources that we require, when we require them, is a potentially time-consuming and frustrating task. Systems that automatically make such resources available when needed are highly desirable, but to produce them presents a significant challenge. Such ideas are not new, there are various recommender systems [1,2], but these are still a long way from being portable, producing meaningful results in real time, and adapting to gradual changes in the user's behaviour.

Context-aware or, perhaps more correctly, context-sensitive systems are an important aspect of Ubiquitous computing. For a review of earlier work see Dey and Abowd [3]. Context-awareness describes the capability of a system to recognise changes in its environment and adapt its behaviour accordingly. However, there is a very large step between collecting values that describe easily measured aspects of the environment, such as location or ambient temperature, and determining a user's current activity and resource needs.

To create such an "activity-sensitive" system, the problem arises of how to capture information about the environment and interpret it in terms that accurately reflect human perception of tasks and needs. Additionally, environmental data is potentially of very high dimensionality, raising another challenge in terms of complexity and data storage, especially as such systems need to be made available on small, portable, resource-constrained devices.

We believe that a system which is capable of fulfilling the above task should be unsupervised, work in real-time, use online learning, and be continuous, noise tolerant, and resource friendly. Having examined the ubiquitous computing

G. Nicosia et al. (Eds.): ICARIS 2004, LNCS 3239, pp. 277–289, 2004.

literature, there seems little evidence to suggest that traditional approaches to such a problem will deliver; see for example [3]. Having investigated the area of Artificial Immune Systems (AIS), we believe that certain immune algorithms may be a good choice to help address some of these challenges facing Ubiquitous computing. AIS have been used for data classification, clustering, and compression, in continuous and online learning systems where adaptability is paramount. They have been applied in areas such as computer security [4] and email classification [5], but not yet to the area of context-aware systems.

It is our goal to develop a system which can support context-aware applications to deliver appropriate resources to users derived from an assessment of their current activity and needs based on the context in which they find themselves.

In Section 2 the paper introduces Ubiquitous systems and relevant work in the field. In Section 3 we present work in the area of Artificial Immune Systems which is relevant to the work proposed in this paper. Section 4 outlines our proposed system, as well as reporting initial experimental work. Section 5 presents our conclusions and future aims.

2   Ubiquitous Computing

Ubiquitous computing, Pervasive computing, and Ambient Intelligence all refer in some way to addressing similar goals based on Mark Weiser's vision that computers should be perfectly integrated in all parts of our lives. Weiser believed that devices should remain largely invisible and the user would interact with them often without realising [6]; if there are differences of emphasis within this community, they lie in details such as the extent of invisibility. In this paper we use the term "ubiquitous computing" to include all these nuances.

An important aspect of ubiquitous computing is context-awareness; Dey *et al.* provide definitions for context and context-aware systems, which are widely accepted in the field:

> "*Context* is any information that can be used to characterize the situation of an entity. An entity is a person, place, or object that is considered relevant to the interaction between a user and an application, including the user and applications themselves."

> "A system is *context-aware* if it uses context to provide relevant information and/or services to the user, where relevancy depends on the users task."

The field of ubiquitous computing began with relatively trivial applications. Some were simple rule-based systems which had a handful of rules, e.g. that the light should be switched off when the last person leaves the house. Others dealt with the automatic presentation of information about places of interest in the user's immediate vicinity, typically using a GPS receiver to detect location and then query a database. However, it was soon realised that these simple systems are not enough to achieve the ambitious goals described above, and that far more sophisticated systems are required whose creation can only be achieved by collaborative effort between ubiquitous computing and other fields.

Ubiquitous computing has a wide range of sub-fields, we highlight the major ones and some existing work which has been carried out. A key area is capturing data from sensors, both worn on the body and distributed throughout the environment. Contextual information captured by sensors comprises attributes which describe relevant details about the environment, e.g. time, location, weather, mood of the user, activity, nearby people, etc.; intuitively, separate sensors may be required for each attribute. Bao and Intille [7], for example, try to detect physical activities by placing five biaxial accelerometers on different parts of the body. Other projects like "The Smart Floor" [8] have integrated sensors in the floor which are used to identify the people walking on it (identification is based on each persons unique walking pattern). Much emphasis has been placed on sensing location information. Determining outdoor location is fairly straightforward using GPS receivers, but indoor location is difficult to determine without significant investment in infrastructure. There are many different technologies for location detection, for a detailed overview see "Location Systems for Ubiquitous Computing" [9].

An area of particular concern in ubiquitous systems is privacy and security. In the early days not much attention was given to security and privacy issues, mainly because it is a difficult problem to resolve and working prototypes where needed first to prove the general concept of ubiquitous computing. Currently a range of privacy enhancing infrastructures are available such as the one developed by Osbakk and Ryan [10].

The storage of data about users and their environment is another important area which is split into two sub-areas, one concerned with storing as much data as possible in order to create a complete memory and develop ways of retrieving useful information based on that data, the other concerned with storing only relevant information. For an example of the former see [11], for an example of the latter see [12]. People in the first field argue that memory is cheap and more or less unlimited, but this might not be a feasible approach for all applications as only the information is stored in a sequential way and connections may be difficult to extract.

Next we focus on projects and frameworks related to classifying and predicting users' behaviour. Mozer's "Neural Network House" tries to learn the behaviour of the inhabitants of a house to save energy, e.g. the light is only switched on when the system expects someone to enter a room. The system is based on a feed-forward neural network and trained with back propagation [13].

Kröner et al. [14] present a mobile personal assistant called SPECTOR. The aim of the system is to assist the user with tasks or problems which occur in a daily life situation, e.g. the user should be alerted when the sum of the prices of the shopping items in his basket is greater than the amount in his bank account to avoid embarrassment at the checkout. A machine learning technique is used to create a decision tree which reflects the user's behaviour (a training set is required to jump-start the system). In order for the system to adapt to changes in user behaviour, or improve the decision making process, they developed two versions of a decision tree editor: one abstracts away from the underlying decision tree and allows the user to tick or untick boxes of attributes related to a certain task; the other allows direct editing of the decision tree.

Mayrhofer *et al.* [15] have developed an interesting framework designed to work on resource limited devices which tries to anticipate the user's behaviour and adapt to her needs in advance. Their framework consists of four major steps. The first is feature extraction which turns raw sensor data into usable context attributes, the second is classification of the input data, the third is the labelling of a set of context attributes to give them real world meaning, and the fourth is the prediction of the user's future context. They put strong emphasis on the exchangeability of individual components by providing well defined interfaces. Currently the classification is done using the Growing Neural Gas algorithm, which produces reasonable results. No quantitative evaluation has been done yet for the prediction step.

3   Immune Networks

The immune memory mechanism proposed by Jerne [16], commonly known as the Immune Network Theory, attempts to explain how the immune system maintains a memory of encounters with antigens (Ag) in the absence of antigenic stimulus. It is based on the assumption that B-cells can, in addition to being able to recognise antigens, recognise each other through interactions of idiotopes [17, 18]. This allows for the formation of a network structure of stimulating and suppressing signals which propagate through the network, boosting or decaying the concentration of a particular B-cell. The network is self-organising and self-regulating and, while not widely accepted from an immunological point of view, has been widely exploited in the area of AIS.

3.1   Artificial Immune Networks

Work by Neal [19] proposed a meta-stable immune network algorithm capable of dynamically identifying new clusters in a continual stream of data. The algorithm was based on the immune network theory (outlined above) and is a result of work in [20] and [21]. The algorithm is divided into two main phases: the first phase creates the initial network, and the second adapts it to a changing environment. The algorithm creates a reduced map of the input data space, where each data item is a vector (in the case of Neal, this was a vector of four real numbers). In the subsections below we explain how the Meta-stable Memory structure works by splitting the algorithm into three parts: network initialisation, network growth, and survival in the network.

Network Initialisation. An initial network is created by randomly selecting a number of vectors from the data set being analysed. The whole data set is referred to as the antigen pool (Ag). The selected vectors are then used to create an Artificial Recognition Ball (ARB) and added to the network. An ARB represents a region of antigen space which is covered by a particular type of B-cell, excluding the need for repetition of individuals [21]. The Ag data items are then matched against each ARB in the network. If the Euclidian distance between two ARBs is less than a pre-defined value, referred to as the Network Affinity Threshold (NAT), they become neighbours by the creation of a link between them. Connected ARBs stimulate each other, which allows them to survive longer. All information regarding connected neighbours and resource levels of the ARBs are stored locally within each ARB.

Network Growth. The primary response is invoked if the nearest ARB to the Ag being presented is further away than the NAT value; in this case the Ag is converted into an ARB and added to the network — this is the growth mechanism in the network. It should be noted that no cloning or mutation in the traditional sense of AIS is being performed here. The secondary response is invoked if the Ag falls beneath the NAT value of any ARB, in this case the Ag will not be added to the network. This is under the assumption that the existing ARB which is the closest already represents to a sufficient degree the region of the input space into which the Ag falls. However, the presence of the Ag will not be forgotten, as the matching between the ARB and Ag will increase the stimulation level of the ARBs in the network inversely proportional to the distance.

Survival in the Network. As mentioned previously, each ARB records a resource level which changes continuously and can increase based on the level of stimulation. The stimulation level is calculated by summing the affinity (match value) between all Ags presented during one iteration of the data, and the affinity between all connected ARBs. The more stimulated an ARB is, the more resources it can claim. The resource level can only grow to a pre-defined upper limit and shrink to a pre-defined lower limit. The shrinking is caused by a decay function, which is applied to all resource levels when a new Ag is presented to the network (in the case of Neal this was a linear decay). When the resource level of an ARB falls below this lower limit it is removed from the network.

3.2   Initial Observations

Before attempting to deploy this algorithm in our application, intensive studies of it where undertaken. We identified a major problem and redundant operations within the algorithm as published. When a new Ag is presented to the network and is within the NAT value of any ARB, it will not be converted into an ARB and therefore not be added to the network. Conversly, when a new Ag is outside the NAT value of any ARB, it will be converted to an ARB and added to the network. However, two ARBs will only become neighbours if they lie within each others NAT value but, as we mentioned above, this cannot be the case, because one cannot lie within the NAT value of another.

The neighbouring ARBs Mark Neal presents have two origins, some are introduced by the random selection of starting ARBs, and the others appear due to a fault in the code of his prototype implementation; the fault is described using the code below:

```
1    result = AIS.present(data[dn]); // Find closest ARB and
                                                  record distance
2    dn++;
3    if (result < (AIS.NAT) )
4    {
5       //secondary response
6       AIS.allocate();
7       AIS.cull(); // only cull
8    }
9    else
10   {
11      // primary response
12      AIS.allocate(); // allocation of resources during
                                          repertoire expansion
13      AIS.clone(data[dn]); // repertoire expansion itself...
14      AIS.relink(); // change !
15      AIS.cull();
16   }
17   // dn++ should be positioned here
```

Where data represents the data array and dn the index number an Ag has in the data array, and result is the distance from data[dn] to the closest ARB.

In line 1 the distance from data[dn] to its closest ARB is stored in result. We will refer to line 2 as dn+1 (this is where the error lies). Line 3 tests if result is less than the NAT value; the true branch is fine. The false branch causes the problem, because when result is larger than NAT, data[dn] is converted to an ARB and added to the network, but instead of adding the data item which was used to calculate result, data[dn + 1] is added; this leads to non-deterministic behaviour. To fix this problem dn++ should be moved to line 17. However, this change introduces a new problem, as it is not possible for two ARBs to be positioned within each others NAT value, so no neighbours will be created. Therefore, a further fix is required: a small change needs to be made to the ImmuneNetwork::addARB(ARB* clone) method in the published code by Neal. An additional, slightly larger NAT value needs to be used to allow two ARBs to fall within a NAT value where they can become neighbours. The modification is shown below:

```
// original:
if (distance(clone->pattern, nodes[others]->pattern) < NAT)

// modified:
if (distance(clone->pattern, nodes[others]->pattern) < NAT * 1.3)
```

The NAT value is incremented by 30% in the second line, which produces sensible results. Furthermore, with these changes there is no need for an initialisation phase — the algorithm can start with an empty structure and the Meta-Stable memory structure gradually evolves.

4   A Context-Aware Immune System: CAIS

Now the two background areas have been reviewed, attention can be turned to our application area. As previously stated, the goal of our system is to assist the user through the provision of a user friendly context-aware system that provides an assessment derived from their current context.

Ideally, as mentioned, the system should be implemented on a resource-constrained device and must be effective even in the absence of connectivity. In practice, context-aware software running on mobile devices needs to work in a range of networking environments with the real possibility that it must spend a proportion of time working with no connectivity. There are some benefits to autonomy and keeping more information locally on the user's device, particularly if privacy of sensitive contextual data is an issue. We have to assume that control is lost over any information which is disclosed. If there is no need for disclosure, then privacy can be assured, however this complicated issue of privacy is beyond the scope of this paper.

We propose to use the feature extractor developed by Mayerhofer, *et al.* (see Section 2), because it supplies a feature vector which consists of individual context attributes. Currently their system only provides support for the user's current context, but this is due only to their choice of sensors. We believe an extension providing a range of possible activities can be implemented with reasonable effort.

An important property of the algorithm is adaptation to a change in the user's behaviour. The adaptation should not happen too fast, but also not too slowly. Petzold *et al.* show with the examples of a 1-State and 2-State Context Predictor that a sudden change from one state to another is not sufficient to reflect the user's behaviour [22].

We believe that the immune inspired algorithm outlined above enables the system to capture the gradual change in humans behaviour. Furthermore, the algorithm's memory structure allows for data compression and adaptability, and online learning enables continuous operation.

4.1   Framework

Work in [18] proposes a framework for Artificial Immune Systems which consists of three components. The first describes the data structure and representation used, the second talks about affinity measures, and the third describes the algorithm. We adopt this framework and explain below our system in terms of these three components.

Representation. The system's inputs consist of the user's context and possible options (e.g. different activities such as "lunch" or "meeting"). The user's context is represented by an attribute vector, $\langle a_1, a_2, ..., a_n \rangle$, which contains attributes along with their attribute identifier — note that attributes can appear in an arbitrary order. Possible options are also represented by attribute vectors, one for each option (options may comprise of an arbitrary number of attributes). An example attribute vector is given below:

```
⟨ GSM.CellID = 04x6,
  Wlan.MacAddress = 0A:40:C3:8D:00:32,
  Location.Building = Library,
  Time.Hour = 18:30 ⟩
```

Where `GSM.CellID`, `Wlan.MacAddress`, `Location.Building`, and `Time.Hour` are attribute identifiers, and `04x6`, `0A:40:C3:8D:00:32`, `Library`, and `18:30` are their respective values.

The output is a list containing a predefined number of options of probable significance to the user in respect to her current context (in descending order of relevance). The list could have the following form:

1. Cinema
2. Lunch with Tom
3. Train home in 30 minutes
4. etc.

Figure 1 shows the input of context and possible options, as well as the list of options as output. Context attributes are stored in the system as ARBs. Every ARB has its own resource level R and current stimulation level L. The same attribute can occur multiple times in the same context and/or different contexts. The notion of ARBs allows us to capture all of the different occurrences of an attribute by storing it in a single ARB.

The representation we are using is an n-dimensional hierarchical network structure, where each dimension represents a different attribute, and is itself a network structure. Figure 2 shows an example of the proposed data structure. The example consists of three dimensions and nine ARBs. Attributes from different dimensions which appear in the same context are connected by cross-dimensional-links, in our example ARB_4 and ARB_2 link D_1 and D_2, and ARB_1 and ARB_6 link D_2 and D_3. These links have a resource level L associated with them which reflects the likelihood that these two attributes occur in the same context. Furthermore, every dimension itself contains a network structure, for example dimension D_1 contains ARB_4 and ARB_5, which are connected with each other. The network structure of each dimension is a Meta-stable memory structure (our improved version) which contains at least one ARB, therefore ARBs in the same dimension can become neighbours if they are similar, as explained in Section 3.2.

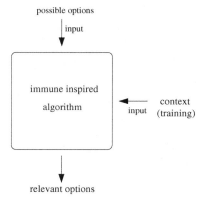

Fig. 1. CAIS

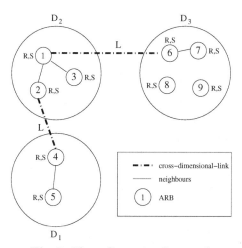

Fig. 2. Three dimensional example

Affinity measures. Affinity is the mechanism by which the distance between two elements is calculated. We use the affinity measure to determine how similar two ARBs are, if they are close enough to be neighbours, and how much one can stimulate the other. Affinity measures have to be chosen carefully in order for the algorithm to work effectively, for a discussion about misuse of affinity functions please refer to [23]. Measuring the distance between GPS co-ordinates is fairly straight-forward as standard Euclidian distance can be used, but measuring the difference between non-numeric attributes is more difficult, e.g. the difference between two mobile phone cell IDs. Mayerhofer, *et al.* have already derived affinity functions for attributes currently supported by their framework [15]; we will adapt these functions for use in our system and develop additional ones as required.

Algorithm. The main part of the algorithm is the process of learning the user's behaviour. At the beginning of its lifetime CAIS is not able to produce resource options that may be made available, as it needs to learn the user's behaviour first. The learning and adaptation of the classification mechanism is achieved by continuously feeding the local context into the system.

To help explain the learning process we define three sets: A is the set of all attributes, e.g. Time, Location, etc.; D_i is the set of ARBs in dimension i, where $i \in A$ (i.e. D_i represents a particular attribute class); and S is the set of all dimensions, $S = \bigcup_{i \in A} \{D_i\}$. In Figure 2, $A = \{1, 2, 3\}$, $D_1 = \{ARB_1, ARB_2\}$, and $S = \{D_1, D_2, D_3\}$. For an attribute i, if D_i is already an element of S, attribute i is stored in D_i. If the dimension is not an element of S, a new dimension, D_i, is created and added to S. The following pseudocode explains the learning process of CAIS:

```
LOOP
    get next input vector
    FOR EACH (attribute i in vector)
        IF (Dᵢ ∈ S)
            stimulate all existing ARBs with the attribute
            IF (distance of attribute to all ARBs > NAT value)
                convert attribute to ARB and add to dimension
            IF (distance of attribute to any ARB < NAT * p)
                make them neighbours
        ELSE
            create dimension and convert attribute to ARB and
                add to dimension
            call decay function on all resource levels
            create cross-dimensional-links between all attributes
        IF (cross-dimensional-link already exists)
            stimulate cross-dimensional-link
```

The user's behaviour is learned from the continuous input of local context. Each attribute in the context attribute vector is presented to the system. First a check is performed to see if the dimension exists to which the attribute belongs, if it does then the attribute stimulates all existing ARBs within this dimension — stimulation depends on the distance to all ARBs within this dimension, which is calculated using the appropriate affinity function. If the distance to all ARBs is greater than the NAT value, it is converted into an ARB and added to the dimension, furthermore if the attribute's distance is within NAT * p of any ARB, where p is the extension to the NAT value within which neighbours are created, it becomes their neighbour. If the dimension does not yet exist, it is created and the attribute is converted into an ARB and stored in the new dimension. After all the attributes have been considered, cross-dimensional-links between them are created or, if they already exist, are stimulated. Both levels decrease due to decay functions, details on the increase and decrease of stimulation levels will be presented in future publications after extensive experiments have been carried out.

In-order to demonstrate the capabilities of the algorithm, creation of a list of appropriate resource options is a possible application. The list of options is generated by taking all possible options as input, CAIS will rate them individually by comparing them to its memory. After all of them have been rated a list is constructed in descending order of rating. Tasks with no match may be included in the list to point out unseen options.

4.2   Prototype

In-order to achieve our goal of a ubiquitous system we have to go through an incremental process. First we identified the requirements, namely continuous operation, high data compression, noise tolerance, and forgetting of redundant patterns. Neal's Meta-stable Memory structure seemed a suitable candidate, as it fulfils the requirements listed. We developed an experimental prototype based on the improved Meta-stable Memory structure described in Section 3 in-order to test the feasibility of using the algorithm in CAIS. The prototype clusters and compresses GPS co-ordinates and displays the current state of the internal memory structure on a map. This allows us to understand and follow the algorithm while running.

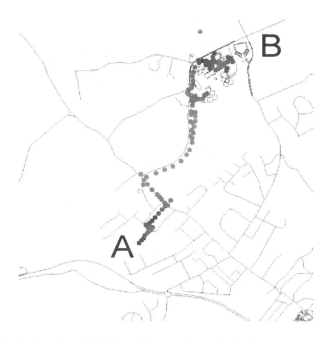

Fig. 3. Tracking GPS Data Using a Meta-Stable Immune Memory

We ran the algorithm with different data sets and different NAT values. Figure 3 shows the output after the algorithm iterated through 200000 points. ARBs are represented by small circles and their resource level is visualised by the darkness of the circle. These points where collected over a period of four months for the same journey from someones house (point A) to the university (point B). The map shows a high activity at point A and point B, and a low to medium activity in between — a standard averaging technique showed a very similar result. The algorithm reduced the points to about 150, and due to the use of ARBs the information about the lost points is retained by the stimulation levels of the ARB. Furthermore, noisy data which was mostly caused by occasional inaccuracies in the GPS measurements is eliminated by the decay function. The time intervals between the capture of individual points ranged from 5 seconds to 5 minutes. The NAT value for this particular example is 15, which corresponds to 15 meters, therefore all points within a 15 meter radius were represented by a single ARB.

The prototype produces promising, and apparently unique results, which we believe justify the usage of the improved Meta-stable Memory structure in CAIS.

5   Conclusion

In general, context-aware systems suffer from a lack of generality and tend to be tailored to a specific set of inputs. In addition, they may require large amounts of data to be of use. In an ideal world we want such systems to be able to generalise, be adaptable, and be able to compress or reduce the amount of data required in-order to function. Immune inspired algorithms appear to be a good candidate for generalisation, adaptability and compression. We believe the immune inspired algorithm presented in this paper has the potential of realising a ubiquitous system that can recognise situations which are of interest to the user, and adapt to a wide variety of user behaviour and environmental inputs. An immune inspired system has been presented that we feel will form the basis of such a ubiquitous system. The first step towards achieving this goal was presented, which was based on tracking GPS data. Clearly more work is needed, but we feel this is an encouraging first step towards a more ambitious goal.

References

1. N. Good, J. Schafer, J Konstan, A Borchers, B Sarwar, J Herlocker, J. Riedl: Combining collaborative filtering with personal agents for better recommendations, in proceedings of the sixteenth national conference on artificial intelligence (1999)
2. Xiaobin Fu, J.B., Hammond, K.J.: Mining navigation history for recommendation, in proc. 2000 conf. on intelligent user interfaces (2000)
3. Abowd, G.D., Dey, A.K.: Towards a better understanding of context and context-awareness, http://www.cc.gatech.edu/fce/contexttoolkit/chiws/dey.pdf (2000)
4. Kim, J., Bentley, P.: The human immune system and network intrusion detection (1999)

5. Secker, A., Freitas, A., Timmis, J.: AISEC: An Artificial Immune System for E-mail Classification. In Sarker, R., Reynolds, R., Abbass, H., Kay-Chen, T., McKay, R., Essam, D., Gedeon, T., eds.: Proceedings of the Congress on Evolutionary Computation, Canberra. Australia, IEEE (2003) 131–139
6. Weiser, M.: The computer for the 21st century. Scientific American (1991)
7. Ling Bao, Stephen S. Intille: Activity recognition from user-annotated acceleration data, in Proceedings of Pervasive Computing 2004,Linz/Vienna,Austria. (2004)
8. Orr, R., Abowd, G.: The smart floor: A mechanism for natural user identification and tracking (2000)
9. Jeffrey Hightower, G.B.: Location systems for ubiquitous computing. IEEE Computer **38** (2001) 57–66
10. Patrik Osbakk, Nick Ryan: A privacy enhancing infrastructure for context-awareness, position paper for the 1st UK-ubinet Workshop, Imperial College, London, UK (2003)
11. Kiyoharu Aizawa, Tetsuro Hori, Shinya Kawasaki, Takayuki Ishikawa: Capture and efficient retrieval of life log, in Proceedings of Pervasive Computing 2004 workshop on memory and sharing of experiences,Linz/Vienna,Austria. (2004)
12. Ashbrook, D., Starner, T.: Learning significant locations and predicting user movement with gps, proceedings of ieee sixth international symposium on wearable computing (iswc02) (2002)
13. M. C. Mozer: The neural network house: An environment that adapts to its inhabitants. in Proceedings of the AAAI 1998 Spring Symposium on Intelligent Environments (1998)
14. Alexander Kroener, Stephan Baldes, Anthony Jameson and Mathias Bauer: Using an extended episodic memory within a mobile companion (2004)
15. Rene Mayerhofer, Harald Radi, Alois Ferscha: Recognizing and predicting context by learning from user behavior, in Proceedings of The International Conference On Advances in Mobile Multimedia (MoMM2003),Austrian Computer Society (OCG) (2003)
16. Jerne, N.: Towards a network theory of the immune system. Ann. Immunol (1979)
17. Farmer, J.D., Packard, N.H., Perelson, A.S.: The immune system, adaptation and machine learning. Phsica **22** (1986) 187–204
18. de Castro, L., Timmis, J.: Artificial Immune Systems: A New Computational Approach. Springer-Verlag, London. UK. (2002)
19. Neal, M.: Meta-stable Memory in an Artificial Immune Network. In Timmis, J., Bentley, P., Hart, E., eds.: Proceedings of the 2nd International Conference on Artificial Immune Systems. Volume 2787 of Lecture Notes in Computer Science., Springer (2003) 229–241
20. Timmis, J., Neal, M.: A resource limited artificial immune system for data analysis. Knowledge Based Systems **14** (2001) 121–130
21. Neal, M.: An artificial immune system for continuous analysis of time-varying data. In Timmis, J., Bentley, P.J., eds.: Proceedings of the 1st International Conference on Artificial Immune Systems (ICARIS). Volume 1., University of Kent at Canterbury, University of Kent at Canterbury Printing Unit (2002) 76–85
22. Jan Petzold, Faruk Bagci, W.T., Theo Ungerer, i.A.I.i.M.S..: Global and local state context prediction (2003)
23. Freitas, A., Timmis, J.: Revisiting the Foundations of Artificial Immune Systems: A Problem Oriented Perspective. In Timmis, J., Bentley, P., Hart, E., eds.: Proceedings of the 2nd International Conference on Artificial Immune Systems. Volume 2787 of Lecture Notes in Computer Science., Springer (2003) 229–241

A Robust Immune Based Approach to the Iterated Prisoner's Dilemma

Oscar M. Alonso, Fernando Nino, and Marcos Velez

National University of Colombia
Computer Science Department
{omalonsom,lfninov,jmvelezc}@unal.edu.co

Abstract. In this paper an artificial immune system approach is used to model an agent that plays the Iterated Prisoner's Dilemma. The learning process during the game is accomplished in two phases: recognition of the opponent's strategy and selection of the best response. Each phase is carried out using an immune network. Learning abilities of the agent are analyzed, as well as its secondary response and generalization capability. Experimental results show that the immune approach achieved on-line learning; the agent also exhibited robust behavior since it was able to adapt to different environments.

1 Introduction

The Prisoner's Dilemma is a game in which two players have to decide between two options: *cooperate*, doing something that is good for both players, and *defect*, doing something that is worse for the other player but better for him/herself. No pre-play communication is permitted between the players. The dilemma arises since no matter what the other does, each player will do better defecting than cooperating, but as both players defect, both will do worse than if both had cooperated. The payoff obtained by each player is given by a payoff matrix, as shown in table 1.

When the game is played several times between the same players, and the players are able to remember past interactions, it is called the Iterated Prisoner's Dilemma (IPD). Each player is said to have an strategy, i.e., a way to decide its next move depending on previous interactions. Accordingly, complex patterns of strategic interactions may emerge, which may lead to exploitation, retaliation or mutual cooperation.

The IPD has been studied as a model of cooperation in social, economic and biological systems [5]. IPD has been modeled in evolutionary and co-evolutionary fashions to analyze the emergence of cooperative behavior among learning selfish agents. Work on the IPD has mainly focused on studying strategies that lead the players to obtain high payoffs. Since the obtained payoff depends not only on a player's own moves but also on those of the opponent, work has been focused on finding robust strategies, i.e., strategies that are good playing against a variety of opponents. This feature is called generalization.

G. Nicosia et al. (Eds.): ICARIS 2004, LNCS 3239, pp. 290–301, 2004.

Table 1. A payoff matrix for the Prisoner's dilemma. The first number in each cell represents the payoff for the row player, and the second value represents the payoff for the column player.

	C	D
C	2 , 2	0 , 3
D	3 , 0	1 , 1

In a first computational approach, Axelrod explored human designed strategies by confronting them through a tournament; in further work, such strategies were compared to strategies obtained through evolution and co-evolution [1].

Further research has been done towards finding strategies that generalize well without human intervention [3,5]. Studies have focused on co-evolutionary approaches, since no human intervention is required in the evaluation process.

Darwen and Yao proposed a speciation scheme in order to get a modular system that played the IPD[3]. Co-evolution and fitness sharing were used in order to get a diverse population. The scheme showed a considerable degree of generalization. Similarly, in this work, an immune agent that plays IPD is proposed, but co-evolution and fitness sharing are replaced with artificial immune systems.

Natural Immune Systems present many interesting features suitable to be applied in computational problems. Some of these features are related to robust behavior of the immune system, as it is able to react to many different antigens, it adapts its response to new antigens, and, additionally, it learns from its interactions with antigens in order to have a faster response in the future. One important model in theoretical immunology is the immune network theory, which explains to some extent the way in which natural immune system achieves immunological memory.

Artificial immune systems have emerged as metaphors of natural immune systems, in order to solve complex computational problems. This field has been a subject of extensive research in the last years. Immune network theory has been used to develop computational models that resemble some features of the natural immune system.

In this paper, an approach based on immune networks is used to model a robust agent that plays the IPD. The structure of the agent is based on two immune networks: the first one attempts to recognize the opponent's strategy, and the second one selects the appropriate next move according to the identified strategy. The resulting behavior of the agent is expected to exhibit some of the features present in natural immune systems, particularly, immunological memory, secondary response and adaptability.

The rest of this paper is organized as follows: Section 2 presents some background on immune networks. In section 3, the internal structure of the proposed immune agent is presented; specifically, the immune networks used are described. Additionally, some modifications to the aiNet algorithm[7] are proposed. In section 4, the experimental setup and results are shown, and then discussed. Finally, some conclusions are devised in section 5.

2   Immune Network Basics

Immune network theory tries to explain the way in which natural immune system achieves immunological memory[8]. B-Cells are stimulated by antigens according to some matching criteria. Thus, a B-Cell is cloned depending on its stimulation level (clonal selection). Additionally, when a B-Cell is cloned, it suffers some mutation depending on its affinity with specific antigens (hypermutation) [9]. The basic idea behind immune network theory is that B-Cells are stimulated not only by antigens, but also by other B-Cells. The relations among B-Cells conform a network structure. Additionally, B-Cells suppress each other in order to control the size of the network.

When an antigen appears for the first time, some matching B-Cells are generated through clonal selection and hypermutation. Once the antigen is no longer present, some of the generated B-Cells are preserved, due to B-Cells co-stimulation. Therefore, when the same antigen reappears, the immune response is faster, since the immune system already contains suitable B-Cells to deal with such antigen.

An Artificial Immune Network (AIN) is a computational model based on immune network theory. Several models for immune networks have been proposed [7,6]. In this work, the aiNet model proposed by De Castro will be used [7]. In such model, the interaction among B-Cells leads to network suppression, i.e., B-Cells that are very similar will suppress each other.

The IPD immune agent proposed in this paper is detailed next.

3   IPD Immune Agent

The basic problem an IPD agent has to deal with consists of deciding the next move it will play given a history of previous moves. The agent should be able to recognize the opponent's strategy during the game, and with the information from such strategy, it should decide what the next move should be. In this work, the process of deciding the next move will be accomplished in two phases: recognizing the opponent's strategy and choosing the appropriate response (see fig 1).

In order to achieve adaptability, memory of previously met opponents and generalization, both phases will be performed by immune networks.

In the first stage, the recognition process will take the recent history of moves of both players, and will attempt to identify the strategy the opponent is playing, i.e., it will try to find a strategy that has a similar behavior to the opponent's. Then, the recognized opponent's strategy will be memorized in order to identify it faster in the future. A suitable model to achieve both, memory and recognition, is the immune network. Thus, for the recognition process an immune network will be used, where the stimulated B-Cells will represent strategies that resemble the opponent's behavior.

On the other hand, the decision process will have to generate new strategies to respond to strategies that have not been seen before, as well as to preserve

---

Algorithm 1 Decision making algorithm

DECISION MAKING

1 **while** *playing*
2   **do**
3   PRESENT HISTORY TO THE RECOGNITION AIN
4   EXTRACT RECOGNIZED STRATEGY FROM THE RECOGNITION AIN
5   PRESENT RECOGNIZED STRATEGY TO THE DECISION AIN
6   EXTRACT BEST PAYOFF STRATEGY FROM THE DECISION AIN
7   OBTAIN SUGGESTED NEXT MOVE FROM THE BEST PAYOFF STRATEGY
8   PLAY NEXT MOVE

---

previously found good strategies. As in the recognition process, an immune network will be used; in this case, a strategy is presented to the decision AIN as an antigen, and stimulated B-Cells will represent strategies with high payoff when confronted with such strategy.

The global IPD decision making process is described in algorithm 1.

3.1   Agent Structure

The proposed IPD agent will consist of two immune networks: a recognition AIN and a decision AIN. In both AINs, B-Cells will represent IPD strategies. The recognition AIN is stimulated by the recent history of moves as an antigen; the network attempts to recognize the strategy that the opponent is playing. On the other hand, the decision AIN will be stimulated by the strategy recognized by the first AIN. The most stimulated B-Cells will be used to determine the next move, since they represent strategies with high payoff when confronted with such antigen.

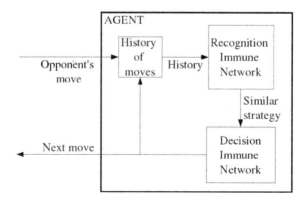

Fig. 1. Agent Structure

Algorithm 2 Modified aiNet algorithm

MODIFIED AINET

```
1   for each antigen
2      do
3          ADD NEW RANDOM B-CELLS TO THE NETWORK
4          CALCULATE ANTIGEN - B-CELLS AFFINITY
5          SELECT N HIGHEST AFFINITY CELLS
6          CLONE AND HYPERMUTATE SELECTED B-CELLS
7          CALCULATE B-CELLS - ANTIGEN AFFINITY
8          RE-SELECT A PERCENTAGE OF HIGHEST AFFINITY CELLS
9          REMOVE LOW AFFINITY B-CELLS
10         CALCULATE SUPPRESSION AMONG B-CELLS
11         REMOVE HIGHLY SUPRESSED B-CELLS
12         ADD RESULTANT CELLS TO THE MEMORY
```

In the aiNet model, all the antigens are known a priori and they are presented to the network many times until the structure of the network adapts to the antigen set. In contrast, the proposed IPD agent, the opponents are not known a priori, and the agent will have to be adapted to the opponents as they appear. Accordingly, to deal with such problem, a slightly modified version of the aiNet algorithm will be used.

The main modification of the aiNet algorithm is introduced in the mechanism the network uses to add B-Cells to the memory. A B-Cell interacts with the B-Cells that have been already memorized. If the suppression it receives from memorized B-Cells is less than the suppression threshold, it is added to the memory and will never be removed. Notice that if a B-Cell is suppressed by the memorized ones, it means that a B-Cell capable of recognizing the antigen that such B-Cell recognizes is already in memory. Thus, in order to avoid redundancy, the B-Cell is not added to the memory.

When a new opponent starts playing a game, there is not enough information to consider that the recognized B-Cells correspond to the opponent, therefore adding the B-Cell in the very early beginning of the game is not a good idea. Additionally, since the agent confronts the same opponent during various moves, it is not necessary to add B-Cells to the memory in each movement given that the history of moves does not change significantly with only one new movement. Thus, in this situation it is more efficient to add the B-Cells that have been periodically generated each k movements. This makes the network more robust, since the network can response even to a change of strategy performed by the same opponent.

The modified version of the aiNet algorithm is summarized in algorithm 2.

3.2   Strategy Representation

The strategies that the immune networks will model as paratopes will be represented as lookup tables. This representation indicates the next move to play, based on the n previous moves of both players. The representation will consist of a vector of moves, where each position in the vector indicates the next move to be done given a specific history of the game. Thus, there are 2^{2n} possibles histories given a memory of n previous moves. Additionally, since there is no initial history, this representation requires $2n$ assumed pre-game moves at the beginning of the game. Hence, the total length of the vector of moves will be $2^{2n} + 2n$, and given that each position of the vector has 2 possible values, cooperate and defect, the number of strategies that can be represented is $2^{2^{2n}+2n}$.

For the process of affinity maturation, strategies will be mutated in two fashions. The first one consists of changing the number of previous interactions remembered by the strategy (memory length), and the second one consists of mutating each position of the vector that defines the strategy according to the mutation rate.

The process of changing the memory length is performed as follows: the new length is selected randomly between one and the maximum allowed memory length. If the new length of the strategy is same as before, nothing has to be done. If it is longer, the new positions of the vector are filled in such a way that the strategy presents the same decision rules as before.

If the new history length is shorter than before, since there are four moves for a history length of k that correspond to one in a history length of k-1, the values of the moves vector will correspond to the move that has the majority in the correspondent moves of the original vector. If there is a tie, it is resolved as *Defect*.

3.3   The Recognition Immune Network

For the recognition immune network, the affinity of the antigen with the B-Cell will be measured by the similarity between the sequence of moves that the paratope would play in the opponent's situation and the moves actually played by the opponent. Such measure is given by the Hamming distance between the two sequences of moves.

Even though some strategies can not be represented completely because of the limitations of lookup table representation, getting a strategy with similar behavior is enough for the recognition process[1]. It will be assumed that any strategy can be approximated with a lookup table representation.

The interaction between B-Cells will lead to suppression, i.e., similar strategies will suppress each other. The similarity of the two strategies will be measured

---

[1] An example of a strategy that can not be represented by a lookup table is GBM Go By Majority, which consists in playing first move randomly an then doing what the opponent has done in the majority of the cases. This strategy can not be represented by a lookup table because it depends of the whole history of moves of the game.

Table 2. Recognition immune network representation

Immune network	Representation
Antigen	History of moves
B-Cell	The paratope represents an IPD Strategy
B-Cell - Antigen Affinity	Similarity of the paratope behavior with opponent's behavior
Co-Stimulation	No co-stimulation will be modeled
Suppression	Similarity of the behavior of B-Cells paratopes

indirectly as follows. Both strategies will play against a randomly generated sequence of moves. The moves of the strategies are compared using the Hamming distance and the percentage of coincidences will determine the suppression value.

A summary of the representation of the elements in the recognition AIN is given in table2.

3.4   The Decision Immune Network

For the decision immune network, the antigen - B-Cell affinity will be given by the payoff obtained by the B-Cell paratope playing a short IPD game against the antigen. The game begins with the current history of the game. The interaction between B-Cells will be calculated as in the recognition immune network.

A summary of the representation in the decision immune network is shown in table 3.

Table 3. Decision immune network representation

Immune network	Representation
Antigen	IPD Strategy
B-Cell	The paratope represents a Strategy
B-Cell - Antigen Affinity	Payoff obtained by the B-Cell paratope playing with the antigen
Co-Stimulation	No co-stimulation will be modeled
Suppression	Similarity of the behavior of B-Cells paratopes

4   Experimental Results

Some experiments were carried out in order to explore the capabilities of the proposed agent. Four experiments were undertaken. First, three experiments were designed to test the immune features presented by the agent. The fourth experiment tests agent's generalization ability.

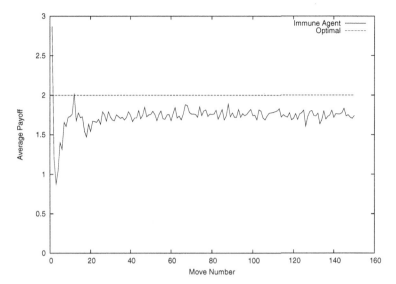

Fig. 2. Agent response against TFT. After a short learning phase, agent's payoff becomes stabilized in a value less than the optimum.

The values of the parameters of the immune networks were set as follows: the suppression threshold was 0.8, and the affinity threshold was 0.9; the number of stimulated B-Cells that were selected in each iteration was 5, and the percentage of stimulated B-Cells that are selected after being cloned and hypermutated was 20%. In each iteration of the immune network, four new random B-Cells were added to the network. In clonal selection, the minimum number of clones that a stimulated B-Cell could generate was 5, and the maximum amount was 10. New B-Cells were added to the memory of each network every 20 moves.

In the recognition process, the length of the history of moves was 10, and the maximum length of the memory of the lookup table representation was set to 3 previous moves. In all the experiments, the payoff matrix shown in table 1 was used.

The first experiment was designed to test the adaptability of the agent to one opponent. Thus, the agent was confronted with an opponent that played Tit For Tat (TFT), which consist in cooperating in the first move and doing whatever the opponent did in the last move, in a game of 150 moves. 200 repetitions of the game were undertaken; the average of the agent's payoff in each move is shown in figure 2.

The results obtained showed that the agent went through a learning process, in which it adapts its behavior to the opponent. This took around 15 moves. After that, the network stabilized, however, the optimal payoff was not reached.

The reasons why the agent did not reach an optimal payoff are hypothesized next. First, as the size of the history of moves is maintained constant, the perception about the opponent is limited. A given history could correspond to

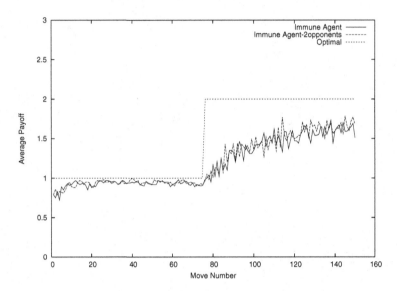

Fig. 3. Agent response to changes in the opponent. The agent detects opponent strategy changes: agent begins to change its behavior and increment its payoff as the opponent changes from ALLD to STFT. The result is similar to the one when the agent is confronted with 2 different opponents.

various opponent strategies, thus, the decision that the agent makes might not be the optimum. Some tests with a longer history size showed a small increase of the agent's payoff reached.

The second experiment was designed to test the agent ability to adapt to a change in the opponent behavior. The agent was confronted with an opponent that changed its strategy in the middle of the game. The opponent began playing the strategy ALLD, that consists in always defecting, and after 75 moves, it changed its strategy to STFT (Suspicious TFT, which is similar to TFT, but begins defecting). This situation was contrasted with the one of having two different opponents with different strategies, playing first against the opponent with strategy ALLD for 75 moves and after that playing with the second opponent for 75 moves, in which the agent knows explicitly that the agent has changed: the average payoff is shown if figure 3.

The results showed that the agent was able to detect the changes in the opponent's strategy. Moreover, there were no significant differences in comparison with the case of a single opponent that changes its strategy in the middle of the game, and the case where there were two opponents with different strategies. Some tests with a longer history size showed a little increase in the payoff the agent reached against the first opponent. However, an increase in the size of the history reduced the adaptability of the agent to changes in the strategy of an opponent, resulting in a slower reaction to changes in the opponent's strategy.

The third experiment was designed to test the agent's ability to adapt its behavior to a new strategy, and agent's secondary response. The agent was

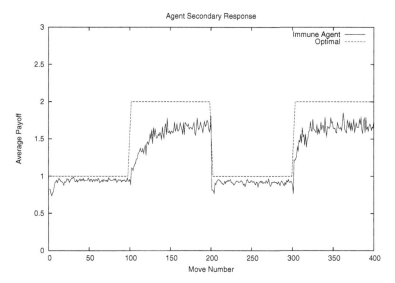

Fig. 4. Agent secondary response. When agent confronts for a second time an opponent playing STFT, the strategy is recognized faster and the overall payoff increases.

confronted with an opponent that played STFT and ALLD alternating them, in games of 100 moves. 100 repetitions of the experiment were done; the average payoff is shown in figure 4.

Results showed that agent response was faster when agent confronts an opponent playing STFT for a second time. The same occurred for ALLD. The experiment showed that the agent responded faster and reached a better total payoff in the game when it was confronted for a second time with an opponent. In figure 4, when STFT was confronted for the second time, the average payoff obtained in each move increased faster than in the first encounter. However, the payoff in which the agent stabilized did not increase.

An interesting phenomenon was observed in this experiment: when the agent was confronted for a second time with ALLD, although the learning phase was shorter, the agent's payoff stabilized in a value slightly lower than in the first encounter. This is hyphotesized to happen because at the beginning of the game the AINs are initialized randomly, and they adapt to play only with one full defective opponent. No cooperative efforts are achieved because the agent has not learned to play cooperatively. However, in the second encounter with ALLD, the agent attempts to induce a cooperative response of the opponent.

The fourth experiment was designed to determine the generalization ability of the agent. The method used in [3] was applied. This is considered a good way to test the generalization by testing the agent behavior with diverse opponents. Accordingly, a large random set of strategies was generated and tested against each other, so that the resultant best strategies in the set were selected as the test opponents. This ensures no favoritism for any special strategy, and that the opponents are good and generalize well as they meet all the other strategies in the set.

Table 4. Results playing against the memory length 2 set of strategies

Player	Wins	Ties	Loses	Own Payoff	Other's Payoff
Immune Agent	40	0	60	1.217	1.175
TFT	0	36	64	1.154	1.173

Table 5. Results playing against the memory length 3 set of strategies

Player	Wins	Ties	Loses	Own Payoff	Other's Payoff
Immune Agent	34	0.13	65.86	1.105	1.272
TFT	0	32	68	1.127	1.148

Table 6. Results playing against the memory length 4 set of strategies

Player	Wins	Ties	Loses	Own Payoff	Other's Payoff
Immune Agent	95.06	0.13	4.08	1.69	0.841
TFT	0	96	4	1.367	1.369

As in [3], three sets of test strategies were generated, each one for a different memory length of previous moves of 2, 3 and 4. The sizes of the sets were 1000 for memory length 2 and 3, and 10000 for memory length 4. In each case, the best 25 strategies in the set were selected, and confronted with the immune based agent and with TFT 30 times per strategy.

Table 4 shows the average payoff per move obtained the agent and TFT being when they where confronted with the test opponents with memory length 2, as well as the percentage of games won, tied and lost against the test opponents. Table 5 and 6 shows the results for the strategies set with memory length 3 and 4, respectively.

In this experiment, the agent showed a better behavior than the simple strategy TFT, when being confronted with a set of test strategies. The results in table 4 and 6 showed not only that it gets an average payoff better that TFT, but also that it won a higher number of games and lost a lower number of games. However, in table 5 (the training set of strategies with memory length 3), the agent did worse than TFT. This was because the testing set contained strategies that were mainly pure defective. As the agent continously tried to test the opponent in search of changes, the agent obtained a worse payoff. Some other experiments with a testing set with memory of three were undertaken in which the agent obtained better payoff as the population was more diverse.

5   Conclusion

In this work, an immune based agent that plays the iterated prisoner's dilemma has been modeled. The immune approach was intended to provide the agent with some features present in the immune system such as adaptability, immune memory and secondary response, in order to achieve agent robustness and generalization.

The agent used two immune networks, one for recognition of the opponent's strategy, and the other one to decide a good way to play the next move.

The agent exhibited the proposed features, i.e., it adapted its behavior to the opponents, memorized opponents previously met and reacted faster when an opponent was confronted for a second time.

Additionally, the agent was shown to generalize well, as it adapted its behavior to not previously seen opponents.

The immune approach resulted in an agent that presented on-line learning, generalization ability and adaptability.

Since the agent is adaptive, further work should be directed to explore co-evolution of immune based agents, as an approach to solve the overspecialization present in co-evolution. Additionally, the proposed approach can be extended to other situations where robust and adaptable agents are desirable.

Acknowledgments. The authors would like to thank Julian Garcia and Fabio Gonzalez at the National University of Colombia for their valuable ideas and helpful comments on previous drafts of this paper.

References

1. Robert M. Axelrod, The evolution of strategies in the iterated prisoner's dilemma, In L. Davis, editor, *Genetic Algorithms and Simulated Annealing*, Chapter 3, pages 32-41, Morgan Kaufmann, CA, 1987.
2. Robert M. Axelrod. *The evolution of Cooperation.* Basic Books, 1984.
3. Paul Darwen and Xin Yao. Automatic modularization with speciation. In *proceedings of the 1996 IEEE Conference on Evolutionary Computing*, pages 166-171,1995.
4. A. M. Colman. *Game Theory and Experimental Games.* Pergamon Press, Oxford, England, 1982.
5. Paul Darwen and Xin Yao, "on evolving robust strategies for the iterated prisoner's dilemma", in Progress in evolutionary computation, Lecture notes in Artificial Intelligence, Vol 956 (X. Yao, ed.), (Heidelberg, Germany), pp. 276 - 292, Springer-Verlag, 1995.
6. Jonathan Ian Timmis, "Artificial Immune Systems: A novel data analysis technique inspired by the immune network theory", doctoral thesis. University of Wales, Aberystwyth. Ceredigion. Wales.
7. de Castro, L. N. & Von Zuben, F. J. (2000), "An Evolutionary Immune Network for Data Clustering", Proc. of the IEEE Brazilian Symposium on Artificial Neural Networks SBRN'00, pp. 84-89.
8. Jerne, N. K. Towards a network theory of the immune system, In Ann. Immunol. (Inst. Pasteur), Vol 125C. pp. 373-389. 1974.
9. de Castro, L. N. & Timmis, J. I. , Artificial Immune Systems: A New Computational Intelligence Approach, Springer-Verlag, London, 2002

Artificial Innate Immune System: An Instant Defence Layer of Embryonics

X. Zhang, G. Dragffy, A.G. Pipe, and Q.M. Zhu

Faculty of Computing, Engineering and Mathematical Sciences
University of the West of England, Bristol
Coldharbour Lane, Bristol, BS16 1QY, United Kingdom
{Xuegong.Zhang,G.Dragffy,Anthony.Pipe,Quan.Zhu}@uwe.ac.uk

Abstract. Will mankind ever be able to construct the elusive 'perpetuum mobile'? We are still far from being able to design systems with a guaranteed finite lifetime, let alone those that we can confidently expect to function unaided in the presence of faults. For example, the Beagle II Mars mission just failed due to malfunction and, worse, the Columbia Space Shuttle suffered the same fate with the loss of many lives. In this context, it is unsurprising that fault tolerance is an increasing emphasis of research into reliable systems. Perhaps if we learn from nature we could design systems, which are tolerant against faults and are able to function properly. Through millions of years of evolution, living things have developed such characteristics. They are cell-based systems that possess an immune system providing an unparalleled defence against faults caused by foreign invaders. It therefore seems intuitive that a generic fault-tolerant hardware system that is inspired by biology should therefore be cell-based and possess some of the immune defence characteristics found in nature. This paper extends the current work on Embryonics (*embryo*logical electro*nics*) at the University of the West of England. It combines internal self-healing characteristics of embryonic cellular array based systems with an instant defence layer, inspired by nature's innate immune system.

1 Introduction

The use of digital techniques is now widespread in almost every area of engineering. The availability of low-cost integrated-circuit devices capable of processing and storing large quantities of data at high speed has led to the development of a wide range of systems for both professional and domestic use. The capabilities of such equipment have increased dramatically while their real cost has been steadily decreasing. Gordon Moore, co-founder of Intel, originally observed this phenomenon in 1965. Widely recognised as Moore's Law, he predicted that the number of transistors per square inch on integrated circuits would be doubled every year. This more or less held true until the mid-80's, although the trend has slightly slowed down, density has still doubled approximately every 18 months. Most experts, including Moore himself, expect Moore's Law to hold for at least another two decades. However with increasing system complexity of VLSI systems it is progressively more difficult to provide comprehensive fault diagnosis to determine its functional validity, when even a simple single

G. Nicosia et al. (Eds.): ICARIS 2004, LNCS 3239, pp. 302–315, 2004.

error could potentially cause it to crash. System reliability therefore is an ever more burning issue and system's ability to function in the presence of faults, to be fault tolerant, is a continuously increasing area of research.

Nature, through hundreds of millions of years of evolution, solved this problem with remarkable efficiency. It builds and can maintain systems, which are far more complex than man has ever made. Animal and the human bodies can survive injury, damage and constant attack from infectious pathogens. In recent years researchers began to investigate artificial systems inspired by biology and apply Phylogeny-Ontogeny-Epigenesis (POE) [1] as well as immunological techniques to build complex and reliable systems with evolutionary, developmental, adaptive and fault tolerant characteristics. In this paper, we will introduce a novel bio-inspired approach to address hardware fault-tolerance in Embryonics (*Embryo*nic Electro*nics*) [2] and Immunotronics (*Immuno*logical Elec*tronics*) [6] based system.

2 Biological Defence Mechanisms: Immunity

The biological defence system has evolved as a surveillance system posited to initiate and maintain protective response against virtually any harmful foreign element the biological body might encounter. In vertebrates, it is called the immune system [7], and is so clever, that is often referred to as a second brain. It is a complex, distributed multilayered system, with each layer providing a different method of fault detection and removal. Physical barriers such as the skin provide defence at the outermost layer. Another barrier is physiological, where conditions such as pH and temperature provide inappropriate living conditions for foreign organisms. Once pathogens enter the body, they are dealt with by the innate immune system and by the acquired immune system. The *innate* immune system primarily consists of the endocytic system, which involves roaming scavenger cells, such as phagocytes, that ingest extracellular molecules and materials, clearing the system of both debris and pathogens. The *acquired* immune response is the most sophisticated and involves a host of cells, chemicals and molecules. It is called acquired because it is responsible for the immunity that is adaptively acquired during the lifetime of the organism.

The immunity in our body against micro-organisms and their products or other foreign substances that may invade the body is divided into two categories: innate or non-specific immunity, and acquired or adaptive immunity.

2.1 Innate Immunity

Most organisms and foreign substances cannot penetrate intact skin but can enter the body if the skin is damaged. Some microorganisms can enter through sebaceous glands and hair follicles. However, the acid pH of sweat and sebaceous secretions, and the presence of various fatty acids and hydrolytic enzymes have some antimicrobial effects, therefore minimising the importance of this route to infection. Once an invading microorganism has penetrated the various physical and chemical barriers, the next line of defence consists of the innate immune system.

Biological protection mechanisms are divided into specific and nonspecific components. Specific or *acquired* immunity is developed during the growth of an individual

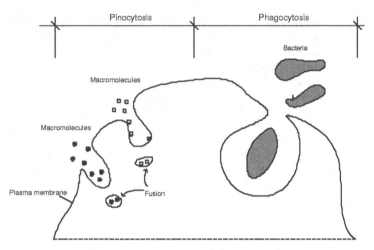

Fig. 1. Endocytic Processes: Pinocytosis and Phagocytosis

through a series of operations, which create a host of specialised cells to counteract invading bacteria and viruses. The nonspecific or *innate* immunity refers to the basic resistance that the individual is born with and is instantly available to defend the body. It operates against almost any substance that threatens the body. Its principle role is to provide an early, nonspecific, first line of defence against pathogens (bacteria, viruses, parasites, or fungi that can cause disease). Most microorganisms encountered daily in the life of a healthy individual are detected and destroyed within minutes to hours by the innate defence system, which uses three defence mechanisms: complement proteins, natural killer cells and phagocytes. All three arms of the innate immune system co-operate with each other and the acquired immune system to ensure efficient defence of the individual.

The first one is the complement system that comprises of approximately twenty-five different complement proteins. They co-operate in a precise sequence to initiate a cascade attack against the invading pathogens. They are highly reactive and can bind and anchor themselves to the wall of the bacterium and by opening up a hole in the surface they destroy it. They circulate in the blood in an inactive form until they are activated.

The second arm of the innate system is the natural killer cell. Natural killer cells kill tumour cells, virus-infected cells, bacteria, parasites, and fungi. They cause the cell to die by forming a membrane attack on the cell surface, like the complement proteins. Natural killer cells also circulate in the blood until they are called.

The last protection mechanism of the innate immune system is provided by various specialised cells whose purpose is to destroy the invader by first ingesting and then destroying it or by killing it extracellularly without ingestion. Two innate immune mechanisms result in the internalisation of foreign macromolecules and cells, and lead to their destruction and elimination. These involve *endocytic* processes called *pinocytosis* and *phagocytosis* (Figure 1).

Endocytosis is the process by which substances are taken into the cell. On contact with e.g. a phagocyte, depression will forms within the cell wall and will deepen until the foreign object is completely engulfed in a pocket. Pinocytosis is the engulfing and digestion of dissolved substances, while phagocytosis is the engulfing and digestion of microscopically visible particles. Phagocytic cells such as a macrophage have surface receptors that can recognise invading foreign particles such as bacteria or virus. The phagocyte plasmalemma will then flow around the invader, until it is enclosed and ingested.

2.2 Acquired Immunity

Under such conditions where an infectious organism is not eliminated by the nonspecific innate immune mechanisms, the acquired immune system will provide the next line of defence. These adaptive responses take more time to develop (> 96 hours) [7] because the rare antigen-specific cells (effector cells) specific for the invading microorganism must undergo clonal expansion before they can differentiate into effector cells to help eliminate the infection.

There are two major types of white blood cells, called lymphocytes, which participate in acquired immunity: B lymphocytes, named after their origination from the bone marrow, and T lymphocytes, named for their differentiation in the thymus. B and T lymphocytes are responsible for the specificity exhibited by the acquired immune response. B lymphocytes synthesise and secret antibodies that bind to pathogens and inactivate them, or identify them to phagocytes and to other innate system defences, thus allowing the innate system to eliminate them. T lymphocytes do not make antibodies but perform various effector functions when antigen-presenting cells or innate immune cells, bring antigens into the secondary lymphoid organs. T lymphocytes also interact with B cells and help the latter to make antibodies. They also activate macrophages and have a central role in the development and regulation of acquired immunity.

Unlike innate immune responses, acquired immune responses are reactions to specific antigenic challenges and display four characteristics [8]:

- Antigenic specificity
- Diversity
- Immunologic memory
- Self/non-self recognition

The *antigenic specificity* of the immune system permits it to distinguish subtle differences among antigens. Antibodies can distinguish between two protein molecules that differ in only a single amino acid. The immune system is capable of generating tremendous *diversity* in its recognition of molecules, allowing it to recognise billions of uniquely different structures of foreign antigens. Because detection is carried out by binding with non-self, the immune system must have sufficient diversity of lymphocytes receptors to ensure that at least some lymphocytes can bind to any given pathogens. Generating sufficiently diverse antibodies is a problem, because the body does not manufacture as many varieties of proteins to build antibodies as there are possible varieties of pathogens. The human body, for example, only makes in the order of 10^6 different proteins, which the immune system must use to construct receptors that can recognise potentially 10^{16} different proteins. However at any given time the actual number of distinct receptors for pathogen recognition is only between 10^8 and 10^{12}. The immune system overcomes this difficulty by using approximate binding and by being very dynamic in producing millions of new and diverse lymphocytes by a pseudo-random process [9] every day.

Once the immune system has recognised and responded to an antigen, it exhibits *immunological memory*. A second encounter with the same antigen induces a heightened state of immune reactivity. Because of this attribute, the immune system can confer life-long immunity to many infectious agents after an initial encounter. Finally, the immune system normally responds only to foreign antigens, indicating that it is capable of *self/non-self recognition*. The ability of the immune system to distinguish self from non-self and respond only to non-self molecules is essential, since the outcome of an inappropriate response to self-molecules can be fatal.

2.3 Collaboration Between Innate and Acquired Immunity

Innate and acquired immunity do not operate in total independence of each other. They cooperate in important ways to produce more effective immunity. They have developed a beautiful interrelationship.

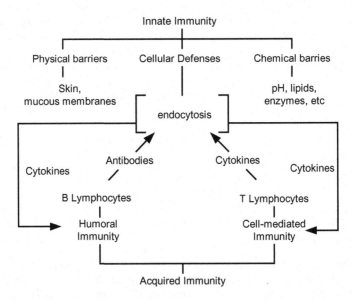

Fig. 2. The interrelationship between innate and acquired immunity

The interrelationship between innate and acquired immunity is shown in Figure 2, where cell-mediated immunity deals with intra-cellular, while humoral immunity with extra-cellular viral infections.

The intricate and ingenious communication system through the various cytokines (proteins made by cells that affect the behaviour of other cells) and cell adhesion molecules allows components of innate and acquired immunity to interact, send each other signals, activate each other, and work together to destroy and eliminate the invading microorganism and its products.

3 Immunotronics and Embryonics

Artificial Immune systems (AIS) are inspired by theoretical immunology and use similar functions and principles of the immune system in addressing complex computational problems [10]. Currently AIS are already used in computer security [11], information system [12], data analysis [13] and fault tolerant embedded systems [6], [15], [16].

3.1 Immunotronics

Immunotronics (*Immuno*logical Elec*tronics*) [14] attempts to create new bio-inspired architectures and to apply AIS mechanisms to build novel fault tolerant electronic systems. It is attracting growing research interest. Of the numerous algorithms and systems researched to date, many use the negative selection algorithm [11] to identify faults within a hardware circuit, specifically a finite state machine (FSM). It is based upon the detection of non-self from self, as found within the immune system. In a hardware system its current state, next state and the current inputs are used to define the current transition of the machine. These are valid operational transitions and can be termed as self. Some transitions however, which are not present in normal, are considered as non-self. Identification of such non-self indicates the presence of an error. This model needs considerable off-line learning time to gather data [17] and large number of self or non-self states needed to be stored in the system. In addition an on-line immunisation cycle [17] is required to distinguish self/non-self. This inevitably increases system complexity and response time. Immuno-Embryonics was first cited by Bradley [18]. He proposed to use adaptive immune system processes for error detection to build fault tolerant hardware systems on an embryonic cellular array. This approach combines two bio-inspired techniques and demonstrates a general architecture of immune–embryonic layer interactions. However it only detects errors in the co-ordinate system and in the memory content of the embryonic cell. Further, although there are no implementation details available it is clear that the proposed system would require high hardware overheads, particularly in terms of routing. Canham [16], [19] suggested a different multi-layer immune system approach. BIST (build-in self-test) is applied at the molecular level. Once the integrity of the molecule's functional module is guaranteed, the innate immune layer is used to verify the validity of inter-modular and inter-cellular communication. Finally, for fault detection and repair, the partial matching ability of the adaptive immune system is used by applying the negative selection algorithm at the system level. The system however needs considerable initial period of learning and there is an assumption that during this time it is fault free and is fully functional. Using this approach, the number of non-self detectors, compared to that of D. W. Bradley, is greatly reduced by applying the negative selection of algorithm at the system level. However, only relatively small systems can be implemented since, as system complexity is increased linearly, the required number of non-self detectors will rise exponentially. Clearly this is, therefore, currently a prohibitive approach for large systems.

3.2 Embryonics

Embryonics (Embryonic Electronics) is inspired by the development of an embryo and attempts to build a multi-cellular system on a two-dimensional embryonic array. It was first discussed by Hugo de Garis in 1991[2]. It is located on the Ontogeny axis of the POE system. In 1994 Daniel Mange [3] described the concept of embryonics in more detail and summarised its three fundamental properties being analogues of nature: multicellular organisation, cellular differentiation and cellular division. He also illustrated a self-repair mechanism [5] using MUXTREE-based cells [20] and proposed a four-layer organisation for the resulting embryonic system [21]: molecular level, cellular level, organismic level and population level. In 1998, Cesar Ortega proposed another embryonic model [22] also based on MUXTREE principles but only using a two-layer structure: cellular level and organism level. The authors of this paper have recently published proposals for an embryonic model [23], [24], [25]. It is based on a reduced DNA memory structure and solves the complexity issue [27], which could limit the size of an embryonic array implemented system. Externally the embryonic cell is governed by cellular division and cellular differentiation, which will define its assigned functionality in the system. Internally it provides the required function, signal routing, error detection using build-in self-test [23] and DNA segment memory repair capability [26] to recover from any fault. However, although it already possesses this intra-cellular repair capability the embryonic cell as a whole would still need additional overall supervision, similar to our immune system, to detect possible malfunction and defence against errors in order to protect the health of the entire organism.

4 Immuno-embryonics

4.1 Innate Immuno-embryonics

As opposed to acquired immunity, innate immunity is presented from birth, no change or adaptation to specific pathogens is needed. It provides a rapid first line of defence, giving the adaptive immune system time to build up a more specific response. Since an embryonic cell [23] is only expected to execute basic logic functions it will comprise of a universal logic element (e.g. a 2:1 multiplexer) and a D-type flip-flop. Furthermore cell simplicity also indicates that only a relatively simple but fast immune system is required as its supervisor. It does not need to analyse the fault and to develop specific antigens for specific errors.

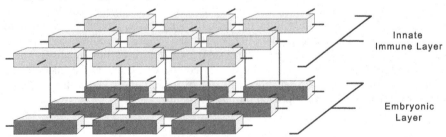

Fig. 3. An innate immuno-embryonics network.

The use of an innate immune system seems to be a better choice in providing an instant error detection mechanism above the embryonic cellular array than an acquired immune system. So this purpose the authors propose a novel innate immune embryonic network (Figure 3).

Following cellular division and cellular differentiation [27], the innate immune system will detect an error in the functionality of an embryonic cell if one exists and will provide a rapid response to trigger a self-repair process within the embryonic array.

The innate immune system demonstrates three basic features:

- Fast response: the innate immune system provides the 'underlying' cell with error detection ability from birth of the embryonic array based system. It requires no learning process, no array reconfiguration and no additional immune cycle for error detection;

- Diversity: Each innate immune cell shares the gene (a 13-bit binary configuration data string) with its collaborative embryonic cell, that through its configuration register [24] also provides inherent diversity. No additional information about the immune cell needs to be stored in the embryonic cell;

- Self/non-self recognition: Every innate immune cell shares the input signals with its embryonic cell and will detect an error in the output of the embryonic cell, if one exists. Unmatched outputs represent a non-self state.

Unlike the case when self-repair is requested by the BIST [23] or by the DNA-repair modules [26] of the embryonic cell, using the innate immune system approach, self-repair -by reconfiguration- can also be triggered by an immune cell. This can guarantee complete error detection of the embryonic cell including its function unit, memory, co-ordinate system, I/O router modules and so on. However, the concept provides yet another advantage. If no immune layer was used and cell 'death' occurs then such an unrecoverable fault would force the embryonic cell to be eliminated [23]. In this case, for signal routing purposes, the cell would be required to operate in the transparent mode. But what if the cell's error is of such nature that it is unable to meet even the requirement of becoming transparent? Such an error could bring the entire system to its knees. Using an innate immune layer can eliminate such situations. Under these conditions, signal routing will be provided by the immune cell rather than by the 'dead' cell.

4.2 Implementation of the Innate Immune System

Four operational modules (Figure 4) make up the innate immune cell. These are the Function unit, Co-ordinate generator, I/O router and the Checker. Both the Function unit of the immune cell and that of the embryonic cell are controlled by the same gene in the DNA-segment memory and therefore both are of the same design. The remaining three modules are unique to the immune cell. The DNA repair unit of the embryonic cell constantly supervises the integrity of its DNA-segment memory against any mutation. Should such mutation occur then the original information will be restored, if the fault is repairable. It would therefore be an unnecessary overhead to duplicate this memory in the immune cell.

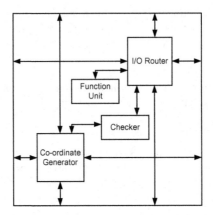

Fig. 4. The structure of an innate immune cell

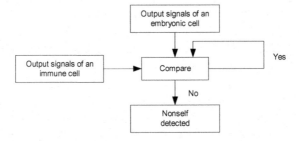

Fig. 5. The negative selection of checker in an innate immune cell

The I/O router and Co-ordinate generator of an immune cell are driven by the same input signals as their counter parts in the embryonic cell. The immune cell will generate it's output signals, which are termed as self or normal signals. Moreover the immune cell will also receive from the embryonic cell the output signals of these modules and will compare them with its own signals for a possible mismatch. Should the Checker uncover any discrepancy a non-self status is set (Figure 5). This in turn will trigger cell elimination and reconfiguration of the array. The I/O router and Co-ordinate generator of the innate immune cell will take over control providing further cell routing and the removal of the faulty embryonic cell from the array.

5 Proposed System and Results

An embryonic array was used to implement a 2-bit binary counter as shown in Figure 6(a). The array has 15 embryonic cells. The configuration also includes a spare row and a spare column for cell-elimination purposes should an error be detected either by the immune cell or by the embryonic cell. A two-layer immuno-embryonic network is shown Figure 6(b). The innate immune layer is placed over the embryonic layer and also has 15 cells. Each immune cell supervises its paired embryonic cell and checks for non-self in its operation.

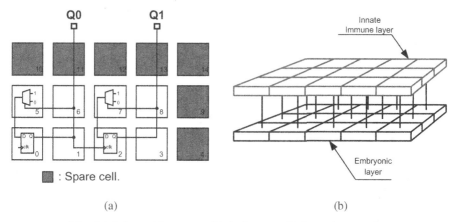

Fig. 6. (a) A two-bit counter, (b) An Immuno-Embryonic network

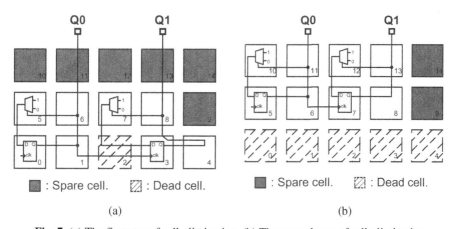

Fig. 7. (a) The first step of cell-elimination, (b) The second step of cell-elimination

The self-repair mechanism in the embryonic module is implemented using cell-elimination strategy. During cell-elimination, spare cells replace faulty cells in two stages. *First*: spares located in the same row replace faulty cells. *Second*: when the number of faulty cells in a row exceeds the number of spare cells assigned to that row, then the whole row is eliminated and cells are logically shifted upwards (row-elimination). In this case a spare row will take over the functionality of the faulty one.

An example of the cell elimination strategy for a 2-bit binary counter, which uses one spare column and one spare row, is shown Figure 7. During the first step of cell-elimination (Figure 7(a)), if cell No.2 in the first row develops an irrecoverable fault then the cell is eliminated. Should any further error develop in the same row then, as shown in Figure 7(b), during the second step of cell-elimination the entire row will be removed. After cell-elimination, signal routing to all neighbouring cells is provided by the associated immune cell of the eliminated embryonic cell.

The simulation results in Figure 8 show what happens when at 42 ns an error is injected into embryonic cell No.2. Its paired immune cell detects a non-self status and an error bit in embryonic cell No.2 will be set. This embryonic cell is now eliminated and embryonic cell No.3 will replace its functionality (gene *3083* of cell No. 3 is replaced by gene *4584* of cell No.2). At the same time functionality of embryonic cell No.3 will also be taken over by embryonic cell No.4 (gene 4097 of cell No. 4 will now be replaced by gene *3083* of cell No.3). The fault is now fully repaired and system functionality can continue unhindered (Figure 7. (a)).

6 Conclusions

We believe that as system complexity increases, the use of conventional design and reliability improvement techniques will no longer offer us safe and extended fault tolerant periods of service. One possible way forward is to draw inspiration from nature, where this problem is solved with remarkable efficiency, thus building artificial systems, that can detect and repair faults while functioning reliably in their presence. This paper discusses and presents such a bio-inspired hardware fault-tolerant system that, like nature, is cellular and possesses innate immune system-like properties. The artificial innate immune system (IAIS) is used as a monitoring device that is overlaid on an embryonic array system to detect and to repair faults if such faults develop. The expected functionality of every cell is contained in its DNA-segment memory. Collectively the cells implement the required functional behaviour of the system. Upon detection of an error, irrespective of whether it was uncovered by the cell itself via its internal repair mechanisms, or by the overlaying immune system, the fault is repaired by 'killing' the faulty cell and by reconfiguring the array. The innate immune repair mechanism provides a fast, instant response to fault detection and unlike the acquired immune system, requires no previous off-line or on-line learning.

To date all applications presented in the literature are software implementations of an artificial immune system with the exception of Immunotronics by Bradley et al. [18] and hardware IAS proposals by Canham et al. [16], [19].

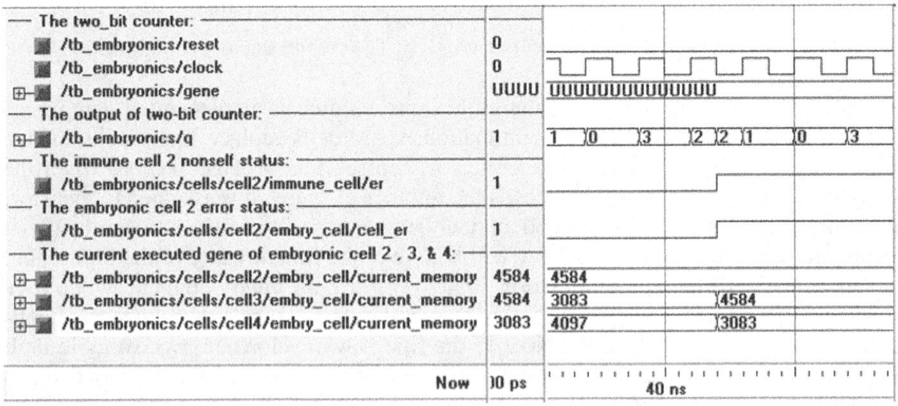

Fig. 8. The simulation results of two-bit counter

There are a number of differences between Bardley's antibody-based and our innate immune system proposals. *Firstly*, from what is known about the immunotronic architecture it does not appear to be sophisticated enough to implement an acquired immune system with on-line learning characteristics. Hence our suggestion to use an innate immune system-like approach for non-self detection. *Secondly*, an overlaid innate immune system can treat the individual embryonic cells as black boxes and monitor the validity of their inputs and corresponding output responses. Unlike the antibody-based approach, over and above configuration memory and co-ordinate register induced faults, it can also detect inter-cell communication errors. *Thirdly*, the antibody cell 'roams' between four embryonic cells. If this is done sequentially then an embryonic cell error may not be detected immediately. In the case of concurrent monitoring the hardware overheads of the antibody cell may became prohibitively large. Our suggestion therefore is the use of one simple innate immune cell for every embryonic cell. *Fourthly*, the monitoring and communication requirements of the antibody-based approach require high routing overheads. By contrast our IAIS approach incurs virtually no routing overhead.

The hardware AIS proposed by R. O. Canham, similar to our body's defences, uses three layers for fault-tolerance. The *first* layer implements built-in self-test (BIST) inside each embryonic cell over its function unit. The *second* layer uses an off-line error checking mechanism by putting the system into a safe mode and concentrates on the routing and switching integrity of the array. The *third* and top level of defence is similar to the biological acquired immune system and uses the negative selection algorithm [11]. The proposal here is to accompany every system by another immune system, which is initially loaded with all possible states of the target system. Then, during a learning period that assumes error-free operation of the system, all valid states found will be eliminated and by the end of the learning period the immune system will contain only non-self (invalid) states. There are a number of issues that need to be considered here: *First*, although the number of "non-self" states for a small system is considerably less than that resulting from from Bradley's approach, as the device gets larger the overheads could become prohibitive. *Second*, the off-line test requires a number of test patterns to be loaded into and run in the array [18]. This process may take some considerable time during the self-repair process, during which no safe control of the system it supervises may be assumed. *Third*, the question of how can the system be brought back after the error checking process into its last error-free state, appears to be left open.

Currently we are considering the use of an integrated embryonic and innate immune layer approach for increased reliability. Our future work lies in expanding this idea to build a multilayered defence structure over an embryonic cell system. This, we hope, will result not only in a fast non-specific immune system, but also in specific immune system with improved response characteristics.

References

1. Sanchez, E., Mange, D., Sipper, M., Tomassini, M., Perez-Uribe, J., and Stauffer, A. "Phylogeny, Ontogeny, and Epigenesis: Three Sources of Biological Inspiration for softening Hardware", on the lecture notes in computer science 1259 "Evolvable Systems: From Biology to Hardware", First International Conference ICES96 proceedings, edited by Tetsuya Higuchi, Masaya Iwata, Weixin Liu, Tsukuba, Japan, October 1996.
2. Garis H. "Genetic Programming: Artificial Nervous System, Artificial embryos and Embryological electronics", in "Parallel Problem Solving from Nature", Lecture Notes in Computer Science 496, Springer Verlag, 1991.

3. Mange, D., Stauffer, A. "Chapter 4. Introduction to Embryonics: Towards New Self-repairing and Self-reproducing Hardware Based on Biological-like Properties", in book "Artificial Life and Virtual reality", edited by Nadia Magnenant Thalmann and Daniel Thalmann, p.p. 61-72, John Wiley & Sons, 1994.

4. Marchal, P., Nussbaum, P., Piguet, C., Durand, S., Mange, D., Sanchez, E., Stauffer, A., and Tempesti, D. "Embryonics: The Birth of Synthetic Life", in book "Towards Evolvable Hardware: The Evolutionary Engineering Approach", edited by Eduardo Sanchez, Marco Tomassini, Springer-Verlag, 1996.

5. Mange, D., Goeke, M., Madon, D., Stauffer, A., Tempesti, D., and Durand, S. "Embryonics: A New Family of Coarse-Grained Field-Programmable Gate Array with Self-Repair and Self-Reproducing Properties", in book "Towards Evolvable Hardware: The Evolutionary Engineering Approach", edited by Eduardo Sanchez, Marco Tomassini, Springer-Verlag, 1996.

6. Tyrrell, A. M. "Computer Know Thy Self!: A Biological Way to Look at Fault-Tolerance", in proceedings of the 25th Euromicro Conference, Volume 2, Pages 129-135, 1999.

7. Coico, R., Sunshine, G., Benjamini, E. "IMMUNOLOGY, A Short Course", the 5th edition, Page 11- 25, A John Wiley & sons, Inc., Publication, 2003.

8. Goldsby, R. A., Kindt, T. J., and Osborne, B. A. "KUBY: IMMUNOLOGY", the 4th edition, pages 3-26, W. H. FREEMAN AND COMPANY, New York, 2002.

9. Hofmeyer, S. A. "An Interpretative Introduction to the Immune System". To Appear in "Design Principles for the Immune System and other Distributed Autonomous Systems". Oxford University Press, Eds, I. Cohen and L. Segel. 2000.

10. Castro, D., L.N. and Timmis, J.I. "Artificial Immune Systems: A New Computational Intelligence Approach", Springer-Verlag, 2002.

11. Forrest, S., Perelson, A. S., Allen, L., and Cherukuri, R. "Self-Nonself Discrimination in a Computer", Symposium on research in Security and Privacy, 1994.

12. Chao, D. L., and Forrest, S. "Information Immune System", the proceedings of 1st International conference on Artificial Immune Systems (ICARIS2002), edited by Jonathan Timmis and Peter J. Bentley, 2002.

13. Morrison, T., and Aickelin, U. "An Artificial Immune System as a Recommender for Web Sites", the proceedings of 1st International conference on Artificial Immune Systems (ICARIS2002), edited by Jonathan Timmis and Peter J. Bentley, 2002.

14. Bradley, D. W., and Tyrrell, A. M. "Immunotronics: Hardware Fault Tolerance Inspired by the Immune System", in proceedings of the 3rd International Conference on Evolvable Systems, Lecture Notes in Computer Science, Springer-Verlag Volume 1801, Pages 11-20, 2000.

15. Bradley, D. W., and Tyrrell, A. M. "The Architecture for a Hardware Immune System", in proceedings of the 3rd NASA/DoD Workshop on Evolvable Hardware, Long Beach, Californian, USA, Pages 193-200, 2001.

16. Canham, R. O., and Tyrrell, A. M. "a Multilayer Immune System for Hardware Fault Tolerance within an Embryonics Array", the proceedings of 1st International conference on Artificial Immune Systems (ICARIS2002), edited by Jonathan Timmis and Peter J. Bentley, 2002.

17. Bradley, D. W., and Tyrrell, A. M. "Immunotronics: Novel Finite-State-Machines Architectures with Built-In Self-Test Using Self-Nonself differentiation" in IEEE Transactions on Evolutionary Computation. Vol. 6, no. 3, pages 227-238, June, 2002.

18. Bradley, D. W., Ortega-Sanchez, C. and Tyrrell, A. M. "Embryonics + Immunotronics: A Bio-Inspired Approach to Fault Tolerance" in proceedings of 2nd NASA/DoD Workshop on Evolvable Hardware Silicon Valley, USA, 2000.

19. Canham, R. O., Tyrrell, A. M. "A Hardware Artificial Immune System and Embryonic Array for Fault Tolerant Systems", Genetic Programming and Evolvable Machine, 4, Pages 359-382, Dec. 2003.

20. Mange, D., Stauffer, A., and Tempesti, G. "Embryonics: A Microscopic View of the molecular Architecture", in the proceedings "Evolvable Systems: From Biology to Hardware" of Second International Conference, ICES98, 1998.
21. Mange, D., Tomassini, M., eds.: Bio-inspired Computing Machines: Towards Novel computational Architectures. Presses Polytechniques et Universitaires Romandes, Lausanne, Switzerland, 1998.
22. Ortega-Sanchez, C., and Tyrell, A. "MUXTREE Revisited: Embryonics as a Reconfiguration Strategy in Fault-Tolerant Processor Arrays", in the proceedings "Evolvable Systems: From Biology to Hardware" of Second International Conference, ICES98, 1998.
23. Zhang, X., Dragffy, G., Pipe, A. G., Gunton, N., Zhu, Q.M. "A Reconfigurable Self–healing Embryonic Cell Architecture", the proceeding of ERSA'03: The 2003 International Conference on Engineering of Reconfigurable Systems and Algorithms, June 2003, Las Vegas, USA.
24. Zhang, X., Dragffy, G., Pipe, A.G., Zhu, Q.M. "Ontogenetic Cellular Hardware for Fault Tolerant Systems", the proceeding of ESA'03: The 2003 International Conference on Embedded Systems and Applications, June. 2003, Las Vegas, USA.
25. Zhang, X., Dragffy,G., Pipe, A.G. "Bio–Inspired Reconfigurable Architecture for Reliable Systems", the proceeding of VLSI'03: The 2003 International Conference on VLSI, June 2003, Las Vegas, USA
26. Zhang, X., Dragffy, G., Pipe, A.G. "Repair of the Genetic Material in Biologically Inspired Embryonic-Cell-Based Systems", the proceeding of VLSI'04: The 2004 International Conference on VLSI, June 2004, Las Vegas, USA
27. Zhang, X., Dragffy, G., Pipe, A.G., Zhu, Q.M. "Partial-DNA Supported Artificial-Life in an Embryonic Array", ", the proceeding of ERSA'04: The 2004 International Conference on Engineering of Reconfigurable Systems and Algorithms, June 2004, Las Vegas, USA.

Immune System Approaches
to Intrusion Detection – A Review

Uwe Aickelin, Julie Greensmith, and Jamie Twycross

School of Computer Science, University of Nottingham, UK
{uxa,jqg,jpt}@cs.nott.ac.uk

Abstract. The use of artificial immune systems in intrusion detection is an appealing concept for two reasons. Firstly, the human immune system provides the human body with a high level of protection from invading pathogens, in a robust, self-organised and distributed manner. Secondly, current techniques used in computer security are not able to cope with the dynamic and increasingly complex nature of computer systems and their security. It is hoped that biologically inspired approaches in this area, including the use of immune-based systems will be able to meet this challenge. Here we collate the algorithms used, the development of the systems and the outcome of their implementation. It provides an introduction and review of the key developments within this field, in addition to making suggestions for future research.

Keywords: Artificial immune systems, intrusion detection systems, literature review

1 Introduction

The central challenge with computer security is determining the difference between normal and potentially harmful activity. For half a century, developers have protected their systems using rules that identify and block specific events. However, the nature of current and future threats in conjunction with ever larger IT systems urgently requires the development of automated and adaptive defensive tools. A promising solution is emerging in the form of biologically inspired computing, and in particular Artificial Immune Systems (AISs): The Human Immune System (HIS) can detect and defend against harmful and previously unseen invaders, so can we not build a similar system for our computers? Presumably, those systems would then have the same beneficial properties as the HIS such as error tolerance, adaptation and self-monitoring [13].

Alongside other techniques for preventing intrusions such as encryption and firewalls, intrusion detection systems (IDSs) are another significant method used to safeguard computer systems. The main goal of IDSs is to detect unauthorised use, misuse and abuse of computer systems by both system insiders and external intruders [23].

In the following sections, we briefly introduce the areas of IDSs and AISs through the examination of core components and basic definition. The research,

G. Nicosia et al. (Eds.): ICARIS 2004, LNCS 3239, pp. 316–329, 2004.

development and implementation of immune-inspired IDSs is catalogued, and is presented in terms of the evolving methodology, algorithmic exploration and system implementation details. An overview of this research area is provided, in conjunction with indications for future areas of study.

2 Background

This section gives a brief introduction to two distinct fields of study - Intrusion Detection Systems (IDSs) and Artificial Immune Systems (AISs), setting the background to and defining the terminology used in the sections that follow. For a detailed discussion readers should consult [29], [23], [30], [13] and [10].

2.1 Intrusion Detection Systems

IDSs are software systems designed to identify and prevent the misuse of computer networks and systems. There are a number of different ways to classify IDSs. Here we focus on two ways: the analysis approach and the placement of the IDS, although there has been recent work [11] on alternative taxonomies. Regarding the former, there are two classes: misuse detection and anomaly detection [29]. The misuse detection approach examines network and system activity for known misuses, usually through some form of pattern-matching algorithm. In contrast, an anomaly detection approach bases its decisions on a profile of normal network or system behaviour, often constructed using statistical or machine learning techniques. Each of these approaches offers its own strengths and weaknesses. Misuse-based systems generally have very low false positive rates but are unable to identify novel or obfuscated attacks, leading to high false negative rates. Anomaly-based systems, on the other hand, are able to detect novel attacks but currently produce a large number of false positives. This stems from the inability of current anomaly-based techniques to cope adequately with the fact that in the real world normal, legitimate computer network and system usage changes over time, meaning that any profile of normal behaviour also needs to be dynamic [30].

A second distinction can be made in terms of the placement of the IDS. In this respect IDSs are usually divided into host-based and network-based systems [29]. Host-based systems are present on each host that requires monitoring, and collect data concerning the operation of this host, usually log files, network traffic to and from the host, or information on processes running on the host. Contrarily, network-based IDSs monitor the network traffic on the network containing the hosts to be protected, and are usually run on a separate machine termed a sensor. Once again, both systems offer the advantages and disadvantages. Host-based systems are able to determine if an attempted attack was indeed successful, and can detect local attacks, privilege escalation attacks and attacks which are encrypted. However, such systems can be difficult to deploy and manage, especially when the number of hosts needing protection is large. Furthermore, these systems are unable to detect attacks against multiple targets of the network. Network-based systems are able to monitor a large number of hosts with relatively little deployment costs, and are able to identify attacks to and from multiple hosts. However, they are unable to detect whether an attempted attack was indeed successful, and are unable to deal with local or encrypted attacks. Hybrid systems, which incorporate host- and network-based elements can offer the best protective capabilities, and systems to protect against attacks from multiple sources are also under development [30].

2.2 Artificial Immune Systems

The Human Immune System (HIS) protects the body against damage from an extremely large number of harmful bacteria and viruses, termed pathogens. It does this largely without prior knowledge of the structure of these pathogens. This property, along with the distributed, self-organised and lightweight nature of the mechanisms by which it achieves this protection [23], has in recent years made it the focus of increased interest within the computer science and intrusion detection communities. Seen from such a perspective, the HIS can be viewed as a form of anomaly detector with very low false positive *and* false negative rates.

An increasing amount of work is being carried out attempting to understand and extract the key mechanisms through which the HIS is able to achieve its detection and protection capabilities. A number of artificial immune systems (AISs) have been built for a wide range of applications including document classification, fraud detection, and network- and host-based intrusion detection [10]. These AISs have met with some success and in many cases have rivalled or bettered existing statistical and machine learning techniques. AISs can be broadly divided into two categories based on the mechanism they implement: network-based models and negative selection models, although this distinction is somewhat artificial as many hybrid models also exist. The first of these categories refers to systems which are largely based on Jerne's idiotypic network theory [19] which recognises that interactions occur between antibodies and antibodies as well as between antibodies and antigens. Negative selection models use negative selection as the method of generating a population of detectors. This latter approach has been by far the most popular when building IDSs, as can be seen from the work described in the next section.

3   Immune System Approaches

In this section, we offer an in-depth review of work relating to the application of AISs to the problem of intrusion detection. Initially, we begin by looking at work comparing broad methodological issues, then move on to describe work which compares the efficacy and advantages and disadvantages of individual AIS algorithms within the context of intrusion detection. Finally, we review complete implementations of immune-based IDSs, firstly from the Adaptive Computation Group at the University of New Mexico and then from other researchers.

3.1 Methodological Issues

Dasgupta and Attoch-Okine [7] compare idiotypic- and negative selection-based approaches to AIS design. Jerne's idiotypic network model [19] is based on idiotypic effects in which antibodies react to each other as well as antigen. In contrast, in the self-nonself model of Forrest et al [34] probabilistic individual antibodies do not interact. The authors consider several applications of AISs, including anomaly detection, fault diagnosis, pattern recognition and computer security. Specifically relating to computer security, they discuss virus detection and process anomaly detection, describing several different approaches. In UNIX processes, changes in behaviour can be detected through short range correlation of process system calls, especially for root processes. Viruses can be detected through detecting changes to files, or through the use of decoys or honeypots, which use a signature-based approach and monitor decoy programs, observe how they were changed, and build signatures from this for main system.

Aickelin et al [1] discuss the application of danger theory to intrusion detection and the possibility of combining research from wet and computer labs in a theoretical paper. They aim to build a computational model of danger theory which they consider important in order to define, explore, and find danger signals. From such models they hope to build novel algorithms and use them to build an intrusion detection system with a low false positive rate. The correlation of signals to alerts, and also of alerts to scenarios, is considered particularly important. Their ideas build on previous work in immunology by Matzinger [28] and work on attack correlation by Kim and Bentley [21]. Their proposed system collects signals from hosts, the network and elsewhere, and correlates these signals with alerts. Alerts are classified as good or bad in parallel to biological cell death by apoptosis and necrosis. Apoptosis is the process by which cells die as a natural course of events, as opposed to necrosis, where cells die pathologically. It is hoped that alerts can also be correlated to attack scenarios. Where these signals originate from is not yet clear, and they will probably be from a mixture of host and network sources. Examples could include traffic normalisers, i.e. a device which sits in the traffic stream and corrects potential ambiguities in this stream, packet sniffers, i.e. a program for collecting live network data, and IDSs such as Snort [32] and Firestorm [26]. The danger algorithm is, however, yet to be specified, as is the correlation algorithm. Whether the system will actively respond to attacks is also not yet clear. Aickelin et al conclude that if this approach works, it should overcome the scaling problems of negative selection, but that a large amount of research still remains to be done. In the future, they intend to implement such a system.

Begnum and Burgess [4] build on previous work by Burgess [6] and combine two anomaly detection models, pH [35] and cfengine [6]. They are motivated by the need to provide a better, automated response mechanism for the pH system, and better detection capabilities for cfengine, as well as the need to collect more detailed data for further research. By the combination of signals from these two systems they hope to provide a more robust, accurate and scalable anomaly detection system. Their approach is to combine the two systems so that pH is able to adjust its monitoring level based on inputs from cfengine, and cfengine is able to adjust its behaviour in response to signals from pH. They discuss the possibility of using the pH/cfengine combination to provide an automated response mechanism which is able to kill misbehaving processes. This work represents an exploration of how to combine the two systems and does not detail any results of experiments, which the authors intend to carry out in the future.

3.2   Algorithmic Explorations

In [21], Kim and Bentley observe that the HIS is more complex than just negative selection and evaluate this with respect to AISs, investigating performance and scaling related to network intrusion detection. The work builds on the LISYS system [18] and proposed work by Kim and Bentley which incorporates a phenotype into the generation and matching process [22]. They do not describe the overall architecture of the system though similar details are presented in their 1999 paper [24]. TCP packet headers are used based on communications between a LAN (local area network) and the external network and internal LAN communications. TCP (Transmission Control Protocol) is a commonly used network communication protocol. These are derived from a given dataset, and profiles from this data are extrapolated as test and training data. Thirteen self profiles are constructed based on this data and detectors are generated using negative selection against these profiles. The encoding of the detectors contains a number of alleles represented by an arbitrary numerical value. The different alleles on a chromosome are related to different properties of the packet. This range of values is then subject to a clustering algorithm. The similarity between the self strings and incoming strings in the case of the test data is measured using an r-contiguous bit scheme, where the value of r is chosen after estimating the expected number of detectors, detector generation trials and expected false negative rate. A matching activation threshold is derived from the number of detectors generated.

The authors compare their results with the negative selection based system described by Hofmeyr [18]. To generate the self profiles they use the Information Exploration Shootout dataset [15]. This data contains five specified attacks. The profile generator extracts the following information from the dataset: connection identifier, known port vulnerabilities, 3-way handshake details and traffic intensity. The feasibility in terms of time and resources of the negative selection algorithm is then assessed by calculating the time taken to produce the detector set. This is coupled with the number of detectors needed for feature space coverage, and from this the time taken for the generation of a comprehensive detector set is calculated. Additionally, the anomaly detection rate is recorded and analysed. The maximum number of detectors was varied for each attack included in the test profile. Non-self detection rates for the various attacks were recorded as less than 16% so the detector coverage in this case was not sufficient. It was estimated that for an 80% detection rate it would take 1,429 years to produce a detector set large enough to achieve this kind of accuracy, using just 20 minutes worth of data, and 6×10^8 detectors would be needed. From these results, they conclude that negative selection produces poor performance due to scaling issues on real-world problems. In their opinion other immune-based algorithms, such as clonal selection, need to be used and a better matching function derived. In the future they intend to evaluate both static and dynamic clonal selection algorithms [23].

Dasgupta and Gonzalez [9] are interested in building a scalable IDS and as a step towards this goal investigate and compare the performance of negative and positive selection algorithms. Positive selection is not found in the selection of T-cells in the natural immune systems, whereas negative selection is. They work from a time-series perspective in terms of scalability and changing self, building on work by Forrest [34] and previous work of their own [8]. Their implementation of the positive selection algorithm generates self using training data and time windows. They use a k-dimensional tree, giving a quick nearest neighbour search. At first, they use only one parameter at once, either bytes per second, packets per second or ICMP packets per second. This is then followed by a combination of all three parameters. An alert is generated when values go beyond a threshold. Their negative selection implementation uses real-valued detectors, with self defined as in their positive selection algorithm. A multi-objective genetic algorithm is used to evolve rules to cover non-self, with fitness correlated to the number of self samples covered, area and overlap with other rules. This allows for niching in the multi-objective problem. They define a variability parameter, v, as the distance from self still considered normal. This results in one rule for time windows equal to 1 and 25 rules for time window equal to 3. These rules are then used to build detectors. The system has two parameters to set manually: the size of the time window and the threshold.

To test the system they use a small subset of the 1999 Lincoln Labs outside tcpdump datasets [25]: week 1 for training, and week 2 for testing. In their results, they seem to concentrate on only five attacks from that week and see how many of these they can find. Using a combination of all three parameters, all five attacks were detected. A single parameter yielded detection in 3 out of 5 cases. Positive selection needs to store all self samples in memory and is not scalable, but has very high detection rates compared to negative selection, which has a rate of 60% and 80% for window sizes of 1 and 3 respectively, using $\frac{1}{100}$ of the memory of positive selection. Overall, the best detection rates they found were 95% and 85% for positive and negative selection respectively. They concluded that it is possible to use negative selection for IDSs, and that in their time series analysis, the choice of time window was imperative. In the future they intend to use more data to comprehensively test their system.

3.3 System Implementations — Developments by the Adaptive Computation Group, University of New Mexico

Early work – analysis. The Adaptive Computation Group at the University of New Mexico, headed by Stephanie Forrest, has been instrumental in the development of intrusion detection systems which employ concepts and algorithms from the field of AISs. Early work from this group is described in Forrest et al [34], and aims to build an intrusion detection system based on the notion of self within a computer system. Their work builds on previous work on an anti-virus system using immune principles [12], and an intrusion detection system called IDES [27]. The system is host-based, looking specifically at privileged processes, and runs on a system which is connected to the network. The system collects information in a training period, which is used to define self. This information is in the form of root user `sendmail` (a popular UNIX mail transport agent) command sequences. A database of normal commands is constructed and further `sendmail` commands are examined and compared with entries in this database. The authors consider the time complexity for this operation be $O(N)$ where N is the length of the sequence. A command-matching algorithm is implemented and new traffic compared with the defined behaviour in the database. Intrusions are detected when the level of mismatches with entries in the database becomes above a predefined level. Subsequent alerts are generated but no direct system changing response is implemented.

Building on previous work by the group [34], the work by Hofmeyr et al [16] is also motivated by the need to improve anomaly-based intrusion detection systems. Misbehaviour in privileged processes was examined through scrutinising the same superuser protocols, but using a different representation. System call traces are presented in a window of system calls, a value of 6 in this case. This window is compared against a database of normal behaviour, stored as a tree structure, compiled during a training period. If a deviation from normal is seen, then a mismatch is generated, with sequence similarity assessed using a Hamming distance metric. A sufficiently high level of mismatches generates an alert, but does nothing to alter the system. No user definable parameters are necessary, and the mismatch threshold is automatically derived from the training data.

In all cases the intrusions were detected by the system. The vast majority of the presented results are evidence of the database scaling well, finding the optimum sequence length and setting the mismatch threshold parameters. With regard to false positives, a bootstrap method was used as a proof of concept, though no actual results were presented. The authors conclude that false positives are reduced with an increase in the training period. It is claimed that their system is scalable, and generates on average four false positives per day, although they did not directly compare their system with any other. The results are suggestive that this approach could work using data from both real and controlled environments, but found that it was difficult to generate live data in a dynamic environment. They also note that issues of efficiency have been largely ignored, but will have to be addressed if this is to work in the real world. In the future they intend to perform more fine-grained experiments, and implement a response which is not just based on user alerts, and to incorporate more immune principles.

Later work – synthesis. The incorporation of some of these suggestions was presented by Hofmeyr and Forrest [17]. The goal of this work was to construct-ing a robust, distributed, error tolerant and self protecting system. Following on from the previous work of Hofmeyr and Forrest [16] and Forrest et al [34], they aimed to implement and test an IDS based on several different components of the HIS. Their system is network-based and examines TCP connections, classifying normal connections as self, and everything else as non-self. Detectors in the form of binary strings are generated using negative selection, and TCP connections are represented in the form of a data-path triplet, and are subsequently matched against sniffed triplets from the network using an r-contiguous bit matching scheme. If a detector matches a number of strings above an activation threshold, an alarm is raised. Detectors that produce many alarms are promoted to memory cells with a lower activation threshold to form a secondary response system. Permutation masks are also implemented to prevent holes in the self definition. Co-stimulation is provided by a user specifying if an alert is genuine, which reinforces true positives. The activation threshold is set according to an adaptive mechanism involving many local activation thresholds, based on match counts of detectors. Their system is distributed across several machines on the network and therefore one central machine does not have to analyse all the traffic on the network [23]. While the focus of the paper is to describe the algorithms and immune concepts, some experiments are briefly described and it was additionally shown that the rate of false positives can be reduced with user aided co-stimulation.

Following criticism by Kim and Bentley in [21] regarding scaling and false positives, Balthrop et al [3] provide an in-depth analysis of the LISYS immune-based IDS, which evolved from some of the research described above. Their work uses a simpler version of LISYS, a system developed by Hofmeyr [18], in addition to work of Kim and Bentley [22]. Balthrop's system monitors network traffic and is deployed on individual hosts. A detector set is distributed to each of the hosts in the network and TCP connections, based on triplets, are monitored using these detectors. Diversity is created through each host independently reacting to self and nonself. The system uses a negative selection algorithm to mature 49-bit binary detectors which are tested against connections collected during a training period. The matured detectors are then deployed on a live network. An anomaly is detected when a detector has matched a number of connections over a threshold parameter, using an r-contiguous matching function. The generality of the detectors is improved through affinity maturation, and once an intrusion is detected, an alert message is generated. Co-stimulation and permutation masks, both present in the original system, are not implemented. In this case, the user is responsible for setting the value of r for the matching function.

Initially, detectors are randomly generated and subject to negative selection so that detectors that match good TCP connections are destroyed. An activation threshold parameter is set automatically by the system, depending upon the number of matches that a detector has made. Additionally, this parameter has a temporal element in the form of a *decay rate*, which is thought to reduce false positive rates. The value for r can be varied manually, as can the total number of detectors allowed, the length of the tolerisation period, and the decay rate for the activation threshold. They compared their system, in terms of components but not in terms of performance, to one described by Kim and Bentley [21], and to the US government CDIS system [36] which also uses negative selection.

The experiments took on two parts: the first stage involved defining the best parameters, the second running attacks on the system. In the first part, the number of detectors was investigated, specifically the effects of detector saturation. In the second part, several attacks were performed through the use of Nessus [31]. They found that once the number of detectors reached a certain point then saturation occurred. At this saturation point, the greater the value of r, the better the detector set coverage. Balthrop et al also found that the longer the tolerisation period, the fewer the false positives, and that increasing the activation threshold reduced the number of false positives. No information was provided as to the statistical significance of the tests. Overall, detection was successful for the attacks in all but one instance, and the tuning of the parameters reduced the false positive rate. Regarding the scaling issue raised by Kim and Bentley, it was noted that the sensitivity of the system has to be investigated before it can be deployed.

The 'light' version of the LISYS system described in Balthrop et al [3] above was used again in [2], though the focus of this research was on improving the representation of the detectors by exploring a richer representation. The dataset and the experimental system used is the same as in [3]. Their experiments investigate the improvement to r-contiguous matching using an r-chunk scheme. In this scheme, only r regions of the whole detector are specified, with the remaining becoming wild-cards. This is thought to reduce the amount of holes that can be present in the detector coverage by the elimination of crossover and length-limited holes during the creation and deployment of detectors.

The effect of permutation masks on the system performance was examined, measured in terms of false positives, and was found to increase the generalisation of the detector coverage. This is based on the observation that an anomaly is likely to produce multiple alerts. Additionally, they found that varying r had little effect, unlike with full length detectors. As the r-chunks scheme performed remarkably well the authors investigated it further, and subsequently found that the dramatic increase in performance was in part due to the configuration of their test network. Nevertheless, it still outperformed the full-length detector scheme. They also found that the incorporation of r-chunks and permutation masking reduced false positives and increased true positives. The results of this series of experiments was compared with the setup described in Balthrop et al [3] above. Balthrop et al conclude that r-chunks is appealing as a matching scheme, and that the addition of permutation masks is useful in controlling the rate of false positives. In the future, they intend to run their system on a larger dataset with more attacks.

3.4 System Implementations — Developments from Other Researchers

The work performed at the University of New Mexico has contributed significantly to the development of AISs for IDSs. However, they are by no means the only researchers to have actually implemented systems in this manner. This section aims to outline system implementations performed by a number of different research groups, with the common goal of implementing various AISs for applications within security.

The AIS described by Kephart [20] is one of the earliest attempts of applying HIS mechanisms to intrusion detection. It focuses on the automatic detection of computer viruses and worms. As interconnectivity of computer systems increases, viruses are able to spread more quickly and traditional signature-based approaches, which involve the manual creation and distribution of signatures, become less effective. Hence they are interested in creating a system which is able to automatically detect and respond to viruses. Their proposed system first detects viruses using either fuzzy matching from a pre-existing signature of viruses, or through the use of integrity monitors which monitor key system binaries and data files for changes. In order to decrease the potential for false positives in the system, if a suspected virus is detected it is enticed by the system to infect a set of decoy programs whose sole function is to become infected. If such a decoy is infected then it is almost certain that the detected program is a virus. In this case, a proprietary algorithm, not described in the paper, is used to automatically extract a signature for the program, and infected binaries are cleaned, once again using a proprietary algorithm not described in the paper. In order to reduce the rapid spread of viruses across networks, systems found to be infected contact neighbouring systems and transfer their signature databases to these systems. No details of testing and performance are given by the author, who claims that some of the mechanisms are already employed in a commercial product, which other are being tested in a laboratory setting.

In [14], Gonzalez and Dasgupta build an anomaly detector that only requires positive samples, not negative ones, and compare this to a self-organising map (SOM) approach. SOMs are a data dimensionality reduction technique using self-organising neural networks. This work explores the issue of scalability, binary versus real value detectors and a fuzzy distinction between self and non-self, building on work in previous papers by the authors [8] and Forrest [34]. Their system uses real-valued negative selection with n-dimensional vectors as detectors. Detectors have a radius r, in other words they represent hyper-spheres. A fuzzy Euclidean matching function is used. In training, detectors are generated randomly and then moved away from self and spaced out. Detectors match if the median distance to their k-nearest neighbours is less than r. After a certain time detectors die of old age and eventually a good set of detectors should be found. These detectors are then used to generate *abnormal* samples. A multi-layer perceptron classifier trained with back-propagation is then used to learn to distinguish between self and nonself, after which real data comes in and is classified. Any abnormalities are reported by the system to an operator. They concluded that scaling is not a problem in negative selection when real values are used rather than binary and r-continuous matching. They also concluded that negative selection could train a classifier effectively without seeing non-self. In the future, they intend to use immune networks rather than artificial neural networks.

Le Boudec and Sarafijanovic [5], [33] build an immune-based system to detect misbehaving nodes in a mobile ad-hoc network. These are wireless networks in which each end-user system, termed a node, acts a both a client and router. As nodes act as routers, their proper functioning is essential for the transmission of information across the network. The authors consider a node to be functioning correctly if it adheres to the rules laid down by the common protocol used to route information, in their case the Dynamic Source Routing (DSR) protocol. Each node in the network monitors its neighbouring nodes and collects one DSR protocol trace per monitored neighbour. Even in low bit-rate networks, the amount of routing traffic becomes large and potentially prohibitive in relation to the negative selection algorithm the authors employ. This lead them to adopt a strategy in which DSR protocol events are sampled over a fixed, discrete time intervals to create a series of data sets.

The protocol events within each data set are then reduced, through the identification of four sequences of protocol events. This creates a binary antigenic representation in which each of the four genes records the frequency of their four sequences of protocol events within each data set. The mapping from raw data to antigen was chosen by the authors in such a way that genes within each antigen correlated in a certain way for nodes behaving correctly, and in a different manner for misbehaving nodes. A negative selection algorithm is then used with the generated antigens and a set of uniformly randomly-generated antibodies to eliminate any antibodies which match using a exact matching function. In this maturation stage all collected protocol events are assumed to be indicative of routing traffic between well-behaved nodes. Once a mature set of detectors has been generated, these antibodies are used to monitor further traffic from the node and, if they match antigens from the node, classify it as suspicious.

4   Discussion and Conclusions

The information presented in sections 3.1 to 3.4 has provided detailed overviews of systems which have been implemented, containing one or more immune-inspired algorithms or concepts. In order to clarify the use of various different types of immune algorithm, we shall concentrate here on 'complete' systems, rather than ideas or partial implementations.

Table 1 presents each of the chosen systems and records, in our opinion, which algorithms were used. Within the context of this table we regard an identification in a column as conforming to the following criteria:

Table 1. Summary of immune-based algorithms used by the systems reviewed

system	self-non-self	gene libraries	negative selection	clonal selection	immune memory	idiotypic networks	response
Kephart [20]	x						x
Forrest [34]	x						
Hofmeyr [16]	x						
Hofmeyr [17]	x		x		x		
Balthrop [3], [2]	x		x				
Gonzalez [14]	x		x				
Le Boudec [5], [33]	x						
Dasgupta [9]	x		x	x			

- Gene libraries mean the system implemented does not initialise random detector genotypes, but does this through the use of an evolutionary method.
- Negative selection refers to the process of selection of detectors based on elimination if binding to self occurs.
- Clonal selection refers to the B-cell based analogy of increasing detector generality and coverage through the process of hypermutaion.
- Immune memory refers to a secondary response, meaning a similar and more rapid response is elicited should the same attack occur again, irrespective of the time between the attacks.
- Networks correspond with an implementation of the idiotypic network theory, where the different immune components have an effect on each other.
- A response within this context does not simply mean the generation of an alert, but an implemented change in the system as the result of a detection.
- Self-nonself refers to the sense of self, as in the system's recognition of what is normal, or belonging to the system, in order to detect the opposite, that is, nonself.

From Table 1 it is evident that the most popular means of implementing an immune system is through the use of a self-nonself model. This approach is used by all systems under review. Furthermore, negative selection is popular, first used by researchers from New Mexico and then adopted by Dasgupta et al We only found one system each that used the comparatively more advanced features of response, immune memory and clonal selection respectively. No system reviewed used idiotypic networks or gene libraries.

Thus, one can conclude that immunologically inspired IDSs still have much room to grow and many areas to explore, as first observed by Kim and Bentley [21]. Experimental results so far have shown that *relatively simple* AIS based IDSs can work on *relatively simple* problems, i.e. selected test data and small to medium sized testbeds. Will larger scale implementations that borrow more heavily from the HIS, i.e. by incorporating aspects such as idiotypic networks, gene libraries and danger theory, be successful. Such work is currently underway by [1] and others. The proof is yet outstanding, but if it works *in vivo*, we ought to be able to make it work *in silico*!

Acknowledgements. This project is supported by the EPSRC (GR/S47809/01), Hewlett-Packard Labs, Bristol, and the Firestorm intrusion detection system team.

References

1. U Aickelin, P Bentley, S Cayzer, J Kim, and J McLeod. Danger theory: The link between ais and ids. In *Proc. of the Second Internation Conference on Artificial Immune Systems (ICARIS-03)*, pages 147–155, 2003.
2. J Balthrop, F Esponda, S Forrest, and M Glickman. Coverage and generaliszation in an artificial immune system. *Proceedings of GECCO*, pages 3–10, 2002.

3. J Balthrop, S Forrest, and M Glickman. Revisiting lisys: Parameters and normal behaviour. *Proceedings of the Congress on Evolutionary Computation*, pages 1045–1050, 2002.
4. K Begnum and M Burgess. A scaled, immunological approach to anomaly countermeasures (combining ph with cfengine). *Integrated Network Management*, pages 31–42, 2003.
5. J Boudec and S Sarafijanovic. An artificial immune system approach to misbehavior detection in mobile ad-hoc networks. Technical Report IC/2003/59, Ecole Polytechnique Federale de Lausanne, 2003.
6. M Burgess. Computer immunology. In *Proc. of the Systems Administration Conference (LISA-98)*, pages 283–297, 1998.
7. D Dasgupta and N Attoh-Okine. Immunity-based systems: A survey. IEEE Int Conference on Systems, Man and Cybernetics, 1997.
8. D Dasgupta and S Forrest. Novelty detection in time series data using ideas from immunology. proceedings of the 5th International Conference on Intelligent Systems, Reno, 1996.
9. D Dasgupta and F Gonzalez. An immunity-based technique to characterize intrusions in computer networks. *IEEE Transactions on Evolutionary Computation*, 6(3):281–291, 2002.
10. L de Castro and J Timmis. *Artificial Immune Systems: A New Computational Intelligence Approach*. Springer, 2002.
11. H Debar, M Dacier, and A Wespi. vised taxonomy of intrusion-detection systems. *Annales des Telecommunications*, 55:83–100, 2000.
12. Stephanie Forrest, Alan S. Perelson, Lawrence Allen, and Rajesh Cherukuri. Self-nonself discrimination in a computer. In *Proceedings of the 1994 IEEE Symposium on Security and Privacy*, page 202. IEEE Computer Society, 1994.
13. Richard A. Goldsby, Thomas J. Kindt, Barbara A. Osborne, and W H Freeman, editors. *Kubi Immunology*. W. H. Freeman and Co., 5th ed edition, 2002.
14. F Gonzalez and D Dasgupta. Anomaly detection using real-valued negative selection. *Journal of Genetic Programming and Evolvable Machines*, 4:383–403, 2003.
15. Georges Grinstein. Information exploration shootout or benchmarks for information exploration. In *Proceedings of the 7th conference on Visualization '96*, pages 449–450. IEEE Computer Society Press, 1996.
16. S Hofmeyr and S Forrest. Intrusion detection using sequences of system calls. *Journal of Computer Security*, 6:151–180, 1998.
17. S Hofmeyr and S Forrest. Immunity by design. *Proceedings of GECCO*, pages 1289–1296, 1999.
18. Steven Hofmeyr. *An immunological model of distributed detection and its application to computer security*. PhD thesis, University Of New Mexico, 1999.
19. N K Jerne. Towards a network theory of the immune system. *Annals of Immunology*, 125:373–389, 1974.
20. J Kephart. A biologically inspired immune system for computers. In *Proceedings of the Fourth International Workshop on Synthesis and Simulatoin of Living Systems, Artificial Life IV*, pages 130–139, 1994.
21. J Kim and P Bentley. Evaluating negative selection in an artificial immune system for network intrusion detection. *Proceedings of GECCO*, pages 1330 – 1337, July 2001.
22. J Kim and P J Bentley. Towards an artificial immune system for network intrusion detection: An investigation of dynamic clonal selection. In *the Congress on Evolutionary Computation (CEC-2001), Seoul, Korea*, pages 1244–1252, 2001.

23. J W Kim. *Integrating Artificial Immune Algorithms for Intrusion Detection*. PhD thesis, University College London, 2002.
24. Jungwon Kim. An artificial immune system for network intrusion detection. In Una-May O'Reilly, editor, *Graduate Student Workshop*, pages 369–370, Orlando, Florida, USA, 13 1999.
25. Lincoln Labs. 1999 dataset. MIT Lincoln Labs, 1999.
26. J Leach and G Tedesco. Firestorm network intrusion detection system. Firestorm Documentation, 2003.
27. T. Lunt, A. Tamaru, F. Gilham, R. Jagannathan, P. Neumann, H. Javitz, A. Valdes, and T. Garvey. A real-time intrusion detection expert system (ides) - final technical report. Technical report, Computer Science Laboratory, SRI International, California, 1992.
28. P Matzinger. An innate sense of danger. *Seminars in Immunology*, 10:399–415, 1998.
29. NIST. Intrusion detection systems. NIST Computer Science Special Reports SP 800-31, November 2001.
30. S Northcutt and J Novak. *Network Intrusion Detection*. New Riders, 3rd edition, 2003.
31. Nessus Project. http://www.nessus.org.
32. M Roesch and C Green. Snort users manual snort release: 2.0.1. Snort Documentation, 2003.
33. S Sarafijanovic and J Boudec. An artificial immune system approach with secondary response for misbehavior detection in mobile ad-hoc networks. Technical Report IC/2003/65, Ecole Polytechnique Federale de Lausanne, 2003.
34. A Somayaji, S Forrest, S Hofmeyr, and T Longstaff. A sense of self for unix processes. *IEEE Symposium on Security and Privacy*, pages 120–128, 1996.
35. Anil B Somayaji. *Operating System Stability and Security Through Process Homeostasis*. PhD thesis, University Of New Mexico, July 2002.
36. P Williams, K Anchor, J Bebo, G Gunsch, and G Lamont. Cdis: Towards a computer immune system for detecting network intrusions. In *In RAID 2001*, volume 2212, pages 117–133, 2001.

Multimodal Search with Immune Based Genetic Programming

Yoshihiko Hasegawa[1] and Hitoshi Iba[2]

[1] The University of Tokyo, Department of Electronics Engineering,
Graduate School of Engineering,
Japan
hasegawa@iba.k.u-tokyo.ac.jp
[2] The University of Tokyo, Department of Frontier Informatics,
Graduate School of Frontier Sciences,
Japan
iba@iba.k.u-tokyo.ac.jp

Abstract. Artificial Immune Systems have become the subject of great interest due to their powerful information processing capabilities. This is because the immune system has some salient features such as memorizing ability, singularity against antigens, flexibility against dynamically changing environments, and diversity of antibodies. Up to now, several algorithms inspired by these immune features have been proposed and applied to many problems such as recognition, computer security, optimization, etc. This paper proposes an optimization algorithm named Multimodal Search Genetic Programming (MSGP), which extends GP by introducing immunological features so as to maintain its diversity for the sake of solving the problems with multimodal fitness landscapes. We empirically show the effectiveness of our approach by applying the algorithm to the artificial ant problem.

1 Introduction

This paper aims to search the multimodal space effectively by Genetic Programming (i.e., GP) with immunological features.

GP has been applied to many applications such as robotics engineering, circuit design, art, financial engineering and so on. Using the traditional GP, only one quasi-optimal solution is searched for in most of these applications. However, it is strongly desired to search for multiple solutions simultaneously. For example, in the field of design engineering, designers have to obtain different solutions from different view points. It would be useful to acquire qualitatively different solutions at the same time. To accomplish this purpose, we employ the immune system's features to maintain diversity.

The immune system is composed of many components, and using them we can survive where many antigens exist. The immune system has the ability to produce various types of antibodies in order to fight against a large number of antigens, whether they are known or unknown. This diversity is well explained by Burnet's clonal selection theory [5].

G. Nicosia et al. (Eds.): ICARIS 2004, LNCS 3239, pp. 330–341, 2004.

Up to now, many immune-based ECs have been proposed. For instance, Genetic Immune Recruitment Mechanism (GIRM) [3] employed the immune mechanism of positive selection. This algorithm inspects newly produced antibodies and adds only the accepted antibody to the antibody population. Immune Algorithm (IA) [19] was based on somatic theory [2] and the network theory [11]. This algorithm calculates the immunological factor, i.e., affinity and concentration to decide which antibody survives in the next generation, mainly for multimodal optimization. Nikolaev et al. extended GA by immune paradigm [20]. They used the concept of antibody concentration change in Idiotypics Networks [15] when calculating the fitness value. However, in most of these studies, the immune approach is used in the context of GA, not GP.

In this paper, we propose Multimodal Search Genetic Programming (MSGP), which employs the immunological feature for the sake of promoting the diversity in the multimodal optimization task. More precisely, in this paper we show the following points:

1. The diversity measure for GP can be explicitly defined in terms of immunological concepts.

2. The extended GP can effectively search for multiple solutions in the artificial ant problem.

3. The search performance is compared to the traditional approach to show the superiority of our approach.

This paper is organized as follows. Section 2 describes previous works on maintaining the population diversity for GA and GP. In Section 3 we explain the proposed diversity measure and the algorithm in detail. Section 4 describes the experimental setups with the artificial ant problem and their results. We discuss the results in Section 5 which is followed by some conclusions in Section 6.

2   Maintaining Diversity for EC

In GA, several methods have been proposed to promote the diversity of the population during the search. 'Sharing' [7] [12] calculates distances between individuals to make common relationship of their fitness values so as to escape convergence. In this method, fitness values are divided by a variable. The variable increases if there are many individuals which resemble the target individual, as a result fitness values become lower. In 'Crowding' [12], a newly added individual is replaced with what resemble the individual. As a result, the population remains diverse. 'Boltzmann Tournament Selection (BTS)' [13] combine Simulated Annealing with GA. In this method, improved tournament selection was employed so that the fitness distribution of individuals obeys the Boltzmann Distribution. Eshelman et al. [10] used Hamming distances between individuals to select individuals for recombination and replacement to improve over hill-climbing type selection strategies for GA. As a result, near relation mating is prohibited in this method. Davidor et al. [6] restricted crossover operation to those which are neighborhoods, resulting in performance improvement.

In GP, many techniques have also been proposed to promote the diversity. Rodriguez proposed Multi-Objective Genetic Programming (MOGP) [22] which applied fitness sharing method to GP. FOCUS (Find Only and Complete Undominated Sets) [8] used the multi-objective method to promote diversity and concentrate on nondominated individuals according to a 3-tuple of *<fitness, size, diversity>*. Ekart et al. [9] applied fitness sharing with a novel tree distance definition and suggested that it may be an efficient measure of structural density.

However, these extensions for maintaining diversity were targeted only at the performance improvement not at getting multiple solutions simultaneously. In order to accomplish this goal, we propose MSGP in which the population diversity is maintained by means of the immunological features.

3 Multimodal Search Genetic Programming

3.1 Calculating Distance Between Two Individuals

It is necessary to define the distance between two individuals and the diversity of the antibody population in order to observe the diversity of antibodies. It is not easy to define the distance between two antibodies because Genetic Programming uses structural gene expressions. Up to now, several definitions have been proposed. The distance definition we used in our algorithm is similar to the definition used in FOCUS. There are other methods like the definition proposed by Ekart [9] and *Edit distance* [17]. However, these definitions cannot take introns into account and consume a lot of computational time. Therefore, we use the affinity-based distance described below. Note that the distance and the affinity are counter part measures.

Affinity between two trees is calculated by Equation (1), (2). $S(T_1,T_2)$ indicates the tentative affinity value. Equation (1) is calculated from the root of the tree. The affinity is calculated with Equation (1) by recursively traversing the trees. T_i represents partial tree of tree i and $T_{i,j}$ represents partial tree rooted at j child of T_i. $node_i$ is a root node of T_i. Fig. 1 shows an example. Our definition doesn't add the number of same nodes under the nodes which are different, the main difference between our algorithm and FOCUS's. We changed this, because our definition is natural when nodes with different arguments are encountered at the same place.

$$S(T_1,T_2) = \begin{cases} 0 & \text{if } node_1 \neq node_2 \\ 1 + \sum_{i=1}^{N} S(T_{1,i},T_{2,i}) & \text{if } node_1 = node_2 \end{cases} . \tag{1}$$

Then, affinity between two antibodies i and j is represented by Equation (2).

$$ay_{i,j} = \frac{S(tree_i,tree_j)}{\min(|tree_i|,|tree_j|)} . \tag{2}$$

The affinity between antigen and antibody is represented by Equation (3). $|tree_i|$ represents the node number of $tree_i$.

$$ax_i = f_a(fitness) . \tag{3}$$

where f_a is the function which normalizes the fitness value to $0 \sim 1$. An antibody of $ax_i = 1$ stands for the fittest antibody of the population. For example, we used Equation (4) in our experiments.

$$f_a(fitness) = \frac{fitness}{maximum\ fitness} \ .$$

(4)

where *maximum fitness* is the highest fitness value in the population.

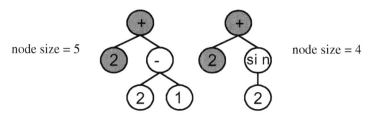

node size = 5   node size = 4

Fig. 1. Example of affinity measure. In this example, the number of same nodes (i.e., + and 2) is 2 and the smaller size of nodes is 4. Then the affinity is calculated 2 / 4 = 0.5.

3.2 Algorithm of Multimodal Search Genetic Programming

In this section, we propose a Multimodal Search Genetic Programming. In this algorithm, the IA [19] approach is extended to be used in conjunction with GP. With MSGP, a search is carried out using the following procedure (Fig. 2, 3).

Step 1 : Production of initial antibody population
An initial antibody population is produced. Initial population is produced randomly.
Step 2 : Calculation of affinity against antigen
The affinity against antigen is calculated. The affinity is calculated by Equation (3).
Step 3 : Calculation of affinity
The affinities between all antibodies are calculated. These values are calculated with Equation (2).
Step 4 : Calculation of concentration
The concentration of every antibody is calculated by Equation (5), (6).

$$c_v = \frac{1}{N} \sum_i^N ac_{v,i} \ .$$

(5)

$$ac_{v,i} = \begin{cases} 1 & ay_{v,i} \ge T_{ac1} \\ 0 & otherwise \end{cases} \ .$$

(6)

N is the number of antibodies in the population, T_{ac1} is a constant value. Equation (6) indicates that if affinity between two trees is larger than T_{ac1}, two trees are regarded as a same tree.
Step 5 : Differentiation to the memory cell
Antibodies whose concentration is higher than T_c differentiate to a memory cell. The number of antibodies which differentiate to memory cell is 1. If there is more than one antibody to differentiate, the antibody which has the maximum affinity with the antigen differentiates. If the affinity between memory cells and the antibody

which is about to differentiate is higher than T_{ac3}, replace the memory cell with the antibody. The size of a memory cell is limited and if it reaches this limit, the memory cell which has highest affinity with the antibody is replaced with that antibody if the affinity with the antigen is higher. If the lowest affinity is lower than T_{ac5}, the memory cell with the highest affinity is replaced with the antibody.

GP always employs the elite selection mechanism. In MSGP, memory cells' antibodies are treated as elite.

With these operations, qualitatively different solutions are stored in the memory cells.

Step 6 : Calculation of probabilities

The probabilities that the antibodies will survive in the next generation are calculated. The probability p_v is represented by Equation (7), (8).

$$p_v = \left(\frac{ax_v \prod_{i=1}^{S} (1 - as_{v,i}^k)}{c_v / c_{min}} \right)^g . \tag{7}$$

$$as_{v,i} = \begin{cases} ay_{v,i} & ay_{v,i} \geq T_{ac2} \\ 0 & otherwise \end{cases} . \tag{8}$$

S stands for the number of memory cells. k is called 'suppressor power' in IA. c_{min} is minimum concentration in the population. For example, $c_{min} = 0.01$ for $N = 100$. g modulates the probability.

Equation (7), (8) indicate that the more the affinity with the memory cell, the lower the probability the antibody survives in the next generation.

Step 7 : Selection of antibodies to erase

In this step, select the antibodies to erase from the population. This selection probability is in proportion to the probability $(1- p_v)$. The antibodies which are selected, survive in the next generation and participate in mutation or crossover. The replacements for the antibodies which are erased are added to the population. These antibodies are randomly produced.

Steps from 2 to 7 are repeated until the termination criteria are met.

After a run, multiple solutions are stored in the memory cells.

4 Experiments

We have applied the above algorithm to the artificial ant problem and the regression problem. This section describes the experimental setups and the results.

4.1 Artificial Ant Problem

Artificial ant problem is a famous benchmark test in Artificial Life [16]. There are several piece of food in an $n \times m$ field. In the field, an artificial ant searches for food with a restriction on energy. The ant's move is determined by a program tree, which

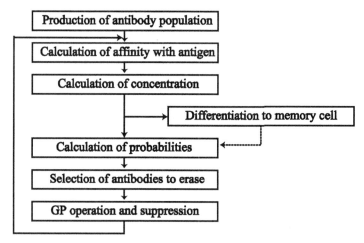

Fig. 2. Flow chart of Multimodal Search Genetic Programming. This figure describes Step 1 - Step 7 illustratively.

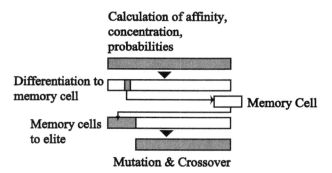

Fig. 3. This figure indicates the operation target in the population. Square stands for the antibody population and the gray square is a target of the operation written near it. For example, "Mutation & Crossover" is operated to the antibodies except the elite.

Table 1. Function and terminal nodes used in ANT problem and their meanings. Zero number of arguments means terminal symbols.

Name	# of arguments	Meaning
If_Food_Ahead	2	If there is food in front of the ant, execute the first argument. Else execute the second argument.
PROG2	2	Execute the first argument and the second argument in order.
PROG3	3	Execute the first argument, the second argument and the third argument in order.
RIGHT	0	Turn right
LEFT	0	Turn left
FORWARD	0	Take a step forward

contains terminal nodes such as 'FORWARD', 'LEFT' and 'RIGHT', and function nodes such as 'PROG2', 'PROG3' and 'If_Food_Ahead' (Table 1). An ant has energy inside and with each move, it consumes energy. The fitness value is defined by the amount of food it picked up. We followed the previous research reports (e.g. [16]) so as to choose these parameter setups.

4.2 Experimental Details of the Artificial Ant Problem

The food maps used in our experiments are shown Fig.4. MAP.1 has a symmetrical food distribution and it has two food groups in the map. MAP.2 has a non-symmetrical food distribution and the two groups are different in size. The parameters we chose are shown below (Table 2). We experimented with many parameters (over 50 experiments) and found these values to be good for accomplishing our purpose. Initial energy $e = 100$ is not enough to pick up all food, so the ant can only get food from one of the group, the upper or the lower.

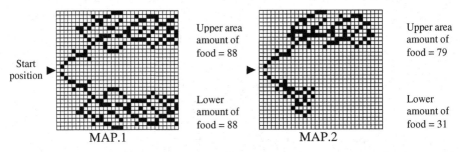

Fig. 4. Food distribution used in our experiments. A black cell stands for food. The cell which the arrow points at is the start point. The direction of the arrow indicates the ant's initial direction. The map has 31×31 cells.

Table 2. Setup of the artificial ant experiments. The parameters listed on the right are used only for MSGP.

Parameter Name	GP	MSGP	Parameter Name	MSGP
Number of individuals	200	200	T_c	0.2
Number of generations	100	100	T_{ac1}	0.9
Mutation probabilities	0.3	0.3	T_{ac2}	0.9
Crossover probabilities	0.7	0.7	T_{ac3}	0.9
Selection method	Tournament	Tournament	T_{ac5}	0.2
Tournament size	4	4	Maximum memory size	4

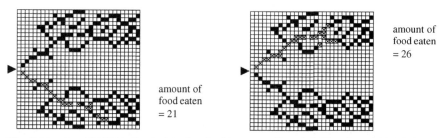

Fig. 5. Results of MAP.1. Food picked up by Memory cell no.2 (left) and no.4 (right). The cells with crosses indicate food picked up. The two programs picked up food from different groups.

4.3 Experimental Results of the Artificial Ant Problem

The results of the artificial ant problem are listed above.

In Fig.5, the cells with crosses indicate food picked up by the memory cell no.2 and no.4. Memory cells no1. and no.3 are omitted because their routes are similar to no 2. and no.4. From Fig.5, we can see MSGP succeeded in finding multiple solutions at a time. Fig. 6 is the change of amount of foods picked up. A dashed line indicates the amount of food which is located at the upper part and a solid line that located in the lower part. These two results were obtained in the same run. Table 3 describes success time. 'Success' means MSGP succeeded in finding the program which picked up more than 15 pieces of food from the group, 'Both', 'Upper', 'Lower'. We experimented 10 times. 'Maximum' indicates the maximum food picked up over 10 runs.

MSGP also succeeded in getting two different types of solutions at once (Fig. 7).

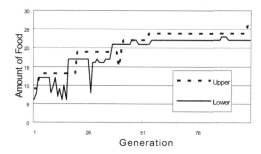

Fig. 6. Relation between generation and amount of foods picked up. The dashed line indicates the maximum amount of food which is located at the upper part and the solid line at the lower part. These two results were acquired in the same run.

Table 3. This table describes the number of success over 10 runs, and the maximum amount of food eaten.

	GP	MSGP
Both	0	6
Only upper	5	0
Only lower	5	4
Failed	0	0
Amount of food	27	28

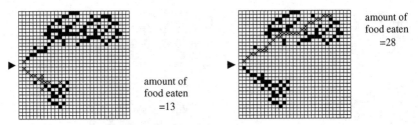

Fig. 7. Results of MAP.2. Food picked up by Memory cell no.1 and no.2. The two programs picked up food from different groups.

4.4 Experimental Details of the Multiple Regression Problem

We also applied our algorithm to the multiple regression problem. This task is different from the ordinary regression problems in the sense that the goal is to identify two different functions $f_1(x)$ and $f_2(x)$ simultaneously. Thus, the validation data are given according to Equation (9).

$$validation = \{(x, y) \mid y = f_1(x) \ or \ y = f_2(x)\} \qquad (9)$$

In the experiment, we used the two functions represented by Equation (10) (Fig. 8).

$$f_1(x) = x^3 \qquad f_2(x) = x \cos(2x) \qquad (10)$$

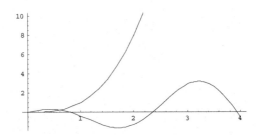

Fig. 8. The shape of the target functions. The upper one indicates $f_1(x)$ and the lower one $f_2(x)$.

The range is $1 \le x < 4$ and the number of sample points is 20. The fitness value is calculated by Equations (11) and (12).

$$fitness\ value = -\sum_{i=1}^{M} error_i^2 \qquad (11)$$

$$error_i = \begin{cases} \mid validation_i - value_i \mid & \mid validation_i - value_i \mid < 2 \\ 2 & \mid validation_i - value_i \mid \ge 2 \end{cases} \qquad (12)$$

where M is the sample points number (i.e., $M=20$ in this experiment).

Table 4. Setup of the multiple regression experiment.

Parameter Name	MSGP	Parameter Name	MSGP
Number of individuals	200	T_c	0.2
Number of generations	100	T_{ac1}	0.9
Mutation probabilities	0.3	T_{ac2}	0.9
Crossover probabilities	0.7	T_{ac3}	0.9
Selection method	Tournament	T_{ac5}	0.2
Tournament size	6	Maximum memory size	4

4.5   Experimental Results of the Multiple Regression Problem

Fig. 9 describes the memory cells of a typical run. Each graph shows the shape of each memory cell. As can be seen, the memory cells no.2 and no.3 showed success in acquiring the target functions. Although the memory cell no.1 seems to show the failure, the acquired trajectory looks like the combination of two functions $f_1(x)$ and $f_2(x)$.

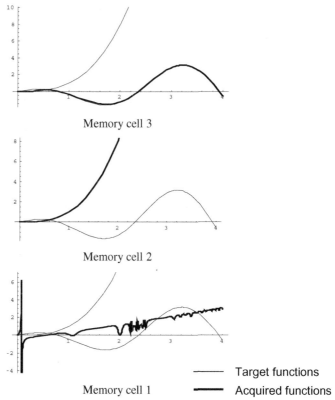

Memory cell 3

Memory cell 2

——— Target functions

━━━ Acquired functions

Memory cell 1

Fig. 9. The shape of obtained functions in the succeeded run.

5 Discussion

In the artificial ant experiment with MAP.1 (Fig. 5), MSGP succeeded in acquiring two different solutions at the same time. As can be seen in Fig. 6, the fitness growth shows that the two different programs evolved effectively. Table 3 describes the number of successful runs compared to those of traditional GP. With the traditional GP, it was almost impossible to evolve two solutions simultaneously, whereas MSGP succeeded 6 out of 10 times. The reason of the MSGP's failure (i.e., 4 times out of 10 times) seems to be that different programs do not necessarily result in different routes. In order to confirm this hypothesis, we looked at the memory cells of the failed run, and found that the stored programs were completely different in shape. By the experiment of MAP.2, we have observed that MSGP is also able to search for a solution whether it is not optimal or quasi-optimal.

The above results seem to be due to the enhancement of the diversity in the antibody population and to the features of the memory cell. Note that the memory cell can store even antibodies with low affinity with the antigen if their affinities with other memory cells are low. Thus, two solutions of MAP.2 will not necessarily be easily obtained with other types of GP extensions.

In the multiple regression experiment, MSGP also succeeded in finding two different solutions at the same time. This result suggests that MSGP is applicable to pattern matching problems with multiple solutions (see [14] for details). This is because figure identification from an image can be taken for the regression problems. For the sake of real-world applications, however, the success ratio should be improved, which we are currently working on.

In this paper, we have calculated the affinity in the form of G-type. However, another plausible approach is to utilize the affinity based on P-type. For example, the distribution of food eaten may be used for calculating the diversity. As mentioned above, the difference in G-type (i.e., different programs) does not necessarily lead to different P-types (i.e., different behaviors). This explains the MSGP's failure in some cases. However, P-type based affinity has the problem that the definition differs from problem to problem. We are in pursuit of this topic in future research.

From the view point of computational time, our algorithm may be relatively inferior to traditional GP because of the affinity calculation in traversing a tree. Furthermore, MSGP requires calculating all affinities between antibodies. More precisely, the computational time is proportional to N^2, where N is the number of antibodies (individuals). We are trying to improve this defect by employing other distance definition.

6 Conclusion

We showed the proposed algorithm is effective for acquiring multiple solutions of the artificial ant problem and the regression problem. This algorithm can keep the diversity of the antibody population high, whereas the ordinary GP cannot. We will apply MSGP to other domains, e.g., circuit design, genome informatics, art and so on. For instance, we have confirmed an immuno-based approach is effective in classification task of bioinformatics [1]. The application of MSGP to such a real-world problem is our future research focus.

References

1. Ando, S. and Iba, H.: Artificial Immune System for Classification of Gene Expression Data, Proc. of Genetic and Evolutionary Computation Conference (GECCO) Lecture Notes in Computer Science Vol. 2723, Springer-Verlag (2003)
2. Atlan, H. and Cohen, I.R.: Theories of Immune Networks , Springer-Verlag (1989)
3. Bersini, H. and Varela, F.J.: The Immune Recruitment Mechanism : A Selective Evolutionary Strategy, Proc. 4th ICGA (1991) pp.520-526
4. Burke, E., Gustafson, S., Kendall, G. and Krasnogor, N.: A Survey and Analysis of Diversity Measures in Genetic Programming. In Proceedings of the Genetic and Evolutionary Computation Conference (2002) pp.716-723
5. Burnet, F.M.: The clonal selection theory of immunity, Vanderbilt and Cambridge Univ. Press (1959)
6. Davidor, Y., Yamada, T. and Nakano, R.: The ECOlogical Framework II: Improving GA Performance At Virtually Zero Cost, Proc. of the Fifth ICGA, pp.171-176, 1993
7. Deb, K. and Goldberg, D.E.: An Investigation of Niche and Species Formation in Genetic Function Optimization, Proc. of the Third ICGA (1989) pp.42-50
8. De Jong, E.D., Watson, R.A. and Pollack, J.B.: Reducing Bloat and Promoting Diversity using Multi-Objective Methods, Proc.GECCO-2001, Morgan Kaufmann, San Francisco (2001) pp.11-18
9. Ekart, A. and Nemeth, S.N.: A metric for genetic programs and fitness sharing, Proceedings of the European Conference on Genetic Programming (2000) pp.259-270
10. Eshelman, L. and Schaffer, J.: Crossover's niche. In S. Forrest (ed.), Proceeding of the Fifth International Conference on Genetic Algorithms (1993) pp.9-14
11. Farmer, J.D., Packard, N.H. and Perelson, A.A.: The Immune System, Adaptation, and Machine Learning, Phisica; 22D (1986) pp.187-204
12. Goldberg, D.E.: Genetic Algorithm in Search, Optimization and Machine Learning, Addison-Wesley Publishing Company, Inc., 1989
13. Goldberg, D.E.: A Note on Boltzmann Tournament Selection for Genetic Algorithms and Population-oriented Simulated Annealing, Complex Systems, Vol.4 (1990) pp.445-460
14. Iba, H., Higuchi, T. and Sato, T.: BUGS:A Bug-based Search Strategy using Genetic Algorithms in Parallel Problem Solving from Nature 2 (PPSN II) (1992) pp.165--174, Elsevier Pub.
15. Jerne, N.K.: The Immune System, Sci. Amer., 229, 1, pp.52-60 (1973)
16. Koza J.R.: Genetic Programming II : Automatic Discovery of Reusable Programs. MIT Press (1994)
17. Lu, S.: A Tree-matching Algorithms based on node splitting and merging, IEEE Transacyion on Pattern Analysis and Machine Intelligence, vol, PAMI-6, no.2 (1984)
18. McKay, R. and Abbass, H.: Anticorrelation measure in genetic programming. In Australasia-Japan Workshop on Intelligent and Evolutionary Systems.
19. Mori, K., Tsukiyama, M. and Fukuda, T. : Multimodal Optimization by Immune Algorithm with Diversity and Learning , 2nd Int. Conf. on Multi Agent Systems, Workshop Notes on Immunity-Based Systems (1996) pp.118-123
20. Nikolaev, N.I., Iba, H. and Slavov, V.: Inductive Genetic Programming with Immune Network Dynamics, in Advance in Genetic Programming 3, Spector, L., et al. (eds.), MIT Press (1996)
21. O'Reilly, U.M.: Using a Distance Metric on Genetic Programs to Understand Genetic Operators, International Conference on Systems, Man, and Cybernetics, Computational Cybernetics and Simulation vol.5 (1997) pp.4092-4097
22. Rodriguez-Vazquez, K., Fonseca, C.M. and Fleming, P.J.: Multi-objective Genetic Programming : A Nonlinear System Identification Application, Proc. Genetic Programming '97 Conference (1997) pp.207-212
23. Ryan's, C.: Pygmies and civil servants. In K. Kinnear, Jr. (ed.) Advances in Genetic Programming, Chapt.11 (1994) pp.243-263, MIT Press

An Artificial Immune System for Misbehavior Detection in Mobile Ad-Hoc Networks with Virtual Thymus, Clustering, Danger Signal, and Memory Detectors

Slaviša Sarafijanović and Jean-Yves Le Boudec

EPFL/IC/ISC/LCA,
CH-1015 Lausanne, Switzerland
{slavisa.sarafijanovic,jean-yves.leboudec}@epfl.ch

Abstract. In mobile ad-hoc networks, nodes act both as terminals and information relays, and they participate in a common routing protocol, such as Dynamic Source Routing (DSR). The networks are vulnerable to routing misbehavior, due to faulty or malicious nodes. Misbehavior detection systems aim at removing this vulnerability. For this purpose, we use an Artificial Immune System (AIS), a system inspired by the human immune system (HIS). Our goal is to build a system that, like its natural counterpart, automatically learns and detects new misbehavior. In this paper we build on our previous work [1,2] and investigate the use of four concepts: (1) "virtual thymus", a novel concept, introduced in this paper, that provides a dynamic description of normal behavior in the system; (2) "clustering", a decision making mechanism for decreasing false positive detections (3) "danger signal", a concept that is, according to the "danger signal theory" of the human immune system [11,12], crucial for correct final decisions making; in our case, the signal is exchanged among nodes, which makes our detection system distributed; (4) "memory detectors", used for achieving faster secondary response of the detection system.
We implement our AIS in a network simulator and test it on two types of misbehavior. We analyze the performance and show the effects of the four concepts on the detection capabilities. In summary: thanks to the virtual thymus, the AIS does not require a preliminary learning phase in which misbehavior should be absent; the use of the clustering and the danger signal is useful for achieving low false positives; the use of memory detectors significantly accelerates the secondary response of the system.

1 Introduction

1.1 Problem Statement: Detecting Misbehaving Nodes in DSR

Mobile ad-hoc networks are self organized networks without any infrastructure other than end-user terminals equipped with radios. Communication beyond the transmission range is made possible by having all nodes act both as terminals and information relays. This in turn requires that all nodes participate in a common routing protocol, such as Dynamic Source Routing (DSR) [17]. A problem is that DSR works well only if all nodes execute the protocol correctly, which is difficult to guarantee in an open ad-hoc environment.

G. Nicosia et al. (Eds.): ICARIS 2004, LNCS 3239, pp. 342–356, 2004.
© Springer-Verlag Berlin Heidelberg 2004

A possible reason for node misbehavior is faulty software or hardware. In classical (non ad-hoc) networks run by operators, equipment malfunction is known to be an important source of unavailability [18]. In an ad-hoc network, where routing is performed by user provided equipment, we expect the problem to be exacerbated. Another reason for misbehavior stems from the desire to save battery power: some nodes may run a modified code that pretends to participate in DSR but, for example, does not forward packets. Last, some nodes may also be truly malicious and attempt to bring the network down, as do Internet viruses and worms. An extensive list of such misbehavior is given in [7]. The main operation of DSR is described in Section 2. In our simulation, we implement faulty nodes that, from time to time, do not forward data or route requests, or do not respond to route requests from their own cache.

We chose DSR as a concrete example, because it is one of the protocols being considered for standardization for mobile ad-hoc networks. There are other routing protocols, and there are parts of mobile ad-hoc networks other than routing that need misbehavior detection, for example, the medium access control protocol. We believe the main elements of our method would also apply there, but a detailed analysis is for further work.

1.2   AIS Problems We Are Solving Here

Eliminating need for preliminary learning phase: In our previous work [1,2] we use a preliminary Artificial Immune System (AIS) operation phase for collecting examples of normal behavior (self). During this phase, misbehavior is absent from the system. This is a drawback of the system for two reasons. First, it is very impractical to provide such a protected environment in a real system. Second, if normal behavior changes over time, the information collected about it in the preliminary phase is not fully adequate. Change of observed normal behavior in our case is caused by changes in traffic and mobility patterns of the nodes. Use of a preliminary learning phase is a common problem of many AISs.

Capability of learning changing self: The human immune system (HIS) becomes self-tolerant to some new antigens produced by the body [12]. We want our AIS to (autonomously) become self-tolerant to changed but normal behavior in the network.

Correct decision making for low false positives: The high false-positives detection rate is a common problem of many AISs, although it seems not to be so with the HIS. High false positives are critical in our system because the aim of detection is to respond; and responding to well behaving nodes could (and should) be observed by other nodes as misbehavior. This could cause instability in our AIS.

Achieving a fast secondary response: We consider the problem of detecting nodes that do not execute the DSR protocol correctly. The actions taken after detecting that a node misbehaves range from forbidding the use of the node as a relay [6] to excluding the node entirely from any participation in the network [8]. In this paper we focus on the detection of misbehavior and do not discuss actions taken after detection. However, the actions do affect the detection function through the need for a secondary response. Indeed, after a node is disconnected (boycotted) because it was classified as misbehaving, it becomes non-observable. Since the protection system is likely to be adaptive, the "punishment" fades out and redemption is allowed [7]. As a result, a misbehaving node is likely to misbehave again, unless it is fixed, for example by a software upgrade. We call primary [resp. secondary] response the classification of a node that misbehaves for the first [resp. second or more] time; thus we need to provide a secondary response that is much faster than the primary response.

1.3   Our Approach for Misbehavior Detection in DSR

We use an Artificial Immune System (AIS) approach, as it promises to overcome some constraints of traditional misbehavior detection approaches (Section 3.1). We map concepts and algorithms of the human immune system (HIS) to a mobile ad-hoc network and build a distributed system for DSR misbehavior detection. Every node runs the same detection algorithm based on its own observations. The nodes also exchange signals among each other (Figure 1).

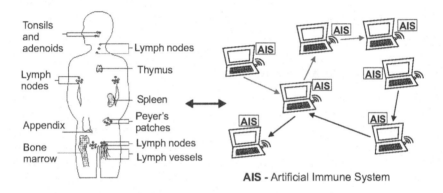

Fig. 1. From the human IS to an AIS: Making DSR immune to node misbehavior.

Our AIS approach and solutions are described in Section 1.4. A detailed description of the detection system components and how it works is given in Section 4.

1.4   Our AIS Approach and Solutions

Dynamic self. Our approach is based on the Danger Signal (DS) model of the HIS [11, 12]. The model can be viewed as a method to protect "dynamic self" in a system. To define "dynamic self" in our system, we extend the notion of self from the behavior specified by the routing protocol (DSR, for example) to any interactive node behavior that does not have negative effects on the normal network trafficking, i.e. does not cause packet losses. As a packet loss, we count any case in which the packet does not arrive at the destination, or the acknowledgment from the destination about receiving the packet does not reach the source, or there is a high delay in any of these packets.

Such a definition of "dynamic self" makes sense, as new interactions that do not cause losses should probably result in some useful traffic, according to the nature of interactions initiated by well behaving nodes. We assume that there are enough nodes that are, for their own reasons (use of the network for own traffic), active in the network for substantial amounts of time. We neglect the effect of those nodes that are present very briefly in the network in order to use it and then turn off for longer time. The active nodes will be overheard, as well as the routes they belong to (this is possible in DSR, see Section 2), and they will be asked by other nodes to carry traffic on these routes. Within such a definition, self will be dynamically determined through the interaction of nodes and feedback in form of losses in cases when some nodes do not cooperate according to the current established network self.

In the context of the danger signal model of the HIS, the feedback in form of packet losses corresponds strongly to the danger signal generated by cells in a process of necrosis, and there is also notion of the current self; for example, new milk protein antigens produced during pregnancy are tolerated and become current self for the body.

We use three concepts to achieve self-tolerance to possibly changing self, and to eliminate the need for a preliminary learning phase: "virtual thymus", "clustering" and "danger signal". To achieve a fast secondary response we use "memory detectors".

Virtual Thymus Model. "Virtual thymus" is a novel concept that introduce in this paper. It uses the danger signal and provides a dynamic description of the normal behavior in the system.

There are two important assumptions for explaining the role of the thymus in self-tolerance induction, which are part of a thymus model described in the literature on immunology ([13], pages 85-87; [14]): (1) both self and non-self antigens are presented in the thymus; the rules about how antigens can enter the thymus from the blood are unclear; (2) the thymic dendritic cells that present antigens survive for only a few days in the thymus, so they present current self antigens; if a non-self antigen is picked up for presentation during an infection, it will be presented only temporarily; once the infection is cleared from the body, freshly made antigens will no longer present the foreign antigen as self.

We use these two assumptions to build two mechanisms that represent what we call a "virtual thymus" in our AIS:

(1) Danger signal used for the virtual thymus. In the case of a danger signal based AIS, we can actually decide on the rules that determine which antigens will enter the virtual thymus and be presented in the process of negative selection (antigen represents observed behavior in our AIS; for more details about our AIS see Section 4). For this, we use a danger signal (which is not its standard use). When the danger signal is present, we forbid antigens that could be related to the signal to enter the virtual thymus. The danger signal in our case is a packet loss in the network, experienced by the source of the packet. The signal is then transmitted along the route on which the loss took place. The signal contains the information about time and nodes that are correlated to the loss, and allows us to forbid correlated antigens that could be non-self (observed for a misbehaving node) to enter the thymus. The information is analogous to the information obtained when a dendritic cell samples antigens that are by time and space related to the damage in the body.

In this way we can provide that sampled antigens that are presented in the virtual thymus are mainly self, and only rarely non-self (there is no guarantee that a danger signal will always be received by a node that samples antigens).

(2) Short time of antigen presentation. We keep collected antigens in the virtual thymus for a time that is finite and short enough to model finite life of thymic dendritic cells and the related effects.

Clustering. Matching between an antigen and an antibody is not enough to cause detection and reaction in the HIS [13,14]. The clustering of the matches on the surface of an immune cell and an additional danger signal are required for detection. These additional requirements can be viewed as decision making control mechanisms.

We also require more matches between AIS antigens and detectors for the detection, which is analogous to the clustering in the HIS(a detector in our AIS correspond to an antibody in the HIS, for details see Section 4).

Danger signal used for detection control. In the HIS, the danger signal is produced by a necrosis (an abnormal cell death) [11,12]. The danger signal in our case is a packet loss. We require a danger signal to be related to the observed node's antigens in order to verify the matchings and cause detection (i.e., classification of the corresponding node as misbehaving).

Memory detectors. In the HIS, the antibodies that are useful in the detection of non-self antigens and that receive a danger signal will undergo clonal selection and become memory. They require a small clustering threshold, and do not require the danger signal for detection. Our AIS also has such educated equivalents, called the memory detectors.

1.5   Organization of the Paper

The rest of the paper is organized as follows. Section 2 gives background on DSR. Section 3 describes the related work. Section 4 gives the mapping from the HIS to the detection system for DSR misbehavior detection, description of the detection system components, and a detailed explanation of how the system works. Section 5 gives simulation specific assumptions and constraints, describes experiments used to evaluate separate and joint effects of the system factors to system performance metrics, and gives simulation results and discussion of the results. Section 6 draws conclusions and describes what we have learned and how we will exploit it in future steps.

2   Background on DSR

The dynamic source routing protocol (DSR) is one of the candidate standards for routing in mobile ad-hoc networks [17]. A "source route" is a list of nodes that can be used as intermediate relays to reach a destination. It is written in the data packet header at the source; intermediate relays simply look it up to determine the next hop.

DSR specifies how sources discover, maintain and use source routes. To discover a source route, a node broadcasts a route request packet. Nodes that receive a route request add their own address in the source route collecting field of the packet, and then broadcast the packet, except in two cases. The first case is if the same route request was already received by a node; then the node discards the packet. Two received route requests are considered to be the same if they belong to the same route discovery, which is identified by the same value of the source, destination and sequence number fields in the request packets. The second case is if the receiving node is destination of the route discovery, or if it already has a route to the destination in its cache; then the node sends a route reply message that contains a completed source route. If links in the network are bidirectional, the route replies are sent over the reversed collected routes. If links are not bidirectional, the route replies are sent to the initiator of the route discovery as included in a new route request generated by answering nodes. The source of the initial route request is the destination of the new route requests. The node that initiates original route request receives usually more route replies, each containing a different route. The replies that arrive earlier than others are expected to indicate better routes, because for a node to send a route reply, it is required to wait first for a time proportional to the number of hops in the route it has as answer. If a node hears that some neighbor node answers during this waiting time, it supposes that the route it has is worse than the neighbor's one, and it does not answer. This avoids route reply storms and unnecessary overhead.

After the initiator of route discovery receives the first route reply, it sends data over the obtained route. While packets are sent over the route, the route is maintained, in such a way that every node on the route is responsible for the link over which it sends packets. If some link in the route breaks, the node that detects that it cannot send over that link should send error messages to the source. Additionally it should salvage the packets destined to the broken link, i.e., reroute them over alternate partial routes to the destination.

The mechanisms just described are the basic operation of DSR. There are also some additional mechanisms, such as gratuitous route replies, caching routes from forwarded or overheard packets and DSR flow state extension [17].

3   Related Work

3.1   Traditional Misbehavior Detection Approaches

Traditional approaches to misbehavior detection [6,8] use the knowledge of anticipated misbehavior patterns and detect them by looking for specific sequences of events. This is very efficient when the targeted misbehavior is known in advance (at system design) and powerful statistical algorithms can be used [9].

To detect misbehavior in DSR, Buchegger and Le Boudec use a reputation system [8]. Every node calculates the reputation of every other node using its own first-hand observations and second-hand information obtained from others. The reputation of a node is used to determine whether countermeasures against the node are undertaken or not. A key aspect of the reputation system is how second-hand information is used, in order to avoid false accusations [8].

The countermeasures against a misbehaving node are aimed at isolating it, i.e., packets will not be sent over the node and packets sent from the node will be ignored. In this way nodes are stimulated to cooperate in order to get service and maximize their utility, and the network also benefits from the cooperation.

Even if not presented by its authors as an artificial immune system, the reputation system in [8,9] is an example of (non-bio inspired) an immune system. It contains interactions between its healthy elements (well-behaving nodes) and detection and exclusion reactions against non-healthy elements (misbehaving nodes). We can compare it to the human *innate* immune system ([14,13]), in the sense that it is hardwired in the nodes and changes only with new versions of the protocol.

Traditional approaches miss the ability to learn about and adapt to new misbehavior. Every target misbehavior has to be imagined in advance and explicitly addressed in the detection system. We use an AIS approach to misbehavior detection as it is promising to overcome these constraints.

3.2 Artificial Immune Systems – Related Work

There are different proposals in the related literature that address the problem of final decision making in AISs. Hofmeyr and Forrest [3] use co-stimulation by a human, which can be viewed as some form of supervised training. Somayaji and Forrest [4] achieve tolerization to new normal behavior in an autonomous way, but their system works only under the assumption that new abnormal behavior always exhibits new patterns that are more clustered than in the case of new normal behavior; if the patterns of a new misbehavior are first sparsely introduced in the system, the system will become tolerant to that misbehavior. Aickelin at all [5] propose the use of the danger signal based on the analogy with the necrosis and apoptosis of the human body cells; with this model, main control signals come from the protected system; the danger signal approach seems to be quite promising for building an autonomous and adaptive AISs.

In our previous work we use a self-nonself model, and define mapping to our AIS. We define representation, matching and the simple use of negative selection and clonal selection algorithms. The system is able to learn normal behavior presented in preliminary training phase and to detect misbehavior afterwards. The drawback is the need for preliminary training phase, and the absence of mechanisms for adaptation to changing self.

For an overview of AIS, see the book by de Castro and Timmis [20] and the paper by de Castro and von Zuben [19].

What is missing in the related literature on AISs is an explicit use of the thymus and a dynamic self presentation; we introduce this concept and incorporate it into a danger signal based AIS.

4   Design of Our Detection System

4.1   Mapping of HIS Elements to Our Detection System

The elements of the natural IS used in our detection system are mapped as follows:

- Body: the entire mobile ad-hoc network
- Self Cells: well-behaving nodes
- Non-self Cells: misbehaving nodes

- Antigen: (AIS) antigen, which is a sequence of observed DSR protocol events recognized in the sequence of packet headers and represented by binary strings as explained in detail in our previous work [1] (representation is adopted from [10]). Examples of events are "data packet received", "data packet received followed by data packet sent", "route request packet received followed by route reply sent".
- Antibody: detector; detectors are binary strings produced in the continuous processes of negative selection and clonal selection; ideally, they "match" non-self antigens (produced by misbehaving nodes) and do not match self antigens.
- Chemical binding of antibodies to antigens: "matching function" between detectors and antigens, as defined in detail in our previous work [1].
- Detection: a node detects a neighbor as misbehaving if the node's detectors match relatively many of the antigens produced by that neighbor (clustering) and if it receives danger signals related to those antigens
- Clustering: clustering of matching antibodies on the immune system cell surface is mapped to the clustering of matches between detectors and antigens in time for a given observed node;
- Necrosis and apoptosis: packet loss
- Danger signal: the danger signal in our framework contains information about the time and nodes correlated with a packet loss
- Antigen presenting cell: transmission of the danger signal
- Thymus: The virtual thymus is a set of mechanisms that provides (as explained in Section 1.4) the presentation of the current self in the system during the continuous negative selection process
- Memory cells: memory detectors; detectors become memory if they prove to be useful in detection; they differ from normal detectors by longer lifetime and lower clustering required for detection.

4.2   How the Detection System Works

The detection system consists of the data and functions shown in the Figure 2, which are present at every node. We explain how the system works by describing a typical series of events at one node. To read this chapter you may need to read first our AIS approach (Section 1.4) and look at the mapping to our concrete problem (Section 4.1).

Observing Antigens. A node overhears the messages exchanged in its neighborhood, during a defined time interval (10s by default), and records separately the routing protocol events of interest (see mapping, Section 4.1) for each of its neighbors. Then it translates the observed data sets into antigens. So, one antigen is created every 10 s for each of the observable neighbors . The antigen represents the behavior of the observed node for the observed time interval.

The collected antigens are buffered (Figure 2, component B) for a time that is greater than the maximum time (64 s by default) needed for the danger signal to be generated and distributed over the route on which a packet has been sent if it got lost. The absence or presence of the danger signal determines whether the related antigen will be presented in the virtual thymus S or not, and whether the matching of the antigens by the detectors will be counted for detection or not.

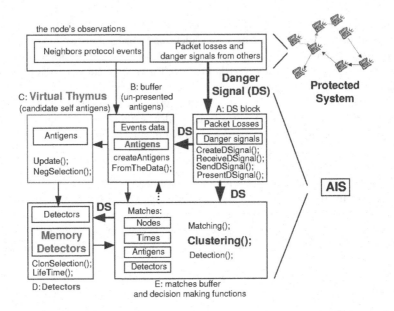

Fig. 2. Components of the detection system.

Generating the Danger Signal. The danger signal is generated by a node when it experiences a packet loss, i.e., when it does not receive an acknowledgment that the packet it sent was received by the destination. The signal is then sent over the route on which the packet loss took place (Figure 3). The signal contains the information about the (approximate) time of the packet loss, and about the nodes on the route over which the lost packet was sent. So, the receivers of the danger signal are able to correlate it with the antigens collected: (1) during the time that is close to the packet loss time; (2) from the nodes that belong to the route on which the loss took place. (There is a strong analogy with the HIS, regarding both the way the danger signal is generated and the information it contains; see Section 1.4.)

Virtual Thymus Mechanisms: (1) Use of the danger signal. When a node causes a packet loss, it also produces an antigen observable by its neighbors. Most of the neighbors that observe the antigen also receive the corresponding danger signal (Figure 3) and consequently forbid the (non-self) antigen to enter the virtual thymus (Figure 2, component *C*). But some of the neighbors will move away from the route over which the danger signal is sent, and not receive the signal, even though they were close enough to collect the non-self antigen at the time of the packet loss; in this case the non-self antigen may enter the virtual thymus. This happens rarely, as the propagation time is relatively short and nodes cannot move very much between a packet loss event and the corresponding danger signal transmission.

    Some of self antigens are forbidden to enter the virtual thymus too, as they were generated from the well-behaving nodes that happen to be on the route on which a packet

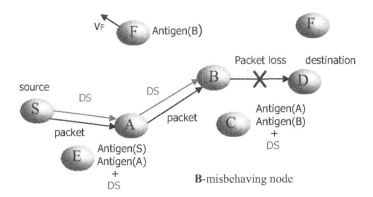

Fig. 3. Generating and transmitting the danger signal: there is packet loss at B; the source S of the packet does not receive the acknowledgment from destination D and sends the danger signal over the route on which the loss took place; the nodes that receive the signal (A,B,C,E) do not present the observed correlated antigens in their thymus; rarely, some nodes (F in this case) move away and do not receive the danger signal, so they present the collected (non-self) antigens.

loss took place. As there are always enough other self antigens that are not correlated to the danger signal, this does not affect the self presentation in the thymus.

From the buffered antigens, those that are not correlated with the danger signal are periodically randomly sampled to enter the virtual thymus (one update every 10 sec, by default). Delay caused by buffering the antigens before presentation in the virtual thymus is significantly greater (300 s by default) than the delay for the antigens to be presented for matching by the detectors (70 s by default). This is done on purpose, in order to postpone deleting useful detectors by non-self antigens that accidently enter virtual bone marrow. It would also make sense to check the antigens by memory detectors before letting them to enter the virtual thymus, but this is currently not implemented (a dashed arrow on the Figure 2).

(2) Finite presentation time. An antigen that enters the virtual thymus stays there for a finite time (500 s by default), ensuring that only the current self is presented during the continuous negative selection process.

Producing Detectors. The detectors are produced in the continuous negative selection process in the thymus (Figure 2, component C): new detectors are generated by random and checked if they match any of the antigens from the thymus; only those that do not match survive, leave the thymus, and update the set of current detectors (Figure 2, component D). Whenever a new antigen enters the thymus, first the detectors (but not the memory detectors) from D that match the new antigen are deleted. The memory detectors are deleted only if they match new antigens from C more times than a given threshold (25 by default). Then, the new detectors are generated in the number needed to replace those deleted. The process of continuous negative selection seems to be computationally more feasible, compared to the standard negative selection.

Matching. Antigens that are presented for detection are checked with current detectors, and if any detector matches an antigen one positive matching score is recorded for the corresponding node; otherwise a negative matching score is recorded. Only a finite number of last matches is stored (maximum 30, by default).

Clustering and Detection. Clustering is realized as a function that operates on scored matches between antigens and detectors, and it enables the detection of the related node if there is enough matching evidence. Clustering means that the matches for a considered node are grouped in time.

Assume we have collected n antigens for the monitored node. Let M_n be the number of antigens (among n) that are matched by detectors. Let θ_{max} be a bound on the probability of false-positive matching (matching a self antigen) that we are willing to accept, i.e. the antigens of well-behaving nodes are matched by detectors with a probability that is less or equal than θ_{max}. We determine a good value by pilot simulation runs ($\theta_{max} = 0.06$). Let α (=0.001 by default) be the false-positive detection that we target. We detect the monitored node (classify it as misbehaving) if

$$\frac{M_n}{n} > \theta_{max}(1 + \frac{\xi(\alpha)}{\sqrt{n}}\sqrt{\frac{1 - \theta_{max}}{\theta_{max}}}) \tag{1}$$

where $\xi(\alpha)$ is the $(1 - \alpha)$-quantile of the normal distribution (for example, $\xi(0.0001) = 3.72$). As long as Equation (1) is not true, the node is classified as well-behaving. With default parameter values, the condition is $\frac{M_n}{n} > 0.06 + 0.88\frac{\xi(\alpha)}{\sqrt{n}}$. The derivation of Equation (1) is given in the appendix.

Co-stimulation by the Danger Signal for Detection. Matching by detectors to an antigen require, in addition, the existence of a related danger signal in order the matching to be counted for the detection.

Memory detectors. The detectors that score the detection (verified by the danger signals) will undergo the process of clonal selection: they are cloned, mutated and (which is not the case in the HIS) checked by negative selection once more. As the maximum number of memory detectors is constrained (50), only those with the best detection score are kept. Matches with memory detectors require less clustering for detection (implemented using a larger value of α, 0.2 by default).

5   Performance Analysis

5.1   Analyzed Factors and Experiments

We analyze the effects of: substitution of the preliminary learning phase by the virtual thymus; clustering; use of the danger signal; use of memory detectors. We first compare the preliminary learning phase versus the virtual thymus. Then we add other components to the solution with virtual thymus and follow the effects onto performance metrics.

5.2   Performance Metrics

The metrics we use are: (1) time until detection of a misbehaving node; (2) true-positive detection, in form of the distribution of the number of nodes which detect a misbehaving node; (3) false-positive detection, in form of the distribution of the number of nodes which detect a well-behaving node. The metrics are chosen from a reputation system perspective; we see the use of a reputation system [7] as a way to add a reactive part to our AIS.

5.3   Description of Simulation

The simulation is done in Glomosim network simulator [15]. The simulation code is available on the Internet [16]. There are 40 nodes, 5-20 nodes are misbehaving. Mobility is the random way point, speed is 1m/s, without pauses. The simulation area is 800x1000 m, and the radio range is 355 m. A node that misbehaves does not forward the packet or does not answer or forward route request messages; this happens with a given probability (0.6 by default) that is also a parameter.

5.4   Simulation Results

The virtual thymus versus the preliminary learning phase: Form the Figures 4 and 5 we see that the preliminary learning phase can be successfully substituted by the virtual thymus. Time until detection and the false positives are similar in both cases, while the false negatives are slightly worse in the case with the virtual thymus.

The danger signal used for detection decision making has a large impact in decreasing false positives (Figures 6(c) and 7(c)).

The use of the memory detectors significantly decreases the time until detection (Figure 7(a)), and also improves true-positive detection (Figures 6(b) and 7(b)).

6   Conclusions, Discussion, and Future Work

From the obtained results we conclude that the examined mechanisms: the virtual thymus, the danger signal and the use of memory detectors can be succesfuly applied for our problem. Moreover, we see "virtual thymus" not only as a solution for eliminating need of the preliminary training phase in our system, but also as a standard component in building the danger signal based AISs.

We do not show here the impact of the clustering separately, because of the lack of the space and because we have shown already in our previous work [1,2] that it has a large impact in both decreasing the false positives and increasing the true positives, but with a cost of longer time until detection; the increase in the time until detection is here partially compensated by the use of the memory detectors.

We did not compare the preliminary learning phase versus the virtual thymus in a case of dynamic self behavior. As the AIS with the virtual thymus collects and presents current self behavior for producing detectors, we expect that, in a dynamic case, this solution will have better performance than the AIS with preliminary learning phase.

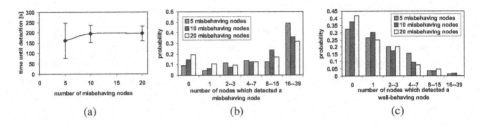

Fig. 4. Use of the preliminary learning phase: (a) time until detection, (b) correct detections and (c) misdetections.

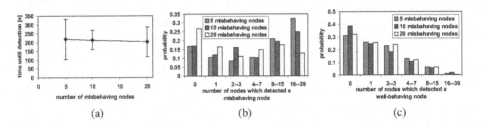

Fig. 5. Use of the virtual thymus instead of the preliminary learning phase: (a) time until detection, (b) correct detections and (c) misdetections.

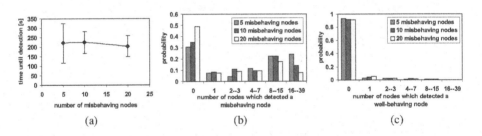

Fig. 6. Use of the danger signal for detection decision making: (a) time until detection, (b) correct detections and (c) misdetections.

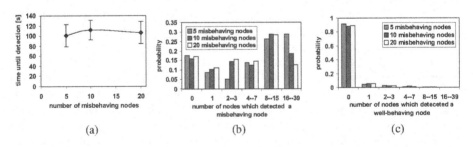

Fig. 7. Use of memory detectors: (a) time until detection, (b) correct detections and (c) misdetections.

Next step in completing our AIS would be adding its reactive part. With a reactive part, it is important to distinguish between a misbehavior and a reaction against a misbehaving node. This may require the information exchange between the nodes. We see the use of a reputation system a possible solution [7]. Here we have shown that the number of nodes that detect a misbehaving node is statistically considerably larger than the number of nodes that miss-detect a well behaving node (Figures 7(b) and 7(c)). This result gives a promise for a successful use of a reputation system within our AIS.

Our future work also includes testing the scalability of our solution with respect to the number of misbehavior types, as well as a more detailed analysis of the impact of system parameters on the detection capabilities.

References

1. J. Y. Le Boudec and S. Sarafijanovic. An Artificial Immune System Approach to Misbehavior Detection in Mobile Ad-Hoc Networks. Proceedings of Bio-ADIT 2004, Lausanne, Switzerland, January 2004, pp. 96-111.
2. S. Sarafijanovic and J. Y. Le Boudec. An Artificial Immune System Approach with Secondary Response for Misbehavior Detection in Mobile Ad-Hoc Networks. TechReport IC/2003/65, EPFL-DI-ICA, Lausanne, Switzerland, November 2003.
3. S. A Hofmeyr and S. Forrest "Architecture for an Artificial Immune System". Evolutionary Computation 7(1):45-68. 2000.
4. A. Somayaji and S. Forrest "Automated Response Using System-Call Delays." Proceedings of the 9th USENIX Security Symposium, The USENIX Association, Berkeley, CA (2000).
5. Aickelin, U., Bentley, P., Cayzer, S., Kim, J. and McLeod, J. (2003) Danger Theory: The Link between AIS and IDS? In Timmis, J., Bentley, P. J. and Hart, E. (Eds) Proc of the Second International Conference on Artificial Immune Systems (ICARIS 2003). Springer LNCS 2787. pp. 147-155.
6. Sergio Marti, T.J. Giuli, Kevin Lai, and Mary Baker. Mitigating routing misbehavior in mobile ad hoc networks. In *Proceedings of MOBICOM 2000*, pages 255–265, 2000.
7. S. Buchegger and J.-Y. Le Boudec. A Robust Reputation System for Mobile ad hoc Networks. Technical Report, IC/2003/50, EPFL-DI-ICA, Lausanne, Switzerland, July 2003.
8. S. Buchegger and J.-Y. Le Boudec. Performance Analysis of the CONFIDANT protocol: Co-operation of nodes - Fairness In Distributed Ad-Hoc Networks. In *Proceedings of MobiHOC, IEEE/ACM*, Lausanne, CH, June 2002.
9. S. Buchegger and J.-Y. Le Boudec. The Effect of Rumor Spreading in Reputation Systems for Mobile Ad-hoc Networks. In *Proceedings of WiOpt '03: Modeling and Optimization in Mobile, Ad Hoc and Wireless Networks*, Sophia-Antipolis, France, March 2003.
10. J. Kim and P.J. Bentley. Evaluating Negative Selection in an Artificial Immune System for Network Intrusion Detection: *Genetic and Evolutionary Computation Conference 2001* (GECCO-2001), San Francisko, pp. 1330-1337, July 7-11.
11. P. Matzinger. Tolerance, Danger and the Extended Family. *Annual Review of Immunology*, 12:991-1045, 1994.
12. P. Matzinger. The Danger Model in it's Historical Contex. *Scandinavian Journal of Immunology*, 54:4-9, 2001.
13. L.M. Sompayrac. How the Immune System Works, 2nd Edition. Blackwell Publishing, 2003.
14. Richard A. Goldsby, Thomas J. Kindt, Barbara A. Osborne, Janis Kuby: Immunology, 5th edition, W. H. Freeman and Company, 2003.

15. Xiang Zeng, Rajive Bagrodia, and Mario Gerla. Glomosim: A library for parallel simulation of large scale wireless networks. *Proceedings of the 12th workshop on Parallel and Distributed Simulations-PDAS'98*, May 26-29, in Banff, Alberta, Canada, 1998.
16. Simulation code: http://lcawww.epfl.ch/ssarafij/ais-code
17. D.B. Johnson and D.A. Maltz. The dynamic source routing protocol for mobile ad hoc networks. *Internet draft, Mobile Ad Hoc Network (MANET) Working Group*, IETF, February 2003.
18. G. Iannaccone C.-N. Chuah, R. Mortier, S. Bhattacharyya, C. Diot. *Analysis of Link Failures in an IP Backbone*. Proceeding of IMW 2002. ACM Press. Marseille, France. November 2002
19. De Castro, L. N. and Von Zuben, F. J. (1999), Artificial Immune Systems: Part I Basic Theory and Application, Technical Report RT DCA 01/99
20. Leandro N. de Castro and Jonathan Timmis, Artificial Immune Systems: A New Computational Intelligence Approach, Springer Verlag, Berlin, 2002

Appendix: Derivation of Equation (1)

We model the outcome of the behavior of a node as a random generator, such that with unknown but fixed probability θ a data set is interpreted as suspicious. We assume the outcome of this fictitious generator is iid. We use a classical hypothesis framework. The null hypothesis is $\theta \leq \theta_{\max}$, i.e., the node behaves well. The maximum likelihood ratio test has a rejection region of the form $\{M_n > K(n)\}$ for some function $K(n)$. The function $K(n)$ is found by the type-I error probability condition: $\mathbb{P}\{M_n > K(n)\}|\theta) \leq \alpha$, for all $\theta \leq \theta_{\max}$, thus the best $K(n)$ is obtained by solving the equation

$$\mathbb{P}(\{M_n > K(n)\}|\theta_{\max}) = \alpha$$

The distribution of M_n is binomial, which is well approximated by a normal distribution with mean $\mu = n\theta$ and variance $n\theta(1 - \theta)$. After some algebra this gives $K(n) = \sqrt{n}\xi\sqrt{\theta_{\max}(1 - \theta_{\max})} + n\theta_{\max}$, from which Equation (1) derives immediately.

Developing Efficient Search Algorithms for P2P Networks Using Proliferation and Mutation*

Niloy Ganguly and Andreas Deutsch

Center for High Performance Computing, Dresden University of Technology, Dresden, Germany.
{niloy, deutsch}@zhr.tu-dresden.de

Abstract. Decentralized peer to peer networks like Gnutella are attractive for certain applications because they require no centralized directories and no precise control over network topology or data placement. The greatest advantage is the robustness provided by them. However, flooding-based query algorithms used by the networks produce enormous amounts of traffic and substantially slow down the system. Recently flooding has been replaced by more efficient k-random walkers and different variants of such algorithms [5]. In this paper, we report immune-inspired algorithms for searching peer to peer networks. The algorithms use the immune-inspired mechanism of affinity-governed proliferation and mutation to spread query message packets in the network. Through a series of experiments, on different types of topologies, we compare proliferation/mutation with different variants of random walk algorithms. The detailed experimental results show message packets undergoing proliferation and mutation spread much faster in the network and consequently proliferation/mutation algorithms produce better search output in $p2p$ networks than random walk algorithms.

1 Introduction

Among different desirable qualities of a search algorithm for $p2p$ networks, robustness is a very important aspect. That is, the performance of a search algorithm should not radically deteriorate in face of the dynamically changing condition of the network. As is known, the big share of Internet users, consequently participants in $p2p$ networks, still use dial-up modems, who besides being slow and unreliable, also leave the community at very short intervals. Thus in order to give robustness a high priority, algorithms generally avoid precise routing algorithms for forwarding query message packets. Instead random forwarding of the message packets forms the basis of their algorithms [5]. The goal of this paper is to study more efficient alternatives to the existing k-random walk. In this connection, we draw our inspiration from the immune system.

Our algorithm has been inspired by the simple and well known mechanism of the humoral immune system where B cells upon stimulation by a foreign agent

---

* This work was partially supported by the Future & Emerging Technologies unit of the European Commission through Project BISON (IST-2001-38923).

G. Nicosia et al. (Eds.): ICARIS 2004, LNCS 3239, pp. 357–371, 2004.

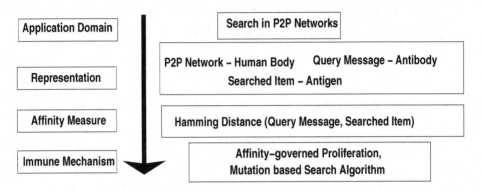

Fig. 1. Immune system concepts used to develop search algorithms

(antigen) undergo proliferation and mutation generating antibodies. Proliferation helps in increasing the number of antibodies while mutation implies a variety of generated antibodies. The antibodies consequently can efficiently track down the antigens (foreign bodies). *Fig. 1* provides an illustration explaining how we have mapped immune system concepts to our search problem. In our problem, the query message packet is conceived as antibody which is generated by the node initiating a search whereas antigens are the searched items hosted by other constituent members (nodes) of the p2p networks. Like in the natural immune system, the packets undergo mutation and proliferation based upon the affinity measure between the message packets and the contents of the node visited which results in an efficient search mechanism.

In the next section, we detail the modeling abstractions upon which the algorithms are based. Moreover, we elaborate our algorithms as well as different variants of k-random walk algorithms. The evaluation metrics used to compare the different schemes are also elaborated. The experimental results are noted next in *Section 3*.

2   Modeling and Evaluation Methodology

It is impossible to model the complete dynamics of a *p2p* system. While our simple models do not capture all aspects of reality, we hope they capture the essential features needed to understand the fundamental qualitative differences between k-random walk and proliferation/mutation algorithms.

2.1   Model Definition

P2p networks are the networks formed through associations of computers, each providing equivalent services, eg. search facility, to the network. Thus each peer can be conceived as both client and server of a particular service [5]. To model search service, we focus on two most important aspects of a *p2p* system: *p2p*

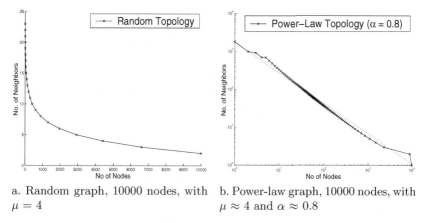

a. Random graph, 10000 nodes, with $\mu = 4$

b. Power-law graph, 10000 nodes, with $\mu \approx 4$ and $\alpha \approx 0.8$

Fig. 2. Distribution of node degrees in the two network topology graphs. Note that we use log scale for the power-law graph, and linear scale for the random graph.

network topology, query and data distribution. For simplicity, we assume the topology and distribution do not change during the simulation of our algorithms. For the purpose of our study, if one assumes that the time to complete a search is short compared to the time of change in network topology and change in query distribution, results obtained from the fixed settings are indicative of performance in real systems.

Network Topology : By network topology, we mean the graph formed by the *p2p* overlay network; each *p2p* member has a certain number of neighbors and the set of neighbor connections form the *p2p* overlay network. We use two different network topologies in our study. The two types of graph - power-law and random graph - best represent the majority of the realistic network topologies formed in the Internet [3,5]. In each of the topologies, we take a representative graph.

(a). Pure Random Graph : A 10000-node graph generated with the help of the topology generator BRITE[4] with mean $\mu = 4$. The distribution is shown in (*Fig. 2(a)*).

(b). Power-law Graph : The node degrees follow a power-law distribution; if one ranks all nodes from the most connected to the least connected, then the ith most connected node has w/i^{α} neighbors, where w is a constant and α is the power-law exponent. The power-law random graph is generated by the topology generator Inet3.0 [2]. The number of nodes in the graph is 10000, the mean in-degree $\mu = 4.3$ and the power-law exponent $\alpha \approx 0.8$ (*Fig. 2(b)*).

Query and data distribution : In order to model query and data distribution, we define two different profiles for each peer - the *informational profile* and the *search profile*. The *informational profile* (P_I) of the peer is formed from the information which it shares with the other peers in the *p2p* network. The *search profile* (P_S) of a peer is built from the informational interest of the user; formally it is represented in the same way as is P_I. In general, the search profile may differ from the information stored on the peer. For simplicity we assume that there are 1024 coarse-grained profiles, and let each of these profiles be represented by a unique 10-bit binary token. The query message packet (M) is also a 10-bit binary token. From now on we interchangeably use the term profile and token. Zipf's distribution[6], is chosen to distribute each of the 1024 unique alternatives in the network. The ranking of tokens in terms of frequency is the same for both information and search profiles.However the profiles are distributed in random nodes with no correlation between similar profiles.

We now describe the proliferation/mutation and random walk algorithms.

2.2   Algorithms

In this section, we explain two proliferation/mutation based as well as three random walk based search algorithms. The important aspects of all these algorithms are that although random walk or proliferation/mutation is exhibited by the message packets, however, the algorithms are independently implemented by each node. And coordinated behavior of the nodes produces the required packet dynamics. All the algorithms can be expressed in terms of the same basic premise which is stated next.

Basic Premise : The search in our $p2p$ network is initiated from the user peer. The user (U) emanates k $(k \geq 1)$ message packets (M) to its neighbors - the packets are thereby forwarded to the surroundings. The message packet (M) is formed from the search profile P_S of U. We next present the search initiation process in algorithmic form.

Algorithm 1 InitiateSearch(U)
Input : Signal to initiate search.
Form Message Packet $(M) = P_S(U)$
Flood k message packets(M) to the neighbors of the user peer.

The message packets travel through the network and when a node (say) A receives a message packet (M), it performs the following two functions.
Function 1 :- It checks whether the P_I of A is equal to the incoming message M. If so, it returns a successful event.
Function 2 :- It forwards the content of the message packet in some *defined* manner to its neighbor(s).

In algorithmic form, we can represent the functions as *Reaction_p2p*:

Algorithm 2 Reaction_p2p(A)
Input : Message packet(M)
*   If $(P_I = M)$ then {Report a successful match /*Function 1*/}*
*   Algorithm Message_Forward(A) /* Function 2*/*

Each of the proliferation/mutation and random walk schemes defines *Algorithm Message_Forward(A)* differently. Elaboration of the algorithms corresponding to each of the schemes follows.
Proliferation/Mutation (PM) : In the proliferation/mutation scheme, the packets undergo proliferation at each node they visit. The proliferation is guided

by a special function, whereby a message packet visiting a node proliferates to form N_{new} message packets which are thereby forwarded to the neighbors of the node. A randomly selected bit of each of these N_{new} messages has a probability β of getting mutated; β is the mutation probability of the system. Mutation is introduced into the system to increase the chance of message packets meeting similar items, which in turn helps in packet proliferation.

However, since mutation changes the content of the packet, it is assumed that the original information is also carried along with the packet. Hence, during the execution of the algorithm *Reaction_p2p*, comparison with P_I (Function 1) is carried out on the basis of the original message, while the input for *Algorithm Message_Forward(A)* (here Algorithm $PM(A)$) is the mutated packet.

Algorithm 3 PM(A)
Input : Message packet(M)
Produce N_{new} message packets(M)
Mutate one randomly selected bit of each of the N_{new} message packets with prob. β
Spread the N_{new} packets to N_{new} randomly selected neighbors of A

The function determining the value of 'N_{new}' ensures that N_{new} is $< n(A)$, where $n(A)$ is the number of neighbors of A and ≥ 1. [Note that if $N_{new} = 1$, proliferation/mutation behaves similar to random walk.]
Restricted Proliferation/Mutation (RPM) : The restricted proliferation/mutation algorithm, similar to PM, produces N_{new} messages and mutates one bit of each of them with probability β. But these N_{new} messages are forwarded only if the node A has $\geq N_{new}$ free neighbors. By 'free', we mean that the respective neighbors haven't been previously visited by message M. If A has $\mathcal{Z}$ 'free' neighbors, where $\mathcal{Z} < N_{new}$, then only $\mathcal{Z}$ messages are forwarded, while the rest are destroyed. However, if $\mathcal{Z} = 0$, then one message is forwarded to a randomly selected neighbor. The rationale behind the restricted movement is to minimize the amount of message wastage. Because, two packets of message M visiting the same peer essentially means wastage of the second packet.

Algorithm 4 RPM(A)
Input : Message packet(M)
Produce N_{new} message packets (M)
Mutate one bit of each of the message packets with probability β
$\mathcal{Z} = No$ of 'free' neighbors
if ($\mathcal{Z} \geq N_{new}$)
     Spread the N_{new} packets in N_{new} randomly selected neighbors of A
else
     if ($\mathcal{Z} > 0$)
          Spread $\mathcal{Z}$ packets in $\mathcal{Z}$ free neighbors of A
          Discard the remaining (N_{new} - $\mathcal{Z}$) packets
     else
          Forward one message packet to a randomly selected neighbor of A
          Discard the remaining (N_{new} - 1) packets

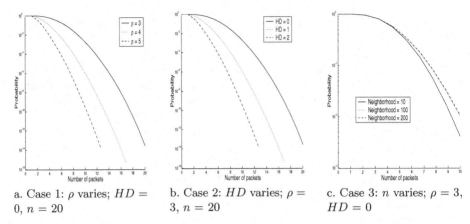

a. Case 1: ρ varies; $HD =$ 0, $n = 20$ b. Case 2: HD varies; $\rho =$ 3, $n = 20$ c. Case 3: n varies; $\rho = 3$, $HD = 0$

Fig. 3. Probability of proliferation of at least η messages (semilog(y) scale)

We now elaborate the function which controls the amount of proliferation. **Proliferation Controlling Function :** The proliferation of message packets at any node A is heavily dependent on the similarity between the message packet (M) and the information profile (P_I) of A. Also care is taken to avoid producing more than $n(A)$ number of messages, where $n(A)$ represents the number of neighbors of A. In this connection we define the following expression p, where $p = e^{-HD} \times \frac{\rho}{n}$, HD is the Hamming distance(M,P_I); ρ represents the proliferation constant; it is same for all nodes. and is generally kept less than the mean indegree of the underlying network. However, since in networks (both random and power-law network), the neighborhood distribution varies widely; if for some particular node (say B) $\rho > n(B)$, then for that node ρ is set to $n(B)$.

With the help of the expression p, we define $P(\eta)$ - the probability of producing at least η packages during proliferation by the following equation.
$$P(\eta) = \sum_{i=\eta}^{n} \binom{n-1}{i-1} \cdot p^{i-1} \cdot (1-p)^{n-i}$$
The significance of the above equation is elaborated through the three figures (*Fig. 3*). The three figures explain the behavior of $P(\eta)$, w.r.t. different HDs, *proliferation constants* and neighborhood sizes. The number of packets is plotted in the x-axis, while the y-axis represents the probability of proliferation of at least those number of packets. All the figures illustrate some commonality. (i). At least one packet necessarily proliferates; (ii). The probability of proliferation of larger number of packets exponentially decreases. *Fig. 3(a)* shows the variation w.r.t. different proliferation constants ρ; three different curves are drawn for $\rho =$ 3, 4, 5. In each of the curves, we find that the probability of proliferating at least η numbers of packets is almost equal to 1 till $\eta = \rho$; if $\eta > \rho$, the probability decreases exponentially. *Fig. 3(b)* shows the variation w.r.t. different Hamming distances; three curves are drawn corresponding to $HD = 0, 1, 2$. It is seen that for $HD > 0$, the probability of proliferation of at least η packets decreases exponentially for $\eta > 1$, which implies that the chance of proliferation is quite low if $HD > 0$. However, the rate of decrease in probability varies inversely to the

value of the *proliferation constant*. The three curves in *Fig. 3(c)*, plotted w.r.t. different neighborhood sizes show that variation of probability of proliferation with respect to different neighborhood sizes is negligible.

We now describe a simple k-random walk algorithm and subsequently two different variations of it.

k-random walk (RW) : In k-random walk, when a peer receives a message packet after performing the task of comparison, as mentioned in *Algorithm 2*, it forwards the packet to a randomly selected neighbor. The algorithm (RW) is quite straightforward and is defined as

Algorithm 5 RW(A)
Input : Message packet(M)
Send the packet M to a randomly chosen neighbor peer

The restricted random walk (RRW) algorithm which is similar to RPM (*Algorithm 4*), is discussed next.

Restricted Random Walk (RRW) : In RRW, instead of passing the message (M) to any random neighbor, we pass on the message to any randomly selected 'free' neighbor. However, if there is no 'free' neighbor, we then pass on the message to any randomly selected neighbor.

Algorithm 6 RRW(A)
Input : Message packet(M)
Send the packet M to a randomly chosen 'free' neighbor peer
If (no 'free' neighbor)
    Send the packet M to a randomly chosen neighbor peer

The next algorithm is a special type of a random algorithm [1] to enhance the speed of simple random walk in a power-law network. The special type of random walk is termed as *high degree restricted random walk (HDRRW)*.

High Degree Restricted Random Walk (HDRRW) : Adamic et. al. in [1] showed that for a single random walker in a power-law network, *high degree random walk* is better than simple random walk. To compare it with our proliferation/mutation scheme, we have simulated the algorithm with k-random walkers participating in the search. In the algorithm, a peer has special affinity to forward the message packet to the neighbors which have higher degree of connection. However, the algorithm also takes into consideration the restricted movement discussed in the previous section.

To balance these two trends, when sending a message packet, a peer checks the first $\mathcal{H}$ most high degree nodes to identify a 'free' node; if it doesn't find, it randomly tries to identify any 'free' node another $\mathcal{L}$ number of times. Even if then a 'free' node is not found, then the message is forwarded to a neighboring node. This forwarding scheme is also biased towards neighbors with high in-degree.

Algorithm 7 HDRRW(A)

Input : Message packet(M)
Find the 'free' neighbor with highest in-degree among the $\mathcal{H}$ most connected
neighbors
If (no 'free' neighbor)
    Randomly try $\mathcal{L}$ times to find a 'free' neighbor among the rest of the peers
If (still no 'free' neighbor found)
    Chose a neighbor through a probability function $f(neigh)$;
        where $f(neigh_1) > f(neigh_2)$ if $n(neigh_1) > n(neigh_2)$
Send the packet M to the chosen peer

2.3   Metrics

In this paper we focus on efficiency aspects of the algorithms solely, and use the following simple metrics in our abstract *p2p* networks. These metrics, though simple, reflect the fundamental properties of the algorithms.

(a). *Success rate:* The number of similar items found by the query messages within a given time period.

(b). *Coverage rate:* The amount of time required by the messages to cover a percentage of the network.

(c). *Cost per search output:* The number of messages required to output a successful search.

(d). *Bad visits:* The number of times the same message re-visits the same node. If a message packet visits the same node more than once, it amounts to wastage of that packet.

3   Simulation Results

The experiments are performed on the two types of topology discussed in *Section 2.1*. As mentioned earlier, each of the above algorithms is distributed in nature and the nodes perform the task independent of the others. However, to assess the speed and efficiency of the algorithm, we have to ensure some sort of synchronous operation among the peers. In this context we introduce the concept of time whereby it is assumed that in one time unit, all the nodes in the network execute the algorithm once. That is, if a peer has some message in its message queue, it will process one message within that time frame. We believe although approximate, it is a fair abstraction of reality of *p2p* networks where each node is supposed to provide equivalent services. The sequence of operation of the peers during one time step is arbitrary. The length of the message queue is considered to be infinite.

In order to assess the efficiency of different algorithms, we have also to ensure fairness of 'power' among them which is explained next.

3.1   Fairness in Power

To ensure fair comparison among all the processes, we must ensure that each process (PM, RPM, RW, RRW, $HDRRW$) should participate in the network with the same 'power'. To provide fairness in 'power' between a proliferation/mutation algorithm (say PM) and a random algorithm (say RW), we ensure that the total number of query packets used is roughly the same in all the cases. Query packets determine the cost of the search; too many packets cause network clogging bringing down the efficiency of the system as a whole. It can be seen that the number of packets increase in the proliferation/mutation algorithms over the generations, while it remains constant in the case of random walk algorithms. Therefore the number of message packets - k in *Algorithm 1* is set in a fashion so that the aggregate number of packets used by each individual algorithm is roughly the same.

To ensure fairness in 'power' between two proliferation/mutation algorithms (say [PM & RPM]), we keep the proliferation constant ρ and the value of k the same for both processes. The value of k for the proliferation/mutation algorithm is generally set as $k = n(U)$, where $n(U)$ is the in-degree of the initiator peer U.

3.2   Experiments

To explore the different properties of the algorithms, two major types of experiments have been performed on different topologies and with different initial conditions. The experiments are noted one by one.

COVERAGE :   In this experiment, upon initiation of a search, the search operation is performed till the message packets cover the entire network. The experiment is repeated 500 times on randomly selected initial nodes.

During the experiment, we collect different statistic at every 10% of coverage of the network that is, we collect statistic at [20%, 30% $\cdots$ 90%, 100%] of coverage of the network. Since the message forwarding algorithms (*Algo. 3 -7*) are non-deterministic in nature, message packets find it increasingly difficult to visit the last 10% of the network. This is true for all the different variants of message forwarding algorithms and also for all types of topologies. Consequently, the results of *Figs. 4, 5, 7* reflect this characteristic.

TIME-STEP :   In this experiment, upon initiation of a search (*Algorithm 1*), the search operation is performed for $\mathcal{N}$ ($= 50$) time steps. The number of search items (n_s) found within 50 time steps from the commencement of the search is calculated. The experiment is repeated for one generation where one generation is defined as a sequence of 100 such searches. The search output (n_s) is averaged over one generation (100 different searches), whereby we obtain N_s, where $N_s = \frac{\sum_{i=1}^{100} n_s}{100}$. The value of N_s, provides the indication of search efficiency.

The above mentioned two experiments have been performed for proliferation/mutation and random walk processes (*Algorithm 3 - 7*). The interesting results derived from such experiments are noted next.

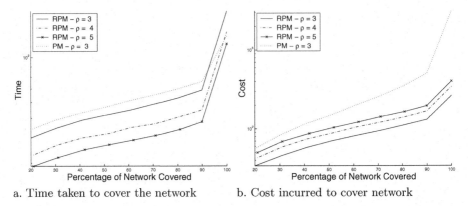

a. Time taken to cover the network   b. Cost incurred to cover network

Fig. 4. Graphs plotting (in semilog(y) scale) the cost and network coverage time of PM [$\rho = 3$] and RPM [$\rho = 3, 4, 5$] algorithms in random networks.

3.3   Experimental Results – Random Network

In this section we report the results obtained by performing the **COVERAGE** experiment on the random network of *Fig. 2(a)*. The results reported below pertains to experiments performed for PM, RPM with different proliferation constants ($\rho = 3, 4, 5$), RRW. In case of the random network, our observation is that mutation does not help in improving the efficiency of *network coverage*. Hence all the proliferation mutation experiments reported here are performed with $\beta = 0$. The major experimental observations are elaborated one by one.

Result I: Comparison between PM and RPM algorithm :   *Fig. 4(a)* shows the network coverage rate of the PM algorithm at $\rho = 3$, and three different instances of the RPM algorithm at $\rho = 3, 4, 5$ respectively. The graph plots the % of network covered in the x-axis, while the time taken to cover corresponding % of network is plotted on the y-axis (semilog scale). It is seen that PM ($\rho = 3$) takes more time to cover up to 90% of the network than RPM with $\rho = 3$. Only while covering the last 10% it overtakes RPM. However, if we increase ρ for RPM, we see that even at 100%, RPM ($\rho = 5$) performs better than PM. An interesting observation to be noted is that RPM ($\rho = 5$) produces a smaller number of packets than PM ($\rho = 3$).

Fig. 4(b) plots the increase in the average number of message packets present in the network (also referred to as cost) in the y-axis with respect to the percentage of network coverage for the four schemes. It is seen that the number of message packets produced in $PM(\rho = 3)$ is about 10 times larger than $RPM(\rho = 3, 4, 5)$. Similarly, in case of random walks, it is found that RRW is much more efficient than RW (the experimental results are not reported here to avoid repetition). So, in our subsequent discussions, we drop PM and RW and concentrate on comparison between RPM and RRW.

Result II: Comparison between RPM and RRW algorithm :   The comparison between RPM and RRW is elaborated through the results highlighted in *Fig. 5*. In case of RRW, we perform three different sets of experiments by

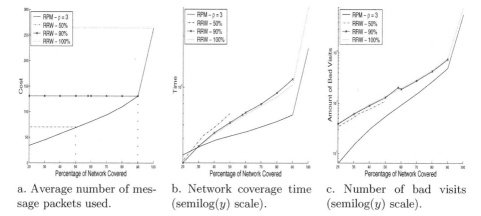

a. Average number of mes-   b. Network coverage time   c. Number of bad visits
sage packets used.   (semilog(y) scale).   (semilog(y) scale).

Fig. 5. Graphs highlighting the (a) average number of message packets used (cost), (b) network coverage time, and (c) number of bad visits by RPM and RRWs (RRW(100%), RRW(90%)   & RRW(50%)) in random network.

varying the initial condition (value of k in *Algorithm 1*). The three different experiments are termed as RRW(50%), RRW(90%), RRW(100%) respectively. The value of k for these experiments are set from collecting information about the average number of packets used by $RPM(\rho = 3)$ to complete coverage of 50%, 90% and 100% of the network respectively. *Fig. 5(a)* plots the average number of packets used by RPM, RRWs (y-axis) vs. network coverage (x-axis).

Fig. 5(b) plots the percentage of the network covered (x-axis) by the four processes RPM($\rho = 3$), RRW(50%), RRW(90%), RRW(100%) against time step (y-axis, in semilog scale). It is seen that the time taken by $RPM(\rho = 3)$ to cover the network is uniformly less than all the other processes beyond the 30% coverage. This is particularly significant because when we are at 30%-40% network coverage zone, the number of message packets used by RPM is significantly lower than RRW algorithms (Refs. Fig. 5(a)). As expected, the time taken to cover the network decreases progressively for RRW(100%), RRW(90%) and RRW(50%). This is because the three processes have an increasing number of message packets. However, as seen the time does not decrease significantly even if we go on adding more messages. The RPM functions are better than RRWs because the packets here exhibit a much smaller probability to visit the same nodes again and again. *Fig. 5(c)* shows the number of *bad visits* (defined on page 364) performed by RPM and RRWs (y-axis) vs. network coverage (x-axis). It is seen that the tendency of RPM to visit the same node again and again is significantly lower.

3.4   Experimental Results – Search Efficiency

To compare the search efficiency of RPM & RRW, we perform the *TIME-STEP* experiment on the random graph for RPM and RRW, each spanning over 100 generations. The graph of *Fig. 6(a)* shows the average value N_s against

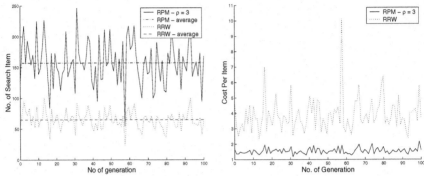

a. Search efficiency of RPM and RRW b. Cost incurred per item searched by
RPM and RRW

Fig. 6. Graphs showing (a). search efficiency, and (b). cost incurred per item searched
by RPM and RRW in random network.

generation number for RPM and RRW. The x-axis of the graph shows the
generation number while the y-axis represents the average number of search items
(N_s) found in the last 100 searches. In this figure we see that the search results
for both RPM and RRW show fluctuations. The fluctuations occur due to the
difference in the availability of the searched items selected at each generation.
However, we see that on the average, search efficiency of RPM is almost 2.5-
times higher than that of RRW. (For RPM, the number of hits ≈ 157, while
it is ≈ 64 for RRW.) The fluctuations in the results help us to understand an
important aspect about cost which is discussed next.

  Fig. 6(b) displays the cost/search item (the number of messages required to
produce a search output) each scheme incurs to generate the performance of
Fig. 6(a). We see that the cost of RPM is hardly changing (it stays constant
at around 1.5) even though the corresponding search output is differing hugely,
while in RRW there is significant fluctuation in terms of cost. This can be easily
understood from the fact that RRW always starts with the same number of
packets irrespective of the availability of the items. While in RPM, the packets
are not generated blindly, but are instead regulated by the availability of the
searched item. Therefore, if a particular searched item is sparse in the network,
RPM produces a lower number of packets and vice versa.

3.5   Experimental Results – Power-Law Graph

In this section, we report the results obtained by performing the COVERAGE
experiment on the power-law graph of *Fig. 2(b)*.

**Result I : Comparison between power-law network and random net-
work :** *Fig. 7* plots % of network coverage in the x-axis, while the time taken
to cover the network space in y-axis (semilog scale). The results for RPM and
RRW are plotted for both random and power-law network, while $HDRRW$
is plotted only for power-law network. It is seen that to cover the power-law

network is almost 10 times more difficult than random network. This happens because in power-law network a few nodes have a huge number of connections while most of the nodes have very few connections (Refs. *Fig. 2(b)*). Hence, to reach a particular node (say x) from another node (say y) (both sparsely connected), the message has to pass through one of the more connected nodes, consequently creating an overload of message on those more connected node. Similar to the results in random networks, the RPM works much better than RRW in power-law networks too. The $HDRRW$ works better than simple RRW however only slightly. The efficiency of $HDRRW$ for multiple random walkers is not as good as in the case of single random walker (as illustrated by Adamic et. al. in [1]).

The next set of results shows that in power-law networks, mutating the proliferated packets indeed helps in improving the coverage rate.

Result II : Effect of mutation on network coverage rate :

Fig. 8(a) plots the time taken to cover the network (y -axis) by RPM at mutation probabilities ($\beta = 0, 0.1, 0.5$) for $\rho = 3$, and at $\rho = 3.5$, $\beta = 0$ vs. % of network coverage (x-axis). It is seen that the performance is best for RPM with ($\beta = 0.1, \rho = 3$). It performs better than even RPM with $\rho = 3.5$. *Fig. 8(b)* plots the number of message packets (y -axis) produced by the corresponding schemes vs. % of network coverage (x-axis). It is

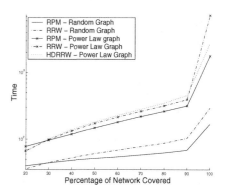

Fig. 7.   Graphs showing network coverage time (semilog(y) scale) by RPM, RRW and $HDRRW$ in random and power-law network.

seen that among the $RPMs$ with $\rho = 3$, RPM with $\beta = 0.1$ produces the largest number of message packets. However, it is less than the number of packets produced by RPM ($\rho = 3.5$). This shows that mutation plays a distinct role in increasing the network coverage efficiency. Merely, by increasing the value of the proliferation constant ρ, we are not able to produce the combined effect of proliferation and mutation.

In power-law networks, a few nodes have a huge number of connections which implies that messages most of the time have to pass through those nodes to reach other nodes. Hence, in order to get a message directed through those nodes more effectively, a high amount of proliferation in their neighboring nodes is desirable. Since the amount of proliferation directly depends on the level of similarity between the message and the information profile (P_I) of the node, a wider variety in the messages improves the chance of similarity between message and information profile. However, these neighboring nodes are only a subset of the total nodes and the frequency distribution of their information profiles are guided by Zipf's law. Excessive mutation tends to make the message packets

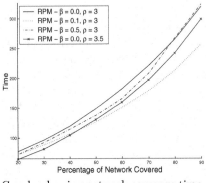
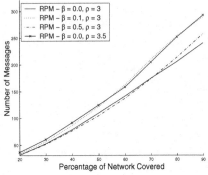

Graphs showing network coverage time   Graphs showing incurred cost

Fig. 8. Graphs showing network coverage time and cost incurred in power-law network by RPMs with ($\rho = 3$, $\beta = 0.0$), ($\rho = 3$, $\beta = 0.1$),($\rho = 3$, $\beta = 0.5$), ($\rho = 3.5$, $\beta = 0.0$).

distribution more uniform and thus the inherent frequency inequality in the distribution of different information profiles cannot be exploited.

3.6 Summarization

The following is the summarization of the results.

(a) RPM is more effective than PM.
(b) RPM is more effective than any random walk algorithm.
(c) RPM has an in-built excellent cost regulatory mechanism.
(d) The search efficiency of RPM is roughly three times higher than RRW.
(e) Coverage is more difficult in power-law networks than random networks.
(f) RPM with mutation probability (β) > 0 functions more effectively in power-law networks, however regulation of mutation probability is important.

4   Conclusion

In this paper, we have produced detailed experimental results showing that the simple immune-inspired concept of proliferation/mutation can be used to cover the network more effectively than random walk. The proliferation/mutation algorithm can regulate the number of packets to be produced during a search operation according to the availability of the searched material, thus improving the efficiency of search. The effectivity of search is demonstrated across the two major types of topologies we have taken into account in this paper. This we believe is a fundamental result and can be applied beyond the domain of the proposed $p2p$ search application. However, a detailed theoretical analysis to explain these interesting results has to be undertaken in the future to explore the full potential of proliferation/mutation algorithms.

References

1. L A Adamic, R M. Lukose, A R. Puniyani, and B A Huberman. Search in Power-Law Networks. *Physical Review E*, 64:046–135, 2001.
2. C Jin, Q Chen, and S Jamin. Inet: Internet Topology Generator. University of Michigan Technical Report CSE-TR-433-00, 2002.
3. M. A. Jovanovic, F. S. Annexstein, and K. A. Berman. Scalability Issues in Large Peer-to-peer Networks - A Case Study of Gnutella. Technical Report University of Cincinnati, 2001.
4. A Medina, A Lakhina, I Matta, and J Byers. BRITE: An Approach to Universal Topology Generation. In *MASCOTS*, August 2001.
5. A. Oram, editor. *Peer-to-Peer: Harnessing the Power of Disruptive Technologies.* O Reilly Books, 2001.
6. G. K. Zipf. *Psycho-Biology of Languages.* Houghton-Mifflin, 1935.

A Game-Theoretic Approach to Artificial Immune Networks

Marcos Velez, Fernando Nino, and Oscar M. Alonso

Department of Computer Science
National University of Colombia, Bogotá
{jmvelezc,lfninov,omalonsom}@unal.edu.co

Abstract. In this paper, a well-known evolutionary dynamics, replicator dynamics, is used to model the dynamics of an immune network. A doubly symmetric game is associated to an immune network by this model, which implies some optimal behavior throughout time under replicator dynamics. Stability of an immune network is guaranteed by such dynamics. Two types of immune networks were modeled. In addition, an algorithm in which perturbation of an immune network by a set of antigens to be recognized is proposed. Some preliminary experiments were carried out to show the potentials of the model.

1   Introduction

Natural immune system is an adaptive learning system that is composed of several parallel and complementary protection mechanisms for defense against foreign pathogens. It is a distributed system, that learns to identify previously unseen invaders, remembering what it has learnt before. It has been the subject of extensive theoretical and experimental research [11].

The field of Artificial Immune Systems (AISs) is a recently created biologically inspired metaphor, subject of research in recent years. Numerous immune algorithms have been proposed, based on processes identified within vertebrate immune systems. These computational techniques have many potential applications, such as pattern recognition, fault detection, computer security, and optimization. A survey of the research in this field can be found in [1]. Despite the wide amount or research on AISs, there is not much theoretical work to study their dynamic behavior to explain the results obtained by such computational models.

On the other hand, Evolutionary Game Theory (EGT) [12] has become an important analytical tool to study evolutionary processes. In EGT, a game is played repeatedly by biologically or socially conditioned players in a large population, who are randomly involved in pairwise strategic interactions. A player is pre-programmed to some strategy, and it is assumed that an evolutionary selection process operates on the distribution of strategies in the population over time [16]. A key aspect of EGT is that fitness of an individual programmed to a strategy depends on the proportions of other strategies in the population [10].

G. Nicosia et al. (Eds.): ICARIS 2004, LNCS 3239, pp. 372–385, 2004.

Interactions between the different elements that belong to the immune system, and between internal elements and external elements, make the immune system to exhibit cognitive abilities [15]. The existence of learning due to these interactions, suggests the idea of modeling such interactions using game theory. In order to introduce the Game Theoretic model, B-cells are thought to be involved in *idiotypic interactions* which may be seen as *pairwise interactions* between them, such as in EGT, where agents are paired to play. Accordingly, payoffs are derived from a B-Cell suppression or stimulation level, which will have effect on the B-Cell proliferation rate.

A representative and widely used evolutionary dynamics in EGT is the replicator dynamics. The replicator dynamics selects agents in a fitness proportional fashion, where fitness is represented by payoff; therefore, subpopulations with better payoffs than the average will grow, while the ones with worse payoffs than the average will be reduced. Accordingly, in this paper, immune networks are analyzed using EGT. Particularly, replicator dynamics is used as a mechanism to describe immune network dynamics. At the end of the immune network stabilization process, a core network of selected B-Cells emerges, which are representatives of the antigens the immune system has been exposed to, this is called immune metadynamics (see [15,14]). A game associated to the immune network is shown to be doubly symmetric, which under the replicator dynamics drives the population towards a social optimum, corresponding to the stability of the immune network.

In Theoretical Immunology, Stadler et al [13] modeled immune networks using second order replicator equations. The EGT metaphor is meaningful to model immune networks; hence, underlying immune concepts in this work and in [13] are similar. However, fundamental differences exist, for instance, the omission of an activation function in the model introduced in this work. The proposed game-theoretic approach seems appropriate because it is a formal abstraction of the behavior of immune networks.

The rest of this paper is organized as follows. In section 2, some remarks on immune network models in Theoretical Immunology are summarized. Then, some fundamental concepts in Evolutionary Game Theory are presented in section 3. The Game Theoretic Immune Network model is explained in detail in section 4. Preliminary experiments are discussed in section 5. Finally, some conclusions are devised in section 6.

2   Immunological Background

Immune network theory was introduced by Jerne[8]; it was hypothesized that the immune system, rather than being a set of discrete clones that responded only when triggered by antigens, is a regulated network of molecules and cells that recognize one another even in the absence of antigens. In this context, the B-cell model is an immune network model that includes only B-cells, and describes the population dynamics of a set of n distinguishable clones that interact in a network [13,11]. All B-cells in a clone i are said to be of type i. For each clone i, the total amount of stimulation is considered to be a linear combination of the populations of other interacting clones j. This linear combination is called the *field* h_i acting on clone i , i. e.,

$$h_i = c \sum_i^n J_{ij} x_j \qquad (1)$$

where J_{ij} specifies the interaction strength (or affinity) between clones i and j; x_j is the relative concentration (share) of clone j; and c is the total concentration of B-cells. The elements of matrix J define the topology of the immune network. For simplicity, the elements of J are typically either 0 or 1; although some authors also use intermediate values to model circumstances closer to Biology[11].

An important feature of the B-cell model is the shape of the activation function $f(h_i)$, which defines the fraction of B-cells that proliferate in terms of the field h_i [11]. Typically, the activation function is assumed to be a log-bell-shaped function.

The population dynamics of the interacting clones in the B-cell model can be described by a set of differential equations. Many variations of these equations have been proposed [11]. Particularly, a relevant dynamical model was presented by Stadler et al [13], which was based on second order replicator equations.

Immune systems exhibit cognitive abilities [15]. The existence of learning due to interactions between the different elements that belong to the immune system, and between internal elements and external elements suggests the idea of modeling such interactions using game theory. In this work, a metaphoric approach to model the dynamics of interacting clones with Evolutionary Game Theory using the replicator dynamics is introduced.

In this approach, immune networks where B-cells only either stimulate or suppress each other are considered. Thus, it is not necessary to consider an activation function. An example of an AIS that only considers stimulation among B-cells is presented in [14]; another AIS in which only suppression is taken into account can be found in [2].

3   Evolutionary Game Theory

The key aspect of EGT is that the fitness of an individual programmed to some strategy depends on the proportions of other strategies in the population [10]. A representative and widely used evolutionary dynamics in EGT is the replicator dynamics, which will be used in this work to model the dynamics of an immune network.

3.1   Fundamentals

Consider a two-player game ∂ in normal form in which both players can play a strategy in the set S of pure strategies. If the payoff to an individual playing $s_i \in S$ is $u(s_i, s_j)$, and the payoff to another individual playing $s_j \in S$ is $u(s_j, s_i)$, such a game is called *symmetric*. In addition to pure strategies, a player can adopt a mixed strategy, which is specified as a probability distribution over the set S of pure strategies. Any pure strategy s_i is a vector e^i, which has at the *i-th* position a value of 1 and 0 at the other coordinates, accordingly, a pure strategy can be seen as a degenerate mixture. The set of all possible mixed strategies is called the mixed strategy simplex which is defined as $\triangle = \{x : x \in R^m, m = |S|, \sum_i^m x_i = 1, x_i \in [0,1]\}$. Pure strategies happen to be the vertices of the simplex $\triangle$; therefore, $\triangle$ is the convex hull of such vertices. Let $A = (a_{ij})$, where $a_{ij} = u(s_i, s_j)$, be the payoff matrix of the symmetric game $\eth$. Given the payoff matrix A, the payoff value $u(x,y)$ with mixed strategies $x, y \in \triangle$ is $x^T A y$. A symmetric game is termed *doubly symmetric* if and only if the payoff matrix A is symmetric $(A = A^T)$, which means that $u(x,y) = u(y,x)$ for any mixed strategies x and y.

From now on, a large population of individuals and symmetric pairwise inter-actions within the population will be considered. In each time period, individuals are randomly *paired* to play the game $\eth$. When an individual uses (or is pro-grammed to play) pure strategy s_i in the game, it is said to be of *type i*. At any point t in time, let $p_i(t) \geq 0$ be the *number of individuals* that are currently *programmed* to play pure strategy $s_i \in S$, and let $p(t) = \sum_{s_i \in K} p_i(t) > 0$ be the total population. Accordingly, the associated population state is defined as the vector $x(t) = (x_1(t), ..., x_k(t))$, where each component $x_i(t)$ is the *population share* programmed to pure strategy s_i at time t, $x_i(t) = p_i(t)/p(t)$. Thus, a *state of the population* may be considered as a *mixed strategy* within the simplex $\triangle$.

When the population is in state $x \in \triangle$, the *expected payoff* to any pure strategy s_i at a random match with another strategy is $u(e^i, x)$; this is true because, for an individual, it is the same to consider its interaction with another individual drawn at random from such a polymorphic population as playing with an individual that has the mixed strategy x. The *population average payoff* (i. e., the payoff to an individual drawn at random from the population) is $u(x,x) = \sum_{s_i \in S} x_i u(e^i, x)$, the same payoff as the mixed *strategy* x earns when it plays against itself.

3.2   The Replicator Dynamics

An evolutionary process based in Darwinian evolution has three fundamental mechanisms, reproduction, mutation and selection, which describe how popula-tions change over time. The replicator dynamics can be seen as a special case of a more general framework based on the equivalence between the replicator mu-tator equation and the Price equation. Adaptive dynamics, evolutionary game dynamics, the Lotka-Volterra equation of ecology and the quasispecies equation of molecular evolution are obtained as special cases of such equations. Therefore, several formulations that appear to be very different, are actually part of a single unified framework [10].

There are many ways in which the emergence of the replicator dynamics can be elicited. For instance, in [6], it was shown that replication may be seen as process to learn of better performing (higher payoff) strategies, when individuals play a game. Typically, replication is seen as a reproduction process where payoffs represent the number of offspring [16].

In its standard setting, the replicator dynamics does not include any mutation mechanism, and it is expressed as a system of ordinary differential equations [16]. If replication takes place continuously over time, the corresponding dynamics for the population shares x_i becomes

$$\dot{x}_i = [u(e^i, x) - u(x, x)]x_i \qquad (2)$$

The replicator dynamics selects agents in a fitness proportional fashion, where payoffs represent fitness; therefore, subpopulations with better payoffs than the average will grow, while those with worse payoffs than the average will be reduced. At any moment in time, the state of population $x(t)$ is contained in the mixed strategy simplex $\triangle$, which means that trajectories of the dynamics are contained in $\triangle$. Clearly, the dynamics will reach a critical point when the growth rate for each population share is 0, which means that all individuals earn the same payoff when confronted with the entire population ($u(e^i, x) = u(e^j, x)$ for any i and j), i.e., all the strategies earn the *average payoff* ($u(e^i, x) = u(x, x)$ for any i).

The discrete version of the replicator dynamics is described by the following equation

$$x_i(t+1) = x_i(t)\frac{u[e^i, x(t)]}{u[x(t), x(t)]} \qquad (3)$$

which can be written in matrix form notation as

$$x_i' = x_i\frac{u_i}{x \cdot u}$$

$$u = Ax$$

where A is the payoff matrix of the game, x is a vector representing the population state, u is a vector that contains the payoffs to each pure strategy.

In some contexts, evolutionary selection induces a monotonic increase over time in the *average* population fitness; this is usually referred to as the fundamental theorem of natural selection (see [5]). In the replicator dynamics, since fittest individuals proliferate throughout time, it can be thought that the average fitness increases monotonically; but this is not always the case. In doubly symmetric games a monotonic increase in the average payoff does happen, as stated in the following proposition [16].

Proposition 1. *In any doubly symmetric game, under the continuous replicator dynamics given by equation 2, $\dot{u}[x(t), x(t)] \geq 0$. Similarly, in any doubly symmetric game, under the discrete replicator dynamics given in equation 3, $u[x(t+dt), x(t+dt)] \geq u[x(t), x(t)]$ and the equality holds if and only if $x(t)$ is a stationary point.*

3.3   Nash Equilibrium

Given a mixed strategy x, the support of x, denoted $C(x)$, is defined as the set of pure strategies with positive share. x is a Nash Equilibrium strategy if and only if all pure strategies in $C(x)$ earn the maximal payoff that can be obtained against x. This implies that all strategies in $C(x)$ earn the same average payoff. Let $\triangle_{NE}$ denote the set of strategies in Nash Equilibrium with themselves. Then, $\triangle_{NE}$ is a subset of the set of stationary points under the replicator dynamics.

Particularly, in doubly symmetric games, evolutionary selection, as modeled by the replicator dynamics, induces a monotonic increase in *social efficiency* over time (proposition 1); hence, given the initial state x^0 in the interior of $\triangle$ (i.e., all the strategies have a positive share), the population converges to some symmetric Nash equilibrium. Also, if a Nash equilibrium is asymptotically stable, then it is an Evolutionarily Stable Strategy (ESS), which has some additional interesting properties that are out of the scope of this paper. Since a doubly symmetric game will be associated to an immune network, replicator dynamics and Nash equilibria will be used to analyze its behavior. Thus, the immune network will exhibit some optimal behavior from the point of view of affinity (suppression) among B-cells; also, the immune network is expected to stabilize at some (at least local) optimal configuration.

4   Modeling Immune Networks with EGT

In this work, an immune network is seen as a population of co-evolving B-Cells, which are involved in idiotypic interactions and the stimulation level of a clone depends on the distribution of other clones in the network. Since there is a correspondence between EGT and co-evolutionary algorithms [3,4,17], it is natural to model immune networks using EGT. It should be noticed that the replicator dynamics is a coevolutionary process, in which the fitness of an individual is not established by an external function, but it rather depends on its interactions with other individuals [17].

4.1   The Transition from EGT to AIS

The natural immune system is a complex system, in which complex tasks such as learning and memory involves cooperation among a large number of components. One goal of immunology modeling is to infer macroscopic properties of immune systems from the properties and interactions between elementary components [11]. Hence, a natural immune system can be modeled as a collection of artificial entities or agents, which interact among them and with their environment [7] and will determine its global behavior.

In order to introduce the GT model, B-cells are thought to be involved in *idiotypic interactions* in a parallel and distributed way; which may be seen as *pairwise interactions* between them, such as in EGT, where agents are paired to play. Accordingly, the payoffs will represent B-Cell suppression or stimulation,

Table 1. Immune network and Evolutionary Game Theory correspondence.

IMMUNE NETWORK	EGT
B-Cell	Individual
B-Cell idiotope	Pure Strategy
Clone i	All individuals with strategy s_i
Clone i relative concentration	Share x_i of individuals with strategy s_i
Idiotypic Interaction between B-cells	Pairwise interaction between individuals
Stimulation level	Payoff
Network repertoire	Population represented by a mixed strategy x
Network stability	Nash Equilibrium
Network dynamics	Replicator dynamics

which will have effect on a B-Cell proliferation rate. In this model, a B-cell is said to be of *type i* if it has an idiotope v^i. All B-cells of type i are said to be part of clone i. Since clones have different amount of B-cells, then the result of the idiotypic interactions between clone i and the other clones can be conceived as the expected stimulation level of the interaction of each B-Cell in clone i and the *immune repertoire* (population). A B Cell of type i will correspond to an individual of type i (programmed to pure strategy s_i) in EGT. In addition, the *population of B-Cells* will be represented as a *mixed strategy* x. Besides, the *stimulation level* of a B-cell of type i will correspond to the *payoff* $u(e^i, x)$ earned by a player with pure strategy s_i when confronted with mixed strategy x. Therefore, the *B-cell population dynamics* as the global behavior in an immune network can be described by the *replicator dynamics* defined in equation 2. This analogy between immune networks and EGT is summarized in table 1.

In this model, as usual, no distinction is made between the representation of the idiotope and the paratope (receptor) of a B-cell. In addition, the replicator dynamics takes care of modeling what is known as a network metadynamics, in which clone selection is performed; clone selection refers to the immune recruitment mechanism as well as the disappearance of not sufficiently stimulated clones. Therefore, when the network stabilizes, the clones present constitute the core immune network. In the proposed approach, the appearance of new clones due to interactions within the network is not considered.

4.2   The Model

Given the random nature of interactions in the replicator dynamics, the population is considered to be completely mixed; this translated to the immune system means that when a B-Cell (individual) with idiotope v^i (strategy s_i) is involved in a idiotypic interaction, the expected stimulation level is obtained by its interaction with all clones in the immune repertoire x, in the EGT context, this values is given by the payoff $u(e^i, x)$. In other words, a B-Cell can be thought of as interacting at the same time with all B-Cells in a completely connected network, because all B-Cells are represented in the population as the mixed strategy x.

The idiotope v^i of a B-Cell of type i may be considered as a real-valued vector in I^n (n-dimensional unit hypercube shape space); thus, the affinity between two B Cells of type i and j is given by $1 - d(v^i, v^j)$, where $d(v^i, v^j)$ is the Euclidean distance between vectors v^i and v^j. Therefore, a symmetric game $\eth$ with set of strategies S may be defined in which each strategy $s_i \in S$ is a vector v^i in I^n that corresponds to a B-Cell idiotope.

Next, two types of immune networks will be modeled. In the first one, it is considered that B-cells only co-stimulate each other (see [14],). In contrast, in the second one only suppression among B-cells will be considered, similar to the one presented in [2].

The selection mechanism in the replicator dynamics is fitness proportional; fitness, as mentioned above, is defined by the payoff to each strategy in a game. By now, the way in which B cells interact under the replicator dynamics is known, however, payoffs attained from these interactions is not known; the game payoff matrix and the distribution of strategies on the population at a certain moment in time will determine the payoffs earned by an individual. Therefore, for an immune network, a payoff matrix needs to be defined. In both cases, payoff matrices will be symmetric, because they are defined in terms of Euclidean distance (i.e., $d(v^i, v^j) = d(v^j, v^i)$ for any i and j) and as said before no distinction is made between the idiotope and the paratope of a B-cell. Thus, the corresponding symmetric game $\eth$ is *doubly symmetric*.

Stimulation network. In this first immune network, only B-cell stimulation is considered. In this case, the stimulation of a B-cell of type i by another B-cell of type j depends on their affinity. The payoff matrix $A = (a_{ij})$ is defined as

$$a_{ij} = \begin{cases} 1 - d(v^i, v^j) & \text{if } d(v^i, v^j) < t, \text{ for } i \neq j \\ 0 & otherwise \end{cases} \tag{4}$$

where t may be considered as a stimulation threshold. Thus a game $\eth$ may be defined using A under the replicator dynamics.

In the game $\eth$, due to the replicator dynamics, highly stimulated individuals are selected throughout time, i.e., B-cells that are close (in Euclidean space) to many other B-Cells will survive coevolution, and will most likely have a positive share in the population when the network reaches stationarity.

The payoff matrix of the game associated to this immune network, is conceptually similar to the matrix J defined in section 2. As mentioned above, the field h_i of clone i, expressed in equation 1, represents the total amount of stimulation for a concentration level c. The value $\frac{h_i}{c}$ for clone i will correspond to the payoff in a stimulation network.

Suppression network. In this second immune network, only B-cell suppression is considered. The suppression of a B-cell of type i by another B-cell of type j depends on their affinity. The payoff matrix $A = (a_{ij})$ is defined as

$$a_{ij} = \begin{cases} d(v^i, v^j) & \text{if } d(v^i, v^j) > t, \text{ for } i \neq j \\ 0 & otherwise \end{cases} \tag{5}$$

where t may be considered as a suppression threshold.

In this model, the less suppressed a B cell is, the higher payoff it obtains, this is why the payoff is the Euclidean distance between two data vectors. Hence, the lesser suppressed clones will prevail under the replicator dynamics.

The concept of a field of a clone, which is given in terms of stimulations does not apply in the context of suppression networks, since A does not represent an affinity matrix.

4.3   Perturbation of an Immune Network

In the model defined above antigens were not considered. In this section, perturbation of immune networks is considered. When an antigen is presented to the immune network, two major phases are performed. In the first phase, the immune network goes into clonal selection, clonal expansion and affinity maturation. This phase constitutes the *exploration* mechanism of the algorithm, and a new starting state for the replicator dynamics is given. In the second phase, the perturbed network stabilizes; this stage constitutes the *exploitation* mechanism of the algorithm. Then, the immune network will deterministically converge to a stationary state, which is a *Nash equilibrium*. Algorithm 1 summarizes this process.

Given an initial population of B-Cells, a vector x^0 represents the shares of each clone, then the network first evolves until it stabilizes. The stabilized network is called the core network (see [14]). In immunology, it is said that when an antigen appears in the immune system, B-Cells which hold higher affinity with the antigen go into clonal expansion and affinity maturation. Therefore, when new B-cells appear in the network, it is perturbed, and the network will evolve until it reaches a stationary point. In addition to clonal expansion, when an network is perturbed, new clones appear; which means in game theoretical terms that new strategies appear, therefore given a new initial state to the replicator dynamics, the trajectory of the dynamical system is in a *new simplex* spanned by strategies in support of such initial state.

Clones that are sufficiently representative of those antigens the network has been exposed to are maintained and they are said to be part of the immune memory. In coevolution, it is common that the population somehow represents the solution to a problem, and that could be the case for artificial immune networks [14,2]. In this model, the population corresponds to the immune repertoire; therefore, the model should ideally guarantee that when the network reaches a stable state, a good solution is attained.

An advantage of the proposed model is that you do not need to worry about the size of the immune network, because the immune network is represented as a vector of shares. Furthermore, each time the immune network stabilizes, clones that are no longer needed disappear, i.e., they vanish in the replicator dynamics.

Algorithm 1

GT-NETWORK($PayoffMatrix, Antigens$)
1   $Shares \leftarrow$ INITIALIZE-POPULATION()
2   $Shares \leftarrow$ REPLICATOR-DYNAMICS($Shares, PayoffMatrix$)
3   **for** $i \leftarrow 0$ **to** $length[Antigens]$
4   **do** $Shares \leftarrow$ PERTURB-NETWORK($Shares, Antigens[i]$)
5   ▷ The network is perturbed
6           $Shares \leftarrow$ REPLICATOR-DYNAMICS($Shares, PayoffMatrix$)
7   ▷ The network is stabilized again
8   **return** $Shares$

---

5   Preliminary Experimental Results

For both the stimulation network and the suppression network some preliminary experiments were undertaken. A data set (IRIS data set) that corresponded to the antigens was considered. In the first experiment, a stimulation network and a suppression network were evolved using the complete data set. In the second set of experiments, both types of networks were initialized with a subset of the data set, and the rest of the data was used to perturb the resulting core networks.

In these experiments, the immune dynamics was implemented using the discrete version of the replicator dynamics 3, and the perturbation mechanism consisted of adding a new clone (with some positive share) to the network for each antigen presented to the network. The added clone resembled the presented antigen. It has to be noticed that population shares are considered to represent states rather than a collection of individuals, therefore, B-cells are not treated as computational units in the AIS, instead the concept of a clone is used, where it represents all B-cells of the same type.

It is reasonable to utilize the idea of achieving a stable representation of the data being learnt by the immune network [14]. The resultant network represents the input data set (antigens) with a smaller number of clones, i.e., it constitutes a simplified approach or compressed image of the universe of antigens [2].

5.1   Stimulation Network Experiments

In figure 1, it is shown how the average payoff evolves through time; the upper curve corresponds to the experiments in which all the data set was used to create the initial immune network. Notice that average payoff between clones monotonically increases, which means that the average affinity between surviving clones increases. The lower curve, shows the average payoff when the network is initialized with a subset of the data. Note that it initially stabilizes, and then, the network is continuously perturbed by presenting the antigens one by one. The initial average affinity to this perturbed state begins on a value lower than the one before being perturbed. It should be emphasized that new clones that

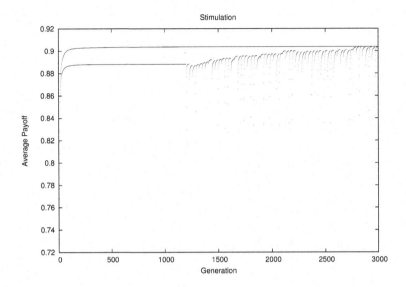

Fig. 1. Stimulation network experiments

increase average affinity appear throughout time. Also notice that when new clones appear stabilization is reached at a similar or higher average payoff.

In the experiments, it was observed that if stimulation among B Cells of the same type is not restricted, the network degenerates and converges to a state where there is only a clone with share value 1.0; thus eliminating any possibility of continuous learning, similar results were reported in [9]. In a context of data analysis, this means that when the network stabilizes, it only represents the central element of the stronger cluster. Figure 1, shows the evolution of the average payoff of the immune network.

5.2 Suppression Network Experiments

In this case, in contrast to the stimulation network, most clones are expected to be positioned in regions of the space containing antigens that are more distant from the center of mass of the distribution [2].

In figure 1, the average payoff is shown; the upper curve corresponds to the experiments in which all the data set was used to create the initial suppression network. Note that average payoff between clones monotonically increases, which means that the average Euclidean distance between surviving clones increases. The lower curve, shows the average payoff when the network is initialized with a subset of the data. Notice that it initially stabilizes, and then, the network is continuously perturbed by presenting the antigens one by one. The initial average distance to this perturbed state begins on a value that may be lower or higher than the one before being perturbed. It should be emphasized that new clones that increase the average distance appear throughout time. Also notice that when new clones appear stabilization is reached at a similar or higher average payoff.

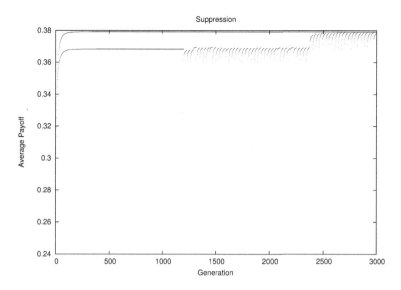

Fig. 2. Suppression network experiments

6   Conclusions

In this work, a well-known evolutionary dynamics, replicator dynamics, was used to model the dynamics of an immune network. The replicator dynamics selects agents in a fitness proportional fashion, where fitness is represented by payoff; therefore, subpopulations with better payoffs than average will grow, while the ones with worse payoffs than average will be reduced. The immune networks are associated to a doubly symmetric game, therefore social efficiency is granted under the replicator dynamics, and the population will be driven towards a social optimum, corresponding to the stability of the immune network.

Two major phases are performed when an antigen is presented to an immune network. In the first phase, the immune network is perturbed and goes into clonal selection, clonal expansion and affinity maturation. This phase constitutes the *exploration* mechanism of the proposed algorithm, and a new initial state for the replicator dynamics is produced. In the second phase, the perturbed network stabilizes; this stage constitutes the *exploitation* mechanism of the algorithm. Given a new initial state to the replicator dynamics, the trajectory of the dynamical system is in a *new simplex* spanned by clones in support of such initial state. Under such dynamics, an immune network is expected to stabilize, i.e., to reach a stationary state, which is a *Nash equilibrium*.

This memory mechanism accumulates a set of clones, that appear through subsequent perturbations of the immune network induced by antigen presentation and represent antigens the immune network has been exposed to and these remaining clones could constitute the answer to a problem. A remarkable preliminary result is that the stability the network reaches through constant perturbations, from antigens that are presented, approaches the quality of Nash equilibrium of a network with initialized clones that represent all antigens.

A simple perturbation mechanism was used to try to explain continuous immune learning in game theoretical terms. However, each time a new perturbed state is given to the replicator dynamics, the trajectory of the dynamics is in a different simplex, which is spanned by the pure strategies (clones) with positive share in the population. In further work, a more sophisticated perturbation mechanism should consider the implementation of a complete clonal selection mechanism.

In future work, other dynamics of great interest in spatial evolutionary game theory should be worth to be explored. Also, pattern recognition and optimization applications of the proposed model should be explored.

References

1. Dipankar Dasgupta, Zhou Ji, and F. Gonzalez, *Artificial immune system (ais) research in the last five years*, Proceedings of the 2003 Congress on Evolutionary Computation CEC2003 (Canberra) (Ruhul Sarker, Robert Reynolds, Hussein Abbass, Kay Chen Tan, Bob McKay, Daryl Essam, and Tom Gedeon, eds.), IEEE Press, 8-12 December 2003, pp. 123–130.

2. Leandro Nunes de Castro, *The immune response of an artificial immune network (ainet)*, Proceedings of the 2003 Congress on Evolutionary Computation CEC2003 (Canberra) (Ruhul Sarker, Robert Reynolds, Hussein Abbass, Kay Chen Tan, Bob McKay, Daryl Essam, and Tom Gedeon, eds.), IEEE Press, 8-12 December 2003, pp. 146–153.

3. S. G. Ficici and J. B. Pollack, *A game-theoretic approach to the simple coevolutionary algorithm*, Parallel Problem Solving from Nature - PPSN VI 6th International Conference (Paris, France) (Günter Rudolph Xin Yao Evelyne Lutton Juan Julian Merelo Hans-Paul Schwefel Marc Schoenauer, Kalyanmoy Deb, ed.), Springer Verlag, September 16-20 2000, LNCS 1917.

4. Sevan G. Ficici, Ofer Melnik, and Jordan B. Pollack, *A game-theoretic investigation of selection methods used in evolutionary algorithms*, Proceedings of the 2000 Congress on Evolutionary Computation CEC00 (La Jolla Marriott Hotel La Jolla, California, USA), IEEE Press, 6-9 July 2000, p. 880.

5. R. A. Fisher, *The genetical theory of natural selection*, Oxford University Press, London, 1930.

6. H. Gintis, *Game theory evolving*, Princeton University Press, 2000.

7. António Grilo, Artur Caetano, and Agostinho Rosa, *Immune system simulation through a complex adaptive system model*, Proceedings of the 3rd. Workshop of Genetic Algorithms and Artificial Life, 1999.

8. N. K. Jerne, *Towards a network theory of the immune system*, Ann. Immunol. (Inst. Pasteur) **125C** (1974), 373–389.

9. Thomas Knight and Jon Timmis, *Assessing the performance of the resource limited artificial immune system aine*, Tech. Report 3-01, University of Kent at Canterbury, 2001.

10. Karen M. Pagen and Martin A. Nowak, *Unifying evolutionary dynamics*, J. Theor. Biol. **219** (2002).

11. A. S. Perelson and G. Weisbuch, *Immunology for physicists*, Rev. Modern Physics **69** (1997), no. 4, 1219–1267.

12. J. Maynard Smith, *Evolution and the theory of games*, Cambridge University Press, Cambridge, 1982.

13. P. Stadler, P. Schuster, and A. Perelson, *Immune networks modeled by replicator equations*, J. Math. Biol. **33** (1994), 111–137.

14. J. Timmis and M. J. Neal, *A resource limited artificial immune system for data analysis*, Research and development in intelligent systems XVII, proceedings of ES2000 (Cambridge, UK), 2000, pp. 19–32.

15. F. Varela, A. Coutinho, B. Dupire, and N. Vaz, *Cognitive networks: immune and neural and otherwise*, Theoretical Immunology: Part Two, SFI Studies in the science of Complexity (1988), 359–371.

16. Jorgen W. Weibull, *Evolutionary game theory*, The MIT Press, 1995.

17. R. Paul Wiegand, William Liles, and Kenneth De Jong, *Analyzing cooperative coevolution with evolutionary game theory*, Proceedings of the 2002 Congress on Evolutionary Computation CEC2002 (David B. Fogel, Mohamed A. El-Sharkawi, Xin Yao, Garry Greenwood, Hitoshi Iba, Paul Marrow, and Mark Shackleton, eds.), IEEE Press, 2002, pp. 1600–1605.

Modelling Immune Memory for Prediction and Computation

W.O. Wilson and S.M. Garrett

Computational Biology Group
Dept. Computer Science
University of Wales, Aberystwyth
Wales, UK. SY23 3DB
{wow93,smg}@aber.ac.uk

Abstract. This paper investigates the concept of immune memory, and the potential for an Artificial Immune System (AIS), in which memory is an emergent property of the antibody population and its dynamics. Inspiration for the implementation of this concept of memory is taken from current biological theories. However, a difficulty lies in the fact that as yet these theories remain unconfirmed; no conclusive explanation has been put forward to explain how immune memory is created and sustained over time. The approach taken here is to investigate and build on two of the basic models of immune memory : (i) the memory cell model, (ii) the residual antigen model, and iii) provide some initial thoughts as to the influence of the immune network model on our theory of immune memory. We show that each model can partially explain how the immune system can remember infections, and respond quickly to re-infections, but we begin to demonstrate that none of them in isolation result in an effective immune memory response. Our initial appraisal is that all three models should be combined, and updated to reflect new biological concepts, we make some suggestions about how this might be achieved, and we illustrate our discussion with some tentative results.

1 Introduction and Motivation

Immunological memory is a vital component of the immune system, allowing it to successfully respond to re-infection, and to ensure the survival of its host. However current understanding of immune memory is primitive at best. Many possible explanations have been proposed but no single theory has been accepted.

In the adaptive immune system, B cells, T cells and plasma cells [1] have all been held to exhibit memory properties. Popular abstractions of immune memory often focus on the interactions between networks of B cells [2], or the complexities of immune memory may be somewhat side-stepped by the use of artificial *memory cells* [3]. It should be noted that these particular studies do not aim to model the immune system, as is our goal, but are inspired by it to create their metaphors. Immunology agrees that these two mechanisms may exist but, in addition, it provides a third possibility: that B cells may be stimulated by residual antigenic material, stimulating B cell activity and ensuring

G. Nicosia et al. (Eds.): ICARIS 2004, LNCS 3239, pp. 386–399, 2004.

that information regarding previously experienced antigen is retained within the population. This residual antigen mechanism has not been widely examined by the Artificial Immune Systems community for its memory properties.

Here we will present a conceptual discussion of how immune memory can be modelled, with some initial simulation results that suggest this line of work has potential. Our findings derive from excerpts from a set of controlled experiments performed, presenting a sample of the results, for the sake of clarity, to draw out the central themes of the research. We also provide some initial theories of how the immune network model could impact on our model of immune memory, a topic for further discussion in subsequent papers. We anticipate that the three mechanisms will be adjusted as this work matures, due to feedback from the results, and due to further investigation into state-of-the-art immunological work on immune memory.

We suggest that any combination of the three memory mechanisms will exhibit dynamics that are *not present in any of the component mechanisms alone*. Such a unified model of immune memory would not only be more accurate when predicting the behaviour of the natural immune system, it is likely to provide new abstractions of immune memory that will have potential in computational systems. Furthermore, a computational model of immune memory may be used by immunologists to help to provide biological insights.

2   Background

As discussed in the previous section, at least three basic models of immune memory exist. It may not be possible, or even necessary, to treat the processes as being separate, but it is useful for our purposes here for explanatory clarity. Each of these theories can be described as follows:

The memory cell model: in which memory is mediated by long-lived 'memory cells', which are differentiated from B cells, and which respond almost immediately to the re-presentation of the antigen that led to their creation. Memory is achieved via the extended life-span of the differentiated B cell.

The residual antigen model: in which small amounts of antigen are retained from every experienced infection to continually stimulate the immune system at a low level, keeping it in a state of readiness if the infection (or one of a similar structure) should ever return in higher concentrations.

The immune network model: in which lymphocytes not only respond to antigenic regions on foreign bodies, they also respond to antigenic regions on other lymphocytes, such as B cells. This can form a loop of stimulation and repression which continues to stimulate the immune system, even in the absence of the antigenic sequence that originally stimulated the response. More importantly in the context of our research, the networking of B cells ensures suppression of identical memory cells localised in different areas of the human body to avoid unnecessary duplication.

Several questions arise after consideration of these three models of memory. How are memory cells originally created, and how do they differ from normal immune cells to obtain longer life spans? How could a small concentration of antigenic material be left behind after an immune response, and is this enough to elicit an adequate immune response? How long can this antigenic material be retained? How can a potentially chaotic network of interactions, between a vast number of immune cells, be controlled and provide useful dynamics? If all three processes do occur in nature, then to what extent to they interact? These are interesting questions and are investigated in turn by building and evolving a model of an artificial immune system that is based on these principles.

Looking first at current implementations of most artificial clonal selection algorithms, we can see that they tend to rely on artificial memory cells to 'remember' an infection [3,4,5]. They evolve a population of antibodies in response to antigen(s), and memory is simply implemented by storing a copy of the best matching antibody. In effect, this creates a separate and distinct immune cell with eternal life that can be used as a reference point to develop a solution to subsequent similar antigen infections. This appears a little contrived, and would, by definition, provide the immune system with a source of memory for as long as the memory cell survived. Unlike these approaches our aim is to model immune memory and as a result this simplistic methodology is not suitable for our purposes. In addition these memory cells are specific to an antigen strain and would limit the ability of the immune memory to generalise across infection types, a desired requirement given the finite number of cells in the immune system. To simulate the emergence of a more natural process of the creation, evolution and maintenance of memory, inspiration was again taken from nature.

3   Memory Cells as an Emergent Property of the Evolution of Lymphocytes

3.1   Biological Inspiration

Each cell in our bodies can reproduce only a predefined number of times, as defined by the length of its *telomeres*, DNA sequences that 'cap' and protect the tips of our chromosomes, which are shorted each time the cell reproduces. Indeed, "... *each cycle of cell division results in a loss of 50 - 100 terminal nucleotides from the telomere end of each chromosome.*" [6]. Given this relationship one could ask, what if the degree of telomere shortening were changed in lymphocytes that match antigenic material? And what if that change were proportional to the strength of the match? In that case strongly matching immune cells would tend to survive longer than weakly matching ones. In either case they would survive considerably longer than non-matching cells.

This principle is not new in immunology—De Boer has suggested a model based on similar concepts [6]—however, it does not appear to have been considered as a memory mechanism in Artificial Immune Systems. Dutton, Bradley and Swain agree that the death rate is a vital component required in establishing robust memory. "*It stands to reason that activated cells must escape cell death if they are to go on to be memory. Thus, factors that promote the survival of otherwise death-susceptible T cells are candidates for memory factors."* [7]. We now look to see how this concept can be implemented in our model.

After an infection has been brought under control, and clonal expansion has ended, immune cells die in accordance with their *death rate*, which corresponds to the length of their telomeres. Crucially, however, cells that are a better match to the infection tend to survive longer. Various possible reasons for this may exist, for example, either because (i) their telomeres have not been shortened as much and they retain their length during reproduction, or (ii) telomerase actually lengthens the telomeres in proportion to the strength of the bind with an antigenic region. Both these possibilities will need investigation as part of our further work, but for the purposes of this paper we have assumed choice (i).

Moving on to consider different types of immune cells, there is clearly a functional difference between naïve cells and memory cells. Grayson, Harrington, Lanier, Wherry and Ahmed state that, *"... memory T cells are more resistant to apoptosis than naïve cells ... Re-exposure of memory cells to antigen through viral infection resulted in a more rapid expansion and diminished contraction compared with those of naïve cells."* [8]. This indicates memory cells would have lower death rates and higher proliferation rates, and so the cell population would naturally contract to long-lived (i.e. high-fitness) cells over time.

Moving on to consider effector or plasma cells, one possibility that has computational value is that the large majority of clonally expanded cells (i.e. effector cells) have their death rates *increased* by the suppression of telomerase for those cells that do not strongly match antigenic sites. Given the dramatic expansion of effector cells during a response, it is not feasible that the population should remain at this peak level. As a result, it is a natural assumption that telomerase suppression in effector cells would lead to high levels of apoptosis within this subset of the population, quickly returning the population size to acceptable levels. This is just an assumption and alternative explanations of telomere behaviour do exist [6,9,10] but whatever the mechanism, telomeres and telomerase influence the life-spans of immune cells.

3.2   Implementing a Preliminary Memory Cell Model

Given the analysis above, we now begin to build a simplistic model of the immune system, with varying death rates. The algorithm implemented for this purpose is detailed in Figure 1.

This model introduces a random antibody population and a specific antigen population (using a Gaussian distribution with minimal standard deviation), reflecting a particular strain of antigen that is to infect the host. The structure of each antibody and antigen are represented by points in three dimensional 'shape space', and the similarity or affinity between these entities is derived using Euclidean distance. This widely used approach has been chosen for the purpose of simplicity, due to the early stage of this research, but alternative representations will be investigated in future work.

The antigen population is considered, cell by cell, identifying the highest affinity antibody for each antigen. The affinity of the best fitting antibody and

1. Load random *Ab* population of naïve cells with low death rates.
2. Load *Ag* population.
3. Loop through each *Ag* until some termination condition:
    − Identify best fitting *Ab* to current *Ag*.
    − If affinity meets threshold criteria:
        (i) Clone parent *Ab* in proportion to bind strength;
        (ii) Mutate clones inversely proportional to bind strength;
        (iii) Mutate the death rate of the clones: those with lower death rates tending to become memory cells, and those with higher death rates tending to become effector cells.
    − Delete bound *Ab* and *Ag* from their populations.
    − For all best fitting *Ab* linked but not bound to *Ag*, mutate *Ab* inversely proportional to bind strength.
    − Initiate natural *Ab* and *Ag* reproduction.
    − Initiate apoptosis based on the death rate of each cell type.
    − Shuffle *Ag* population.
4. Print results.

Fig. 1. An algorithm for immune memory that draws on established immunological theories of immune memory to vary the death-rate of its population members.

antigen is then calculated and compared to a predetermined 'bind threshold', and if successful the current antibody will clone and proliferate. These clones then undergo mutation in an attempt to become a better fit to the antigen in question. During this process the clones differentiate into either plasma / effector cells or memory cells. Studies performed [11,12], show that after proliferation, 90% of the expanded population is eliminated, leaving a 10% memory pool. In accordance with this theory we assume that 10% of clones differentiate into memory cells. In an attempt to improve affinity and move towards a bind in the following generation, immune cells that were unsuccessful in the current bind process undergo mutation, using a Gaussian distribution, weighted by the affinity fit and the bind threshold. Antibody and antigen populations undergo natural reproduction and apoptosis, based on a death rate associated with each cell type. Finally the antigen population is randomly shuffled to prevent favourable bias occurring towards antigen located early on in the population. Preliminary results from this algorithm can be seen in Figure 2.

Figure 2 shows plots of the size of an immune cell population versus the size of an antigen population, beginning at the point of infection and continuing until several generations after the infection has been removed. The drop seen in the antibody population is entirely caused by immune cell death, and the cells that survive longest naturally tend to be those that were good matches for the infection. The reason for this is that memory cells have been created with a strong affinity to the antigen strain and these are retained over longer periods compared to other cells. These memory cells have emerged, by evolution from

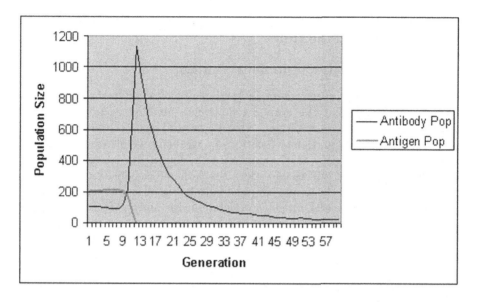

Fig. 2. Death rate alone cannot maintain a stable population of memory cells. Both prior to the immune response's activation, and after it has ended, the population size is shrinking towards zero.

the general population, without the model artificially creating and sustaining a separate memory cell sub-population on a permanent basis.

Here a 'memory cell' is simply a more evolved effector cell that happens to have developed a longer life, and each clone has the same probability of differentiating into such a memory cell. In this particular case the effectiveness of the immune response is also improved because the immune system has only experienced one antigen strain and therefore the post-infection antibody population as a whole would not have had the chance to deviate away in 'shape space' from the vicinity of the original antigen strain.

However, there is a problem. It is fairly clear from Figure 2 that the immune cell population size will eventually fall to zero, because even with a longer lifespan, all cells will eventually die. This resulting memory pool is therefore not sufficient by itself to explain the persistence of memory. This is confirmed by Harty [11] "*When only 10 percent of a small expansion population survives, that memory population might not be sufficient to help defend against the disease, or to provide long term protection.*" In reality the immune system is repopulated with naïve cells, and although naïve cells are being born continually, which can maintain a constant *overall* population size, a naïve cell cannot replace a dying memory cell's memory of an infection—at least, not without first forming an immune response. Therefore, a further mechanism is required to explain how memory cells can be retained in the long term.

4   Residual Antigen as an Emergent Property of Lymphocyte Function

4.1   Biological Theories of Residual Antigen

Several reports suggest that protein antigens can be retained in the lymph node (e.g. [13]), implying that the normal lymphocyte function cannot remove *all* traces of a particular class of antigen. This is a natural result of the immune system being focussed on particular locations in the body. Whilst most antigenic material will be cleared by the immune system, causing an immune response, some antigenic material will escape a localised immune response long enough to reproduce. In so doing, the immune system quickly establishes a steady state between immune response and antigenic population size, and the immune system's population is stimulated by the normal hypermutation response.

An alternative theory for persistent antigen suggests, *"The prevailing view is that maintenance of B cell memory ... is a function of the persistence of antigen on FDCs [follicular dendric cells] ... only a few hundred picograms of antigen are retained in the long term on FDCs, but these small amounts are sufficient to sustain durable and efficient memory response."* [1]. Either of these biological processes could provide the inspiration to allow us to preserve memory cells for the given antigen in our model, via the low level stimulation they provide.

Some may ask whether this residual antigen phenomenon may explain immune memory on its own. Perhaps we do not need to concern ourselves with death rates and telomeres, or other life prolonging measures at all? However, it does not explain why better matching cells tend to survive and worse matching cells tend to die off; nor does it explain how memory cells can naturally emerge as a result of immune cell evolution. As a result, both apoptosis-reduction via telomerase, and re-stimulation via residual antigen, are required to evolve an effective immune response.

4.2   Modelling Residual Antigen

We now modify our earlier algorithm (Figure 1) to accommodate the residual antigen effect. We do this by stimulating the immune model with a single instance of the residual antigen every n generations. Here $n = 1$, but other values are possible. Figure 3 illustrates the effect of re-stimulating the immune response in this manner, and illustrates that this process is sufficient to prevent the population of memory cells from dissipating over time.

It may seem clear that antigen persistence is important for our model, to ensure that the high affinity memory cells are sustained over long periods, but there is another related possibility. Perhaps memory cells do not need stimulation by antigen; they simply proliferate periodically. Would this represent another evolutionary step for an immune cell in order for it to differentiate into a memory cell? Grayson, Harrington, Lanier, Wherry and Ahmed identified the discrepancy between the long term behaviour of memory cells and naïve cells and state that, *"... memory cells undergo a slow homeostatic proliferation, while naïve cells*

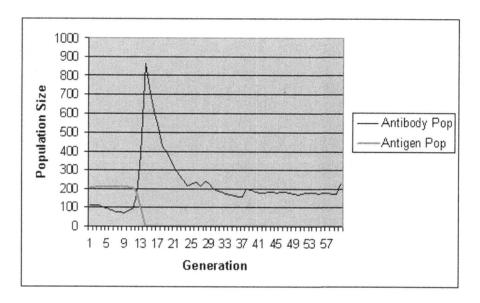

Fig. 3. In combination with the residual antigen model, the memory cell model is better able to maintain a stable population of memory cells.

undergo little or no proliferation." [8] (our emphasis). If this is the case, do memory cells actually need persistence of the antigen to survive?

Even if re-exposure is not necessary, Antia, Pilyugion and Ahmed conclude "*... estimates for the half-life of immune memory suggest that persistent antigen or repeated exposure to antigen may not be required for the maintenance of immune memory in short-lived vertebrates; however, ... repeated exposure may play an additional role in the maintenance of memory of long-lived vertebrates.*" [14]. Considering these points it appears reasonable that antigen persistence plays an important role in our model, and provides a solution to the problems highlighted in Section 3.2. For these reasons, our model, adjusted to include antigen persistence, will be used as a basis for all further investigation in this paper. Further work is proposed to repeat all experiments without antigen persistence to investigate the validity of its inclusion here.

4.3   Multiple Infections

So far we have only considered the elimination of an initial infection, but the effectiveness of the immune system is measured by its response to *repeated* exposures to different antigen strains. To examine this phenomenon, we now explore the effects of multiple infections on our model with antigen persistence.

Firstly the *same* antigen strain is reintroduced to the system (during generation 30) when the original antigen has been eliminated. The results of this re-infection can be seen in Figure 4.

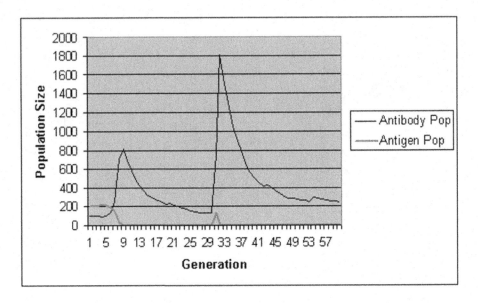

Fig. 4. Primary and secondary response phases to an antigen strain

There is a clear, characteristic secondary response, such that the antibody population increases to just over 1800 cells compared to 800 cells for the primary response. This faster, greater reaction eliminated the antigen infection within 2 generations, compared to the 8 generations required during the primary phase. Measurements were taken from generations 25 and 50 respectively, after both the infections were eliminated, and at these points the affinity of the antibody population as a whole improved from 57% to 64%, measured as the percentage of the population within 1 Euclidean distance from the antigen strain. Given the bind threshold of 1, this shows a high proportion of the population would now be able to immediately eliminate the antigen if it were to be reintroduced again. Between generations 25 and 50, the percentage of the population consisting of memory cells increased from 33% to 55%, whilst that of the effector cells remained constant at 42-43%.

It is important to consider here however that the effectiveness of the immune system is strengthened by the fact that there were no intervening alternative infections between the primary and secondary responses. As a result not only was memory retained within memory cells themselves, but also within the antibody population as a whole, as it's members converged in 'shape space' on the antigen strain. In reality this situation is unrealistic, as an immune system would be subjected to varying antigen strains over its lifetime causing the antibody population to divert away from the initial infection source. To model this behaviour we now introduce a new antigen strain to the AIS and examine the impact this has on the quality of the immune memory.

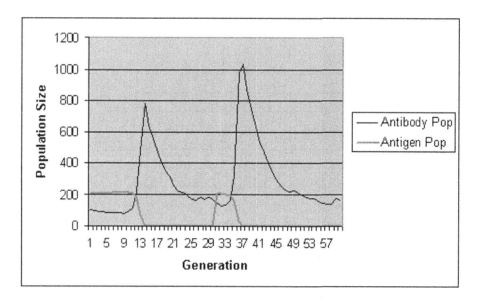

Fig. 5. Immune response to an alternative antigen strain

Figure 5 illustrates the response to an antigen infection with an alternative structure. Previously the antigen strain introduced has been represented by the element array [5.5,5.5,5.5], corresponding to a point in three dimensional 'shape space'. We now introduce a second antigen strain [3.3,3.3,3.3] at generation 30. The Euclidean distance between these two antigen is 3.81: a significant difference in 'structure', given a bind threshold of 1.0. The population trend for this new infection (the second peak) is similar to that of the original infection (the first peak). The growth in the antibody population is slightly larger by 200 cells, and it still takes time (6 generations) to eliminate the new infection. This shows that there is a clear distinction between the response to a new infection and a re-infection of an experienced antigen (Figure 4). Effectively the immune system is having to start from scratch to deal with this new infection, as it has no prior experience of this infection source.

However, this new infection has had a big impact on the affinity of the final antibody population to the original infection. It has caused the antibody population to divert away from the original infection source and converge on the new antigen, causing the percentage of the population within 1.0 Euclidean distance from the original antigen strain to decline from 32% to 25% between generations 25 and 50. More significantly at an Euclidean distance of 3.0, the percentage falls from 65% to 42%. This shows as the antibody population shifts its focus to the new infection source, the affinity to the original infection source is reduced. However the affinity is maintained at some minimal level by the memory cells still in existence from the primary response and those generated via the small scale proliferation arising from the persistent antigen in the system. An obvious

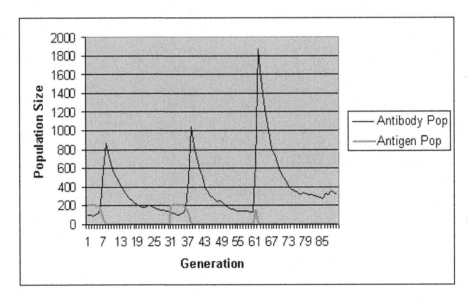

Fig. 6. Immune response to a re-infection with an intervening alternative infection

question to raise at this point is, are these limited memory cells sufficient to elicit an effective immune response given the antibody population as a whole is no longer strongly attuned to the antigen strain?

Figure 6 extends Figure 5 and reintroduces the original infection in generation 60, to model the situation where we have an intervening infection between a reoccurring infection of the same type. Even though the intervening infection diverted the antibody population away from the original infection source, a strong secondary response to the first infection is clearly evident. Here the antibody population reaches a new high of over 1800 cells, compared to the primary response of only 800. This is an identical response to that of Figure 4, thus the intermediate infection has had little impact on the effectiveness of the immune response, because the memory retained via antigen persistence is sufficient to elicit an effective immune response to the re-infection. This is clearly evident when we examine the affinity of the antibody populations during generations 25, 50 and 75, after each of the infections have been eliminated. During generation 25, 69% of the population are within 3.0 Euclidean distance of the original antigen strain, after the new infection at generation 50, this falls to 38%, but after generation 75 this rises to 89%. This shows that even when the antibody population diverts away to handle a new infection, as happens in reality, the memory cells generated via antigen persistence are sufficient to elicit an effective and successful immune response. Given these findings, an interesting experiment would be to repeatedly introduce new infections one at a time to identify the critical point at which the largest number of antigen types can be accommodated whilst still maintaining memory of the first infection. The robustness of this form of memory will be investigated in future work.

To summarise at this point, Section 4.2 indicates antigen persistence is extremely helpful in retaining knowledge of an antigen's structure. Now we have shown this antigen persistence is sufficient to elicit a secondary response from our model, over an intervening infection. Therefore antigen persistence, when combined with the earlier apoptosis reduction mechanism, does explain a form of immune memory. However, what is not clear, in this model at least, is how different immune responses interact with each other. Given the current model, each infection would lead to an immune response, and to the generation of evolved memory cells. Infections of the same strain in different locations would therefore result in a duplication of memory cells across those locations. This represents a waste of resources the immune system can ill afford, given the finite resources available. A further modification to the model will use immune network theory to explore these issues.

5   Immune Network Interactions

This third mechanism is the most well-studied in AIS: the immune network. The first study of this mechanism was undertaken by Farmer, Packard and Perelson [15]. It defined a set of dynamically changing, differential equations for the interactions that might occur between B cells if they were activated by each other, as well as by antigenic binding surfaces. They showed that a circuit of stimulation and repression could be formed that would continue even in the absence of antigenic stimulation. Recently this theory, as a biological representation, has fallen out of favour in the AIS community to some extent, and it does not seem likely that this mechanism alone can be the major source of immune memory. However, it does provide us with an alternative perspective that explains the interrelationships between immune cells that has not been considered in our model thus far, and this is its main use here.

We suggest that the main purpose of the immune network is to regulate the relationships *between* memories of infections. There is no point storing memories of several, very similar infections located in one or many alternative locations within the body, when one would cover them all. This duplication represents a waste of resources and given memory cells comprise a limited sub-set of the finite number of immune cells we have in our bodies, it is evolutionarily sensible to maximise the effect of each memory cell. Our hypothesis is that the immune network would tend to focus its suppressive effects on groups of memory cells that are similar, since this would elicit an immune(-like) response against those cells. This in turn would cause an expansion of other cells, but if those cells are not further stimulated it is likely that their offspring will not form long-lived cells and the unsuccessful strain would be eliminated. The result of this process is that the network of memory cells has been kept as lean as possible to sustain an effective immune response. At this stage this hypothesis has not been implemented, but the theoretical implications of its incorporation appear sound and reasonable. Another effect of the immune network would be to suppress *any* accumulation of immune cells, helping to quickly remove the swelled population of effector cells.

6   Conclusions

6.1   Discussion

Our study of the three basic hypotheses of immune memory is still in its infancy, but we have already demonstrated that there are several exciting possibilities. We have shown that each model, considered alone, can partially explain how the immune system can remember infections, and respond quickly to re-infections, but we have begun to demonstrate that none of them in isolation result in an effective immune memory response. It is hypothesized that when these models are combined together, a more optimal immune response is revealed, and the success of the response is dependent on the degree of interaction. We have also shown some tentative results that support our suggestions, and these are upheld by biological findings. Furthermore, there are subtleties in our findings, such as emergent memory and residual on-line training, that appear to be useful in machine learning.

6.2   Future Work

So far, this investigation has been course-grained; future work will refine the following aspects of our investigation.

- The implementation of memory will require extensive evaluation of the various possible combinations of the three memory mechanisms described in Section 2. Their relative contributions will be explored, and the results will be compared to the behaviour of the natural immune system.
- Gaussian mutation is currently used to produce the representation of new antibodies in 3D Euclidean shape space; a more biological gene library approach will be investigated, to see if it adds biological realism to the results, and machine learning usefulness to the computer science.
- The models were small scale; the next developmental step will be to increase the number of elements involved.
- Further development and investigation of the immune network model will be conducted in relation to our model to evaluate whether the theories introduced here are valid.
- Experiments will be re-performed without antigen persistence to further assess the validity of its inclusion in our model.
- Variations in death rate implementation will be investigated to represent the alternative theories of telomeres and telomerase behaviour.

The ultimate aim is to produce a model of immune memory that is useful for the prediction of immune system dynamics, and to abstract new mechanisms from that model that are computationally able to perform tasks faster, better or uniquely.

References

1. Zanetti, M., Croft, M.: Immunological memory. In: Encyclopedia of Life Sciences. (2001) http://www.els.net.
2. Timmis, J., Neal, M.J.: A resource limited artificial immune system for data analysis. In: Proceedings of ES2000, Cambridge, UK. (2000) 19–32
3. de Castro, L.N., Von Zuben, F.J.: Artificial immune systems: Part I—basic theory and applications. Technical Report DCA-RT 01/99, School of Computing and Electrical Engineering, State University of Campinas, Brazil (1999)
4. Fukuda, T., Mori, K., Tsukiyama, M.: Immune networks using genetic algorithm for adaptive production scheduling. In: 15th IFAC World Congress. Volume 3. (1993) 57–60
5. White, J.A., Garrett, S.M.: Improved pattern recognition with artificial clonal selection. In: Proceedings of the Second International Conference on Artificial Immune Systems (ICARIS-03). (2003) Springer-Verlag Lecture Notes in Computer Science No.2787, pages 181–193, Edinburgh, Sept 1st-3rd, 2003.
6. De Boer, R.J., Noest, A.J.: T cell renewal rates, telomerase, and telomere length shortening. Journal of Immunology **22** (1998) 5832–5837
7. Dutton, R.W., Bradley, L.M., Swain, S.L.: T cell memory. Ann. Rev. Immunol **16** (1998) 201–223
8. Grayson, J., Harrington, L.E., Lanier, J.G., Wherry, E.J., Ahmed, R.: Differential sensitivity to naive and memory cd8+ t cells to apoptosis in vivo. J. Immunol **169** (2002) 3760–3770
9. Yates, A., Callard, R.: Cell death and the maintenance of immunological memory. Discrete and Continuous Dynamical Systems **1** (2001) 43–59
10. N. P. Weng, L.G., Hodes, R.J.: Telomere lengthening and telomerase activation during human B cell differentaion. Immunology **94** (1997) 10827–10832
11. Harty, J.: U.I. study investigates molecular events that control immune memory (2003) Available from
http://www.uiowa.edu/ournews/2002/june/0603immune-memory.html.
12. DeNoon, D.J.: Immunology: How long will memory last (1998) AEGiS-AIDSWeekly, Available from
http://www.aegis.com/pubs/aidswkly/1998/AW981213.html.
13. Perelson, A.S., Weisbuch, G.: Immunology for physicists. Rev. Modern Phys. **69** (1997) 1219–1267
14. Antia, R., Pilyugin, S.S., Ahmed, R.: Models of immune memory: On the role of cross-reactive stimulation, competition, and homeostasis in maintaining immune memory. PNAS **95** (1998) 14926–14931
15. Farmer, J., Packard, N., Perelson, A.: The immune system, adaptation and machine learning. Physica D **22** (1986) 187–204

Immunity Through Swarms: Agent-Based Simulations of the Human Immune System

Christian Jacob[1,2], Julius Litorco[1], and Leo Lee[1]

[1] Department of Computer Science, Faculty of Science
[2] Dept. of Biochemistry and Molecular Biology, Faculty of Medicine University of Calgary, Calgary, Alberta, Canada T2N 1N4
{jacob,litorcoj}@cpsc.ucalgary.ca
http://www.cpsc.ucalgary.ca/~jacob/ESD/

Abstract. We present a swarm-based, 3-dimensional model of the human immune system and its response to first and second viral antigen exposure. Our model utilizes a decentralized swarm approach with multiple agents acting independently—following local interaction rules—to exhibit complex emergent behaviours, which constitute externally observable and measurable immune reactions. The two main functional branches of the human immune system, humoral and cell-mediated immunity, are simulated. We model the production of antibodies in response to a viral population; antibody-antigen complexes are formed, which are removed by macrophages; virally infected cells are lysed by cytotoxic T cells. Our system also demonstrates reinforced reaction to a previously encountered pathogen, thus exhibiting realistic memory response.

1 Introduction

Major advances in systems biology will increasingly be enabled by the utilization of computers as an integral research tool, leading to new interdisciplinary fields within bioinformatics, computational biology, and biological computing. Innovations in agent-based modelling, computer graphics and specialized visualization technology, such as the CAVE® Automated Virtual Environment, provide biologists with unprecedented tools for research in 'virtual laboratories' [4,8,13].

However, current models of cellular and biomolecular systems have major shortcomings regarding their usability for biological and medical research. Most models do not explicitly take into account that the measurable and observable dynamics of cellular/biomolecular systems result from the interaction of a (usually large) number of 'agents', such as cytokines, antibodies, lymphocites, or macrophages. With our agent-based models [10,17], simulations and visualizations that introduce swarm intelligence algorithms [2,5] into biomolecular and cellular systems, we develop highly visual, adaptive and user-friendly innovative research tools, which, we think, will gain a much broader acceptance in the biological and life sciences research community—thus complementing most of

G. Nicosia et al. (Eds.): ICARIS 2004, LNCS 3239, pp. 400–412, 2004.

the current, more abstract and computationally more challenging[1] mathematical and computational models [3,14]. We propose a model of the human immune system, as a highly sophisticated network of orchestrated interactions, based on relatively simple rules for each type of immune system agent. Giving these agents the freedom to interact within a confined, 3-dimensional space results in emergent behaviour patterns that resemble the cascades and feedback loops of immune system reactions.

This paper is organized as follows. In section 2, we present a brief synopsis of the immune system as it is currently understood in biology. In section 3, we discuss our agent- or swarm-based implementation of the immune system, highlighting the modelled processes and structures. Section 4 gives a step-by-step description of both simulated humoral and cell-mediated immunity in response to a viral antigen. Memory response, which we analyze in more detail in Section 5, shows the validity of our model in reaction to a second exposure to a virus. We conclude with a brief discussion of future applications of our agent-based immune system modelling environment.

2   The Immune System: A Biological Perspective

The human body must defend itself against a myriad of intruders. These intruders include potentially dangerous viruses, bacteria, and other pathogens it encounters in the air and in food and water. It must also deal with abnormal cells that have the capability to develop into cancer. Consequently, the human body has evolved two cooperative defense systems that act to counter these threats: (1) a nonspecific defense mechanism, and (2) a specific defense mechanism. The nonspecific defense mechanism does not distinguish one infectious agent from another. This nonspecific system includes two lines of defense which an invader encounters in sequence. The first line of defense is external and is comprised of epithelial tissues that cover and line our bodies (e.g., skin and mucous membranes) and their respective secretions. The second line of nonspecific defense is internal and is triggered by chemical signals. Antimicrobial proteins and phagocytic cells act as effector molecules that indiscriminately attack any invader that penetrates the body's outer barrier. Inflammation is a symptom that can result from deployment of this second line of defense.

The specific defense mechanism is better known as the *immune system* (IS), and is the key subject of our simulations. This represents the body's third line of defense against intruders and comes into play simultaneously with the second line of nonspecific defense. The characteristic that defines this defense mechanism is that it responds specifically to a particular type of invader. This immune response includes the production of antibodies as specific defensive proteins. It also involves the participation of white blood cell derivatives (lymphocytes).

---

[1] For example, many differential equation models of biological systems, such as gene regulatory networks, are very sensitive to initial conditions, result in a large number of equations, and usually require control parameters that have no direct correspondence to measurable quantities within biological systems [3].

While invaders are attacked by the inflammatory response, antimicrobial agents, and phagocytes, they inevitably come into contact with cells of the immune system, which mount a defense against specific invaders by developing a particular response against each type of foreign microbe, toxin, or transplanted tissue.

2.1   Humoral Immunity and Cell-Mediated Immunity

The immune system mounts two different types of responses to antigens — humoral response and cell-mediated response (Fig. 1). *Humoral immunity* results in the production of antibodies through plasma cells. The antibodies circulate as soluble proteins in blood plasma and lymph. *Cell-mediated immunity* depends upon the direct action of certain types of lymphocytes rather than antibodies. The circulating antibodies of the humoral response defend mainly against toxins, free bacteria, and viruses present in body fluids. In contrast, lymphocytes of the cell-mediated response are active against bacteria and viruses inside the host's cells. Cell-mediated immunity is also involved in attacks on transplanted tissue and cancer cells, both of which are perceived as non-self.

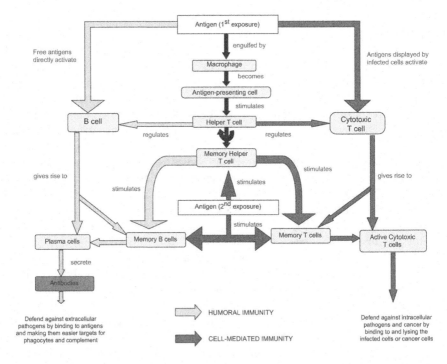

Fig. 1. Schematic summary of immune system agents and their interactions in response to a first and second antigen exposure. The humoral and cell-mediated immunity interaction networks are shown on the left and right, respectively. Both immunity responses are mostly mediated and regulated by macrophages and helper T cells.

2.2   Cells of the Immune System

There are two main classes of lymphocytes: B cells, which are involved in the humoral immune response, and T cells, which are involved in the cell-mediated immune response. Lymphocytes, like all blood cells, originate from pluripotent stem cells in the bone marrow. Initially, all lymphocytes are alike but eventually differentiate into the T cells or B cells. Lymphocytes that mature in the bone marrow become B cells, while those that migrate to the thymus develop into T cells. Mature B and T cells are concentrated in the lymph nodes, spleen and other lymphatic organs where the lymphocytes are most likely to encounter antigens. Both B and T cells are equipped with antigen receptors on their plasma membranes. When an antigen binds to a receptor on the surface of a lymphocyte, the lymphocyte is activated and begins to divide and differentiate. This gives rise to effector cells, the cells that actually defend the body in an immune response. With respect to the humoral response, B cells activated by antigen binding give rise to plasma cells that secrete antibodies, which help eliminate a particular antigen (Fig. 1, left side). Cell-mediated response, however, involves cytotoxic T cells (killer T cells) and helper T cells. Cytotoxic T cells kill infected cells and cancer cells. Helper T cells, on the other hand, secrete protein factors (cytokines), which are regulatory molecules that affect neighbouring cells. More specifically, through helper T cells cytokines regulate the reproduction and actions of both B cells and T cells and therefore play a pivotal role in both humoral and cell-mediated responses. Our immune system model incorporates most of these antibody-antigen and cell-cell interactions.

2.3   Antigen-Antibody Interaction

Antigens are mostly composed of proteins or large polysaccharides. These molecules are often outer components of the coats of viruses, and the capsules and cell walls of bacteria. Antibodies do not generally recognize an antigen as a whole molecule. Rather, they identify a localized region on the surface of an antigen called an antigenic determinant or epitope. A single antigen may have several effective epitopes thereby stimulating several different B cells to make distinct antibodies against it. Antibodies constitute a class of proteins called immunoglobulins.

An antibody does not usually destroy an antigen directly. The binding of antibodies to antigens to form an antigen-antibody complex is the basis of several effector mechanisms. Neutralization is the most common and simplest form of inactivation because the antibody blocks viral binding sites. The antibody will neutralize a virus by attaching to the sites that the virus requires in order to bind to its host cell. Eventually, phagocytic cells destroy the antigen-antibody complex. This effector mechanism is part of our simulation.[2]

---

[2] Another effector mechanism is the *agglutination* or clumping of antigens by antibodies. The clumps are easier for phagocytic cells to engulf than are single bacteria. A similar mechanism is *precipitation* of soluble antigens through the cross-linking of

One of the most important effector mechanisms of the humoral responses is the activation of the *complement* system by antigen-antibody complexes. The complement system is a group of proteins that acts cooperatively with elements of the nonspecific and specific defense systems. Antibodies often combine with complement proteins, activating the complement proteins to produce lesions in the antigenic membrane, thereby causing lysis of the cell. *Opsonization* is a variation on this scheme whereby complement proteins or antibodies will attach to foreign cells and thereby stimulate phagocytes to ingest those cells. Cooperation between antibodies and complement proteins with phagocytes, opsonization, and activation of the complement system is simulated in our IS model.

Another important cooperative process occurs with macrophages. Macrophages do not specifically target an antigen but are directly involved in the humoral process which produces the antibodies that will act upon a specific antigen. A macrophage that has engulfed an antigen will present it to a helper T cell. This activates the helper T cell which in turn causes B cells to divide and differentiate through cytokines. A clone of memory B cells, plasma cells, and secreted antibodies will be produced as a result (Fig. 1, bottom left). These aspects are also part of our IS model, which is described in the following section.

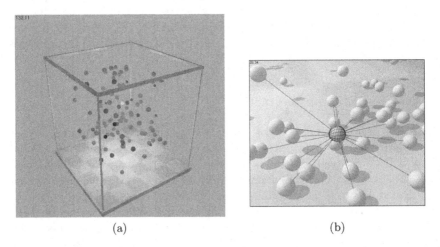

(a)   (b)

Fig. 2. Interaction space for immune system agents: (a) All interactions between immune system agents are simulated in a confined 3-dimensional space. (b) Actions for each agent are triggered either by direct collision among agents or by the agent concentrations within an agent's spherical neighbourhood space. Lines illustrate which cells are considered neighbours with respect to the highlighted cell.

---

numerous antigens to form immobile precipitates that are captured by phagocytes. This aspect is not yet built into our current IS model.

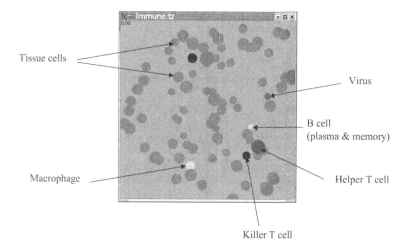

Tissue cells

Virus

B cell
(plasma & memory)

Macrophage

Helper T cell

Killer T cell

Fig. 3. The immune system agents as simulated in 3D space: tissue cells (light blue), viruses (red), macrophages (yellow), killer T cells (blue), helper T cells (purple), plasma and memory B cells (green).

3   A Biomolecular Swarm Model

Our computer implementation[3] of the immune system and its visualization incorporates a swarm-based approach with a 3D visualization (Fig. 2a), where we use modeling techniques similar to our other agent-based simulations of bacterial chemotaxis, the lambda switch, and the lactose operon [4,8,9,13]. Each individual element in the IS simulation is represented as an independent agent governed by (usually simple) rules of interaction. While executing specific actions when colliding with or getting close to other agents, the dynamic elements in the system move randomly in continuous, 3-dimensional space. This is different to other IS simulation counter parts, such as the discrete, 2D cellular automaton-based versions of IMMSIM [6,11]. As illustrated in Figure 3, we represent immune system agents as spheres of different sizes and colours. Each agent keeps track of other agents in the vicinity of its neighbourhood space, which is defined as a sphere with a specific radius. Each agent's next-action step is triggered depending on the types and numbers of agents within this local interaction space (Fig. 2b).

Confining all IS agents within a volume does, of course, not take into account that the actual immune system is spread out through a complicated network within the human body, including tonsils, spleen, lymph nodes, and bone marrow; neither do we currently—for the sake of keeping our model computationally manageable—incorporate the exchange of particles between the lymphatic vessels, blood capillaries, intestinal fluids, and tissue cells.

Each agent follows a set of rules that define its actions within the system. As an example, we show the (much simplified) behaviours of macrophages and B

---

[3] We use the BREVE physics-based, multi-agent simulation engine [16].

Table 1. Simplified rules governing the behaviours of macrophages and B cells as examples of immune system agents.

Macrophage	B Cell
| ```
if collision with virus:
    if virus is opsonized:
        Kill virus.
    else:
        Kill virus with prob. p.
    Create new macrophage.

if collision with tissue cell:
    if cell is infected:
        if sufficient macrophages:
            Create new B cell.
        Create new macrophage.
``` | ```
state = passive.
if collision with virus:
    state = active.

if collision with virus & active:
    Increment vir-collision counter.
    if vir-collision counter > TH:
        if enough helper T cells:
            Secrete antibodies.
            Create new B cell.
``` |

cells in Table 1. The simulation system provides each agent with basic services, such as the ability to move, rotate, and determine the presence and position of other agents. A scheduler implements time slicing by invoking each agent's Iterate method, which executes a specific, context-dependent action. These actions are based on the agent's current state, and the state of other agents in its vicinity. Consequently, our simulated agents work in a decentralized fashion with no central control unit to govern the interactions of the agents.

4   Immune Response After Exposure to a Viral Antigen

We will now describe the evolution of our simulated immune response after the system is exposed to a viral antigen. Figure 4 illustrates key stages during the simulation. The simulation starts with 80 tissue cells (light blue), two killer T cells (dark blue), a macrophage (yellow), a helper T cell (purple), and a naive B cell (light green). In order to trigger the immune system responses, five viruses (red) are introduced into the simulation space (Fig. 4b). The viruses start infecting tissue cells, which turn red and signal their state of infection by going from light to dark red (Fig. 4c). The viruses replicate inside the infected cells, which eventually lyse and release new copies of the viruses, which, in turn, infect more and more of the tissue cells (Fig. 4d). The increasing concentration of viral antigens and infected tissue cells triggers the reproduction of macrophages (yellow), which consequently stimulate helper T cells (purple) to divide faster (Fig. 4e; also compare Fig. 1). The higher concentration of helper T cells then stimulates more B cells (green) and cytotoxic T cells (killer T cells; dark blue) to become active (Fig. 4f). Whenever active B cells collide with a viral antigen, they produce plasma and memory B cells (dark green) and release antibodies

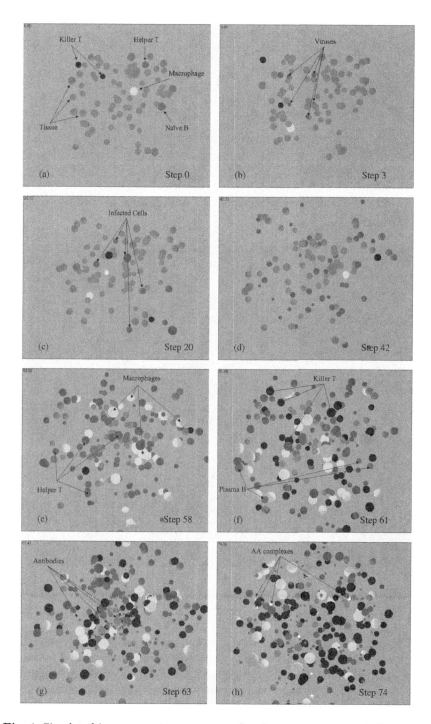

Fig. 4. Simulated immune system response after first exposure to a viral antigen.

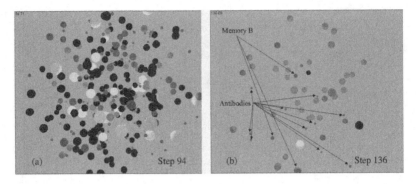

Fig. 5. Simulated immune system response after first exposure to a viral antigen (continued from Fig. 4).

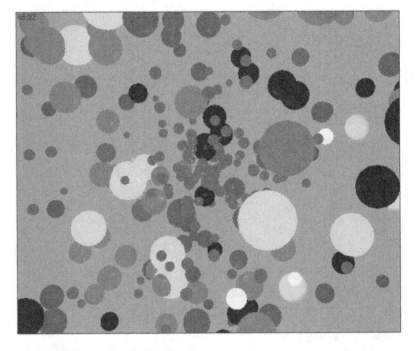

Fig. 6. Release of antibodies after collision of an activated B cell with a viral antigen.

(small green; Fig. 4g). Figure 6 shows a closeup with an antibody-releasing B cell in the center. Viruses that collide with antibodies are opsonized by forming antigen-antibody complexes (white; Fig. 4h), which labels viruses for elimination by macrophages and prevents them from infecting tissue cells. Eventually, all viruses and infected cells have been eliminated (Fig. 5a), with a large number of helper and cytotoxic T cells, macrophages, and antibodies remaining. As all IS agents are assigned a specific life time, the immune system will eventually restore

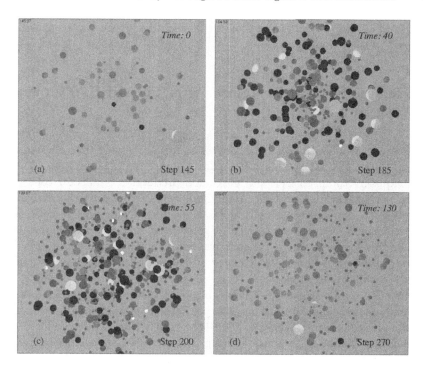

Fig. 7. Faster and more intense response after second exposure to viral antigens. (a) Five viruses are inserted into the system, continuing from Step 136 after the first exposure (Fig. 5b). (b) The production of antibodies now starts earlier (at $time = 40$, instead of $time = 60$ for the first antigen exposure). (c) Five times more antibodies are released compared to the first exposure. (d) After 130 time steps the system falls back into a resting state, now with a 10- to 12-fold higher level of antibodies (compare Fig. 8) and newly formed memory B cells. The time steps in the top right corners make it easier to see the increased progression speed of the immune response as compared to the first viral exposure in Figure 4.

to its initial state, but now with a reservoir of antibodies, which are prepared to fight a second exposure to the now 'memorized' viral antigen (Fig. 5b).

The described interactions among the immune system agents are summarized in Figure 8a, which shows the number of viruses and antibodies as they evolve during the simulated humoral and cell-mediated immune response. This graph is the standard way of characterizing specificity and memory in adaptive immunity [1,7,12,15]. After the first antigen exposure the viruses are starting to get eliminated around iteration $time = 50$, and have vanished from the system at $time = 100$. The number of antibodies decreases between time step 50 and 100 due to the forming of antigen-antibody complexes, which are eliminated by macrophages. Infected tissue cells are lysed by cytotoxic T cells, which delete all cell-internal viruses. After all viruses have been fought off, a small amount of antibodies remains in the system, which will help to trigger a more intense and faster immune response after a second exposure to the same antigen, which is described in the following section.

5   Immune System Response After Second Exposure to Antigen

The selective proliferation of lymphocytes to form clones of effector cells upon first exposure to an antigen constitutes the primary immune response. Between initial exposure to an antigen and maximum production of effector cells, there is a lag period. During this time, the lymphocytes selected by the antigen are differentiating into effector T cells and antibody-producing plasma cells. If the body is exposed to the same antigen at some later time, the response is faster and more prolonged than the primary response. This phenomenon is called the secondary immune response, which we will demonstrate through our simulated immune system model (Fig. 8b).

The immune system's ability to recognize a previously encountered antigen is called immunological memory. This ability is contingent upon long-lived memory cells. These cells are produced along with the relatively short-lived effector cells of the primary immune response. During the primary response, these memory cells are not active. They do, however, survive for long periods of time and proliferate rapidly when exposed to the same antigen again. The secondary immune response gives rise to a new clone of memory cells as well as to new effector cells.

Figure 7 shows a continuation of the immune response simulation of Figure 5b. About 10 time steps later, we introduce five copies of the same virus the system encountered previously. Each virus, which is introduced into the system, receives a random signature $s \in [0, 10]$. We keep track of all viruses inserted into the system and can thus reinsert any previous virus, for which antibodies have been formed. Once memory B cells collide with a virus, they produce antibodies with the same signature, so that those antibodies will only respond to this specific virus. Consequently, after a second exposure to the same viral antigen at $t = 145$, the highest concentration of antibodies is increased by five times (to about 250), only after a lag time of 25 steps (Fig. 8b). Consequently, the virus is eliminated much faster, as more antigen-antibody complexes are formed, which get eliminated quickly by the also increased number of macrophages. Additionally, an increased number of helper and killer T cells contributes to a more effective removal of infected cells (Fig. 7). Not even half the number of viruses can now proliferate through the system, compared to the virus count during the first exposure. After the complete elimination of all viruses, ten to fifteen times more antibodies (about 130) remain in the system after this second exposure. This demonstrates that our agent-based model—through emergent behaviour resulting from agent-specific, local interaction rules—is capable of simulating key aspects of both humoral and cell mediated immune responses.

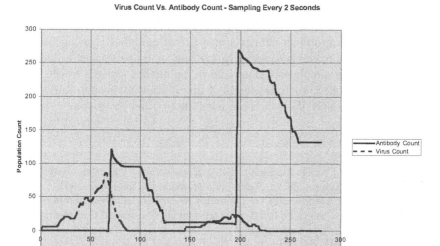

Fig. 8. Immunological Memory: The graph shows the simulated humoral immunity response reflected in the number of viruses and antibodies after a first and second exposure to a viral antigen. (a) During the viral antigen exposure the virus is starting to get eliminated around iteration $time = 70$, and has vanished from the system at $time = 90$. The number of antibodies decreases between time step 70 and 125 due to the forming of antigen-antibody complexes, which are then eliminated by macrophages. A small amount of antibodies (10) remains in the system. (b) After a second exposure to the viral antigen at $t = 145$, the antibody production is increased in less than 50 time steps. Consequently, the virus is eliminated more quickly. About 13 times more antibodies (130) remain in the system after this second exposure.

6   Conclusions and Future Research

From our collaborations with biological and medical researchers, we are more and more convinced that a decentralized swarm approach to modelling the immune system closely approximates the way in which biologists view and think about living systems. Although our simulations have so far only been tested for a relatively small number of (hundreds of) interacting agents, the system is currently being expanded to handle a much larger number of immune system agents and other biomolecular entities (such as cytokines), thus getting closer to more accurate simulations of massively-parallel interaction processes among cells that involve hundreds of thousands of particles. Our visualizations, developed as a 2D projection on a normal computer screen are further enhanced through stereoscopic 3D in a CAVE® immersive environment, as we have already done for a simulation of the lactose operon gene regulatory system [4]. On the other hand, we are also investigating in how far noise and the number of biomolecular and cell agents actually affect the emergent behaviour patterns, which we observe in our simulations and can be measured *in vivo* in wet-lab experiments.

A swarm-based approach affords a measure of modularity, as agents can be added and removed from the system. In addition, completely new agents can be introduced into the simulation. This allows for further aspects of the immune system to be modelled, such as effects of immunization through antibiotics or studies of proviruses (HIV), which are invisible to other IS agents.

References

1. A. K. Abbas and A. H. Lichtman. *Basic Immunology - Functions and Disorders of the Immune System*. W. B. Saunders Company, Philadelphia, 2001.
2. E. Bonabeau, M. Dorigo, and G. Theraulaz. *Swarm Intelligence: From Natural to Artificial Systems*. Santa Fe Institute Studies in the Sciences of Complexity. Oxford University Press, New York, 1999.
3. J. M. Bower and H. Bolouri, editors. *Computational Modeling of Genetic and Biochemical Networks*. MIT Press, Cambridge, MA, 2001.
4. I. Burleigh, G. Suen, and C. Jacob. Dna in action! a 3d swarm-based model of a gene regulatory system. In *ACAL 2003, First Australian Conference on Artificial Life*, Canberra, Australia, 2003.
5. S. Camazine, J.-L. Deneubourg, N. R. Franks, J. Sneyd, G. Theraulaz, and E. Bonabeau. *Self-Organization in Biological Systems*. Princeton Studies in Complexity. Princeton University Press, Princeton, 2003.
6. F. Castiglione, G. Mannella, S. Motta, and G. Nicosia. A network of cellular automata for the simulation of the immune system. *International Journal of Modern Physics C*, 10(4):677–686, 1999.
7. J. Clancy. *Basic Concepts in Immunology - A Student's Survival Guide*. McGraw-Hill, New York, 1998.
8. R. Hoar, J. Penner, and C. Jacob. Transcription and evolution of a virtual bacteria culture. In *Congress on Evolutionary Computation*, Canberra, Australia, 2003. IEEE Press.
9. C. Jacob and I. Burleigh. Biomolecular swarms: An agent-based model of the lactose operon. *Natural Computing*, 2004. (in print).
10. S. Johnson. *Emergence: The Connected Lives of Ants, Brains, Cities, and Software*. Scribner, New York, 2001.
11. S. H. Kleinstein and P. E. Seiden. Simulating the immune system. *Computing in Science & Engineering*, (July/August):69–77, 2000.
12. P. Parham. *The Immune System*. Garland Publishing, New York, 2000.
13. J. Penner, R. Hoar, and C. Jacob. Bacterial chemotaxis in silico. In *ACAL 2003, First Australian Conference on Artificial Life*, Canberra, Australia, 2003.
14. S.L. Salzberg, D.B. Searls, and S. Kasif, editors. *Computational Methods in Molecular Biology, volume 32 of New Comprehensive Biochemistry*. Elsevier, Amsterdam, 1998.
15. L. Sompayrac. *How the Immune System Works*. Blackwell Science, London, 1999.
16. L. Spector, J. Klein, C. Perry, and M. Feinstein. Emergence of collective behavior in evolving populations of flying agents. In E. Cantu-Paz et al., editor, *Genetic and Evolutionary Computation Conference (GECCO-2003)*, pages 61–73, Chicago, IL, 2003. Springer-Verlag.
17. S. Wolfram. *A New Kind of Science*. Wolfram Media, Champaign, IL, 2002.

Studies on the Implications of Shape-Space Models for Idiotypic Networks

Emma Hart and Peter Ross

Napier University, Scotland, UK
{e.hart,p.ross}@napier.ac.uk

Abstract. Despite the flood of practical work in the AIS area over the past few years, unlike in other fields derived from biological paradigms, there has yet to emerge a concise view of what an artificial immune system actually is, although most interpretations of the metaphor possess a set of common elements. In this conceptual paper, we argue that one of the components of an AIS algorithm that most distinguishes it from other paradigms is the matching aspect (although memory, as argued by [9], is clearly also a defining feature of AIS algorithms). However, for the most part, the implications of choosing a suitable matching rule and the likely effects on the algorithm from an engineering point of view have not been well studied. We present some results obtained using freely available software that simulates an idiotypic network with various models of shape-space, in the hope of illustrating the importance of selecting a suitable shape-space and matching rule in *practical* implementations of AISs. We raise some interesting questions and encourage others to experiment with the tool also in order to better understand the performance of their algorithms and to be able to design better ones.

1 Introduction

The field of AIS, although vibrant and productive, is relatively young when compared against more established biological metaphors such as evolutionary algorithms or neural networks. Examining the literature reveals a wide variety of interpretations of what an AIS actually is, and an equally wide variety of application domains to which it has been applied. Recently, attempts have been made to unify the field, for example [11] who attempt to introduce a common architecture, and by [5] who provide a general-purpose framework for engineering an AIS. This frame work is shown in figure 1, taken from [5] and expanded to show some possible components of each layer. We argue that many of the processes found in the Representation Layer and Immune Algorithm layer bear considerable resemblance to other algorithms and it is the Affinity Layer that really distinguishes the AIS from its competitors. For example, clonal selection algorithms show strong resemblances to classifier systems, which use the notion of strength to decide which classifier is selected to fire, and also to the selection methods of some variants of evolutionary algorithms (although admittedly the classical EA does not tend to make multiple copies of candidate solutions during

G. Nicosia et al. (Eds.): ICARIS 2004, LNCS 3239, pp. 413–426, 2004.

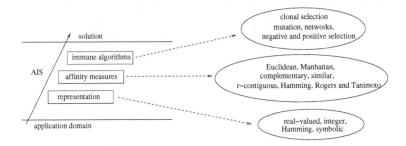

Fig. 1. The AIS framework proposed by De Castro and Timmis

selection). Mutation is also a common component of evolutionary algorithms, and all paradigms have an issue with representation. This paper therefore concerns the role played by the affinity measure layer, and suggests that much of the effort of designing an AIS ought to be directed at getting this component right — we present the results of some simulations which illustrate the impact that this layer can have. The paper is organised as follows: first we briefly review the concept of shape-space and its relevance for idiotypic network models. A shape-space simulator is then described, and then we present the results of three sets of experiments using different shape-space models in an idiotypic network. The experiments lead to a number of interesting observations, most of which are as yet unexplained. We hope that in the foreseeable future, providing answers to these questions will lead to a better understanding of AIS that not only places the field on a more solid scientific foundation but also leads to the design of better algorithms. Note that although the observations presented are gleaned from simulating an idiotypic immune network, the general principles have implications for all AIS algorithms, as according to the framework, all implement an affinity-measure layer of one kind or another. The type of matching used has a direct impact on the performance of the algorithm. Previous studies have considered the impact of choice of matching rule in negative-selection algorithms (e.g. [8]), but there has been little work involving other forms of AIS algorithm. Note also that this work concerns the practical implementation of AIS algorithms and does not suppose to offer any insight into theoretical immunology.

2   The Notion of Shape-Space

The biological immune system consists of lymphocyte cells (producing antibodies) which respond to pathogenic molecules (antigens) — the notion of shape-space was introduced by Perelson and Oster [13] in order to provide a formal model which quantitatively described the interactions between these molecules. The model is based on the classical "lock and key" analogy that two molecules can bind together if they contain sufficient complementary shaped regions on their surfaces to allow the molecules to "fit" together; in reality the molecules are bound by electrostatic and other interactions as a result of the chemical groups and charge distributions arranged on the surface of the molecules which effectively comprise their shape. Assuming an antibody can be described by a set of L parameters (for example denoting the width, height, and charge on a combining site), then a point in a L-dimensional shape-space will specify the generalised shape of an antigen that can bind to the antibody in question, [5]. Thus, mathematically speaking, the generalised shape of an molecule can be represented by a vector of L attributes, where the attributes themselves can be real-valued, integers, binary, symbols, or a combination, depending on the application. If the shape of an antigen is also represented by another vector of length L, then a degree of affinity can be calculated for any antibody-antigen pair by defining a measure of distance between the two vectors.

2.1   Applying Shape-Space Ideas to AIS

This is actually a somewhat simplified picture of binding between real molecules. In reality, antibodies exhibit special binding sites called *paratopes* which bind to complementary *epitopes* on the antigen molecules. Furthermore, in a somewhat controversial view, Jerne [12] suggested that antibodies can also display epitopes, which permits binding between the paratope of one antibody and the epitope of another, resulting in an *idiotypic* network. Using the shape-space model defined above, many successful AIS applications have been produced, however it useful to note the following general points about the methods in which biological cells perform recognition which are rarely, if ever, modelled in practical AIS applications, and yet can have far-reaching impacts.

1. *Epitopes are not paratopes*
   Most AIS models tend to simplify the epitopes and paratopes of a molecule into a single vector — this is coined the Single Vector Assumption (SVA) by Garret [7], who addresses some of the implications of this in his recent paper. In fact, one of the seminal works in this area by Farmer [6] did use binary vectors which contained distinct paratopes and epitopes but his approach has generally not been adopted. One of the striking observations of this simplification is that if some molecule x has an affinity a with another molecule y, then the reciprocal situation is also true, i.e. y also has an affinity a with x. This is not typically the case for real molecules.

2. *Molecules can contain multiple epitopes and/or paratopes*
   The SVA also implies that molecules have a single binding site; in reality, an antibody may have multiple paratopes and epitopes, thus leading to the possibility of it binding to several different, antigens and antibodies at the same time. This will impact the dynamics of any resulting network, for example, a molecule binding to both an antigen and another antibody of similar type of the antigen will increase the rate of eradication of the antigen [7].

3. *Complementarity is not the same as Similarity*
   Although in the biological immune system, affinity between two molecules arises due to the presence of complementary regions between the molecules,

in many AIS applications, e.g [15] this is inverted in that a measure of similarity is instead defined between two vectors, which then determines the interactions. Surprisingly, this seems to have little effect. It appears most commonly in applications which use real-valued vector representations; in cases where binary representations are used, complementary matching is observed, as it is perhaps more obvious how this can be implemented (e.g. [4,10]).

In the remainder of this paper, we describe some simulations using an idiotypic network which try to analyse the effects of making some of the above decisions in order to better understand *why* the manner in which shape-space is defined affects the behaviour of systems, and how we as engineers, can alter the behaviour of such systems to suit our own purposes.

3   A Simulated Idiotypic Network

Varela and Coutinho [16] and later Bersini [2] proposed a radical interpretation of the idiotypic network discussed above in which a self-sustaining autonomous network can be produced even in the absence of any antigenic activity. In such a network, the boundaries separating cells that are tolerated from those that are not tolerated (i.e. pathogens in the classical view) are entirely self-defined by the activity of the network, and not by any pre-categorization of cells into distinct types. The software we describe is based on code kindly provided to us by Bersini [1] which had been used in for example [2] in order to illustrate their claims about self-assertive networks. The code has been re-written in C++ and considerably extended in order to be able to analyse the resulting networks, and provide alternative models of shape-space. It is freely available from [14]. The following section describes the algorithm used in the simulator.

3.1   Cell Dynamics

Assume that cells (i.e antibodies) are randomly recruited to points on a 2-D grid of size 100x100. One new cell P is created at each iteration, placed randomly and with initial concentration of $P_c = 10$. Then, at each cycle, the total affinity P_a of each cell is calculated as follows. If the cell P is at (x, y), then the contents of a region S of radius r centered at the complementary point $Q = (100 - x, 100 - y)$ are deemed to be an adequately close complement to the cell and influence the value of P_a as follows:

$$P_a = \sum_{\text{antigens } A \in S} A_c(r - ||A - Q||) \qquad \text{or}$$

$$P_a = \sum_{\text{antigens } A \in S} A_c(r - ||A - Q||) + \sum_{\text{cells } E \in S} E_c(r - ||E - Q||)$$

depending on whether the user chooses to let cells 'see' just antigens or both cells and antigens in the complementary region. Thus, antigens (and maybe cells) closest to the centre of the complementary region have potentially much more effect on the affinity than those close to the edge of the region.

If a cell P's total affinity P_a satisfies $L \leq P_a \leq U$ then its concentration is increased by 1, otherwise it is decreased by 1 (Bersini used $L = 100, U = 10,000$). A cell dies, and is removed, if its concentration falls to 0.

This means that if there is a reasonable, but not excessive, amount and concentration of antigens and (maybe) cells, in the complementary region the cell's concentration rises. If the complementary region contains too much or too little, the cell's concentration falls.

3.2   Antigen Dynamics

During the simulation, antigens are created by the user. A newly-created antigen has an initial concentration A_c of 1000. At each cycle, the total affinity A_a of an antigen A at (x, y) is computed in a somewhat similar way by looking at the cells in the complementary region S centered at the complementary point $B = (100 - x, 100 - y)$:

$$A_a = \sum_{\text{cells } E \in S} E_c(r - ||E - B||)$$

If $A_a \leq L$ the concentration of A is unaffected, but if $A_c > L$ then the concentration decreases by an amount $A_c/(100L)$. If the concentration falls to 0 the antigen dies and is removed. Thus, antigens never *increase* in concentration, their concentration either stays the same, or decreases. This means that if the amount and concentration of cells in the complementary region is low, the antigen survives; but if the amount and concentration of cells in that region is high enough, the antigen starts to die.

3.3   Software

In the simulation software, each cells computes the total compatibility it receives; if this lies between a lower limit (default 100) and upper limit (default 10000) its concentration increases, otherwise it decreases. A cell's concentration is represented as a shade of grey, from dark to white. Various refinements allow specific details of the simulation to be examined at any point in the simulation:

- Antigens can be added by the user and as with network-cells, are shaded to represent concentration.
- Limits can be interactively modified during the simulation
- Antigens can be forcibly removed from the system
- The boundary of the complementary-region of any individual cell can be displayed. These boundaries are provided to attempt to understand why the frontiers that appear in the simulation have the shape that they do.
- Simulations can either be seeded randomly from the clock, or started with a given seed to aid demonstrations.

These features are detailed in full in a document accompanying the software, [14].

4   Some Simulation Results

In this section, some results of simulations using various shape-space model are presented. First, results using the shape-space model depicted in figure 2 are given. Note that the work in this section is essentially a replication of Bersini's original work from [2]. However, a number of additional interesting observations are made which raise pertinent questions not addressed by Bersini. Following this, two additional novel shape-space models are examined with the simulator: the first of which models the possibility of cells containing multiples binding sites, and the second considers the implications of non-symmetrical complementary regions.

Note that unless specifically noted, in the following experiments, the simulations are in absence of antigens, therefore the networks formed are entirely self-assertive. In several cases however, antigens have been added to the diagrams when the simulator is not actually running in order to illustrate the different tolerant zones (i.e in which antigens can persist) and reactive zones (in which antigens rapidly die) that form. Unless otherwise stated, the threshold limits remain fixed at values of 100 and 10000. The grid is always of size 100x100 and a fixed radius of 15 is used for the radius of the complementary regions, whatever their shape, for consistency. The screen shots have been edited and annotated from those originally captured in order to ensure they are reproducible in print.

4.1   Model 1: The Basic Shape-Space Model

The first shape-space model used in the simulation is a simple 2-D shape-space model, in which an immune cell is represented by a point on a 2-D grid, and is considered to exert an affinity in some zone which lies in a complementary region

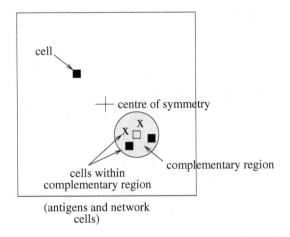

Fig. 2. A Cell, and its complementary region of affinity

of the space. In the simplest case, in practice, this means that the zone of affinity of cell x lies in the symmetrical space centered on the reflection of x, i.e x'. The zone of affinity extends around the reflected point x' within a region of radius R, as illustrated in figure 2. Note that this model suffers from the drawbacks mentioned previously, i.e. it effectively utilises a single binding site and implies a mutual recognition between two cells, i.e if A recognises B then B recognises A. Using Model 1, the following observations are made:

Observation 1: Tolerant and non-tolerant zones emerge that are not pre-determined. Figure 3 show the results of several different simulations. In these simulations, antigens, marked as circles, are clearly tolerated in certain regions of the space. These regions vary in shape and position across simulations. Recall that an antigen will decrease in concentration if it is bound by sufficient network cells. Figure 3(d) illustrates the matching region of tolerated antigens:- clearly no network cells exist in these regions. In contrast, figure 3(e) shows the matching region of an antigen placed in a non-tolerated zone just before it is eliminated from the system. In this case, it is clear that a number of network cells exist within the region that allow it to be eliminated. Furthermore, these figures illustrate the result of several different simulations which clearly emphasises the fact that the tolerated and non-tolerated region emerge solely from the system dynamics. As noted by Bersini in his original paper, this is qualitatively in agreement with the clonal selection theory of [3] which suggests that the emergence of zones reflects the history of the system: if recruitment initially favoured some zone X, then this zone will tend to become tolerant.

Observation 2: The zones are unsymmetrical. Figure 3 also shows that the zones are unsymmetrical in nature, despite the symmetrical nature of the stimulation function. Again, as noted by Bersini, this is simply an artifact of the random nature of the system.

Observation 3: The boundaries are generally lines. Note that for the threshold limits given above, the boundaries between regions are always narrow *lines*, effectively one cell wide. Despite running numerous simulations, boundaries consisting of closely-related clustered cells never emerge. Experimentation shows that by altering the value of the upper limit, then wider boundaries emerge (see figure 4 which shows 3 experiments run from the same seed but with increasing upper bounds on the stimulation level), and the networks take longer to stabilise — however the general shape of the boundaries remains consistent across all experiments. Understanding this properly seems an important issue for AIS research.

Observation 4: The set of cells S that lie in the complementary region of any persistent cell x lying on a zone-boundary occur only around the boundaries of the complementary region of x. A further interesting observation can be seen by examining figure 3(c). If we use the simulator to examine the matching regions of cells occurring on the zone-boundary, it can be seen that the persistent cells

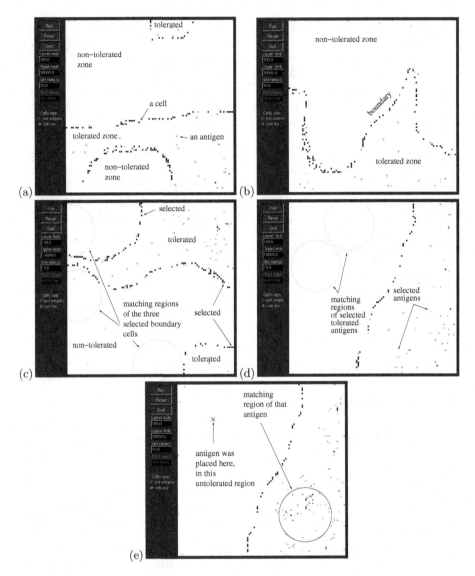

Fig. 3. Simulation results using shape-space model 1

that fall within this region occur *only* close to the boundaries of the matching region, and therefore also on the zone-boundary. This result is consistent for a variety of threshold limits, i.e. even when the boundaries are several cells thick.

Recall that the stimulation received by some cell x from another cell y is proportional to the distance between y and the complement x' of x — x receives maximum stimulation from those cells closest to x' and minimum stimulation from those on the boundary of its complementary region. Yet, the simulations

Upper limit = 10,000   Upper limit = 17,500   Upper limit = 50,000

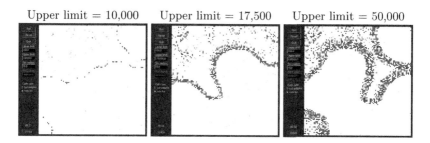

Fig. 4. Simulations in which the upper bound on stimulation level is varied. The figures show snapshots of simulations starting from the same seed after 10000 iterations

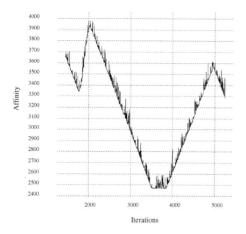

Fig. 5. The affinity of one long-lived cell

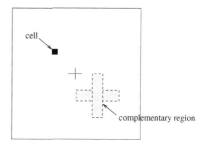

Fig. 6. A Complementary Region which models multiple binding sites

show that it is those cells on the boundaries that persist. A cell only increases in concentration if its total stimulation lies *between* an upper and lower limit. It appears that cells in the centre of the complementary region would cause so much stimulation to x that its concentration is driven above the upper threshold, thus causing its concentration to decrease. Clearly, a balancing act exist which must result in just sufficient stimulation for a cells concentration to remain between the thresholds. Figure 5 shows a plot of the affinity for a chosen long-lived cell over several thousand iterations, starting from the cell's creation. The 'noise' arises from short-lived randomly-created cells; the see-saw appears to be due to the waxing and waning of other long-lived cells.

Observation 5: The emergence of stable regions is dependent on the size of the recognition radius. Experiments in which the recognition radius is varied shows that stable regions and boundaries only emerge readily when the recognition radius is large enough, which in these experiments means a value of 10 or greater. This is plausible; if the complementary region is small, fewer cells will be created by chance within it to 'fan the flames' (as it were) to encourage the development of a long-lived cell. However, the transition (as the radius is increased) between a regime in which it takes a long time to form stable regions and a regime in which such regions form easily, is quite sharp. There appears to be a 'critical sand-pile' effect at work; long-lived cells encourage each other.

4.2   Model 2: Incorporating Multiple Binding Sites

Our second shape-space model attempts to include the notion of an antibody containing multiple binding sites. In this case, the complementary region of antibody is defined as shown in figure 6 has a different-shaped complementary region: that is, one co-ordinate must match the complement closely and the other matches within the specified recognition radius. The radii of the respective axes can be altered within the simulator.

Observation 1: Tolerated and Non-tolerated regions still emerge. As in model 1, boundaries also emerge which separate regions in which antigens are tolerated from those in which they are not; again, the location and shape of these regions is an emergent property of the system.

Observation 2: The boundaries are lines. Again, as in model 1, the boundaries separating distinct regions are *lines* of individual antibodies. As in model 1, the width of the boundary defined by the persistent cells is controlled by the value of the upper limit on stimulation level. A limit of 10000 results in boundary lines 1 cell wide — higher levels increase the width of the boundaries but do not alter the shape.

Observation 3: Enclosed Tolerated Regions Appear. Although the boundaries between regions are still lines, the lines tend to *enclose* regions of the space, rather than just bisecting it. This is illustrated in figure 7 which shows examples of 2 different simulations.

Observation 4: Persistent cells only appear at 1 binding site. Figure 7 illustrates that as in Model 1, the persistent cells again tend to lie at the extremes of the complementary regions. Again, no persistent cells lie in the centre of the region, and a further observation in this case is that the persistent cells lie only within *one* of the binding regions; the antibodies do not exhibit multiple binding.

Observation 5: The emergence of boundaries is dependent on the recognition radius. In these simulations, it was observed that a minimum recognition radius of 11 was required in order for stable regions to appear.

5   Non-symmetrical Binding

Finally, we have incorporated two other models into the simulator. In the first model, shown in figure 8(a), the complementary regions are engineered such that

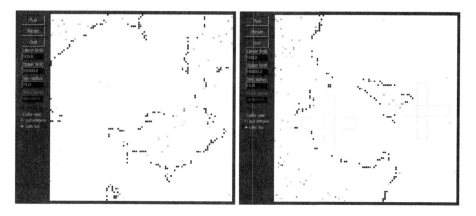

Fig. 7. Example Simulations using Model 2

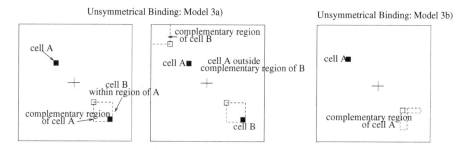

Fig. 8. Models with Unsymmetrical Binding Regions

there is not necessarily mutual recognition between a pair of cells; thus, if cell B lies in the complementary region of cell A, then cell A does *not necessarily* also lie in the complementary region of cell B. The complementary regions in this case essentially consist of a square of radius R positioned at a point in the space dependent on the coordinates of the cell. In the model shown in figure 8(b), the effect of a complementary region which is itself unsymmetrical in shape is modelled. In this case, an L shaped complementary region is used, in which the L always has its arms extending to the east and to the south. The complementary point is centred in the square common to both arms of the L-shape. Due to space limitations, only brief investigations with model 3a) are presented here. However, it is clear that using both of these modes the behaviour that emerges is very different to those described earlier in this paper; we intend to describe these behaviours in more detail in forthcoming work. In order that these results can be directly compared to the earlier examples where the complementary region was a circle of radius 15, the length of the box sides has been set to 26.57 which ensures that the area of the complementary regions are equivalent.

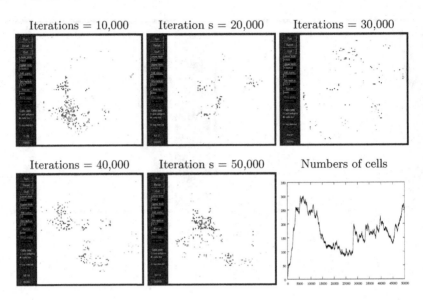

Fig. 9. The arrangement of persistent cells is dynamic when non-symmetric binding is enforced. The graph shows number of cells (0 to 350) vs iterations (0 to 50000)

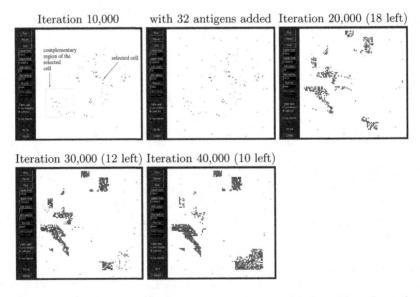

Fig. 10. Tolerant zones emerge when using unsymmetric binding. The tolerated antigens "fossilize" the emergent network

Observation 1: The arrangement of persistent cells in the network fluctuates much more over time. Figure 9 also indicates that unlike in the other models, the networks that appear are not so stable over time; clumps of persistent cells tend to appear and disappear over time, hence the resulting tolerated and non-tolerated zones also change.

Observation 2: The persistent cells do not occur on line-boundaries. Figures 9 and 10 illustrate that persistent cells tend to occur in clumps, and that that these clumps appears in many regions of the space, unlike the other models which resulted in clear boundaries defining regions of space.

Observation 3: Tolerant and non-tolerant zones still emerge. Figure 10 shows an example of a simulation in which antigens were added randomly at iteration 10000. Tolerant zones emerge, as in previous cases. Many of these antigens are still tolerated after a further 30000 iterations. The figure also shows that the addition of these antigens tends to "fossilise" the pattern of persistent cells, so that clumps of cells become stable across many thousands of iterations.

6   Conclusions

In this paper we have argued that matching should be seen as one of the particularly distinctive aspects of AISs and we have presented a series of observations of the effect of different sorts of matching within a simple form of shape-space. In these experiments stable regions do emerge, but the cells that form the boundaries can be far more transient than the regions themselves. The general structure of the stable regions that form depend on the nature of the matching and in particular having multiple binding sites or non-symmetric binding between cells appears to alter the characteristic behaviour significantly. Clearly the collective behaviour of the set of cells within the kinds of shape-spaces considered in this paper is a sophisticated dynamical system. Although this paper has perhaps served to raise questions rather than answer them, it seems important that AIS research should try to develop a good understanding of the behaviour of such systems.

References

1. H. Bersini. Personal Communication.
2. H. Bersini. Self-assertion vs self-recogntion: A tribute to francisco varela. In *Proceedings of ICARIS 2002*, 2002.
3. F.M. Burnet. *The Clonal Slection Theory of Acquired Immunity*. Cambridge University Press, 1959.
4. D. E. Cooke and J.E Hunt. Recognising promoter sequences using an artificial immune system. In *Proceedings of Intelligent Systems in Molecular Biology*, pages 89–97, CA, 1995. AAAI Press.
5. L. De Castro and J. Timmis. *Artificial Immune Systems: A new Computational Intelligence Approach*. Springer, 2002.

6. J.D Farmer, H Packard N, and A.H Perelson. The immune system, adaption and machine learning. *Physica D*, 22:187–204, 1986.
7. S. Garret. An epitope is not a paratope. In *Proceedings of ICARIS 2003*. Springer, 2003.
8. F. Gonzalez, D. Dasgupta, and J. Gomez. The effect of binary matching rules in negative selection. In *Proceedings of the Genetic and Evolutionary Computation Conferemce, GECCO 2003*, 2003.
9. D. Goodman, L. Boggess, and A. Watkins. An investigation into the source of power of airs, an immune classification system. In *Proceedings of IJCNN03 - International Joint Conference on Neural Networks*, 2003.
10. P.K. Hermer and G.B. Lamont. An agent based architecture for a computer virus immune system. In *Proceedings of GECCO 2000*, 2000.
11. S. Hofmeyr and S. Forrest. An architecture for an artificial immune system. *Evolutionary Computing*, 8(4):443–473, 2000.
12. N.K. Jerne. Towards a network theory of the immune system. *Annals of Immunology (Institute Pasteur)*, 1974.
13. A. Perelson and G.F. Oster. Theoretical studies of clonal selection: Minimal antibody repertoire size and reliability of self-nonself discrimination in the immune system. *J. Theoretical Biology*, 158, 1979.
14. Peter Ross. http://www.dcs.napier.ac.uk/~peter/.
15. Jon Timmis and Mark Neal. A resource limited artificial immune system for data analysi s. *Knowledge Based Systems*, 14(3-4):121–130, June 2001.
16. F.J. Varela and A. Coutinho. Second generation immune networks. *Immunology Today*, 12(5), 1991.

Exploiting Parallelism Inherent in AIRS, an Artificial Immune Classifier

Andrew Watkins[1,2] and Jon Timmis[1]

[1] Computing Laboratory, University of Kent, UK
{abw5,jt6}@kent.ac.uk
http://www.cs.kent.ac.uk/~abw5/
[2] Department of Computer Science and Engineering, Mississippi State University,
USA

Abstract. The mammalian immune system is a highly complex, inherently parallel, distributed system. The field of Artificial Immune Systems (AIS) has developed a wide variety of algorithms inspired by the immune system, few of which appear to capitalize on the parallel nature of the system from which inspiration was taken. The work in this paper presents the first steps at realizing a parallel artificial immune system for classification. A simple parallel version of the classification algorithm Artificial Immune Recognition System (AIRS) is presented. Initial results indicate that a decrease in overall runtime can be achieved through fairly naïve techniques. The need for more theoretical models of the behavior of the algorithm is discussed.

1   Introduction

Among the oft-cited reasons for exploring mammalian immune systems as a source of inspiration for computational problem solving include the observations that the immune system is inherently parallel and distributed with many diverse components working simultaneously and in cooperation to provide all of the services that the immune system provides [1,2]. Within the AIS community, there has been some exploration of the distributed nature of the immune system as evidenced in algorithms for network intrusion detection (e.g., [3,4]) as well as some ideas for distributed robot control (e.g., [5,6]), to name a couple of examples. However, very little has been done in the realm of parallel AIS–that is, applying methods to parallelize existing AIS algorithms in the hopes of efficiency (or other) gains. While just parallelizing AIS algorithms is, admittedly, venturing fairly far afield from the initial inspiration found in the immune system, the computational gains through this exercise could well be worth the (possible) side-track. Additionally, this exploration may provide some insight into other relevant areas of AIS, such as ways to incorporate diversity or even understanding the need for such.

The exploitation of parallelism inherent in many algorithms has provided definite gains in efficiency and lent insight into the limitations of the algorithms [7,8]. One example of this within the field of AIS was a very basic study of a

G. Nicosia et al. (Eds.): ICARIS 2004, LNCS 3239, pp. 427–438, 2004.
© Springer-Verlag Berlin Heidelberg 2004

parallel version of the CLONALG algorithm [9]. That study took advantage of the embarrassingly parallel nature of this basic AIS algorithm and demonstrated that parallel techniques can be effectively applied to AIS. This paper builds upon the lessons learned in the parallelization of CLONALG to parallelize another immune learning algorithm: AIRS. While some theoretical results are hinted, the results discussed here are very much of an empirical nature with most of the required theoretical analysis still needing to be performed.

The remainder of this paper details these initial results in parallelizing AIRS. Section 2 gives a brief overview of the serial version of the AIRS algorithm. Section 3 discusses the issues involved with parallelizing this algorithm and provides results from an initial method for this parallelization. Section 4 discusses the role of memory cells in AIRS, the impact of the initial parallel technique on the number of memory cells produced, and a possible way to overcome this apparent issue. Section 5 presents a third memory cell merging technique and the results obtained from adopting this method for solving the memory cell issue. Finally, section 6 offers some concluding remarks about this initial study of parallel AIRS.

2   Overview of the AIRS Algorithm

Developed in 2001, the Artificial Immune Recognition System (AIRS) algorithm was introduced as one of the first immune-inspired supervised learning algorithms and has subsequently gone through a period of study and refinement [10,11,12,13,14,15,16,17,18,19,20][1]. To use classifications from [1], AIRS is a bone-marrow, clonal selection type of immune-inspired algorithm, and, as with many AIS algorithms, immune-**inspired** is the key word. We do not pretend to imply that AIRS directly models any immunological process, but rather AIRS employs some components that can metaphorically relate to some immunological components. In the AIS community, AIRS has two basic precursor algorithms: CLONALG [21] and AINE [22]. AIRS resembles CLONALG in the sense that both algorithms are concerned with developing a set of memory cells that give a representation of the learned environment. AIRS also employs affinity maturation and somatic hypermutation schemes that are similar to what is found in CLONALG. From AINE, AIRS has borrowed population control mechanisms and the concept of an abstract B-cell which represents a concentration of identical B-cells (referred to as Artificial Recognition Balls in previous papers). AIRS has also adopted from AINE the use of an affinity threshold for some learning mechanisms. It should be noted that while AIRS does owe some debt of

---

[1] There is a debate concerning the label of supervised learning for AIRS. The authors are of the view that supervised learning is any learning system which utilizes knowledge of a training example's actual class in the building of its representation of the problem space. While AIRS does not use this information to directly minimize some error function (as seen with neural networks), it does utilize classification information about the training instances to create its world-view. Therefore, we feel that the label of supervised learning is more apt than that of reinforcement learning.

inspiration to AINE, AIRS is a population based algorithm and not a network algorithm like AINE.

While we will not detail the entire algorithm here, we do want to highlight the key parts of AIRS that will allow for understanding of the parallelization[2]. Like CLONALG, AIRS is concerned with the discovery/development of a set of memory cells that can encapsulate the training data. Basically, this is done in a two-stage process of first evolving a candidate memory cell and then determining if this candidate cell should be added to the overall pool of memory cells. This process can be outlined as follows:

1. Compare a training instance with all memory cells of the same class and find the memory cell with the best affinity for the training instance[3]. We will refer to this memory cell as mc_{match}.
2. Clone and mutate mc_{match} in proportion to its affinity to create a pool of abstract B-Cells.
3. Calculate the affinity of each B-Cell with the training instance.
4. Allocate resources to each B-Cell based on its affinity.
5. Remove the weakest B-Cells until the number of resources returns to a preset limit.
6. If the average affinity of the surviving B-Cells is above a certain level, continue to step 7. Else, clone and mutate these surviving B-Cells based on their affinity and return to step 3.
7. Choose the best B-Cell as a candidate memory cell (mc_{cand}).
8. If the affinity of mc_{cand} for the training instance is better than the affinity of mc_{match}, then add mc_{cand} to the memory cell pool. If, in addition to this, the affinity between mc_{cand} and mc_{match} is within a certain threshold, then remove mc_{match} from the memory cell pool.
9. Repeat from step 1 until all training instances have been presented.

Once this training routine is complete, AIRS classifies instances using k-nearest neighbor with the developed set of memory cells.

3   Parallelizing AIRS

Having reviewed the serial version of AIRS, we turn our attention to our initial strategies for parallelizing this algorithm. Our primary motivation for these experiments is computational efficiency. We would like to employ mechanisms of harnessing the power of multiple processors applied to the same learning task rather than relying solely on a single processor. This ability will, in theory, allow us to apply AIRS to problem sets of a larger scale without sacrificing some of the appealing features of the algorithm. Secondary goals of this work include gaining more insight into the processes necessary to parallelize immune algorithms, in

---

[2] See [14] for the pseudocode of AIRS.

[3] Affinity is currently defined as Euclidean distance. We are looking for the closest memory cell of the same class as the training instance.

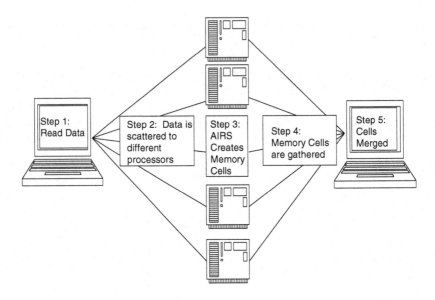

Fig. 1. Overview of Parallel AIRS

general, as well as the implication of such work for the study of the role of diversity and distributedness in AIS.

Our initial approach to parallelizing this process is the same as the approach to parallelizing CLONALG presented in [9]: we partition the training data into np (number of processes) pieces and allow each of the processors to train on the separate portions of the training data. Figure 1 depicts this process. Unfortunately, unlike CLONALG which simply evolves one memory cell for each training data item, AIRS actually employs some degree of interaction between the candidate cells and the previously established memory cells. Partitioning the training data and allowing multiple copies of AIRS to run on these fractions of the data in essence creates np separate memory cell pools. It introduces a (possibly) significant difference in behavior from the serial version. So, when studying this parallelism, we must examine not only the computational efficiency we gain through this use of multiple processors, but we must also learn how evolving these memory cell pools in isolation of one another effects the overall performance of the algorithm.

Algorithmically, based on what is described in section 2, the parallel version behaves in the following manner:

1. Read in the training data at the root process.
2. Scatter the training data to the np processes.
3. Execute, on each process, steps 1 through 9 from the serial version of the algorithm on the portion of the training data obtained.
4. Gather the developed memory cells from each processes back to the root.
5. Merge the gathered memory cells into a single memory cell pool for classification.

Table 1. Iris Results: Concatenation

NP	Test Set Accuracy	Memory Cells	Overall Runtime(s)	Parallel Efficiency
1	95.600%(3.591)	64.380(4.295)	0.346(0.010)	1.000
2	95.800%(3.973)	74.920(4.642)	0.393(0.084)	0.441
4	96.133%(2.886)	86.960(4.785)	0.282(0.092)	0.307
8	95.400%(3.222)	97.280(5.474)	0.282(0.057)	0.153
16	95.333%(3.869)	104.920(5.279)	0.372(0.083)	0.058
24	95.533%(3.665)	108.300(4.879)	0.499(0.065)	0.029

Table 2. Pima Diabetes Results: Concatenation

NP	Test Set Accuracy	Memory Cells	Overall Runtime(s)	Parallel Efficiency
1	73.084%(4.564)	277.050(9.314)	3.540(0.091)	1.000
2	73.347%(5.200)	316.960(13.153)	2.668(0.120)	0.663
4	73.362%(5.186)	359.470(15.344)	1.848(0.104)	0.479
8	74.115%(4.866)	402.270(22.718)	1.557(0.057)	0.284
16	74.494%(4.802)	448.270(26.608)	1.362(0.057)	0.162
24	74.451%(4.605)	475.590(31.687)	1.330(0.082)	0.111

Table 3. Sonar Results: Concatenation

NP	Test Set Accuracy	Memory Cells	Overall Runtime(s)	Parallel Efficiency
1	85.144%(8.097)	172.885(4.074)	57.141(3.582)	1.000
2	84.615%(8.946)	179.038(3.463)	34.738(3.277)	0.822
4	83.894%(8.341)	183.546(2.883)	20.189(1.539)	0.708
8	85.288%(8.731)	186.677(2.589)	12.141(1.261)	0.588
16	84.904%(9.396)	189.038(1.914)	7.255(0.867)	0.492
24	84.567%(8.602)	189.838(1.656)	5.769(0.873)	0.413

Since this method of parallelism creates np separate memory cell pools and since our classification is performed using a single memory cell pool, we must devise a method for merging the separate memory cell pools into one pool.

Initially, we simply gathered each of the np memory cell pools at the root processor and concatenated these into a single large memory cell pool. While this is an extremely naïve approach, as tables 1, 2, and 3 demonstrate, we were still able to achieve overall speedup in the process[4]. On a technical note, for the experiments presented in this paper, we used the Iris, Pima Diabetes, and Sonar data sets that were used in previous studies of AIRS [14]. For all of these we took an average over 10 cross-validated runs and tested the parallel version on an increasing number of processors. A cluster of dual-processor 2.4Ghz Xeons were used. The Message Passing Interface (MPI)[23] was used as the communication library and communication took place over a Gigabit Ethernet network.

There are a couple of observations to be made from this initial set of experiments. Foremost, for our current purposes, there is a gain in overall

---

[4] Values in parentheses represent standard deviation.

runtime of the algorithm by parallelizing it, and this speedup is achieved without any loss in classification accuracy. The iris data set is somewhat anomalous to this general observation The results indicate that for this data set some amount of gain can be had by utilizing more processing power; however, at some point this gain is no longer achieved. This point is probably where the communication and setup time involved in this type of parallelization outstrips the usefulness of having more processors evaluating the training data. Being able to predict what this point is in general will be the focus of our future theoretical/analytical work as we explore this parallel version of AIRS more thoroughly. However, looking at the parallel efficiency, there appears to be something subtler occurring than just a simple speedup from more processing power.

Parallel efficiency can be defined as:

$$E(P) = \frac{T(1)}{P * T(P)}$$

where P is the number or processors, $T(1)$ is the time for the serial version of the algorithms, and $T(P)$ is the time for the parallel version of the algorithm to run on P processors. Ideally, we would have a parallel efficiency of 1. However, this can rarely be achieved due to issues such as communication time and setup. For AIRS, we might initially assume that the more feature vectors in the training set, the greater the parallel efficiency. However, this is not the case. The pima diabetes data set has 691 training items in it whereas the sonar data set has only 192 data items in the training set. Yet, examining the parallel efficiency results for these two data sets reveals that the sonar data set has much more to gain from parallelization than does the pima diabetes data. The explanation for this seeming discrepancy is in the number of features in each feature vector. The pima diabetes data has only eight features per feature vector, whereas the sonar data has 60 (iris has 4 features, incidentally). That our overall runtime (and its parallel efficiency) is predicated on the number of features in the data set should not be surprising. As with parallel GAs [7], the parallel version of AIRS is essentially dividing up the work of fitness (or affinity) evaluations. For the current version of AIRS, affinity is determined based on Euclidean distance which is a metric whose evaluation grows linearly with the number of features. Thus, more gain will be seen from data sets with both a large number of features and a large number of training instances when applying the parallel version of AIRS.

4   Memory Cells

The results in the previous section exhibited another side-effect of note: with parallelization comes an increase in memory cells. One of the hallmarks of AIRS has been its data reduction capabilities. As presented in [14], AIRS has been shown to reduce the amount of data needed to classify a given data set up to 75%. This data reduction is measured in the number of memory cells present in the final classifier. To get an empirical sense of how the size of the memory cell set effects the classification time, we ran a set of experiments in which we

Table 4. Comparison of Runtimes for KNN and AIRS

Tr	Test	MC	T_{test}(KNN)	T_{test}(AIRS)	T(KNN)	T(AIRS)
692	77	277.850	0.149	0.072	1.290	3.521
615	153	254.040	0.276	0.115	1.181	3.048
512	256	217.433	0.373	0.154	1.012	2.468

compared AIRS to k-nearest neighbor (k-nn). Recall, that basic k-nn simply takes all of the training instances as examples and then classifies the test set through a majority voting scheme. AIRS first grows a set of memory cells which are then used to classify the test set. The results from these basic experiments on the pima diabetes data set are given in table 4 and provides a comparison between the number of training and test cases used, the number of memory cells developed by AIRS, and the difference in testing and overall runtime for the k-nn and AIRS. Not surprisingly, when AIRS has greatly reduced the data set, there is a speed up in time to classify the test set[5].

Since the classification speed of AIRS is based on the number of memory cells in the final pool, it is important to understand what impact parallelizing AIRS would have on the size of this set. In the serial version of AIRS, the minimum number of memory cells allowed is the number of classes that exist in the data set (one memory cell per class), and the maximum number is the number of data items in the training set, n, (one memory cell per training vector). For the parallel version, assuming that each process has examples of each class, the minimum at each process is the number of classes (nc); whereas, the maximum would be n/np. So, in the concatenation version of merging, the minimum number of memory cells in the final classifier increases from nc to $nc * np$. While one might suppose that the number of memory cells obtained through either the serial or parallel versions should be the same, it should be remembered that step 1 and (by implication) step 8 of the serial version depend on interaction with the entire memory cell pool. This interaction is not available in the current parallel version.

Our second approach to the merging stage is an attempt to minimize the number of memory cells that resulted from the pure concatenation approach. This method uses an affinity-based technique similar to step 8 in the serial version to reduce the size of the final memory cell pool. After gathering all the memory cells to the root process, they were then separated by class. Within each class grouping, a pairwise calculation of affinity between the memory cells was performed. If the affinity between two memory cells was less than the affinity threshold multiplied by the affinity threshold scalar, then only one of the memory cells was maintained in the final pool. That is, if this relation:

$$\text{affinity}(mc_i, mc_j) < AT * ATS \tag{1}$$

---

[5] In all fairness, it should be mentioned that the time to train in k-nn is virtually nothing, whereas the time to train in AIRS can be significant (when compared to 0). However, once the classifier is trained, it is the classification time that becomes most important as this is the task for which the classifier has been trained.

Table 5. Iris Results: Affinity-Based Merging

NP	Test Set Accuracy	Memory Cells	Overall Runtime(s)	Parallel Efficiency
1	95.867%(3.535)	62.520(4.687)	0.379(0.218)	1.000
2	95.200%(3.698)	68.020(3.771)	0.379(0.047)	0.500
4	95.267%(3.815)	72.740(5.620)	0.264(0.067)	0.359
8	95.333%(3.159)	79.600(7.025)	0.279(0.072)	0.170
16	95.267%(4.046)	84.720(9.630)	0.381(0.070)	0.062
24	94.867%(3.822)	88.380(13.351)	0.514(0.090)	0.031

Table 6. Pima Diabetes Results: Affinity-Based Merging

NP	Test Set Accuracy	Memory Cells	Overall Runtime(s)	Parallel Efficiency
1	73.321%(4.908)	276.090(10.363)	3.739(0.086)	1.000
2	73.806%(4.921)	305.350(14.519)	2.944(0.177)	0.635
4	73.504%(4.444)	340.660(13.444)	2.160(0.107)	0.433
8	73.766%(4.731)	373.150(23.934)	1.891(0.100)	0.247
16	74.280%(4.585)	412.600(31.110)	1.776(0.140)	0.132
24	73.961%(4.811)	429.570(41.682)	1.768(0.174)	0.088

Table 7. Sonar Results: Affinity-Based Merging

NP	Test Set Accuracy	Memory Cells	Overall Runtime(s)	Parallel Efficiency
1	84.808%(8.523)	172.585(4.124)	58.320(3.057)	1.000
2	83.846%(8.934)	179.346(3.258)	35.291(4.128)	0.826
4	85.625%(8.895)	184.008(2.610)	20.407(1.863)	0.714
8	84.712%(8.668)	186.754(2.392)	12.419(1.157)	0.587
16	85.000%(8.403)	188.992(1.882)	7.489(0.692)	0.487
24	84.375%(9.282)	189.862(1.529)	5.996(0.837)	0.405

(where mc_i and mc_j are two memory cells of the same class, the affinity threshold (AT) had been calculated across all of the training antigens as shown in equation 2, and the affinity threshold scalar (ATS) is set by the user) holds true, then mc_j is removed from the memory cell pool.

$$AT = \frac{\sum_{i=1}^{n} \sum_{j=i+1}^{n} \text{affinity}(ag_i, ag_j)}{\frac{n(n-1)}{2}} \tag{2}$$

This merging technique was an initial attempt to compensate for the lack of global interaction the parallelizing process introduced. Tables 5, 6, and 7 give results when using this affinity-based merging.

5   Affinity-Based Merging Revisited

As seen in Section 4, the basic affinity-based merging technique employed did not significantly reduce the increase in memory cells present in the final classifier.

Clearly, the serial version of AIRS does not need as many memory cells to classify as accurately, so we would like to find a way to capture this further reduction in data while still employing our parallel techniques. Examining the increase in memory cells, there appears to be a roughly logarithmic increase with respect to an increase in the number of processors used. One method of remedying this increase in memory cells would be to alter the memory cell replacement criterion used in the affinity-based merging scheme by a logarithmic factor of the number of processors. That is, the criterion for removing a given memory cell is no longer as specified in equation 1, but now the following relation must hold true for the removal of a memory cell:

$$\text{affinity}(mc_i, mc_j) < AT * ATS + \text{factor} \tag{3}$$

and factor is defined as:

$$\text{factor} = AT * ATS * \text{dampener} * log(np) \tag{4}$$

With the "dampener" referred to in equation 4 being a number between 0 and 1, this change to the merging scheme relaxes the criterion for memory cell removal in the affinity-based merging scheme by a small fraction in logarithmic proportion of the number of processors used[6]. Tables 8, 9, and 10 below present results when employing this logarithmic factor to the criterion used in the affinity-based merging scheme[7].

Table 8. Iris Results: Processor Dependent, Affinity-Based Merging

NP	Test Set Accuracy	Memory Cells	Overall Runtime(s)	Parallel Efficiency
1	95.533%(3.726)	63.200(4.607)	0.356(0.012)	1.000
2	95.933%(3.943)	63.720(4.953)	0.358(0.069)	0.497
4	95.467%(3.913)	64.220(4.679)	0.229(0.123)	0.388
8	95.467%(3.913)	63.520(6.234)	0.387(0.126)	0.115
16	95.067%(3.450)	64.440(10.643)	0.495(0.098)	0.045
24	95.333%(3.434)	63.160(13.872)	0.502(0.092)	0.030

Table 9. Pima Diabetes Results: Processor Dependent, Affinity-Based Merging

NP	Test Set Accuracy	Memory Cells	Overall Runtime(s)	Parallel Efficiency
1	73.356%(4.827)	274.430(9.580)	3.734(0.172)	1.000
2	73.359%(4.731)	283.170(12.588)	2.888(0.159)	0.647
4	74.113%(4.524)	283.380(17.528)	1.934(0.141)	0.483
8	73.935%(5.162)	274.890(18.706)	1.589(0.081)	0.294
16	74.066%(4.794)	263.640(31.849)	1.297(0.126)	0.180
24	72.984%(5.433)	261.800(43.940)	1.203(0.165)	0.129

---

[6] Obviously, the scheme presented in section 4 is just a variation on this new formulation with a "dampener" value of 0.

[7] An arbitrary value of 0.1 was used for the "dampener" value for these experiments.

Table 10. Sonar Results: Processor Dependent, Affinity-Based Merging

NP	Test Set Accuracy	Memory Cells	Overall Runtime(s)	Parallel Efficiency
1	83.654%(8.954)	172.692(4.112)	58.499(3.138)	1.000
2	84.519%(9.633)	175.877(3.783)	35.231(3.286)	0.830
4	84.135%(9.213)	179.600(2.863)	20.230(1.310)	0.723
8	84.760%(9.208)	182.292(2.868)	12.386(1.421)	0.590
16	84.087%(8.808)	183.523(3.211)	7.413(0.676)	0.493
24	85.529%(9.209)	185.108(3.071)	5.806(0.746)	0.420

The results from this new merging scheme are somewhat inconclusive. Looking at the iris results (table 8), we appear to have achieved our goal of maintaining the number of memory cells in the parallel classifier at a similar level to the serial version. (As a side-note, we again see the same timing behavior with this data set that we mentioned in section 3.) However, the other two sets of results are not as obvious. While the experiments on the pima diabetes set (table 9) do exhibit a reduction in the number of memory cells in the final classifier, it is unclear if this reduction would have continued unbounded if we had tested on more and more processors. Eventually, with a significant decrease in memory cells, classification accuracy would decrease as well. And, with the sonar data set experiments (table 10), our new scheme appears to have had virtually no impact on the rate of growth of the number of memory cells. What all of this indicates may be simply that we have introduced another parameter (the "dampener" in equation 4) and that we need to determine the appropriate setting for this parameter for each classification task at hand.

6   Conclusion

Our goal with this study was to explore ways of exploiting parallelism inherent in an artificial immune system for decreased overall runtime. Using a very basic mechanism for this parallelism, we have shown that there are definite benefits (computationally, at least) from this exploration. However, more questions were raised than were answered here. Ideally, we would like a way to predict the number of processors to employ to provide the most benefit. In other words, there is the need for a run-time prediction model based on input size as well as feature size.

One side-effect of our parallelization of AIRS was that its final predictive model increased in size. We explored mechanisms for reducing this size to something more comparable with the serial version. While our technique for tackling this might ultimately be the correct approach, currently its use provides inconclusive results (at best). One logical place to look for other ways of solving this problem would be the immune system itself. The immune system is inherently distributed, yet the number of memory cells in the system remains fairly constant. Examining the mechanisms used for this in nature might lend insight into how to address this problem in parallel AIRS.

In addition to some of the algorithmic and theoretical questions that need to be answered, we would also like to expand the use of AIRS and parallel AIRS to more application domains. Any good learning technique attempts to exploit domain knowledge. Given this, we also want to find ways to incorporate domain knowledge into our current learning model.

References

1. de Castro, L., Timmis, J.: Artificial immune systems: A new computational approach. Springer-Verlag, London. UK. (2002)
2. Dasgupta, D., ed.: Artificial Immune Systems and Their Applications. Springer, Berlin (1998)
3. Hofmeyr, S., Forrest, S.: Arichitecture for an aritifcial immune system. Evolutionary Computation $7(1)$ (2000) 45–68
4. Kim, J.W.: Integrating Artificial Immune Algorithms for Intrusion Detection. PhD thesis, Department of Computer Science, University College London (2002)
5. Lee, D.W., Jun, H.B., Sim, K.B.: Artificial immune system for realisation of co-operative strategies and group behaviour in collective autonomous mobile robots. In: Proceedings of Fourth International Symposium on Artificial Life and Robotics, AAAI (1999) 232–235
6. Lau, H.Y., Wong, V.W.: Immunologic control framework for automated material handling. In Timmis, J., Bentley, P., Hart, E., eds.: Proceedings of the 2nd International Conference on Artificial Immune Systems. Number 2787 in Lecture Notes in Computer Science, Springer-Verlag (2003) 57–68
7. Cantú-Paz, E.: Efficient and Accurate Parallel Genetic Algorithms. Kluwer Acadeimic Publishers (2000)
8. Chattratichat, J., Darlington, J., Ghanem, M., Guo, Y., Hunning, H., Kohler, M., Sutiwaraphun, J., Wing To, H., Yang, D.: Large scale data mining: Challenges and responses. In: KDD-97. (1997) 143–146
9. Watkins, A., Bi, X., Phadke, A.: Parallelizing an immune-inspired algorithm for efficient pattern recognition. In Dagli, C., Buczak, A., Ghosh, J., Embrechts, M., Ersoy, O., eds.: Intelligent Engineering Systems through Artificial Neural Networks: Smart Engineering System Design: Neural Networks, Fuzzy Logic, Evolutionary Programming, Complex Systems and Artificial Life. Volume 13. ASME Press, New York (2003) 225–230
10. Watkins, A.: AIRS: A resource limited artificial immune system. Master's thesis, Mississippi State University (2001)
11. Watkins, A., Boggess, L.: A new classifier based on resource limited artificial immune systems. In: Proceedings of Congress on Evolutionary Computation, Part of the 2002 IEEE World Congress on Computational Intelligence held in Honolulu, HI, USA, May 12-17, 2002, IEEE (2002) 1546–1551
12. Watkins, A., Boggess, L.: A resource limited artificial immune classifier. In: Proceedings of Congress on Evolutionary Computation, Part of the 2002 IEEE World Congress on Computational Intelligence held in Honolulu, HI, USA, May 12-17, 2002, IEEE (2002) 926–931
13. Watkins, A., Timmis, J.: Artificial immune recognition system (AIRS): Revisions and refinements. In: Proceedings of the 1st International Conference on Artificial Immune Systems (ICARIS). (2002)

14. Watkins, A., Timmis, J., Boggess, L.: Artificial immune recognition system (AIRS): An immune inspired supervised machine learning algorithm. Genetic Programming and Evolvable Machines **5** (2004) 291–317
15. Marwah, G., Boggess, L.: Artificial immune systems for classification: Some issues. In: Proceedings of the 1st International Conference on Artificial Immune Systems (ICARIS). (2002)
16. Goodman, D., Boggess, L., Watkins, A.: Artificial immune system classification of multiple-class problems. In Dagli, C.H., Buczak, A.L., Ghosh, J., Embrechts, M.J., Ersoy, O., Kercel, S.W., eds.: Intelligent Engineering Systems Through Artificial Nerual Networks: Smart Engineering System Design: Neural Netwokrs, Fuzzy Logic, Evolutionary Programming, Data Mining, and Complex Systems. Volume 12. ASME Press, New York (2002) 179–184
17. Goodman, D., Boggess, L., Watkins, A.: An investigation into the source of power for AIRS, an artificial immune classification system. In: Proceedings of the International Joint Conference on Neural Networks 2003, Portland, OR, USA, The International Neural Network Society and the IEEE Neural Networks Society (2003) 1678–1683
18. Goodman, D., Boggess, L.: The role of hypothesis filter in AIRS, an artificial immune classifier. In Dagli, C., Buczak, A., Ghosh, J., Embrechts, M., Ersoy, O., eds.: Intelligent Engineering Systems through Artificial Neural Networks: Smart Engineering System Design: Neural Networks, Fuzzy Logic, Evolutionary Programming, Complex Systems and Artificial Life. Volume 13. ASME Press (2003) 243–248
19. Greensmith, J., Cayzer, S.: An artificial immune system approach to semantic document classification. In Timmis, J., Bentley, P., Hart, E., eds.: Proceedings of the 2nd International Conference on Artificial Immune Systems. Number 2787 in Lecture Notes in Computer Science, Springer-Verlag (2003) 136–146
20. Hamaker, J., Boggess, L.: Non-euclidean distance measures in AIRS, an artificial immune classification system. In: Proceedings of the 2004 Congress on Evolutionary Computing. (2004)
21. de Castro, L.N., von Zuben, F.: Learning and optimization using the clonal selction principle. IEEE Transactions on Evolutionary Computation **6** (2002) 239–251
22. Timmis, J., Neal, M.: A Resource Limited Artificial Immune System. Knowledge Based Systems **14** (2001) 121–130
23. Gropp, W., Lusk, E., Skjellum, A.: Using MPI: Portable Parallel Programming with the Message Passing Interface. 2nd edn. MIT Press (1999)

An Overview of Computational and Theoretical Immunology

Alan S. Perelson

Theoretical Division
Los Alamos National Laboratory
Los Alamos, NM 87545 USA

In this talk, I will give an overview of the operating principles of the immune system emphasizing its role as a pattern recognizer. The fundamental algorithm that the immune system uses to recognize foreign cells and molecules is called clonal selection. The basic idea is to generate cells each of which has many copies of a unique receptor on its surface. In the case of B lymphocytes, which are the cells in the immune system that secrete antibody, the receptor is a membrane associated form of antibody called surface immunoglobulin (sIg). Each lymphocyte during its development expresses a pseudo random set of genes, which code for its surface Ig. The diversity of Ig genes is such that potentially about 10^{10} different sIg molecules could be made. A mouse, for example, only has 10^8 lymphocytes so that at any given time only a small fraction of its potential repertoire of receptor types can be found in the animal. This is called the expressed repertoire. When a foreign molecule (antigen) is encountered, one hopes the diversity of receptor types is sufficiently large that one or more lymphocytes will recognize the antigen. If this occurs, the lymphocyte will be triggered to proliferate and make copies of itself, as well as to differentiate into cells that secrete high levels of antibody. The antibody they secrete is a soluble form of their sIg. Thus, in essence antigen selects the lymphocytes that can recognize it and causes those cells to expand into a clone, hence the name clonal selection. Given this scenario and assuming a random repertoire of size N such that each receptor has a probability p of recognizing a random antigen, one can easily see that the probability of an antigen not being recognized by any receptor is $(1-p)^N = \exp[N \ln(1-p)]$, which for $p \ll 1$ is approximately e^{-pN}, and the probability of recognizing an antigen is $1-e^{-pN}$. Note that if $p=1$, the immune system would only need one receptor, but since this receptor would also recognize self molecules it would not be useful. Consequently, one must also require that the immune discriminate between self and non-self.

These ideas have been made more concrete and placed in a form that is easy to implement computationally by the introduction of the idea of shape-space and the representation of the shapes of receptors and epitopes (the parts of an antigen recognized by a receptor) with bitstrings and digit strings. If one represents a receptor with a 32 bit binary string then the potential repertoire is $2^{32} \sim 10^9$, which is close to the size seen in mice. Much larger repertoire sizes can be represented using strings with letters chosen from larger alphabets. The idea of a receptor recognizing an epitope is then implemented as a string match rule, and the probability of recognition, p, can be calculated for any potential rule. Different match rules have been implemented and different rules give rise to immune systems with different properties. For example, in the case of real antibody responses, B cells after they recognize an antigen and begin

G. Nicosia et al. (Eds.): ICARIS 2004, LNCS 3239, pp. 439–441, 2004.
© Springer-Verlag Berlin Heidelberg 2004

proliferating can then mutate their receptor genes and evolve receptors that better match the antigen. Most such mutations are found to be deleterious with improvement mutations that greatly enhance the match being rare. This feature can be mimicked by a match rule that quantifies the strength of a match by the length of the longest matching substring, whereas a match rule such as XOR used for binary strings does not have this property since each mutation can only change the score by 1/the string length.

Simulation models of the immune system have been developed that utilize different shape space representation. In order to efficiently simulate realistic size immune systems, methods such as lazy evaluation and stage-structured stochastic simulation methods have been developed. In lazy evaluation, rather than initializing a simulation of the immune system with a set of cells representing the diversity of the expressed repertoire, one only initially creates the set of cell that given the match rule being used could potentially interact with the antigen or antigens being studied. As more antigens are encountered or as B cell mutate their receptors additional B cells are brought into the simulation as needed. In stage-structured simulation models, all cells with the same receptor specificity and in the same developmental stage are considered identical. The population of such cells is then followed with stochastic transitions between states.

Lastly, the ideas of immune protection have been carried over to developing algorithms for the protection of a computer or a network of computers. The adaptive immune system generates both humoral (B cell) and cell mediated (T cell) immune responses. One can think of B cell responses with their generation of antibody as examining a system from the outside. Antibodies only bind to the surface of pathogens or proteins and can not detect what is inside of them. On the other hand T cells only recognize degradation products of proteins and other cellular components. Thus T cell examine the interior of antigens. By analogy one could view detecting infection of a computer by seeing anomalous system calls or other anomalous behavior as the venue of the humoral response, whereas looking at the innards of a program for a viral signature pattern as the equivalent of a T cell response. Both types of responses are needed by the immune system and both might be needed for computer/network security.

Stephanie Forrest, University of New Mexico, and I have pursued these analogies as well as the algorithms for self-non self discrimination that the immune systems use in order to build virus and anomaly detection systems. Briefly, if one takes a program and parses it into strings, one can think of these strings as self components. Then randomly generate other strings, which represent randomly made immunological receptors, which for simplicity I will call antibodies. Given a match rule, if these antibodies match self, delete them, so one is left with a repertoire of antibodies which does not recognize self. If this repertoire is sufficiently diverse and random, then it could be used as a computer immune system recognizing the presence of infection when these antibodies match strings within the program space. Calculations, such as those given earlier, can be used to determine the probability a computer virus could be detected given a repertoire of size N and a match rule that recognizes random strings with probability p. The immune system for each machine can be made unique. For example, if a program is encrypted using a unique key for each machine before being parsed into strings that define self-components and in the subsequent generation of strings for examination by the computer immune system, one would expect the set of antibodies generated for each machine to be different. This is somewhat analogous to how MHC molecules operate both in the generation of the T cell repertoire and in the presentation of antigens to T cells

Lastly, it is important to emphasize that the field of artificial immune systems is a two way street where facts from immunology can be translated into algorithms that may have significance in other fields, but also as we develop principles that guide the operation of artificial immune system we need to be aware that we may uncover insights into how natural immune systems operate.

Author Index

Lecture Notes in Computer Science

For information about Vols. 1–3114

please contact your bookseller or Springer

Vol. 3170: P. Gardner, N. Yoshida (Eds.), CONCUR 2004 - Concurrency Theory. XIII, 529 pages. 2004.

Vol. 3166: M. Rauterberg (Ed.), Entertainment Computing – ICEC 2004. XXIII, 617 pages. 2004.

Vol. 3163: S. Marinai, A. Dengel (Eds.), Document Analysis Systems VI. XII, 564 pages. 2004.

Vol. 3162: R. Downey, M. Fellows, F. Dehne (Eds.), Parameterized and Exact Computation. X, 293 pages. 2004.

Vol. 3160: S. Brewster, M. Dunlop (Eds.), Mobile Human-Computer Interaction – MobileHCI 2004. XVIII, 541 pages. 2004.

Vol. 3159: U. Visser, Intelligent Information Integration for the Semantic Web. XIV, 150 pages. 2004. (Subseries LNAI).

Vol. 3158: I. Nikolaidis, M. Barbeau, E. Kranakis (Eds.), Ad-Hoc, Mobile, and Wireless Networks. IX, 344 pages. 2004.

Vol. 3157: C. Zhang, H. W. Guesgen, W.K. Yeap (Eds.), PRICAI 2004: Trends in Artificial Intelligence. XX, 1023 pages. 2004. (Subseries LNAI).

Vol. 3156: M. Joye, J.-J. Quisquater (Eds.), Cryptographic Hardware and Embedded Systems - CHES 2004. XIII, 455 pages. 2004.

Vol. 3155: P. Funk, P.A. González Calero (Eds.), Advances in Case-Based Reasoning. XIII, 822 pages. 2004. (Subseries LNAI).

Vol. 3154: R.L. Nord (Ed.), Software Product Lines. XIV, 334 pages. 2004.

Vol. 3153: J. Fiala, V. Koubek, J. Kratochvíl (Eds.), Mathematical Foundations of Computer Science 2004. XIV, 902 pages. 2004.

Vol. 3152: M. Franklin (Ed.), Advances in Cryptology – CRYPTO 2004. XI, 579 pages. 2004.

Vol. 3150: G.-Z. Yang, T. Jiang (Eds.), Medical Imaging and Augmented Reality. XII, 378 pages. 2004.

Vol. 3149: M. Danelutto, M. Vanneschi, D. Laforenza (Eds.), Euro-Par 2004 Parallel Processing. XXXIV, 1081 pages. 2004.

Vol. 3148: R. Giacobazzi (Ed.), Static Analysis. XI, 393 pages. 2004.

Vol. 3146: P. Érdi, A. Esposito, M. Marinaro, S. Scarpetta (Eds.), Computational Neuroscience: Cortical Dynamics. XI, 161 pages. 2004.

Vol. 3144: M. Papatriantafilou, P. Hunel (Eds.), Principles of Distributed Systems. XI, 246 pages. 2004.

Vol. 3143: W. Liu, Y. Shi, Q. Li (Eds.), Advances in Web-Based Learning – ICWL 2004. XIV, 459 pages. 2004.

Vol. 3142: J. Diaz, J. Karhumäki, A. Lepistö, D. Sannella (Eds.), Automata, Languages and Programming. XIX, 1253 pages. 2004.

Vol. 3140: N. Koch, P. Fraternali, M. Wirsing (Eds.), Web Engineering. XXI, 623 pages. 2004.

Vol. 3139: F. Iida, R. Pfeifer, L. Steels, Y. Kuniyoshi (Eds.), Embodied Artificial Intelligence. IX, 331 pages. 2004. (Subseries LNAI).

Vol. 3138: A. Fred, T. Caelli, R.P.W. Duin, A. Campilho, D.d. Ridder (Eds.), Structural, Syntactic, and Statistical Pattern Recognition. XXII, 1168 pages. 2004.

Vol. 3137: P. De Bra, W. Nejdl (Eds.), Adaptive Hypermedia and Adaptive Web-Based Systems. XIV, 442 pages. 2004.

Vol. 3136: F. Meziane, E. Métais (Eds.), Natural Language Processing and Information Systems. XII, 436 pages. 2004.

Vol. 3134: C. Zannier, H. Erdogmus, L. Lindstrom (Eds.), Extreme Programming and Agile Methods - XP/Agile Universe 2004. XIV, 233 pages. 2004.

Vol. 3133: A.D. Pimentel, S. Vassiliadis (Eds.), Computer Systems: Architectures, Modeling, and Simulation. XIII, 562 pages. 2004.

Vol. 3132: B. Demoen, V. Lifschitz (Eds.), Logic Programming. XII, 480 pages. 2004.

Vol. 3131: V. Torra, Y. Narukawa (Eds.), Modeling Decisions for Artificial Intelligence. XI, 327 pages. 2004. (Subseries LNAI).

Vol. 3130: A. Syropoulos, K. Berry, Y. Haralambous, B. Hughes, S. Peter, J. Plaice (Eds.), TeX, XML, and Digital Typography. VIII, 265 pages. 2004.

Vol. 3129: Q. Li, G. Wang, L. Feng (Eds.), Advances in Web-Age Information Management. XVII, 753 pages. 2004.

Vol. 3128: D. Asonov (Ed.), Querying Databases Privately. IX, 115 pages. 2004.

Vol. 3127: K.E. Wolff, H.D. Pfeiffer, H.S. Delugach (Eds.), Conceptual Structures at Work. XI, 403 pages. 2004. (Subseries LNAI).

Vol. 3126: P. Dini, P. Lorenz, J.N.d. Souza (Eds.), Service Assurance with Partial and Intermittent Resources. XI, 312 pages. 2004.

Vol. 3125: D. Kozen (Ed.), Mathematics of Program Construction. X, 401 pages. 2004.

Vol. 3124: J.N. de Souza, P. Dini, P. Lorenz (Eds.), Telecommunications and Networking - ICT 2004. XXVI, 1390 pages. 2004.

Vol. 3123: A. Belz, R. Evans, P. Piwek (Eds.), Natural Language Generation. X, 219 pages. 2004. (Subseries LNAI).

Vol. 3122: K. Jansen, S. Khanna, J.D.P. Rolim, D. Ron (Eds.), Approximation, Randomization, and Combinatorial Optimization. IX, 428 pages. 2004.

Vol. 3121: S. Nikoletseas, J.D.P. Rolim (Eds.), Algorithmic Aspects of Wireless Sensor Networks. X, 201 pages. 2004.

Vol. 3120: J. Shawe-Taylor, Y. Singer (Eds.), Learning Theory. X, 648 pages. 2004. (Subseries LNAI).

Vol. 3119: A. Asperti, G. Bancerek, A. Trybulec (Eds.), Mathematical Knowledge Management. X, 393 pages. 2004.

Vol. 3118: K. Miesenberger, J. Klaus, W. Zagler, D. Burger (Eds.), Computer Helping People with Special Needs. XXIII, 1191 pages. 2004.

Vol. 3116: C. Rattray, S. Maharaj, C. Shankland (Eds.), Algebraic Methodology and Software Technology. XI, 569 pages. 2004.

Vol. 3115: P. Enser, Y. Kompatsiaris, N.E. O'Connor, A.F. Smeaton, A.W.M. Smeulders (Eds.), Image and Video Retrieval. XVII, 679 pages. 2004.